KV-638-147

150 LEADING CASES

Law of the European Union

SECOND EDITION

ALINA KACZOROWSKA
BCL, DEA, PhD, Barrister at the Paris Bar

OLD BAILEY PRESS

OLD BAILEY PRESS
at Holborn College, Woolwich Road,
Charlton, London, SE7 8LN

First published 1999
Second edition 2002

ISBN 1 85836 453 1

British Library Cataloguing-in-Publication

A catalogue record for this book is available from the British
Library.

Printed and bound in Great Britain

Contents

Acknowledgements

Extracts from the Treaties and documents of the European Economic Communities, and of the judgments and decisions of the European Court of Justice and the European Court of Human Rights, have been reproduced, free of charge, with the kind permission of the European Commission, the European Court of Justice, the European Court of Human Rights and the European Law Centre.

The publishers and editor would also like to thank the Incorporated Council of Law Reporting for England and Wales for their kind permission to reproduce extracts from the Weekly Law Reports, and Butterworths for their kind permission to reproduce extracts from the All England Law Reports.

Preface

The selection of 150 Leading Cases on the Law of the European Union involves difficult choices. The authoress, in selecting 150 of the most significant cases emanating from the courts of the European Communities, had in mind two perspectives. Accordingly, the book examines, on the one hand, recent cases (up to December 2001) which take account of new developments, of changes in the law and of the Community courts' clarifications of essential issues, and, on the other, examines earlier 'landmark' cases in the light of subsequent events.

The comments, elucidating the nuances of the various judgments, are intended to ensure that this publication can be used as an educative work which stands on its own. Additionally, the inclusion of verbatim quotations of important extracts from judgments makes it an ideal companion to the Old Bailey Press Textbook on the *Law of The European Union.*

The reader should note: first, that with the entry into force of the Treaty of Amsterdam on 1 May 1999 the numbering of almost all Articles of the Treaty on European Union and the EC Treaty was changed. Most of the cases/judgments dealt with in this book refer only to the pre-Treaty of Amsterdam numbering. In order to assist the reader, the authoress has, in the facts of the case and her comments, set out in brackets the new numbering. Additionally, this book has an appendix containing a correlation table for certain Treaty Articles.

Second, that the manner of referring to each Treaty was changed after 1 May 1999. Now only two letters are used to indicate the Treaty concerned:

EU for the Treaty on European Union
EC for the EC Treaty
CS for the ECSC Treaty
EA for the Euratom Treaty

Therefore, for example, 'art 81 EC' refers to Article 81 of that Treaty as numbered after 1 May 1999. Where reference is made to an Article of a Treaty as it stood before 1 May 1999, for example 'art 85', the number of the Article is followed by the words 'EC Treaty'. Thus, 'art 85 EC Treaty' refers to art 85 of that Treaty before 1 May 1999.

Third, that certain recent cases, although unreported, can be found at the website of the courts of the European Communities: http://europa.eu.int/cj/en/index.htm.

Fourth, that many quotations from judgments do not read well but they are precise quotations.

I must thank the following individuals who greatly contributed to the creation of this work: my friends from the Old Bailey Press, Professor Cedric Bell and Vanessa Osborne; and Christopher Ireland, of Irelands Commercial Lawyers in Hampshire.

Alina Kaczorowska
2002

Table of Cases

Cases in bold type are the leading cases. Page numbers in bold indicate the main references to them.

1 The Birth, Development and Legal Status of the European Union

Continued expanding membership

R v Secretary of State for the Home Department, ex parte Gloszczuk and Gloszczuk Case C–63/99 [2001] 3 CMLR 1035; [2001] ECR I–6369; ***R v Secretary of State for the Home Department, ex parte Barkoci and Malik*** Case C–257/99 [2001] ECR I–6557; ***R v Secretary of State for the Home Department, ex parte Kondova*** Case C–235/99 [2001] 3 CMLR 1077; [2001] ECR I–6427
European Court of Justice

- *Association Agreements – external relations – freedom of establishment – equality of treatment – leave to enter obtained fraudulently*

Facts
In the above cases the High Court referred to the ECJ a number of questions concerning the interpretation of the Association Agreements concluded between the EEC, on the one side, and Poland (which entered into force on 1 February 1994), the Czech Republic (which entered into force on 1 February 1995) and Bulgaria (which entered into force on 1 February 1995), on the other side. A Polish couple, two Czech nationals and one national of Bulgaria, all of whom were refused leave to remain in the United Kingdom under the relevant Association Agreement, argued that the refusal was in breach of the relevant Agreements.

The Association Agreements provide a framework for the gradual integration of the Associated States into the European Union with a view to preparing these States for their accession to the EU. The Association Agreements contain, inter alia, provisions dealing with the movement of workers, the right of establishment and the right to provide services. The Association Agreements also provide for the application of the principle of non-discrimination on grounds of nationality to nationals of the Associated States who are self-employed, or setting up and managing companies. The Association Agreements clearly state that they do not prevent the Member States from applying their laws and regulations regarding entry and stay, work, labour conditions, establishment of natural persons and supply of services unless such national rules are applied in such a manner as to nullify or impair the benefit accruing to any party under the terms of the relevant Agreement. Following the entry into force of these Agreements the United Kingdom enacted immigration legislation, that being the Immigration Rules 1994, defining the conditions governing leave to reside in the United Kingdom for persons covered by the above Agreements.

In respect of the Polish couple, they entered the UK in 1989 and 1991 as tourists for a period of six months. Their entry visas contained an express condition prohibiting them from entering employment or engaging in any business or profession in a self-employed capacity. When their visas expired they did not leave the UK. Whilst they remained unlawfully in the UK the husband started to work in the building industry. He claimed that he become established as a self-employed building contractor in 1995. After his wife gave birth to their son, the couple sought to regularise their stay. They applied to the Secretary of State for 'recognition' of their right to establish themselves in the UK under the relevant provision of the Association Agreement and consequently for leave to remain in the UK. The Secretary of State rejected their application on the ground that only persons lawfully present in the UK could benefit from rights conferred by the relevant Association Agreement. In addition the husband was also in breach of the express condition attached to his leave to enter the UK by working before applying for recognition of his right to become established under the Association Agreement. The Polish couple sought judicial review of the above decision, arguing that they did not need 'leave' to enter or remain in the UK because they could rely on directly applicable rights granted under the Association Agreement.

In the case of Julius Barkoci and Marcel Malik, both members of the Roma community and nationals of the Czech Republic, after their arrival in the UK they applied for political asylum. When the Secretary of State refused the applications they submitted an application to remain in the UK pursuant to the relevant Association Agreement.

Mr Barkoci wished to establish himself as a self-employed gardener whilst Mr Malik wanted to provide domestic and commercial cleaning services. The UK authorities chose to treat these applications as applications for initial leave to enter, although both were already present in the territory of the UK. Upon the examination of their business plans, the UK immigration authority refused to grant them leave to enter the UK under the relevant Association Agreement on the ground that those plans were not satisfactory in terms of their financial viability. Mr Barkoci and Mr Malik challenged these decisions.

With regard to Ms Kondova, a Bulgarian veterinary student, she arrived in 1993 in the UK after being granted a single entry visa for a period of three months to work as a farm labourer. Once in the UK she applied for political asylum. Although her application was refused she remained unlawfully in the UK. She admitted that she intentionally misled the UK authorities as to the reason for her stay in the UK, as she had always intended to seek political asylum. In the meantime she married a Mauritian national who had indefinite leave to remain in the UK. In 1996 she started to work as a self-employed cleaner. In 1996 she applied for leave to remain in the UK pursuant to the relevant Association Agreement. Although she claimed that her income would be supplemented by funds provided by her husband, the business plans were considered unsatisfactory in terms of profitability by the relevant authorities and consequently she was refused leave to remain in the UK. In July 1996 the Secretary of State issued instructions to proceed with her removal from the territory of the UK. In September 1996 she was arrested and detained for one month. During her detention she challenged the decision of the Secretary of State refusing her leave to remain in the UK. In October 1996 the Secretary of State invited her to provide a more realistic assessment of the profitability of her intended business. In the light of new calculations provided by her, the Secretary of State decided that Ms Kondova's business would be profitable and was ready to grant her leave to remain in the UK under the provisions of the relevant Association Agreement, even though her entry was illegal. She was also invited to withdraw her application for judicial review of his previous decision. In response she submitted a list of terms under which she was prepared to withdraw her application. This was rejected by the Secretary of State. Before the High Court Ms Kondova sought both a declaration that at all material times she was entitled to leave to remain in the UK by virtue of the provisions on the right of establishment under the relevant Association Agreement, and compensation for the damage caused to her by the denial of her directly applicable rights under the above Agreement and by her unlawful detention in breach of those rights.

The High Court referred a number of questions to the ECJ regarding the direct applicability and the scope of the right of establishment under the Association Agreements in the context of the above cases.

Held

The ECJ held that the principle of non-discrimination under the Association Agreements was sufficiently unconditional and precise to be directly effective. The right of establishment under the relevant Agreement means that rights of entry and residence, as corollaries of the right of establishment, are conferred on nationals of an Associated State. However, the rights of entry and residence are not absolute privileges, inasmuch as their exercise may be limited by the rules of a host Member State governing the entry and stay and establishment of nationals of an Associated State. Further, nationals of an Associated State who fraudulently obtain leave to enter place themselves outside the sphere of protection recognised by the Association Agreements. For that reason a Member State may reject applications made pursuant to the Agreement and may require that the applicants submit a new application in due and proper form for establishment on the basis of that Agreement by applying for an entry visa to the competent authorities in their country of origin or, as the case may be, in another country, provided that this does not prevent them from having their situation reviewed at a later date.

Judgment

'[*R* v *Secretary of State for the Home Department, ex parte Gloszczuk and Gloszczuk* Case C–63/99]
[*Whether the restrictions imposed on the right of establishment by the host Member State's immigration legislation are compatible with the condition set out in art 58(1) of the Association Agreement*]
It is necessary in this regard to determine whether the immigration rules applied by the competent national authorities are appropriate for achieving the objective in view or whether they constitute, in regard to that objective, measures which would strike at the very substance of the rights which art 44(3) of the Association Agreement grants to Polish nationals by making exercise of those rights impossible or excessively difficult.

It should first be noted that, since art 44(3) of the Association Agreement is applicable only to those persons who are exclusively self-employed, in accordance with the final sentence of art 44(4)(a)(i) of that Agreement, it is necessary to determine whether the activity contemplated in the host Member State by persons covered by that provision is an activity performed in an employed or a self-employed capacity.

Application of a national system of prior control to check the exact nature of the activity contemplated by the applicant has a legitimate objective in so far as it makes it possible to restrict the exercise of rights of entry and residence by Polish nationals invoking art 44(3) of the Association Agreement to persons to whom that provision applies.

However, as follows from arts 44(3) and 58(1) of the Association Agreement, the host Member State cannot refuse to a Polish national admission and residence for the purpose of that person's establishment in the territory of that State, for instance on grounds of the nationality of the person concerned or his country of residence, or because the national legal system provides for a general limitation on immigration, or make the right to take up an activity as a self-employed person in that State subject to confirmation of a proven need in the light of economic or labour-market considerations.

With particular regard to the substantive requirements, such as those set out in paras 217 and 219 of the Immigration Rules, these, as the United Kingdom Government and the Commission have pointed out, pursue the objective of allowing the competent authorities to verify that a Polish national wishing to become established in the United Kingdom genuinely intends to take up an activity as a self-employed person without at the same time entering into employment or having recourse to public funds, and that he possesses, from the outset, sufficient financial resources and has reasonable chances of success. Further, substantive requirements such as those set out in paras 217 and 219 of the Immigration Rules are appropriate to ensure that such an objective is achieved.

Furthermore, as the United Kingdom Government has correctly pointed out, following the entry into force of the Association Agreement and the other Europe Association Agreements concluded with the countries of Central and Eastern Europe, the national rules on immigration of nationals of non-Member countries intending to establish themselves as self-employed persons were re-examined and amended. Thus, in particular, the requirement of possession of investment capital of GBP 200,000 continues to be imposed on persons who cannot invoke rights under Europe Association Agreements, but this requirement is no longer applicable to Polish nationals.

In addition, the national legislation at issue in the main proceedings includes rules allowing a person intending to become established in the host Member State under the provisions of a Europe Association Agreement to request leave to remain in that State as a self-employed worker notwithstanding the fact that the person had originally been admitted for a different purpose. Consequently, provisions such as those contained in paras 217 and 219 of the Immigration Rules facilitate the establishment of Polish nationals in the host Member State and must be regarded as being compatible with the Association Agreement.

It ought, however, to be borne in mind that, as indicated in para 24 above, the applications for leave to remain submitted by Mr and Mrs Gloszczuk pursuant to the Association Agreement were rejected by the Secretary of State on grounds not related to the substantive requirements laid down by the national immigration legislation for the establishment of Polish nationals. That decision of refusal by the Secretary of State was

based on para 322(2) and (3) of the Immigration Rules, in so far as Mr and Mrs Gloszczuk had made false representations in order to be admitted to the United Kingdom and had failed to comply with the expiry dates and conditions attached to their initial leave to enter.

It is therefore necessary to examine whether art 58(1) of the Association Agreement allows the competent authorities of the host Member State to refuse leave to remain, applied for by a Polish national invoking art 44(3) of that Agreement, on the ground that the applicant's presence within the territory of that State is irregular by reason of false representations made for the purpose of obtaining initial leave to enter or by reason of the breach of an express condition attached to that entry and relating to the authorised duration of that person's stay in that Member State, where that irregularity occurred before that person became self-employed and claimed the right of establishment under the Association Agreement.

That was indeed the situation of Mr and Mrs Gloszczuk, who had remained unlawfully in the United Kingdom since 1989 and 1991 respectively and claimed a right of establishment under the Association Agreement only in January 1996.

[*The power of the competent authorities of the host Member State to refuse leave to remain, applied for by a Polish national invoking art 44(3) of the Association Agreement, on the sole ground that his presence within the territory of that State was unlawful*]

Mr and Mrs Gloszczuk argue that, unlike art 37(1) of the Association Agreement, which concerns the movement of workers, art 44(3) of the Agreement does not make lawful residence a precondition. There is, therefore, nothing in art 44 to suggest that a right of establishment cannot be conferred on Polish nationals because of an infringement of the immigration legislation of the Member State concerned.

Consequently, a Member State may reject an application submitted under art 44(3) of the Association Agreement by a person whose presence within its territory is otherwise unlawful only after it has taken into account the substantive requirements established by that Agreement.

In order to rule on whether this argument is well founded, it is necessary to bear in mind that, as pointed out in paras 57 to 62 above, a system of prior control, such as that established by the Immigration Rules, under which the host Member State makes the granting of entry clearance and leave to remain subject to verification by the competent immigration authorities that the applicant genuinely intends to pursue in that Member State a viable activity as a self-employed person and no other, is in principle compatible with art 44(3) of the Association Agreement, read in conjunction with art 58(1) thereof.

Under such a system of prior control, if it turns out that a Polish national who submitted in due and proper form a prior request for leave to reside for purposes of establishment satisfied the substantive requirements laid down for that purpose by the immigration legislation of the host Member State, compliance with the express condition set out in art 58(1) of the Association Agreement obliges the competent national authorities to recognise that person as having a right of establishment in a self-employed capacity and to grant that person, for that purpose, leave to enter and remain.

However, should it turn out that, as in the case in the main proceedings, the requirement concerning submission of a prior request for leave to remain for purposes of establishment has not been met, the competent immigration authorities of the host Member State may in principle refuse that leave to a Polish national invoking art 44(3) of the Association Agreement, irrespective of whether the other substantive conditions laid down by the national legislation have been satisfied.

Furthermore, as the Commission has correctly pointed out, the effectiveness of such a system of prior control rests in very large measure on the correctness of the declarations made by the persons concerned at the time when they apply for an entry visa from the competent authorities in their State of origin or when they arrive in the host Member State.

In those circumstances, as the Advocate-General indicates in point 75 of his Opinion, if Polish nationals were allowed at any time to apply for establishment in the host Member State, notwithstanding a previous breach of the condition relating to the authorised duration of their initial stay as tourists in that State, such nationals might be encouraged to remain illegally within the territory of that State and submit to the national system of control only once the substantive requirements set out in immigration legislation had been satisfied.

An applicant might then rely on the clientele and business assets which he may have built up during his unlawful stay in the host Member State, or on funds accrued there, perhaps through taking employment, and so present himself to the national authorities as a self-employed person now engaged in, or likely to be engaged in, a viable activity, whose rights ought to be recognised pursuant to the Association Agreement.

Such an interpretation would risk depriving art 58(1) of the Association Agreement of its effectiveness and opening the way to abuse through endorsement of infringements of national legislation on admission and residence of foreigners.

Consequently, a Polish national who intends to take up an activity in a Member State as an employed or self-employed person but who gets round the relevant national controls by falsely declaring that he is entering that Member State for the purpose of tourism places himself outside the sphere of protection afforded to him under the Association Agreement (see, by analogy, in relation to circumvention of national law by Community nationals improperly or fraudulently invoking Community law, *Centros Ltd* v *Erhvervs-og Selskabsstyrelsen* Case C–212/97 [1999] ECR I–1459, at para 24 and the case law cited therein).

The fact that the infringement of the host Member State's immigration legislation was committed by the Polish national at a date prior to the entry into force of the Association Agreement is irrelevant where, as in the present case, the irregular situation had not ended at that time and was still continuing when the application for establishment was made. Moreover, as indicated in para 24 above, the Secretary of State treated the applications made by Mr and Mrs Gloszczuk under the Association Agreement as if they were applications for leave to remain and rejected them on the ground that Mr and Mrs Gloszczuk were in an irregular situation when he took his decision.

Consequently, it is compatible with art 58(1) of the Association Agreement for the competent authorities of the host Member State to reject an application made under art 44(3) of that Agreement on the ground that, when that application was made, the applicant was residing illegally within its territory by reason of false representations made to those authorities for the purpose of obtaining initial leave to enter that Member State on a separate basis or of the failure to comply with an express condition attached to that entry and relating to the authorised duration of his stay in that Member State.

[*Whether the requirement for a new application for establishment to be submitted in due and proper form is compatible with the rule of equal treatment laid down in art 44(3) of the Association Agreement and with the condition mentioned in art 58(1) thereof*]

In considering the question whether the requirement that a Polish national whose presence within the host Member State's territory is irregular must submit a new establishment application in due and proper form in his State of origin or, as the case may be, in another country is compatible with the rule of equal treatment laid down in art 44(3) of the Association Agreement, where such a requirement could not be imposed on the host Member State's own nationals, it is important to bear in mind that the Court has held, with regard to the free movement of workers, that the reservation contained in art 48(3) of the EC Treaty

(now, after amendment, art 39(3) EC) allows Member States, on the grounds set out in that provision, and in particular grounds justified by requirements of public policy, to take measures against nationals of other Member States which they could not apply to their own nationals, inasmuch as they have no authority to expel the latter from the national territory or deny them access to it (see, in this regard, *Van Duyn* v *Home Office* Case 41/74 [1974] ECR 1337, para 22; *Adoui and Cornvaille* v *Belgian State* Joined Cases 115 and 116/81 [1982] ECR 1665, para 7; *R* v *Immigration Appeal Tribunal and Surinder Singh, ex parte Secretary of State for the Home Department* Case C–370/90 [1992] ECR I–4265, para 22; *R* v *Secretary of State for the Home Department, ex parte Shingara and Radiom* Joined Cases C–65/95 and C–111/95 [1997] ECR I–3341, para 28; and *Rui Alberto Pereira Rogue* v *His Excellency the Lieutenant Governor of Jersey* Case C–171/96 [1998] ECR I–4607, para 37).

This difference in treatment between a Member State's own nationals and those of other Member States derives from a principle of international law which precludes a Member State from refusing its own nationals the right to enter its territory and remain there for any reason, and which the Treaty cannot be assumed to disregard in the context of relations between Member States (*Van Duyn*, cited above, para 22, and *Pereira Roque*, cited above, para 38).

For the same reasons, such a difference in treatment in favour of nationals of the host Member State cannot be considered to be incompatible with art 44(3) of the Association Agreement.

There is also the question whether, in a situation such as that of Mr and Mrs Gloszczuk, the requirement to submit a new establishment application in due and proper form in the Polish national's State of origin or, as the case may be, in another country is compatible with art 44(3) of the Association Agreement and with the condition set out at the end of the first sentence of art 58(1), read together.

The making of false representations

breaches the obligation to declare one's intentions honestly. As indicated in para 71 above, that obligation is incumbent on any person applying to become established in the host Member State and compliance with it is necessary to enable the competent national authorities to check that the activity in which the Polish national intends to engage in that State in a self-employed capacity will be exclusive and viable. In view of the seriousness of its breach, the requirement that a new application to become established be submitted by that national in due and proper form in his State of origin or, as the case may be, in another country, which may be laid down by the immigration legislation of the host Member State, cannot be regarded as being unjustified.

On the same grounds as those indicated in paras 68 to 77 above, the interpretation of the Association Agreement advocated by Mr and Mrs Gloszczuk, which would allow any illegalities to be regularised in consideration of the fact that the substantive conditions governing establishment imposed by the immigration legislation of the host Member State would then be satisfied, would compromise the effectiveness and reliability of the national system of prior control.

However, even in a situation such as that prevailing in the present case, due regard for the condition set out at the end of the first sentence of art 58(1) of the Association Agreement must mean that the actions of the competent authorities of the host Member State should have neither the purpose nor the effect of striking at the very substance of the rights of entry, residence and establishment which the Association Agreement grants to Polish nationals.

It follows that the decision by the competent authorities of the host Member State to reject an application for establishment submitted by a Polish national on the basis of art 44(3) of the Association Agreement, because of false representations made to them for the purpose of obtaining initial leave to enter or the failure to comply with a condition attaching to the granting of that leave to enter or leave to stay, and the requirement that he submit, in due and proper form, a new application for establishment on the basis of that Agreement by applying for an entry visa to the competent authorities in his State of origin or, as the case may be, in another country, can never have the effect of preventing that national from having his situation reviewed at a later time when he submits that new application. Moreover, such measures must be adopted without prejudice to the obligation to respect that national's fundamental rights, such as the right to respect for his family life and the right to respect for his property, which follow, for the Member State concerned, from the European Convention for the Protection of Human Rights and Fundamental Freedoms of 4 November 1950 or from other international instruments to which that State may have acceded.'

Comment

In each of the above three cases the reasoning of the ECJ is identical. First, the ECJ confirmed that the principle of non-discrimination under the Association Agreements is directly effective and therefore can be relied on by an individual before a national court of the Member State concerned. However, its interpretation under the Association Agreements is different from that under art 43 EC, taking into account the fact that the purpose of an Association Agreement is to create an appropriate framework for an Associated State's gradual integration into the EU, whilst the main objective of art 43 EC is to create an internal market. Consequently, a Member State is allowed to apply its national rules regarding entry, stay and establishment in the context of an Association Agreement, providing that such rules do not nullify or impair the benefits accruing to the nationals of an Associated State. Second, the ECJ examined the compatibility of UK immigration legislation with the requirements of the above Association Agreements. In this respect the ECJ established the following principles.

1. A host Member State is entitled to set up

a system of prior control as to the exact nature of the activity intended by a national of an Associated State, in particular to ensure that the applicant wishing to establish himself in a host Member State shows that he genuinely intends to take up an activity as a self-employed person without at the same time entering employment or having recourse to public funds, and that he possesses, from the outset, sufficient financial resources and has reasonable chances of success.

2. A host Member State is entitled to refuse a request for leave to reside for purposes of establishment in respect of nationals of Associated States who make false representations when they apply for an entry visa or fail to comply with conditions attaching to the granting of that visa. Therefore the requirement to submit a new establishment application in due and proper form in a State of origin or in another State is justified, provided that this does not prevent them from having their situation reviewed at a later date.

The legal nature of the European Union

EC Commission v EC Council (Re the European Road Transport Agreement) Case 22/70 [1971] ECR 263; [1971] CMLR 335 European Court of Justice

• *Legal personality of the EC – external relations – capacity of the EC to conclude agreements with third countries – implied powers of the EC – action for annulment under art 173 EC Treaty [art 230 EC] – reviewable acts under art 173 EC Treaty [art 230 EC] – common transport policy – distribution of powers amongst institutions*

Facts
In 1962 five of the original Member States of the Community entered into an international agreement (AETR) with several non-Community states designed to establish a legal regime for the organisation of road transportation throughout Europe.

Prior to the entry into force of the agreement, the European Commission drafted proposals for the implementation of the Community transport policy, as required by art 75 of the EC Treaty [art 71 EC]. These proposals were enacted by the Council of Ministers as Council Regulation 543/69 (1969).

At a meeting in March 1970, the Council of Ministers discussed the shape of Community policy for imminent negotiations for the revision of the AETR, due to be held in April 1970. A common position was agreed in the Council, and subsequent negotiations were to be conducted in the light of the general policy framework.

The Commission took the view that the discussions held in the Council encroached upon its area of responsibility. The Commission brought an action in the Court of Justice of the European Communities (ECJ) to annul the Council proceedings on the grounds that the Member States no longer exercised the capacity to enter into negotiations for international agreements in matters which fell within the scope of the Community Treaties.

Held
The ECJ held that, if a particular subject matter falls within the scope of the Community Treaties, Member States can no longer exercise the capacity to conduct negotiations on any subject which would interfere with the formulation of policy. The Court defined the competence of the Community by reference to the general principles of the EC Treaty. Member States therefore, no longer possess the right, acting individually or collectively, to enter international obligations with third countries which would affect the proper exercise of the functions assigned to

the Community acting through the European Commission. In relation to the substance of the dispute, the ECJ held that the AETR agreement had been in the process of negotiation since 1962, a considerable time before the issue of Regulation 543/69. Despite the Commission's claim that the Council had infringed art 75 EC Treaty [art 71 EC], the Commission had in fact made no attempt to make any submission to the Council under art 75(1)(c) EC Treaty [art 71(1)(c) EC] nor did the Commission make any application to the Council in pursuance of its right to carry out these negotiations under art 228(1) EC Treaty [art 300(1) EC]. In the light of the above and the fact that a shift in the negotiating power may have jeopardised the successful outcome of the negotiations, the ECJ dismissed the application.

Judgment

'[*Implied powers*]
In the absence of specific provisions of the Treaty relating to the negotiation and conclusion of international agreements in the sphere of transport policy – a category into which the AETR falls by its very nature – one must turn to the general system of Community law in the sphere of relations with third countries.

Article 210 provides that: "The Community shall have legal personality".

This provision, placed at the head of Part Six of the Treaty, devoted to "General and Final Provisions", means that in its external relations the Community enjoys the capacity to establish contractual links with third countries over the whole field of objectives defined in Part One of the Treaty, which Part Six supplements.

To determine in a particular case the Community's authority to enter into international agreements, regard must be had to the whole scheme of the Treaty no less than to its substantive provisions.

Such authority arises not only from an express conferment by the Treaty – as is the case with arts 113 and 114 for tariff and trade agreements and with art 238 for asso-

ciations agreements – but may equally flow from other provisions of the Treaty and from measures adopted, within the framework of those provisions, by the Community institutions.

In particular, each time the Community, with a view to implementing a common policy envisaged by the Treaty, adopts provisions laying down common rules, whatever form these may take, the Member States no longer have the right, acting individually or even collectively, to undertake obligations with third countries which affect those rules.

As and when such common rules come into being, the Community alone is in a position to assume and carry out contractual obligations towards third countries affecting the whole sphere of application of the Community legal system.

With regard to the implementation of the provisions of the Treaty the system of internal Community measures may not therefore be separated from that of external relations.

Under art 5, the Member States are required on the one hand to take all appropriate measures to ensure fulfilment of the obligations arising out of the Treaty or resulting from action taken by the institutions and, on the other hand, to abstain from any measure which might jeopardise the attainment of the objectives of the Treaty.

If these two provisions are read in conjunction, it follows that to the extent to which Community rules are promulgated for the attainment of the objectives of the Treaty, the Member States cannot, outside the framework of the Community institutions, assume obligations which might affect those rules or alter their scope.

According to art 74, the objectives of the Treaty in matters of transport are to be pursued within the framework of a common policy.

With this view, art 75(1) directs the Council to lay down common rules and, in addition, "any appropriate provisions".

By the terms of subparagraph (a) of the same provision, those common rules are applicable "to international transport to or from the territory of a Member State or passing across the territory of one or more Member States".

This provision is equally concerned with transport from or to third countries, as regards that part of the journey which takes place on Community territory.

It thus assumes that the powers of the Community extend to relationships arising from international law, and hence involve the need in the sphere in question for agreements with the third countries concerned.

Although it is true that arts 74 and 75 do not expressly confer on the Community authority to enter into international agreements, nevertheless the bringing into force, on 25 March 1969, of Regulation No 543/69 of the Council on the harmonisation of certain social legislation relating to road transport (OJ L77 p49) necessarily vested in the Community power to enter into any agreements with third countries relating to the subject matter governed by that regulation.

The grant of power is moreover expressly recognized by art 3 of the said regulation which prescribes that: "The Community shall enter into any negotiations with third countries which may prove necessary for the purpose of implementing this regulation".

Since the subject matter of the AETR falls within the scope of Regulation No 543/69, the Community has been empowered to negotiate and conclude the agreement in question since the entry into force of the said Regulation.

These Community powers exclude the possibility of concurrent powers on the part of Member States, since any steps taken outside the framework of the Community institutions would be incompatible with the unity of the Common Market and the uniform application of Community law.

[Reviewable act]
The Council considers that the proceedings of 20 March 1970 do not constitute an act, within the meaning of the first sentence of the first paragraph of art 173, the legality of which is open to review.

Neither by their form nor by their subject matter or content, it is argued were these

proceedings a regulation, a decision or a directive within the meaning of art 189 ...

... Under art 173, the Court has a duty to review the legality "of acts of the Council ... other than recommendations or opinions".

Since the only matters excluded from the scope of the action for annulment open to the Member States and the institutions are "recommendations or opinions" – which by the final paragraph of art 189 are declared to have no binding force – art 173 treats as acts open to review by the Court all measures adopted by the institutions which are intended to have legal force.

... An action for annulment must therefore be available in the case of all measures adopted by the institutions, whatever their nature or form, which are intended to have legal effects ...

... It thus seems that in so far as they [Council's proceedings] concerned the objective of the negotiations as defined by the Council, proceedings of 20 March 1970 could not have been simply the expression or the recognition of a voluntary co-ordination, but were designed to lay down a course of action binding on both the institutions and the Member States, and destined ultimately to be reflected in the tenor of the regulation.

In the part of its conclusions relating to the negotiating procedure, the Council adopted provisions which were capable of derogating in certain circumstances from the procedure laid down by the Treaty regarding negotiations with third countries and the conclusion of agreements.

Hence, the proceedings of 20 March 1970 had definite legal effects both on relations between the Community and the Member States and on the relationship between institutions.'

Comment

In this case the Court not only settled the first dispute brought by the Commission against the Council but also adopted a radical approach towards the expansion of Community competence by establishing important general principles in this area, first, on the attribution of powers to the EC and, second, on their exclusive nature. With regard to attributed powers, the ECJ stated that in order to determine in a particular case the Community competence to enter into international agreements 'regard must be had to the whole scheme of the Treaty no less than its substantive provisions'. The ECJ endorsed the doctrine of parallelism under which the external competence is not limited to express provisions of the Treaty but may also derive from other provisions of the Treaty and from internal measures adopted within the framework of those provisions.

On the exclusive nature of Community powers the ECJ stated that where the Community has adopted Community rules within the framework of a common policy, the Member States are not allowed, individually or collectively, to enter into agreements with third States in the areas affected by those rules.

In the present case the ECJ considerably extended the category of reviewable acts under art 173 EC Treaty [art 230 EC]. The Court held that any act which has binding legal effect, irrespective of its form and nature, may be challenged under art 173 EC Treaty [art 230 EC].

Re ILO Convention 170 on Chemicals at Work Opinion 2/91 [1993] 3 CMLR 800 European Court of Justice

• *Compatibility of an international treaty with the EC Treaty – Community external competence – treaty-making powers of the EC – extension to all areas where there are common policies or positive measures – joint action   minimum standards – art 118a EC Treaty [art 138 EC]*

Facts
All the members of the European Community are members of the International Labour Organisation. The Community is not a full member of this organisation in its own right. An international convention on safety in the use of chemicals at work was negotiated within the ILO.

Since competence for matters covered by the Convention was spread among the Member States and the EC/EU, the European Commission requested an opinion from the ECJ as to whether the EC/EU had status to adhere to the Convention. This question goes to the heart of the nature of the competence conferred on the EC.

Held
The treaty-making powers of the Community operated in all spheres falling inside a 'common policy' and also in those areas where there were positive measures enacted by the Community. Where competence was shared between the Member States, on the one hand, and the Community on the other, the Community's approval was required. Hence, the negotiation and conclusion of an international agreement in such areas required joint action on the part of the Community and the Member States.

Judgment
'... Convention 170 concerns safety in the use of chemicals at work. According to the preamble, its essential objective is to prevent or reduce the incidence of chemically induced illnesses and injuries at work by ensuring that all chemicals are evaluated to determine their hazards, by providing employers and workers with the information necessary for their protection, and finally, by establishing principles for protective programmes.

The field covered by Convention 170 falls within the "social provisions" of the [EC] Treaty which constitute Chapter 1 of Title III on social policy.

Under art 118a [EC], Member States are required to pay particular attention to encouraging improvements, as regards the health and safety of workers, and to set as their objective the harmonisation of conditions in this area, while maintaining the improvements made. In order to help achieve this objective, the Council has the power to adopt minimum requirements by means of directives. It follows from art 118a(3) [EC] Treaty that the provisions adopted pursuant to that article are not to prevent any Member State from maintaining or introducing more stringent measures for the protection of working conditions compatible with the Treaty.

The Community thus enjoys an internal legislative competence in the area of social policy. Consequently, Convention 170, whose subject matter coincides, moreover, with that of several directives adopted under art 118a [EC], falls within the Community's area of competence.

For the purpose of determining whether this competence is exclusive in nature, it should be pointed out that the provisions of Convention 170 are not of such a kind as to affect rules adopted pursuant to art 118a [EC]. If, on the one hand, the Community decides to adopt rules which are less stringent than those set out in an ILO convention, Member States may, in accordance with art 118a(3), adopt more stringent measures for the protection of working conditions or apply for that purpose the provisions of the relevant ILO convention. If, on the other hand, the Community decides to adopt more stringent measures than those provided for under an ILO convention, there is nothing to prevent the full application of Community law by the Member States under art 19(8) of the ILO Constitution, which allows Members to adopt more stringent measures than those provided for in conventions or recommendations adopted by that organisation.

The Commission notes, however, that it is sometimes difficult to determine whether a specific measure is more favourable to workers than another. Thus, in order to avoid being in breach of the provisions of an ILO convention, Member States may be tempted not to adopt provisions better suited to the social and technological conditions which are specific to the Community. The Commission therefore takes the view, in so far as this attitude risks impairing the devel-

opment of Community law, the Community itself ought to have exclusive competence to conclude Convention 170.

That argument cannot be accepted. Difficulties, such as those referred to by the Commission, which might arise for the legislative function of the Community cannot constitute the basis for exclusive Community competence.

Nor, for the same reasons, can exclusive competence be founded on the Community provisions adopted on the basis of art 100 [EC] Treaty, such as, in particular, Council Directive 80/1107 on the protection of workers from the risks related to exposure to chemical, physical and biological agents at work and individual directives adopted pursuant to art 8 of Directive 80/1107, all of which lay down minimum requirements.

A number of directives adopted in the areas covered by Part III of Convention 170 do, however, contain rules, which are more than minimum requirements. This is the case, for instance, with regard to Council Directive 67/548 on the approximation of laws, regulations and administrative practices relating to the classification, packaging and labelling of dangerous substances adopted pursuant to art 100 [EC] and amended by, inter alia, Directive 79/831 and Directive 88/379 on the approximation of the laws, regulations and administrative provisions of the Member States relating to the classification, packaging and labelling of dangerous preparations, adopted pursuant to art 100a [EC].

Those directives contain provisions which in certain respects constitute measures conferring on workers, in their conditions of work, more extensive protection than that accorder under the provisions contained in Part III of Convention 170. This is so, in particular, in the case of the very detailed rules on labelling set out in the above-mentioned Directive 88/379.

The scope of Convention 170, however, is wider than that of the directives mentioned. The definition of chemicals (art 2(a)), for instance, is broader than that of products covered by the directives. In addition (and in contrast to the provisions contained in the directives), arts 6(3) and 7(3) of the Convention regulate the transport of chemicals.

While there is no contradiction between these provisions of the Convention and those of the directives mentioned, it must nevertheless be accepted that Part III of Convention 170 is concerned with an area which is already covered to a large extent by Community rules progressively adopted since 1967 with a view to achieving an ever greater degree of harmonisation and designed, on the one hand, to remove barriers to trade resulting from differences in legislation from one Member State to another and, on the other hand, to provide, at the same time, protection for human health and the environment.

In those circumstances, it must be considered that the commitments arising from Part III of Convention 170, falling within the area covered by the directives cited above are of such a kind as to affect the Community rules laid down in those directives and that consequently Member States cannot undertake such commitments outside the framework of the Community institutions.

… It follows from all the foregoing considerations that the conclusion of ILO Convention 170 is a matter which falls within the joint competence of the Member States and the Community.'

Comment

In the present opinion the ECJ made a distinction between common rules and minimum rules. In many areas the Community harmonisation measures are based on minimum standards with a possibility for a Member State to apply higher standards (for example in environmental matters). The ILO Convention contains minimum rules on safety in the use of chemicals at work which will not affect any national or Community legislation providing for more favourable protection of workers. Under art 118a EC Treaty [art 138 EC] the Community is entitled to adopt measures in respect of health and safety of workers. Under this provision, Member States are permitted to maintain and introduce more stringent require-

ments for the protection of working conditions than the minimum standards adopted by the Council in this area.

In relation to exclusive competence of the Community in this area the ECJ stated that Convention 170, as containing the 'minimum rules' would not affect rules adopted at the Community level. Therefore, if national rules were more stringent than both the Community measures and Convention 170, national rules prevail. This is expressly authorised by both instruments. The Commission argued that the Community should have exclusive competence in the matter for two reasons. First, that sometimes it is difficult to determine which rule is more favourable to the workers, which may prevent Member States from adopting measures under art 118a EC Treaty [art 138 EC] as being contrary to the Convention and, second, in the event that a Community rule was below the standard contained in the Convention, Member States would be in breach of Community law if they applied the Convention. The ECJ rejected those arguments and stated such difficulties cannot constitute the basis for exclusive Community competence and that, for the same reason, such a competence cannot be founded on Community rules which lay down minimum requirements.

Re Uruguay Round Agreements
Opinion 1/94 [1994] ECR I–5267
European Court of Justice

• *Exclusive competence of the EC – common commercial policy – TRIPs and GATS agreements – scope of implied external powers of the EC – duty of co-operation between Member States and the Community institutions in the area of shared competence*

Facts

The Commission requested the opinion of the ECJ under art 228(6) EC Treaty [art 300(6) EC] as to the exclusive competence of the Community to conclude a number of multilateral agreements, in particular GATS and TRIPs of the Uruguay round of negotiations conducted within the framework of the General Agreement on Tariffs and Trade (GATT).

The GATS and TRIPs agreements are modelled on GATT rules. GATS applies to trade in all services apart from services supplied in the exercise of governmental authority and regulates four forms of services, that is, cross-border supply of services, consumption abroad, commercial presence and movement of persons. As a result, it covers not only supply of services but also establishment of the supply of services. The TRIPs agreement encompasses all intellectual property rights. The Commission asked the following questions:

1. whether the EC has exclusive competence to conclude Multilateral Agreements on Trade in Goods, in so far as those Agreements covered products under the ESCS and Euratom Treaties;
2. whether the EC has exclusive competence under art 113 EC Treaty [art 133 EC] or alternatively under other provisions of EC Treaty, to conclude the General Agreement on Trade in Services (GATS) and the Agreement on Trade-related Aspects of Intellectual Property Rights (TRIPs) within the framework of the GATT agreements.

Held

The ECJ held that the EC had exclusive competence under art 113 EC Treaty [art 133 EC] to conclude Multilateral Agreements on Trade in Goods, including the Agreement on Agriculture and goods subject of the Euratom and ESCS Treaties. In relation to the Multilateral Agreements on Trade in Goods (the Tokyo Round Agreement on Technical Barriers to Trade was concluded jointly by the EEC and the Member States), the ECJ confirmed the exclusive competence of the EC in this area. On trade in ESCS and Euratom products with third countries the ECJ restated its previous position that this is covered under art

113 [art 133 EC] and as such is within the exclusive competence of the EC, apart from agreements relating specifically to ESCS products.

The ECJ held that many areas were excluded from the scope of art 113 EC Treaty [art 133 EC]: international transport; all services except the cross-frontier supplies of services; the TRIPs agreement apart from its provisions regarding the prohibition of the release into free circulation of counterfeit goods already governed by Regulation 3842/86. The Court stated that competence to conclude GATS and TRIPs is shared between the EC and the Member States.

Judgment

'[*Article 113 of the EC Treaty, GATS and TRIPs*]

Relying essentially on the non-restrictive interpretation applied by the Court's case law to the concept of the common commercial policy (see Opinion 1/78, paragraphs 44 and 45), the links or overlap between goods and services, the purpose of GATS and the instruments used, the Commission concludes that services fall within the common commercial policy, without any need to distinguish between the different modes of supply of services and, in particular, between the direct, cross-frontier supply of services and the supply of services through a commercial presence in the country of the person to whom they are supplied. The Commission also maintains that international agreements of a commercial nature in relation to transport (as opposed to those relating to safety rules) fall within the common commercial policy and not within the particular title of the Treaty on the common transport policy.

It is appropriate to consider, first, services other than transport and, subsequently, the particular services comprised in transport.

As regards the first category, it should be recalled at the outset that in Opinion 1/75 the Court, which had been asked to rule on the scope of Community competence as to the arrangements relating to a local cost standard, held that "the field of the common commercial policy, and more particularly that of export policy, necessarily covers systems of aid for exports and more particularly measures concerning credits for the financing of local costs linked to export operations" ([1975] ECR 1362). The local costs in question concerned expenses incurred for the supply of both goods and services. Nevertheless, the Court recognized the exclusive competence of the Community, without drawing a distinction between goods and services.

In its Opinion 1/78 (para 44), the Court rejected an interpretation of art 113 "the effect of which would be to restrict the common commercial policy to the use of instruments intended to have an effect only on the traditional aspects of external trade". On the contrary, it considered that "the question of external trade must be governed from a wide point of view", as is confirmed by "the fact that the enumeration in art 113 of the subjects covered by commercial policy ... is conceived as a non-exhaustive enumeration" (Opinion 1/78, para 45).

The Commission points out in its request for an opinion that in certain developed countries the services sector has become the dominant sector of the economy and that the global economy has been undergoing fundamental structural changes. The trend is for basic industry to be transferred to developing countries, whilst the developed economies have tended to become, in the main, exporters of services and of goods with a high value-added content. The Court notes that this trend is borne out by the WTO Agreement and its annexes, which were the subject of a single process of negotiation covering both goods and services.

Having regard to this trend in international trade, it follows from the open nature of the common commercial policy, within the meaning of the Treaty, that trade in services cannot immediately, and as a matter of principle, be excluded from the scope of art 113, as some of the governments which have submitted observations contend.

In order to make that conclusion more specific, however, one must take into account the definition of trade in services given in GATS in order to see whether the overall scheme of the Treaty is not such as to limit the extent to which trade in services can be included within art 113.

Under art 1(2) of GATS, trade in services is defined, for the purposes of that Agreement, as comprising four modes of services: (1) cross-frontier supplies not involving any movement of persons; (2) consumption abroad, which entails the movement of the consumer into the territory of the WTO member country in which the supplier is established; (3) commercial presence, ie the presence of a subsidiary or branch in the territory of the WTO member country in which the service is rendered; (4) the presence of natural persons from a WTO member country, enabling a supplier from one member country to supply services within the territory of any other member country.

As regards cross-frontier supplies, the service is rendered by a supplier established in one country to a consumer residing in another. The supplier does not move to the consumer country; nor, conversely, does the consumer move to the supplier's county. This situation is, therefore, not unlike trade in goods, which is unquestionably covered by the common commercial policy within the meaning of the Treaty. There is thus no particular reason why such a supply should not fall within the concept of the common commercial policy.

The same cannot be said of the other three modes of supply of services covered by GATS, namely, consumption abroad, commercial presence and the presence of natural persons.

As regards natural persons, it is clear from art 3 of the Treaty, which distinguishes between "a common commercial policy" in para (b) and "measures concerning the entry and movement of persons" in para (d), that the treatment of nationals of non-Member countries on crossing the external frontiers of Member States cannot be regarded as falling within the common commercial policy. More generally, the existence in the Treaty of specific chapters on the free movement of natural and legal persons shows that those matters do not fall within the common commercial policy.

It follows that the modes of supply of services referred to by GATS as "consumption abroad", "commercial presence" and the "presence of natural persons" are not covered by the common commercial policy.

Turning next to the particular services comprised in transport, these are the subject of a specific title (Title IV) of the Treaty, distinct from Title VII on the common commercial policy. It was precisely in relation to transport policy that the Court held for the first time that the competence of the Community to conclude international agreements "arises not only from an express conferment by the Treaty – as is the case with arts 113 and 114 for tariff and trade agreements and with art 238 for association agreements – but may equally flow from other provisions of the Treaty and from measures adopted, within the framework of those provisions, by the Community institutions" (Case 22/70 *EC Commission* v *EC Council (Re ERTA)* [[1971] ECR 263], para 16, the "AETR judgment"). The idea underlying that decision is that international agreements in transport matters are not covered by art 113.

The scope of the AETR judgment cannot be cut down by drawing a distinction between agreements on safety rules, such as those relating to the length of driving periods of professional drivers, with which the AETR judgment was concerned, and agreements of a commercial nature.

The AETR judgment draws no such distinction. The Court confirmed that analysis in Opinion 1/76 concerning an agreement intended to rationalise the economic situation in the inland waterways sector – in other words, an economic agreement not concerned with the laying down of safety rules. Moreover, numerous agreements have been concluded with non-Member countries on the basis of the Transport Title; a long list of such agreements was given by the United Kingdom in its observations.

In support of its view the Commission has further cited a series of embargoes based on

art 113 and involving the suspension of transport services: Measures against Iraq: Council Regulation 2340/90 preventing trade by the Community as regards Iraq and Kuwait, Council Regulation 3155/90 extending and amending Regulation 2340/90 preventing trade by the Community as regards Iraq and Kuwait, and Council Regulation 1194/91 amending Regulations 2340/90 and 3155/90 preventing trade by the Community as regards Iraq and Kuwait; measures against the Federal Republic of Yugoslavia (Serbia and Montenegro); measures against Haiti: Council Regulation 1608/93 introducing an embargo concerning certain trade between the European Economic Community and Haiti. Those precedents are not conclusive. As the European Parliament has rightly observed, since the embargoes related primarily to the export and import of products, they could not have been effective if it had not been decided at the same time to suspend transport services. Such suspension is to be seen as a necessary adjunct to the principal measure. Consequently, the precedents are not relevant to the question whether the Community has exclusive competence pursuant to art 113 to conclude international agreements in the field of transport.

In any event, the Court has consistently held that a mere practice of the Council cannot derogate from the rules laid down in the Treaty and cannot, therefore, create a precedent binding on Community institutions with regard to the correct legal basis (see Case 68/86 *United Kingdom* v *EC Council (Re Hormones)* [[1988] ECR 855], para 24).

It follows that only cross-frontier suppliers are covered by art 113 of the Treaty and that international agreements in the field of transport are excluded from it.

[TRIPs]

The Commission's argument in support of its contention that the Community has exclusive competence under art 113 is essentially that the rules concerning intellectual property rights are closely linked to trade in the products and services to which they apply.

It should be noted, first, that s4 of Part III of TRIP's, which concerns the means of enforcement of intellectual property rights, contains specific rules as to measures to be applied at border crossing points. As the United Kingdom has pointed out, that section has its counterpart in the provisions of Council Regulation (EEC) No 3842/86 laying down measures to prohibit the release for free circulation of counterfeit goods. Inasmuch as that regulation concerns the prohibition of the release into free circulation of counterfeit goods, it was rightly based on art 113 of the Treaty: it relates to measures to be taken by the customs authorities at the external frontiers of the Community. Since measures of that type can be adopted autonomously by the Community institutions on the basis of art 113 of the EC Treaty, it is for the Community alone to conclude international agreements on such matters.

However, as regards matters other than the provisions of TRIPs on the release into free circulation of counterfeit goods, the Commission's arguments cannot be accepted.

Admittedly, there is a connection between intellectual property and trade in goods. Intellectual property rights enable those holding them to prevent third parties from carrying out certain acts. The power to prohibit the use of a trade mark, the manufacture of a product, the copying of a design or the reproduction of a book, a disc or a video-cassette inevitably has effect on trade. Intellectual property rights are moreover specifically designed to produce such effects. That is not enough to bring them within the scope of art 113. Intellectual property rights do not relate specifically to international trade; they affect internal trade as much as, if not more than, international trade.

As the French government has rightly observed, the primary objective of TRIPs is to strengthen and harmonise the protection of intellectual property on a word-wide scale. The Commission has itself conceded that, since TRIPs lays down rules in fields in which there are no Community harmonisa-

tion measures, its conclusion would make it possible at the same time to achieve harmonisation within the Community and thereby to contribute to the establishment and functioning of the Common Market.

It should be noted here that, at the level of internal legislation, the Community is competent, in the field of intellectual property, to harmonise national laws pursuant to art 100 and may use art 235 as the basis for creating new rights superimposed on national rights, as it did in Council Regulation (EC) No 40/94 on the Community trade mark. Those measures are subject to voting rules (unanimity in the case of art 100 and 235) or rules of procedure (consultation of the Parliament in the case of arts 100 and 235, the joint decision-making procedure in the case of art 100a) which are different from those applicable under art 113.

If the Community were to be recognised as having exclusive competence to enter into agreements with non-member countries to harmonise the protection of intellectual property and, at the same time, to achieve harmonization at Community level, the Community institutions would be able to escape the internal constraints to which they are subject in relation to procedures and rules as to voting.

Institutional practices in relation to autonomous measures or external agreements adopted on the basis of art 113 cannot alter this conclusion.

... it must be held that, apart from those of its provisions which concern the prohibition of the release into free circulation of counterfeit goods, TRIPs does not fall within the scope of the common commercial policy.

[The Community's implied external powers, GATS and TRIPs]
In the event of the Court rejecting its main contention that the Community has exclusive competence pursuant to art 113, the Commission maintains in the alternative that the Community's exclusive competence to conclude GATS and TRIPs flows implicitly from the provisions of the Treaty establishing its internal competence, or else from the need to enter into international commit-

ments with a view to achieving an internal Community objective. The Commission also argues that, even if the Community does not have adequate powers on the basis of specific provisions of the Treaty or legislative acts of the institutions, it has exclusive competence by virtue of arts 100a and 235 of the Treaty. The Council and the Member States which have submitted observations acknowledge that the Community has certain powers, but deny that they are exclusive.

[*GATS*]

With particular regard to GATS, the Commission cites three possible sources for exclusive external competence on the part of the Community: the powers conferred on the Community institutions by the Treaty at internal level, the need to conclude the agreement in order to achieve a Community objective, and, lastly, arts 100a and 235.

The Commission argues, first, that there is no area or specific provision in GATS in respect of which the Community does not have corresponding powers to adopt measures at internal level. According to the Commission, those powers are set out in the chapter on the right of establishment, freedom to provide services and transport. Exclusive external competence flows from those internal powers.

This argument must be rejected.

It was on the basis of art 75(1)(a) which, as regards that part of a journey which takes place on Community territory, also concerns transport from or to non-Member countries, that the Court held in the AETR judgment (at para 27), that "the powers of the Community extend to relationships arising from international law, and hence involve the need in the sphere in question for agreements with the third countries concerned".

However, even in the field of transport, The Community's exclusive external competence does not automatically flow from its power to lay down rules at internal level. As the Court pointed out in the AETR judgment (paras 17 and 18), the Member States, whether acting individually or collectively, only lose their right to assume obligations with non-Member countries as and when

common rules which could be affected by those obligations come into being. Only insofar as common rules have been established at internal level does the external competence of the Community become exclusive. However, not all transport matters are already covered by common rules.

... Unlike the chapter on transport, the chapters on the right of establishment and on freedom to provide services do not contain any provision expressly extending the competence of the Community to "relationships arising from international law". As has rightly been observed by the Council and most of the Member States which have submitted observations, the sole objective of those chapters is to secure the right of establishment and freedom to provide services for nationals of Member States. They contain no provisions on the problem of the first establishment of nationals of non-member countries and the rules governing their access to self-employed activities. One cannot therefore infer from those chapters that the Community has exclusive competence to conclude an agreement with non-member countries to liberalise the subject of cross-border supplies within the meaning of GATS, which are covered by art 113.

Referring to Opinion 1/76 (paras 3 and 4), the Commission submits, second, that the Community's exclusive external competence is not confined to cases in which use has already been made of internal powers to adopt measures for the attainment of common policies. Whenever Community law has conferred on the institutions internal powers for the purposes of attaining specific objectives, the international competence of the Community implicitly flows, according to the Com-mission, from those provisions. It is enough that the Community's participation in the international agreement is necessary for the attainment of one of the objectives of the Community.

The Commission puts forward here both internal and external reasons to justify participation by the Community, and by the Community alone, in the conclusion of GATS and TRIPs. At internal level, the

Commission maintains that, without such participation, the coherence of the internal market would be impaired. At external level, The European Community cannot allow itself to remain inactive on the international stage: the need for the conclusion of the WTO Agreement and its annexes, reflecting a global approach to international trade (embracing goods, services and intellectual property), is not in dispute.

That application of Opinion 1/76 to GATS cannot be accepted.

Opinion 1/76 related to an issue different from that arising from GATS. It concerned rationalisation of the economic situation in the inland waterways sector in the Rhine and Moselle basins, and throughout all The Netherlands inland waterways and the German inland waterways linked to the Rhine basin, by elimination of short-term over-capacity. It was not possible to achieve that objective by the establishment of autonomous common rules, because of the traditional participation of vessels from Switzerland in navigation on the waterways in question. It was necessary, therefore, to bring Switzerland into the scheme envisaged by means of an international agreement (see Opinion 1/76, para 2). Similarly, in the context of conservation of the resources of the seas, the restriction, by means of internal legislative measures, of fishing on the high seas by vessels flying the flag of a Member State would hardly be effective if the same restrictions were not to apply to vessels flying the flag of a non-member country bordering on the same seas. It is understandable, therefore, that external powers may be exercised, and thus become exclusive, without any internal legislation having first been adopted.

That is not the situation in the sphere of services: attainment of freedom of establishment and freedom to provide services for nationals of the Member States is not inextricably linked to the treatment to be afforded in the Community to nationals of non-Member countries or in non-member countries to nationals of Member States of the Community.

Third, the Commission refers to arts 100a and 235 of the Treaty as the basis of exclusive external competence.

As regards art 100a, it is undeniable that, where harmonising powers have been exercised, the harmonisation measures thus adopted may limit, or even remove, the freedom of the Member States to negotiate with non-member countries. However, an internal power to harmonise which has not been exercised in a specific field cannot confer exclusive competence in the field on the Community.

Article 235, which enables the Community to cope with any insufficiency in the powers conferred on it, expressly or by implication, for the achievement of its objectives, cannot in itself vest exclusive competence in the Community at international level. Save where internal powers can only be effectively exercised at the same time as external powers (see Opinion 1/76 and para 85 above) internal competence can give rise to exclusive external competence only if it is exercised. This applies a fortiori to art 235.

… It follows that competence to conclude GATS is shared between the Community and the Member States.

[TRIPs]

In support of its claim that the Community has exclusive competence to conclude TRIPs, the Commission relies on the existence of legislative acts of the institutions which could be affected within the meaning of the AETR judgment if the Member States were jointly to participate in its conclusion, and, as with GATS, on the need for the Community to participate in the agreement in order to achieve one of the objectives set out in the Treaty (the "Opinion 1/76 doctrine"), as well as on arts 100a and 235.

The relevance of the reference to Opinion 1/76 is as just disputable in the case of TRIPs as in the case of GATS: unification or harmonisation of intellectual property rights in the Community context does not necessarily have to be accompanied by agreements with non-Member countries in order to be effective.

Moreover, arts 100a and 245 of the Treaty

cannot in themselves confer exclusive competence on the Community, as stated above.

It only remains, therefore, to consider whether the subordinate legislative acts adopted in the Community context could be affected within the meaning of the AETR judgment if the Member States were to participate in the conclusion of TRIPs, as the Commission maintains.

Suffice it to say on that point that the harmonisation achieved within the Community in certain areas covered by TRIPs is only partial and that, in other areas, no harmonisation has been envisaged. There has been only partial harmonisation as regards trade marks, for example: it is apparent from the third recital in the preamble to the First Council Directive 89/104 to approximate the laws of the Member States relating to trade marks that it is confined to the approximation of national laws "which most directly affect the functioning of the internal market". In other areas covered by TRIPs, no Community harmonisation measures have been adopted. That is the position as regards the protection of undisclosed technical information, as regards industrial designs, in respect of which proposals have merely been submitted, and as regards patents. With regard to patents, the only acts referred to by the Commission are conventions which are intergovernmental in origin, and not Community acts: the Munich Convention of 5 October 1973 on the Grant of European Patents and the Luxembourg Agreement of 15 December 1989 relating to Community Patents, which has not yet, however, entered into force.

Some of the governments which have submitted observations have argued that the provisions of TRIPs relating to measures to be adopted to secure the effective protection of intellectual property rights, such as those ensuring a fair and just procedure, the rules regarding the submission of evidence, the right to be heard, the giving of reasons for decision, the right of appeal, interim measures and the award of damages, fall within the competence of the Member States. If that argument is to be understood as meaning that all those matters are within

some sort of domain reserved to the Member States, it cannot be accepted. The Commission is certainly competent to harmonise national rules on those matters, insofar as, in the words of art 100 of the Treaty, they "directly affect the establishment or functioning of the Community Market". But the fact remains that the Community institutions have not hitherto exercised their powers in the field of the "enforcement of intellectual property rights", except in Regulation No 3842/86 (para 55) laying down measures to prohibit the release for free circulation of counterfeit goods.

It follows that the Community and its Member States are jointly competent to conclude TRIPs.

[*The duty of co-operation between the Member States and the Community institutions*]
… it must be stressed, first, that any problems which may arise in implementation of the WTO Agreement and its annexes as regards the co-ordination necessary to ensure unity of action where the Community and the Member States participate jointly cannot modify the answer to the question of competence, that being a prior issue. As the Council has pointed out, resolution of the issue of the allocation of competence cannot depend on problems which may possibly arise in administration of the agreements.

Next, where it is apparent that the subject matter of an agreement or convention falls in part within the competence of the Community and in part within that of the Member States, it is essential to ensure close co-operation between the Member States and the Community institutions, both in the process of negotiation and conclusion and in the fulfilment of the commitments entered into. That obligation to co-operate flows from the requirement of unity in the international representation of the Community (Ruling 1/78, paras 34 to 36, and Opinion 2/99, para 36).'

Comment

The distinction between exclusive external

competence of the Community and competence which it shares with the Member States is very important. If the external competence is exclusive, Member States are prevented from acting unilaterally or collectively in this area. They are confined to the processes available within the Community institutional system in relation to the adoption of external measures. Exclusive competence of the Community may be based on express EC Treaty provisions conferring upon the Community external powers (for example art 133 EC in relation to the common commercial policy), and on express provisions in internal measures (regulations, directives, etc). It may also be implied from internal provisions adopted by Community institutions, and finally it may be implied if, taking into account particular circumstances, internal powers can only be effectively exercised at the same time as external powers. In particular, the last-mentioned possibility has been examined by the ECJ in the present opinion.

In respect of implied exclusive external competence the Court stated that such a competence did not automatically flow from the Community's internal power. Such competence results only when there are common rules which could be affected by continued Member State external competence. The external competence of the Community becomes exclusive without internal legislation where the conclusion of an international agreement is necessary to achieve Treaty objectives which cannot be achieved by internal rules, that is, without third part participation. However, until the competence is exercised, the Member States may enter into international agreements.

2 The Institutions of the European Union

The Commission

Connolly v EC Commission Case C–274/99 [2001] 3 CMLR 58 European Court of Justice

• *Staff of the European Communities – duties and responsibilities – the protection of the rights of EC institutions – the European Convention on Human Rights – the individual's right to freedom of expression – breach of mutual trust between the employee and the employer*

Facts

Mr Connolly was an employee of the European Commission, a high-ranking Community official in charge of a unit in the Directorate for Monetary Affairs. When he was on leave on personal grounds he published (in June 1995) a book entitled *The Rotten Heart of Europe: The Dirty War for Europe's Money* in which he severely criticised the working of the EC in general, and ridiculed and undermined the creation of economic and monetary union.

When he returned to work in October 1995 disciplinary proceedings were brought against him for infringement of his obligations under the staff regulations. The Commission argued that Mr Connolly was in breach of the regulations which require staff to obtain prior permission in respect of their publications, and that his book was particularly prejudicial to the achievement of economic and monetary union since Mr Connolly was responsible for its

implementation, and his book undermined the image and reputation of the EC.

On 16 January 1996 the Disciplinary Board removed Mr Connolly from his office. Mr Connolly brought an action before the Court of First Instance (CFI) for annulment of that decision. The CFI rejected Mr Connolly's action by two judgments dated 19 May 1999.

On 20 July 1999 Mr Connolly appealed against those judgments to the ECJ. He argued that under art 10 of the European Convention on Human Rights (ECHR) he was entitled to express his opinion and therefore had merely exercised his right to freedom of expression.

Held

The ECJ dismissed Mr Connolly's appeal and upheld the judgments of the Court of First Instance.

Judgment

'First, according to settled case law, fundamental rights form an integral part of the general principles of law, whose observance the Court ensures. For that purpose, the Court draws inspiration from the constitutional traditions common to the Member States and from the guidelines supplied by international treaties for the protection of human rights on which the Member States have collaborated or to which they are signatories. The ECHR has special significance in that respect.

Those principles have, moreover, been restated in art 6(2) of the Treaty on European Union, which provides:

"The Union shall respect fundamental rights, as guaranteed by the European

Convention for the Protection of Human Rights and Fundamental Freedoms signed in Rome on 4 November 1950 and as they result from the constitutional traditions common to the Member States, as general principles of Community law."

As the Court of Human Rights has held:

"Freedom of expression constitutes one of the essential foundations of [a democratic society], one of the basic conditions for its progress and for the development of every man. Subject to para 2 of art 10 [of the ECHR], it is applicable not only to 'information' or 'ideas' that are favourably received or regarded as inoffensive or as a matter of indifference, but also to those that offend, shock or disturb; such are the demands of that pluralism, tolerance and broadmindedness without which there is no 'democratic society'."

Freedom of expression may be subject to the limitations set out in art 10(2) of the ECHR, in terms of which the exercise of that freedom:

"... since it carries with it duties and responsibilities, may be subject to such formalities, conditions, restrictions or penalties as are prescribed by law and are necessary in a democratic society, in the interests of national security, territorial integrity or public safety, for the prevention of disorder or crime, for the protection of health or morals, for the protection of the reputation or rights of others, for preventing the disclosure of information received in confidence, or for maintaining the authority and impartiality of the judiciary."

Those limitations must, however, be interpreted restrictively. According to the Court of Human Rights, the adjective "necessary" involves, for the purposes of art 10(2), a "pressing social need" and, although "[t]he contracting States have a certain margin of appreciation in assessing whether such a need exists", the interference must be "proportionate to the legitimate aim pursued" and "the reasons adduced by the national authorities to justify it" must be "relevant and sufficient".

Furthermore, the restrictions must be prescribed by legislative provisions which are worded with sufficient precision to enable interested parties to regulate their conduct, taking, if need be, appropriate advice.

As the Court has ruled, officials and other employees of the European Communities enjoy the right of freedom of expression (see *Oyowe and Traore v EC Commission* [Case C–100/88 [1989] ECR 4285], para 16), even in areas falling within the scope of the activities of the Community institutions. That freedom extends to the expression, orally or in writing, of opinions that dissent from or conflict with those held by the employing institution.

However, it is also legitimate in a democratic society to subject public servants, on account of their status, to obligations such as those contained in arts 11 and 12 of the Staff Regulations. Such obligations are intended primarily to preserve the relationship of trust which must exist between the institution and its officials or other employees.

It is settled that the scope of those obligations must vary according to the nature of the duties performed by the person concerned or his place in the hierarchy.

In terms of art 10(2) of the ECHR, specific restrictions on the exercise of the right of freedom of expression can, in principle, be justified by the legitimate aim of protecting the rights of others. The rights at issue here are those of the institutions that are charged with the responsibility of carrying out tasks in the public interest. Citizens must be able to rely on their doing so effectively.

That is the aim of the regulations setting out the duties and responsibilities of the European public service. So an official may not, by oral or written expression, act in breach of his obligations under the regulations, particularly arts 11, 12 and 17, towards the institution that he is supposed to serve. That would destroy the relationship of trust between himself and that institution and make it thereafter more difficult, if not impossible, for the work of the institution to be carried out in cooperation with that official.

In exercising their power of review, the

Community Courts must decide, having regard to all the circumstances of the case, whether a fair balance has been struck between the individual's fundamental right to freedom of expression and the legitimate concern of the institution to ensure that its officials and agents observe the duties and responsibilities implicit in the performance of their tasks.

As the Court of Human Rights has held in that regard, it must: "[be borne in mind] that whenever civil servants' right to freedom of expression is in issue the duties and responsibilities' referred to in art 10(2) assume a special significance, which justifies leaving to the national authorities a certain margin of appreciation in determining whether the impugned interference is proportionate to the above aim" (see ECHR *Vogt* v *Germany* [(1995) 21 EHRR 205]; *Ahmed* v *United Kingdom* [(2000) 29 EHRR 1], Reports of Judgments and Decisions 1998–VI, p2378, 56; and *Wille* v *Liechtenstein* [Judgment of 28 October 1999, No 28396/95, Reports of Judgments and Decisions 1999–VII]).

The second paragraph of art 17 of the Staff Regulations must be interpreted in the light of those general considerations, as was done by the Court of First Instance in paras 148 to 155 of the contested judgment.

The second paragraph of art 17 requires permission for publication of any matter dealing with the work of the Communities. Permission may be refused only where the proposed publication is liable "to prejudice the interests of the Communities". That eventuality, referred to in a Council regulation in restrictive terms, is a matter that falls within the scope of "the protection of the rights of others", which, according to art 10(2) of the ECHR as interpreted by the Court of Human Rights, is such as to justify restricting freedom of expression. Consequently, the appellant's allegations that the second paragraph of art 17 of the Staff Regulations does not pursue a legitimate aim and that the restriction of freedom of expression is not prescribed by a legislative provision must be rejected.

The fact that the restriction at issue takes the form of prior permission cannot render it contrary, as such, to the fundamental right of freedom of expression, as the Court of First Instance held in para 152 of the contested judgment.

The second paragraph of art 17 of the Staff Regulations clearly provides that, in principle, permission is to be granted, refusal being possible only in exceptional cases. Indeed, in so far as that provision enables institutions to refuse permission to publish, and thus potentially interfere to a serious extent with freedom of expression, one of the fundamental pillars of a democratic society, it must be interpreted restrictively and applied in strict compliance with the requirements mentioned in para 41 above. Thus, permission to publish may be refused only where publication is liable to cause serious harm to the Communities' interests.

Furthermore, as their scope is restricted to publications dealing with the work of the Communities, the rules are designed solely to allow the institution to keep itself informed of the views expressed in writing by its officials or other employees about its work so as to satisfy itself that they are carrying out their duties and conducting themselves with the interests of the Communities in mind and not in a way that would adversely reflect on their position.

Remedies against a decision refusing permission are available under arts 90 and 91 of the Staff Regulations. There is thus no basis for the appellant to claim, as he does, that the rules in art 17 of the Staff Regulations are not amenable to effective judicial review. Review of that kind enables the Community Courts to ascertain whether the appointing authority has exercised its power under the second paragraph of art 17 of the Staff Regulations in strict compliance with the limitations to which any interference with the right to freedom of expression is subject.

Such rules reflect the relationship of trust which must exist between employers and employees, particularly when they discharge high-level responsibilities in the public service. The way in which the rules are applied can be assessed solely in the light of all the relevant circumstances and the implications thereof for the performance of public duties. In that respect, the rules meet the criteria set out in para 41 above for the acceptability of interference with the right to freedom of expression.

It is also clear from the foregoing that, when applying the second paragraph of art 17 of the Staff Regulations, the appointing authority must balance the various interests at stake and is in a position to do so by taking account, in particular, of the gravity of the potential prejudice to the interests of the Communities.

In the present case, the Court of First Instance found, in para 154 of the contested judgment, that:

"... the appointing authority maintained, in its decision removing the applicant from his post, that he had failed to comply with [the second paragraph of art 17 of the Staff Regulations] on the grounds that, first, he had not requested permission to publish his book, second, he could not have failed to be aware that he would be refused permission on the same grounds as those on which permission had previously been refused in respect of articles of similar content, and, finally, his conduct had seriously prejudiced the Communities' interests and damaged the institution's image and reputation."

In relation to the latter infringement, the Court of First Instance observed first, in para 125 of the contested judgment, that:

"... the book at issue contains numerous aggressive, derogatory and frequently insulting statements, which are detrimental to the honour of the persons and institutions to which they refer and which have been extremely well publicised, particularly in the press."

The Court of First Instance was thus entitled to reach the conclusion, on the basis of an assessment which cannot be challenged on appeal, that those statements constituted an infringement of art 12 of the Staff Regulations.

The Court of First Instance then referred,

in para 128 of the contested judgment, not only to Mr Connolly's high-ranking grade but also to the fact that the book at issue:

"... publicly expressed ... the applicant's fundamental opposition to the Commission's policy, which it was his responsibility to implement, namely bringing about economic and monetary union, an objective which is, moreover, laid down in the Treaty."

Finally, the Court of First Instance made it clear, in para 155 of the contested judgment, that it had not been established:

"that the finding that he had infringed the second paragraph of art 17 of the Staff Regulations would have been made even if the Communities' interests had not been prejudiced."

The foregoing observations of the Court of First Instance, based on the statement of reasons in the preamble to the contested decision (see, in particular, the fifth, sixth, ninth, tenth, twelfth and fifteenth recitals to that decision), make it clear that Mr Connolly was dismissed not merely because he had failed to apply for prior permission, contrary to the requirements of the second paragraph of art 17 of the Staff Regulations, or because he had expressed a dissentient opinion, but because he had published, without permission, material in which he had severely criticised, and even insulted, members of the Commission and other superiors and had challenged fundamental aspects of Community policies which had been written into the Treaty by the Member States and to whose implementation the Commission had specifically assigned him the responsibility of contributing in good faith. In those circumstances, he committed "an irremediable breach of the trust which the Commission is entitled to expect from its officials" and, as a result, made "it impossible for any employment relationship to be maintained with the institution" (see the fifteenth recital to the decision removing Mr Connolly from his post).

As to the measures intended to prevent distribution of the book, which, the appellant claims, the Commission should have adopted in order to protect its interests effectively, suffice it to say that the adoption of such measures would not have restored the relationship of trust between the appellant and the institution and would have made no difference to the fact that it had become impossible for him to continue to have any sort of employment relationship with the institution.

It follows that the Court of First Instance was entitled to conclude, as it did in para 156 of the contested judgment, that the allegation of breach of the right to freedom of expression, resulting from the application thereto of the second paragraph of art 17 of the Staff Regulations, was unfounded.

The first ground of appeal must therefore be rejected.'

Comment

The decision of the ECJ is not surprising. Indeed, it is difficult to envisage Mr Connolly's reinstatement to the Commission in the light of his opinions presented in the book. No employer would want him reinstated. The ECJ held that Mr Connolly destroyed the relationship of trust with his employer by publishing, without authorisation, a book which severely criticised the functioning of the EC, insulted members of the Commission and challenged fundamental aspects of Community policy, the implementation of which he was directly responsible for.

In respect of the argument submitted by Mr Connolly regarding his right to freedom of expression, the ECJ stated that fundamental rights, including freedom of expression, form an integral part of the general principles of law, whose observance the Court ensures. The right to freedom of expression is also enjoyed by officials and other servants of the European Communities even in areas falling within the scope of the work of the Community institutions. Nevertheless, this right is not unconditional. The case law of the European Court of Human Rights shows that there are limitations imposed upon freedom of expression in a democratic society. It is legitimate in a demo-

cratic society to subject public servants to obligations intended to preserve the relationship of trust between an institution and its employees. Otherwise, the work of the institution would not be possible. Therefore, the obligation to request permission before publishing any material dealing with the work of the Communities must be regarded as being within the scope of the protection of the rights of the institutions. The ECJ stated that the importance of the protection of the rights of the institutions, which are responsible for carrying out tasks in the public interest, is such as to justify (in accordance with the European Convention on Human Rights) restrictions on an individual's right to freedom of expression.

The ECJ emphasised that permission for the publication of material concerning the Communities may be refused only in exceptional cases where such publication is liable to cause serious harm to the interests of the Communities. In addition, such a decision is subject to appeal.

In determining whether or not permission is to be granted, a fair balance must be struck between the individual's right to freedom of expression and the legitimate concern of the institutions to ensure that their officials and employees observe the duties and responsibilities implicit in their work.

EC Commission v EC Council (Re Generalised System of Tariff Preferences) Case 45/86 [1987] ECR 1493 European Court of Justice

• *Absence of a precise legal basis – measures based on a twin legal basis – single legal basis sufficient – arts 113 and 235 EC Treaty [arts 133 and 308 EC] – objective factors – common commercial policy – Community system of generalised tariffs*

Facts

The Commission challenged the legality of two Council regulations dealing with the issue of tariff preferences for products from third world countries on the ground that they were adopted without their legal basis being expressly stated as required by art 190 EC Treaty [art 254 EC]. In addition, the fact that the Council had resorted to unanimous voting in relation to the adoption of the measures implied that art 235 EC Treaty [art 308 EC] was the legal basis the Council had in mind. The Commission argued that the measure should have been adopted on the authority of art 113 EC Treaty [art 133 EC] alone.

Held

The ECJ sustained the arguments of the Commission and found the measures in question void. Where the illegality was not merely formal, the fact that a measure was adopted on the incorrect legal basis was sufficient to render it void.

Judgment

'Article 190 of the Treaty provides that "Regulations, directives and decisions of the Council and of the Commission shall state the reasons on which they are based". According to the case law of the Court (in particular the judgment in Case 158/80 *Rewe-Handelsgesellschaft Nord mbH* v *Hauptzollamt Kiel* [1981] ECR 1805), in order to satisfy the requirements to state reasons, Community measures must include a statement of facts and the law which led the institution in question to adopt them, so as to make possible review by the Court and so that the Member States and the nationals concerned may have knowledge of the conditions under which the Community institutions have applied the Treaty.

It is therefore necessary to consider whether the contested regulations satisfy those requirements.

In that connection the Council contends that, although the indication of the legal basis is not precise, the recitals in the preambles to the regulations, taken as a whole, provide sufficient alternative information as to the aims pursued by the Council, that is to say both commercial aims and aims of development-aid policy.

However, those indications are not sufficient to identify the legal basis by virtue of which the Council acted. Although the recitals on the preambles to the regulations do refer to improving access for developing countries to the markets of the preference-giving countries, they merely state that adaptations to the Community system of generalised preferences have proved to be necessary in the light of experience in the first 15 years. Moreover, according to information given to the Court by the Council itself, the wording "having regard to the Treaty" was adopted as a result of differences of opinion about the choice of the appropriate legal basis. Consequently, the wording chosen was designed precisely to leave the legal basis of the regulations in questions vague.

Admittedly, failure to refer to a precise provision of the Treaty need not necessarily constitute and infringement of essential procedural requirements when the legal basis for the measure may be determined from other parts of the measure. However, such explicit reference is indispensable where, in its absence, the parties concerned and the Court are left uncertain as to the precise legal basis.

In answer to a question put by the Court the Council has stated that when it adopted the contested regulations it intended to base them on both arts 113 and 235 of the [EC] Treaty. It has explained that it departed from the Commission's proposal to base the regulations on art 113 alone because it was convinced that the contested regulations had not only commercial policy aims, but also major development policy aims. The implementation of development policy goes beyond the scope of art 113 of the Treaty and necessitates recourse to art 235.

It must also be observed that in the context of the organisation of the powers of the Community the choice of the legal basis for a measure may not depend simply on an institution's conviction as to the objective pursued but must be based on objective factors which are amenable to judicial review.

In this case, the dispute as to the correct

legal basis was not purely formal in scope since arts 113 and 235 of the [EC] Treaty lay down different rules governing the Council's decision-making process, and the choice of the legal basis was therefore liable to affect the determination of the content of the contested legislation.

It follows from the very wording of art 235 that its use as the legal basis for a measure is justified only where no other provision of the Treaty gives the Community institutions the necessary power to adopt the measure in question.

It must therefore be considered whether in this case the Council was competent to adopt the contested regulations pursuant to art 113 of the Treaty alone, as the Commission maintains.'

After due consideration of this question, the ECJ concluded that art 113 EC Treaty [art 133 EC] would have been a sufficient basis for the regulations and the Council was not justified in adopting the measure on the basis of art 235 EC Treaty [art 308 EC], and continued:

'It is clear from the foregoing that the contested regulations do not satisfy the requirements laid down in art 190 of the Treaty with regard to the statement of reasons and that, moreover, they were not adopted on the correct legal basis. Consequently, they must be declared void.'

Comment

Article 235 EC Treaty [art 308 EC] provides that if action by the Community is necessary in order to achieve one of the objectives of the common market but the Treaty has not assigned appropriate competences to the EC in this area, the Council is empowered to take that necessary measure acting unanimously on a proposal from the Commission and after consulting the European Parliament. Article 235 EC Treaty [art 308 EC] provides the EC with residual legislative powers which were used extensively to take measures in important areas outside the scope of the founding Treaty (such as environmental protection, regional aid, research and technology). On the basis of art 235 EC Treaty [art 308 EC] the

Community extended its competences without revising the Treaty itself.

In the past, the Council leant, probably, too frequently, upon art 235 EC Treaty [art 308 EC] for two reasons. First, the Paris summit in October 1972 decided that in order to establish an economic and monetary union, as well as promote the social dimension of the Community, all provisions of the EC Treaty, including art 235 [art 308 EC], should be widely used. As a result, in the 1970s the Council referred to art 235 EC Treaty [art 308 EC] extensively and systematically. On 15 March 1992, 677 measures both internal and external were adopted on the basis of this provision, and 407 are still operational (Question No 1130/92, OJ C285 of 3.11.1992). The second reason is that art 235 EC Treaty [art 308 EC] requires unanimity and thus the Member States felt well protected in adopting measures as none of them were contrary to their vital national interests.

The Commission has challenged before the ECJ the legal basis of certain measures adopted by the Council under art 235 EC Treaty [art 308 EC]. In the present case the ECJ held that a measure can only be adopted under art 235 [art 308 EC] if there is no other appropriate provision in the Treaty which would provide a legal basis for Community action.

Amendments to the founding Treaty have considerably extended the competences of the Community and thus limited the role of art 235 EC Treaty [art 308 EC]. In Opinion 2/94 (ECHR) ([1996] ECR I–1759, para 30) the ECJ held that:

'Article 235 [art 308 EC], cannot be used as a basis for the adoption of provisions whose effect would, in substance be to amend the Treaty without following the procedure which it provides for that purpose.'

EC Commission v *Federal Republic of Germany* Case C–191/95 [1998] ECR I–5449 European Court of Justice

• *Action for failure to act – reasoned opinion – principle of collegiate responsibility of the Commission – company law – Directives 68/151 and 78/660 – annual accounts – penalties for failure to disclose companies' annual accounts – different grounds of complaint in the letter of formal notice and the application for a declaration under art 169 EC Treaty [art 226 EC]*

Facts

The Commission decided to issue a reasoned opinion against the government of the Federal Republic of Germany for failure to provide for appropriate penalties in cases where companies limited by shares failed to disclose their annual accounts, as prescribed in particular by the First Council Directive 68/151/EEC of 9 March 1968 and the Fourth Council Directive 78/660/EEC of 25 July 1978. When Germany did not comply with the opinion the Commission decided, in conformity with art 169 EC Treaty [art 226 EC], to bring proceedings before the ECJ against the German government. Both decisions were challenged by the German government as not being the subject of collective deliberations by the college of Commissioners. Germany argued that the issue of the reasoned opinion and commencement of proceedings were delegated. In addition, Germany maintained that the action was inadmissible because the contents of the application for a declaration of its failure to fulfil obligations under art 169 EC Treaty [art 226 EC] differed from those of the letter of formal notice.

Held

The plea of inadmissibility submitted by the government of Germany was rejected by the ECJ.

Judgment

'[*Principle of collegiality*]
It is important to remember, at the outset, that the functioning of the Commission is governed by the principle of collegiate responsibility.

It is common ground that the decisions to issue the reasoned opinion and to commence proceedings are subject to that principle of collegiate responsibility.

The principle of collegiality is based on the equal participation of the Commissioners in the adoption of decisions, from which it follows in particular that decisions should be the subject of collective deliberation and that all the members of the college of Commissioners should bear collective responsibility at political level for all decisions adopted.

Nevertheless, the formal requirements for effective compliance with the principle of collegiality vary according to the nature and legal effects of the acts adopted by that institution.

The issue of a reasoned opinion constitutes a preliminary procedure, which does not have any binding legal effect for the addressee of the reasoned opinion. The purpose of that pre-litigation procedure provided for by art 169 of the Treaty is to enable the Member State to comply of its own accord with the requirements of the Treaty or, if appropriate, to justify its position.

If that attempt at settlement is unsuccessful, the function of the reasoned opinion is to define the subject matter of the dispute. The Commission is not, however, empowered to determine conclusively, by reasoned opinions formulated pursuant to art 169, the rights and duties of a Member State or to afford that State guarantees concerning the compatibility of a given line of conduct with the Treaty. According to the system embodied in arts 169 to 171 of the Treaty, the rights and duties of Member States may be determined and their conduct appraised only by a judgment of the Court.

The reasoned opinion therefore has legal effect only in relation to the commencement of proceedings before the Court so that where a Member State does not comply with that opinion within the period allowed, the Commission has the right, but not the duty, to commence proceedings before the Court.

The decision to commence proceedings before the Court, whilst it constitutes an indispensable step for the purpose of enabling the Court to give judgment on the alleged failure to fulfil obligations by way of a binding decision, nevertheless does not per se alter the legal position in question.

Both the Commission's decision to issue a reasoned opinion and its decision to bring an action for a declaration of failure to fulfil obligations must be the subject of collective deliberation by the college of Commissioners. The information on which those decisions are based must therefore be available to the members of the college. It is not, however, necessary for the college itself formally to decide on the wording of the acts which give effect to those decisions and put them in final form.

In this case it is not disputed that the members of the college had available to them all the information they considered would assist them for the purposes of adopting the decision when the college decided, on 31 July 1991, to issue the reasoned opinion, and approved, on 13 December 1994, the proposal to bring the present action.

In those circumstances, it must be held that the Commission complied with the rules relating to the principle of collegiality when it issued the reasoned opinion with regard to the Federal Republic of Germany and brought the present action.

[Inadmissibility based on the difference between the content of the application and the letter of formal notice]
The fact that the Commission did not persist in the complaints based on the fact that a large proportion of companies limited by shares were failing to comply with the disclosure requirements, whilst it detailed the complaints based on the need to provide appropriate sanctions, which it had already set out more generally in the letter of formal

notice, merely limited the subject matter of the action.'

Comment
The Commission is a collegiate body. This means that each member of the Commission is not empowered to take any decision on his own and that once he makes a decision, issues a declaration etc he expresses the position of the entire Commission. This principle entails that each measure must be formally approved by the college, its violation may render that measure invalid (*EC Commission* v *BASF* Case C–137/92P [1994] ECR I–2555 in which the ECJ confirmed the decision of the CFI (*BASF* Cases T–79, 84–86, 91–92, 94, 96 and 98/89 [1992] ECR II–315)).

In the present case the ECJ held that compliance with the principle of collegiality varies according to the nature and legal effect of the act. In the case of acts which have no binding legal effect it is not necessary for the college 'itself formally to decide on the wording of the acts which give effect to those decisions and put them in final form'.

The Council of the European Union

United Kingdom v *EC Council (Re Hormones)* Case 68/86 [1988] 2 CMLR 453 European Court of Justice

• *Legal basis for the adoption of measures – objective criteria determining the choice of legal basis – arts 100 and 43 EC Treaty [arts 94 and 37 EC] – voting in the Council – agriculture – use of hormones*

Facts
The United Kingdom brought an action for annulment of a Council directive prohibiting the use of particular types of hormones in the rearing of livestock. The measure had been adopted by the Council despite the votes of the United Kingdom and Denmark against its

adoption. The United Kingdom argued that the legal authority for the adoption of the measure was art 100 EC Treaty [art 94 EC], which requires unanimity. In the Council, the other Member States claimed that art 43 EC Treaty [art 37 EC] was the correct legal basis for the measure. This provision permitted the adoption of legislation by means of a qualified majority. If the proper legal basis for the measure was art 100 [art 94 EC], the measure was void due to the negative votes of the UK and Denmark, but if the measure could be justified under art 43 [art 37 EC], the measure would be validly constituted.

Held

The ECJ held that the Council acted properly in adopting the measure under art 43 EC Treaty [art 37 EC]. This provision was sufficiently broad as to permit legislation which dealt not only directly, but also indirectly, with issues relating to agriculture. The choice of the legal basis for legislation must be made on objective criteria, which may be subject to judicial review. The fact that, in the past, the Council had followed a practice of citing a double basis for the adoption of such measures could not constitute a precedent capable of modifying the express terms of a Treaty provision.

Judgment

'... in order to determine whether the submission based on the alleged insufficiency of the legal basis of the directive at issue is well-founded it is necessary to consider whether the Council had the power to adopt it on the basis of art 43 alone.

By virtue of art 38 of the Treaty, the provisions of arts 30 to 46 apply to the products listed in Annex II of the Treaty. Article 43, moreover, must be interpreted in the light of art 39, which sets out the objectives of the Common Agricultural Policy, and art 40, which governs its implementation, providing inter alia that in order to attain the objectives set out in art 39 a common organisation of agricultural markets is to be estab-lished and that organisation include all measures required to attain those objectives.

The agricultural policy objectives set out in art 39 of the Treaty include in particular the increasing of productivity by promoting technical progress and by ensuring the rational development of agricultural production and the optimum utilisation of the factors of production. Moreover, art 39(2)(b) and (c) provide that in working out the Common Agricultural Policy account must be taken of the need to effect the appropriate adjustments by degrees and the fact that in the Member States agriculture constitutes a sector closely linked with the economy as a whole. It follows that agricultural policy objectives must be conceived in such a manner as to enable the Community institutions to carry out their duties in the light of developments in agriculture and in the economy as a whole.

Measures adopted on the basis of art 43 of the Treaty with a view to achieving those objectives under a common organisation of the market as provided for in art 40(2) may include rules governing conditions and methods of production, quality and marketing of agricultural products. The common organisation of the market contain many rules in that regard.

Efforts to achieve objectives of the Common Agricultural Policy, in particular under common organisations of the markets, cannot disregard requirements relating to the public interest such as the protection of consumers or the protection of the health and life of humans and animals, requirements which the Community institutions must take into account in exercising their powers.

Finally, it must be observed that according to art 42 of the Treaty the rules on competition are to apply to production of and trade in agricultural products only to the extent determined by the Council within the framework of provisions adopted pursuant to art 43. Consequently, in adopting such provisions the Council must take into consideration the requirements of competition policy.

It follows from the provisions discussed above, taken as a whole, that art 43 of the Treaty is the appropriate legal basis for any legislation concerning the production and marketing of agricultural products listed in Annex II of the Treaty which contributed to the achievement of one or more of the objectives of the Common Agricultural Policy set out in art 39 of the Treaty. There is no need to have recourse to art 100 of the Treaty where such legislation involves the harmonisation of provisions of national laws in that field.

As the Court pointed out (in earlier cases), art 38(2) of the Treaty gives precedence to specific provisions in the agricultural field over general provisions relating to the establishment of the common market. Consequently, even where the legislation in question is directed both to objectives of agricultural policy and to other objectives which, in the absence of specific provisions, are pursued on the basis of art 100 of the Treaty, that article, a general one under which directives may be adopted for the approximation of the laws of the Member States, cannot be relied on as a ground for restricting the field of application of art 43 of the Treaty.

It is on the basis of the foregoing considerations that it must be determined whether or not the contested directive falls within the scope of art 43 of the Treaty as described above.

In that regard, it must first be observed that there are common organisations of the markets in the sectors of beef and veal, pigmeat and sheepmeat and goatmeat, and that (the regulations establishing these organisations) provide for the adoption of Community measures designed to promote better organisation of production, processing and marketing, and to improve quality.

The directive at issue essentially contains, on the one hand, rules on the administration of certain substances having a hormonal action on farm animals whose meat is covered by the aforementioned common organisations of the markets and, on the other hand, rules concerning the requisite control measures. Those measures relate in particular to trade between Member States in live animals and meat and to imports of those products into the Community.

The aim of the directive, according to the recital in its preamble, is to protect human health and consumers interests with a view to eliminating the distortion of conditions of competition and bringing about an increase in "consumption of the production in question".

In view of the content and objectives of the directive, it must be found that, in regulating conditions for the production and marketing of meat with a view to improving its quality, it comes into the category of measures provided for by the aforementioned common organisations of the markets in meat and thus contributes to the achievement of the objectives of the Common Agricultural Policy which are set out in art 39 of the Treaty.

It follows from the foregoing that the directive at issue falls within the sphere of the Common Agricultural Policy and that the Council had the power to adopt it on the basis of art 43 alone. That finding cannot be affected by the fact, on which the applicant places some reliance, that the Council departed from its practice of basing measures in the field in question on arts 43 and 100 of the Treaty.

On that point, it should be borne in mind, as the Court held in its judgment in Case 45/86 *EC Commission* v *EC Council*, in the context of the organisation of the powers of the Community that the choice of the legal basis for the measure must be based on objective factors which are amenable to judicial review. A mere practice on the part of the Council cannot derogate from the rules laid down in the Treaty. Such a practice cannot therefore create a precedent binding on Community institutions with regard to the correct legal basis.

The applicant's first submission must therefore be rejected.'

Comment

The choice of a legal basis for a particular measure must be based on objective factors which are amenable to judicial review. The aim and content of that measure should be taken into account in order to select a proper legal basis (*EC Commission* v *EC Council* Case C–155/91 [1993] ECR I–939, *European Parliament* v *EC Council* Case C–42/97 [1999] ECR I–869). In the present case, the primary objective of the measure is a common organisation of agricultural markets and the secondary objective is the harmonisation of provisions of national law in the area of agriculture. Consequently the theory of the principal and accessory should be applied in order to select the proper legal basis for the adoption of that measure.

The choice of a legal basis determines the mode of voting in the Council. Article 43 EC Treaty [art 37 EC] permits the adoption of a measure by means of a qualified majority whilst art 100 EC Treaty [art 94 EC] requires unanimity. Therefore, the choice of legal basis has important implications. In the present case the UK and Denmark voted against its adoption which means that if the proper legal basis had been art 100 EC Treaty [art 94 EC], the measure would have never been adopted.

The European Parliament

European Parliament v *Council of the European Union* Joined Cases C–164 and 165/97 [1999] ECR I–1139 European Court of Justice

• *Parliament's prerogatives – choice of legal basis – arts 43 and 130s EC Treaty [arts 37 and 175 EC] – environment – protection of forests against atmospheric pollution and fire*

Facts
The European Parliament (EP) brought proceedings against the Council for annulment of two Regulations, Nos 307/97 and 308/97, concerning the protection of forests against pollution and fire. The EP argued that both Regulations were adopted on an inappropriate legal basis, ie art 43 EC Treaty [art 37 EC] instead of art 130s EC Treaty [art 175 EC]. Consequently, the EP prerogatives in respect of the procedure involving its participation in the drafting of legislation were undermined.

Held
The ECJ annulled both Regulations. It held that the challenged Regulations should continue to have effect pending the adoption, within a reasonable time, of regulations enacted on the proper legal basis.

Judgment
'It must be borne in mind that in the context of the organisation of the powers of the Community, the choice of a legal basis for a measure must be based on objective factors which are amenable to judicial review. Those factors include, in particular, the aim and content of the measure.

It is clear from the provisions of the amended regulations that the aims of the Community schemes for the protection of forests are partly agricultural since they are intended in particular to contribute to safeguarding the productive potential of agriculture, and partly of a specifically environmental nature since their primary objective is to maintain and monitor forest ecosystems.

With more particular reference to the common agricultural policy and the Community environmental policy, there is nothing in the case-law to indicate that, in principle, one should take precedence over the other. It makes clear that a Community measure cannot be part of Community action on environmental matters merely because it takes account of requirements of protection referred to in art 130r(2) of the EC Treaty. Articles 130r and 130s leave intact the powers held by the Community under other provisions of the Treaty and provide a legal basis only for specific action on environmental matters. In contrast, art 130s of the Treaty must be the basis for provisions which fall specifically within the environmental policy, even if they have an impact on the functioning of the internal market or if their objective is the improvement of agricultural production.

In this case, although the measures referred to in the regulations may have certain positive repercussions on the functioning of agriculture, those indirect consequences are incidental to the primary aim of the Community schemes for the protection of forests, which are intended to ensure that the natural heritage represented by forest ecosystems is conserved and turned to account, and does not merely consider their utility to agriculture. Measures to defend the forest environment against the risks of destruction and degradation associated with fires and atmospheric pollution inherently form part of the environmental action for which Community competence is founded on art 130s of the Treaty.

The contested regulations do not constitute rules on the production and marketing of agricultural products for which, to the extent to which those rules contribute to the attainment or one or more objectives of the common agricultural policy set out in art 39 of the Treaty, art 43 of the Treaty would have been the appropriate legal basis.

The Parliament is therefore correct in its assertion that, by basing the contested regulations on art 43 of the Treaty although art 130s was the appropriate legal basis, the Council has infringed essential procedural requirements and undermined its prerogatives.'

Comment
The ECJ confirmed its position as to the choice of a legal basis in respect of a Community measure. The ECJ stated that when the aims of contested regulations are partly agricultural and partly of a specifically environment nature then in order to determine the appropriate legal basis the Council has to apply the theory of the principal and accessory (see *European Parliament* v *EC Council (Re Tchernobyl)* Case C–70/88 [1990] ECR 2041; [1992] 1 CMLR 91) unless the measure is intended to pursue both objectives. In that

case the measure must be based on two legal basis (see *European Parliament* v *EC Council* Case C–360/96 [1996] ECR I–1195).

The choice of a legal basis determines the participation of the EP in the adoption of a measure. In the present case both regulations should have been based on art 130s of the EC Treaty [art 175 EC] and therefore adopted by the Council under the procedure for co-operation with the Parliament provided for in art 189c of that Treaty [art 252 EC]. Their adoption on the basis of art 43 EC Treaty [art 37 EC] means that the Parliament was merely consulted.

The European Parliament's prerogatives in external relations

European Parliament v *Council of the European Union* Case C–189/97 [1999] ECR I–4741 European Court of Justice

• *EC/Mauritania fisheries agreement – agreement with important budgetary implications for the Community – the European Parliament's prerogatives in external relations – arts 37 and 300(3) EC*

Facts
The European Parliament brought an action for annulment of Council Regulation 408/97 regarding the conclusion on 24 February 1999 of an Agreement of co-operation in the sea fisheries sector between the EC and Mauritania, under which EC vessels are allowed to fish off the coast of Mauritania in exchange for payments from the Community budget. The European Parliament (EP) contested the legal basis of the Regulation, arguing that the agreement had important budgetary implications for the Community and therefore should be concluded under art 300(3) EC, which requires the EP's assent,

instead of art 37 EC whereby the Council is required to obtain the EP's opinion within the simple consultation procedure.

Held
The ECJ dismissed the application.

Judgment

'Article 228(3) of the Treaty provides that:

> "The Council shall conclude agreements after consulting the European Parliament, except for the agreements referred to in art 113(3), including cases where the agreement covers a field for which the procedure referred to in art 189b or that referred to in art 189c is required for the adoption of internal rules …
>
> By way of derogation from the previous subparagraph, agreements referred to in art 238, other agreements establishing a specific institutional framework by organising cooperation procedures, agreements having important budgetary implications for the Community and agreements entailing amendment of an act adopted under the procedure referred to in art 189b shall be concluded after the assent of the European Parliament has been obtained."

The Parliament argues first of all that the Treaty on European Union has substantially increased its involvement in the conclusion of international agreements, especially by enlarging the scope of the assent procedure. Its position is therefore closer to that of the parliaments of the Member States, whose powers in the matter should serve as a frame of reference for the interpretation of the second subparagraph of art 228(3) of the Treaty.

The Parliament maintains, secondly, that by requiring its assent for the conclusion of agreements with important budgetary implications, that provision is intended to safeguard its internal powers as a constituent part of the budgetary authority. In the light of that objective, it proposes that, in determining whether an agreement has important budgetary implications, the criteria to be taken into account should include the fact that expenditure under the agreement is spread over several years, the relative share of such expenditure in relation to expenditure of the same kind under the budget heading concerned, and the rate of increase in expenditure under the agreement in question in relation to the financial section of the previous agreement.

The Parliament goes on to state that the fisheries agreement with Mauritania undoubtedly satisfies those three criteria. First, it makes provision for financial compensation split into five annual tranches, the amounts of which vary between ECU 51,560,000 and ECU 55,160,000. Second, that financial compensation represents, for each of the years in question, more than 20 per cent of the appropriations entered under the budget heading concerned (heading B7–8000, "International fisheries agreements"). Finally, the financial outlay in favour of the Islamic Republic of Mauritania has increased more than fivefold in relation to the previous agreement, or has more than doubled if only the year 1995, which included exceptional supplementary compensation, is used as the point of reference.

The Council, supported by the Spanish Government, contends that the second subparagraph of art 228(3) of the Treaty must be strictly interpreted, since it constitutes a derogation from the rule laid down by the first subparagraph, whereby the Council is to conclude agreements after consulting the Parliament.

The Council considers, in that respect, that the criteria put forward by the Parliament are inoperative. First, the fact that expenditure is spread over several years is not decisive, because the budget is, by definition, annual. Nor is the extent of the financial impact of the agreement in relation to expenditure of the same kind under the budget heading in question significant, given that budgetary nomenclature is capable of being altered under the budget procedure and that the amount of available appropriations may always be adapted by means of transfers or supplementary budgets. Finally, the rate of increase in expenditure is not very revealing, since a high rate may very well correspond to minimal expenditure.

The Council therefore maintains that, in order to assess whether an agreement has important budgetary implications, it is necessary to refer to the overall budget of the Community, and that it did not act in a manifestly erroneous and arbitrary manner in seeking merely an opinion of the Parliament for a fisheries agreement under which annual expenditure amounted to 0.07 per cent of that budget.

In the context of the organisation of powers in the Community, the choice of a legal basis for a measure must be based on objective factors which are amenable to judicial review (see, in particular, Case 45/86 *EC Commission* v *EC Council (Re Generalised Tariff Preferences)* [1987] ECR 1493, para 11; Case C–22/96 *European Parliament* v *EC Council* [1998] ECR I–3231, para 23; and Joined Cases C–164 and 165/97 *European Parliament* v *Council of the European Union* [1999] ECR I–1139, para 12).

In order to assess whether an agreement has important budgetary implications within the meaning of the second subparagraph of art 228(3) of the Treaty, the Council has referred to the overall budget of the Community. It should be pointed out, however, that appropriations allocated to external operations of the Community traditionally account for a marginal fraction of the Community budget. Thus, in 1996 and 1997, those appropriations, grouped under subsection B7, "External operations", barely exceeded 5 per cent of the overall budget. In those circumstances, a comparison between the annual financial cost of an agreement and the overall Community budget scarcely appears significant, and to apply such a criterion might render the relevant wording of the second subparagraph of art 228(3) of the Treaty wholly ineffective.

The Council maintains, however, that the criterion upon which it relies does not have the effect of excluding the use of that legal basis altogether. In support of that view, it cites the Agreement on cooperation in the sea fisheries sector between the European

Community and the Kingdom of Morocco (OJ 1997 L30, p5), the financial implications of which, amounting to 0.15 per cent of the Community budget annually, it acknowledged were important.

The Council has not, however, explained in any way how such a small percentage could render the financial implications of an Agreement important, when the scarcely more insignificant figure of 0.07 per cent is said to be insufficient in that respect.

As regards the three criteria proposed by the Parliament, the Court finds that the first of them may indeed contribute towards characterising an Agreement as having important budgetary implications. Relatively modest annual expenditure may, over a number of years, represent a significant budgetary outlay.

The second and third criteria put forward by the Parliament do not, however, appear to be relevant. In the first place, budget headings, which can moreover be altered, vary substantially in importance, so that the relative share of the expenditure under the Agreement may be large in relation to appropriations of the same kind entered under the budget heading concerned, even though the expenditure in question is small. Moreover, the rate of increase in expenditure under the Agreement may be high in comparison with that arising from the previous agreement, whilst the amounts involved may still be small.

As has been pointed out in para 26 of this judgment, a comparison between the annual financial cost of an international Agreement and the overall budget scarcely appears significant. However, comparison of the expenditure under an Agreement with the amount of the appropriations designed to finance the Community's external operations, grouped under subsection B7 of the budget, enables that Agreement to be set in the context of the budgetary outlay approved by the Community for its external policy. That comparison thus offers a more appropriate means of assessing the financial importance which the Agreement actually has for the Community.

Where, as in this case, a sectoral

Agreement is involved, the above analysis may, in appropriate cases, and without excluding the possibility of taking other factors into account, be complemented by a comparison between the expenditure entailed by the Agreement and the whole of the budgetary appropriations for the sector in question, taking the internal and external aspects together. Such a comparison makes it possible to determine, from another angle and in an equally consistent context, the financial outlay approved by the Community in entering into that Agreement. However, since the sectors vary substantially in terms of their budgetary importance, that examination cannot result in the financial implications of an Agreement being found to be important where they do not represent a significant share of the appropriations designed to finance the Community's external operations.

In this case, the fisheries Agreement with Mauritania was concluded for five years, which is not a particularly lengthy period. Moreover, the financial compensation for which it makes provision is split into annual tranches the amounts of which vary between ECU 51,560,000 and ECU 55,160,000. In respect of previous budgetary years, those amounts, whilst exceeding 5 per cent of expenditure on fisheries, represent barely more than 1 per cent of the whole of the payment appropriations allocated for external operations of the Community, a proportion which, whilst far from negligible, can scarcely be described as important. In those circumstances, if the Council had taken that comparison into account, it would also have been entitled to take the view that the fisheries Agreement with Mauritania did not have important budgetary implications for the Community within the meaning of the second subparagraph of art 228(3) of the Treaty.

Furthermore, the scope of that provision, as set out in the Treaty, cannot, despite what the Parliament suggests, be affected by the extent of the powers available to national parliaments when approving international Agreements with financial implications.

It follows from all the foregoing consider-ations that the Council was right to conclude the fisheries Agreement with Mauritania on the basis, inter alia, of the first subparagraph of art 228(3) of the Treaty. This action must therefore be dismissed.'

Comment

This case marks an important victory for the EP in its struggle for more power, even though its application was dismissed.

The participation of the EP in the external relations of the EC takes place within the framework of two procedures: consultation and assent. In respect of the consultation procedure, art 300(3) EC provides that the Council is required to consult the EP before concluding international Agreements, except for the Agreements referred to in art 133(3) EC, which include cases 'where the Agreement covers a field for which the procedure referred to in art 251 EC or that referred to in art 252 EC is required for the adoption of internal rules'. Therefore, the EP's right to be consulted applies to all international Agreements apart from the above-mentioned exceptions. Taking into account the fact that whatever the opinion of the EP, the Council of the European Union is entitled to proceed, and that the requirement of an opinion is a mere formality, the participation of the EP in shaping international relations within the consultation procedure is of no real significance. However, this is not the case under the assent procedure. The Single European Act 1986 gave the EP the power of assent in respect of the admission of new Members and the conclusion of association Agreements with non-Member States, whilst art 300(3) EC added three new areas for which the assent of the EP is required. They are: in Agreements establishing a specific institutional framework by organising co-operation procedures; Agreements having important budgetary implications for the EC; and Agreements necessitating an amendment of an act adopted under the procedure provided for in art 251 EC. The assent procedure is in fact a co-decision procedure, as it allows the EP to be an equal partner of the Council in concluding international Agreements.

In the present case the ECJ was asked to define the notion of 'important budgetary implications for the Community', following on from which the EP's powers would be either greater or lesser, depending upon what is included within the definition. In order to assess the budgetary implications of international Agreements, the EP laid down three criteria: the first based on a comparison between the annual financial cost of an international Agreement; the second referring to the relative share of the expenditure under the Agreement in relation to appropriations of the same kind entered under the budget heading concerned; and the third based on the rate of increase in expenditure under the Agreement as compared to the previous Agreement. The EP concluded that the application of these criteria to the Agreement between the Community and Mauritania showed that it had important budgetary implications for the Community, because the payments from the Community budget would represent 20 per cent of the budgetary outlay approved by the Community for its external policy. The Council rejected the assessment made by the EP and referred to the overall budget of the Community, under which payments to Mauritania represent only 0.07 per cent of the budget and therefore could not be considered as having important financial implications for the EC.

The ECJ had to resolve two very important political and legal questions, namely: assessing the balance of power between the EP and the Council, and the possible judicial revision of the EC Treaty in respect of the external powers of the EP. If the ECJ had approved the arguments of the EP, the latter would have been entitled to negotiate and conclude Agreements having important budgetary implications for the Community, including Agreements regarding common commercial policy which are expressly excluded from the participation of the EP by art 303(3) EC.

The ECJ rejected the arguments of the EP but did not follow the reasoning of the

Council. In this respect the ECJ held that relatively modest annual expenditure may, over a number of years, represent a significant budgetary outlay. Although the ECJ did not strengthen the external prerogatives of the EP, it warned the Council that if the Council had taken into consideration the comparison of the expenditure under the Agreement with the amount of the appropriations designed to finance the Community's external operations (the criterion favoured by the ECJ) it 'would also have been entitled to take the view that the fisheries Agreement with Mauritania did not have important budgetary implications for the Community within the meaning of the second subparagraph of art 228(3) of the EC Treaty [art 300(3) EC]'. This means that the ECJ will approach each case separately in order to assess whether an Agreement in question has important budgetary implications. This will force the Council to increase co-operation with the EP in respect of international Agreements having important budgetary implications for the Community. Consequently, the EP has indirectly achieved its objective.

European Parliament v *EC Council (Re Common Transport Policy)* Case 13/83 [1985] ECR 1513; [1985] 1 CMLR 138 European Court of Justice

• *Action for failure to act – right of the European Parliament to commence proceedings under art 175 EC Treaty [art 232 EC] – objections raised by the Council against the right of Parliament to initiate such proceedings – challenge dismissed – common transport policy*

Facts

The European Parliament (EP) brought an action under art 175(1) EC Treaty [art 232 EC] against the EC Council, alleging that the Council had infringed the terms of the EC Treaty by failing to introduce a common policy for transport, in particular to establish a framework for the negotiation of such a policy.

The Council objected to the admissibility of the action arguing, inter alia, that the EP had no locus standi under art 175 EC Treaty [art 232 EC] to initiate such proceedings. Article 175 EC Treaty [art 232 EC] merely refers to 'other institutions of the Community' in relation to competence to raise an action in the ECJ for failure to act. No express reference is made to the position of the EP in such proceedings. In addition, the Council also alleged that the conditions laid down in art 175 EC Treaty [art 232 EC] for bringing such an action had not been satisfied.

Held

The ECJ rejected the contention that the EP possessed no competence to bring an action under art 175 EC Treaty [art 232 EC]. The fact that the EP lacked capacity to commence actions under other provisions of the Treaty was irrelevant in construing art 175 EC Treaty [art 232 EC] which conferred rights of action to the 'other institutions of the Community', other than the Council and the Commission. The ECJ also rejected the allegations that the procedure followed in the raising of the action did not satisfy the conditions set out in art 175 EC Treaty [art 232 EC].

Judgment

'[*Capacity of the EP to bring proceedings under art 175 EC Treaty*]
The Council explains first of all that in its opinion the present action is to be seen as part of the Parliament's efforts to increase its influence in the decision-making process within the Community. Those efforts, although legitimate, should not seek to exploit the action for failure to act provided for by art 175 since collaboration between the Community institutions is not governed by that provision. The political aims of the Parliament must be pursued by other means.

In the light of that the Council, while recognising that art 175 gives a right of action in respect of omissions of the Council

and Commission to Member States and the "other institutions of the Community", enquires whether the right of review conferred on the Parliament by the Treaty is not exhausted by the powers provided for in arts 175, 143 and 144 of the Treaty, which govern the ways in which the Parliament may exercise influence on the activities of the Commission and the Council. If so, the Parliament can have no right of review over the Council which may exercised by means of an action for failure to act.

The Council adds that upon systematic interpretation of the Treaty the Parliament has no capacity to bring proceedings. The Parliament has no right of action under art 173, which enables a review of the legality of measures of the Council and Commission to be obtained by means of an action for annulment. In so far as the Treaty deprives the Parliament of the right to review the legality of measures of the two institutions it would be illogical to allow it a right of action in the case of unlawful failure by one of those institutions to act. Accordingly, only through an express attribution of powers would it have been possible to confer on the Parliament a right to bring an action for failure to act.

The European Parliament and the Commission contest that argument on the basis of the actual wording of art 175, which in their view does not lend itself to any interpretation which would prevent the Parliament from bringing an action for failure to act. Both institutions also consider that recognition of such a power is in no way incompatible with the division of powers provided for by the Treaty.

The Court would emphasise that the first paragraph of art 175, as the Council recognised, expressly gives a right of action for failure to act against the Council and Commission, inter alia, to "the other institutions of the Community". It this gives the same right of action to all the Community institutions. It is not possible to restrict the exercise of that right by one of them without adversely affecting its status as an institution under the Treaty, in particular art 4(1).

The fact that the European Parliament is

at the same time the Community institution whose task is to exercise a political review of the activities of the Commission, and to a certain extent those of the Council, is not capable of affecting the interpretation of the provisions of the Treaty on the rights of action of the institutions.

Accordingly the first objection of inadmissibility must be rejected.'

Comment

The ECJ confirmed that the EP may bring an action against the Council or Commission for failing to act under the terms of art 175 EC Treaty [art 232 EC].

European Parliament v *EC Council (Re Tchernobyl)* Case C–70/88 [1990] ECR 2041; [1992] 1 CMLR 91 European Court of Justice

• *Action for annulment under art 173 EC Treaty [art 230 EC] – no express right granted to the European Parliament to initiate such an action – locus standi – a semi-privileged applicant – the prerogatives of the European Parliament*

Facts

Before the present case, the European Parliament (EP) had brought a number of actions in an attempt to establish its locus standi under art 173 EC Treaty [art 230 EC] to bring an action for annulment against the other institutions of the Community, particularly the Council and the Commission (see *European Parliament* v *EC Council (Re Comitology)* Case 302/87 [1988] ECR 5615). Article 173 EC Treaty [art 230 EC] (before its amendment by the Treaty of Maastricht) expressly reserved the right to bring actions for annulment of the acts of Community institutions to the Council, the Commission and the Member States as privileged applicants.

In the present case the EP challenged an act of the Council. During the consultation stage of the legislative process, Parliament had

expressed its disagreement over the legal basis proposed by the Commission for enacting such legislation. Despite these reservations, the Council proceeded to adopt the regulation on the contested legal basis.

The EP brought an action for annulment of the regulation on the ground that it had been adopted on the basis of inappropriate legal authority. However, technically the action was raised under art 146 Euratom Treaty [art 146 EA] and art 173 EC Treaty [art 230 EC], although both provisions are worded in identical terms.

Held

The ECJ reversed its earlier jurisprudence in a dramatic turnabout, and found that the European Parliament did possess sufficient standing under art 173 EC Treaty [art 230 EC] to bring an action to challenge the disputed regulation.

Judgment

It was appropriate to observe, as a preliminary ruling matter, that since the disputed measure was based upon a provision of the Euratom Treaty, the admissibility of the action seeking the annulment of that measure was to be assessed in the light of that Treaty.

It was clear from the judgment in Case 302/87 *Comitology* that the Parliament had no right to bring an action for annulment under the provisions of art 173 EC Treaty or those of art 146 Euratom Treaty which was identically worded.

As pointed out by that judgment, not only did the Parliament have the right to bring an action for failure to act but also the Treaties provided various means by which acts of the Council or the Commission adopted in infringement of the prerogatives of the Parliament could be reviewed by the Court. None the less the background and the arguments had revealed that however useful and varied the various means of redress laid down by the Euratom and EC Treaty might be, they could prove to be inefficient or uncertain.

In the first place, an action for failure to

act could not be used to dispute the legal basis of an act which had already been adopted. Moreover, the submission of a preliminary question relating to the validity of a given act or the bringing of acts before the Court by states or individuals with a view to annulment of such an act, were mere possibilities upon which the Parliament could not rely. Finally, although it was for the Commission to ensure the observance of the powers of the Parliament, that task could not go so far as to require the Commission to accept a position of the Parliament and to present an application for annulment which for its own part, it might view as ill-founded.

It followed from the foregoing that the existence of the various legal remedies was not sufficient to guarantee in all circumstances, the annulment of an act of the Council or of the Commission which had infringed the powers of the Parliament. These powers were one of the elements in the institutional balance established by the Treaties. The Treaties had established a system of division of powers between the various institutions of the Community, which conferred upon each of them its own task in the institutional structure of the Community and in the achievement of the tasks conferred upon it.

Respect for the institutional balance implied that each institution should be able to exercise its powers while observing those of the others. It required also that any infringement of that rule, should it arise, should be able to be punished.

The Court, which was responsible pursuant to the Treaties for ensuring the observance of the law in their interpretation and application, had therefore to ensure that he institutional balance was maintained and consequently had to provide judicial review over the observation of the powers of the Parliament where a case was brought before it by the latter, by means of an action suitable to the objective which it was seeking to attain.

In carrying out that task, the Court obviously could not include the Parliament among the institutions which might bring an action

pursuant to art 173 EC Treaty or art 146 Euratom Treaty, without having to demonstrate a specific interest in the proceedings.

It was, however, for it to ensure the full application of the provisions of the Treaty relating to the institutional balance and to act in such a way that the European Parliament, like the other institutions, could not have its powers infringed without having the possibility of a legal action provided for by the Treaties and which could be used in a certain and effective manner.

The absence from the Treaties of a provision enabling the Parliament to bring an action for annulment might constitute a procedural lacuna; however, that could not prevail over the fundamental interest in the maintenance and observation of its institutional balance laid down by the Treaties establishing the European Communities.

Consequently, an action for the annulment of an act of the Council or the Commission brought before the Court by the Parliament was admissible provided that that action sought only to safeguard its powers and that it was based exclusively on grounds based upon the infringement of those powers. Subject to that reservation, an action for annulment by the European Parliament was to be brought in accordance with the rules laid down in the Treaties for an action for annulment brought by other institutions.

The various powers conferred upon the Parliament by the Treaties included participation in the procedure for drawing up legislative acts in the context of the co-operation procedure laid down in the EC Treaty.

In the present case, the Parliament maintained that the disputed regulation was based on art 31 Euratom Treaty, which provided only for consultation of the Parliament, although it ought to have been based on art 100a EC Treaty which required the opening of the co-operation procedure with the Parliament.

The Parliament therefore concluded that the choice by the Council of the legal basis for the disputed regulation had resulted in a failure to observe its powers by depriving it of the possibility, provided for in the co-operation procedure, of taking a more active part in the drawing up of the act than was possible in the context of the consultation procedure.

The Parliament having raised the question of an infringement of its powers following the choice of the legal basis of the disputed act, it follows from the foregoing that the present action is admissible.

Comment

Until the entry into force of the TEU the EP was denied locus standi under art 173 EC Treaty [art 230 EC]. It was logical in the sense that acts adopted by the EP were not reviewable under art 173 EC Treaty [art 230 EC]. However, once the ECJ permitted acts of the EP to be reviewed (*Partie Ecologiste 'Les Verts'* v *European Parliament* Case 294/83 [1986] ECR 1339 and *EC Council* v *European Parliament (Budget)* Case 34/86 [1986] ECR 2155), the EP argued that its locus standi under art 173 EC Treaty [art 230 EC] should be recognised. In *European Parliament* v *EC Council (Comitology)* Case 302/87 the ECJ had refused to confer the EP even limited locus standi although Advocate-General Darmon suggested that the EP should have limited locus standi to maintain the institutional balance of power, especially in cases where its interests or rights were directly affected by acts of the Commission or the Council since in such circumstances the position of the EP would be worse than that of a non-privileged applicant.

Two years later the ECJ reversed its position. In the present case the ECJ referred to the suggestions of Advocate-General Darmon and decided that the action of the EP was admissible under art 173 EC Treaty [art 230 EC] taking into account that the EP prerogatives (which in this case concerned the right of the EP to influence the legislative process leading to the adoption of a measure) were infringed. In the present case the ECJ imposed an important restriction upon the EP. This is that the EP may submit an application for annulment only in order to protect its prerogatives and based solely on the violation of its prerogatives.

France v *European Parliament* Case C–345/95 [1997] ECR I–5215 European Court of Justice

• *Seat of the European Parliament – periods of monthly plenary ordinary sessions – Edinburgh Decision*

Facts

The French government supported by Luxembourg brought an action for annulment of the vote of the European Parliament (EP) of 20 September 1995 adopting the calendar for its part-sessions for 1996 which reduced the number of plenary part-sessions to be held in Strasbourg in 1996 from 12 to 11. The French government argued that the vote in question was adopted in breach of the Edinburgh Decision, in breach of essential procedural requirements and was also contrary to art 190 EC Treaty [art 253 EC]. The Edinburgh Decision adopted by the European Council on 12 December 1992 was intended to determine the location of the seats of the Community institutions and of certain bodies and departments of the European Communities. Article 1(a) of that decision specified that:

'The European Parliament shall have its seat in Strasbourg where the 12 periods of monthly plenary sessions, including the budget session, shall be held. The periods of additional plenary sessions shall be held in Brussels. The Committees of the European Parliament shall meet in Brussels. The General Secretariat of the European Parliament and its departments shall remain in Luxembourg' (OJ C341 23.12.92 p1).

The Edinburgh Decision was confirmed and complemented by the European Council Decision adopted at the Brussels meeting on 29–30 October 1993 (OJ C323 30.11.93 p1).

Held

The ECJ annulled the vote of the EP of 20 September 1995 adopting the calendar of its part-time sessions for 1996 to the extent that it did not provide for 12 ordinary plenary part-sessions in Strasbourg in 1996.

Judgment

'By adopting the Edinburgh Decision, therefore, the governments of the Member States have now discharged their obligation by definitively locating the seat of the Parliament in Strasbourg, whilst maintaining several places of work for that institution.

   Given a plurality of working places, the exercise of that competence involved not only the obligation to determine the location of the seat of the Parliament but also the implied power to give precision to that term by indicating the activities which must take place there ...

   ... The Edinburgh Decision must thus be interpreted as defining the seat of the Parliament as the place where 12 ordinary plenary part-sessions must take place on a regular basis, including those during which the Parliament is to exercise the budgetary powers conferred upon it by the Treaty. Additional plenary part-sessions cannot therefore be scheduled for any other place of work unless the Parliament holds the 12 ordinary plenary part-sessions in Strasbourg, where it has its seat.

   Contrary to the Parliament's contention, the governments of the Member States have not, by so defining its seat, encroached upon the power of the Parliament to determine its own internal organization, conferred by arts 25 of the ECSC Treaty, 142 of the EC Treaty and 112 of the EAEC Treaty.

   Whilst the Parliament is authorised, under that power of internal organisation, to take appropriate measures to ensure the proper functioning and conduct of its proceedings, its decisions in that regard must respect the competence of the governments of the Member States to determine the seat of the institutions ...

   ... Whilst it is true that the Edinburgh Decision does place certain constraints on the Parliament as regards the organisation of its work, those constraints are inherent in the need to determine its seat while maintaining several places of work for the institution.'

Comment

Articles 216 EC Treaty [art 289 EC], 77 CS and 189 EA provide that the seat of Community institutions should be determined by common accord of the Member States. In practice, the determination of the permanent seats of the Community institutions has always been subject to fierce competition among the Member States. The Decision of 8 April 1965 (OJ L152 13.7.67 p18) offered a temporary solution by locating the seats of the institutions in three different places: Luxembourg, Brussels and Strasbourg. This compromise led to many political, financial and legal difficulties, especially with respect to where the session of the EP were to be held (*Luxembourg* v *European Parliament* Case 230/81 [1983] ECR 255; *Luxembourg* v *European Parliament* Case 108/83 [1984] ECR 1945; *France* v *European Parliament* Cases 358/85 and 51/86 [1988] ECR 4821; *Luxembourg* v *European Parliament* Cases C–213/88 and C–39/89 [1991] ECR I–5643).

   It seemed that the Edinburgh Decision had settled all controversies regarding the seat of the EP. This is not, however, the case as the EP did not hesitate to challenge the Edinburgh Decision arguing that the latter was adopted in breach of art 216 EC Treaty [art 289 EC] as it encroached upon the power of the EP to determined its own internal organisation conferred by art 142 EC Treaty [art 199 EC].

   The ECJ held that by adopting the Edinburgh Decision the Member States discharged their obligation consisting of definitely locating the seat of the EP in Strasbourg whilst maintaining several places of work for that institution.

The Court of Justice of the European Communities (ECJ)

Re the Draft Treaty on a European Economic Area Opinion 1/91 [1992] 1 CMLR 245 European Court of Justice

• *Consultative jurisdiction – infringement of the powers of the ECJ – international agreement between the EC and EFTA – creation of the European economic area – modifications required for approval of the EEA agreement*

Facts
The European Community and the European Free Trade Association (EFTA) entered into an international agreement to create the European Economic Area. This agreement extended the scope of the EC Treaty's four freedoms and the existing principles of competition law to the Member States of the EFTA on a reciprocal basis.

The agreement also established a separate Court to supervise the implementation and enforcement of these provisions. This Court was to consist of judges of the ECJ and other appointees named by the contracting parties to the agreement. This Court was required to take into consideration all the jurisprudence of the ECJ to the date of the signing of the agreement, but not necessarily after that date. The Court would also have the power to refer a matter to the ECJ for a preliminary ruling but any decision was not necessarily binding on the referring judge.

The judges of the ECJ expressed a number of reservations about the legal implications of such an agreement, especially on the competence of the ECJ. As a result, the Commission requested an opinion from the ECJ on the compatibility of the agreement with the EC Treaty.

Held
The ECJ rejected some parts of the agreement on the ground that they undermined the ECJ's authority as conferred by the EC Treaty. In particular, the ECJ stressed that the two treaties sought to achieve separate purposes. For that reason, homogeneity of the rules of law throughout the EEA is not secured by the fact that the provisions of Community law and those of the corresponding provisions of the agreement are identical in their content or wording

The EEA Treaty was accordingly suspended and subsequently amended to take into consideration the concerns of the ECJ.

Judgment
'The EEA is to be established on the basis of an international treaty which, essentially, merely creates rights and obligations as between the Contracting parties and provides for no transfer of sovereign rights to the intergovernmental institutions which it sets up.

In contrast, the [EC] Treaty, albeit concluded in the form of an international agreement, none the less constitutes the constitutional charter of the Community based on the rule of law. As the Court of Justice has consistently held, the Community treaties established a new legal order for the benefit of which the States limited their sovereign rights, in even wider fields, and the subject of which comprise not only Member States but also their nationals. The essential characteristics of the Community legal order which has thus been established are in particular its primacy over the law of the Member States and the direct effect of a whole series of provisions which are applicable to their nationals and to the Member States themselves.

It follows from those considerations that homogeneity of the rules of law throughout the EEA is not secured by the fact that the provisions of Community law and those of the corresponding provisions of the agreement are identical in their content or wording.

It must therefore be considered whether the agreement provides for other means of guaranteeing that homogeneity.

Article 6 of the Agreement pursues that objective by stipulating that the rules of the Agreement must be interpreted in conformity with the case law of the Court of Justice on the corresponding provisions of Community law.

However, for two reasons that interpretation mechanism will not enable the desired legal homogeneity to be achieved.

First, art 6 is concerned only with rulings of the Court of Justice given prior to the date of signature of the Agreement. Since the case law will evolve, it will be difficult to distinguish the new case law from the old and hence the past from the future.

Secondly, although art 6 of the Agreement does not clearly specify whether it refers to the Court's case law as a whole, and in particular the case law on the direct effect and primacy of Community law, it appears from Protocol 35 to the agreement that, without recognising the principles of direct effect and primacy which that case law entails, the Contracting parties undertake merely to introduce into their respective legal orders a statutory provision to the effect that EEA rules are to prevail over contrary legislative provisions.

It follows that compliance with the case law of the Court of Justice, as laid down in art 6 of the Agreement, does not extend to essential elements of that case law which are irreconcilable with the homogeneity of the law throughout the EEA, either as regards the past or for the future.

It follows from the foregoing considerations that the divergencies which exist between the aims and context of the Agreement, on the one hand, and the aims and context of Community law, on the other, stand in the way of the achievement of the objective of homogeneity in the interpretation and application of the law in the EEA.

It is in light of the contradiction which has just been identified that it must be considered whether the proposed system of courts may undermine the authority of the Community legal order in pursuing its particular objectives.

The interpretation of the expression "Contracting party" which the EEA Court will have to give in the exercise of its jurisdiction will be considered first, followed by the effect of the case law of that court on the interpretation of Community law.

As far as the first point is concerned, it must be observed that the EEA Court has jurisdiction under art 96(1)(a) of the Agreement with regard to settlement of dispute between the Contracting parties and that, according to art 117(1) of the Agreement, the EEA Joint Committee or a Contracting Party may bring such a dispute before the EEA Court.

The expression "Contracting parties" is defined in art 2(c) of the Agreement. As far as the Community and its Member States are concerned, it covers the Community and the Member States, or the Community, or the Member States, depending on the case. Which of the three possibilities is to be chosen is to be deduced in each case from the relevant provisions of the Agreement and from the respective competencies of the Community and the Member States as they follow from the [EC] Treaty and the ECSC Treaty.

This means that, when a dispute relating to the interpretation or application of one or more provisions of the Agreement is brought before it, the EEA Court may be called upon to interpret the expression "Contracting party" within the meaning of art 2(c) of the Agreement, in order to determine either, for the purposes of the provision at issue, the expression "Contracting party" means the Community, the Community and the Member States, or simply the Member States. Consequently, the EEA Court will have to rule on the respective competencies of the Community and the Member States as regards matters governed by the provisions of the Agreement.

It follows that the jurisdiction conferred on the EEA Court under art 2(c), art 96(1)(a) and art 117(1) of the Agreement is likely adversely to affect the allocation of responsibilities defined in the Treaties and, hence, the autonomy of the Community legal order, respect for which must be assured by the Court of Justice pursuant to art 164 of the [EC] Treaty. This exclusive jurisdiction of the Court of Justice is confirmed by art 219 of the [EC] Treaty under which Member States undertake not to submit a dispute concerning the interpretation or application of that Treaty to any method of settlement other than those provided for in the Treaty.

Consequently, to confer that jurisdiction on the EEA Court is incompatible with Community law.

As for the second point, it must be observed in limine that international agreements concluded by means of the procedure set out in art 228 of the Treaty are binding on the institutions of the Community and its Member States and that, as the Court of Justice has consistently held, the provisions of such agreements and the measures adopted by institutions set up by such agreements become an integral part of the Community legal order when they enter into force.

In this connection, it must be pointed out that the agreement is an act of one of the institutions of the Community within the meaning of indent (b) of art 117(1) [EC] and that therefore the court has jurisdiction to give preliminary rulings on its interpretation. It also has jurisdiction to rule on the Agreement in the event that the Member States of the Community fail to fulfil their obligations under the Agreement.

Where, however, an international agreement provides for its own system of courts, including a court with jurisdiction to settle disputes between the Contracting parties to the agreement, and, as a result, to interpret its provisions, the decisions will also be binding on the Community institutions, including the Court of Justice. Those decisions will also be binding in the event that the Court of Justice is called upon to rule, by way of preliminary ruling or in a direct action, on the interpretation of the international agreement, in so far that agreement is an integral part of the Community legal order.

An international agreement providing for such a system of courts is in principle compatible with Community law. The Community's competence in the field of international relations and its capacity to conclude international agreements necessarily entail the power to submit to the decisions of a court which is created or designated by such an agreement as regards the interpretation and application of its provisions.

However, the Agreement at issue takes over an essential part of the rules – including the rules of secondary legislation – which govern economic and trading relations within the Community and which constitute, for the most part, fundamental provisions of the Community legal order.

Consequently, the Agreement has the effect of introducing into the Community legal order a large body of rules which is juxtaposed to a corpus of identically-worded Community rules.

Furthermore, in the preamble to the Agreement and in art 1, the Contracting parties express the intention of securing the uniform application of the provisions of the Agreement throughout their territory.

However, the objective of uniform application and equality of conditions of competition which is pursued in this way and reflected in art 6 and art 104(1) of the Agreement necessarily covers the interpretation both of the provisions of the Agreement and of the corresponding provisions of the Community legal order.

Although, under art 6 of the Agreement, the EEA Court is under a duty to interpret the provisions of the Agreement in the light of the relevant rulings of the Court of Justice given prior to the date of signature of the Agreement, the EEA Court will no longer be subject to any such obligation in the case of decisions given by the Court of Justice after that date.

Consequently, the Agreement's objective of ensuring homogeneity of the law throughout the EEA will determine not only the interpretation of the rules of the Agreement but also the interpretation of the corresponding rules of Community law.

It follows that in so far as it conditions the future interpretation of the Community rules on free movement and competition the machinery of courts provided for in the Agreement conflicts with art 164 of the [EC] Treaty and, more generally, with the very foundations of the Community.'

Comment

Unlike its name the consultative jurisdiction of the ECJ results in binding decisions although it is not necessary that a dispute exists on the matter brought to the attention of the ECJ even though in practice this is often the case. The consultative jurisdiction is provided for all three Communities: arts 95(3) and (4) CS, arts 103 and 104 EA and art 300(6) EC. The Council, the Commission or a Member State may ask the ECJ for its opinion as to whether the envisaged agreement is compatible with the provisions of the Treaty. If the ECJ considers that the agreement in question is contrary to EC law the only possibility for that agreement to enter into force, apart from its renegotiation, is to revise the Treaty in accordance with art 48 EU. The consultative jurisdiction of the ECJ has become quite popular in recent years.

In the context of the present case it is interesting to note that the EEA Agreement is the most important and the most sophisticated agreement concluded under art 300 EC as it has created a sui generis form of integration.

EFTA was the biggest commercial partner of the EC but after the accession of Austria, Finland and Sweden to the EU on 1 January 1995, which resulted in their desertion from EFTA, the latter has become an obscure and insignificant organisation.

The Treaty establishing the European Economic Area (EEA) was signed on 2 May 1992 in Oporto between the 12 Member States of the European Economic Communities (EC, SC but not the EA) and the seven Members of the European Free Trade Area: Austria, Finland, Iceland, Liechtenstein, Norway, Sweden and Switzerland. Its main objective was the creation of the biggest trade area in the world which would account for 46 per cent of the world trade. It was beneficial for both parties: for EFTA countries it secured access to a single market which was essential for their economic survival; for the EC it ensured the expansion of its economy and constituted a counterbalance for the influence of NAFTA (North American Free Trade Agreement) and Japan in international markets.

There were a number of obstacles to the ratification of the original EEA Treaty.

First, the ECJ challenged the creation of the EEA in the present opinion.

Second, the Swiss rejected the EEA in a referendum held in December 1992. The non-participation of Switzerland in the EEA necessitated amendments to the original agreement. The Commission presented a modified text of the EEA Treaty on 9 March 1993 which was embodied in a Protocol annexed to the Treaty and signed on 17 March 1993. The EEA Treaty as amended entered into force on 1 January 1995.

Under the EEA six institutions were set up: the EEA Council, the EEA Joint Committee, the EEA Joint Parliamentary Committee, the EEA Consultative Committee, the EEA Surveillance Authority and the EFTA Court. The main difference in the functioning of the EEA bodies and the EU is that the decision-making procedures of the EEA institutions are based upon consensus between the EU and its Member States and the EFTA countries. Furthermore, the EEA institutions are classical inter-governmental bodies as they have no legislative power.

Presently, there are only three EFTA countries within the EEA: Iceland, Liechtenstein and Norway.

Public access to documents of the institutions

Bavarian Lager Co Ltd v Commission of the European Communities Case T–309/97 [1999] 3 CMLR 544 Court of First Instance

• *Access to information – transparency – Commission Decision 94/90/EC/ECSC/ Euratom on public access to Commission documents – scope of the exception relating to protection of the public interest – draft reasoned opinion – art 226 EC*

Facts

The Bavarian Lager Company lodged a complaint with the Commission concerning the UK legislation relating to the purchase of beer, under which a large number of pubs in the UK are bound by exclusive purchasing agreements requiring them to obtain their supplies of beer from particular breweries. The Bavarian Lager Company argued that the UK legislation was contrary to art 28 EC as it constituted a measure having an equivalent effect to a quantitative restriction on imports. The Commission decided, after investigation, to start infringement proceedings and to send a reasoned opinion to the government of the UK. In the meantime, the UK announced a proposal to amend the challenged legislation. As a result, the Commission has never sent a reasoned opinion to the UK, and informed the Bavarian Lager Company that the infringement proceedings had been suspended and would be closed after entry into force of the amended legislation.

The Bavarian Lager Company requested a copy of the 'reasoned opinion'. The Commission refused on the grounds that disclosure of the reasoned opinion could undermine the protection of the public interest and, in particular, the Commission inspections and investigation tasks. The Bavarian Lager Company challenged this decision.

Held

The Court of First Instance (CFI) approved the Commission's refusal.

Judgment

'Decision 94/90 is a measure which grants citizens a right of access to documents held by the Commission (*WWF UK* v *Commission* [Case T–105/95 [1997] ECR II–313], para 55, Case T–83/96 *Van der Wal* v *Commission* [1998] ECR II–545, para 41, and Case T–124/96 *Interporc* v *Commission* [1998] ECR II–231, para 46). It is intended to give effect to the principle of the widest possible access for citizens to information with a view to strengthening the democratic character of the institutions and the trust of the public in the administration (see, with regard to the corresponding provisions of Council Decision 93/731/EC of 20 December 1993 on public access to Council documents (OJ 1993 L340, p43, Case T–174/95 *Svenska Journalistförbunder* v *Council* [1998] ECR II–2289, para 66).

Furthermore, the Court has previously held that it is clear from the scheme of Decision 94/90 that that Decision applies generally to requests for access to documents and that any person may ask for access to any unpublished Commission document without being required to give a reason for the request (*Interporc*, cited above, para 48, and see, with regard to the corresponding provisions of Decision 93/731, *Svenska Journalistförbunder*, para 109).

However, two categories of exceptions to the general principle that citizens are to have access to Commission documents are set out in the Code of Conduct adopted by the Commission in Decision 94/90. The first category, which includes the exception relied on by the Commission in the present case, is worded in mandatory terms, providing that:

"the institutions will refuse access to any document where disclosure could undermine [inter alia] the protection of the public interest (public security, international relations, monetary stability, court proceedings, inspections and investigations)."

It is to be remembered that the exceptions to access to documents fall to be interpreted and applied restrictively so as not to frustrate application of the general principle of giving the public "the widest possible access to documents held by the Commission" (*WWF*, para 56, *Van der Wal*, para 41, and *Interporc*, para 49).

In the contested decision, the Commission states that disclosure of the reasoned opinion "could undermine the protection of the public interest, in particular Commission inspections and investigation tasks". It expressly mentions that "in the matter of investigation of infringements, sincere cooperation and a climate of mutual confidence between the Commission and the Member State concerned are required, which allow for both parties to engage in a process of negotiation and compromise with the search for a settlement to a dispute at a preliminary stage". In so doing, the Commission refers principally to the *WWF* judgment.

However, contrary to the Commission's assertions, it does not follow from the case law, in particular the *WWF* judgment, that all documents linked to infringement procedures are covered by the exception relating to protection of the public interest. According to that judgment, the confidentiality which the Member States are entitled to expect of the Commission warrants, under the heading of protection of the public interest, a refusal of access to documents relating to investigations which may lead to an infringement procedure, even where a period of time has elapsed since the closure of the investigation (*WWF*, para 63).

In that regard, it is wrong in fact and in law to classify the document to which the applicant seeks access as a "reasoned opinion". The Commission has stated, in reply to a written question put by the Court, that the members of the Commission did not have before them a draft of the reasoned opinion when, on 26 June 1996, they adopted the decision to deliver that reasoned opinion. The draft was in fact drawn up by the administration, under the Commissioner responsible for the area in question, after the Commission had adopted the decision to deliver a reasoned opinion. Thus, it was the Commission staff who drew up the document to be sent to the United Kingdom as a reasoned opinion. Subsequently, on 19 March 1997, the Commission suspended its decision to send a reasoned opinion to the United Kingdom and that document was, in the end, never signed by the Commissioner responsible or communicated to that Member State. The procedure initiated under art 169 of the Treaty thus never reached the stage where the Commission "deliver[s] a reasoned opinion"; the opinion therefore remained a purely preparatory document.

Although the Commission has not disputed the classification of the document at issue in the present case as a "reasoned opinion", it appears necessary to correct that misclassification. The action cannot be determined on the basis of a misrepresentation of the document at issue. A misrepresentation of that kind would amount to an error of law and consequently vitiate the Court's judgment (see the judgments in Case C–53/92P *Hilti AG* v *Commission (No 2)* [1994] ECR I–667, para 42, and in Case C–362/95P *Blackspur DIY and Others* v *Council and Commission* [1997] ECR I–4775, para 29, and the orders in Case C–55/97P *AIUFFASS and AKT* v *Commission* [1997] ECR I–5383, para 25, and in Case C–140/96P *Dimitriadis* v *Court of Auditors* [1997] ECR I–5635, para 35).

It follows that the question of access must be considered having regard to the preparatory nature of the document at issue. It will be remembered that according to Communication 94/C 67/03 of 4 March 1994, "anyone may ... ask for access to any unpublished Commission document, including preparatory documents and other explanatory material".

Taking account of those matters, it is therefore necessary to consider whether the Commission is entitled to rely on the exception relating to protection of the public interest and, if so, to what extent, in order to refuse to grant access to the document requested by the applicant.

In the present case, having regard to the preparatory nature of the document at issue and to the fact that, when access to it was requested, the Commission had suspended its decision to deliver the reasoned opinion, it is clear that the procedure under art 169 of the Treaty was still at the stage of inspection and investigation. As the Court stated in the *WWF* judgment, the Member States are entitled to expect confidentiality from the Commission during investigations which may lead to an infringement procedure (para 63). The disclosure of documents relating to the investigation stage, during the negotiations between the Commission and the Member State concerned, could undermine the proper conduct of the infringement procedure inasmuch as its purpose, which is to enable the Member State to comply of its own accord with the requirements of the Treaty or, if appropriate, to justify its position (see Case C–191/95 *EC Commission* v *Germany* [1998] ECR I–5449, para 44), could be jeopardised. The safeguarding of that objective warrants, under the heading of protection of the public interest, the refusal of access to a preparatory document relating to the investigation stage of the procedure under art 169 of the Treaty.

It follows from all of the foregoing that the sole plea cannot be upheld and, therefore, that the application must be dismissed.'

Comment

The CFI held that the exception to the right of access to Commission documents based on the protection of the public interest does not apply to all documents which deal with the infringement procedure. Only documents relating to inspection and investigations are covered by the exception, since their disclosure could undermine the proper conduct of the infringement procedure and the duty of confidentiality imposed upon the Commission. Indeed, the very nature of the procedure itself reflects the philosophy of art 226 EC, that is, that the

action should not be brought unless there is no other possibility of enforcing Community law. The use of non-contentious means in the proceedings under art 226 EC constitutes one of its dominant features.

In the proceedings under art 226 EC two stages can be distinguished: the informal stage prior to the formal procedure, and the latter itself which comprises the administrative and the judicial stage.

In this case the documents in question were prepared during the informal stage. At that stage the Commission enjoys a double discretion: first, it decides whether or not a Member State is in breach of art 226 EC; and, second, it assesses various aspects of the situation in question, especially by placing it in political context in order to determine whether to commence proceedings against the defaulting State. Advocate-General Roemer in *EC Commission* v *France* Case 7/71 [1971] ECR 1003 suggested that in certain circumstances the Commission should abstain from initiating proceedings under art 226 EC: when there is a possibility of reaching a settlement; when the effect of the breach of Community law is minor; when the proceedings of the Commission would exacerbate a major political crises in the defaulting Member State, especially in the context of a minor violation of Community law by that Member State; or when there is a possibility that the provision in question would be modified or annulled in the near future.

All complaints are registered by the General Secretariat of the Commission and are the subject of reports concerning the situation of the presumed violations of the Treaties. These reports are periodically examined by the chief of the private office or cabinet of each Commissioner and their observations are forwarded to the Commission. Once there is sufficient evidence that a Member State is in breach of Community law the appropriate Directorate-General initiates proceedings. At this stage the Commission invites the Member State concerned to provide some explanations, and that Member State is reminded that it has an obligation to co-operate under arts 10 and 211 EC: *EC Commission* v *Italy* Case 147/77 [1978] ECR 1307. The request for information takes the form of a 'letter pre-226' proceeding which fixes a time limit for the reply. Usually, the Commission and representatives of that Member State discuss the matter. Sometimes the negotiations between them take a considerable amount of time; on other occasions both parties will settle the matter immediately. The informal proceedings emphasise the non-punitive nature of art 226 EC. The objective of the provision is to terminate the violation of Community law and not to exacerbate the dispute.

The CFI rightly emphasised that in the present case there was no 'reasoned opinion'. It was in fact a draft reasoned opinion drawn up by the Commission in order to be sent to the UK. This document was never signed by the Commissioner responsible or sent to the UK. As a result, the CFI held this was a purely preparatory document.

Hautala v *Council of the European Union* Case C–353/99P [2002] 1 CMLR 421 European Court of Justice

• *Access to Council documents – Decision 93/731/EC – exceptions to the principle of access to documents – protection of public interest concerning international relations – partial access*

Facts
The Council of the EU refused Ms Heidi Hautala, a Member of the European Parliament (EP), access to a report on conventional arms' export drawn up by a working group within the framework of the common foreign and security policy under the COREU special European correspondence system. Documents written under the COREU system are for internal use by the Council, and in this case the contested report contained the exchange of views of the Member States on

the protection of human rights in the recipient countries of exported conventional arms. Ms Hautala learnt of the existence of the report when, on 14 November 1996, she put a written question to the Council seeking clarification of the common criteria for arms exports, defined by the European Council in Luxembourg in June 1991 and in Lisbon in June 1992.

The Council refused access to the contested report on the ground that it contained sensitive information, the disclosure of which would harm the European Union's relations with non-Member States. The Court of First Instance (CFI) annulled the Council's Decision refusing the applicant access to the contested report (Case T–14/98 [1999] 3 CMLR 528). The Council appealed from the judgment of the CFI.

Held
The ECJ upheld the judgment of the CFI.

Judgment
'As the Court of First Instance observed in para 78 of the contested judgment, while Decision 93/731 does not expressly require the Council to consider whether partial access to documents may be granted, it does not expressly prohibit such a possibility either.

In the context of its interpretation of Decision 93/731, the Court of First Instance first correctly pointed out the origin of that decision, in paras 80 and 81 of the contested judgment. Thus in Declaration No 17, "Declaration on the right of access to information", the conference of the representatives of the Governments of the Member States considered that "transparency of the decision-making process strengthens the democratic nature of the institutions and the public's confidence in the administration" and recommended that the Commission should submit to the Council no later than 1993 a report on measures designed to improve "public access to the information" available to the institutions. That commitment was reaffirmed at the European

Council in Copenhagen on 22 June 1993, which invited the Council and the Commission to "continue their work based on the principle of citizens having the fullest possible access to information". Moreover, in the preamble to the Code of Conduct, the Council and the Commission referred expressly to Declaration No 17 and the conclusions of the European Council in Copenhagen as the basis for their initiative. Finally, the Code of Conduct states the general principle that the public will have "the widest possible access to documents held by the Commission and the Council".

It is therefore apparent even from the context in which Decision 93/731 was adopted that the Council and the Spanish Government are wrong in submitting that that decision concerns only access to "documents as such rather than to the information contained in them".

Next, as the Court of First Instance observed in para 82 of the contested judgment, the Court of Justice stressed in para 35 of its judgment in *Netherlands* v *Council* [Case C–58/94 [1996] ECR I–2169] the importance of the public's right of access to documents held by public authorities and noted that Declaration No 17 links that right with the "democratic nature of the institutions".

The aim pursued by Decision 93/731, as well as being to ensure the internal operation of the Council in conformity with the interests of good administration (*Netherlands* v *Council*, para 37), is to provide the public with the widest possible access to documents held by the Council, so that any exception to that right of access must be interpreted and applied strictly (see, to that effect, with reference to Commission Decision 94/90/ECSC, EC, Euratom of 8 February 1994 on public access to Commission documents (OJ L46, p58), Joined Cases C–174/98P and C–189/98P *Netherlands and Van der Wal* v *Commission* [2000] ECR I–1, para 27).

The interpretation put forward by the Council and the Spanish Government would have the effect of frustrating, without the slightest justification, the public's right of

access to the items of information contained in a document which are not covered by one of the exceptions listed in art 4(1) of Decision 93/731. The effectiveness of that right would thereby be substantially reduced.

Finally, contrary to the submissions of the Council and the Spanish Government, the Court of First Instance did not err in law by holding that the principle of proportionality also requires the Council to consider partial access to a document which includes items of information whose disclosure would endanger one of the interests protected by art 4(1) of Decision 93/731.

On this point, the Court of First Instance correctly referred, in para 85 of the contested judgment, to the case law of this Court holding that the principle of proportionality requires that derogations remain within the limits of what is appropriate and necessary for achieving the aim in view.

Beside the fact that no reason has been put forward to show why an institution should be able to keep secret the items of information in a document which are not covered by the exceptions laid down in art 4(1) of Decision 93/731, a refusal to grant partial access would be manifestly disproportionate for ensuring the confidentiality of the items of information covered by one of those exceptions. As the Court of First Instance observed in para 85 of the contested judgment, the aim pursued by the Council in refusing access to the contested report could be achieved even if the Council did no more than remove, after examination, the passages in the report which might harm international relations.

The Court of First Instance also applied the principle of proportionality correctly when, in para 86 of the contested judgment, in response to the Council's argument based on the excessive administrative burden which would be entailed by an obligation to ensure partial access to the documents it holds, it reserved the possibility of safeguarding the interests of good administration in particular cases.

Accordingly, without its being necessary to consider whether, as the Council and the

Spanish government submit, the Court of First Instance was wrong in basing itself on the existence of a "principle of the right to information", that Court was right to hold in para 87 of the contested judgment that art 4(1) of Decision 93/731 must be interpreted as meaning that the Council is obliged to examine whether partial access should be granted to the information not covered by the exceptions, and to annul the contested decision on finding that the Council had not made such an examination since, in its opinion, the principle of access to documents applied only to documents as such and not to the information contained in them.

The appeal must therefore be dismissed.'

Comment

The most important aspects of the judgment are that, first, it specifies the exceptions to the principle of access to documents and, second, it endorses the principle of partial access to such documents. The Court held that art 4(1) of Decision 93/731, which lists the exceptions to access to the Council's documents, should be interpreted and applied strictly so as not to undermine the principle of access to such documents.

However, the CFI and subsequently the ECJ imposed an important restriction upon the duty of the Council to proceed to such an examination in each individual case based on the principle of proportionality and the necessity to safeguard the interests of good administration. The CFI held that: '... in particular cases where the volume of the document or the passages to be removed would give rise to an unreasonable amount of administrative work' the Council is allowed to 'balance the interest in public access to those fragmentary parts against the burden of work so caused'. Therefore, the Council is still entitled to refuse partial access to its documents, claiming that this would impose an unreasonable amount of work upon it. It seems that the Council has a duty to examine whether or not partial access should be granted, but it will also decide whether this will impose an unreasonable burden of work upon the Council.

Rothmans International BV v *Commission of the European Communities* Case T–188/97 [1999] 3 CMLR 66 Court of First Instance

• *Access to public documents – Commission Decision 94/90/EC/ECSC/ Euratom on public access to Commission documents – decision refusing access to documents – authorship of the contested documents – comitology committees*

Facts

The applicant, a company incorporated under Netherlands law, and a branch of the multinational Rothmans group which manufactures, distributes and sells tobacco products, in particular cigarettes, challenged the Commission's decision refusing it access to the minutes of the Customs Code Committee on the ground that the Commission was not its author, although the contested minutes were in its possession.

Held

The Court of First Instance (CFI) annulled the contested decision refusing the applicant access to the minutes of the Customs Code Committee.

Judgment

'It should be borne in mind at the outset, first, that Declaration No 17 and the Code of Conduct lay down the general principle that the public should have the greatest possible access to documents held by the Commission and the Council and, second, that Decision 94/90 is a measure conferring on citizens the right of access to documents held by the Commission (*WWF UK* v *Commission* [Case T–105/95 [1997] ECR II–313], para 55).

Next, it is important to note that where a general principle is established and exceptions to that principle are laid down, those exceptions must be construed and applied strictly, so as not to frustrate the application of the general principle (*WWF UK* v

Commission, cited above, para 56, and *Interporc* v *Commission* [Case T–124/96 [1998] ECR II–231], para 49).

In this connection, the rule on authorship, howsoever described, lays down an exception to the general principle of transparency in Decision 94/90. It follows that this rule must be construed and applied strictly, so as not to frustrate the application of the general principle of transparency.

It is in the light of these observations that the Court must appraise the argument that "comitology" committees are entirely distinct from and independent of the Commission and that the documents in question are consequently not Commission documents.

"Comitology" committees have their origin in art 145 of the EC Treaty (now art 202 EC), which provides that the Council may confer on the Commission, in the acts which the Council adopts, powers for the implementation of the rules which the Council lays down. These committees established pursuant to the "comitology" decision are composed of representatives of the Member States and are presided over by a Commission representative.

According to the "comitology" decision, the committees established under that decision, such as the Customs Code Committee, assist the Commission in performing the tasks conferred on it. Furthermore, under the terms of the Committee's internal regulation, the Commission provides the secretarial services for the Committee, which means that it draws up the minutes which the Committee adopts. In addition, it appears that this Committee, in common with the other "comitology" committees, does not have its own administration, budget, archives or premises, still less an address of its own.

In light of the above findings, the Committee cannot be regarded as being "another Community institution or body" within the meaning of the Code of Conduct adopted by Decision 94/90. Since it is also not a natural or legal person, a Member State or any other national or international body, such a committee does not belong to any of the categories of third-party authors listed in that Code.

At the Court's request, the Council confirmed that "comitology" committees are not working groups set up for the purpose of supporting it in its activity, but are, on the contrary, established for the purpose of assisting the Commission in the exercise of the powers conferred on it. Moreover, the Council stated that it was only exceptionally that it held copies of the documents produced by those committees. The Council concluded that the minutes of a "comitology" committee are not documents belonging to it and that it therefore does not have the power to grant access to those minutes. Finally, it pointed out that an application for access to the minutes of a "comitology" committee should be made to the Commission, since it is the Commission that provides the chairman of and the secretarial services for such a committee.

Furthermore, refusal of access to the minutes of the numerous "comitology" committees would amount to placing a considerable restriction on the right of access to documents, the importance of which was confirmed by the Court of Justice in its judgment in Case C–58/94 *Netherlands* v *Council* [1996] ECR I–2169, and by the Court of First Instance, most recently, in its judgment in Case T–174/95 *Svenska Journalistförbunder* v *Council* [1998] ECR II–2289. Such a restriction is not compatible with the very objective of the right of access to documents.

In those circumstances, it must be held that, for the purposes of the Community rules on access to documents, "comitology" committees come under the Commission itself. It is therefore the Commission which is responsible for ruling on applications for access to documents of those committees, such as the minutes here in question.

The Commission was therefore not entitled, in this case, to refuse access to the minutes of the Committee by invoking the rule on authorship set out in the Code of Conduct adopted by Decision 94/90. It follows that it infringed that Decision in adopting the contested decision.

It follows that the second plea in law must be upheld and that the contested decision must be annulled without its being necessary to examine the alternative submission put forward by the applicant.'

Comment

In this case the CFI clarified two important points: first, the nature of comitology, that is the relationship between the Commission and various executive committees; and, second, it defined the concept of an author of a document in the light of the principle of access to documents.

By virtue of art 211 EC the Commission exercises the powers conferred on it by the Council for the implementation of measures adopted by the latter. The Commission must act within the limits of authority delegated by the Council, although the ECJ has given a broad interpretation to such delegated implementation powers, as it recognises the wide discretion of the Commission in this respect, including the possibility of imposing sanctions and authorising derogations: *ACF Chemiefarma NV* v *EC Commission* Case 41/69 [1970] ECR 661; *Westzuker* Case 57/72 [1973] ECR 321; *Eridanea* Case 230/78 [1979] ECR 2749; *France and Ireland* v *EC Commission* Case C–296/93 [1996] ECR I–795 and *Ireland* v *EC Commission* Case C–307/93 [1993] ECR I–4191.

The drawback to the delegated implementing powers conferred on the Commission is that a system of procedural mechanisms has been established by the Member States in order to supervise the way the Commission exercises those powers.

In the present case, the Commission argued that, taking into account the nature of comitology, the Custom Code Committee, as one of the executive committees established under the Comitology legislation (Council Regulation 2913/92 (OJ L302 p1)), is entirely distinct from, and independent of, the Commission. The CFI decided otherwise. It held that for the purposes of the Community rules on access to documents, 'comitology' committees come under the Commission itself, mainly because they have no separate infrastructure: that is, they have no budget, no offices, no archives and no postal address of their own. Furthermore, they cannot be regarded as Community institutions or Community bodies. They are neither natural nor corporate persons. They are neither Member States, nor other international or national bodies. However, in the context of access to public documents they must belong somewhere. The CFI decided that they belong to the Commission. The decision of the CFI is surprising taking into account the purposes of 'comitology', although by virtue of art 7 of Decision 99/468/EC adopted on 28 June 1999 (OJ L184 17 July 1999, p23) the Commission is in charge of transmitting documents and preparing annual reports regarding the works of committees.

The Commission argued that it could not be considered as an author of the contested document because: first, the Commission only acted in its secretarial capacity; second, the contested minutes were adopted by the Customs Code Committee which is therefore their author; and, third, under the Commission Code of Conduct adopted on 8 February 1994, when a document is held by the Commission but its author is a natural or a legal person, a Member State or an EC institution or other Community, national or international body, the application regarding access to such a document must be addressed to its author.

Once the CFI decided that for the purposes of the Community rules on access to documents the Customs Code Committee came under the Commission itself, the Commission was regarded as the author of the contested minutes. Therefore, the Commission decision refusing the applicant access to the minutes was in breach of the principle of transparency.

3   The Sources of Community Law

Primary sources

See Chapter 8: Fundamental Principles of Community Law.

Treaties entered into by the European Community with third states

Hauptzollamt Mainz v *Kupferberg*
Case 104/81 [1982] ECR 3641; [1983] 1 CMLR 1 European Court of Justice

• *International agreements between the EC and third states – free trade agreement – conflict between national law and international agreements concluded by the EC with third states and national law of a Member State – supremacy of international agreements – direct effect of international agreements*

Facts
Prior to the accession of Portugal to the European Community, Kupferberg, a German undertaking, imported Portuguese wine into Germany. Duty was charged on these imports by the German customs authorities. Article 21 of the Portugal-EEC Free Trade Agreement contains provisions similar to those in the EC Treaty abolishing customs charges and charges having an equivalent effect. The plaintiff sought to have these charges abolished, arguing that art 21 of the Free Trade Agreement had direct effect in Community law and therefore prevailed over the inconsis-

tent statute of German national law. If direct effect could be given to the provision, no customs duties would be payable on the imported wine from Portugal.

In fact, the German court of first instance (the Finanzgericht Rheinland-Pfalz) did give direct effect to art 21 and removed the duties accordingly. The German tax authorities, however, appealed the decision of this court to a higher court (the Bundesfinanzhof) which subsequently referred the matter to the ECJ for a preliminary ruling.

Held
The ECJ held that the relevant provisions of the Portugal-EEC Free Trade Agreement produced direct effect on the ground that international obligations assumed by the Community must be respected within the national legal systems of the Member States. However, such provisions must satisfy conditions similar to those for direct effect of provisions of Community Treaties, namely that the particular provision must be unconditional, sufficiently precise, and must not require legislative intervention on the part of the Community institutions or the Member States.

Judgment
'The Treaty establishing the Community has conferred upon the institutions the power not only of adopting measures applicable in the Community but also of making agreements with non-Member countries and international organisations in accordance with the provisions of the Treaty. According to art 228(2) these agreements are binding on the institutions of the Community and on Member States. Consequently, it is incumbent upon the Community institutions, as well as upon the Member States, to ensure

compliance with the obligations arising from such agreements.

The measures needed to implement the provisions of an agreement concluded by the Community are to be adopted, according to the state of Community law for the time being in the areas affected by the provisions of the agreement, either by the Community institutions or by the Member States. That is particularly true of agreements such as those concerning free trade where the obligations entered into extend to may areas of a very diverse nature.

In ensuring respect for commitments arising from an agreement concluded by the Community institutions the Member States fulfil an obligation not only in relation to the non-Member country concerned but also and above all in relation to the Community which has assumed responsibility for the due performance of the agreement. That is why the provisions of such an agreement, as the Court has already stated in its judgment in Case 181/73 *Haegeman* [1974] ECR 449, form an integral part of the Community legal system.

It follows from the Community nature of such provisions that their effect in the Community may not be allowed to vary according to whether their application is in practice the responsibility of the Community institutions or the Member States and, in the latter case, according to the effects in the internal legal order of each Member State which the law of that State assign to international agreements concluded by it. Therefore it is for the Court, within the framework of its jurisdiction in interpreting the provisions of agreements, to ensure their uniform application throughout the Community.

... Nevertheless the question whether such a stipulation is unconditional and sufficiently precise to have direct effect must be considered in the context of the Agreement of which it forms part. In order to reply to the question on the direct effect of the first paragraph of art 21 of the Agreement between the Community and Portugal it is necessary to analyse the provision in the light of both the object and purpose of the Agreement and its context.

The purpose of the Agreement is to create a system of free trade in which rules restricting commerce are eliminated in respect of virtually all trade in products originating in the territory of the parties, in particular by abolishing customs duties and charges having equivalent effect and eliminating quantitative restrictions and measures having equivalent effect.

Seen in context the first paragraph of art 21 of the Agreement seeks to promote the liberalisation of the trade in goods, through the abolition of customs duties and charges having equivalent effect and quantitative restrictions and measures having equivalent effect, from rendered nugatory by fiscal practices of the contracting parties. This would be so if the product imported from one party were taxed more heavily than the similar domestic products which it encounters on the market on the other party.

It appears from the foregoing that the first paragraph of art 21 of the Agreement imposes on the contracting parties un unconditional rule against discrimination in matters of taxation, which is dependent only on a finding that the products affected by a particular system of taxation are of like nature, and the limits of which are the direct consequence of the purpose of the Agreement. As such this provision may be applied by a court and thus produces direct effects throughout the Community.

The first part of the first question should be answered to the effect that the first paragraph of art 21 of the Agreement between the Community and Portugal is directly applicable and capable of conferring upon individual traders rights which the courts must protect.'

Comment

By virtue of art 228(2) EC Treaty [art 300(7) EC] international agreements entered into by the Community and third countries or international organisations are binding upon the EC institutions and Member States. This provision has been inserted to underline that the principle of public international law, according to which only contracting parties to an international agreement are bound by its provisions. This principle does not apply in the context of the Community. In addition, the principle of supremacy of Community law strengthens the peculiar position of the Member States vis-à-vis international agreements concluded between the Community and third countries. In *Haegeman* v *Belgian State* Case 181/73 [1974] ECR 449 the ECJ held that the provisions of international agreements, from their entry into force, form an integral part of the Community legal order. It means that international agreements acquire ipso facto, (ie solely because they are international agreements) and from the date of their entry into effect the force of law in the Community legal order. No express incorporation into Community law is required

In the hierarchy of sources of EC law international agreements concluded between the Communities and third countries or international organisations are situated below primary sources and general principles of EC law but above the secondary sources. Their secondary position vis-à-vis primary sources is justified on the grounds of art 228(2) EC [art 300(7) EC] (*Schroeder KG* v *The Federal Republic of Germany* Case 40/72 [1973] ECR 125).

In the present case the ECJ held that neither the nature nor the structure of an international agreement can prevent an individual from relying on its provisions in proceedings before national courts.

Secondary legislation

EC regulations

Bussone v *Ministry of Agriculture*
Case 31/78 [1978] ECR 2429; [1979] 3 CMLR 18 European Court of Justice

• *EC regulations – binding force – direct applicability – art 189 EC Treaty [art 249*

EC] – national rules implementing EC directives

Facts
The Council enacted a number of regulations concerning the marketing of eggs throughout the Community. These regulations were incorporated into Italian law by a domestic statute. One of the regulations specified a requirement that packs containing eggs were to have a band or a label, which could not be reused, to inform the consumer of certain important details, such as the sell-by date, the producer's name, the weight of the goods and the quality of the product. Under the Italian law, 'packing centres' were authorised to conduct this activity and only the government was entitled to issue these labels or bands.

An Italian businessman ran an egg-packing centre, and was required to pay considerable sums to the Italian Ministry of Agriculture in order to acquire the labels. The businessman paid these charges, but challenged their legality under Community law, arguing that the regulation did not specify that a charge should be made for this service. In fact, the Italian legislation permitted the government to charge sums far in excess of the costs of supplying these bands and labels.

Held
The ECJ confirmed that direct applicability of regulations should not be compromised by implementing provisions of national law but did not believe that this effect had occurred in this particular case. The ECJ pointed out that the principle of direct applicability implies that the legal force of a regulation lies in the measure itself, independently of any implementing legislation.

Judgment
'The following third question is asked (by the Italian court):

"Must the said regulations be interpreted to mean that their direct applicability must not be jeopardised by the adoption of the national provisions which, whilst purporting to implement the regulations in question, introduce additional conditions, such as those reserving to the public authorities the right to prepare and distribute bands and labels and making the issue of such bands and labels subject to the payment of a pecuniary consideration?"

That question raises the point as to whether the fact that the preparation and distribution of labels is reserved to the public authorities and their issue is made conditional on payment of a pecuniary consideration is contrary to the directly applicable nature of the regulation, which would be prejudiced by the introduction of "additional considerations purporting to implement the regulation in question".

According to the second paragraph of art 189 of the Treaty a regulation shall have general application and shall be directly applicable in all Member States. By reason of its nature and its function in the system of sources of Community law, therefore, a regulation has direct effect. The direct applicability of a regulation requires that its entry into force and its application in favour of or against those subject to it must be independent of any measure of reception into national law. Proper compliance with that duty precludes the application of any legislative measure, even one adopted subsequently, which is incompatible with the provisions of that regulation.

That prohibition is, however, relaxed to the extent to which the regulation in question leaves it to the Member States themselves to adopt the necessary legislative, regulatory, administrative and financial measures to ensure the effective application of the provisions of that regulation.

The position is that established Regulations 1619/68 and 95/69, which provide inter alia that "large packs ... shall be provided with a band or label ... which shall be issued by or under the supervision of the official agencies ... appointed for the purpose in each Member State ... a list of [which] shall be forwarded to other Member States and to the Commission" (arts 17 and

26 of Regulation 1619/68) and that the latter shall be provided with "one or more specimens of the band or label ... which may be numbered [and] shall bear an official marking laid down by the competent authority" (art 5 of Regulation 95/69).

Nor is it ruled out that in that case the costs of printing and distributing the bands and labels, and those arising from the implementation of the specific checks required by the basic regulations, should be regarded as a service rendered to the user such as to justify the imposition of a pecuniary charge, on condition that it does not exceed the real costs of the supervisory system in question. Indeed, the fact that a Member State reserves to its public authorities the preparation of the bands and labels in no way disrupts the functioning of the common organisation and does not obstruct and is not of such a nature as to obstruct the free movement of the products.

The reply should therefore be given that the directly applicable nature of Regulation 1619/68, replaced by Regulation 2771/75 and Regulation 95/69, is not affected by the adoption of national rules required by the said regulations for their application which comply with the aim and objectives of the regulations by introducing additional conditions such as reserving to the public authorities the preparation and distribution of the bands and labels and making the issue thereof conditional on payment of a pecuniary consideration, on condition that the consideration is not disproportionate to the costs of the supervisory system in question.'

Comment

An EC regulation is binding in its entirety which means that its incomplete (*EC Commission* v *Italy* Case 39/72 [1973] ECR 101) or selective (*Granaria* Case 18/72 [1972] ECR 1163) application is prohibited under EC law. Also, the modification (*Norddeutsches Vieh- und Fleischkontor* Case 3/70 [1971] ECR 49) or introduction of any national legislation susceptible to affect its content or scope of application is contrary to EC law (*Bollmann* Case 40/69 [1970] ECR 69). These well established principles acquire a special importance in the case of an incomplete regulation. EC regulations are incomplete in the sense that they require Member States to adopt necessary measures to ensure their full application. Sometimes this requirement is expressly stated in a regulation itself, sometimes this obligation is based on art 5 EC Treaty [art 10 EC] which provides that Member States shall take all necessary measures to fulfil their obligations deriving out of the Treaty. In the present case the ECJ confirmed the principle that national measures enacted in relation to an incomplete EC regulation are subordinate to the provisions contained in that regulation and must neither alter them nor hinder their uniform application throughout the Community.

EC directives

Inter-Environnemental Wallonie ASBL v Région Wallonne Case C–129/96 [1998] 1 CMLR 1057 European Court of Justice

• *EC directives – obligations of Member States based on arts 5 and 189 EC Treaty [arts 10 and 249 EC] before expiry of transposition period – adoption of national measures during a directive's transposition period likely to seriously compromise the result prescribed by the directive – entry into force of a directive at the time of its notification to the Member State concerned – broad interpretation of 'waste' under art 1(a) of Directive 75/442 as amended by Directive 91/156*

Facts
In the framework of proceedings instituted by Inter-Environmental Wallonie ASBL (a non-profit-making organisation) requesting the Belgian Conseil d'Etat to annul the Decree of the Regional Council of 9 April 1992 on toxic or hazardous waste, the Belgian Conseil d'Etat (highest administrative court in Belgium)

referred to the ECJ for a preliminary ruling under art 177 EC Treaty [art 234 EC] questions:

1. concerning the interpretation of art 5 and 189 EC Treaty [arts 10 and 249 EC] and, in particular, whether those provisions preclude Member States from adopting national legislation contrary to an unimplemented EC directive before the period for its transposition has expired; and

2. concerning the interpretation of art 1(a) of Council Directive 75/442 of 15 July 1975 on waste as amended by Council Directive 91/156 of 18 March 1991.

Held
The ECJ held that a Member State to which an EC directive is addressed is required, during the period prescribed for its transposition, to refrain from adopting national measures liable to seriously compromise the result prescribed by that directive.

It also stated that a substance is not excluded from the definition of 'waste' contained in art 1(a) of Directive 75/44 as amended by Directive 91/156 merely because it directly or indirectly forms an integral part of an industrial production process.

Judgment
'It should be recalled at the outset that the obligation of a Member State to take all the measures necessary to achieve the result prescribed by a directive is a binding obligation imposed by the third paragraph of art 189 of the Treaty and by the directive itself.

The next point to note is that it follows from the second paragraph of art 191 of the [EC] Treaty, applicable at the material time, that a directive has legal effect with respect to the Member State to which it is addressed from the moment of its notification.

Here, and in accordance with current practice, Directive 91/156 itself laid down a period by the end of which the laws, regulations and administrative provisions necessary for compliance are to have been brought into force.

Since the purpose of such a period is, in particular, to give Member States the necessary time to adopt transposition measures, they cannot be faulted for not having transposed the directive into their internal legal order before expiry of that period.

Nevertheless, it is during the transposition period that the Member States must take the measures necessary to ensure that the result prescribed by the directive is achieved at the end of that period.

Although the Member States are not obliged to adopt those measures before the end of the period prescribed for transposition, it follows from the second paragraph of art 5 in conjunction with the third paragraph of art 189 of the Treaty and from the directive itself that during that period they must refrain from taking any measures liable seriously to compromise the result prescribed.

It is for the national court to assess whether that is the case as regards the national provisions whose legality it is called upon to consider.

If the provisions in issue are intended to constitute full and definitive transposition of the directive, their incompatibility with the directive might give rise to the presumption that the result prescribed by the directive will not be achieved within the period prescribed if it is impossible to amend them in time.

Conversely, the national court could take into account the right of a Member State to adopt transitional measures or to implement the directive in stages. In such cases, the incompatibility of the transitional national measures with the directive, or the non-transposition of certain of its provisions, would not necessarily compromise the result prescribed.'

Comment

The opportunities which individuals possess to enforce Community rights at the national level have been enriched by the ECJ in the present case. The practical implication of the ECJ decision in this case is that an individual is entitled, at a time when the period allowed by the directive for its transposition has not yet expired, to challenge national measures enacted during that period (whether or not they are intended to implement an EC directive) in the event of their incompatibility with the result prescribed by that directive. However, in relation to measures which purport to implement an EC directive a distinction must be made between national provisions intended to constitute full and definitive transposition of the directive and national provisions which introduce transitional measures or measures designed to implement the directive in stages. The ECJ addressed this question and held that in the case of the first-mentioned measures their incompatibility might indicate that the result prescribed by the directive would not be achieved within the prescribed time-limit as it would be impossible for a Member State to amend them in time and thus they should be struck down by a national court. In the case of the second-mentioned measures their incompatibility may only be temporary and therefore a national court should not declare them invalid before the end of the directive's transposition period.

This is a very important case as it specifies obligations imposed on Member States by EC directives before the expiry of the period for their transposition, and in particular the obligation of Member States to refrain from adopting measures which are likely to seriously compromise the result required by the directive. In the present case the ECJ has confirmed two important points.

First, that EC directives, whether published in the Official Journal of the European Communities or those not requiring publication (all other directives), enter into force (which means they are directly applicable) from the moment of their notification to Member States to which they are addressed, and not at the end of the transposition period laid down in the directive itself.

Second, the decision of the ECJ in the present case confirmed that a directive is directly applicable from the time of its notification to a Member State concerned, although it only becomes legally effective from the expiry of the implementation period. It has been well established (at least until this decision) that before the expiry of the prescribed time-limit no obligations or rights arise for a Member State or for individuals from a directive (*Pubblico Ministero* v *Ratti* Case 148/78 [1979] ECR 1629). For that reason, it has been widely accepted that until the transposition of directives into national law or the expiry of the time-limit prescribed for their implementation, they do not exist from a legal point of view. They were not considered until this case as being directly applicable. This view has been seriously challenged by the decision of the ECJ in the present case.

General principles of law

Accession of the European Community to the European Convention for the Protection of Human Rights and Fundamental Freedoms Opinion 2/94 [1996] ECR I–1759 European Court of Justice

• *European Convention on Human Rights – admissibility of the request for an opinion – art 228(6) EC Treaty [art 300(6) EC] – compatibility of accession with the EC Treaty – arts 164 and 219 EC Treaty [arts 220 and 292 EC] – competence of the EC to accede to the ECHR – art 235 EC Treaty [art 308 EC]*

Facts
The Council requested the opinion of the ECJ under art 228 EC Treaty [art 300 EC] on the question whether the accession of the EC to the ECHR would be compatible with the EC Treaty. Fourteen governments submitted observations; the majority were in favour of accession, and against it were France, Ireland, Portugal, Spain and the UK. The ECJ had to answer three questions: first, concerning the admissibility of the request taking into account that the conclusion of an agreement

was hypothetical as there had been no negotiation of any kind nor a draft; second, on the compatibility of accession with EC Treaty, in particular with rules on jurisdiction of the ECJ; and, third, on the competence of the Community to accede to the ECHR.

Held
The ECJ held that it had jurisdiction under art 228 EC Treaty [art 300 EC] to deliver an opinion. The ECJ held it had no sufficient information to decide whether accession by the EC to the ECHR would infringe its jurisdiction under arts 164 and 219 EC Treaty [arts 220 and 292 EC]. The Court stated that the Community had no competence to accede to the ECHR.

Judgment
'[*Admissibility of the request for an opinion*] … As regards the question of competence, in para 35 of Opinion 1/78 the Court held that, where a question of competence has to be decided, it is in the interests of the Community institutions and of the States concerned, including non-member countries, to have that question clarified from the outset of negotiations and even before the main points of the agreement are negotiated.

The only condition which the Court referred to in that Opinion is that the purpose of the envisaged agreement be known before negotiations are commenced.

There can be no doubt that, as far as this request for an opinion is concerned, the purpose of the envisaged agreement is known. Irrespective of the mechanism by which the Community might accede to the Convention, the general purpose and subject matter of the Convention and the institutional significance of such accession for the Community are perfectly well known.

The admissibility of the request for an opinion cannot be challenged on the ground that the Council has not yet adopted a decision to open negotiations and that no agreement is therefore envisaged within the meaning of art 228(6) of the Treaty.

While it is true that no such decision has

yet been taken, accession by the Community to the Convention has been the subject of various Commission studies and proposals and was on the Council's agenda at the time when the request for an Opinion was lodged. The fact that the Council has set the art 228(6) procedure in motion presupposes that it envisaged the possibility of negotiating and concluding such an agreement. The request for an opinion thus appears to be prompted by the Council's legitimate concern to know the exact extent of its powers before taking any decision on the opening of negotiations.

Furthermore, insofar as the request for an opinion concerns the question of Community competence, its import is sufficiently clear and a formal Council decision to open negotiations was not indispensable in order further to define its purpose.

Finally, if the art 228(6) procedure is to be effective it must be possible for the question of competence to be referred to the Court not only as soon as negotiations are commenced (Opinion 1/78, paragraph 35) but also before negotiations have formally begun.

... It follows that the request for an Opinion is admissible insofar as it concerns the competence of the Community to conclude an agreement of the kind envisaged.

[*Compatibility of accession with arts 164 and 219 EC Treaty*]
... In order fully to answer the question whether accession by the Community to the Convention would be compatible with the rules of the Treaty, in particular with arts 164 and 219 relating to the jurisdiction of the Court, the Court must have sufficient information regarding the arrangements by which the Community envisages submitting to the present and future judicial control machinery established by the Convention.

As it is, the Court has been given no detailed information as to the solutions that are envisaged to give effect in practice to such submission of the Community to the jurisdiction of an international court.

It follows that the Court is not in a position to give its opinion on the compatibility of Community accession to the Convention with the rules of the Treaty.

[*Competence of the Community to accede to the Convention*]
... Article 235 is designed to fill the gap where no specific provisions of the Treaty confer on the Community institutions express or implied powers to act, if such powers appear none the less to be necessary to enable the Community to carry out its functions with a view to attaining one of the objectives laid down by the Treaty.

That provision, being an integral part of an institutional system based on the principle of conferred powers, cannot serve as a basis for widening the scope of the Treaty as a whole and, in particular, by those that define the task and the activities of the Community. On any view, art 235 cannot be used as a basis for the adoption of provisions whose effect would, in substance, be to amend the Treaty without following the procedure which it provides for that purpose.

It is in the light of those considerations that the question whether accession by the Community to the Convention may be based on art 235 must be examined.

It should first be noted that the importance of respect for human rights has been emphasised in various declarations of the Member States and of the Community institutions ... Reference is also made to respect for human rights in the preamble to the Single European Act and in the preamble to, and in art F(2), the fifth indent of art J.1(2) and art K.2(1) of, the Treaty on European Union. Article F provides that the union is to respect fundamental rights, as guaranteed, in particular, by the Convention. Article 130u(2) of the EC Treaty provides that Community policy in the area of development co-operation is to contribute to the objective of respecting human rights and fundamental freedoms.

Furthermore, it is well settled that fundamental rights form an integral part of the general principles of law whose observance the Court ensures. For that purpose, the Court draws inspiration from the constitutional traditions common to the Member States and from the guidelines supplied by international treaties for the protection of human rights on which the Member States have collaborated or to which they are signatories. In that regard, the Court has stated that the Convention has special significance.

Respect for human rights is therefore a condition of the lawfulness of Community acts. Accession to the Convention entails a substantial change in the present Community system for the protection of human rights in that it would entail the entry of the Community into a distinct international institutional system as well as integration of all the provisions of the Convention into the Community legal order.

Such a modification of the system for the protection of human rights in the Community, with equally fundamental institutional implications for the Community and for the Member States, would be of constitutional significance and would therefore be such as to go beyond the scope of art 235. It could be brought about only by way of Treaty amendment.

It must therefore be held that, as Community law now stands, the Community has no competence to accede to the Convention.'

Comment

The importance of fundamental human rights has prompted the Council, the Commission and the European Parliament to sign a Joined Declaration on 5 April 1977 which expresses their attachment to the protection of human rights. Although the Declaration is solely a political statement it has initiated a new approach, that is the need for the Community to incorporate the European Convention on human rights into Community law. This initiative was blocked by the Member States at the Maastricht Conference and in the present Opinion 2/94 the ECJ held that the EC had no competence to accede to the ECHR without a Treaty amendment.

In the present opinion the ECJ clarified the extent to which art 235 EC Treaty [art 308 EC] can be used to extend the implied external competence of the Community. The ECJ stated that art 235 EC Treaty [art 308 EC] cannot constitute a legal base for accession to the ECHR since such accession being of constitutional significance is beyond its scope of application.

In this context it is interesting to note that the substantive action in respect of the protection of human rights within the EU was initiated by the Cologne European Council held in June 1999, which decided to draw up a charter of the basic human rights of EU citizens by December 2000. The Tampere European Council, held in October 1999, reached an agreement on the composition of, and method of work and practical arrangements for, a body (referred to as 'the Convention') entrusted with this task. The Convention was made up of 62 members: 15 personal representatives of the Heads of State and Government, 16 members of the European Parliament and 30 members of national parliaments. The Convention commenced its work in November 1999, electing as its chairman the former president of the Federal Republic of Germany, Roman Herzog. It completed its work on 20 October 2000 and sent its draft Charter to the European Council.

The Nice European Council held on 7, 8 and 9 December 2000, which concluded the Intergovernmental Conference on the Reform of European Institutions (IGC), adopted a declaration on the Charter of the Fundamental Human Rights of the European Union and welcomed the proclamation made jointly by the Council, the European Parliament and the Commission of the Charter, but decided that it would examine the matter of its binding force later (a new Intergovernmental Conference will be set up in 2004). As matters stand at the time of writing, the Charter is not binding but many Member States wish the Charter to be incorporated into the treaties. The Charter, even as a non-binding document, has some impact on EU law: the three Institutions which proclaimed the Charter have committed themselves to respect it and the Court of Justice of the European Communities will take it into consideration when deciding cases.

The Charter contains 50 Articles. Its main purpose is to make fundamental rights and freedoms more visible, more explicit and more familiar to EU citizens. The Charter expresses the fundamental human values shared by all Member States. The Charter, contrary to the European Convention on Human Rights, contains not only civil and political but also economic, social and societal rights. The Charter of Fundamental Rights was published in the OJ (OJ (2000) C 364).

Danisco Sugar AB v *Almänna Ombudet* Case C–27/96 [1997] ECR I–6653 European Court of Justice

• *Principles of international law – principle of good faith – accession of the Kingdom of Sweden to the European Union – common organisation of the markets in the sugar sector – national levy on sugar stocks*

Facts
Danisco Sugar AB, the only Swedish sugar producer and the largest importer of sugar, entered into a two-year agreement with the Swedish beet growers' association (SBC) which entitled the latter, in the event of accession of Sweden to the EU, to more than one-half of the difference between the 'minimum' Community price for sugar for the marketing year 1994/95 and the reference price for sugar applicable in Sweden during previous marketing years. When Danisco made a declaration in December 1994 that it held in stock 267,134 tonnes of sugar the Swedish government introduced new legislation which imposed a levy on sugar being held in stock in Sweden. Under the Sugar Law, Danisco was liable to pay approximately SKR 435 million in sugar tax. Danisco challenged the Sugar Law arguing that Sweden was in breach of Community law since the legislation in question was in fact a

transitional measure which under art 149 of the Act of Accession could be adopted only by Community institutions. Furthermore, Sweden was not permitted, on the eve of its accession to the EU, to adopt measures liable to affect the functioning of the common organisation of the market in the sugar sector.

Held
The ECJ held that arts 137(2) and 145(2) of the Act of Accession of Austria, Finland, Norway and Sweden and the adjustment to the EU Treaties, in particular arts 39 and 40 EC Treaty [arts 33 and 34 EC], Council Regulation 1785/81 of 30 June 1981 on the common organisation of the markets in the sugar sector as well as the Commission Regulation 3330/94 of 21 December 1994 containing transitional measures in the sugar sector following the accession of Austria, Finland and Sweden did not preclude Sweden from adopting, on the eve of its accession to the EU, legislation imposing a levy on sugar stored within that State.

Judgment
'In order to establish whether a law introducing a levy on sugar stocks, such as the Lageravgiftslag, is contrary to the provisions of Community law concerning the common organisation of the markets in the sugar sector, it must be determined whether that law concerns an area for which the Community rules make exhaustive provision or interferes with the proper functioning of the mechanisms provided by the common organisation of the markets, in particular through its influence on price formation or on the structure of agricultural holdings.

As regards the sugar forming part of the normal carryover stocks, Regulation No 3300/94 provides that the provisions of Regulation No 1785/81 concerning the self-financing of the sector or the system of export refunds are not to apply to quantities of sugar produced before 1 July 1995 in the new Member States, since the entire sugar output of those States was produced under national arrangements and much of the sugar produced had already been disposed of before 1 January 1995.

As regards pricing, the levy on sugar stocks could not have had any effect on the position of sugar producers whose storage costs, including taxes, undoubtedly rose because of the levy, but whose selling price for the product increased commensurately by reason of accession, to come into line with the higher Community selling price for sugar. The impact of the levy on such persons was therefore neutral.

On the contrary, failure to charge a levy on sugar stocks at the time of accession would have placed Swedish sugar producers at an advantage compared with Community sugar producers, since they would have been able to benefit from the higher Community selling prices without, however, having contributed to the self-financing arrangements for the sector.'

Comment
The question raised in national proceedings concerned the compatibility of a Swedish law (which entered into force on 31 December 1994, that is one day before the accession of the Kingdom of Sweden to the European Union) with Community law. In the event that the legislation in question was contrary to the Act of Accession and the provisions of Community law concerning the common organisation of the markets in sugar, the Kingdom of Sweden was in breach of the principle of good faith contained in art 18 of the Vienna Convention on the Law of Treaties adopted on 23 May 1969 according to which a State, prior to the entry into force of an international treaty to which it is a contracting party, must refrain from adopting acts which would defeat that treaty's object and purpose. Unfortunately, in the present case it was not necessary for the ECJ to decide whether the Swedish law in question was contrary to the principle of good faith as the Court held that Swedish law was not in breach of EC law. This case leaves open the question whether the principle of good faith is to be considered

as a general principle of EC law. In this respect it is interesting to note that in *Opel Austria GmbH* v *Council of the European Union* Case T–115/94 [1997] ECR II–39, points 90 and 91 the Court of First Instance recognised the principle of good faith as a general principle of Community law. The Court stated that the principle of good faith is: 'the corollary in public international law of the principle of protection of legitimate expectations which, according to the case law, forms part of the Community legal order [and on which] any economic operator to whom an institution has given justified hopes may rely'.

Emsland-Stärke GmbH v *Hauptzollamt Hamburg-Jonas* Case C–110/99 [2000] ECR I–11569 European Court of Justice

• *General principle of EC law – abuse of rights – agriculture – export refunds – goods immediately re-imported into the EU – the principle of lawfulness*

Facts
Emsland-Stärke, a German undertaking, exported several consignments of products based on potato starch to Switzerland. Their recipients were Fuga AG and Lukova AG, both established in Switzerland, and managed and represented by the same group of people. The invoice was addressed in each case to Lukova. Immediately after the release of the exported products for home use in Switzerland they were transported back to Germany (on one occasion to Italy) unaltered, and after the payment of relevant import duties released for home use in Germany. Emsland-Stärke had been granted export refunds for its products by virtue of Regulation 2730/79 which lays down common detailed rules for the application of the system of export refunds on agricultural products: OJ L317 (1979). The Hauptzollamt Hamburg-Jonas (the HZA) revoked the decision granting export refunds and demanded repayment of DM 66,722,89.

Emsland-Stärke challenged that revocation before the Finanzgericht (German Financial Court) on the basis that all the products had left the territory of the EU and had been released for home use in a non-Member State, and that in that State the goods had been sold by Fuga to Lukova before being re-imported. Emsland-Stärke claimed that it had no idea what the purchasers intended to do with the goods. The Finanzgericht dismissed the appeal. Emsland-Stärke appealed to the Bundesfinanzhof (Federal Financial Court) claiming that there had been a breach of Regulation 2730/79. The Bundesfinanzhof referred two questions to the ECJ.

1. Whether under Regulation 2730/79 the exporter loses his right to payment of an export refund if the product in respect of which the export refund was paid, and which is sold to a purchaser in a non-Member State, is, immediately after its release for home use in that non-Member State, transported back to the territory of the EU and is there released for home use on payment of import duties without any infringement being established.
2. Would the answer be different if, before the product was re-imported into the Community, the purchaser in a non-Member State sold it to an undertaking with which he was personally and commercially connected, which was established in that non-Member State.

Held

The ECJ held that under Regulation 2730/79 the exporter can forfeit his right to payment of an export refund if:

1. the product in respect of which the export refund was paid, and which is sold to a purchaser in a non-Member State, is, immediately after its release for home use in that non-Member State, transported back into the territory of the EU and is there released for home use on payment of import duties, without any infringement being established; and
2. that operation constitutes an abuse on the part of the Community exporter.

The ECJ stated that an abuse presupposes an intention on the part of the Community exporter to benefit from an advantage as a result of the application of the Community rules by artificially creating the conditions for obtaining it. Evidence of this must be placed before the national court in accordance with the rules of national law, for instance by establishing that there was collusion between the exporter and the importer of the goods into the non-Member State. The fact that the product, before being re-imported into the EU, was sold by the importer established in a non-Member State to an undertaking established in a non-Member State with which it had personal and commercial links should be taken into account by the national court when determining whether the Community exporter should repay refunds.

Judgment

'... it is clear from the case law of the Court that the scope of Community regulations must in no case be extended to cover abuses on the part of a trader (Case 125/76 *Cremer v Balm* [1977] ECR 1593). The Court has also held that the fact that importation and re-exportation operations were not realised as bona fide commercial transactions but only in order wrongfully to benefit from the grant of monetary compensatory amounts, may preclude the application of positive monetary compensatory amounts (Case C–8/92 *General Milk Products* v *Hauptzollamt Hamburg-Jonas* [1993] ECR I–779).

A finding of an abuse requires, first, a combination of objective circumstances in which, despite formal observance of the conditions laid down by the Community rules, the purpose of those rules has not been achieved.

It requires, second, a subjective element consisting in the intention to obtain an advantage from the Community rules by creating artificially the conditions laid down for obtaining it. The existence of that subjective element can be established, inter alia, by evidence of collusion between the

Community exporter receiving the refunds and the importer of the goods in the non-member country.

It is for the national court to establish the existence of those two elements, evidence of which must be adduced in accordance with the rules of national law, provided that the effectiveness of Community law is not thereby undermined.

The Bundesfinanzhof considers that the facts described in the first question referred for a preliminary ruling establish that the objective of the Community rules has not been achieved. It is therefore for that Court to establish, in addition, the existence of an intention on the part of the Community exporter to benefit from an advantage as a result of the application of the Community rules by carrying out an artificial operation.

Contrary to the assertions of Emsland-Stärke, the obligation to repay refunds received in the event that the two constituent elements of an abuse are established would not breach the principle of lawfulness. The obligation to repay is not a penalty for which a clear and unambiguous legal basis would be necessary, but simply the consequence of a finding that the conditions required to obtain the advantage derived from the Community rules were created artificially, thereby rendering the refunds granted undue payments and thus justifying the obligation to repay them.

Moreover, the argument that a demand for repayment cannot be addressed to the Community exporter on the ground that he did not re-import the goods cannot be accepted either. The re-importation of the goods is only one of the circumstances which demonstrate that the objective of the rules has not been achieved. Moreover, it is the exporter who enjoys the undue advantage of the grant of export refunds when he carries out an artificial operation in order to benefit from that advantage.

As regards the second question referred by the national court, it must be observed that the fact that, before being re-imported into the Community the product was resold by the purchaser established in the non-Member country concerned to an undertak-

ing also established in that country with which it has personal and commercial links does not preclude the export to the non-Member country at issue from being an abuse attributable to the Community exporter. On the contrary, it is one of the factual elements which can be taken into account by the national court to establish the artificial nature of the operation concerned.

In the light of these factors, the answer to the questions referred should be that arts 9(1), 10(1) and 20(2) to (6) of Regulation No 2730/79 must be interpreted as meaning that a Community exporter can forfeit his right to payment of a non-differentiated export refund if (a) the product in respect of which the export refund was paid, and which is sold to a purchaser established in a non-Member country, is, immediately after its release for home use in that non-Member country, transported back to the Community under the external Community transit procedure and is there released for home use on payment of import duties, without any infringement being established and (b) that operation constitutes an abuse on the part of that Community exporter.

A finding that there is an abuse presupposes an intention on the part of the Community exporter to benefit from an advantage as a result of the application of the Community rules by artificially creating the conditions for obtaining it. Evidence of this must be placed before the national court in accordance with the rules of national law, for instance by establishing that there was collusion between that exporter and the importer of the goods into the non-Member country.

The fact that, before being re-imported into the Community, the product was sold by the purchaser established in the non-Member country concerned to an undertaking also established in that country with which he has personal and commercial links, is one of the facts which can be taken into account by the national court when ascertaining whether the conditions giving rise to an obligation to repay refunds are fulfilled.'

Comment

For the Commission the situation in the main proceedings constituted an example of the abuse of rights by a Community exporter. The Commission noted that in the starch sector, at the material time, the amount of the export refund was twice that of the production refund. In addition, import duties were very low. All those factors combined made a three-way transaction very profitable. In addition, the time between the export and the return of the product was very short. Indeed, the same means of transport were used. As a result, the Community exporter obtained a substantial financial gain from the transactions.

In order to combat this kind of abuse, Regulation 2988/95 on the protection of the European Communities' financial interests (OJ L312 (1995)) was adopted on 18 December 1995. Article 4(3) of the above Regulation provides:

'... [acts] which are established to have as their purpose the obtaining of an advantage contrary to the objectives of the Community law applicable in the case by artificially creating the conditions required for obtaining that advantage shall result, as the case shall be, either in failure to obtain the advantage or in its withdrawal.'

Unfortunately, at the material time, the above Regulation did not apply. Nevertheless, the Commission emphasised that it could be cited as expressing a general principle of law in the Community legal order.

The above case is of considerable importance with regard to the recognition of the principle of the abuse of rights as a fundamental principle of EC law. The ECJ has applied the principle of abuse of rights in a number of cases in various areas of EC law, although the Court has never expressly recognised it as a general principle of EC law: *Cremer* v *Balm* Case 125/76 [1977] ECR 1593; *Anklagemyndighen* v *Töepfer and Others* Case 250/80 [1981] ECR 2465; *General Milk Products* v *Hauptzollamt Hamburg-Jonas* Case C–8/92 [1993] ECR I–779 and the Opinion in *Pafitis*

and Others v *Trapeza Kentrikis Ellados* Case C–441/93 [1996] ECR I–1347. In the case under consideration the ECJ has, however, moved closer than ever towards recognising the principle of abuse of rights.

In the commented case the ECJ specified the conditions in which an abuse of rights may be found. It requires a combination of objective and subjective elements, evidence of which must be ascertained by a national court in accordance with the rules of national law, provided that the effectiveness of Community law is not undermined.

In respect of the objective element the ECJ held that:

'A finding of an abuse requires ... a combination of objective circumstances in which despite formal observance of the conditions laid down by the Community rules, the purpose of those rules has not been achieved.'

This is exactly what the referring court found in the commented case. No infringement of Regulation 2730/79 was established. The exporter submitted a customs entry certificate which proved that the customs formalities for release of the product for home use were completed; the transport documents showed that in each case products were physically brought to a non-Member State although they were immediately forwarded from there.

The subjective element refers to the intention of the Community exporter to obtain an advantage from the Community rules by artificially creating the conditions laid down for obtaining it. The ECJ added that the subjective element can be established, inter alia, by evidence of collusion between the Community exporter obtaining the refunds and the importer of the product established in a non-Member State. In the commented case it was obvious that the Community exporter carried out an artificial operation with the intention of obtaining substantial financial advantage under the Community rules. In commercial language 'if he had not been so blatant he might have got away with it'!

Nold and Others v EC Commission
Case 4/73 [1974] ECR 491; [1974] 2
CMLR 338 European Court of Justice

• *General principle of EC law – source of EC law – human rights – European Convention on Human Rights – relationship between EC law and human rights – ECSC Treaty*

Facts
In accordance with a Community decision made under the authority of the ECSC Treaty [CS Treaty], coal wholesalers were prohibited from directly purchasing Ruhr coal from the regional selling agency unless they purchased a certain minimum quantity. The applicant was a wholesale coal trader. The decision of the Commission prevented him from purchasing coal from the wholesale agency because he could not meet the minimum purchase requirement. As a result, he was forced to purchase coal via an intermediary and thereby incurred additional expenses.

The applicant argued that the Commission's decision was in breach of his fundamental human rights and sought to annul that decision. However, the Community Treaties do not refer to fundamental human rights as a source of law.

Held
The ECJ held that fundamental human rights form an integral part of the general principles of Community law and that the Court was the guardian of these principles insofar as they were adopted into Community law. The source of these principles of human rights was declared to be the constitutional traditions common to the Member States, together with the international agreements entered into by the Member States.

Judgment
'The applicant asserts finally that certain of its fundamental rights have been violated, in that the restrictions introduced by the new trading rules authorised by the Commission have the effect, by depriving it of direct supplies, of jeopardising both the profitability of the undertaking and the free development of its business activity to the point of endangering its very existence.

In this way the decision is said to violate, in respect of the applicant, a right akin to a proprietary right, as well as its right to the free pursuit of business activity, as protected by the Grundgesetz of the Federal Republic of Germany and by the Constitutions of other Member States and various international treaties, including in particular the Convention for the Protection of Human Rights and Fundamental Freedoms of 4 November 1950, and the Protocol to that Convention of 20 March 1952.

As the Court already stated, fundamental rights form an integral part of the general principles of law, the observance of which it ensures.

In safeguarding these rights, the Court is bound to draw inspiration from constitutional traditions common to the Member States, and it cannot therefore uphold measures which are incompatible with fundamental rights recognised and protected by the Constitutions of those States.

Similarly, international treaties for the protection of human rights on which the Member States have collaborated, or of which they are signatories, can supply guidelines which should be followed within the framework of Community law.

The submissions of the applicant must be examined in the light of these principles.

The rights of ownership are protected by the constitutional laws of all Member States and if similar guarantees are given in respect of their right freely to choose and practise their trade or profession, the rights thereby guaranteed, far from constituting unfettered prerogatives, must be viewed in the light of the social function of the property and activities protected thereunder.

For this reason, rights of this nature are protected by law subject always to limitations laid down in accordance with the public interest.

Within the Community legal order it likewise seems legitimate that these rights should, if necessary be subject to certain limits justified by the overall objectives pursued by the Community, on condition that the substance of these rights is left untouched.

As regards the guarantees accorded to a particular undertaking, they can in no respect be extended to protect mere commercial interests or opportunities, the uncertainties of which are part of the very essence of economic activity.

The disadvantages claimed by the applicant are in fact the result of economic change and not of the contested decision.

It was for the applicant, confronted by the economic changes brought about by the recession in coal production, to acknowledge the situation itself and carry out the necessary adaptations.

The submission must be dismissed for all the reasons outlined above.'

Comment

In the present case the ECJ, for the first time, made reference to the European Convention on Human Rights and Fundamental Freedoms signed in Rome on 4 November 1950 to which all Member States are contracting parties. The ECJ emphasised that the European Convention on Human Rights can supply guidelines which should be followed within the framework of Community law. However, the ECJ held that these rights are not absolute and 'far from constituting unfettered prerogatives, [they] must be viewed in the light of the social function'. Thus it is legitimate that 'these rights should, if necessary, be subject to certain limits justified by the overall objectives pursued by the Community, on condition that the substance of these rights is left untouched'. Although the ECJ has incorporated an important number of human rights within the general principle of Community law, the uneasy relationship between EC law and human rights persists (see Opinion 2/94 above).

United Kingdom v *EC Council (Re Working Time Directive)* Case C–84/94 [1996] ECR I–5758 European Court of Justice

• *Principles of subsidiarity and proportionality – legal base – Directive 93/104/ EC – arts 118A(2), 100 and 235 EC Treaty [arts 138(2), 94 and 308 EC] – misuse of powers – infringement of essential procedural requirements – social policy – working time – fixing of Sundays as the weekly rest day – annulment of the second paragraph of art 5 of the Directive*

Facts

The UK brought an action for either annulment of Council Directive 93/104 concerning certain aspects of the organisation of working time; or, for annulling its art 4, the first and second sentences of art 5 and all of arts 6(2) and art 7. The UK challenged the legal base of the Directive. First, the UK argued that the Directive should have been adopted under art 100 EC Treaty [art 94 EC] or art 235 EC Treaty [art 308 EC] which require unanimity within the Council instead of art 118A(2) [art 138(2) EC] which imposes only qualified majority voting (QMV) within the Council. Second, the UK claimed that the Directive was in breach of the principles of proportionality and subsidiarity since the Council failed to demonstrate that the objective of the Directive could better be achieved at Community level than at a national level. Finally, the UK contended that the Directive infringed essential procedural requirements by not providing sufficient reasons for its adoption in the preamble.

Held

The ECJ held that art 118A(2) EC Treaty [art 138 EC] was an appropriate legal base for the Directive since it refers to 'working environment', 'health' and 'safety' which should be interpreted broadly. In respect of the principles of subsidiarity and proportionality the ECJ confirmed that the principle of subsidiarity could be relied upon by the applicant, although in this case it was invoked to support the main claim and not as an autonomous ground for annulment. Thus, all disputes as to whether or not subsidiarity as such can be invoked before the ECJ seem settled. The ECJ annulled only the second sentence of art 5 of Directive 93/104 which stated that Sunday could be chosen as the weekly rest day. Taking into account cultural, ethnic and religious diversity in Member States the ECJ decided to leave to their discretion the choice of the weekly rest period. The remainder of the applicant was dismissed by the ECJ.

Judgment

'In support of its action, the applicant relied on four pleas, alleging, respectively, that the legal base of the directive is defective, breach of the principle of proportionality, misuse of powers, and infringement of essential procedural requirements.

[The plea that the legal base of the directive is defective]
The applicant contends that the directive should have been adopted on the basis of art 100 of the EC Treaty, or art 235 of the Treaty, which require unanimity within the Council.

The scope of art 118A
Article 118A(2), read in conjunction with art 118A(1), empowers the Council to adopt, by means of directives, minimum requirements for gradual implementation, having regard to the conditions and technical rules obtaining in each of the Member States, with a view to "encouraging improvements, especially in the working environment, as regards the health and safety of workers" by harmonising conditions in this area, while maintaining the improvements made.

There is nothing in the wording of art 118A to indicate that the concepts of "working environment", "safety" and "health" as used in that provision should, in the absence of other indications, be inter-

preted restrictively, and not as embracing all factors, physical or otherwise, capable of affecting the health and safety of the worker in his working environment, including in particular certain aspects of the organisation of working time. On the contrary, the words "especially in the working environment" militate in favour of a broad interpretation of the powers which art 118A confers upon the Council for the protection of the health and safety of workers. Moreover, such an interpretation of the words "safety" and "health" derives support in particular from the preamble to the Constitution of the World Health Organisation to which all the Member States belong. Health is there defined as a state of complete physical, mental and social well-being that does not consist only in the absence of illness or infirmity.

It follows that, where the principal aim of the measure in question is the protection of the health and safety of workers, art 118A must be used, albeit such a measure may have ancillary effects on the establishment and functioning of the internal market.

Finally, it is to be remembered that it is not the function of the Court to review the expediency of measures adopted by the legislature. The review exercised under art 173 must be limited to the legality of the disputed measure.

[The choice of legal basis for the directive]
As part of the system of Community competence, the choice of the legal basis for a measure must be based on objective factors which are amenable to judicial review. Those factors include, in particular, the aim and content of the measure.

As regards the aim of the directive, the sixth recital in its preamble states that it constitutes a practical contribution towards creating the social dimension of the internal market. However, it does not follow from the fact that the directive falls within the scope of Community social policy that it cannot properly be based on art 118A, so long as it contributes to encouraging improvements as regards the health and safety of workers. Indeed, art 118A forms part of Chapter 1, headed "Social Provisions", of Title VIII of the Treaty, which deals in particular with "Social Policy". This led the Court to conclude that that provision conferred on the Community internal legislative competence in the area of social policy.

Furthermore, the organisation of working time is not necessarily conceived as an instrument of employment policy.

The approach taken by the directive, viewing the organisation of working time essentially in terms of the favourable impact it may have on the health and safety of workers, is apparent from several recitals in its preamble.

While it cannot be excluded that the directive may affect employment, that is clearly not its essential objective.

As regards the content of the directive, the applicant argues that the connection between the measures it lays down, on the one hand, and health and safety, on the other, is too tenuous for the directive to be based on art 118A of the Treaty.

A distinction must be drawn between the second sentence of art 5 of the directive and its other provisions.

As to the second sentence of art 5, whilst the question whether to include Sunday in the weekly rest period is ultimately left to the assessment of Member States, having regard, in particular, to the diversity of cultural, ethnic and religious factors in those States, the fact remains that the Council has failed to explain why Sunday, as a weekly rest day, is more closely connected with the health and safety of workers than any other day of the week. In those circumstances, the applicant's alternative claim must be upheld and the second sentence of art 5, which is severable from the other provisions of the directive, must be annulled.

The other measures laid down by the directive, which refer to minimum rest periods, length of work, night work, shift work and the pattern of work, relate to the "working environment"and reflect concern for the protection of "he health and safety of workers".

Since, in terms of its aim and content, the directive has as its principal objective the protection of the health and safety of workers by the imposition of minimum requirements for gradual implementation, neither art 100 nor art 100a could have constituted the appropriate legal basis for its adoption.

It must therefore be held that the directive was properly adopted on the basis of art 118A, save for the second sentence of art 5, which must accordingly be annulled.

[The plea of breach of the principle of proportionality]

… a measure will be proportionate only if it is consistent with the principle of subsidiarity. The applicant argues that it is for the Community institutions to demonstrate that the aims of the directive could better be achieved at Community level than by action on the part of the Member States. There has been no such demonstration in this case.

The argument of non-compliance with the principle of subsidiarity can be rejected at the outset. It is said that the Community legislature has not established that the aims of the directive would be better served at Community level than at national level. But that argument, as so formulated, really concerns the need for the Community action, which has already been examined [above].

As regards the principle of proportionality, the Court has held that, in order to establish whether a provision of Community law complies with that principle, it must be ascertained whether the means which it employs are suitable for the purpose of achieving the desired objective and whether they do not go beyond what is necessary to achieve it.

So far as concerns the first condition, it is sufficient that the measures on the organisation of working time which form the subject matter of the directive, save for that contained in the second sentence of art 5, contribute directly to the improvement of health and safety protection for workers within the meaning of art 118A, and cannot therefore be regarded as unsuited to the purpose of achieving the objective pursued.

The second condition is also fulfilled.

Contrary to the view taken by the applicant, the Council did not commit any manifest error in concluding that the contested measures were necessary to achieve the objective of protecting the health and safety of workers.

[*The plea of infringement of essential procedural requirements*]

As to those arguments, whilst the reasoning required by art 190 of the EC Treaty must show clearly and unequivocally the reasoning of the Community authority which adopted the contested measure so as to enable the persons concerned to ascertain the reasons for it and to enable the Court to exercise judicial review, the authority is not required to go into every relevant point of fact and law.

In the case of the directive, the preamble clearly shows that the measures introduced are intended to harmonise the protection of the health and safety of workers.

The argument that the Council should have included in the preamble to the directive specific references to scientific material justifying the adoption of the various measures which it contains must be rejected.

[*The plea of misuse of powers*]

... As is apparent from the court's examination of the plea of defective legal base, the Council could properly found the directive on art 118A of the Treaty. The applicant has failed to establish that the directive was adopted with the exclusive or main purpose of achieving an end other than the protection of the health and safety of workers. In those circumstances, the plea of misuse of powers must be rejected.'

Comment

The principle of subsidiarity is not only a socio-political concept but also a fundamental principle of EC law. No special procedure has been established to bring an issue of subsidiarity before the ECJ although this solution was supported by the European Parliament.

In the present case the ECJ made a clear distinction between the principle of proportionality and the principle of subsidiarity. Advocate-General Leger emphasised that the principle of subsidiarity answers the question at which level, Community or national, the adoption of a legislative measure is more appropriate, while the principle of proportionality governs the intensity of the Community action. In the other words, the ECJ on the ground of subsidiarity would examine whether a measure adopted by a Member State would achieve the desired Community objective. Under the principle of proportionality the ECJ would examine whether less onerous, less restrictive measures adopted by the Community would achieve the aims pursued.

4　Enforcement Actions against Member States

Actions against a Member State by the European Commission under art 226 EC

Commission of the European Communities v Hellenic Republic
Case C–387/97 [2000] ECR I–5047
European Court of Justice

• *Failure of a Member State to fulfil its obligations – judgment of the ECJ establishing such failure – non-compliance – art 228 EC – financial penalties – daily penalty payment – Directives 1975/442/ EEC and 1978/319/EEC*

Facts
Greece did not implement Directive 75/442/EEC on waste and Directive 78/319/EEC on toxic and dangerous waste within the prescribed time limit. The Commission brought proceedings against Greece under art 228 EC in which the ECJ found that Greece failed to fulfil its obligations deriving from the above-mentioned Directives: *EC Commission v Greece* Case C–45/91 [1992] ECR I–2509. Greece did not comply with that judgment. The Commission, after exchanging letters with the Greek government in respect of the failure of Greece to comply with the above judgment, and after following the procedure provided for in art 228 EC, submitted an application for:

1. a declaration that by failure to take necessary measures to comply with the above judgment Greece was in breach of art 228 EC; and
2. an order requiring Greece to pay the Commission (into the account 'EC own resources') a daily penalty payment of EUR 24,600, commencing from notification of the present judgment, for each day of delay in implementing the measure necessary to comply with the judgment in Case C–45/91.

Held
The ECJ declared Greece in breach of art 228 EC and ordered Greece to pay the Commission a penalty payment of EUR 20,000 for each day of delay in implementing the measures necessary to comply with the judgment in Case C–45/91. Payment to commence upon delivery of the present judgment and continue until the judgment in Case C–45/91 had been complied with.

Judgment
'[*Setting of the penalty payment*]
Relying on the method of calculation set out in its memorandum 96/C242/07 of 21 August 1996 on applying art 171 of the EC Treaty (OJ 1996 C242, p6) and its communication 97/C63/02 of 28 February 1997 on the method of calculating the penalty payments provided for pursuant to art 171 of the EC Treaty (OJ 1997 C63, p2), the Commission has proposed that the Court should, in respect of failure to comply with the judgment in Case C–45/91, impose a penalty payment of EUR 24,600 for each day of delay from the date of notification of the present judgment until the breach of

obligations has been remedied. The Commission contends that a financial penalty in the form of a periodic penalty payment is the most appropriate means of achieving the objective of compliance with the judgment as soon as possible.

The Greek government claims that the Court should set the penalty payment on the basis of coefficients of seriousness and duration which are more favourable to the Hellenic Republic than those applied by the Commission. It contends that the coefficient relating to the duration of the infringement, determined unilaterally by the Commission without considering the extent to which the judgment has been complied with, does not reflect the existing situation and would be unfair to the Hellenic Republic. While the Commission has a discretion to determine coefficients relating to seriousness, duration and the Member States' ability to pay, without their assent, it is exclusively for the Court to assess what is just, proportionate and equitable.

As to that, art 171(1) of the Treaty provides that, if the Court finds that a Member State has failed to fulfil an obligation under the Treaty, that State is required to take the necessary measures to comply with the Court's judgment.

Article 171 of the Treaty does not specify the period within which a judgment must be complied with. However, in accordance with settled case law, the importance of immediate and uniform application of Community law means that the process of compliance must be initiated at once and completed as soon as possible (Case 131/84 *EC Commission* v *Italy* [1985] ECR 3531, para 7; Case 169/87 *EC Commission* v *France* [1988] ECR 4093, para 14, and Case C–334/94 *EC Commission* v *France* [[1996] ECR I–1307]).

If the Member State concerned has not taken the necessary measures to comply with the Court's judgment within the time-limit laid down by the Commission in the reasoned opinion adopted pursuant to the first subparagraph of art 171(2) of the Treaty, the Commission may bring the case before the Court. As provided in the second subparagraph of art 171(2), the Commission is to specify the amount of the lump sum or penalty payment to be paid by the Member State concerned which it considers appropriate in the circumstances.

In the absence of provisions in the Treaty, the Commission may adopt guidelines for determining how the lump sums or penalty payments which it intends to propose to the Court are calculated, so as, in particular to ensure equal treatment between the Member States.

Memorandum 96/C242/07 states that decisions as to the amount of a fine or penalty payment must be taken with an eye to their purpose, namely the effective enforcement of Community law. The Commission therefore considers that the amount must be calculated on the basis of three fundamental criteria: the seriousness of the infringement, its duration and the need to ensure that the penalty itself is a deterrent to continuation of the infringement and to further infringements.

Communication 97/C63/02 identifies the mathematical variables used to calculate the amount of penalty payments, that is to say a uniform flat rate amount, a coefficient of seriousness, a coefficient of duration, and a factor intended to reflect the Member State's ability to pay while ensuring that the penalty payment is proportionate and has a deterrent effect, calculated on the basis of the gross domestic product of the Member States and the weighting of their votes in the Council.

Those guidelines, setting out the approach which the Commission proposes to follow, help to ensure that it acts in a manner which is transparent, foreseeable and consistent with legal certainty and are designed to achieve proportionality in the amounts of the penalty payments to be proposed by it.

The Commission's suggestion that account should be taken both of the gross domestic product of the Member State concerned and of the number of its votes in the Council appears appropriate in that it enables that Member State's ability to pay to be reflected while keeping the variation between Member States within a reasonable range.

It should be stressed that these suggestions of the Commission cannot bind the Court. It is expressly stated in the third paragraph of art 171(2) of the Treaty that the Court, if it "finds that the Member State concerned has not complied with its judgment … may impose a lump sum or a penalty payment on it". However, the suggestions are a useful point of reference.

First, since the principal aim of penalty payments is that the Member State should remedy the breach of obligations as soon as possible, a penalty payment must be set that will be appropriate to the circumstances and proportionate both to the breach which has been found and to the ability to pay of the Member State concerned.

Second, the degree of urgency that the Member State concerned should fulfil its obligations may vary in accordance with the breach.

In that light, and as the Commission has suggested, the basic criteria which must be taken into account in order to ensure that penalty payments have coercive force and Community law is applied uniformly and effectively are, in principle, the duration of the infringement, its degree of seriousness and the ability of the Member State to pay. In applying those criteria, regard should be had in particular to the effects of failure to comply on private and public interests and to the urgency of getting the Member State concerned to fulfil its obligations.

In the present case, having regard to the nature of the breaches of obligations, which continue to this day, a penalty payment is the means best suited to the circumstances.

As regards the seriousness of the infringements and in particular the effects of failure to comply on private and public interests, the obligation to dispose of waste without endangering human health and without harming the environment forms part of the very objectives of Community environmental policy as set out in art 130r of the EC Treaty (now, after amendment, art 174 EC). The failure to comply with the obligation resulting from art 4 of Directive 75/442 could, by the very nature of that obligation,

endanger human health directly and harm the environment and must, in the light of the other obligations, be regarded as particularly serious.

The failure to fulfil the more specific obligations of drawing up a waste disposal plan and drawing up, and keeping up-to-date, plans for the disposal of toxic and dangerous waste, imposed by art 6 of Directive 75/442 and art 12 of Directive 78/319 respectively, must be regarded as serious in that compliance with those specific obligations was necessary in order for the objectives set out in art 4 of Directive 75/442 and art 5 of Directive 78/319 to be fully achieved.

Thus, contrary to the Commission's submissions, the fact that specific measures have been taken, in accordance with art 5 of Directive 78/319, to reduce the quantities of toxic and dangerous waste cannot have a bearing on the seriousness of the failure to comply with the obligation, under art 12 of Directive 78/319, to draw up, and keep up to date, plans for the disposal of toxic and dangerous waste.

In addition, account should be taken of the fact that it has not been proved that the Hellenic Republic has failed fully to comply with the obligation to dispose of toxic and dangerous waste from the area of Chania in accordance with art 5 of Directive 78/319.

As regards the duration of the infringement, suffice it to state that it is considerable, even if the starting date be that on which the Treaty on European Union entered into force and not the date on which the judgment in Case C–45/91 was delivered.

Having regard to all the foregoing considerations, the Hellenic Republic should be ordered to pay to the Commission, into the account "EC own resources", a penalty payment of EUR 20,000 for each day of delay in implementing the measures necessary to comply with the judgment in Case C–45/91, from delivery of the present judgment until the judgment in Case C–45/91 has been complied with.'

Comment

For the first time the ECJ ordered a Member State to pay daily penalty payments for non-compliance with its judgment. In the above judgment the ECJ provided important clarifications in respect of pecuniary sanctions introduced by the Treaty on European Union (TEU) 1992.

The ECJ approved the method of calculating the pecuniary sanctions adopted by the Commission in the Communication of 5 June 1996, which was further elaborated on in the Communication of 8 January 1997. However, the ECJ is not bound by the figure suggested by the Commission. It may increase or reduce the fine, or may decide not to impose any penalty at all, as only the ECJ is entitled in each case to decide what is just, proportionate and equitable. Also, in different circumstances, the ECJ may decide to impose a lump sum penalty instead of a daily penalty payment. In the above case the ECJ held that a daily penalty payment was the means best suited to the circumstances.

The ECJ in determining the amount of the fine took into consideration the duration of the infringement, its degree of seriousness and the ability of the Member State concerned to pay. The Court held that, in applying those criteria, regard should be had to the effect of failure to comply on private and public interests and to the urgency of getting the Member State concerned to comply with the previous judgment. However, the ECJ reduced the amount of the daily penalty payment suggested by the Commission on the ground that the Commission had not proved that Greece failed fully to comply with the obligations imposed by Directive 78/319.

EC Commission v Belgium (Re Failure to Implement Directives)
Case C–225/86 [1988] ECR 579; [1989] 2 CMLR 797 European Court of Justice

• *Action against Belgium for failure to comply with Community law – defence based on constitutional fetters – defence rejected – immediate remedial action required*

Facts

In February 1982, the ECJ ruled that Belgium was in violation of its Treaty obligations by failing to adopt a number of Community directives within the prescribed period. By July 1985, Belgium has still not complied with the judgment of the ECJ. The directives were still not implemented. The Commission brought another action before the ECJ, this time requiring the Court to compel Belgium to comply with the judgment and adopt the appropriate legislation. The Belgian government claimed that its failure to comply with the judgment of the ECJ was attributable to the constitutional limitations placed on the central government by the Belgian constitution. In particular, the central government had no power to compel provincial governments to comply with the judgments of the ECJ as far as the implementation of legislation was concerned.

Held

The ECJ held that the fact that a government is constitutionally unable to compel a constituent part of its territory to comply with a judgment of the ECJ did not absolve that Member State of its responsibilities under Community law. The ECJ stated that although the Community Treaties did not specify a period within which a Member State must comply with judgment of the ECJ, remedial action must be commenced immediately after the judgment had been rendered.

Judgment

'The Belgian government states that the delay is the result of special difficulties arising out of the transfer of a substantial number of powers to the new regional institutions created by the Loi Speciale de Reforms Instititionelles of 8 August 1980.

In reply to the question asked by the Court, the Belgian government stated that the national authorities has power to implement only part of Directive 78/176. At the hearing the Agent of the Belgian government stated that the Royal Decree on the discharge of waste water into surface water had been adopted on 4 August 1986, and therefore at the level of the powers of the national authorities all the measures had been adopted to comply with the aforesaid judgments.

In so far as the regional level was concerned the Belgian government informed the Court that on 2 July 1981, the Flemish region had adopted a decree on the management of waste and had issued a series of implementing decrees which covered the four directives. However, the Belgian government admitted that the directives still had not been wholly implemented in the Walloon region and the Brussels region in spite of the efforts made by those two regions to that end. In that connection, the Agent of the Belgian government stated at the hearing that the Belgian legislation did not empower the State to compel the regions to implement Community legislation or to substitute itself for them and directly implement the directives in the event of persistent delay on their part.

As the Court stated in its judgment in Case 96/81 *EC Commission* v *The Netherlands*, [[1982] ECR 1791] each Member State is free to delegate powers to its domestic authorities as it considers fit and to implement directives by means of measures adopted by regional or local authorities. That division of powers does not however release it from the obligation to ensure that the provisions of the directive are properly implemented in national law.

Furthermore, the Court has consistently held that a Member State may not plead provisions, practices or circumstances existing in its internal legal system in order to justify failure to comply with its obligations under Community law.

In its judgment of 2 February 1982, the Court held that by not adopting within the prescribed periods the provisions needed to comply with the directives, the Kingdom of Belgium had failed to fulfil its obligations

under the Treaty. The Kingdom of Belgium was required under art 171 of the Treaty to take the necessary measures to comply with judgments of the Court. Article 171 does not specify the period within which such measures must be adopted. However, action to comply with a judgment must be commenced immediately and must be completed as soon as possible, which was not the case here since several years have passed since the judgments in question were delivered.

It must therefore be held that the Kingdom of Belgium has failed to fulfil its obligations under the Treaty.'

Comment
The ingeniousness of Member States in constructing defences under art 169 EC Treaty [art 226 EC] is astonishing. Over the years, they have attempted to plead every justification imaginable for their failure to fulfil their obligations under the Treaty. In the present case, the ECJ rejected a defence based on a Member State's constitutional and institutional organisation. The ECJ stated that a Member State cannot invoke provisions, practices or circumstances existing in its internal legal system in order to justify its failure to fulfil an obligation arising under Community law.

EC Commission v *Belgium* Case C–263/96 [1997] ECR I–7453 European Court of Justice

• *Action against a Member State – failure to implement a directive – defence based on circumstances existing in the Community legal order – defence rejected*

Facts
Belgium failed to implement Directive 89/106 on construction products within the prescribed time-limit. Belgium argued that Directive 89/106 required the adoption of further implementing measures at the Community level. This point has been confirmed by the Moliter group charged which the task of simplifying

legislative and administrative acts adopted by the Community institutions and the organisation responsible for the pilot project SLIM concerning the simplification of legislation affecting the functioning of the internal market. The government of Belgium stated that the delays in the adoption of further implementing measures by the Community institutions justified non-implementation of the Directive, and that its failure did not adversely affect the creation of the internal market in construction products taking into account the fact that the latter due to the delays on the part of the Community had not yet been established.

Second, the government of Belgium stated that the difficulties it faced with respect to the implementation of the Directive originated from circumstances existing in the Community legal order, namely because further implementing measures based on non-binding Community acts were necessary in order to complete the Directive in question. Therefore, implementation of the Directive would be very difficult because the Directive as it stood then was incomplete. As a result, the failure to transpose it into national law was justified.

Finally, the Belgian government argued that the Directive in question had been modified by subsequent directives on several occasion and that its final version would be adopted by Belgium in the light of the recommendations adopted within the framework of the SLIM programme.

Held

The ECJ held that a Member State is in breach of its obligation arising out of the Treaty even though difficulties regarding the implementation of the directive in question within the prescribed time-limit result from circumstances existing in the Community legal order. The ECJ held Belgium in breach of Community law.

Judgment

'In its defence the Belgian government states, first that a draft Royal decree has now been drawn up but that a number of problems concerning recognition and supervision, notification of bodies and the creation of fund in accordance with art 7 of the Law of 25 March 1996 remain to be resolved. In that connection a working group bringing together representatives of the Ministry of Economic Affairs and of the Ministry of Transport and Infrastructure is in the process of being set up and the measures necessary for the transposition of the directive should be adopted within six months.

Secondly, the Belgian government emphasises that the directive has still not been implemented at Community level. It refers in that connection to certain documents. First, a report drawn up by the group of experts on legislative and administrative simplification (Molitor Group) indicates that, seven years after adoption of the directive, the construction sector is still not in a position to use the EC trade mark for construction products. Moreover, in a report on the directive submitted on 15 May 1996 under art 23 thereof, the Commission itself acknowledged that there were still obstacles to the practical implementation of the directive and concluded that for a large number of products harmonised standards would not be available for five years. In the same vein the Economic and Social Committee in its opinion on "Technical standards and mutual recognition" (OJ 1996 C212 p7) cited the poor operation of the directive and the lack of harmonised standards. Finally, the Council has supported the setting up of the pilot project known as SLIM (simpler legislation for the single market) whose objective is to examine whether the obligations and burdens weighting on undertakings and which constitute an impediment on account of their over complexity may be eased by simplifying legislative or administrative provisions.

The Belgian government concludes that the delay in the transposition of the directive has had no ill consequence on the process of achieving the single market or on the process of implementing the directive.

The Commission objects that, even though there has been a delay in the application of the directive, that does not prevent its transposition. Referring to the judgment in *EC Commission* v *Italy* Case C–182/94 [1995] ECR I–1465, it also emphasised the fact that the possibility of an amendment to a directive in the near future cannot justify the failure to transpose.

Thirdly, the Belgian government stresses that some of the problems connected with the transposition of the directive stem from Community law itself.

In its resolution of 21 December 1989 on a global approach to conformity assessment (OJ 1990 C10 p1), for instance, the Council advocated systematic recourse to European standards (EN 45000) for the approval of certification and inspection and testing laboratories. That resolution led to the drawing up of a guide on the application of Community directives on technical harmonisation drawn up on the basis of the provisions of the new approach and the global approach (first version – 1994) and the general procedures were laid down in the document on methods of co-ordination for procedures for notification and management of bodies notified. Effect was given to the Council resolution and the documents cited, as regards the directive, by means of the document "Construct 95/149" of 3 November 1995, approved in December 1995 by the Standing Committee on construction referred to in art 19 of the directive.

According to the Belgian government, since these documents had no binding force, the Community legal basis is insufficient to permit the directive to be transposed in such a way as to take account both of the Council Resolution of 21 December 1989 and of the technical approval guide of 3 November 1995. In those circumstances the directive needs to be amended.

Fourthly, the Belgian Government points out that the directive has already been modified by Council Directive 93/68/EEC of 22 July 1993 amending Directives 87/404/EEC (simple pressure vessels), 88/378/EEC (safety of toys), 89/106/EEC (construction products), 89/336/ EEC (electromagnetic compatibility) 89/392/EEC (machinery),

89/686/EEC (personal protective equipment), 90/384/EEC (non-automatic weighing instruments), 90/385/EEC (active implantable medicinal devices), 90/396/ EEC (appliances burning gaseous fuels), 91/263/EEC (telecommunications terminal equipment), 92/42/EEC (new hot-water boilers fired with liquid or gaseous fuels) and 73/23/EEC (electrical equipment designed for use within certain voltage limits) (OJ 1993 L220 p1). Article 14 thereof required the Member States to transpose the directive by 1 July 1994.

Moreover, the Belgian government observes that the SLIM report, submitted to the Council on 26 November 1996, could also result in an amendment to the directive.

It concludes that, under those conditions, the solution adopted by the Kingdom of Belgium, namely the adoption of an enabling law accompanied by a Royal decree, is the most appropriate method of transposition. Those legal instruments enable a swift and flexible response to changes in circumstances without the need for a cumbersome procedure of legislative amendment.

The Court notes that, after expiry of the period prescribed by the reasoned opinion, no provision had been adopted by the Kingdom of Belgium in order to meet its obligation to transpose the directive.

Although it is true, as the Kingdom of Belgium has pointed out, that a law was adopted on 25 March 1996 with that intention, it should be observed that, since it contains no substantive provisions transposing the directive but merely empowers an authority subsequently to adopt the requisite substantive provisions, that law cannot be regarded as effecting a complete and accurate transposition of the directive.

With regard to the first argument relied on by the Belgian government, the Court has consistently held that a Member State may not rely on circumstances in its internal legal system to justify its failure to comply with obligations and time-limits laid down in a directive (*EC Commission* v *Greece* Cases C–109, 207 and 225/94 [1995] ECR I–1791, para 11).

As to the second argument, non-implementation of the directive at Community level cannot prevent the Kingdom of Belgium from adopting the laws and regulations necessary for transposition of the directive.

Furthermore, the binding force conferred on directives by the third paragraph of art 189 of the Treaty precludes any calling in question by a Member State, for opportunistic reasons, of the period prescribed by any directive for its transposition.

Finally, where the finding of a failure by a Member State to fulfil its obligations is not bound up with a finding as to the damage flowing there from, a Member State may not rely on the argument that the failure to adopt measures to transpose a directive has had no adverse consequences for the functioning of the internal market or of that directive.

As to the third argument that the Council Resolution of 21 December 1989 and the technical approval guide of 3 November 1995 were without binding force, suffice it to state that the failure alleged against that State is constituted by the failure to transpose the directive. The fact that those documents are of no binding effect is therefore of no relevance to the alleged failure to fulfill obligations.

As to the fourth argument, concerning the various amendments made to the directive, Directive 93/68 neither amends nor abrogates the obligation to transpose it. The adoption of the latter directive therefore has no effect on the alleged failure to fulfil obligations. The same is true a fortiori of the purely putative adoption of another amending directive.

As regards the choice of a framework law accompanied by a Royal decree, it should be recalled that, in regard to the implementation of directives, art 189 of the Treaty leaves to the Member States the choice of forms and methods, provided that the result prescribed by the directive is achieved. However, in the present case, the framework law was not accompanied by any Royal decree, notwithstanding standing the flexibility afforded, according to the Belgian government, by such a legal instrument.

It must therefore be concluded that the result prescribed by the directive was not achieved, since an essential component of its transposition is lacking

Consequently, it must be held that, by not adopting all the laws, regulations and administrative provisions necessary to comply with the directive, the Kingdom of Belgium has failed to fulfil its obligations under that directive.'

Comment

The originality of the defences submitted by Belgium requires a comment. Notwithstanding arguments submitted by Belgium, the ECJ held that non-adoption on the part of the Community institutions of further implementing measures cannot justify a failure to transpose a directive by a Member State to which it is addressed. The ECJ rejected the defence based on circumstances existing in the Community legal order. In this respect, the ECJ emphasised that the obligation of implementation which results from art 189 EC Treaty [art 249 EC] cannot be modified according to the circumstances, even though difficulties have their root in the Community legal order. The ECJ underlined that the obligations arising out of the EC Treaty are assessed objectively, that is they are not conditional upon the existence of loss and therefore a Member State may not rely on the argument that the failure to adopt measures to transpose a directive has had no adverse impact on the functioning of the internal market or of that directive. The failure to fulfil an obligation results solely from non-implementation of a directive within a prescribed time-limit. It also means that a directive must be transposed as it stands, regardless of the fact that it may be subject to future modifications and amendments.

EC Commission v *French Republic*
Case C–144/97 [1998] ECR I–613
European Court of Justice

• *Action against a Member State – failure*

Enforcement Actions against Member States 83

to implement a directive – defence based on internal legislative difficulties – dissolution of French Parliament – defence rejected

Facts

The Commission brought proceedings against the French Republic for failure to implement Directive 92/74/ECC of 22 September 1992 widening the scope of Directive 81/85/ECC on the approximation of provisions laid down by law, regulation or administrative action relating to veterinary medicinal products and homeopathic veterinary medicinal products. The French government stated that it had already prepared a draft law and a draft decree transposing Directive 92/74/EEC but it was impossible to enact legislation in this respect because, by decree of 21 April 1997, the President of the French Republic dissolved the French Parliament.

Held

The ECJ held that the dissolution of a national Parliament which made it impossible for a Member State to implement the directive in question within the prescribed time-limit cannot amount to a defence under art 169 EC Treaty [art 226 EC]. The ECJ held France in breach of Community law.

Judgment

'Under the Directive the Member States had to bring into force the laws, regulations and administrative provisions needed in order to comply with the Directive by 31 December 1993 and to inform the Commission thereof forthwith.

The French Republic states that a draft law and a draft decree transposing the Directive have been drawn up. It adds that the draft law could not be put to a parliamentary vote because, by decree of 21 April 1997, the President of the French Republic decided to dissolve the National Assembly.

It is, however, settled case-law that a Member State cannot rely on provisions, practices or circumstances existing in its internal legal order in order to justify its failure to respect the obligations and time-limits laid down by a directive.

Since the Directive was not transposed within the period prescribed therein, the infringement pleaded by the Commission in that regard must be considered to be established.'

Comment

The interest of this case lies in the fact that the French government decided to justify its failure to implement the Directive in question on internal legislative difficulties knowing that the ECJ has been very consistent in rejecting this defence (see *EC Commission* v *Luxembourg* Case 58/81 [1982] ECR 2175; *EC Commission* v *Belgium* Case 77/69 [1970] ECR 237; *EC Commission* v *Belgium* Case C–133/94 [1996] ECR I–2323).

EC Commission v *Greece (Re Electronic Cash Registers)* Case C–137/91 [1992] 3 CMLR 117 European Court of Justice

• *Obligation to co-operate with the Commission during investigations under art 169 EC Treaty [art 226 EC] – breach of arts 5 and 30 EC Treaty by Greece [arts 10 and 28 EC] – separate proceedings based on art 5 EC Treaty [art 10 EC]*

Facts

In 1988 Greece enacted a law requiring certain retailers to use electronic cash registers. All such registers were to be approved by the appropriate national authorities which adopted a policy of refusing to certify any register containing less than 35 per cent add-on value from Greece. Another Member States complained to the Commission that this policy obstructed imports of cash registers made by its manufacturers and was therefore in breach of art 30 EC Treaty [art 28 EC].

The Commission began an investigation and, in the course of its initial stage, sent two telex messages to the Greek Permanent Representation in Brussels, requesting further information. No reply was received in response and the Commission issued a formal notice under art 169 EC Treaty [art 226 EC] informing Greece of the alleged breach of EC law and asking it to submit its observations on the compatibility of the national law with its Community obligations in respect of the disputed matter.

Again no reply was received by the Commission and, as a final step, the Commission delivered the formal pre-litigation reasoned opinion as required by art 169(1) EC Treaty [art 226(1) EC] prior to bringing Court proceedings. Once again, Greece failed to respond. The Commission instituted proceedings before the ECJ based on art 5 EC Treaty [art 10 EC].

Held

The ECJ held that Greece had violated art 5 EC Treaty [art 10 EC] merely by failing to co-operate with the Commission during the investigation. Article 5 EC Treaty [art 10 EC] imposes a positive duty on Member States to assist the Commission in its investigations into alleged violations of Community law, and failure to do so is itself a breach of Community law.

Judgment

'The Commission states that, following a complaint from the authorities of a Member State concerning the arrangements in force in Greece relating to the purchase of electronic cash registers by commercial enterprises, it sent two telexes on December 7, 1988 and February 23, 1989, respectively, to the defendant's Permanent Representation to the European Communities asking for information and explanations concerning such arrangements. As the Hellenic Republic never replied to those telexes, the Commission considers that it infringed art 5 [EC] Treaty.

Greece rejects this complaint. It points out that the Greek government gave the Commission all the necessary information concerning the arrangements in question at a meeting in Athens in September 1990. It adds that in January 1991 it sent the Commission the text of Act 1914/1990, which is said to put an end to the infringement by the defendant of art 30 [EC] Treaty. Therefore, the Commission was fully informed before the action was brought and it had no further interest in applying to the Court for a declaration that art 5 had been infringed.

In this connection it should be observed that the defendant did not supply the information in question until almost two years after it was requested and, in any case, after expiry of the time limit fixed by the reasoned opinion.

The failure to reply to the Commission's questions within a reasonable period made the task which it has to perform more difficult and therefore amounts to a violation of the obligation of co-operation laid down by art 5 [EC] Treaty.

The defendant does not dispute the Commission's complaint that Act 1809/1988 is contrary to art 30 [EC] Treaty because it requires, as a condition for the approval of electronic cash registers by the Greek authorities, that not less than 35 per cent of the cost of the machine should consist of national value added. An Act which is said to rectify the position was brought in only after the time-limit fixed by the reasoned opinion had expired.

It follows that Greece has failed to fulfil its obligations under arts 5 and 30 [EC] Treaty by not providing the Commission with the information which it had asked for and by imposing an obligation on enterprises to purchase exclusively electronic cash registers comprising in their manufacture not less than 35 per cent value added in Greece.'

Comment

Article 5 EC Treaty [art 10 EC] was considered for a long time as an interpretive device requiring Member States to act in good faith. Gradually, its scope of application has been extended. First, art 5 EC Treaty [art 10 EC] has served to strengthen the binding effect of

Community obligations imposed upon Member States. Second, the ECJ has imposed, by virtue of art 5 EC Treaty [art 10 EC], an obligation on national courts to interpret national law in conformity with Community law; and, finally, art 5 EC Treaty [art 10 EC] has become an independent and autonomous source of obligation. As a result, a breach of art 5 EC Treaty [art 10 EC] gives rise to the liability of the Member States under art 169 EC Treaty [art 226 EC]. In the present case the ECJ explained the autonomous function of art 5 EC Treaty [art 10 EC].

Article 5 EC Treaty [art 10 EC] imposes a positive duty on Member States to co-operate with the Commission in its investigations into alleged violations of Community law. Failure to do so is in itself sufficient reason to give rise to the liability of a Member State under art 169 EC Treaty [art 226 EC] (*EC Commission v Italy* Case C–33/90 [1991] ECR I–5987; *EC Commission v Greece* Case C–65/91 [1992] ECR I–5245) regardless of whether a Member State refuses or simply ignores the request of the Commission for information (*EC Commission v Greece* Case 272/86 [1988] ECR 4875; *EC Commission v Spain* Case C–375/92 [1994] ECR I–923) or omits to forward necessary indications allowing the Commission to exercise its control of the observance by the Member States of Community law (*EC Commission v United Kingdom* Case C–40/92 [1994] ECR I–989).

Action by a Member State against another Member State under art 227 EC

France v *United Kingdom (Re Fishing Mesh)* Case 141/78 [1979] ECR 2923; [1980] 1 CMLR 6
European Court of Justice

• *Direct action by one Member State against another Member State – incompatibility of national measures with EC law – the duty of co-operation – art 5 EC Treaty [art 10 EC] – conservation of fishing stock*

Facts
The United Kingdom enacted an Order in Council which regulated the size of the mesh of fishing nets in an attempt to conserve fishing stocks. Fishing policy is a matter within the competence of the Community and the Council of the European Union had earlier passed a resolution allowing Member States to introduce conservation measures, but only on the condition that prior consultations were held with the Commission. The United Kingdom failed to enter into such consultations prior to the enactment of the Order.

France complained to the Commission that the order had been enacted without the prior approval of the Commission and was therefore contrary to Community law. The Commission delivered a reasoned opinion which supported the contentions of the French government, but did not assume responsibility for continuing the action. The French government brought the matter before the ECJ in the form of a direct action against the United Kingdom based on art 170 EC Treaty [art 227 EC].

Held
The ECJ held that the British Order in Council had indeed been enacted without the necessary formalities being observed and consequently the United Kingdom was held in breach of Community law.

Judgment
'The French Republic claims in particular that the disputed order, which was adopted in a matter reserved for the competence of the Community, was brought into force in disregard of the requirements set out in Annex VI to the Resolution adopted by the Council at The Hague at its meetings on 30 October and 3 November 1976, under which, pending the implementation of the appropriate Community measures, Member

States might, as an interim measure, adopt unilateral measures to ensure the protection of fishery resources on condition that they had first consulted the Commission and sought its approval. As these requirements were not observed by the government of the United Kingdom the measure adopted is contrary to Community law. In the alternative, the French government also claims that the disputed order is, with regard to the measure adopted, excessive and thus does not constitute a reasonable measure of protection.

... The Commission has rightly claimed that that resolution, in particular field to which it applies, makes specific the duties of co-operation which the Member States assumed under art 5 of the [EC] Treaty when they acceded to the Community. Performance of these duties is particularly necessary in a situation in which it has appeared impossible, by reason of divergences of interest which it has not yet been possible to resolve, to establish a common policy and in a field such as that of the conservation of the biological resources of the sea in which worthwhile results can only be attained thanks to the co-operation of all Member States.

It follows from the foregoing that the institution of measures of conservation by a Member State must first be notified to the other Member States and to the Commission and that such measures are in particular subject to the requirements laid down by Annex VI to the Hague Resolution. In other words, a Member State proposing to bring such measures into force is required to seek the approval of the Commission, which must be consulted at all stages of the procedure.

It is common ground that these requirements have not been satisfied in this case. The government of the United Kingdom, however, claims that it was not required to follow that procedure since it applies exclusively in the case of "unilateral measures" of conservation of resources adopted by a Member State and that the measures which are subject of the disputed order are not "unilateral measures", inasmuch as they

were adopted in order to ensure, within the jurisdiction of the United Kingdom, the undertakings arising for the United Kingdom from the North-East Atlantic Fisheries Convention and the resolutions adopted thereunder.

Annex VI of the Hague Resolution, in the words of which "the Member States will not take any unilateral measures in respect of the conservation of resources", except in certain circumstances and with due observance of the requirements set out above must be understood as referring to any measure of conservation emanating from the Member States and not from the Community authorities. The duty of consultation arising under that resolution thus covers measures adopted by a Member State to comply with one of its international obligations in this matter. Such consultation was all the more necessary in this case since it is common ground, as has been emphasised by the French government and the Commission and accepted by the government of the United Kingdom itself, that the order in question, although carrying our certain recommendations of the North-East Atlantic Fisheries Convention, nevertheless in some respects goes beyond the requirements flowing from those recommendations.

It follows from the foregoing that, by not previously notifying the other Member States and the Commission of the measure adopted and seeking the approval of the Commission, the United Kingdom has failed to fulfil its obligations under art 5 of the [EC] Treaty, Annex VI to the Hague Resolution and arts 2 and 3 of Regulation 101/76.'

Comment

Articles 170 EC Treaty [art 227 EC] and 142 Euratom Treaty [art 142 EA], recognise the autonomous right of a Member State to act against another Member State that has failed to fulfil its obligations arising from Community law. The Commission is very much involved in such proceedings: first, before a Member State brings an action, the

Commission must be seised of the disputed matter; and second, the Commission must proceed in exactly the same manner as under art 169 EC Treaty [art 226 EC], ie it investigates the matter, gives both parties an opportunity to submit their arguments orally and in writing and finally delivers a reasoned opinion within three months of the date on which the matter was brought to its attention.

The involvement of the Commission serves two purposes. On the one hand the Commission during the period of three months acts as an intermediary between the Member States concerned; it attempts to settle the case and find an acceptable solution to the crisis. Indeed, hostility between two Member States undermines the unity of the Community as a whole and may even paralyse its proper functioning. The period of three months is in reality the 'cooling off' period during which the Commission endeavours to resolve the matter in the light of the Community interest. On the other hand, the participation of the Commission in proceedings under art 170 EC Treaty [art 227 EC] emphasises its privileged role as a 'guardian' of the Treaty as well as the exceptional nature of an action against a Member State by another Member State. The case law in respect of art 170 EC Treaty [art 227 EC] confirms this point. Actions under art 170 EC Treaty [art 227 EC] are extremely rare and in general never reach the ECJ. So far the ECJ has delivered only one judgment under art 170 EC Treaty [art 227 EC] and that was in the present case.

5   Direct Actions against Community Institutions

Article 230 EC: individual and direct concern

Codorniu SA v *Council of the European Union* Case C–309/89 [1994] ECR I–1853; [1995] 2 CMLR 561 European Court of Justice

• *Action for annulment – individual concern – locus standi – possibility to challenge 'real' regulation under art 173 EC Treaty [art 230 EC] – regulation reserving the use of the term 'crémant' to sparkling quality wines produced in two specific Member States – proprietor of a trade mark containing such a term traditionally using it for sparkling wines produced in another Member State*

Facts
Codorniu, a Spanish producer of quality sparkling wines has been a holder of a graphic trade mark since 1924 in relation to one of its wine's designed as 'Gran Crémant de Codorniu'. In certain regions of French and Luxembourg the word 'crémant' was also used for certain quality wine. The producers in those countries asked the Community to adopt a regulation which would reserve the word 'crémant' only for their sparkling wine. Council Regulation 2045/89 restricted the use of the word 'crémant' to wines originated in France and Luxembourg in order to protect the traditional description used in those areas. Codorniu challenged the Regulation.

Held
The ECJ held that Codorniu was differentiated from other producers of wine since it had registered and used the word 'crémant' since 1924. Although Regulation 2045/89 was a true Regulation it did not prevent it from being of individual concern to Codorniu which was badly affected by the Regulation. Also the restriction of the word 'crémant' to wine originating from certain regions of France and Luxembourg could not be objectively justified, and in addition it was contrary to art 7(1) EEC [art 12 EC] which prohibits discrimination based on nationality.

Judgment
'Codorniu alleges that the contested provision [of Regulation 2045/89] is in reality a decision adopted in guise of a regulation. It has no general scope but affects a well determined class of producers which cannot be altered. Such producers are those who on 1 September 1989 traditionally designated their sparking wines with the term 'crémant'. For that class the contested provision has no general scope. Furthermore, the direct result of the contested provision will be to prevent Codorniu from using the term 'Gran Crémant' which will involve a loss of 38 per cent of its turnover. The effect of that damage is to distinguish it, within the meaning of the second paragraph of art 173 of the Treaty, from any other trader. Codorniu alleges that the Court has already recognised the admissibility of an action for annulment brought by a natural or legal person against a regulation in such circumstances.

Under the second paragraph of art 173 of the Treaty the institution of proceedings by a natural or legal person for a declaration that a regulation is void is subject to the condition that the provision of the regulation at issue in the proceedings constitutes in reality a decision of direct and individual concern to that person.

As the Court has already held, the general applicability, and thus the legislative nature of a measure, is not called into question by the fact that it is possible to determine more or less exactly the number or even the identity of the persons to whom it applies at any given time, as long as it is established that it applies to them by virtue of an objective legal or factual situation defined by the measure in relation to its purpose.

Although, it is true that according to the criteria in the second paragraph of art 173 of the Treaty, the contested provision is, by nature and by virtue of its sphere of application, of a legislative nature in that it applies to the traders concerned in general, that does not prevent it from being of individual concern to some of them.

Natural or legal persons may claim that a contested provision is of individual concern to them only if it affects them by reason of certain attributes which are peculiar to them or by reason of circumstances in which they are differentiated from all other persons.

Codorniu registered the graphic trade mark 'Gran Crémant de Codorniu' in Spain in 1924 and traditionally used that mark both before and after registration. By reserving the right to use the term 'crémant' to French and Luxembourg producers, the contested provision prevents Codorniu from using its graphic trade mark.

It follows that Codorniu has established the existence of a situation which from the point of view of the contested provision differentiates it from all other traders.'

Comment

The restrictive interpretation of individual concern has been widely criticised. It was argued that the ECJ should take a more realistic approach and carry out an economic analysis of the situation of an undertaking, its degree of dependence vis-à-vis the effect that the measure in question had on the market in order to assess whether that measure differentiates and individualises the applicant from other undertakings. It was thought that the present case represented the real breakthrough. In the present case the applicant was prevented from using its trade mark which, from a point of view of its economic interests, resulted in putting it in such a disadvantageous position that it was differentiated from other undertakings and thus individually concerned by the contested Regulation. Unfortunately, it seems that a more liberal approach toward locus standi in general and individual concern in particular has been rejected (see especially *Stichting Greenpeace Council* v *EC Commission* Case C–321/95 [1998] ECR I–1651; *Weber* v *EC Commission* Case T–482/93 [1996] ECR II–609; *Terres Rouges Consultant SA* v *EC Commission, supported by the Council, Spain and France* Case T–47/95 [1997] ECR II–481, etc). It seems that the present case constitutes an exception justified on the ground of ownership of a trade mark.

Plaumann v EC Commission Case 25/62 [1964] ECR 95; [1964] CMLR 29 European Court of Justice

• *Action for annulment – locus standi – individual concern – definition of individual concern – the 'closed class' test*

Facts

Plaumann was an importer of clementines. Under the Common Customs tariff he paid 13 per cent customs duty as any importer of clementines from outside the Community. The government of Germany asked the Commission for authorisation under art 25(3) EC Treaty [now repealed] to suspend this duty. The Com-mission refused and issued a decision in this respect. Plaumann challenged this decision.

Held

The ECJ held that Plaumann was not individually and directly concerned by the Commission's decision, although he was affected as any importer of clementines by the decision. His commercial activities were such as may be practised at any time by any person and thus he did not distinguish himself from others in relation to the challenged directive as in the case of the addressee. Individual concern may only be invoked if persons other than the addressees of the decision demonstrate that 'that decision affects them by reason of certain attributes which are peculiar to them or by reason of circumstances in which they are differentiated from all other persons by virtue of these factors distinguishing them individually just as in the case of the person addressed'.

Judgment

'Under the second paragraph of art 173 of the Treaty private individuals may institute proceedings for annulment against decisions which, although addressed to another person, are of direct and individual concern to them, but in the present case the defendant denies that the contested decision is of direct and individual concern to the applicant.

It is appropriate in the first place to examine whether the second requirement of admissibility is fulfilled because, if the applicant is not individually concerned by the decision, it becomes unnecessary to enquire whether he is directly concerned.

... Persons other than those to whom a decision is addressed may only claim to be individually concerned if that decision affects them by reason of certain attributes which are peculiar to them or by reason of circumstances in which they are differentiated from all other persons and by virtue of these factors distinguishes them individually just as in the case of the person addressed. In the present case the applicant is affected by the disputed decision as an importer of clementines, that is to say, by reason of a commercial activity which may at any time

be practised by any person and is not therefore such as to distinguish the applicant in relation to the contested decision as in the case of the addressee.

For these reasons the present action for annulment must be declared inadmissible.'

Comment

The most confusing and complicated question under art 173 EC [art 230 EC] is the issue of individual concern, mostly because of inconsistency in the decisions of Community courts in this area. In the present case the ECJ defined individual concern. The ECJ has restrictively interpreted 'certain peculiar attributes' or 'circumstances which differentiate' the applicant challenging a decision addressed to another person or a regulation in the form of a decision. As a result, the ECJ refused to recognise that a person was individually concerned in the following situations: in the *Plaumann* case when the Decision concerned specific activities, that is importers of clementines, when the number of the affected persons was limited, ie only 30 importers of clementines; when an undertaking was the only one concerned by a measure in a particular Member State (*Spijker Kwasten BV* v *EC Commission* Case 231/82 [1983] ECR 259; *Union Deutsche Lebensmittelwerke* Case 97/85 [1987] ECR 2265); when an undertaking operated in a determined zone and the regulation expressly applied to that geographically delimited zone (*Molitaria Immolese* Case 30/67 [1968] ECR 172); when an undertaking was a direct competitor of another undertaking to which the decision was addressed (*Eridania* v *EC Commission* Cases 10 and 18/68 [1969] ECR 459); when the number of undertakings concerned was limited to three undertakings in a Member State but potential producers would not be in a position to enter the market for at least two years taking into account the technological requirements involving the production of isoglucose (*KSH NV* v *EC Council and EC Commission* Case 101/76 [1977] ECR 797).

In all those cases the applicants were considered as being members of the 'open class', that is anyone may at any time practice the commercial activity in question and potentially join the group of producers of particular goods. The case law of the ECJ indicates that in order to be individually concerned a person must prove that at the time the measure was passed it was possible to identify all potential applicants. It only happens if the membership of that class was fixed at that time which means, in practice, that only in respect of retrospective measures is it possible to invoke individual concern.

Stichting Greenpeace Council (Greenpeace International) and Others v EC Commission Case C–321/95 [1998] ECR I–1651 European Court of Justice

- *Action for annulment – direct and individual concern – locus standi of a nature conservancy foundation on behalf of its members – environment – appeal*

Facts
Greenpeace International, a nature conservancy foundation with its headquarters in The Netherlands, brought an appeal against the order of the Court of First Instance (CFI) of 9 August 1995 which declared inadmissible their action for annulment of the Commission's decisions taken between 7 March 1991 and 29 October 1993 to disburse to the Kingdom of Spain ECU 12,000,000 from the European Regional Development Fund pursuant to Council Decision C(91) 440 concerning financial assistance for the construction of two power stations in the Canary Islands. The applicant argued: first, that the CFI erred in the interpretation and application of art 173(4) EC Treaty [art 230(4) EC] as it failed to take into consideration the nature and specific character of the environmental interests underpinning its action; second, that the CFI was wrong to take the view that reference to national laws on locus standi was irrelevant

for the purposes of art 173 EC Treaty [art 230 EC]; third, that the order of the CFI was contrary to the case law of the ECJ as well as the declaration of EC institutions and Member States on environmental matters; and, fourth, the applicant set up its own criteria for locus standi for a non-privileged applicant in environmental matters which criteria, according to the applicants, were satisfied in the present case.

Held
The ECJ confirmed the order of the CFI rejecting the action for annulment brought by Greenpeace International.

Judgment
'The interpretation of the fourth paragraph of art 173 of the Treaty that the Court of First Instance applied in concluding that the appellants did not have locus standi is consonant with the settled case law of the Court of Justice.

As far as natural persons are concerned, it follows from the case law, cited at paragraph 48 of the contested order, that where, as in the present case, the specific situation of the applicant was not taken into consideration in the adoption of the act, which concerns him in a general and abstract fashion and, in fact, like any other person in the same situation, the applicant is not individually concerned by the act.

The same applies to associations which claim to have locus standi on the basis of the fact that the persons whom they represent are individually concerned by the contested decision. For the reasons given in the preceding paragraph, that is not the case.

In appraising the appellants' arguments purporting to demonstrate that the case law of the Court of Justice, as applied by the Court of First Instance, takes no account of the nature and specific characteristics of the environmental interests underpinning their action, it should be emphasised that it is the decision to build the two power stations in question which is liable to affect the environmental rights arising under Directive 85/337 that the appellants seek to invoke.

In those circumstances, the contested decision, which concerns the Community financing of those power stations, can affect those rights only indirectly.

As regards the appellants' argument that application of the Court's case law would mean that, in the present case, the rights which they derive from Directive 85/337 would have no effective judicial protection at all, it must be noted that, as is clear from the file, Greenpeace brought proceedings before the national courts challenging the administrative authorisations issued to Unelco concerning the construction of those power stations.

Although the subject matter of those proceedings and of the action brought before the Court of First Instance is different, both actions are based on the same rights afforded to individuals by Directive 85/337, so that in the circumstances of the present case those rights are fully protected by the national courts which may, if need be, refer a question to this Court for a preliminary ruling under art 177 of the Treaty.

The Court of First Instance did not therefore err in law in determining the question of the appellants' locus standi in the light of the criteria developed by the Court of Justice in the case law set out at para 7 of this judgment.'

Comment

This is the first decision of the ECJ following *Codorniu SA* v *Council of the European Union* Case C–309/89 [1994] ECR I–1853 in respect of locus standi of non-privileged applicants under art 173(4) EC Treaty [art 230(4) EC]. The ECJ decided to apply the restrictive approach based on a 'closed class' test introduced by *Plaumann* v *EC Commission* Case 25/62 [1964] ECR 95. The ECJ rejected the opinion of Advocate-General Cosmas suggesting the evolution of conditions of admissibility in respect of actions brought by non-privileged applicants under art 173(4) EC Treaty [art 230(4) EC] in matters relating to the protection of environment. Also, the ECJ confirmed its case law in respect of the right of associations, including those active in the field

of the protection of the environment, to bring an action for annulment under art 173 EC Treaty [art 230 EC]. In conformity with the opinion of the Advocate-General the ECJ rejected the possibility for an association to have locus standi under art 173 EC Treaty [art 230 EC]. According to the ECJ this possibility would lead to the development of an actio popularis contrary to the philosophy of art 173 EC Treaty [art 230 EC].

Timex Corporation v *EC Council and EC Commission* Case 264/82 [1985] ECR 849 European Court of Justice

• *Action for annulment – locus standi – regulation introducing anti-dumping duties – participation of the applicants in the adoption of contested act*

Facts

Timex challenged Regulation 3017/79 which had imposed an anti-dumping duty on cheap mechanical watches coming from the Soviet Union. The Regulation was adopted as a result of a complaint lodged on behalf of Timex and taking into account information forwarded by the applicant. Timex sought to annul Regulation 3017/79, arguing that the new duty was too low.

Held

The ECJ held that Timex was individually concerned because its complaint led to the opening of the investigation procedure and subsequently to the adoption of Regulation 3017/79. The challenged Regulation constituted a decision in respect of Timex as the anti-dumping duty was fixed on the basis of 'the extent of the injury caused to Timex by the dumped importers'.

Judgment

'Timex and the parties intervening in its support contend that the action is admissible because the contested Regulation constitutes in reality a decision which is of direct and individual concern to Timex within the meaning of the second paragraph of art 173 of the [EC] Treaty. They submit that the Regulation was adopted as a result of a complaint lodged on behalf of Timex, amongst others, and that it therefore constitutes the culmination of an administrative proceedings initiated at Timex's request. Its interest in bringing proceedings is all the more evident in so far as it is the only remaining manufacturer of mechanical wristwatches in the United Kingdom and the anti-dumping duty was fixed exclusively by reference to its economic situation.

The question of admissibility raised by the Council and the Commission must be resolved in the light of the system established by Regulation 3017/79 and, more particularly, of the nature of the anti-dumping measures provided for by that Regulation, regard being had to the provisions of the second paragraph of art 173 of the [EC] Treaty.

Article 13(1) of Regulation 3017/79 provides that "Anti-dumping or countervailing duties, whether provisional or definitive, shall be imposed by Regulation." In the light of the criteria set out in the second paragraph of art 173, the measures in question are, in fact, legislative in nature and scope, inasmuch as they apply to traders in general; nevertheless, their provisions may be of direct and individual concern to some of those traders. In this regard, it is necessary to consider in particular the part played by the applicant in the anti-dumping proceedings and its position on the market to which the contested legislation applies.

It should be pointed out first of all that the complaint under art 5 of Regulation No 3017/79 which led to the adoption of Regulation No 1882/82 was lodged by the British Clock and Watch Manufacturers' Association Limited on behalf of manufacturers of mechanical watches in France and the United Kingdom, including Timex. According to the documents before the Court, that association took action because a complaint which Timex had lodged in April 1979 had been rejected by the Commission on the ground that it came from only one Community manufacturer.

The complaint which led to the opening of the investigation procedure therefore owes its origin to the complaint originally made by Timex. Moreover, it is clear from the preamble to Commission Regulation No 84/82 and the preamble to Council Regulation No 1882/82 that Timex's views were heard during that procedure.

It must also be remembered that Timex is the leading manufacturer of mechanical watches and watch movements in the Community and the only remaining manufacturer of those products in the United Kingdom. Furthermore, as is also clear from the preambles to Regulations Nos 84/82 and 1882/82, the conduct of the investigation procedure was largely determined by Timex's observations and the anti-dumping duty was fixed in the light of the effect of the dumping on Timex. More specifically, the preamble to Regulation No 1882/82 makes it clear that the definitive anti-dumping duty was made equal to the dumping margin which was found to exist "taking into account the extent of the injury to Timex by the dumping imports". The contested Regulation is therefore based on the applicant's own situation.

It follows that the contested Regulation constitutes a decision which is of direct and individual concern to Timex within the meaning of the second paragraph of art 173 of the [EC] Treaty. As the Court held in its judgment of 4 October 1983 in *EEC Seed Crushers' and Oil Processors' Federation (FEDIOL)* v *EC Commission* Case 191/82 [1983] ECR 2913, the applicant is therefore entitled to put before the Court any matters which would facilitate a review as to whether the Commission has observed the procedural guarantees granted to complainants by Regulation No 3017/79 and whether or not it has committed manifest errors in its assessment of the facts, has omitted to take any essential matters into consideration or has based the reasons for its decision on considerations amounting to a misuse of powers. In that respect, the Court is required to exercise its normal powers of review over a discretion granted to a public authority, even though it has no jurisdiction to intervene in the exercise of the discretion reserved to the Community authorities by the aforementioned Regulation.'

Comment

Non-contentious procedures involve more or less direct participation of undertakings in the adoption of the measures. If an applicant assists the Commission in the preparation of the measure then his association with the adoption of the measure differentiates him from others and his individual concern is self-evident. This is mostly used in competition, anti-dumping and State-aid cases. In the context of the common market, dumping occurs when a non-EC undertaking sells its products below domestic market prices and at the same time at a price below the real cost of the goods. This strategy is used to penetrate the market and eliminate the existing competitors. The undertaking affected by such dumping can complain to the Commission which may adopt a provisional regulation and request the Council to issue a definite regulation imposing an anti-dumping duty to counterbalance the competitive advantage of the foreign undertaking and which is determined in the light of the effect of the dumping on EC undertakings, especially the one that lodged a complaint.

It is interesting to mention that in *Métropole Télévision and Others* v *EC Commission* Cases T–528, 542, 543 and 546/93 [1996] ECR II–649 the Com-mission argued that the applicant was not individually concerned as it did not participate in the preparation of the measure. The CFI replied that effective participation in the adoption of a measure cannot be required in order to establish an individual concern as it would amount to the introduction of an additional requirement which is not provided for in art 173 EC Treaty [art 230 EC]. Therefore, the CFI has rightly indicated that the participation in the adoption of a measure constitutes solely a factor facilitating the recognition of an individual concern but it is not a necessary requirement.

Toepfer (Alfred) and Getreide-Import Gesellschaft v *EC Commission* Joined Cases 106 and 107/63 [1965] ECR 525; [1966] CMLR 111 European Court of Justice

• *Action for annulment – locus standi – applications by individuals against a decision addressed to another person – decision of direct concern to them – concept*

Facts

Toepfer applied for an import licence for maize on 1 October 1962, being the very day on which the German authorities mistakenly reduced the levy for imports of maize from France to zero. The German intervention agency realised the mistake and refused to grant licences from 2 October 1962. Three days later the Commission authorised German authorities to impose the levy as from 2 October 1962. Toepfer challenged the Commission's decision on the grounds that he was individually and directly concerned.

Held

The ECJ held that Toepfer was individually concerned because the number and identity of those individually concerned 'had become fixed and ascertainable before the contested decision was made'.

Judgment

'The only persons concerned by the said measures were importers who had applied for an import licence during the course of the day of 1 October 1962. The number and identity of these importers had already become fixed and ascertainable before 4 October, when the contested decision was made. The Commission was in a position to know that its decision affected the interests and the position of the said importers alone.

The factual situation thus created differentiates the said importers, including the applicants, from all other persons and distinguishes them individually just as in the case of the person addressed.

Therefore, the objection of inadmissibility which has been raised is unfounded and the applications are admissible.'

Comment

The applicant was a member of a 'closed group' as the decision affected his interests and position in a significantly different way from other importers who might wish to apply for a licence after the adoption of the decision but during the remaining period of the ban. Therefore, only those who applied on 1 October were individually concerned since from 2–4 October applications were refused and on the 4 October the Commission issued its decision. As a result, Toepfer was within the closed group who applied on 1 October; the larger group, that is those who applied between 2–4 October, was open since they were refused licences and could reapply thereafter without loss to them as the levy would be the same after 2 October.

Union Nazionale Importatori e Commercianti Motoviecoli Esteri (UNICME) and Others v *EC Council* Case 123/77 [1978] ECR 845 European Court of Justice

• *Action for annulment – locus standi – direct concern – Regulation 1692/77 – protective measures on the importation of motorcycles from a third country – discretion of a Member State in relation to import licences*

Facts

Under Council Regulation 1692/77 (EEC) concerning protective measures on the importation of motorcycles originating in Japan into Italy, Italian authorities were to issue a limited number of import authorisations. The applicants, Italian importers of such motorcycles and their trade association, UNICME, challenged the Regulation.

Held

The ECJ held that the applicants were not directly concerned since the Italian government had a discretion as to the grant of import licences. As a result, they were concerned not by the Regulation but by the subsequent refusal of import licences by the Italian authorities.

Judgment

'The system [introduced by Regulation 1692/77] would only affect the interests of the importers in the event of the necessary authorisation being refused them.

Consequently Regulation No 1692/77 would only be of concern to the applicants if, pursuant to that measure, they were refused an import authorisation.

In that case they will be able to raise the matter before the national court having jurisdiction, if necessary raising before that court their questions concerning the validity of the Regulation, which the court will, if it thinks fit, be able to deal with by means of the procedure under art 177 of the Treaty.

In the present case the condition laid down in art 173, to the effect that the contested measure must be of direct and individual concern to the applicants, is not fulfilled.

The applicants claim that, taken together, they represent all the importers affected by the import system introduced for motorcycles originating in Japan.

They state that even before Regulation No 1692/77 was adopted it could have been established that they were the only persons concerned and that they were all concerned.

The possibility of determining more or less precisely the number or even the identity of the persons to whom a measure applies by no means implies that it must be regarded as being of individual concern to them.

In the present case the fact that all the applicants might possibly be refused an import authorisation pursuant to Regulation No 1692/77 does not provide a sufficient basis for regarding the regulation as being of individual concern to them in the same way as if a decision had been addressed to them.

On the contrary the Regulation will not produce effects in individual cases until it is implemented by the Italian authorities.

Consequently, the second condition laid down by art 173 likewise remains unfulfilled.'

Comment
In the present case the application was rejected on the ground of lack of direct concern. Italian authorities enjoyed a large measure of discretion in the implementation of a Community measure.

Time-limit under art 230 EC

Bayer AG v *EC Commission* Case T–12/90 [1991] ECR II–219; [1993] 4 CMLR 30 Court of First Instance

• *Action for annulment – time-limit for initiating proceedings – excuses for failing to raise proceedings in time – regularity of notification – excusable error – unforeseeable circumstances and force majeure*

Facts
The Commission sent notification to the applicant company fining it for a number of infringements of art 85 EC Treaty [art 81 EC].

The company brought an action under art 173(2) EC Treaty [art 230(2) EC] to have Commission's decision judicially reviewed. In response, the Commission argued that the application was inadmissible as time-barred under art 173(3) EC Treaty [art 230(3) EC] and the ECJ's rules of procedure.

The applicant argued that the action was not time-barred and relied on three separate contentions to support this argument. First, it was submitted that the Commission was guilty of a number of irregularities in the notification. In particular, the Commission notified

the decision to the company and not to the company's legal department with which it had conducted all previous correspondence. Second, the company claimed that its internal organisational breakdown was an excusable error. Finally, the applicants pleaded unforeseeable circumstances in order to justify the delay in submitting the application under art 173 EC Treaty [art 230 EC].

Held
The Court of First Instance rejected all three arguments submitted by the applicants. The Court stated that the Commission was not guilty of any procedural irregularities in the notification and had complied with the necessary formalities contained in its rules of procedure. Both the arguments relating to excusable error and force majeure were also rejected as the delay had been caused by fault on the part of the applicants.

Judgment
'[*Irregularity of the notification*]
With regard to the regularity of the notification, this Court notes that, according to the settled case law of the Court of Justice, a registered letter with acknowledgment of receipt is a suitable method of giving notice insomuch as it enables the date from which time begins to run to be determined. Furthermore, a decision is duly notified once it has been communicated to the person to whom it is addressed and that person is in a position to take cognisance of it.

In the present case, this Court has found that the Commission sent the decision to Bayer by registered letter with postal acknowledgment of receipt and that letter duly arrived at Bayer's registered office at Leverkusen on December 28, 1989. It follows that Bayer was in position on that date to take cognisance of the contents of the letter and thus of the tenor of the decision ...

It follows from the foregoing that the applicant's first plea in law in defence must be dismissed.

[*Excusable error*]
The Court considers, first of all, in view of
the obligations incumbent on any normally
experienced trader, that the fact that the
Commission notified the contested decision
to the applicants registered office, whereas it
had previously addressed all its communications directly to the applicant's legal department, cannot constitute an exceptional circumstance such as to render excusable the
applicant's error.

Secondly, the Court finds that the argument that Bayer had taken every step within
its power to avoid any error in the forward-
ing of mail addressed to it is, assuming it is
true, entirely irrelevant in the present case
insomuch as it is clear from the documents
before the Court, and it is not denied, that
errors were in fact committed within the
undertaking when the registered letter was
received.

... It follows from the foregoing that
Bayer may not rely either on the inadequate
functioning of its internal organisation or
on a failure to apply its own internal instructions in support of its claim that the error
which is committed was excusable, insomuch as it is undisputed that those instructions were not followed and that, in any
event, the Commission in no way contributed to the inadequate functioning of
Bayer's organisation.

[*Unforeseeable circumstances and force
majeure*]
Finally, Bayer considers that it may rely on
the existence of unforeseeable circumstances or force majeure within the meaning
of the second paragraph of art 42 of the rules
of procedure of the Court of Justice. Having
fulfilled in all respects its obligations of
organisation and control, it cannot be held to
have been at fault or, therefore, in view of
the Commission's conduct as a whole, to
have been responsible for the failure to
comply within the prescribed period.

The Court observes that, for the purpose
of determining whether the applicant has
established the existence of unforeseeable
circumstances or force majeure, there must,
as the Court of Justice has consistently held,
be abnormal difficulties, independent of the
will of the person concerned and apparently
inevitable, even if all due care is taken.

Bayer, however, in support of that plea in
law, has relied on arguments identical to
those put forward in support of its plea
based on the existence in the circumstances
of excusable error on its part. In view of
what has bee stated above in connection
with the alleged existence of excusable
error, it appears clearly, and a fortiori, that
the above-mentioned conditions for the
existence of unforeseeable circumstances or
force majeure, within the meaning of art 42
of the rules of procedure of the Court of
Justice, such as to justify the transgression
of the time-limit for initiating proceedings,
are not fulfilled in this case.

It follows from the foregoing that the
three pleas in law submitted by Bayer in its
defence must be dismissed.'

Comment

The time-limit is one month under the ECSC
Treaty [CS Treaty] and two months under the
EC and Euratom Treaties [EC and EA
Treaties]. It is regrettable from the point of
view of legal certainty that the various amendments to the founding Treaties have omitted to
provide a situation where all three have the
same time-limit for bringing an action for
annulment.

The time-limit begins to run from the date
of publication of an act in the Official Journal
of the European Communities, or from its
notification to the applicant. If the act was
published, by virtue of art 81 of the Rules of
Procedure of the ECJ and the CFI, the commencement of the time-limit is extended by 15
days, and further extension is granted to take
into consideration the distance of the applicant
from the Community courts. In the case of an
applicant from the United Kingdom the extension amounts to an additional ten days.
Therefore, for a UK applicant the time-limit
is two months, plus 15 days, plus ten days. In
the absence of publication or notification the
time-limit starts at the day when the act came
to the knowledge of the applicant (*Tezi Textiel*

v *EC Commission* Case 59/84 [1986] ECR 887). However, in the absence of a formal notification and provided that the applicant knew the content of the final position adopted by an EC institution, the time-limit starts to run at the time the definite decision came to his knowledge (*Pesqueria Vasco-Montanesa SA and Another* v *EC Commission* Cases T–452 and 453/93R [1994] ECR II–229).

The time-limit is rigorously enforced by the Community courts. Once it elapses, the application is deemed inadmissible d'office, that is the act is immune from annulment. This is justified by the principle of legal certainty and equality in the administration of justice (*Ferriera Valsabbia SpA* v *EC Commission* Case 209/83 [1984] ECR 3089).

In *Simet* Cases 25 and 26/65 [1967] ECR 40 the ECJ accepted an exception to the strict observance of the time-limit based on force majeure.

Glencore Grain Ltd v *Commission*
Case T–509/93 [2000] ECR II–3697
Court of First Instance

• *Action for annulment – time-limit – locus standi – emergency aid provided by the Community to the States of the former Soviet Union – invitation to tender – legal interest in bringing proceedings under art 230 EC*

Facts
In the context of aid granted to the Republics of the former Soviet Union by the EU (in this case in the form of loans) for food and medical supplies, the Commission adopted rules for the implementation of aid under which the loans granted to the Republics were to finance only the purchase of supplies under contracts that had been approved by the Commission. The approval was given only if the contract offered the most favourable terms of purchase in relation to the price normally obtained on the international markets.

The applicant, Glencore Grain Ltd, for-

merly trading as Richco Commodities Ltd, submitted four offers for the supply of wheat (the prices of which varied depending upon the time allowed for delivery) to Ukrimpex, an organisation acting on behalf of the government of the Ukraine. Ukrimpex accepted only one offer which guaranteed delivery of wheat by 15 June 1993. The offer was not the most advantageous in terms of price. The Commission decided not to approve the contract. Notwithstanding this decision, a contract was concluded on 26 May 1993 and notified by the State Export-Import Bank (the SEIB), the financial agent of the government of the Ukraine, to the Commission for approval.

On 10 June 1993 the Commission informed the Vice-Prime Minister of the Ukraine that it was unable to approve the contract submitted to it by the SEIB.

On 11 June 1993 Ukrimpex informed the applicant of the Commission's refusal and requested it to defer the transportation of goods. The applicant replied that it had already delivered the wheat to the Ukraine.

By a letter of 12 July 1993 the Agriculture Commissioner officially informed the SEIB of the Commission's refusal to approve the contract.

On 10 September 1993 the applicant brought an action before the CFI for annulment of the Commission's decision of 12 July 1993. This action was dismissed as inadmissible by the CFI: *Richco Commodities* v *EC Commission* Case T–509/93 [1996] ECR II–1181. The applicant appealed against that decision to the ECJ, which set aside the judgment of the CFI and referred the case back to the CFI for judgment on the substance: *Glencore Grain* v *Commission* Case C–404/96P [1998] ECR I–2435. By order of the President of the second Chamber of the CFI of 19 January 2000, Cases T–485, 491 and 494/93, 61/98 and 509/93 were joined.

Held
The CFI dismissed the action.

Judgment

'It is settled case law that the time-limits for bringing proceedings are a matter of public policy (see, in particular, Joined Cases T–121/96 and T–151/96 *Mutual Aid Administration Services* v *EC Commission* [1997] ECR II–1355, para 38). Consequently, the Court may examine of its own motion a plea of inadmissibility based on the action being allegedly time-barred.

In that regard, it should be recalled that an action for annulment of a decision which merely confirms a previous decision not contested within the time-limit for bringing proceedings is inadmissible (order of the Court of Justice in Case C–12/90 *Infortec* v *EC Commission* [1990] ECR I–4265, para 10).

It is apparent from a comparison of the letters produced to the Court, dated 10 June 1993 and 12 July 1993, that the second of those letters contains nothing new in relation to the first letter and, in particular, that the reasons stated in them are the same. Moreover, neither the documents in the case file nor the letter of 12 July 1993 show that there was any re-examination of the matter prior to the adoption of the decision contained in that second letter.

However, whilst it is apparent from the documents before the Court that the applicant already knew of the existence of the letter of 10 June 1993 on the following day, the case file does not show that the applicant was informed of the reasons on which it was based.

Moreover, whilst it is true, as the Commission has pointed out, that the loan agreement does not expressly state the identity of the person to whom a decision refusing to approve a contract was to be addressed, it should be observed that, according to the loan agreement, it was for the SEIB to send to the Commission both the requests for approval of contracts and the requests for disbursement of the loan. Similarly, a notice of confirmation of a supply contract which has been notified is defined in the loan agreement as a "notice of approval to the Agent [the SEIB] from the Lender [the European Community]". It must be inferred from this that the decision not to issue a notice of confirmation was also intended to be addressed to the SEIB. Since it was only by the letter of 12 July 1993 that the Commission informed the SEIB, the applicant was legitimately entitled to consider that only that official notification constituted the final decision.

In those circumstances, the present action cannot be rejected as time-barred.

As regards the alleged lack of interest in bringing proceedings, it must be recalled, first, that such an interest must be assessed as at the date on which the action is brought (see, in particular, the judgment of the Court of Justice in Case 14/63 *Forges de Clabecq* v *High Authority* [1963] ECR 357, at 371). It cannot be contested that, on that date, the applicant had an interest in bringing proceedings.

Moreover, to accept the Commission's argument would be tantamount to anticipating the consequences to be drawn by the Commission, pursuant to art 176 of the EC Treaty (now art 233 EC), from the judgment to be given in the case.

Lastly, it is not impossible that the annulment of a decision such as that contested in the present case may be capable, of itself, of having legal consequences, in particular that of preventing a repetition of the Commission's practice (see the order in Case T–256/97 *BEUC* v *EC Commission* [1999] ECR II–169, para 18, and the case law cited therein).

Consequently, the objections raised against the admissibility of the action must be rejected.'

Comment

In the above cases the CFI provided interesting clarifications as to the determination of the time-limit for bringing an action for annulment.

The CFI stated that the time-limit for bringing proceedings was a matter of public policy and therefore it was entitled to examine of its own motion a plea of inadmissibility based on that ground. The CFI agreed that from a comparison of both letters it emerged that the letter of 12 July 1993 contained no new elements as compared to the letter of 10 June 1993, and that the reason for refusal stated in them was the same. The CFI held that, although from 11 June 1993 the applicant knew of the existence of the letter of 10 June 1993, 'the case file does not show that the applicant was informed of the reasons on which it was based'.

Additionally, the CFI noted that the letter of 10 June 1993 was addressed to the government of the Ukraine. The SEIB only received the letter of 12 July 1993. However, under the loan agreement, the SEIB being the addressee of a 'notice of approval to the Agent (the SEIB) from the Lender (the European Community)', should also have been an addressee of a decision not to issue a notice of confirmation of a supply contract. In those circumstances the CFI held that: 'Since it was only by the letter of 12 July 1993 that the Commission informed the SEIB, the applicant was legitimately entitled to consider that only that official notification constituted the final decision'.

The CFI decided that the application was not time-barred.

Article 232 EC

Lord Bethell v EC Commission Case 246/81 [1982] ECR 2277; [1982] 3 CMLR 300 European Court of Justice

• *Action for failure to act – meaning of 'failure to act' – locus standi – conditions of admissibility – relationship between arts 173 and 175 EC Treaty [arts 230 and 232 EC]*

Facts
Lord Bethell, a Member of the European Parliament and Chairman of the Freedom of the Skies Committee, complained to the Commission about anti-competitive practices of a number of European airlines in relation to passenger fares. He argued that the Commission was under a duty to submit proposals under art 89 EC Treaty [art 85 EC] in order to curtail those practices. Dissatisfied with the answer from the Commission he brought an action against the Commission under art 175 EC Treaty [art 232 EC] for failure to act, claiming that the Commission's reply amounted in fact to a failure to act, and alternatively under art 173 EC Treaty [art 230 EC] arguing that this answer should be annulled.

Held
The ECJ held that Lord Bethell had neither locus standi to challenge the Commission's alleged failure to act under art 175 EC Treaty [art 232 EC] nor to seek annulment of the Commission's answer under art 173 EC Treaty [art 230 EC].

Judgment
'It appears from the provisions quoted [art 175 EC Treaty] that the applicant, for his application to be admissible, must be in a position to establish either that he is the addressee of a measure of the Commission having specific legal effects with regard to him, which is, as such, capable of being declared void, or that the Commission, having been duly called upon to act in pursuance of the second paragraph of art 175, has failed to adopt in relation to him a measure which he was legally entitled to claim by virtue of the rules of Community law.

In reply to a question from the Court the applicant stated that the measure to which he believed himself to be entitled was "a response, an adequate answer to his complaint saying either that the Commission was going to act upon it or saying that it was not and, if not, giving reasons". Alternatively the applicant took the view that the letter addressed to him on 17 July 1981 by the Director-General for Compet-ition was to be described as an act against which proceedings may be instituted under the second paragraph of art 173.

The principal question to be resolved in this case is whether the Commission had, under the rules of Community law, the right and the duty to adopt in respect of the applicant a decision in the sense of the request made by the applicant to the Commission in his letter of 13 May 1981. It is apparent from the content of that letter and from the explanations given during the proceedings that the applicant is asking the Commission to undertake an investigation with regard to the airlines in the matter of the fixing of air fares with a view to a possible application to them of the provisions of the Treaty with regard to competition.

It is clear therefore that the applicant is asking the Commission, not to take a decision in respect of him, but to open an inquiry with regard to third parties and to take decisions in respect of them. No doubt the applicant, in his double capacity as a user of the airlines and a leading member of an organisation of users of air passenger services, has an indirect interest, as other users may have, in such proceedings and their possible outcome, but he is nevertheless not in the precise legal position of the actual addressee of a decision which may be declared void under the second paragraph of art 173 or in that of the potential addressee of a legal measure which the Commission has a duty to adopt with regard to him, as is the position under the third paragraph of art 175.

It follows that the application is inadmissible from the point of view of both art 175 and art 173.'

Comment

The ECJ held that the application of Lord Bethell would be admissible only if the Commission 'having been duly called upon ... has failed to adopt in relation to him a measure which he was legally entitled to claim by virtue of the rules of Community law'. Lord, Bethell, although indirectly concerned by the measure as a user of the airlines and Chairman of the Freedom of the Skies Committee which represented users, was nevertheless not in the legal position of a potential addressee of a decision and therefore the Commission had

no duty to adopt such a decision with regard to him. Also, his application under art 173 EC Treaty [art 230 EC] was rejected for the same reason. The analogy between locus standi of non-privileged applicants under arts 173 EC and 175 EC Treaty [arts 230 and 232 EC] was confirmed by the ECJ in the present case.

The similarity between arts 173 EC and 175 EC Treaty [arts 230 and 232 EC] means that an application under art 175 EC Treaty [art 232 EC] is admissible if the applicant is directly and individually concerned by a measure which an EC institution failed to adopt, including a decision addressed to a third party but of individual and direct concern to the applicant. In *ENU* v *EC Commission* Case C–107/91 [1993] ECR I–599 the ECJ recognised this possibility within the framework of the Euratom Treaty and in *Ladbroke Racing Ltd* v *EC Commission* Case T–32/93 [1994] ECR II–1015 the Court of First Instance extended it to the EC Treaty).

Actions for damages against European Community institutions: art 288(2) EC

Adams v *EC Commission* Case 145/83 [1985] ECR 3539 European Court of Justice

• *Action for non-contractual liability of European Commission – requirements of art 214 EC Treaty [art 287 EC] – duty of confidentiality, fault or negligence – damage – contributory negligence*

Facts

Adams was employed by the Swiss-based multinational Hoffman-La Roche. He forwarded confidential information to the Commission concerning breaches of art 86 EC Treaty [art 82 EC] by his employer for which the latter was heavily fined. During the proceedings Hoffman-La Roche asked the

Commission to disclose the name of the informant. The Commission refused but forwarded to Hoffman-La Roche certain documents which enabled them to identify Adams as the source of leaked information which was contrary to the duty of confidentiality contained in art 214 EC Treaty [art 287 EC]. In the meantime Adams moved to Italy where he set up his own business. Hoffman-La Roche due to its international connections destroyed the business established by Adams in Italy. The Commission failed to inform Adams that his former employer was planning to persecute him. On his return to Switzerland Adams was arrested by the Swiss police for economic espionage and held in solitary confinement. His wife committed suicide. Adams brought proceedings before the ECJ against the Commission for loss of earnings and loss of reputation as a result of his conviction and imprisonment.

Held

The ECJ held that the Commission was liable for the breach of duty of confidentiality as it had allowed Adams to be identified as an informer, and awarded Adams £200,000 in damages for his mental anguish and lost earnings, and £176,000 for costs, half the sum he had demanded. The reason for the reduction was Adams' contributory negligence. The ECJ held that Adams contributed to the resulting damage by failing to warn the Commission that he could be identified from the confidential documents, and by failing to enquire about progress of proceedings especially before returning to Switzerland.

Judgment

'[*Duty of confidentiality*]
… As regards the existence of a duty of confidentiality it must be pointed out that art 214 of the [EC] Treaty lays down an obligation, in particular for the member and the servants of the institutions of the Community "not to disclose information of the kind covered by the obligation of professional secrecy, in particular information about undertakings, their business relations

or their cost components". Although that provision primarily refers to information gathered from undertakings, the expression "in particular" shows that the principle in question is a general one which applies also to information supplied by natural persons, if that information is "of the kind" that is confidential. That is particularly in the case of information supplied on a purely voluntary basis but accompanied by a request for confidentiality in order to protect the informant's anonymity. An institution which accepts such information is bound to comply with such a condition.

As regards the case before the Court, it is quite clear from the applicant's letter of 25 February 1973 that he requested the Commission not to reveal his identity. It cannot therefore be denied that the Commission was bound by a duty of confidentiality towards the applicant in that respect. In fact the parties disagree not so much as to the existence of such a duty but as to whether the Commission was bound by a duty of confidentiality after the applicant had left his employment with Roche.

In that respect it must be pointed out that the applicant did not qualify his request by indicating a period upon which the expiry of which the Commission would be released from its duty of confidentiality regarding the identity of its informant. No such indication can be inferred from the fact that the applicant was prepared to appear before any court after he had left Roche. The giving of evidence before a court implies that the witness has been summoned, that he is under a duty to answer the questions put to him, and is, in return, entitled to all guarantees provided by a judicial procedure. The applicant's offer to confirm the accuracy of his information under such conditions cannot therefore be interpreted as a general statement releasing the Commission from its duty of confidentiality. Nor can any such intention be inferred from the applicant's subsequent conduct.

It must therefore be stated that the Commission was under a duty to keep the applicant's identity secret even after he had left his employer.

[*Damages*]
It must therefore be concluded that in principle the Community is bound to make good the damage resulting from the discovery of the applicant's identity by means of the documents handed over to Roche by the Commission. It must however be recognised that the extent of the Commission's liability is diminished by reason of the applicant's own negligence. The applicant failed to inform the Commission that it was possible to infer his identity as the informant from the documents themselves, although he was in the best position to appreciate and to avert that risk. Nor did he ask the Commission to keep him informed of the progress of the investigation of Roche, and in particular of any use that might be made of the documents for that purpose. Lastly, he went back to Switzerland without attempting to make any inquiries in that respect, although he must have been aware of the risks to which his conduct towards his former employer had exposed him with regard to Swiss legislation.

Consequently, the applicant himself contributed significantly to the damage which he suffered. In assessing the conduct of the Commission on the one hand and that of the applicant on the other, the Court considers it equitable to apportion responsibility for that damage equally between the two parties.

It follows from all the foregoing considerations that the Commission must be ordered to compensate the applicant to the extent of one half of the damage suffered by him as a result of the fact that he was identified as the source of information regarding Roche's anti-competitive practice. For the rest, however, the application must be dismissed. The amount of the damages is to be determined by agreement between the parties or, failing such agreement, by the Court.'

Comment

There is an important distinction between the liability of Community institutions for unlawful conduct and liability for legislative acts adopted by them. In the present case the Commission was found liable for breach of the principle of confidentiality. Consequently, the applicant had to establish that the action of the Community was contrary to law, that he suffered damage as a result of the wrongful conduct of the Commission and that there was a causal link between the conduct of the institution and the alleged damage (see *SGEEM and Etroy* v *European Investment Bank* Case C–370/89 [1993] ECR I–2583).

Community law recognises contributory negligence. In the present case the ECJ held that the applicant through his own negligence contributed to the resulting damage and reduced the amount of damages proportionally to his responsibility for the loss.

Aktien-Zuckerfabrik Schöppenstedt v *EC Council* Case 5/71 [1971] ECR 975 European Court of Justice

• *Non-contractual liability of EC institutions – autonomous nature of action under art 215(2) EC Treaty [art 288(2) EC] – wrongful act – conditions for liability for legislative acts involving measures of economic policy – Regulation 769/68 – damages*

Facts

A German sugar producer argued that Regulation 769/68 on sugar prices infringed art 40(3) EC Treaty [art 34(3) EC] according to which any common price policy should be based on common criteria and uniform methods of calculation. He claimed damages under art 215(2) EC Treaty [art 288(2) EC].

Held

The ECJ dismissed the claim.

Judgment

'In the present case the non-contractual liability of the Community presupposed at the very least the unlawful nature of the act alleged to be the cause of the damage. Where legislative action involving measures of economic policy is concerned, the

Community does not incur non-contractual liability for damage suffered by individuals as a consequence of that action, by virtue of the provisions contained in art 215, second paragraph, of the Treaty, unless a sufficiently flagrant violation of a superior rule of law for the protection of individuals has occurred. For that reason the Court, in the present case, must first consider whether such a violation has occurred.

Regulation No 769/68 was adopted pursuant to art 37(1) of Regulation No 1009/67 which requires the Council to adopt provisions concerning the measures needed to offset the difference between national sugar prices and prices valid from 1 July 1968, and it authorises the Member States in which the price of white sugar is higher than the target price to grant compensation for such quantities of white sugar and raw sugar which are in free circulation in its territory at 0.00 hours on 1 July 1968. The applicant points out that as regards Member States with a low price this regulation provides for the payment of dues on sugar stocks only if the previous prices were less than the intervention price valid from 1 July 1968 and concludes from this that by adopting different criteria for the right to compensation of sugar producers in a Member State with high prices, the regulation infringes the provision of the last subparagraph of art 40(3) of the Treaty according to which any common price policy shall be based on common criteria and uniform methods of calculation.

The difference referred to does not constitute discrimination because it is the result of a new system of common organisation of the market in sugar which does not recognise a single fixed price but has a maximum and minimum price and lays down a framework of prices within which the level of actual price depends on the development of the market. Thus it is not possible to challenge the justification of transitional rules which proceeded on the basis that where the previous prices were already within the framework set up they must be governed by market forces and which therefore required the payment of dues only in cases where the

previous prices were still too low to come within the new framework of prices and authorised compensation only in cases where the previous prices were too high to come within the said framework.

In addition, having regard to the special features of the system established with effect from 1 July 1968, the Council by adopting Regulation No 769/68 satisfied the requirements of art 37 of Regulation No 1009/67.

It is also necessary to dismiss the applicant's claim that Regulation No 769/68 infringed the provisions of art 40 of the Treaty because the method of calculating the compensation and dues for the raw sugar stocks was derived from that adopted for white sugar, which could, according to the applicant, result in the unequal treatment of the producers of raw sugar. Although, relying on hypothetical cases, the applicant stated that the calculation methods selected did not necessarily lead to uniform results with regard to producers of raw sugar, it was not proved that this could have been the case on 1 July 1968.

The applicant's action founded upon the Council's liability does not therefore satisfy the first condition mentioned above and must be dismissed.'

Comment

In the present case the ECJ established additional conditions for liability of Community institutions for legislative acts in the following terms:

'When legislative action involving measures of economic policy is concerned, the Community does not incur non-contractual liability for damage suffered by individuals as a consequence of that action, by virtue of the provisions contained in art 215 [art 288 EC], second paragraph, of the Treaty, unless a sufficiently flagrant violation of a superior rule of law for the protection of the individual has occurred.'

This is referred to as the Schöppenstedt formula. It means that the applicant must establish three general conditions and three special conditions. The three general conditions are: unlawful conduct on the part of the Community; damage to the applicant; and a causal link between the conduct of the Community institution and the alleged damage. The three special conditions are that there must be a breach of a superior rule of law, the breach must be sufficiently serious and the superior rule must be one for the protection of individuals.

This formula enhances the fact that EC institutions are particularly protected against actions in damages under art 215(2) EC Treaty [art 288(2) EC], for the very simple reason that all legislative acts imply that their authors enjoy a large margin of discretion. Indeed, it is not important whether a legislative act concerns economic policies sensu stricto or other areas such as transport, social policy etc, what is important is that an institution has a wide discretion and must exercise it in the interest of the Community. It must make choices in conducting the Community policies in the areas of competences of the Community in order to attain the objectives which are essential for integration of national policies and especially to harmonise national laws in specific areas regardless of the fact that those legislative measures may adversely affect individual interests. The prospect of continual applications for damages must not hinder the Community in its policy-making. For that reason the requirements contained in the Schöppenstedt formula are very restrictive and rigorous.

Embassy Limousines & Services SA v European Parliament Case T–203/96 [1999] 1 CMLR 677 Court of First Instance

• *Jurisdiction of the CFI based on an arbitration clause – existence of a contract – art 238 EC – contractual and non-contractual liability of the Community institution – legitimate expectations – assessment of damage*

Facts

The European Parliament (EP) published in the Official Journal of the European Communities a tender notice in respect of a contract for the transport of members of the EP using chauffeur-driven vehicles. The applicant, Embassy Limousines & Services SA, submitted its tender and on 4 December 1995 received a favourable opinion of the Advisory Committee on Procurements and Contracts (ACPC) of the EP. On 12 December 1995 the applicant informed the EP of measures it had taken to respond to the urgency of the situation in which the EP found itself, consisting of entering into contracts for leasing cars and renting mobile telephones, engaging drivers and attending to their social security, health insurance and tax situation. However, the opinion of the ACPC was not confirmed by the EP which decided to renew a contract with a company that previously provided these services, annulled the invitation to tender and reopened a new invitation to tender. The applicant requested the EP not to annul the contested invitation to tender and to award it the contract or to pay it satisfactory compensation. The EP rejected the requests.

Held

The CFI held that the EP was liable for damages suffered by the applicant.

Judgment

'In this case, it has been established that the fault committed by the Parliament gives rise to non-contractual liability on the part of the Community. On the other hand, no contractual liability has been incurred. In the circumstances the applicant is not justified in claiming compensation for its loss of profit, since that would result in giving effect to a contract which never existed.

Next, it is clear from art 4 of the General Terms and Conditions that the contracting institution is not liable for any compensation with respect to tenderers whose tenders have not been accepted. It follows that the charges and expenses incurred by a tenderer in connection with his participation in a tendering procedure cannot in principle constitute damage which is capable of being remedied by an award of damages (see Case T–13/96 *TEAM* v *EC Commission* [1998] ECR I–4073, para 71). In this case the applicant has provided no evidence that would permit derogation from that principle. The applicant is therefore not justified in claiming reimbursement of the expenses relating to the preparation of the tender.

It remains, therefore, to determine the damage which is connected with the investments made by Embassy by reason of the information received on 4 December 1995 showing that the ACPC had delivered an opinion in its favour.

On that subject, it is clear from the file that, after receiving that information, the applicant immediately took the measures necessary for the performance of the contract. In a letter dated 5 December 1995 Mr Hautot expresses himself in these terms:

"I will take responsibility for all recruitment ... and all the working meetings with [the Parliament] ... bringing together the necessary fleet is the responsibility of [Mr Heuzer] and his assistants. ... I would ask everyone to make the effort required to put in place a flawless organisation for 1.1.96 ..."

Next, a letter of 6 December 1995 from Budget Rent a Car reads:

"... further to your express request, we confirm that we are proceeding with the official order and, thereafter, with the registration of the vehicles requested for 1996. ... to avoid duplication of effort we would remind you again that we are currently proceeding with the acquisition of the telecommunications infrastructure (GSM) needed for the proper conduct of your business."

In addition the applicant, in its letter of 12 December 1995, reported on the measures it had taken in order to be capable of dealing with the urgency of the situation announced by the Parliament. In that letter the applicant therefore mentioned the contracts for leasing cars and GSM rental, the recruitment of drivers and attending to the latters' social security, health insurance and tax situation (see para 7 above).

It follows that the aforementioned investments show a direct causal link with the telephone conversation of 4 December 1995.

In addition, by making those investments, Embassy did not exhibit a lack of prudence. First, it has already been established that its certainty of winning the contract had not been removed at the meeting in Strasbourg on 13 December 1995 (see para 82 above). Secondly, the Parliament has put forward no argument which casts doubt on the truthfulness of the version of the facts given by the Embassy representatives, under oath, according to which the investments mentioned in the letter of 12 December 1995 had all been made in December 1995. Thirdly, it is clear from the testimony of the Parliament officials that Embassy did not receive any information to indicate that it might not eventually win the contract (see paras 82 to 85 above).

It goes without saying that, in the absence of a clear refusal to award it the contract, the applicant had no reason to annul, during the first months of 1996, the contracts already concluded. It is useful to recall, in that regard, the minutes of 19 December 1995 in which the ACPC, while giving an opinion in favour of a contract from 1 January 1996 to 31 January 1996 with Company A, invites the authorising officer to do everything necessary in order for the contract with Embassy to be signed as soon as possible. That confirms that the Parliament itself intended, at that juncture, to award the contract to Embassy.

In view of the foregoing, the compensable damage can be considered to be made up of the damage pleaded by the applicant and mentioned above at para 89(a), "expenses and charges incurred by reason of its certainty of winning the contract", and those mentioned under (b), "expenses of recruitment, medical examinations, training and familiarisation expenses for the drivers" and "preparation, negotiation for fleet of vehicles, telephone contract and parking".

In that regard the Court rejects the argument of the Parliament according to which the applicant's invoices do not show that the expenses were incurred in connection with their relations. No document in the file goes to disprove the fact that those invoices correspond to the measures which Embassy took in order to respond to the urgency of the situation in which the Parliament found itself, measures on which Embassy had already reported in its letter of 12 December 1995.

However, it is clear from the file produced by the applicant that the GSM rental costs (BEF 424,450) cover the period from 19 January 1996 to 18 October 1996. The fact that the rental began to run only on 19 January 1996 is said to be due to a special offer of a rent-free period. However, the Court finds it reasonable to limit the recoverable costs to those relating to the period from 19 January 1996 to 31 March 1996. Inasmuch as the applicant did not relinquish that contract at the end of March 1996, at which point it should have realised that it was very likely that the Parliament contract would not be awarded to it, it must itself bear the costs incurred thereafter. The sum recoverable for GSM rental, including the estimated cost for breaking off the contract, can therefore be assessed at BEF 200,000.

Since the Parliament has not disputed the correctness of the sums claimed by the applicant, it is appropriate to assess Embassy's loss on the basis of the figures it has supplied (see para 89 above). Compensation for the damage suffered by the applicant therefore amounts to the total sum of BEF 5,579,593 (including VAT). However, since the VAT paid by the undertaking can be reclaimed and is not, consequently, borne by Embassy, it cannot be taken into account in calculating the damages. It is therefore necessary to take into consideration the sums claimed exclusive of VAT, namely, according to Embassy's invoices, BEF 1,875,000 + BEF 829,583 for car rental, BEF 947,917 for breaking off the contract, BEF 524,880 for the parking of cars, and BEF 103,275 for the file relating to cars and telephone costs. To

that must be added the sum for GSM rental, earlier calculated at BEF 200,000, and the flat-rate sum relating to the recruitment of drivers, amounting to BEF 200,000. The sum of the material damage suffered by the applicant amounts therefore to BEF 4,680,655.

Given the circumstances of this case it is also necessary to compensate the applicant for the non-material damage it has suffered. It has certainly neither shown that its reputation has been damaged nor proved that the Parliament was responsible for causing such damage. However, it is clear from the file that, although, from December 1995, Embassy took preparatory measures in order to respond to the urgency of the situation outlined by the Parliament officials, it did not know until 19 June 1996 that the contract would not be awarded to it (see para 19 above). In those circumstances, by sending it no information – which had however been requested on many occasions – concerning the outcome of the tendering procedure, the Parliament placed Embassy in a position of uncertainty and forced it to make useless efforts with a view to responding to the urgency of the situation.

Consequently, the Court considers it equitable to quantify the damage, both material and non-material, suffered by the applicant at a total sum of BEF 5,000,000.'

Comment

It is interesting to note that the CFI confirmed its restrictive approach to damages. The applicant could neither claim compensation for its loss of profit, since there was no valid contract between the parties, nor any compensation in respect of its participation in a tendering procedure, as those expenses are incurred by any tenderer whose tender is not accepted. As a result the compensatable damage included 'expenses and charges incurred by reason of [the applicant's] certainty of winning the contract', 'expenses of recruitment, medical examinations, training and familiarisation expenses for the drivers' and 'preparation, negotiation for fleet of vehicles, telephone contract and parking'. Also, the CFI compensated the applicant for moral damage it had suffered caused by the uncertainty of the situation, as well as for the efforts made in order to respond to the urgency of the situation in which the EP found itself.

Fresh Marine Company SA v EC Commission Case T–178/98 [2000] ECR II–3331 Court of First Instance

• *Non-contractual liability of the Community – autonomy of an action based on art 288(2) EC – unlawful conduct of the Commission – duty of diligence and good administration – the causal link between damage and the wrongful conduct of the Commission – contributory negligence – provisional anti-dumping and countervailing duties*

Facts
Following anti-dumping and anti-subsidy proceedings initiated by the Commission in respect of imports of farmed Atlantic salmon originating in Norway, the applicant offered undertakings not to sell its products above a minimum price. By a Decision of 26 September 1997 the Commission accepted the undertakings and terminated anti-dumping and anti-subsidy proceedings with regard to the applicant. On the same day, the Council adopted two regulations, one imposing a definitive anti-dumping duty and the other imposing a definitive countervailing duty on imports of farmed Atlantic salmon originating in Norway. Under both regulations the applicant was exempted from these duties on the basis of the acceptance of its undertakings by the Commission. The applicant's undertakings entered into force on 1 July 1997. On 22 October 1997 the applicant submitted a report to the Commission (the October 1997 report) relating to its export of farmed Atlantic salmon to the Community covering the third quarter of 1997. On the basis of the report the Commission decided that the applicant was in breach of its undertakings.

On 16 December 1997 the Commission adopted Regulation 2529/97 which imposed provisional anti-dumping and countervailing duties upon the applicant who complained to the Commission, arguing that the Commission misinterpreted its report by deleting a number of lines which were intended to cancel lines containing errors. Following the complaint the Commission carried out an investigation at the applicant's premises on 26 and 27 January 1998.

By a letter of 2 February 1998 the Commission acknowledged that the applicant's complaint was justified and that it intended to lift the provisional anti-dumping and countervailing duties. However, the Commission adopted a relevant regulation in this respect on 23 March 1998 and 'reinstated' the applicant's undertakings with effect from 25 March 1998.

The applicant brought proceedings against the Commission under art 288(2) EC claiming damages for loss of profit in respect of the period between 18 December 1997 and 25 March 1998.

Held
The CFI held that the Commission was in breach of its duty of diligence and good administration and was liable for one-half of the loss of profit suffered by the applicant between 18 December 1997 and 31 January 1998 and for all the loss caused to the applicant from 1 February to 25 March 1998.

Judgment
'It is necessary to examine first whether the applicant has proved that it suffered actual loss or damage to its business, as it claims.

So far as concerns, first, loss of profit between 18 December 1997 and 25 March 1998, it must be observed that the figures given by the Commission for exports of farmed Atlantic salmon by the applicant to the Community between July 1997 and September 1998 show that the applicant wholly suspended its exports during the period from approximately mid-December

1997 to the end of March 1998. That suspension of the applicant's business activities on the Community market is confirmed by the auditing firm's certificate appended as annex 6 to the application, which states:

"[W]e hereby confirm that according to the books of the [applicant], no sales of Atlantic salmon have been made to the Community in the period 18 December 1997 and 25 March 1998."

There is nothing in the case file to show that, during that period, the applicant was in a position to make up, even in part, for the total absence of exports to the Community market by a corresponding increase in its sales on other world markets. The Commission has, moreover, never made such an argument, either in its written submissions or at the hearing.

On the contrary, the mission report drawn up by the Commission after the inspection at the applicant's premises on 26 and 27 January 1998 (see para 18 above) shows that following the imposition of the provisional duties the applicant's business activity was extremely reduced and that its directors stated that they would probably have to close if the duties were confirmed. That report goes on to state that the applicant effectively exported only to Japan following the entry into force of the provisional measures. However, that last indication, read in the light of the preceding statements, must be understood as referring to the applicant's exploitation of an opening on the Japanese market and cannot be taken as an indication that the focus of the applicant's business activities had shifted towards that market in order to make up for the total absence of sales by it on the Community market.

In light of those circumstances, it is necessary to assess the amount of the loss of profit suffered by the applicant as a result of the suspension of its exports to the Community between 18 December 1997 and 25 March 1998. That loss of profit must be considered to equate to the profit which it would have made if it had continued to export to the Community during that period.

In order to do so, it is necessary first to determine at what rate the applicant's exports to the Community fell following the entry into force on 1 July 1997 of its undertaking, which would in any event still have applied if it had continued to export to the Community during the period in question. For a reliable calculation, the trends in the applicant's sales within the Community between 1996 and 1997 during the period from 1 July to 17 December have to be examined.

In that respect, it appears from the figures sent on 14 April 2000 by the applicant to the Court in reply to a written question that, during the period from 1 July to 17 December, it exported to the Community 1,271,304kg of farmed Atlantic salmon in 1997 instead of the 2,030,883kg of 1996, which represents a reduction of 759,579kg, or a fall in the order of 37 per cent of its sales on the Community market.

On that basis, it may thus be held that, if the applicant had continued exporting to the Community within the framework of its undertaking between 18 December 1997 and 25 March 1998, its sales of farmed Atlantic salmon would have been 63 per cent (100 per cent – 37 per cent) of those realised on the Community market in the previous year during the corresponding period. The figures set out in the abovementioned reply provided by the applicant make it clear that it exported to the Community approximately 450,000kg of farmed Atlantic salmon from 18 December 1996 to 31 January 1997, 210,000kg in February 1997 and 230,000kg from 1 to 25 March 1997.

It can therefore be estimated that the applicant's sales of farmed Atlantic salmon on the Community market would have amounted to approximately 284,000kg (63 per cent of 450,000kg) during the period between 18 December 1997 and 31 January 1998, 132,000kg (63 per cent of 210,000kg) in February 1998 and 145,000kg (63 per cent of 230,000kg) during the period from 1 to 25 March 1998.

From the information provided in the abovementioned reply by the applicant, it is apparent that between 1 July and 17

December 1997, when it exported its products to the Community within the framework of its undertaking, the applicant made an average profit of NOK 1,307,539/ 1,271,304kg, that is to say NOK 1.028/kg. It may thus be inferred that, if it had continued to export on the basis of that undertaking between 18 December 1997 and 25 March 1998, it would have made a profit equivalent to NOK 292,000 (284,000kg x NOK 1.028/kg), NOK 135,000 (132,000kg x NOK 1.028/kg) and NOK 150,000 (145,000kg x NOK 1.028/kg) between 18 December 1997 and 31 January 1998, in February 1998 and between 1 and 25 March 1998 respectively.

The loss of profit suffered by the applicant will therefore be fixed at NOK 292,000 in respect of the period between 18 December 1997 and 31 January 1998, NOK 135,000 in respect of February 1998 and NOK 150,000 in respect of the period from 1 to 25 March 1998.

So far as concerns, secondly, the costs incurred in re-establishing its position on the Community market, it must be stated, as the Commission points out, that, contrary to the requirement laid down in the case law (see Case C–237/98P *Dorsch Consult* v *EC Council* [2000] ECR I–4549, para 23, and the case law cited), the applicant does not adduce any evidence to prove that it has actually incurred such costs and that it will continue to do so. Moreover, it must be pointed out that, according to the figures provided by the Commission in annex 5 to the defence, which were not disputed by the applicant in its reply, the applicant has largely recovered its share of the market in the Community since June 1998. Its exports of farmed Atlantic salmon to the Community during that month, in proportion to the total exports of salmon originating in Norway to the Community, in fact represented 1.60 per cent of the market whereas, according to the same Commission figures, the applicant's share of the market had been, on average, 1.38 per cent during the five months prior to the entry into force of Regulation No 2529/97. Accordingly, the

Court holds that that head of damage alleged by the applicant has not been proved.

It is necessary now to determine whether there is a causal link between the loss or damage to the applicant's business, as established by the analysis set out in paras 105 to 116 above, and the wrongful conduct of the Commission, confirmed by Regulation No 2529/97, which is clear from the examination carried out in paras 73 to 82 and 91 above.

There is a causal link for the purposes of the second paragraph of art 215 of the Treaty where there is a direct causal nexus between the fault committed by the institution concerned and the injury pleaded, the burden of proof of which rests on the applicant (Case T–149/96 *Coldiretti and Others* v *EC Council and EC Commission* [1998] ECR II–3841, para 101, and the cited case-law). The Community cannot be held liable for any damage other than that which is a sufficiently direct consequence of the misconduct of the institution concerned (see, in particular, Joined Cases 64/76 and 113/76, 167/78 and 239/78, 27/79, 28/79 and 45/79 *Dumortier and Others* v *EC Council* [1979] ECR 3091, para 21; Case T–168/94 *Blackspur and Others* v *EC Council and EC Commission* [1995] ECR II–2627, para 52, and *TEAM* v *EC Commission* [Case T–13/96 [1998] ECR II–4073] para 68).

In the present case, it is clear from the certificate issued by the firm of auditors analysed in para 106 above that the period during which the applicant suspended its exports to the Community coincides with that during which the provisional measures imposed by Regulation No 2529/97 applied to imports of its products. That must be interpreted as evidence of the existence of a causal link between the irregularities, in particular those committed by the Commission, giving rise to the imposition of provisional measures, on the one hand, and the loss of profit, on the other.

It is, indeed, undeniable that, were it not for such irregularities and the provisional measures which followed them, the applicant would have continued its exports to the

Community in compliance with its under-taking. It would thus have suffered no loss of profit on the Community market. The misconduct of the Commission, when analysing the October 1997 report, and which was confirmed by Regulation No 2529/97, is therefore causally linked, within the meaning of the case law referred to in para 118 above, with the loss or damage to the applicant's business.

The evidence mentioned in para 119 above cannot however be considered in itself to prove that the whole of the appli-cant's loss of profits, as determined in para 115 above, was caused exclusively by the irregularities, in particular those of the Commission, which gave rise to the adop-tion of the provisional measures. In that regard, it is necessary to ascertain whether, as the case law requires, the applicant showed reasonable diligence in limiting the extent of the damage which it claims to have suffered, a matter which the Commission disputes (see, Joined Cases C–104/89 and C–37/90 *Mulder and Others* v *EC Council and EC Commission* [1992] ECR I–3061, para 33; Joined Cases C–46/93 and C–48/93 *Brasserie du Pêcheur and Factortame* [1996] ECR I–1029, para 85; and Case C–284/98P *European Parliament* v *Bieber* [2000] ECR I–1527, para 57).

The Commission's argument is that, in view of the fact that the duties imposed by Regulation No 2529/97 were provisional, the applicant could, by providing a modest amount for the setting-up of a bank guaran-tee, have continued to export to the Community at unchanged prices.

In that regard, the parties do not dispute that, at the time, the applicant exported its products to the Community mainly under the DDP system. Under that system, it would have been obliged to pay the provi-sional anti-dumping and countervailing duties imposed by Regulation 2529/97 to the relevant customs authorities, if it had exported to the Community market during the period when the provisional measures were in force. For that reason, it would have been for the applicant, and not for its cus-tomers within the Community, to provide a

bank guarantee for that type of sale to cover such provisional duties, and on which art 7(3) of Regulation No 384/96 and art 12(2) of Regulation No 2026/97 predicate the free circulation of the products in question within the Community.

However, even supposing that the appli-cant, which has not disputed the Commission's statements regarding the cost of such a bank guarantee, had obtained one, the Court holds that it would have run an unusual commercial risk, beyond the level of risk inherent in any commercial enter-prise, by exporting to the Community during the period when Regulation No 2529/97 was applicable to imports of its products. If, once that bank guarantee had been issued, it had, as the Commission sug-gests, decided to export to the Community at unchanged prices without passing on to its Community customers the amount of the provisional duties through the prices it charged, it would have run the risk of having to bear on its own the burden of those duties should they ever have been collected defini-tively. Since it was not able to tell at that time whether that would eventually be the case, it therefore had no option but to increase its export prices by the amount of those provisional duties. Having regard in particular to competition from Community companies selling salmon and from the numerous Norwegian exporters which had been able to continue to sell on the Community market within the terms of their undertakings during the period in question, the applicant could reasonably have taken the view that there was no chance of finding an outlet for its products on that market during that period.

In view of those circumstances, the absence of any attempt by the applicant to export its products to the Community during the period in question cannot be regarded as a failure to fulfil the obligation, laid down in the case law referred to in para 121 above, to show reasonable diligence in mitigating the extent of the damage which it claims to have suffered.

The Commission maintains that it gave the applicant an early assurance that its undertaking would be reinstated and that the provisional duties imposed by Regulation No 2529/97 on imports of its products would not be confirmed.

None the less, the Court observes that in its letter of 5 January 1998 (see para 11 above) the Commission stated that it was prepared to reconsider its position vis-à-vis the applicant in the light of any new data which the latter sent it in good time. It did not however offer it any certainty as to the reinstatement of its undertaking or the non-confirmation of the provisional duties imposed by Regulation No 2529/97.

It is true that in its letter of 30 January 1998, mentioned in para 19 above, the Commission informed the applicant that it no longer had any reason to believe that it had breached its undertaking, that the provisional duties imposed on imports of its products were expected to be repealed and that the undertaking would be reinstated as soon as that repeal took effect or by 19 April 1998, whichever was the earlier. However, in its letter of 2 February 1998, the Commission – which, during the hearing, did not dispute that that letter constituted the reply to the applicant's inquiry regarding the conditions under which it could resume exporting to the Community pending the reinstatement of its undertaking – after recalling the content of art 7(3) of Regulation No 384/96 (see para 123 above), stated:

> "As it is intended to propose to the Council to make a negative determination, i.e. not to impose definitive duties, the provisional duties imposed by Regulation (EC) No 2529/97 are expected not to be confirmed, pursuant to art 10(3) of Regulation (EC) No 384/96. Article 10(2) of Regulation (EC) No 384/96 provides that amounts of provisional duties shall be released in so far as there is no decision by the Council to definitively collect all or part of the provisional duties."

Whatever the reason for them, the last words of that passage, which suggest that the Commission's intention not to propose the imposition of definitive duties on the

applicant's products did not mean that the Council would not decide to collect definitively all or part of the amounts paid by way of provisional duties, left the applicant's directors with the prospect of the unusual commercial risk described in para 124 above, if it resumed exports to the Community while the provisional measures imposed by Regulation No 2529/97 remained in force.

Although it was not possible, at the material time, to find any actual cases of provisional duties being collected definitively where they had not been replaced by definitive duties, the applicant cannot be reproached for continuing, upon reading such a statement, to refrain from exporting to the Community until 25 March 1998, when it knew for certain, with the entry into force of Regulation No 651/98, that its undertaking had been reinstated and the provisional duties imposed by Regulation No 2529/97 on imports of its products had been repealed.

On the other hand, the Court holds, on reading the letters of 30 January and 2 February 1998 analysed in para 128 above, that the Commission did not take the necessary and appropriate measures which the party causing the damage must take where damage, such as that at issue here, is ongoing (see, to that effect, *European Parliament v Bieber*, cited in para 121 above, para 57) in order to limit the extent of the damage to which its misconduct, when it was verifying compliance by the applicant with its undertaking, had contributed.

It is clear from the case file that, following the explanations provided by the applicant at the beginning of January 1998 (see paras 12 and 13 above) and the investigation carried out at its premises at the end of that month (see para 18 above), the Commission had become convinced, at least as from 30 January 1998, as attested by its letter of that date, that the applicant had complied with its undertaking in the course of the third quarter of 1997. However, the Commission, which, in its own words (see para 102 above) and as is shown moreover by the fact that it adopted Regulation No 651/98, was alone entitled in the present case to lift the provisional measures imposed on imports of the applicant's products by Regulation No 2529/97, for no obvious reason delayed until 25 March 1998 before giving the applicant, by means of Regulation No 651/98, the formal legal reassurance which it could have given at the end of January 1998. Although it could have realised during the abovementioned investigation at the applicant's premises that the applicant was suffering considerable commercial loss as a result of the application of those provisional measures (see para 108), by its letter of 2 February 1998 it unjustifiably perpetuated the doubts as to the final outcome regarding the provisional duties imposed by Regulation No 2529/97. It thus dissuaded the applicant from resuming commercial activities on the Community market.

The fact that the Commission was faced at the same time with several similar cases, which prompted it to check the information necessary for the purposes of definitively determining whether undertakings had been breached, and the fact that the period of validity of Regulation No 2529/97 had been set at four months, did not exonerate it from the duty to regularise the applicant's own situation as soon as it was finally convinced that the applicant had complied with its undertaking during the period in question.

For having thus failed to take the necessary measures as soon as the irregularities giving rise to the imposition of provisional measures on imports of the applicant's products were definitively rectified, the Commission must be held solely responsible for the applicant's loss of profit, at least as from the end of January 1998.

It must therefore be held that, although, as is apparent from the grounds set out in paras 73 to 92 above, the applicant contributed to the same extent as the Commission in causing loss or damage to its business, continuation of that loss after the end of January 1998 is, on the other hand, exclusively due to a failure by the Commission to exercise due care; even though the explanations which it had obtained from the applicant had definitely made it possible to correct their

respective prior errors and removed any reason to continue to believe that the undertaking had been breached, the Commission delayed, for no apparent reason, in regularising the applicant's situation by withdrawing the provisional measures originally imposed against it.

It follows that the Commission must be held to be liable for one half of the loss of profit suffered by the applicant between 18 December 1997 and 31 January 1998 and for all the loss caused to the applicant from 1 February to 25 March 1998 (see para 115 above).

In conclusion, the Commission will be ordered to pay to the applicant, first, one half of NOK 292,000 in respect of the applicant's loss of profit between 18 December 1997 and 31 January 1998 and, second, NOK 285,000 (NOK 135,000 + NOK 150,000) as compensation for the damage caused to the applicant from 1 February to 25 March 1998, that is a total amount of NOK 431,000. The remainder of the application will be dismissed.'

Comment

In the commented case the act challenged by the applicant was of an administrative nature as it concerned the misinterpretation by the Commission of the October 1997 report. That interpretation did not involve any choices of economic policy and conferred on the Commission only very little or no discretion. In these circumstances mere infringement of Community law was sufficient to establish the non-contractual liability of the Commission. Any administrative authority exercising ordinary care and diligence would not have committed the error which the Commission had committed when dealing which the October 1997 report. Consequently, the CFI found the Commission in breach of its duty of diligence and good administration. However, the CFI decided that the applicant contributed through its own negligence to the resulting damage. The lack of experience in drafting the October 1997 report was not considered as an excuse. In this respect the CFI stated that the applicant should have annexed to the October 1997 report the explanations required for a correct understanding of certain parts of it, since any trader exercising ordinary care and diligence would have done so. As a result the Commission and the applicant were equally at fault. The CFI held that the applicant contributed through his negligence to the resulting damage and therefore reduced by half the amount claimed for the period between 18 December 1997 and 31 January 1998.

In respect of the duty to mitigate loss, neither the Commission nor the CFI suggested that the applicant was in a position to make up for the loss of profit, that is that it could reasonably have replaced the lost profit from alternative activities or by a corresponding increase in its sales in other world markets.

Mulder and Others v *EC Council and EC Commission* Joined Cases C–104/89 and C–37/90 [1992] ECR I–3061 European Court of Justice

• *Action for non-contractual liability of the Council and the Commission – legislative measure involving economic policy choices – common agricultural policy – sufficiently serious breach – principle of protection of legitimate expectations – duty to mitigate any loss – abnormal and special damage*

Facts
Mulder and other farmers submitted an application under art 215(2) EC Treaty [art 288(2) EC] claiming that they suffered loss as a result of various Community regulations dealing with over-production and cuts-back in dairy products. Under Regulation 1078/77 (1977) they were paid a premium for five years for not selling milk and milk products. At the end of this five years period they applied for 'special reference quantities' which would have allowed them to come back into the market. Under Regulation 857/84 they failed to obtain the 'special reference quantities'.

They were unable to sell any milk, and consequently, they were put out of business. They successfully challenged Regulation 857/84 under art 173 EC Treaty [art 230 EC] (*Mulder* v *Ministry of Agriculture and Fisheries* Case 120/86 [1988] ECR 2321). The farmers argued that the failure to obtain 'special reference quantities' upon the expiry of the scheme was contrary to Community law on the ground that such action contravened the principle of legitimate expectations.

Held
The ECJ held that the Community incurred liability in relation to the regulation allocating 'special reference quantities' but not in respect of the second regulation. In the case of the regulation concerning the allocation of 'special reference quantities', although the ECJ held that the group of people affected was clearly defined, it comprised more than 12,000 farmers who were entitled to claim approximately ECU 250 million. The ECJ reduced the damages awarded by the amount of profit which the producers could reasonably have earned from alternative activities on the grounds of the duty to mitigate any loss.

Judgment
'[*Wrongful acts – general legislative measures*]
The second paragraph of art 215 of the Treaty provides that, in the case of non-contractual liability, the Community in accordance with the general principles common to the laws of the Member States, is to make good any damage caused by its institutions in the performance of their duties. The scope of that provision has been specified in the sense that the Community does not incur liability on account of a legislative measure involving choices of economic policy unless a sufficiently serious breach of a superior rule of law for the protection the individuals occurred (see in particular, the judgment in *HNL* v *EC Council and EC Commission* Joined Cases 83 and 94/76, 4, 15 and 40/77 [1978] ECR 1209, paras 4,5, and 6). More specifically, in a legislative field such as the

one in question, which is characterised by the exercise of a wide discretion essential for the implementation of the Common Agricultural Policy, the Com-munity cannot incur liability unless the institution concerned has manifestly and gravely disregarded the limits on the exercise of its powers (see in particular the judgment in *HNL v EC Council and EC Commission*, para 6).

The Court has also consistently held that, in order for the Community to incur non-contractual liability, the damage alleged must go beyond the bounds of the normal economic risks inherent in the activities in the sector concerned.

... Those conditions are fulfilled in the case of Regulation No 857/84 as supplemented by Regulation No 1371/84.

In contrast, contrary to the applicants' assertions, the Community cannot incur liability on account of the fact that Regulation No 764/89 introduced the 60 per cent rule.

Admittedly, that rule also infringes the legitimate expectation of the producers concerned with regard to the limited nature of their non-marketing or conversion undertaking, as the Court held in the judgments in *Spagl* and *Pastätter* [*Spagl* v *Haumpzollamt Rosenheim* Case C–189/89 [1990] ECR I–4359 and *Pastätter* v *Hauptzollamt Bad Reichenhall* Case C–217/89 [1990] ECR I–4585]. However, the breach of the principle of the protection of legitimate expectations which was held to exist cannot be described as being sufficiently serious within the meaning of the case law on the non-contractual liability of the Community.

In that regard, it must be borne in mind first that, unlike the 1984 rules, which made it impossible for the producers concerned to market milk, the 60 per cent rule enabled those traders to resume their activities as milk producers. Consequently, in the amending regulation, Regulation No 764/89, the Council did not fail to take the situation of the producers concerned into account.

Secondly, it must be observed that, by adopting Regulation No 764/89 following

the judgment of 28 April 1988 in *Mulder* and *Von Deetzen* [*Mulder* Case 120/86 [1988] ECR 2321 and *Von Deetzen* Case 170/86 [1988] ECR 2355], the Community legislature made an economic policy choice with regard to the manner in which it was necessary to implement the principles set out in those judgments. That was based, on the one hand, on the "overriding necessity of not jeopardising the fragile stability that currently obtains in the milk products sector" (fifth recital in the preamble to Regulation No 764/89) and, on the other, on the need to strike a balance between the interests of the producers concerned and the interests of the other producers subject to the scheme. The Council made that choice in such a way as to maintain the level of other producers' reference quantities unchanged while increasing the Community reserve by 600,000 tonnes, or 60 per cent of aggregate foreseeable applications for the allocation of special reference quantities, which, in its view, was the highest quantity compatible with the aims of the scheme. Accordingly the Council took account of a higher public interest, without gravely and manifestly disregarding the limits of its discretionary power in this area.

In the light of the foregoing, it must therefore be held that the Community is bound to make good the damage suffered by the applicants as a result of the application of Regulation No 857/84, as supplemented by Regulation No 1371/84, cited above, but not the damage resulting from the application of Regulation No 764/89, cited above.

[*Duty to mitigate any loss*]
As regards the extent of the damage which the Community should make good, in the absence of particular circumstances warranting a different assessment, account should be taken of the loss of earnings consisting in the difference between, on the one hand, the income which the applicants would have obtained in the normal course of events from the milk deliveries which they would have made if, during the period between 1 April 1984 (the date of entry into force of Regulation No 857/84) and 29

March 1989 (the date of entry into force of Regulation No 764/89), they had obtained the reference quantities to which they were entitled and, on the other hand, the income which they actually obtained from milk deliveries made during that period in the absence of any reference quantity, plus any income which they obtained, or could have obtained, during that period from any replacement activities.

... As regards income from any replacement activities which is to be deducted from the hypothetical income referred above, it must be noted that that income must be taken to include not only that which the applicants actually obtained from replacement activities, but also that income which they could have obtained had they reasonably engaged in such activities. This conclusion must be reached in the light of a general principle common to the legal systems of the Member States to the effect that the injured party must show reasonable diligence in limiting the extent of his loss or risk having to bear the damage himself. Any operating losses incurred by the applicants in carrying out such a replacement activity cannot be attributed to the Community, since the origin of such losses does not lie in the effects of the Community rules.

It follows that the amount of compensation payable by the Community should correspond to the damage which it caused. The defendant institutions' contention that the amount of the compensation should be calculated on the basis of the amount of the non-marketing premium paid to each of the applicants must therefore be rejected. It must be noted in this regard that that premium constitutes the quid pro quo for the non-marketing undertaking and has no connection with the damage which the applicants suffered owing to the application of the rules on the additional levy, which were adopted at a later date.'

Comment

The ECJ confirmed the Schöppenstedt formula. The Court held that in relation to leg-

islative acts involving choices in economic policy the Community institutions enjoyed a wide discretion and thus they were liable only if they had manifestly and gravely disregarded the limits of the exercise of their powers. As a result, in order to incur non-contractual liability the damage must go beyond the bounds of normal economic risks inherent in the activities relevant to a particular sector. However, in the present case the ECJ softened its approach towards the assessment of the criterion of sufficiently serious breach.

The restrictive interpretation reached its apogee in *Amylum (GR) NV and Tunnel Refineries Ltd* v *EC Council and EC Commission* Cases 116 and 124/77 [1979] ECR 3497 and *Koninklijke Scholten Honig NV* v *EC Council and EC Commission* Case 43/77 [1979] ECR 3583, the so-called *Isoglucose* cases in which a regulation imposing levies on the production of isogluose, successfully challenged under art 173 EC Treaty [art 230 EC] prior to the application for damages, had such effect on the remaining three or four isoglucose undertakings in the Community that, for example, Koninklijke had to close down its business. The ECJ held that only if the conduct of an EC institution was 'verging on the arbitrary' (which was not the case) it would be considered as a sufficiently serious breach. The ECJ refused to award damages. The interests of the Community prevailed. The EC was entitled to limit the production of isoglucose and stabilise the market although some mistakes were made which resulted in the annulment of the Regulation.

In the present case the Court held that in the absence of 'the peremptory public interest' the Community cannot justify a measure which is gravely illegal and thus the Community would incur liability in such circumstances. Nevertheless, the change of approach of the Community courts in application of the Schöppenstedt formula has not eliminated the requirement that only grave illegality, in the absence of the peremptory public interest of the Community, would permit applicants to successfully claim damages under art 215(2) EC Treaty [art 288(2) EC] (*Odigitria AAE* v *EC Council and EC Commission* Case T–572/93 [1995] ECR II–2025).

As to the amount of damages, it is generally negotiated between the parties. In the case of a large number of applicants, the Commission and the Council submit a collective offer of indemnification as happened in the present case (the Council and the Commission adopted a regulation regarding the modality of indemnification OJ C198, p4).

However, the ECJ reduced the amount of damages. The Court justified the reduction on the basis of the duty upon the applicants to mitigate any loss, although the Court made no suggestion as to alternative activities but the term 'reasonable' implies that fundamentally different activities from their previous business were not considered as alternatives.

6 The Preliminary Reference Procedure

Preliminary ruling on interpretation of Community law

Foglia v *Novello (No 1)* Case 104/79 [1980] ECR 745; [1981] 1 CMLR 45 European Court of Justice

• *Discretionary referral – genuine dispute between the parties to national proceedings – charges having equivalent effect to custom duties – art 30 EC Treaty [art 28 EC]*

Facts

Foglia, an Italian wine merchant, entered into a contract with Novello, an Italian national, for the delivery of liqueur wine to a person residing in France. They inserted an express clause providing that Novello would not pay any unlawfully levied taxes. The French authorities imposed a tax on the importation of the wine to France which Foglia paid although his contract which a shipper Danzas also provided that he should not be liable for any charges imposed in breach of the free movement of goods. Foglia brought proceedings against Novello who refused to reimburse the French tax levied on wine.

Held

The ECJ declined to exercise jurisdiction under art 177 EC Treaty [art 234 EC] on the ground that there was no real dispute between the parties to national proceedings. The Court held that the parties were concerned to obtain

a ruling that the French tax system was invalid in relation to liqueur wine.

Judgment

'In their written submissions to the Court of Justice the two parties to the main action have provided an essentially identical description of the tax discrimination which is a feature of the French legislation concerning the taxation of liqueur wines; the two parties consider that the legislation is incompatible with Community law. In the course of the oral procedure before the Court Foglia stated that he was participating in the procedure before the Court in view of the interest of his undertaking as such and as an undertaking belonging to a certain category of Italian traders in the outcome of the legal issues involved in the dispute.

It thus appears that the parties to the main action are concerned to obtain a ruling that the French tax system is invalid for liqueur wines by the expedient of proceedings before an Italian court between two private individuals who are in agreement as to the result to be attained and who have inserted a clause in their contract in order to induce the Italian court to give a ruling on the point. The artificial nature of this expedient is underlined by the fact that Danzas did not exercise its rights under French law to institute proceedings over the consumption tax although it undoubtedly had an interest in doing so in view of the clause in the contract by which it was bound and moreover by the fact that Foglia paid without protest that undertaking's bill which included a sum paid in respect of that tax.

The duty of the Court of Justice under art

177 of the [EC] Treaty is to supply all courts in the Community with the information on the interpretation of Community law which is necessary to enable them to settle genuine disputes which are brought before them. A situation in which the Court was obliged by the expedient of arrangements like those described above to give rulings would jeopardise the whole system of legal remedies available to private individuals to enable them to protect themselves against tax provisions which are contrary to the Treaty.

This means that the questions asked by the national court, having regard to the circumstances of this case, do not fall within the framework of the duties of the Court of Justice under art 177 of the Treaty.

The Court of Justice accordingly has no jurisdiction to give a ruling on the questions asked by the national court.'

Comment

The ECJ held that the parties to national proceedings were concerned to obtain a ruling on the legality of the French legislation by the expedient of proceedings before an Italian court. Both parties had the same interest in the outcome of the dispute which was to obtain a ruling on the invalidity of the French legislation and, since under their contracts they were not liable for any unlawful charges imposed by France, their action was a collusive and artificial device aimed at obtaining a ruling and not a genuine dispute which the ECJ could settle.

When the Italian court asked the ECJ to provide clarification on its preliminary judgment in *Foglia* v *Novello* Case 104/79, the ECJ accepted the second reference in the same case but once again declined its jurisdiction to give a preliminary ruling on the same grounds (*Foglia* v *Novello (No 2)* Case 244/80 [1981] ECR 3045). The existence of a real dispute in the proceedings before a national court is determined from the point of view of art 177 EC Treaty [art 234 EC]. Thus, neither the fact that the parties challenge national legislation of one Member State before a court of another Member State, nor their agreement

to 'organise' the proceedings before a national court leading to the preliminary ruling, is sufficient to exclude a real dispute from the scope of art 177 EC Treaty [art 234 EC] (see *Société d'Importation Edouard Leclerc-Siplec* v *TFI Publicité SA* Case C–412/93 [1995] ECR I–179; *Bosman* Case C–141/93 [1995] ECR I–4921, *Eau de Cologne* v *Provide* Case C–150/88 [1989] ECR 3891).

Pretore di Salo v *Persons Unknown*
Case 14/86 [1989] 1 CMLR 71
European Court of Justice

• *Preliminary ruling – jurisdiction of the ECJ – determination of a court or tribunal – timing of the reference – framing of the question referred – Directive 78/659/EEC*

Facts
The Italian authorities instituted criminal proceedings against unidentified persons responsible for the pollution of a river in Italy. The prosecution was based on provisions of the Italian Criminal Code, and the question was raised whether this statute was consistent with Council Directive 78/659 which regulated the quality of water and the amount of pollution that may be released into water sources.

The Pretore asked the ECJ for a preliminary ruling under art 177 EC Treaty [art 234 EC] as to whether the Italian laws for the protection of waters from pollution were consistent with the Directive. This gave rise to a number of issues, including the necessary status of the referring court to obtain a preliminary ruling, the proper timing of such request, and the role of the ECJ in ascertaining the facts of a dispute.

Held
The ECJ held that: (1) the reference from the magistrate came from 'a court or tribunal' within the meaning of art 177 EC Treaty [art 234 EC]; (2) the reference was not premature and did not preclude a later reference if such a request was subsequently received from the

tribunal; (3) the question of compatibility of Italian law with Community law was too generally framed but, in such cases, the ECJ is empowered to reformulate the question; and (4) Directive 78/659 could not aggravate liability of a person violating the Directive.

Judgment

'[*First question*]

Without expressly arguing that the Court does not have jurisdiction to reply to the questions referred to it, the Italian government draws the Court's attention to the nature of the function performed in this case by the Pretore, which are both those of a public prosecutor and those of an examining magistrate. The Pretore carries out preliminary investigations in his capacity as public prosecutor and, where these disclose no grounds for continuing the proceedings, makes an order accordingly in the place of an examining magistrate. That order is not a judicial act because it cannot acquire the force of res judicata or create an irreversible procedural situation and because no reason need be given for it, whereas art 111 of the Italian Constitution imposes an obligation to state reasons in the case of judicial acts.

It must be observed that the Pretori are judges who, in proceedings such as those in which the questions referred to the Court in this case were raised, combine the functions of a public prosecutor and an examining magistrate. The Court has jurisdiction to reply to a request for a preliminary ruling if that request emanates from a court or tribunal which has acted in the general framework of its task as judging, independently and in accordance with law, cases coming within the jurisdiction conferred on it by law, even though certain functions of that court or tribunal in the proceedings which give rise to the reference for a preliminary ruling are not, strictly speaking, of a judicial nature.

[*Second question*]

At the hearing, the Italian government also maintained that, having regard to the present stage of the proceedings, at which the facts have not been sufficiently established and those who may be responsible have not yet been identified, a reference for a preliminary ruling is premature.

The European Commission considers that the reference for a preliminary ruling is inadmissible because in criminal proceedings against persons unknown it is possible that a decision may never be given on the substance of the case. All that is required for that to be the case is for those responsible never to be identified. At the hearing, the Commission also relied on another argument in support of the proposition that the Court does not have jurisdiction: if, after the Court's decision, the persons responsible were identified, they would be prevented from defending before the Court the interpretation of Community law most in conformity with their interests. That would constitute a violation of the right to a fair hearing.

It must be pointed out first that, as the Court decided in Joined Cases 36 and 71/80 *Irish Creamery Milk Supplier's Association* v *Ireland* [1981] ECR 735, if the interpretation of Community law is to be use to the national court, it is essential to define the legal context in which the interpretation requested should be placed. In that perspective, it might be convenient in certain circumstances for the facts of the case to be established and for questions of purely national law to be settled at the time when the reference is made to the Court of Justice so as to enable the latter to take cognisance of all the matters of fact and law which may be relevant to the interpretation of Community law which it is called upon to give.

However, as the Court already held, those considerations do not in any way restrict the discretion of the national court, which alone has a direct knowledge of the facts of the case and of the arguments of the parties, which will have to take responsibility for giving judgment in the case and which is therefore in the best position to appreciate at what stage of the proceedings it requires a preliminary ruling from the Court of Justice. The decision at what stage in the proceedings a question should be referred to the Court of Justice for a preliminary ruling is therefore dictated by considerations of procedural economy and efficiency to be weighed only by the national court and not the Court of Justice.

It should be pointed out that the Court consistently held that the fact that judgments delivered on the basis of references for a preliminary ruling are binding on the national court does not preclude the national court to which such a reference is addressed from making a further reference to the Court of Justice if it considers it necessary in order to give judgment in the main proceedings. Such a reference may be justified when the national court encounters difficulties in understanding or applying the judgment, when it refers a fresh question of law to the Court, or again, when it submits new considerations which might lead the Court to give a different answer to a question submitted earlier.

It follows that where the accused are identified after the reference for a preliminary ruling and if one of the above mentioned conditions arises, the national court may once again refer a question to the Court of Justice and thereby ensure that due respect is given to the right to a fair hearing.

In those circumstances, the objections raised by the Commission and the Italian government concerning the jurisdiction of the Court must be rejected.

[Third question]
As the Court consistently held, it may not, in proceedings under art 177 [EC] Treaty, rule on the conformity of national measures with Community law. The Court may, however, extract from the wording of the question formulated by the national court, and having regard to the facts stated by the latter, those elements which concern the interpretation of Community law for the purpose of enabling that court to resolve the legal problems before it. In this case, however, in view of the generality of the question and the absence of any specific elements which would make it possible to identify the doubts entertained by the national court, it is not possible for the Court to reply to the first question referred to it.

[Fourth question]
According to the national court's order for reference, the Community rules are relevant to the questions of criminal law raised before it:

"… in view of the fact that such rules constitute an essential basis for the criteria to be applied in the investigations, in view of the decisive importance for the purpose of the requirements laid down by the rules of criminal law in force and in view of the undeniable possibilities which may emerge from the directive of broadening the sphere of the protection afforded by the criminal law."

The national court is therefore essentially seeking to ascertain whether Directive 78/659 may, of itself and independently of the internal law of a Member State, have the effect of determining or aggravating the liability in criminal law of persons who act in contravention of that directive.

In that regard, the Court already held in Case 152/84 *Marshall* v *Southampton and South-West Hampshire Area Health Authority* [1986] ECR 723 that "a directive may not of itself impose obligations on an individual and that a provision of a directive may not be relied upon as such against such a person". A directive which has not been transposed into the internal legal order of a Member State may not therefore give rise to obligations on individuals either in regard to other individuals or, a fortiori, in regard to the State itself.

Consequently, the reply to the [fourth] question must be that Council Directive 78/659 cannot, of itself and independently of a national law adopted by a Member State for its implementation, have the effect of determining or aggravating the liability in criminal law of persons who act in contravention of the provisions of that directive.'

Comment

In the present case the ECJ held that a body which exercises not only a judicial function but also other tasks may be considered as a court or tribunal within the meaning of art 177 EC Treaty [art 234 EC]. An Italian Pretore, a magistrate who initially acts as a public prosecutor and then as an examining magistrate, was considered as a court or a tribunal within the meaning of art 177 EC Treaty [art 234 EC] on the ground that the request emanated from a body that acted in the general framework of its task of judging, independently and in accordance with the law, despite the fact that certain functions performed by that body were not sensu stricto of a judicial nature.

Court or tribunal within the meaning of art 234 EC

Victoria Film A/S Case C–134/97 [1999] 1 CMLR 279 European Court of Justice

• *Preliminary ruling – lack of jurisdiction of the ECJ – court or tribunal under art 177 EC Treaty [art 234 EC] – act of accession of the Kingdom of Sweden – transitional provisions – exemptions – services provided by authors, artists and performers*

Facts
There was a tax dispute between Victoria Film A/S and Swedish tax authorities concerning certain transitional exemptions relating to turnover tax provided for in art 28(3)(b) of the Sixth Council Directive 77/388/EEC and the application of arts 2(1), 6(1) and 17 of that Directive allowing the suppliers of exclusive rights to exhibit motion pictures to deduct the VAT component of goods and services included in the price charged on the assignment of those rights. The Skatterättsnämnden (Swedish Revenue Board), which assesses the situation of the applicant from the point of view of internal taxation and delivers only preliminary decisions prior to binding decisions of the Swedish tax authorities, referred the above-mentioned questions for a preliminary ruling to the ECJ. The European

Commission argued that the ECJ had no jurisdiction because the Swedish Revenue Board was not a court or a tribunal within the meaning of art 177 EC Treaty [art 234 EC] as its activities were administrative in nature.

Held
The ECJ held that it had no jurisdiction to answer the questions referred by the Swedish Revenue Board.

Judgment
'By decision of 20 February 1997, Skatterättsnämnden (Revenue Board) referred to the Court for a preliminary ruling under art 177 of the EC Treaty three questions on the interpretation of the Act concerning the conditions of accession of the Republic of Austria, the Republic of Finland and the Kingdom of Sweden and the adjustments to the Treaties on which the European Union is founded, in conjunction with art 28(3)(b) of Sixth Council Directive (77/388/EEC) of 17 May 1977 and point 2 of Annex F thereto.

Those questions have been raised in the context of an application for a preliminary decision submitted by Victoria Film A/S ("Victoria") to Skatterättsnämnden.

Skatterättsnämnden can, upon application by a taxable person, give a preliminary decision on matters of taxation.

The Commission submits that the Court has no jurisdiction to reply to the questions referred by Skatterättsnämnden. In particular, it submits that the latter is not a court or tribunal for the purposes of art 177 of the Treaty, since its activities seem to be rather administrative in nature.

In this connection, it should be observed that it has been consistently held that a national court may refer a question to the Court only if there is a case pending before it and if it is called upon to give judgment in proceedings intended to lead to a decision of a judicial nature.

It should be borne in mind, in particular, that at the time when an application for a preliminary decision is lodged with

Skatterättsnämnden the taxpayer's situation has not been the subject of any decision by the tax authorities. Skatterättsnämnden does not therefore have as its task to review the legality of the decisions of the tax authorities but rather to adopt a view, for the first time, on how a specific transaction is to be assessed to tax.

Where, upon application by a taxable person, Skatterättsnämnden gives a preliminary decision on a matter of assessment or taxation, it performs a non-judicial function which, moreover, in other Member States is expressly entrusted to the tax authorities.'

Comment

In most cases the question whether or not a particular body is a court or a tribunal is self-evident. However, on a few occasions the ECJ has to determine the status of a referring body in the context of art 177 EC Treaty [art 234 EC]. The uniformity in the application of Community law throughout the Community requires that the definition of a court or a tribunal for the purposes of art 177 EC Treaty [art 234 EC] is independent from national concepts, which vary from one Member State to another, and has an autonomous, Community meaning. The case law of the ECJ has gradually determined the criteria permitting identification of a body which is considered as 'a court or a tribunal' under art 177 EC Treaty [art 234 EC]. Apart from all judicial bodies expressly recognised as such under national law of Member States, the ECJ held that other bodies can refer under art 177 EC Treaty [art 234 EC] provided they meet certain requirements. In *Vassen-Göbbels* Case 61/65 [1966] ECR 377 the ECJ held that technical factors – such as whether the type of procedure is adversarial or not, the involvement of national authorities in the appointments of the members of that body, the mandatory jurisdiction of that body imposed by national law upon the parties to the dispute – were all relevant for the purpose of art 177 EC Treaty [art 234 EC].

In the present case the ECJ confirmed its case law in respect of determination of a court

or tribunal within the meaning of art 177 EC Treaty [art 234 EC]. The fact that the Swedish Revenue Board did not exercise judicial function excluded it from the scope of art 177 EC Treaty [art 234 EC]. Similarly, in *Borker* Case 138/80 [1980] ECR 1975, Paris Conseil de l'Ordre des Avocats à la Cour (Paris Bar Council) was not considered as a court or tribunal within the meaning of art 177 EC Treaty [art 234 EC] because that body was not exercising any judicial function but in fact 'made a request for a declaration relating to a dispute between a member of the Bar and the courts or tribunals of another Member State'.

Compulsory reference

CILFIT v *Ministry of Health* Case 283/81 [1982] ECR 3415; [1983] 1 CMLR 472 European Court of Justice

• *Compulsory reference – court or tribunal of last resort – question previously referred – doctrine of acte clair – health inspection levy in breach of art 30 EC Treaty [art 28 EC] – interpretation of EC law*

Facts

The Italian Ministry of Health imposed an inspection levy on imports of wool coming from other Member States. An Italian importer of wool challenged the levy. The Italian court considered that the case law on this matter was reasonably clear but as a court of final instance it was uncertain whether or not it should refer the question of legality of this fixed health inspection levy to the ECJ. The Italian court asked the ECJ whether it was obliged to refer under art 177(3) EC Treaty [art 234(3) EC] when the Community law was sufficiently clear and precise and there were no doubts as to its interpretation.

Held

The ECJ held that courts of last resort like any other courts or tribunals have the discretion to assess whether a referral is necessary to enable them to give judgment They are not obliged to refer if a question concerning the interpretation of Community law raised before them is not relevant to the dispute, that is, if it can in no way affect the outcome of the case.

The ECJ confirmed the principle that if the ECJ had already dealt with a point of law in question, even though the questions were not strictly identical, the court of last resort is not obliged to refer. Finally, the ECJ held that there is no obligation to refer if the correct application of Community law may be so obvious as to leave no scope for any reasonable doubt as to the manner in which the question raised is to be resolved. Before it comes to the conclusion that such is the case, the national court or tribunal must be convinced that the matter is equally obvious to the courts of the other Member States and to the Court of Justice.

Judgment

'In order to answer that question, it is necessary to take account of the system established by art 177, which confers jurisdiction on the Court of Justice to give preliminary rulings on, inter alia, the interpretation of the Treaty and the measures adopted by the institutions of the Community.

The second paragraph of that Article provides that any court or tribunal of a Member State may, if it considers that a decision on a question of interpretation is necessary to enable it to give judgment, request the Court of Justice to give a ruling thereon. The third paragraph of that Article provides that, where a question of interpretation is raised in a case pending before a court or tribunal of a Member State against whose decision there is no judicial remedy under national law, the court or tribunal shall bring the matter before the Court of Justice.

That obligation to refer a matter to the Court of Justice is based on co-operation, established with a view to ensuring the proper application and uniform interpretation of Community law in all Member States, between national courts, in their capacity as courts responsible for the application of Community law, and the Court of Justice. More particularly, the third paragraph of art 177 seeks to prevent the occurrence within the Community of divergencies in judicial decisions on question of Community law. The scope of that obligation must therefore be assessed, in view of those objectives, by reference to the powers of the national courts, on the one hand, and those of the Court of Justice, on the other, where such a question of interpretation is raised within the meaning of art 177.

In this connection, it is necessary to define the meaning for the purposes of Community law of the expression "where any such question is raised" in order to determine the circumstances in which a national court or tribunal against whose decision there is no judicial remedy under national law is obliged to bring a matter before the Court of Justice.

In this regard, it must in the first place be pointed out that art 177 does not constitute a means of redress available to the parties to a case pending before a national court or tribunal. Therefore the mere fact that a party contends that the dispute gives rise to a question concerning the interpretation of Community law does not mean that the court or tribunal concerned is compelled to consider that a question had been raised within the meaning of art 177. On the other hand, a national court or tribunal may, in an appropriate case, refer a matter to the Court of Justice of its own motion.

Secondly, it follows from the relationship between the second and third paragraphs of art 177 that the courts or tribunals referred to in the third paragraph have the same discretion as any other national court or tribunal to ascertain whether a decision on a question of Community law is necessary to enable them to give judgment. Accordingly, those court or tribunals are not obliged to refer to the Court of Justice a question concerning the interpretation of Community law raised before them if that question is not relevant, that is to say, if the answer to that question, regardless of what it may be, can in no way affect the outcome of the case.

If, however, those courts or tribunals consider that recourse to Community law is necessary to enable them to decide a case, art 177 imposes an obligation on them to refer to the Court of Justice any question of interpretation which may arise.

The question submitted by the [Italian court] seeks to ascertain whether, in certain circumstances, the obligation laid down in the third paragraph of art 177 might nonetheless be subject to certain restrictions.

It must be remembered in this connection that in its judgment in *Da Costa* v *Netherlands* (Cases 28–30/62 [1963] CMLR 224), the Court ruled that:

"Although the third paragraph of art 177 unreservedly requires courts or tribunals of Member States against whose decision there is no judicial remedy under national law … to refer to the Court every question of interpretation raised before them, the authority of an interpretation under art 177 already given by the Court may deprive the obligation of its purpose and thus empty it of its substance. Such is the case especially when the question raised is materially identical with a question which has already been the subject of a preliminary ruling in a similar case."

The same effect, as regards the limits set to the obligation laid down by the third paragraph of art 177, may be produced where previous decisions of the Court have already dealt with the point of law in question, irrespective of the nature of the proceedings which led to those decisions, even though the questions at issue are not strictly identical.

However, it must not be forgotten that in all such circumstances national courts and tribunals, including those referred in the third paragraph of art 177, remain entirely at liberty to bring a matter before the Court of Justice if they consider it appropriate to do so.

Finally, the correct application of Community law may be so obvious as to leave no scope for any reasonable doubt as to the manner in which the question raised is to be resolved. before it comes to the conclusion that such is the case, the national court or tribunal must be convinced that the matter is equally obvious to the courts of the other Member States and to the Court of Justice. Only if those conditions are satisfied may the national court or tribunal refrain from submitting the question to the Court of Justice and take upon itself the responsibility for resolving it.

However, the existence of such a possibility must be assessed on the basis of the characteristic features of Community law and the particular difficulties to which its interpretation gives rise.

To begin with, it must be borne in mind that Community legislation is drafted in several languages and that different language versions are equally authentic. An interpretation of a provision of Community law thus involves a comparison of the different language versions.

It must also be borne in mind, even where the different language versions are entirely in accord with one another, that Community law uses terminology which is peculiar to it. Furthermore, it must be emphasised that legal concepts do not necessarily have the same meaning in Community law and in the law of the various Member States.

Finally, every provision of Community law must be placed in its context and interpreted in the light of the provisions of Community law as a whole, regard being had to the objectives thereof and to the state of its evolution at the date on which the provision in question is to be applied.

In the light of all those considerations, the answer to the question submitted by the [Italian court] must be that the third paragraph of art 177 of the [EC] Treaty is to be interpreted as meaning that a court or tribunal against whose decision there is no judicial remedy under national law is required, where a question of Community law is raised before it, to comply with its obligation to bring the matter before the Court of Justice, unless it has established that the question is irrelevant or that the Community provision in question has already been interpreted by the Court or that the correct application of Community law is so obvious as to leave no scope for any reasonable doubt. The existence of such a possibility must be assessed in the light of the specific characteristics of Community law, the particular difficulties to which its interpretation give rise and the risk of divergences in judicial decisions within the Community.'

Comment

The ECJ endorsed the French doctrine of acte clair, according to which the court before which the exception prejudicielle is raised concerning the interpretation or validity of a particular provision must refer it to a competent court in order to resolve that question, but only if there is real difficulty concerning its interpretation or validity or if there is a serious doubt in this respect. However, if this provision is clear, if its validity is obvious, the court may apply it immediately.

It stems from *CILFIT* that it is not necessary for a court of last resort to refer if:

1. the question of Community law is irrelevant to the dispute;
2. the question of Community law has already been interpreted by the ECJ even though it may not be identical. However, it does not mean that national courts whatever their position in the hierarchy of national courts are prevented from referring an identical or a similar question to the ECJ. In *CILFIT* the ECJ clearly stated that all courts remain entirely at liberty to refer a matter before them if they consider it appropriate to do so.
3. the correct application of Community law is so obvious as to leave no scope for reasonable doubt, this incorporates the French theory of acte clair. However, the ECJ added that before a national court concludes that such is the case it must be convinced that the question is equally obvious to courts in other Member States and to the ECJ itself. Furthermore, the ECJ added three requirements which a national court must take into consideration when deciding that the matter is clear and free of doubts. Firstly, it must assess such possibility in the light of the characteristic features of Community law and especially the

difficulties that its interpretation raise, ie that it is drafted in several languages and all version are equally authentic. Secondly, it must be aware that Community law uses peculiar terminology and has legal concepts which have different meaning in different Member States. Finally, a national court must bear in mind that every provision of Community law must be placed in its context and interpreted in the light of the provisions of Community law as a whole, its objectives and the state of its evolution at the date on which that provision is to be applied.

In practice the endorsement by the ECJ of the doctrine of acte clair has sensibly extended the discretion of the courts of last resort. It has also increased the risk of conflicting decisions being rendered by the highest courts in each Member State.

Preliminary rulings on validity of Community acts

Eurotunnel SA and Others v *SeaFrance* Case C–408/95 [1997] ECR I–6315; [1998] 2 CMLR 293 European Court of Justice

• *Administrative law – assessment of validity of transitional arrangements for tax-free shops – conditions for a natural or legal person to challenge the validity of Community acts in the context of preliminary rulings when no action for annulment has been brought pursuant to art 173 EC Treaty [art 230 EC] within the prescribed time-limit – obligation to consult again the European Parliament if the Council substantially amends a proposal after receiving the Parliament's opinion within the consultation procedure*

Facts

French companies (Eurotunnel SA and France Manche SA) and English companies (Eurotunnel plc and the Channel Tunnel Group Ltd), joint operators of the Channel Tunnel railway link (Eurotunnel), brought proceedings against SeaFrance, a cross-channel maritime transport company and a subsidiary of SNCF acting under the trade mark 'Sealink', for infringement of EC competition law consisting of selling goods free of tax and excise duty on board its vessels and thus offsetting transport charges at below cost price. SeaFrance had already been found guilty of unfair competition by a French court in previous proceedings instituted by Eurotunnel. Consequently, Eurotunnel felt that anti-competitive practices of SeaFrance could only be stopped if art 28k of the Sixth Directive 77/388 of 17 May 1977 (on the harmonisation of the laws of the Member States relating to turnover taxes-Common system of value added tax) and art 28 of Directive 92/12 of 25 February 1992 were to be declared invalid by the ECJ. Those Articles authorise Member States to grant exemptions from value added tax and excise duty for supplies by tax-free shops located within an airport, port or Channel Tunnel terminal until 30 June 1999. The French Republic made use of this opportunity while implementing the Directives in question. The Parisian commercial court (tribunal de commerce) referred three questions to the ECJ:

1. the possibility for Eurotunnel to challenge the validity of arts 28k and 28 within the framework of art 177 EC Treaty [art 234 EC], notwithstanding the fact that the plaintiffs did not bring an action for annulment under art 173 EC Treaty [art 230 EC] within the prescribed time-limit;
2. the assessment of validity of the challenged provisions; and
3. in the case of invalidity of the provisions, the consequences of a declaration of invalidity with respect to SeaFrance.

Held

The ECJ clarified its decision in *TWD*

Textilwerke Deggendorf GmbH v *Germany* Case C–188/92 [1994] ECR I–833 regarding the conditions for a natural or legal person to challenge the validity of Community acts in the context of a preliminary ruling when no action for annulment has been brought pursuant to art 173 EC Treaty [art 230 EC] within a prescribed time-limit. In this respect the ECJ held that a natural or legal person may bring proceedings before a national court challenging the validity of a Community act, even though:

1. the act in question has not been addressed to that person;
2. that person has not brought an action for annulment pursuant to art 173 EC Treaty [art 230 EC]; and
3. a court of another Member State has already given judgment in separate proceedings.

The ECJ upheld the validity of transitional arrangements for tax-free shops based on Directive 91/680 and 92/12. In relation to the requirement for the European Parliament to be consulted again when the Council adopts a measure which substantially alters the Commission's proposal, the ECJ stated that such a consultation is not necessary if amendments correspond to the wishes of the European Parliament.

Judgment

'[*Question 1*]
By its first question the national court essentially asks whether a natural or legal person, such as Eurotunnel, may challenge before a national court the validity of provisions in directives, such as arts 28 and 28k, even though that person has not brought an action for annulment of those provisions pursuant to art 173 of the Treaty and even though a court of another Member State has already given judgment in separate proceedings.

In the case of Community directives whose contested provisions are addressed in general terms to Member States and not to natural or legal persons, it is not obvious that an action by Eurotunnel challenging arts 28 and 28k under art 173 of the Treaty would have been admissible.

In any event, Eurotunnel cannot be directly concerned by arts 28 and 28k. The exemption arrangements introduced by those provisions constitute no more than an option open to Member States. It follows that arts 28 and 28k are not directly applicable to the operators concerned, namely passenger transporters and travellers ...

[*Question 2*]

The reasoning of the judgment making the reference and the wording of the second question make it clear that the only grounds of invalidity raised by the national court relate to the possibility that the procedure whereby arts 28 and 28k were adopted may have been irregular by reason of the alleged lack of a proposal from the Commission and failure to consult the Parliament again.

[*The lack of proposal from the Commission*]

As to that point, by virtue of its power to amend under, at that time, art 149(1) of the EEC Treaty (now art 189a(1) of the EC Treaty) the Council could amend the proposal from the Commission provided it acted unanimously, that requirement being imposed in any case by the legal basis of those directives, namely art 99 of the Treaty.

Moreover, the maintenance for a limited period of the system of exemption from value added tax and excise duty of supplies of goods by the tax-free shops, notwithstanding the Commission's opposition to that maintenance in the context of intra-Community travel, falls within the scope of Directives 91/680 and 92/12, which are intended to ensure that the conditions necessary for the movement of goods and services subject to value added tax or excise duty within an internal market without fiscal frontiers are implemented as from 1 January 1993.

Consequently, to the extent that the Council's amendments to the proposals for Directives 91/680 and 92/12 remained within the scope of those directives as defined in the original proposals from the Commission, the Council did not exceed its power to make amendments under art 149 of the Treaty.

[*The requirement for the Parliament to be consulted again*]

... It is to be remembered that due consultation of the Parliament in the cases provided for by the Treaty constitutes an essential formal requirement, breach of which renders the measure concerned void.

It is settled law that the requirement to consult the European Parliament in the legislative procedure, in the cases provided for by the Treaty, means that it must be consulted again whenever the text finally adopted, taken as a whole, differs in essence from the text on which the Parliament has already been consulted, except in cases in which the amendments substantially correspond to the wishes of the Parliament itself.

It must therefore be considered whether the amendments referred to by Eurotunnel and the Parliament go to the essence of the measures considered as a whole.

The purpose of the Commission's proposals for Directives 91/680 and 92/12 presented to the Parliament was to adjust the systems of value added tax and excise duty to the existence of an internal market, defined as an area without internal frontiers.

The object of arts 28 and 28k is to permit a pre-existing system to be maintained if the Member States so wish. Those Articles must therefore be interpreted as optional exceptions of limited scope. The possibility of tax free sales is reserved for certain categories of traders and is limited in extent (ECU 90) and time (30 June 1999).

It follows that the changes made by arts 28 and 28k are not such as to affect the intrinsic tenor of the provisions introduced by Directives 91/680 and 92/12 and thus cannot be classed as changes in the essence of the measures.

In any event, the Parliament not only had an opportunity to express its opinion on the question of tax-free sales, it recommended that they should be maintained.

Consequently, by deciding to maintain tax-free sales until 30 June 1999 in order to deal with the social repercussions in that sector, the Council responded in substance to the wishes of the Parliament.

In those circumstances, it was not necessary for the Parliament to be consulted again on arts 28 and 28k.

It follows from all the foregoing that consideration of the questions raised has not disclosed any factor of such a kind as to affect the validity of art 28 and 28k.'

Comment

In the present case the ECJ clarified its decision in *TWD Textilwerke Deggendorf GmbH v Germany* Case C–188/92 [1994] ECR I–833: if a Community act is addressed to natural or legal persons and thus they are directly and individually concerned they would be precluded from challenging the validity of those acts in the context of a preliminary ruling if they have not brought an action for annulment pursuant to art 173 EC Treaty [art 230 EC] within the prescribed time-limit. In this respect the ECJ transposes its solution regarding EC regulation to EC directives (*Accrington Beef* Case C–241/95 [1996] ECR 6699). In the present case the challenged Community directives are addressed in general terms to Member States as they offer an option open to them which a priori excludes the existence of any link between the challenged directives and the applicants. As arts 28 and 28k are not directly applicable to the operators concerned, namely passenger transporters and travellers, it would be extremely difficult for Eurotunnel to establish locus standi under art 173 EC Treaty [art 230 EC] even though in some cases the ECJ has accepted an action for annulment challenging EC directives addressed to the Member States provided the applicants were directly and individually concerned (*Gibraltar v EC Council* Case C–298/89 [1993] ECR I–3605; *Asocarne v EC Council* Case C–10/95P [1995] ECR I–4149).

In respect of the validity of arts 28 and 28k the ECJ held that the Council's amendments to the original proposals from the Commission remained within the scope of those Directives. Consequently, the Council did not exceed its powers to amend such proposals since under art 189a(1) EC Treaty [art 250(1) EC] the Council could amend the proposal provided it acted unanimously, which in fiscal matters is required anyway.

The requirement for the Parliament to be consulted again if the Commission's original proposal is substantially amended by the Council is essential from the point of view of the legality of an adopted act. Its infringement renders the adopted measure void. However, if substantial amendments made by the Council correspond to the wishes of the Parliament there is no need for the Parliament to be consulted again (this requirement has been clearly stated in *European Parliament v EC Council* Case C–65/90 [1992] ECR I–4593 and repeated in *Driessen en Zonen and Others v Minister van Verkeer en Waterstaat* Cases C–13–16/92 [1993] ECR I–4751 and *European Parliament v EC Council (Cabotage II)* Case C–388/92 [1994] ECR I–2067).

Firma Foto-Frost v Hauptzollamt Lubeck-Ost Case 314/85 [1987] ECR 4199 European Court of Justice

• *Referral on validity of Community acts – national courts have no jurisdiction to annul a Community act – exclusive jurisdiction of the ECJ to declare an act invalid*

Facts

Frost applied to a German municipal court to declare a decision issued by the Commission invalid on the grounds that it was in breach of the requirements set out in the Council regulation which delegated authority to the Commission to adopt decisions. The German court requested a preliminary ruling as to whether it could review the validity of the decision in question.

Held

The ECJ held that for the uniformity of Community law it is especially important that there are no divergences between Member States as to the validity of Community acts since they would jeopardise the very unity of the Community legal order as well as detract from the fundamental requirement of legal certainty. The ECJ drew comparison between its exclusive jurisdiction under art 173 EC Treaty [art 230 EC] and the preliminary ruling on validity of Community acts. It stated that the coherence of the system requires that where the validity of Community measures is challenged before a national court the jurisdiction to declare the act invalid must also be reserved to the ECJ. As a result the ECJ held that 'national courts have no jurisdiction themselves to declare the acts of Community Institutions invalid'.

Judgment

'In enabling national courts against whose decisions there is judicial remedy under national law to refer to the Court for a preliminary ruling questions on interpretation or validity, art 177 did not settle the question whether those courts themselves may declare that acts of Community institutions are invalid.

Those courts may consider the validity of a Community act and, if they consider that the grounds put forward before them by the parties in support of invalidity are unfounded, they may reject them, concluding that the measure is completely valid. By taking that action they are not calling the existence of the Community measure into question.

On the other hand, those courts do not have the power to declare acts of the Community institutions invalid. As the Court emphasised in the judgment of 13 May 1981 (Case 66/80 *International Chemical Corporation* v *Amministrazione delle Finanze* [1981] ECR 1191), the main purpose of the powers accorded to the Court by art 177 is to ensure that Community law is applied uniformly by national courts. That requirement of uniformity is particularly imperative when the validity of a Community act is in question. Divergencies between courts in the Member States as to the validity of Community acts would be

liable to place in jeopardy the very unity of the Community legal order and detract from the fundamental requirement of legal certainty.

The same conclusion is dictated by consideration of the necessary coherence of the system of judicial protection established by the Treaty. In that regard it must be observed that requests for preliminary rulings, like actions for annulment, constitute means for reviewing the legality of acts of the Community institutions. As the Court pointed out in its judgment of 23 April 1986 (Case 294/83 *Partie Ecologiste Les Verts* v *European Parliament* [1986] ECR 1339), "in arts 173 and 184, on the one hand, and in art 177, on the other, the Treaty established a complete system of legal remedies and procedures designed to permit the Court of Justice to review the legality of measures adopted by the institutions".

Since art 173 gives the Court exclusive jurisdiction to declare void an act of a Community institution, the coherence of the system requires that where the validity of a Community act is challenged before a national court the power to declare the act invalid must also be reserved to the Court of Justice.

It must also be emphasised that the Court of Justice is in the best position to decide on the validity of Community acts. Under art 20 of the Protocol on the Statute of the Court of Justice of the [EC], Community institutions whose acts are challenged are entitled to participate in the proceedings in order to defend the validity of the acts in question. Furthermore, under the second paragraph of art 21 of that Protocol the Court may require the Member States and institutions which are not participating in the proceedings to supply all information which it considers necessary for the purpose of the case before it.

It should be added that the rule that national courts may not themselves declare Community acts invalid may have to be qualified in certain circumstances in the case of proceedings relating to an application for interim measures; however, that case is not referred to in the national court's question.

The answer to the first question must therefore be that national courts have no jurisdiction themselves to declare that acts of Community institutions are invalid.'

Comment

This case confirmed that the ECJ has exclusive jurisdiction to declare an act of a Community institution invalid. There is no distinction between national courts in matters relating to validity. Lower courts and the courts of final resort must refer to the ECJ if there are some doubts as to the validity of a Community measure.

7 State Liability – the Creation of a Community Remedy

Brasserie du Pêcheur SA v Federal Republic of Germany; R v Secretary of State for Transport, ex parte Factortame Ltd (No 4) Joined Cases C–46 and 48/93 [1996] 1 CMLR 889 European Court of Justice

- *Non–contractual liability of a Member State – acts and omissions of the national legislature – conditions of liability, fault – supremacy of Community law*

Facts

Brasserie du Pêcheur v Germany Case C–46/93
Brasserie, a French brewer, was forced to cease exports to Germany as its beer did not comply with the purity standards imposed by the Biersteuergesets (Law on Beer Duty, BGBI.I p144). In *EC Commission v Germany* Case 178/84 [1987] ECR 1227 the ECJ had already ruled that such a ban was incompatible with art 30 EC Treaty [art 28 EC].

R v Secretary of State for Transport, ex parte Factortame (No 4) Case C–48/93
The United Kingdom government enacted the Merchant Shipping Act 1988 which made the registration of fishing vessels dependent upon conditions as to the nationality, residence and domicile of their owners. Factortame, being a Spanish-owned company, were deprived of their right to fish. In *R v Secretary of State for Transport, ex parte Factortame Ltd and Others (No 3)* Case C–221/89 [1991] ECR I–3905 the ECJ held such regulations as contrary to EC law, this was confirmed in *EC Commission v United Kingdom* Case C–246/89 [1991] ECR I–4585.

Held

The ECJ held that Member States could be liable under Community law for breaches of EC Treaty and Community measures in certain defined circumstances. The breach itself must be manifest and serious, and the injury sustained by the individual must have been caused by an illegal act committed by the authorities of a Member State. However, an applicant suing a Member State need not prove that the authorities were at fault.

It is for the national courts to determine the types of injury for which reparation may be awarded, as well as the criteria for quantifying the loss or damage. Nevertheless, under no circumstances could a Member State, in determining the measure of damages, apply criteria which are less favourable to EC cases than to equivalent domestic cases. The manner in which damages are assessed must not be such as to make it impossible or excessively difficult for full compensation to be obtained.

Judgment

'[*State liability for acts and omissions of the national legislature contrary to Community law (first question in both cases)*]
The German, Irish and Netherlands governments contend that Member States are required to make good loss or damage caused to individuals only where the provisions breached are not directly effective: in *Francovich and Others* [*Francovich and Bonifaci v Italian Republic* Joined Cases C–6 and 9/90 [1991] ECR I–5357] the Court simply sought to fill a lacuna in the system for safeguarding rights of individuals. In so far as national law affords individuals a right of action enabling them to assert their

rights under directly effective provisions of Community law, it is unnecessary, where such provisions are breached, also to grant them a right to reparation founded directly on Community law.

This argument cannot be accepted.

The Court consistently held that the right of individuals to rely on the directly effective provisions of the Treaty before national courts is only a minimum guarantee and is not sufficient in itself to ensure the full and complete implementation of the Treaty (see, in particular, Case 168/85 *EC Commission* v *Italy* [1986] ECR 2945, [1988] 1 CMLR 580, para 11; Case C–120/88 *EC Commission* v *Italy* [1991] ECR I–621, para 10; and C–119/89 *EC Commission* v *Spain* [1991] ECR I–641; [1993] 1 CMLR 41). The purpose of that right is to ensure that provisions of Community law prevail over national provisions. It cannot, in every case, secure for individuals the benefit of the rights conferred on them by Community law and, in particular, avoid their sustaining damage as a result of a breach of Community law attributable to a Member State. As appears from para 33 of the judgment in *Francovich and Others*, the full effectiveness of Community law would be impaired if individuals were unable to obtain redress when their rights were infringed by a breach of Community law.

This will be so where an individual who is a victim of the non-transposition of a directive and is precluded from relying on certain of its provisions directly before the national court because they are insufficiently precise and unconditional, brings an action for damages against the defaulting Member State for breach of the third paragraph of art 189 of the Treaty. In such circumstances, which obtained in the case of *Francovich and Others*, the purpose of reparation is to redress the injurious consequences of a Member State's failure to transpose a directive as far as beneficiaries of that directive are concerned.

It is all the more so in the event of infringement of a right directly conferred by a Community provision upon which individuals are entitled to rely before the national courts. In that event, the right to reparation is the necessary corollary of the direct effect of the Community provision whose breach caused the damage sustained.

In this case, it is undisputed that the Community provisions at issue, namely art 30 of the Treaty in Case C–46/93 and art 52 in Case C–48/93, have direct effect in the sense that they confer on individuals rights upon which they are entitled to rely directly before the national courts. Breach of such provisions may give rise to reparation.

… It must, however, be stressed that the existence and extent of State liability for damage ensuing as a result of a breach of obligations incumbent on the State by virtue of Community law are questions of Treaty interpretation which fall within the jurisdiction of the Court.

In this case, as in *Francovich and Others*, those questions of interpretation have been referred to the Court by national courts pursuant to art 177 of the Treaty.

Since the Treaty contains no provision expressly and specifically governing the consequences of breaches of Community law by Member States, it is for the Court, in pursuance of the task conferred on it by art 164 of the Treaty of ensuring that in the interpretation and application of the Treaty the law is observed, to rule on such a question in accordance with generally accepted methods of interpretation, in particular by reference to the fundamental principles of the Community legal system and, where necessary, general principles common to the legal systems of the Member States.

Indeed, it is to the general principles common to the laws of the Member States that the second paragraph of art 215 of the Treaty refers as the basis of the non-contractual liability of the Community for damage caused by its institutions or by its servants in the performance of their duties.

The principle of non-contractual liability of the Community expressly laid down in art 215 of the Treaty is simply an expression of the general principles familiar to the legal systems of the Member States that an unlawful act or omission gives rise to an obligation to make good the damage caused.

That provision also reflects the obligation on public authorities to make good damage caused in the performance of their duties.

In any event, in many national legal systems the essentials of the legal rules governing State liability have been developed by the courts.

In view of the foregoing considerations, the Court held in *Francovich and Others* at para 35, that the principle of State liability for loss and damage caused to individuals as a result of breaches of Community law for which it can be held responsible is inherent in the system of the Treaty.

It follows that the principle holds good for any case in which a Member State breaches Community law, whatever be the organ of the State whose act or omission was responsible for the breach ...

Consequently, the reply to the national courts must be that the principle that Member States are obliged to make good damage caused to individuals by breaches of Community law attributable to the State is applicable where the national legislature was responsible for the breach in question.

[*Conditions under which the State may incur liability for acts or omission of the national legislature contrary to Community law (second question in Case C–46/93 and first question in Case C–48/93)*]
... Although Community law imposes State liability, the conditions under which that liability gives rise to reparation depend on the nature of the breach of Community law giving rise to the loss and damage (*Francovich and Others*).

In order to determine those conditions, account should be taken of the principles inherent in the Community legal order which form the basis for State liability, namely, first, the full effectiveness of community rules and the effective protection of the rights which they confer and, second, the obligation to co-operate imposed on Member States by art 5 of the Treaty (*Francovich and Others*).

In addition, as the Commission and the several governments which submitted observations have emphasised, it is perti-nent to refer to the Court's case law on non-contractual liability on the part of the Community.

First, the second paragraph of art 215 of the Treaty refers, as regards the non-contractual liability of the Community, to the general principles common to the laws of the Member States, from which, in the absence of written rules, the Court also draws inspiration in other areas of Community law.

Second, the conditions under which the State may incur liability for damage caused to individuals by breach of Community law cannot, in the absence pf particular justification, differ from those governing the liability of the Community in like circumstances. The protection of the rights which individuals derive from Community law cannot vary depending on whether a national authority or a Community authority is responsible for the damage.

The system of rules which the Court has worked out with regard to art 215 of the Treaty, particularly in relation to liability for legislative measures, takes into account, inter alia, the complexity of the situations to be regulated, difficulties in the application or interpretation of the texts and, more particularly, the margin of discretion available to the author of the act in question.

Thus, in developing its case law on the non-contractual liability of the Community, in particular as regards legislative measures involving choices of economic policy, the Court has had regard to the wide discretion available to the institutions in implementing Community policies.

The strict approach taken towards the liability of the Community in the exercise of its legislative activities is due to two considerations. First, even where the legality of measures is subject to judicial review, exercise of the legislative function must not be hindered by the prospect of actions for damages whenever the general interest of the Community requires legislative measures to be adopted which may adversely affect individual interest. Second, in a legislative context characterised by the exercise of a wide discretion, which is essential for implementing a Community policy, the Community cannot incur liability unless the institution concerned has manifestly and gravely disregarded the limits on the exercise of its powers (Joined Cases 83 and 94/76, and 4, 15 and 40/77 *HNL and Others* v *EC Council and EC Commission* [1978] ECR 1209, paras 5 and 6).

That said, the national legislature – like the Community institutions – does not systematically have a wide discretion when it acts in a field governed by Community law. Community law may impose upon it obligations to achieve a particular result or obligations to act or refrain from acting which reduce its margin of discretion, sometimes to a considerable degree. This is so, for instance, where, as in the circumstances to which the judgment in *Francovich an Others* relates, art 189 of the Treaty places the Member States under an obligation to take, within a given period, all the measures needed in order to achieve the result required by a directive. In such a case, the fact that it is for national legislature to take the necessary measures has no bearing on the Member State's liability for failing to transpose the directive.

In contrast, where a Member State acts in a field where it has a wide discretion, comparable to that of the Community institutions in implementing Community policies, the conditions under which it may incur liability must, in principle, be the same as those under which the Community institutions incur liability in a comparable situation.

In the case which gave rise to the reference in Case C–46/93, the German legislature had legislated in the field of foodstuffs, specifically beer. In the absence of Community harmonization, the national legislature had a wide discretion in that sphere in laying down rules on the quality of beer put on the market.

As regards the facts in Case C–48/93, the United Kingdom legislature also had a wide discretion. The legislation at issue was concerned, first with the registration of vessels, a field which, in view of the state of development of Community law, falls within the jurisdiction of the Member States and, secondly, with regulating fishing, a sector in which implementation of the common fisheries policy leaves a margin of discretion to the Member States.

Consequently, in each case the German and United Kingdom legislatures were faced with situations involving choices comparable to those made by the Community institutions when they adopt legislative measures pursuant to a Community policy.

In such circumstances, Community law confers a right to reparation where three conditions are met: the rule of law infringed must be intended to confer rights on individuals; the breach must be sufficiently serious; there must be a direct causal link between the breach of the obligation resting on the State and the damage sustained by the injured parties.

Firstly, those conditions satisfy the requirements of the full effectiveness of the rules of Community law and of the effective protection of the rights which those rules confer.

Secondly, those conditions correspond in substance to those defined by the Court in relation to art 215 in its case law on liability of the Community for damage caused to individuals by unlawful legislative measures adopted by its institutions.

The first condition is manifestly satisfied in the case of art 30 of the Treaty, the relevant provision in Case C–46/93, and in the case of art 52, the relevant provision in Case C–48/93. Whilst art 30 imposes a prohibition on member States, it nevertheless gives rise to rights for individuals which the national courts must protect (Case 74/76 *Iannelli and Volpi SpA* v *Meroni* [1977] ECR 557; [1977] 2 CMLR 688, para 13). Likewise, the essence of art 52 is to confer rights on individuals (Case 2/74 *Reyners (Jean)* v *Belgian State* [1974] ECR 631; [1974] 2 CMLR 305, para 25).

As to the second condition, as regards both Community liability under art 215 and Member States' liability for breaches of Community law, the decisive test for finding that a breach of Community law is sufficiently serious is whether the Member

State or the Community institution concerned manifestly and gravely disregarded the limits on its discretion.

The factors which the competent court may take into consideration include the clarity and precision of the rule breached, the measure of discretion left by that rule to the national or Community authorities, whether the infringement and the damage caused was intentional or involuntary, whether any error of law was excusable or inexcusable, the fact that the position taken by a Community institution may have contributed towards the omission, and the adoption or retention of national measures or practices contrary to Community law.

On any view, a breach of Community law will clearly be sufficiently serious if it has persisted despite a judgment finding the infringement in question to be established, or a preliminary ruling or settled case law of the Court on the matter from which it is clear that the conduct in question constituted an infringement.

While, in the present cases, the Court cannot substitute its assessment for that of the national courts, which have sole jurisdiction to find the facts in the main proceedings and decide how to characterise the breaches of Community law at issue, it will be helpful to indicate a number of circumstances which the national courts might take into account ...

[*The possibility of making reparation conditional upon the existence of fault*]
... where a breach of Community law is attributable to a Member State acting in a field in which it has a wide discretion to make legislative choices, a finding of a right to reparation on the basis of Community law will be conditional, inter alia, upon the breach having been sufficiently serious.

So, certain objective and subjective factors connected with the concept of fault under a national legal system may well be relevant for the purposes of determining whether or not a given breach of Community law is serious.

The obligation to make reparation for loss or damage caused to individuals cannot,

however, depend upon a condition based on any concept of fault going beyond that of a sufficiently serious breach of Community law. Imposition of such a supplementary condition would be tantamount to calling in question the right to reparation founded on the Community legal order.

Accordingly, the reply to the question from the national court must be that, pursuant to the national legislation which it applies, reparation of loss or damage cannot be made conditional upon fault (intentional or negligent) on the part of the organ of the State responsible for the breach, going beyond that of a sufficiently serious breach of Community law.'

Comment

In the present cases the ECJ elucidated many outstanding questions left unanswered in *Francovich*. First, the Court abolished the disparity between the conditions governing liability of the Community institutions based on art 215(2) EC Treaty [art 288(2) EC] and the conditions under which the Member State may incur liability for damage caused to individuals in like circumstances. Second, the ECJ clarified the conditions of liability:

1. the rule of law which has been infringed must be one which is intended to confer rights on individuals;
2. the breach must be sufficiently serious to merit an award of damages. To be held liable a Member State must have 'manifestly and gravely' disregarded its obligation to be held liable. In order to assess whether this condition is satisfied, national courts should take into consideration a number of factors such as: the clarity and precision of the EC rule breached; the element of discretion in the adoption of normative acts by national authorities; whether or not the infringement was intentional or accidental; whether any error of law was excusable; and whether any action or advice on the part of the Commission had contributed to the breach, etc;
3. there must be a direct causal link between

the Member State's default and the loss suffered by the applicant.

These conditions of State liability apply to all breaches of Community law, whether legislative, executive or administrative. A State is liable regardless of the organ of State whose act or omission infringed Community law. Also, it is irrelevant whether the provision in question is directly effective or not. Whichever is breached, a Member State may be liable. The ECJ emphasised that direct effect constitutes a minimum guarantee and thus *Francovich* liability is a necessary corollary of the effet utile of Community law.

The ECJ has placed the onus upon national courts to uphold such rights under national rules for public tortious liability by imposing upon them the duty to 'verify whether or not the conditions governing state liability for a breach of Community law are fulfilled'. The court laid down the criteria which might be used by national courts in order to determine the measure of damage. National courts are charged with ensuring that the protection of Community law rights is given equal status and may not be less favourable than the protection afforded to similar rights arising under domestic law. National courts may not impose any procedure that makes it more difficult or even impossible for an individual to rely upon those rights. The UK's rule on the award of exemplary damages against a public official for oppressive, arbitrary or unconstitutional behaviour should be carried over to claims for breaches of EC law.

Dillenkofer and Others v *Federal Republic of Germany* Joined Cases C–178, 179, 188, 189 and 190/94 [1996] ECR I–4845 European Court of Justice

• *Non-contactual liability of a Member State – non-implementation of Directive 90/314/EEC*

Facts
Erich Dillenkofer and others brought proceed-

ings against Germany for non-implementation of Directive 90/314/EEC on package travel, package holidays and package tours within the prescribed time-limit. The plaintiffs had to make an 'advance payment' of 10 per cent towards the travel price, with a maximum of DM 500 to the travel organiser. The travel organiser became insolvent and they lost the deposit. The requirement of a deposit is contrary to Directive 90/314/EEC intended to protect customers against the risk of the organiser's insolvency. The plaintiffs suffered damages because of the failure of Germany to transpose the Directive within the prescribed time-limit and asked for compensation.

Held
The ECJ held that non-implementation of a directive within the prescribed time limit constitutes per se a serious breach of Community law and consequently gives rise to a right of reparation for individuals suffering injury if the result prescribed by the directive entails the grant to individuals of rights whose content is identifiable and a causal link exists between the breach of the State's obligation and the loss and damage suffered. Germany was liable for damages suffered by the plaintiffs.

Judgment
'[*Conditions under which a Member State incurs liability*]
The crux of these questions is whether a failure to transpose a directive within the prescribed period is sufficient per se to afford individuals who have suffered injury a right to reparation or whether other conditions must also be taken into consideration. In order to reply to those questions, reference must first be made to the Court's case law on the individual's right to reparation of damage caused by a breach of Community law for which a Member State can be held responsible.

The Court has held that the principle of State liability for loss and damage caused to individuals as a result of breaches of Community law for which the State can be held responsible is inherent in the system of the Treaty (*Francovich*, *Brasserie du Pêcheur*, *Factortame*, *British Telecommunications* and *Hedley Lomas*). Furthermore, the Court has held that the conditions under which State liability gives rise to a right to reparation depend on the nature of the breach of Community law giving rise to the loss and damage.

When the Court held that the conditions under which State liability gives rise to a right to reparation depended on the nature of the breach of Community law causing the damage, that meant that those conditions are to be applied according to each type of situation.

On the one hand, a breach of Community law is sufficiently serious if a Community institution or a Member State, in the exercise of its rule-making powers, manifestly and gravely disregards the limits on those powers. On the other hand, if, at the time when it committed the infringement, the Member State in question was not called upon to make any legislative choices and had only considerably reduced, or even no, discretion, the mere infringement of Community law may be sufficient to establish the existence of a sufficiently serious breach.

So where, as in *Francovich*, a Member State fails, in breach of the third paragraph of art 189 of the Treaty, to take any of the measures necessary to achieve the result prescribed by a directive within the period it lays down, that Member State manifestly and gravely disregards the limits on its discretion.

Consequently, such a breach gives rise to a right to reparation on the part of individuals if the result prescribed by the directive entails the grant of rights to them, the content of those rights is identifiable on the basis of the provisions of the directive and a causal link exists between the breach of the State's obligation and the loss and damage suffered by the injured parties: no other conditions need be taken into consideration.

In particular, reparation of that loss and damage cannot depend on a prior finding by the Court of an infringement of Community law attributable to the State, nor on the existence of intentional fault or negligence on the part of the organ of the State to which the infringement is attributable.'

Comment

In the present case the ECJ clarified the conditions for non-contractual liability of a Member State. The Court confirmed that when a Member State is not called upon to make any legislative choices and has only considerably reduced, or even no, discretion, the mere breach of EC law may be sufficient to establish the existence of a breach sufficiently serious to give rise to non-contractual liability (see *R* v *HM Treasury, ex parte British Telecommunications plc* Case C–392/93 [1996] ECR I–1631). In the case of non-implementation of a directive within the prescribed time-limit a Member State 'manifestly and gravely' disregards the limits of its discretion and therefore will be held liable.

Francovich and Bonifaci v *Italian Republic* Joined Cases C–6 and 9/90 [1991] ECR I–5357; [1993] 2 CMLR 66 European Court of Justice

• *Non-contractual liability of a Member State – failure to implement a directive – injury to private party – conditions of liability*

Facts

As a result of the bankruptcy of his employer, Francovich lost 6,000,000 lira. He sued his former employer but could not enforce judgment against him (the latter was insolvent). He decided to commence proceedings against the Italian State for sums due under Council Directive 80/987, which was not implemented in Italy, although the prescribed time-limit had already elapsed, or for compensation in lieu. Directive 80/987 on protection of employees in the event of the insolvency of their employers required that the Member State set up a scheme under which employees of insolvent companies would receive at least some of their outstanding wages. In *EC Commission* v *Italy* Case 27/87 [1989] ECR 143 the ECJ under art 169 EC Treaty [art 226 EC] held Italy in breach of EC law for non-implementation of Directive 80/987. The Italian court made reference to the ECJ under art 177 EC Treaty [art 234 EC] to determine whether the provision of the Directive in relation to payment of wages was directly effective, and whether the Italian State was liable for damages arising from its failure to implement the Directive.

Held

The ECJ held that the provision in question was not sufficiently clear to be directly effective . However, the ECJ stated that while the plaintiff could not rely on the direct effect of the Directive to establish liability, he could succeed against the State on the ground that Member States are liable to private individuals for injury caused to them by failing to properly implement a Community measure.

This liability was not absolute. In particular, in order to establish liability, the Directive had to confer rights on individuals and the content of these rights had to be identified within the context of the measure. The third condition for liability was the existence of a causal link between the failure of the Member State to comply with its Community obligations and the injury suffered by the individual.

Judgment

'[*The existence of State liability as a matter of principle*]

It must be recalled first of all that the [EC] Treaty has created its own legal system which is an integral part of the legal systems of the Member States and which courts are bound to apply; the subjects of that legal system are not only Member States but also their nationals. Just as it imposes obligations on individuals. Community law is also intended to create rights which become part of their legal patrimony; those rights arise not only where they are expressly granted

by the Treaty but also by virtue of obligations which the Treaty imposes in a clearly defined manner both on individuals and on the Member States and the Community institutions (see the judgment in Case 26/62 *Van Gend en Loos* v *Netherlands* [1963] ECR 1 and Case 6/64 *Costa* v *ENEL* [1964] ECR 585).

Furthermore, it has been consistently held that the national courts whose task it is to apply the provisions of Community law in cases within their jurisdiction must ensure that those rules have full effect and protect the rights which they confer on individuals (see in particular the judgment in Case 106/77 *Amministrazione delle Finanze dello Stato* v *Simmenthal* [1978] ECR 629, para 16, and Case C–213/89 *R* v *Secretary of State for Transport, ex parte Factortame* [1990] ECR I–2433, para 19).

It must be held that the full effectiveness of Community rules would be impaired and the protection of the rights which they grant would be weakened if individuals were unable to obtain compensation when their rights are infringed by a breach of Community law for which a member State can be held responsible.

The possibility of compensation by the Member State is particularly indispensable where, as in this case, the full effectiveness of Community rules is subject to prior action on the part of the state and consequently individuals cannot, in the absence of such action, enforce the rights granted to them by Community law before the national courts.

It follows that the principle of State liability for harm caused to individuals by breaches of Community law for which the State can be held responsible is inherent in the system of the Treaty.

Further foundation for the obligation on the part of Member States to pay compensation for such harm is to be found in art 5 of the Treaty, under which the Member States are required to take all appropriate measures, whether general or particular, to ensure fulfilment of their obligations under Community law. Among these is the obligation to nullify the unlawful consequences of a breach of Community law (see, in relation to the analogous provision of art 86 of the ECSC Treaty, the judgment in Case 6/60 *Humblet* v *Belgium* [1960] ECR 1125).

It follows from all the foregoing that it is a principle of Community law that the Member States are obliged to pay compensation for harm caused to individuals by breaches of Community law for which they can be held responsible.

[*Preconditions of State liability*]
Although State liability is thus required by Community law, the conditions under which that liability gives rise to a right to compensation depend on the nature of the breach of Community law giving rise to the harm.

Where, as in this case, a Member State fails to fulfil its obligation under the third paragraph of art 189 of the Treaty to take all the measures necessary to achieve the result prescribed by a directive the full effectiveness of that rule of Community law requires that there should be a right to compensation where three conditions are met.

The first of those conditions is that the result prescribed by the directive should entail the grant of rights to individuals. the second condition is that it should be possible to identify the content of those rights on the basis of the provisions of the directive. Finally, the third condition is the existence of a causal link between the breach of the State's obligation and the harm suffered by the injured parties.

Those conditions are sufficient to give rise to a right on the part of individuals to obtain compensation, a right which is founded directly on Community law.

Subject to that reservation, it is in accordance with the rules of national law on liability that the State must make reparation for the consequences of the harm caused. In the absence of any Community legislation, it is a matter for the internal legal order of each Member State to determine the competent court and lay down the detailed procedural rules for legal proceedings intended fully to safeguard the rights which individuals derive from Community law (see the judgments in Case 60/75 *Russo* v *AIMA*

[1976] ECR 45, Case 33/76 *Rewe-Zentralfinanz eG and Rewe-Zentrale AG* v *Landwirtschaftskammer für das Saarland* [1976] ECR 1989 and Case 158/80 *Rewe* v *Hauptzollamt Kiel* [1981] ECR 1805).

It must also be pointed out that the substantive and procedural conditions laid down by the national law of the various Member Stated on compensation for harm may not be less favourable than those relating to similar internal claims and may not be so framed as to make it virtually impossible or excessively difficult to obtain compensation (see, in relation to the analogous issue of the repayment of taxes levied in breach of Community law, inter alia, the judgment in Case 199/82 *Amministrazione delle Finanze dello Stato* v *San Giorgio* [1983] ECR 3595).

In this case, the breach of Community law by a Member State by virtue of its failure to transpose Directive 80/987 within the prescribed period has been confirmed by a judgment of the Court. The result required by that directive entails the grant to employees of a right to a guarantee of payment of their unpaid wage claims. As is clear from the examination of the first part of the first question, the content of that right can be identified on the basis of the provisions of the directive.

Consequently, the national court must, in accordance with the rules of national law on liability, uphold the right of employees to obtain compensation for harm caused to them as a result of the failure to transpose the directive.

The answer to be given to the national court must therefore be that a Member State is required to pay compensation for the harm suffered by individuals as a result of the failure to implement Directive 80/987.'

Comment

The principle that a Member State should be liable in damages to individuals who have suffered loss as a result of its infringement of Community law is today one of the cornerstones of Community law. Its origin can be found in *Russo* v *Aima* Case 60/75 [1976]

ECR 45 in which the ECJ held that a Member State should compensate damage caused by its own breach of Community law but referred to national law to lay down the necessary conditions applicable to tortious liability.

In the present case the ECJ for the first time established Member States' liability in tort. The ECJ justified the new principle on the basis of supremacy of Community law, effet utile and art 5 EC Treaty [art 10 EC] which requires Member States to take all appropriate measure to ensure the fulfilment of their obligations arising out of the Treaty. The less obvious justification, not mentioned in the present case, is that many Member States in the late 1980s delayed the implementation of EC directives which were mainly used to complete the internal market. There was no effective remedy since penalties against defaulting Member States were introduced in the amended art 171 EC Treaty [art 228 EC] by the TEU. The best way to ensure implementation of an EC directive was to allow individuals to enforce their rights before national courts, that is to permit them to sue a defaulting Member State for loss that they had suffered, especially in cases where the EC directives were not directly effective or when individuals had no remedy based on indirect horizontal effect.

In this case the ECJ has established three conditions necessary to give rise to liability in the case of total failure of a Member State to implement a directive:

1. the result required by the directive must include the conferring of rights for the benefit of individuals;
2. the content of those rights must be clearly identifiable by reference to the directive;
3. there must be a causal link between the breach of the State's obligation and the damage suffered by the individual.

Haim v *Kassenzahnärztliche Vereinigung Nordrhein* Case C–424/97 [2000] ECR I–5123 European Court of Justice

• *Supremacy of EC law – Member State liability in the event of a breach of Community law – breaches attributable to a public body – sufficiently serious breach of Community law – compatibility of a language requirement with freedom of establishment*

Facts

This case is a sequel to *Haim* v *Kassenzahnärztliche Vereinigung Nordrhein* Case C–319/92 [1994] ECR I–425. Salomone Haim, an Italian national, obtained his qualification in dentistry in 1946 in Turkey, where he practised as a dentist until 1980. In 1981 he obtained permission to practise in Germany as a self-employed dentist. In 1982 his Turkish diploma was recognised in Belgium and subsequently he practised for eight years in Belgium under a Belgian social security scheme. Between November 1991 and August 1992 he interrupted his work in Belgium in order to work in his son's dental practice in Germany. In 1988 he applied to the Association of Dental Practitioners of Social Security Schemes in Norderhein (KVN) in Germany to be enrolled on the register of dental practitioners in order to practise under a social security scheme. He was refused permission to work on a social security scheme unless he completed a further two-year preparatory training course. He argued that his professional experience in Belgium should be taken into account by the German authorities.

The ECJ agreed. The Court held that, although a Member State was not required to recognise the equivalence of a qualification obtained in a non-Member State, since Directive 78/686/EEC did not cover such situations, a Member State was, nevertheless, obliged to take into account professional experience gained in another Member State. Therefore, taking into account that he was authorised to practise, and had practised, his profession in Belgium and Germany, it was contrary to art 43 EC to refuse his appointment as a dental practitioner under a German social security scheme on the ground that he had not completed the preparatory training required under German legislation without examining whether, and to what extent, the experience already established corresponded to the requirements set out by that legislation.

Following the judgment Haim was enrolled on the register of dental practitioners of KVN on 4 January 1995 but, on account of his age, did not conclude the necessary formalities to be appointed as a dental practitioner under a social security scheme.

In the above context Haim brought further proceedings against KVN for compensation for the loss of earnings he had suffered between 1 September 1988 and the end of 1994. He argued that his earnings were lower than those he could have expected if he had practised as a dental practitioner under a social security scheme in Germany. The referring court asked, inter alia, the following questions:

1. whether an official or legally independent public body of a Member State can be held jointly liable with a Member State for a breach of Community law;
2. whether there was a sufficiently serious breach of Community law in the situation where a national official, who did not have any discretion when taking a decision, either applied national law contrary to EC law or applied national law in a manner inconsistent with EC law.

Held

With regard to the first question the ECJ held that a public body, in addition to the Member State, may be held liable to make reparation for loss and damage to individuals as a result of measures it took which were in breach of EC law.

In respect of the second question the ECJ

held that in order to determine whether there is a serious breach of EC law reference must be made to the discretion enjoyed by the Member State concerned and not by reference to national law.

Judgment

'[*The first question*]

By its first question, the national court is asking essentially whether Community law precludes a public law body, in addition to the Member State itself, from incurring liability to make reparation for loss and damage caused to individuals as a result of measures which it took in breach of Community law.

First of all, it should be recalled that liability for loss and damage caused to individuals as a result of breaches of Community law attributable to a national public authority constitutes a principle, inherent in the system of the Treaty, which gives rise to obligations on the part of the Member States (see Joined Cases C–6/90 and C–9/90 *Francovich and Bonifaci* v *Italian Republic* [1991] ECR I–5357, para 35; Joined Cases C–46/93 and C–48/93 *Brasserie du Pêcheur SA* v *Federal Republic of Germany; R* v *Secretary of State for Transport, ex parte Factortame Ltd* [1996] ECR I–1029, para 31; Case C–392/93 *R* v *Her Majesty's Treasury, ex parte British Telecommunications plc* [1996] ECR I–1631, para 38; Case C–5/94 *R* v *Ministry of Agriculture, Fisheries and Food, ex parte Hedley Lomas (Ireland) Ltd* [1996] ECR I–2553, para 24; Joined Cases C–178/94, C–179/94, C–188/94, C–189/94 and C–190/94 *Dillenkofer and Others* v *Federal Republic of Germany* [1996] ECR I–4845, para 20; and Case C–127/95 *Norbrook Laboratories Ltd* v *Minister of Agriculture, Fisheries and Food* [1998] ECR I–1531, para 106).

As in substance all the governments which submitted observations to the Court and the Commission have pointed out and as is clear from the case law of the Court, it is for each Member State to ensure that individuals obtain reparation for loss and damage caused to them by non-compliance with Community law, whichever public authority is responsible for the breach and whichever public authority is in principle, under the law of the Member State concerned, responsible for making reparation (Case C–302/97 *Konle (Klaus)* v *Austria* [1999] ECR I–3099, para 62).

Member States cannot, therefore, escape that liability either by pleading the internal distribution of powers and responsibilities as between the bodies which exist within their national legal order or by claiming that the public authority responsible for the breach of Community law did not have the necessary powers, knowledge, means or resources.

However, in the judgments cited in paras 26 and 27 above there is nothing to suggest that reparation for loss and damage caused to individuals by national measures taken in breach of Community law must necessarily be provided by the Member State itself in order for its obligations under Community law to be fulfilled.

As regards Member States with a federal structure, the Court has held that, if the procedural arrangements in the domestic system enable the rights which individuals derive from the Community legal system to be effectively protected and it is not more difficult to assert those rights than the rights which they derive from the domestic legal system, reparation for loss and damage caused to individuals by national measures taken in breach of Community law need not necessarily be provided by the federal State in order for the Community law obligations of the Member State concerned to be fulfilled (*Konle*, paras 63 and 64).

That is also true for those Member States, whether or not they have a federal structure, in which certain legislative or administrative tasks are devolved to territorial bodies with a certain degree of autonomy or to any other public law body legally distinct from the State. In those Member States, reparation for loss and damage caused to individuals by national measures taken in breach of Community law by a public law body may therefore be made by that body.

Nor does Community law preclude a public law body, in addition to the Member State itself, from being liable to make reparation for loss and damage caused to individuals as a result of measures which it took in breach of Community law.

It is well settled that, subject to the existence of a right to obtain reparation which is founded directly on Community law where the conditions for Member State liability for breach of Community law are met, it is on the basis of rules of national law on liability that the State must make reparation for the consequences of the loss and damage caused, with the proviso that the conditions for reparation of loss and damage laid down by national legislation must not be less favourable than those relating to similar domestic claims and must not be so framed as to make it in practice impossible or excessively difficult to obtain reparation.

In view of the foregoing, the answer to the first question must be that Community law does not preclude a public law body, in addition to the Member State itself, from being liable to make reparation for loss and damage caused to individuals as a result of measures which it took in breach of Community law.

[The second question]

By its second question, the national court asks whether, where a national official has either applied national law conflicting with Community law or applied national law in a manner not in conformity with Community law, the mere fact that he did not have any discretion in taking his decision gives rise to a serious breach of Community law, within the meaning of the case law of the Court.

It is clear from the case law of the Court that three conditions must be satisfied for a Member State to be required to make reparation for loss and damage caused to individuals as a result of breaches of Community law for which the State can be held responsible: the rule of law infringed must have been intended to confer rights on individuals; the breach must be sufficiently serious; and there must be a direct causal link between the breach of the obligation resting on the State and the loss or damage sustained by the injured parties. Those conditions are to be applied according to each type of situation (*Norbrook Laboratories*, para 107).

Those three conditions must be satisfied both where the loss or damage for which reparation is sought is the result of a failure to act on the part of the Member State, for example in the event of a failure to implement a Community directive, and where it is the result of the adoption of a legislative or administrative act in breach of Community law, whether it was adopted by the Member State itself or by a public law body which is legally independent from the State.

As regards, more particularly, the second of those conditions, the Court has held that a breach of Community law is sufficiently serious where a Member State, in the exercise of its legislative powers, has manifestly and gravely disregarded the limits on its powers (see *Brasserie du Pêcheur and Factortame*, para 55; *British Telecommunications*, para 42; and *Dillenkofer and Others*, para 25) and that where, at the time when it committed the infringement, the Member State in question had only considerably reduced, or even no, discretion, the mere infringement of Community law may be sufficient to establish the existence of a sufficiently serious breach (see *Hedley Lomas*, para 28; and *Norbrook Laboratories*, para 109).

The obligation to make reparation for loss or damage caused to individuals cannot, however, depend upon a condition based on any concept of fault going beyond that of a sufficiently serious breach of Community law (*Brasserie du Pêcheur and Factortame*, para 79).

The discretion referred to in para 38 above is that enjoyed by the Member State concerned. Its existence and its scope are determined by reference to Community law and not by reference to national law. The discretion which may be conferred by national law on the official or the institution responsible for the breach of Community law is therefore irrelevant in this respect.

It is also clear from the case law cited in para 38 that a mere infringement of Community law by a Member State may, but does not necessarily, constitute a sufficiently serious breach.

In order to determine whether such an infringement of Community law constitutes a sufficiently serious breach, a national court hearing a claim for reparation must take account of all the factors which characterise the situation put before it.

Those factors include, in particular, the clarity and precision of the rule infringed, whether the infringement and the damage caused was intentional or involuntary, whether any error of law was excusable or inexcusable, and the fact that the position taken by a Community institution may have contributed towards the adoption or maintenance of national measures or practices contrary to Community law (see *Brasserie du Pêcheur and Factortame*, para 56, as regards the conditions under which the State may incur liability for acts and omissions of its national legislature contrary to Community law).

As regards the application of those criteria in the present case, it is clear from the case law of the Court that, in principle, they must be applied by the national courts (*Brasserie du Pêcheur and Factortame*, para 58) in accordance with the guidelines laid down by the Court (*Konle*, para 58).

In this respect, it should be noted that the rule of Community law concerned is a Treaty provision which has been directly applicable since the transitional period laid down by the Treaty came to an end, long before the facts in the main proceedings arose.

However, when the German legislature adopted para 3 of the ZOK and the KVN then refused to enrol Mr Haim on the register of dental practitioners, the Court had not yet given judgment in the *Vlassopoulou* case [*Vlassopoulou* v *Ministerium für Justiz, Bundesund Europaangelegenheiten Baden-Würtemburg* Case C–340/89 [1991] ECR I–2357], in para 16 of which it held for the first time that a Member State which receives a request to admit a person to a profession to which access, under national law, depends upon the possession of a diploma or a professional qualification must take into consideration the diplomas, certificates and other evidence of qualifications which the person concerned has acquired in order to exercise the same profession in another Member State by making a comparison between the specialised knowledge and abilities certified by those diplomas and the knowledge and qualifications required by the national rules.

The Court applied the same principle when it held, in para 29 of *Haim I*, that it is not permissible under art 52 of the Treaty for the competent authorities of a Member State to refuse appointment as a dental practitioner under a social security scheme to a national of another Member State who has none of the qualifications mentioned in art 3 of Directive 78/686, but who has been authorised to practise, and has been practising, his profession both in the first and in another Member State, on the ground that he has not completed the preparatory training period required by the legislation of the first State, without examining whether, and, if so, to what extent, the experience already established by the person concerned corresponds to that required by that provision.

In the light of the criteria and observations referred to in paras 43 to 47 above, it is for the national court to examine whether or not, in the case before it, there is a serious breach of Community law.

The answer to the second question must therefore be that, in order to determine whether there is a serious breach of Community law, within the meaning of the case law of the Court, account must be taken of the extent of the discretion enjoyed by the Member State concerned. The existence and the scope of that discretion must be determined by reference to Community law and not by reference to national law.'

Comment

The above questions referred by the German court to the ECJ for a preliminary ruling are of considerable interest.

In respect of a Member State's liability for loss and damage caused to individuals as a result of that State's infringement of Community law, the ECJ restated its previous case law. It is for each Member State to ensure that individuals obtain compensation whichever public body is responsible for the breach and whichever public body is in principle, under the law of the Member State concerned, responsible for making reparation: *Konle (Klaus)* v *Austria* Case C–302/97 [1999] ECR I–3099. Consequently, a Member State cannot avoid that liability, either by invoking the autonomy of the public body responsible for the breach of EC law, or by relying upon the internal division of competences between the bodies which exist within their national legal system, or by claiming that the public body responsible for the breach of EC law did not have necessary powers, knowledge, means or resources. However, EC law does not require that reparation for loss and damage caused to individuals must necessarily be provided by the Member State itself. In particular, in respect of a Member State with a federal structure, reparation may not necessarily be made by a federal State provided that members of the federation have a legal system which enables the rights conferred on individuals by Community law to be effectively protected, and their enforcement is similar to that required at federal level. Also, reparation may be made by a public body which was in breach of EC law in any Member State 'in which certain legislative or administrative tasks are devolved to territorial bodies with a certain degree of autonomy or to any other public body legally distinct from the State'. Consequently, a Member State, a Member State jointly with its public body or a public body of a Member State alone may make reparation for loss and damage caused to individuals as a result of measures which had been taken in breach of EC law.

The second question referred to the ECJ concerned the conditions for liability of a Member State (*Brasserie du Pêcheur SA* v *Federal Republic of Germany*; *R* v *Secretary of State for Transport, ex parte Factortame Ltd* Joined Cases C–46 and 48/93 [1996] 1 CMLR 889), in particular the second condition requiring that the breach of EC law must be sufficiently serious to merit an award of damages. To be held liable a Member State must have 'manifestly and gravely' disregarded its obligation. In order to assess whether this condition is satisfied, national courts should take into consideration a number of factors such as: the clarity and precision of the EC rule breached; the element of discretion in the adoption of legislative acts by national authorities; whether or not the infringement was intentional or accidental, whether any error of law was excusable; whether any action or advice on the part of the Commission had contributed to the breach, etc.

In relation to the second question the ECJ emphasised that the discretion which may be conferred by national law on the official or the body responsible for the infringement of Community law is irrelevant in the determination of whether a breach of Community law is sufficiently serious to merit an award of damages. Indeed, the second condition of liability refers to the discretion enjoyed by the Member State concerned. In this respect the ECJ held that the existence and scope of such discretion are to be determined under Community law and not under national law.

However, the ECJ declined to determine whether in the case under consideration a Member State had committed an infringement of EC law sufficiently serious for it to incur liability, although the referring court expressly asked the ECJ for assistance in this respect. Even though the ECJ may consider that Community law is sufficiently clear on the matter and therefore the referring court would be able to decide whether or not, in the case before it, there was a serious breach of Community law, it would certainly be advantageous from the perspective of uniformity of Community law to have a clear answer from the ECJ. This would be even more helpful taking into account the fact that the Advocate-

General, the Commission and all Member States which submitted their observations (Greece, Spain, Italy, Sweden and the UK) considered that the breach of Community law by Germany did not constitute a sufficiently serious breach.

Rechberger and Greindl v *Austria*
Case C–140/97 [1999] ECR I–3499
European Court of Justice

• *Liability in tort – sufficiently serious breach of Community law – Directive 90/314/EEC on package travel – package holidays and package tours – travel offered at a reduced price to the subscribers of a daily newspaper – implementation*

Facts
The plaintiffs were subscribers to the Austrian daily newspaper, *Neue Kronenzeitung*, which wanted to reward their loyalty to its newspaper by offering them, by a way of gift, a four- or seven-day trip to one of four European destinations. The offer was generally free of charges for the subscribers (save for airport taxes), but there was a charge of ATS 500 if they travelled alone. A person travelling with a subscriber was required to pay the price set out in the brochure. Subscribers who accepted the offer were required to pay the organiser a deposit of 10 per cent of the relevant charges, the balance being payable no later than ten days before the scheduled departure date. The offer was so successful that the travel organiser Arena-Club-Reisen could not cope with the demand and went bankrupt. In the meantime the advertising campaign organised by the newspaper was held by the Austrian Supreme Court to be in breach of Austrian competition law.

Under the Act of Accession the Republic of Austria had to implement Council Directive 90/314/EEC by 1 January 1995. Article 7 of Directive 90/314 provides that the organiser of a package tour or holiday is to provide 'sufficient evidence of security for the refund of money paid over and for the repatriation of the consumer in the event of insolvency'.

When the subscribers asked to be reimbursed they faced two problems. The first was that the bank guarantee issued by the travel organiser in conformity with national law implementing Directive 90/314 was insufficient to reimburse the travel cost they paid. The second was that some subscribers had made bookings in 1994 but the legislation implementing Directive 90/314 applied only to packages booked after 1 January 1995 with a departure date of 1 May 1995 or later. Even the 'lucky' subscribers who were covered by the legislation could only recover from the bank guarantee 25.38 per cent of the amount paid.

In these circumstances the plaintiffs brought an action against the Republic of Austria before an Austrian court for failure to implement art 7 of Directive 90/314 correctly and in good time.

The referring court asked, inter alia, the ECJ:

1. whether defective transposition of art 7 constituted a sufficiently serious breach of Community law giving rise to a right to compensation;
2. for some clarifications as to the causal link between the failure of a Member State to implement a directive correctly and the damage sustained by the individuals, in particular whether a State's liability in tort can be precluded by imprudent conduct on the part of the travel organiser or by force majeure.

Held

The ECJ held that art 7 of Directive 90/314 applied to public relations trips even though they were part of an advertising campaign that contravened national competition law. The Court stated the following.

1. Austria failed to correctly implement art 7 of Directive 90/314 by not protecting travellers who had booked package travel after

1 January 1995 intending to travel after 1 May 1995 or later.
2. This alone constituted a sufficiently serious breach of Community law.
3. Irrespective of the actual implementing measures, art 7 of Directive 90/314 required that travellers should obtain the full refund of money paid.
4. Once a direct causal link was established, a Member State's liability for breach of art 7 of Directive 90/314 could not be precluded by imprudent conduct of the travel organiser or by the occurrence of exceptional or unforeseeable events.

Judgment

'[*The fourth question*]

By its fourth question the national court is essentially asking whether such defective transposition of art 7 of the Directive constitutes a sufficiently serious breach of Community law to give rise to a right to reparation where, as is the case here, all the other provisions of the Directive have been implemented.

According to the case law of the Court, a breach is sufficiently serious where, in the exercise of its legislative powers, an institution or a Member State has manifestly and gravely disregarded the limits on the exercise of its powers. Factors which the competent court may take into consideration include the clarity and precision of the rule breached (Case C–392/93 *R v Her Majesty's Treasury, ex parte British Telecommunications plc* [1996] ECR I–1631, para 42).

In the present case it must be held that neither art 7 nor any other provision of the Directive may be interpreted as conferring a right upon the Member States to limit the application of art 7 to trips taken on a date later than the time-limit prescribed for transposition of the Directive. The Member State in question here enjoyed no margin of discretion as to the entry into force, in its own law, of the provisions of art 7. That being so, the limitation of the protection prescribed by art 7 to trips with a departure date of 1 May 1995 or later is manifestly incompatible with the obligations under the Directive and thus constitutes a sufficiently serious breach of Community law.

The fact that the Member State has implemented all the other provisions of the Directive does not alter that finding.

In view of the foregoing the answer to the fourth question must be that transposition of art 7 of the Directive in a way that limits the protection prescribed by that provision to trips with a departure date four months or more after the expiry of the period prescribed for transposing the Directive constitutes a sufficiently serious breach of Community law, even where the Member State has implemented all the other provisions of the Directive.

[*The sixth question*]

By its sixth question the national court is essentially asking whether, where there is a direct causal link between the conduct of the State which has only partially transposed the directive and the loss or damage suffered by individuals, that causal link might not render that State liable if it shows that there was imprudent conduct on the part of the travel organiser or that exceptional or unforeseeable events occurred.

The plaintiffs in the main action maintain that unlawful conduct on the part of the travel organiser or any other third party cannot exempt the Member State concerned from liability. The question concerning exceptional and unforeseeable increase in risk is irrelevant in the present case since a substantial increase in turnover can never be unforeseeable and provision for it should in any event have been made by the national legislature.

The Republic of Austria argues that, in any event, there is no direct causal link between late or incomplete transposition of art 7 of the Directive and the loss or damage suffered by consumers if the date and scope of the implementing measures can have contributed to the occurrence of the loss or damage only as a result of a chain of wholly exceptional and unforeseeable events.

According to the United Kingdom and Swedish Governments, it is for the national

court to determine, according to the principles applicable under its national law, whether, in any given case, there is a direct causal link between, on the one hand, a Member State's failure to transpose art 7 within the prescribed period or to do so adequately and, on the other hand, the loss or damage suffered by the consumer, such as to render the Member State liable and to require it to reimburse the unsecured sums in full.

According to the Commission, that causal link should be held to exist even when the organiser's insolvency and its extent are to be attributed to wholly exceptional and unforeseeable causes.

In this connection, it should be observed that, as the Court held in Joined Cases C–46/93 and C–48/93 *Brasserie du Pêcheur SA v Federal Republic of Germany; R v Secretary of State for Transport, ex parte Factortame Ltd* [1996] ECR I–1029, at para 65, it is for the national courts to determine whether there is a direct causal link between the breach of the obligation resting on the State and the damage sustained by the injured parties.

In the present case, it should first be observed that the national court found that there was such a direct causal link between the conduct of the Member State which had failed to transpose the Directive in full and the damage sustained by the individuals.

Next, it should be pointed out that art 7 of the Directive imposes an obligation of result, namely to guarantee package travellers the refund of money paid over and their repatriation in the event of the travel organiser's bankruptcy. Such a guarantee is specifically aimed at arming consumers against the consequences of the bankruptcy, whatever the causes of it may be.

In those circumstances, the Member State's liability for breach of art 7 of the Directive cannot be precluded by imprudent conduct on the part of the travel organiser or by the occurrence of exceptional and unforeseeable events.

Such circumstances, in as much as they would not have presented an obstacle to the refund of money paid over or the repatriation of consumers if the guarantee system had been implemented in accordance with art 7 of the Directive, are not such as to preclude the existence of a direct causal link.

Consequently, the answer to the sixth question must be that once a direct causal link has been established a Member State's liability for breach of art 7 of the Directive cannot be precluded by imprudent conduct on the part of the travel organiser or by the occurrence of exceptional or unforeseeable events.'

Comment

There are two interesting aspects raised in the present case. First, the matter regarding the conditions under which State liability gives rise to a right to compensation, in particular whether the Austrian authorities committed a sufficiently serious breach. In *Dillenkofer and Others* v *Federal Republic of Germany* Cases C–178, 179 and 189/94 [1996] ECR I–4845 the ECJ held that non-implementation of a Directive within the prescribed time limit constitutes, per se, a serious breach of Community law, and consequently gives rise to a right of reparation for individuals suffering injury. In that case the ECJ clarified the conditions for the non-contractual liability of a Member State. The Court confirmed that when a Member State is not called upon to make any legislative choices and has only considerably reduced, or even no, discretion, the mere breach of EC law may be sufficient to establish the existence of a breach sufficiently serious to give rise to non-contractual liability: see *R* v *Her Majesty's Treasury, ex parte British Telecommunications plc* Case C–392/93 [1996] ECR I–1631. In the case of non-implementation of a directive within the prescribed time limit, a Member State 'manifestly and gravely' disregards the limits of its discretion and therefore will be held liable. However, in the present case, only art 7 of Directive 90/314 was incorrectly implemented. In this respect, the ECJ held that art 7 of the Directive leaves no discretion to a Member State, and thus Austria could not

limit its application to package travel booked after 1 January 1995 with a departure date of 1 May 1995 or later, since art 7 applies to all contracts for package travel entered into from 1995 onwards and relating to trips to be taken after that date. The ECJ clearly stated that:

'The limitation of the protection prescribed by art 7 to trips with a departure date of 1 May 1995 or later is manifestly incompatible with the obligations under the Directive and thus constitutes a sufficiently serious breach of Community law.'

Also, the reimbursement of 25.38 per cent of the amount paid by the plaintiffs is in breach of the Directive, since art 7 clearly states that there should be a 'refund of money paid over'.

Third, the referring court asked the ECJ a question regarding the causal link between the breach of the State's obligation and the harm suffered by the injured parties, in particular whether this link can be interrupted by imprudent conduct on the part of the travel organiser or the occurrence of exceptional or unforeseeable events. The ECJ rejected the possibility of exoneration or attenuation of a State's liability on the grounds of force majeure or the imprudent conduct of the travel organiser. In this respect the ECJ held:

'... art 7 of the Directive imposes an obligation of result, namely to guarantee package travellers the refund of money paid over and their repatriation in the event of the travel organiser's bankruptcy. Such a guarantee is specifically aimed at arming consumers against the consequences of the bankruptcy, whatever the causes of it may be.'

This solution is fully justified, taking into account the fact that a State's liability is based on its failure to fulfil an obligation arising from EC law, and thus different and separate from the liability of the parties to a contract made between them. In the present case the referring court has already established the existence of such a link.

8 Fundamental Principles of Community Law

Supremacy of EC law

Amministrazione delle Finanze dello Stato v Simmenthal SpA Case 106/77 [1978] ECR 629; [1978] 3 CMLR 263 European Court of Justice

- *Supremacy of EC law – national law subsequent to EC law – preliminary rulings – art 177 EC Treaty [art 234 EC] – charges equivalent to customs duties – art 12 EC Treaty [art 25 EC] – charges for veterinary and health inspection – art 30 EC Treaty [art 28 EC] – quantitative restrictions and measures having equivalent effect*

Facts

Simmenthal imported a consignment of beef from France to Italy. He was asked to pay for veterinary and public health inspections carried out at the frontier. He paid, but sued in the Italian court for reimbursement of money, arguing that the fees were contrary to Community law. After reference to the ECJ, which held that the inspections were contrary to art 30 EC Treaty [art 28 EC] as being of equivalent effect to quantitative restriction and consequently charges were unlawful under art 12 EC Treaty [art 25 EC] being charges equivalent to customs duties, the Italian court ordered the Italian Ministry to repay the fees. The ministry refused to pay claiming that the national statute of 1970 under which Simmenthal was liable to pay fees was still preventing any reimbursement and could only be set aside by the Italian Constitutional court.

The question was referred once again to the ECJ under art 177 EC Treaty [art 234 EC].

Held

The ECJ confirmed that in the event of incompatibility of a subsequent legislative measure enacted by a Member State with Community law all national judges must apply Community law in its entirety and must set aside any provision of national law, prior or subsequent, in conflict with Community law. National courts should not request or await the prior setting aside of an incompatible national provision by legislation or other constitutional means but of its own motion, if necessary, refuse the application of conflicting national law and instead apply Community law.

Judgment

'In accordance with the principle of the precedence of Community law, the relationship between provisions of the Treaty and directly applicable measures of the institutions on the one hand and the national law of the Member States on the other is such that those provisions and measures not only by their entry into force render automatically inapplicable any conflicting provision of current national law but – in so far as they are an integral part of, and take precedence in, the legal order applicable in the territory of each of the Member States – also preclude the valid adoption of new national legislative measures to the extent to which they would be incompatible with Community provisions.

Indeed any recognition that national legislative measures which encroach upon the field within which the Community exercises it legislative power or which are otherwise incompatible with the provisions of Community law had any legal effect would amount to a corresponding denial of the effectiveness of obligations undertaken unconditionally and irrevocably by Member States pursuant to the Treaty and would thus imperil the very foundations of the Community.

The same conclusion emerges from the structure of art 177 of the Treaty which provides that any court or tribunal of a Member State is entitled to make a reference to the Court whenever it considers that a preliminary ruling on a question of interpretation or validity relating to Community law is necessary to enable it to give judgment.

The effectiveness of that provision would be impaired if the national court were prevented from forthwith applying Community law in accordance with the decision or the case law of the Court.

It follows from the foregoing that every national court must, in a case within its jurisdiction, apply Community law in its entirety and protect rights which the latter confers on individuals and must accordingly set aside any provision of national law which may conflict with it, whether prior or subsequent to the Community rule.

Accordingly any provision of a national legal system and any legislative, administrative or judicial practice which may impair the effectiveness of Community law by withholding from the national court having jurisdiction to apply such law the power to do everything necessary at the moment of its application to set aside national legislative provisions which might prevent Community rules from having full force and effect are incompatible with those requirements which are the very essence of Community law.

This would be the case in the event of a conflict between a provision of Community law and a subsequent national law if the solution of the conflict were to be reserved for an authority with a discretion of its own, other than the court called upon to apply Community law, even if such an impediment to the full effectiveness of Community law were only temporary.

The first question should therefore be answered to the effect that a national court which is called upon, within the limits of its jurisdiction, to apply provisions of Community law is under a duty to give full effect to those provisions, if necessary refusing of its own motion to apply any conflicting provision of national legislation, even if adopted subsequently, and it is not necessary for the court to request or await the prior setting aside of such provision by legislative or other constitutional means.'

Comment

The obligation to give full effectiveness to Community law, and thus to protect rights which it confers upon individuals, empowers a national judge to suspend, as an interim measure, the application of national law which he suspects is in conflict with Community law although it might be contrary to national law to do so.

On the basis of supremacy of Community law national judges are able to resolve any difficulties which they may encounter while facing a conflict between national law and Community law. Similarly, administrative authorities are required to set aside any national provision incompatible with Community law (*Fratelli Costanzo SpA v Comune di Milano* Case C–103/88 [1989] ECR 1839). In relation to sanctions, especially of a penal nature, ordered by virtue of national law and incompatible with Community law, those sanctions are considered as devoid of any legal base (*Minister for Fisheries v CA Schonenberg and Others* Case 88/77 [1978] ECR 473; *R v Robert Tymen* Case 269/80 [1981] ECR 3079).

Costa v ENEL Case 6/64 [1964] ECR 585; [1964] CMLR 425
European Court of Justice

• *Supremacy of Community law – conflict between provisions of the constitutional treaties and national law – pre-existing national law*

Facts

Costa was a shareholder of one of the private undertakings nationalised by the Italian government on 6 September 1962 when the assets of some private undertakings were transferred to ENEL. Costa who was also a lawyer refused to pay an electricity bill for £1 sent by ENEL and was sued by the latter. He argued, inter alia, that the nationalisation legislation was contrary to various provisions of EC Treaty. The Milanese Giudice Conciliatore referred this question to the ECJ under art 177 EC Treaty [art 234 EC]. The Italian government claimed that the referral was 'absolutely inadmissible' since a national court which is obliged to apply national law cannot avail itself of art 177 EC Treaty [art 234 EC].

Held

The ECJ rejected the arguments of the Italian government. The Court stated that the EC Treaty created a new legal order which was an integral element of the legal systems of the Member States. The national courts were required to apply Community law in all proceedings. Where a provision of national law was inconsistent with Community law, Community law took precedence, regardless of whether the national provision was enacted prior or subsequent to the date the EC Treaty took effect. The ECJ held that Community law because of its special and original nature, could not be overridden by domestic provisions, however framed, without being deprived of its character as Community law and without the legal basis of the Community itself being called into question.

Judgment

'By contrast with ordinary international treaties, the [EC] Treaty has created its own legal system which, on the entry into force of the Treaty, became an integral part of the legal systems of the Member States and which their courts are bound to apply.

By creating a Community of unlimited duration, having its own institutions, its own personality, its own legal capacity and capacity of representation on the international plane and, more particularly, real powers stemming from a limitation of sovereignty or a transfer of powers from the States to the Community, the Member States have limited their sovereign rights, albeit within limited fields, and have thus created a body of law which binds both their nationals and themselves.

The integration into the laws of each Member State of provisions which derive from the Community, and more generally the terms and the spirit of the Treaty, make it impossible for the States, as a corollary, to accord precedence to a unilateral and subsequent measure over a legal system accepted by them on a basis of reciprocity. Such a measure cannot therefore be inconsistent with that legal system. The executive force of Community laws, without jeopardising the attainment of the objectives of the Treaty set out in art 5(2) and giving rise to the discrimination prohibited by art [6].

The obligations undertaken under the Treaty establishing the Community would not be unconditional, but merely contingent, if they could be called in question by subsequent legislative acts of the signatories. Wherever the Treaty grants the States the right to act unilaterally, it does this by clear and precise provisions (for example arts 15, 93(3), 223, 224 and 225). Applications by Member States for authority to derogate from the Treaty are subject to a special authorisation procedure (for example arts 8(4), 17(4), 25, 26, 73, the third subparagraph of 93(2) and 226) which would lose their purpose if the Member States could renounce their obligations by means of an ordinary law.

The precedence of Community law is confirmed by art 189, whereby a regulation "shall be binding" and "directly applicable in all Member States". This provision, which is subject to no reservation, would be quite meaningless if a State could unilaterally nullify its effects by means of a legislative measure which could prevail over Community law.

It follows from all these observations that the law stemming from the Treaty, an independent source of law, could not, because of its special and original nature, be overridden by domestic legal provisions, however framed, without being deprived of its character as Community law and without the legal basis of the Community itself being called into question.

The transfer by the States from their domestic legal system to the Community legal system of the rights and obligations arising under the Treaty carries with it a permanent limitation of their sovereign rights, against which a subsequent unilateral act incompatible with the concept of the Community cannot prevail.'

Comment

In the present case the ECJ established the most important principle of Community law: the supremacy of EC Law. The ECJ based its reasoning on three arguments.

1. Direct applicability and direct effect of Community law would be meaningless if a Member State were permitted by subsequent legislation to nullify unilaterally its effects by means of a legislative measure which could prevail over Community law.
2. By transferring certain competences to the Community institutions the Member States have limited their sovereignty.
3. Uniformity of application of Community law, which ensures homogeneity of the Community legal order, requires that EC law prevails over conflicting national law.

The ECJ has summarised its reasoning in the following terms:

'... the law stemming from the Treaty, an independent source of law, could not, because of its special and original nature, be overridden by domestic legal provisions, however framed, without being deprived of its character as Community law and without the legal basis of the Community itself being called into question.'

This statement constitutes the essence of supremacy of Community law. The position of the ECJ has not changed since its decision in *Costa*. If anything, the ECJ has become more radical in confirming obvious implications of supremacy of Community law vis-à-vis the Member States. Indeed, whatever the reaction of the Member States, and no matter how long it takes to gain full recognition of this principle by the Member States, for the Community supremacy is a necessary requirement of its existence.

In the present case the ECJ resolved the conflict between national law enacted prior to the entry into force of the Treaties in favour of Community law. All pre-dating national law is deemed to be abrogated, or at least devoid of its legal effect, insofar as it is contrary to Community law.

Criminal Proceedings against Nunes and de Matos Case C–186/98 [1999] 2 CMLR 1403 European Court of Justice

• *Supremacy of EC law – penalties under Community law and national law – criminal sanction for civil breach of Community law – financial assistance granted from the European Social Fund – improper use of funds*

Facts

Criminal proceedings were brought under the Portuguese Criminal Code against Maria Nunes, for forgery, and Evangelina de Matos, for forgery and corruption, committed in connection with a vocational training initiative financed from the European Social Fund. At the material time under art 6(1) of Council Regulation 2950/83 the improper use of Community funds was not a criminal offence, whilst its art 6(2) provided that sums paid which were used improperly were recoverable. The defendants argued that since the sanctions under Community law were of a civil nature they could not be charged with criminal proceedings.

Held

The ECJ held that under art 10 EC Member

States are required to take effective measures to sanction conduct which affects the financial interests of the Community, including criminal penalties even where EC law provides only for civil sanctions. However, national sanctions must be analogous to those applicable to similar infringements of national law and must be effective, proportionate and dissuasive.

Judgment

'[*The first question*]
It is clear from art 6 of Regulation No 2950/83 that the consequences of using ESF assistance in breach of the conditions set out in the decision of approval are not in the nature of criminal sanctions.

Consequently the answer to the first question must be that Community legislation does not classify the improper use of ESF assistance as a criminal offence.

[*The second question*]
Where a Community regulation does not specifically provide any penalty for an infringement or refers for that purpose to national laws, regulations and administrative provisions, art 5 of the EC Treaty (now art 10 EC) requires the Member States to take all measures necessary to guarantee the application and effectiveness of Community law (see, in particular, Case 68/88 *EC Commission* v *Greece* [1989] ECR 2965, para 23).

For that purpose, while the choice of penalties remains within their discretion, the Member States must ensure in particular that infringements of Community law are penalised under conditions, both procedural and substantive, which are analogous to those applicable to infringements of national law of a similar nature and importance and which, in any event, make the penalty effective, proportionate and dissuasive (*EC Commission* v *Greece*, para 24).

Moreover, the national authorities must proceed, with respect to infringements of Community law, with the same diligence as that which they bring to bear in implement-

ing corresponding national laws (*EC Commission* v *Greece*, para 25).

The same reasoning applies where a Community regulation lays down particular penalties for infringement, but does not exhaustively list the penalties that the Member States may impose, as is the case with the regulation on the ESF.

The nature of the obligation imposed by art 5 of the EC Treaty is underlined, as Advocate-General Jacobs observed in point 9 of his Opinion, by the first paragraph of art 209a of the EC Treaty (now, after amendment, art 280(2) EC), which expressly requires Member States to take the same measures to counter fraud affecting the financial interests of the Community as they take to counter fraud affecting their own financial interests.

Consequently the answer to the second question must be that art 5 of the Treaty requires the Member States to take all effective measures to penalise conduct harmful to the financial interests of the Community. Such measures may include criminal penalties even where the Community legislation only provides for civil ones. The penalty provided for must be analogous to those applicable to infringements of national law of similar nature and importance, and must be effective, proportionate and dissuasive.'

Comment

The decision of the ECJ is not surprising in the light of art 280(2) EC which requires that Member States should take the same measures to counter fraud affecting the financial interests of the Community as they take to combat fraud affecting their own financial interests.

The ECJ held that when Community law does not expressly provide for any penalty for an infringement of Community law, or refers to national laws in this respect, art 10 EC imposes an obligation on Member States to take all necessary measures to ensure the application and effectiveness of Community law, in particular in relation to measures intended to counter fraud affecting Community financial interests as defined in

EC Commission v *Greece* Case 68/88 [1989] ECR 2965. When Community law provides for civil sanctions, as in the present case, without exhaustively listing the penalties that the Member States could impose, and therefore the choice of penalties remains within their discretion, the Member States are entitled to include criminal penalties. In such a case the criminal sanctions for infringements of Community law must satisfy two requirements which derive from the supremacy of Community law. First, national rules, both procedural and substantive, must be analogous to those applicable to infringements of national law of similar nature and importance, and, second, they must be effective, proportionate and dissuasive.

International Handelsgesellschaft GmbH v *EVGF* Case 11/70 [1970] ECR 1125; [1970] CMLR 255
European Court of Justice

• *Supremacy of EC law – conflict between provisions of the constitutional treaties and the German constitution – conflict avoided by interpreting both European and German constitutional law as enshrining the same constitutional safeguards – fundamental human rights*

Facts
EC regulations set up a system of export licences, guaranteed by a deposit, for certain agricultural products and required that the products were exported during the validity of the licence, failing which the deposit would be forfeited. The plaintiffs lost a deposit of DM 17,000 and argued that the system introduced by EC regulations, which was run by the West German National Cereals Intervention Agency, was in breach of the fundamental human rights' provisions contained in the German constitution and especially the principle of proportionality as it imposed obligations (the forfeited deposit) which were not necessary in order to achieve the objectives

pursued by EC regulations, that is the regulation of the cereals market. The Frankfurt administrative court took the view that this type of deposit regulation was unconstitutional because it infringed the reasonable freedom of an individual to carry on business, and also contravened a fundamental principle of German legal theory that the compulsory payment of money cannot be imposed in the absence of fault on the part of the individual concerned. Nevertheless, the German court did refer the matter to the ECJ under art 177 EC Treaty [art 234 EC].

Held
The ECJ held that Community law prevails over national constitutional law, including fundamental human rights enshrined in the constitution of a Member State. In order to avoid direct confrontation between EC law and fundamental human rights contained in the German constitution, the ECJ stated that fundamental human rights were a part of Community law and could therefore be enforced through the Community legal system. The ECJ upheld the regulation in question and declared the system of deposits as appropriate methods of attainment of the objectives of arts 40(3) EC and 43 EC Treaty [arts 34(3) and 37 EC] concerning the common organisation of the agricultural markets.

Judgment
'Recourse to the legal rules or concepts of national law in order to judge the validity of measures adopted by the institutions of the Community would have an adverse effect on the uniformity and efficacy of Community law. The validity of such measures can only be judged in the light of Community law. In fact, the law stemming from the Treaty, an independent source of law, cannot because of its very nature be overridden by rules of national law, however framed, without being deprived of its character as Community law and without the legal basis of the Community itself

being called in question. Therefore, the validity of a Community measure or its effect within a Member State cannot be affected by allegations that it runs counter to either fundamental rights as formulated by the constitution of that State or the principles of a national constitutional structure.

However, an examination should be made as to whether or not any analogous guarantee inherent in Community law has been disregarded. In fact, respect for fundamental human rights forms an integral part of the general principles of law protected by the Court of Justice. The protection of such rights, whilst inspired by the constitutional traditions common to the Member States, must be ensured within the framework of the structure and objectives of the Community.'

Comment

The ECJ confirmed that supremacy of Community law is unconditional and absolute, all Community law prevails over all national law.

It means that all sources of Community law, the provisions of the Treaties and secondary legislation – regulations (*Politi* v *Italian Ministry of Finance of the Italian Republic* Case 43/71 [1971] ECR 1039; *Marimex SpA* v *Italian Finance Administration* Case 29/72 [1972] ECR 1309), directives (*Rewe-Handelsgesellschaft Nord mbH* v *Hauptzollamt Kiel* Case 158/80 [1981] ECR 1805; *Becker (Ursula)* v *Finanzamt Münster-Innenstadt* Case 8/81 [1982] ECR 53), decisions (*Salumificio di Cornuda* Case 130/78 [1979] ECR 867), general principles of Community law (*Wachauf* v *Germany* Case 5/88 [1989] ECR 2609), international agreements concluded between the Community and third countries (*Nederlandse Spoowegen* Case 38/75 [1975] ECR 1439; *SPI and SAMI* Cases 267–269/81 [1983] ECR 801) – irrespective whether or not they are directly effective, prevail over all national law. Also Community law is superior to all provisions of national law: legislative, administrative, jurisdictional and constitutional.

Ministero delle Finanze v *IN.CO.GE.'90 SRL and Others*
Joined Cases C–10–22/97 [1998] ECR I–6307 European Court of Justice

• *Supremacy of EC law – direct applicability of EC law – preliminary ruling – recovery of sums paid but not due – treatment of national charge incompatible with EC law*

Facts

IN.CO.GE.'90 and 12 other Italian limited liability companies paid a special annual administrative charge for entering them on the register of companies (tassa do concessione governativa). This charge was declared unlawful by the ECJ in *Ponente Carni* Cases C–71 and 178/91 [1993] ECR I–1915. The companies subject to the charge sought to recover their payments. The Italian authorities refused the reimbursement. They argued that the Italian courts had no jurisdiction over fiscal matters and that the claims were time-barred. The Italian district magistarate's court at Rome referred to the ECJ the question relating to the consequences arising under Italian law from the incompatibility of the domestic charge with EC law. The questions of classification of the charge and of procedural law were at issue. If a national judge had to disapply national law which implemented EC law, including its provisions on the classification of the charge in question as contrary to EC law and classified the charge on the basis of Italian law, the charge in question would cease to be of a fiscal nature and would fall within the general rules for recovery of amounts paid but not due with a consequence of depriving the charge of any existence in law.

Held

The ECJ held that the incompatibility with EC law of a subsequently adopted rule of national law did not render that rule of national law non-existent. The national court must disapply that rule but uphold claims for repayment of a charge contrary to Community law. The national court may apply national procedural rules to any rights which are conferred by EC law, providing that they impose conditions no less favourable than for equivalent actions not involving EC law and that they do not make impossible or excessively difficult the exercise of rights conferred by Community law.

Judgment

'[*Jurisdiction*]

The Court has power to explain to the national court points of Community law which may help to solve the problem of jurisdiction with which that court is faced. To that end, it may, if appropriate, extract the relevant points from the wording of the question submitted and the facts set forth by the national court.

It appears from the order for reference that the Pretura di Roma is uncertain as to the consequences arising under national law from the incompatibility of a domestic charge with Community law. The Pretura bases its opinion that the disputes pending before it are not of a fiscal nature but fall, under Italian law, within the general rules for recovery of amounts paid but not due on the fact that such incompatibility, inasmuch as its effect is to disapply the relevant national provisions in their entirety and deprive the charge in question of any existence in law, necessarily has the effect of divesting it of its fiscal nature.

It follows that the Court does have jurisdiction to reply to the question submitted.

[*The question of supremacy*]

The Commission points out that, in its judgment in Case 106/77 *Amministrazione delle Finanze dello Stato* v *Simmenthal*, the Court held, inter alia, that the provisions of the Treaty and the directly applicable measures of the institutions have the effect, in their relationship with the domestic law of the Member States, not only of rendering automatically inapplicable any conflicting provision of national law in force but also of precluding the valid adoption of new national

legislative measures which would be incompatible with Community provisions. From this, the Commission infers that a Member State has no power whatever to adopt a fiscal provision that is incompatible with Community law, with the result that such a provision and the corresponding fiscal obligation must be treated as non-existent.

That interpretation cannot be accepted.

It cannot therefore, contrary to the Commission's contention, be inferred from the judgment in *Simmenthal* that the incompatibility with Community law of a subsequently adopted rule of national law has the effect of rendering that rule of national law non-existent. Faced with such a situation, the national court is, however, obliged to disapply that rule, provided always that this obligation does not restrict the power of the competent national courts to apply, from among the various procedures available under national law, those which are appropriate for protecting the individual rights conferred by Community law.

It remains to be considered whether non-application, as the result of a judgment given by the Court, of national legislation which introduced a levy contrary to Community law has the result of depriving that levy retroactively of its character as a charge and thereby divesting of its fiscal nature the legal relationship established when that charge was levied between the national tax authority and the companies liable to pay it.

Entitlement to the recovery of sums levied in breach of Community law is a consequence of, and an adjunct to, the rights conferred on individuals by the relevant Community provisions as interpreted by the Court. A Member State is therefore in principle required to repay charges levied in breach of Community law.

In the absence of Community rules governing the matter, such repayment may be claimed only if the substantive and formal conditions laid down by the various national laws are complied with. Community law does not in principle preclude the legislation of a Member State from laying down, alongside a limitation period applicable under the ordinary law to actions between private individuals for the recovery of sums paid but not due, special detailed rules governing claims and legal proceedings to challenge the imposition of charges and other levies.

The possibility thus recognised by the Court of applying those special detailed rules to the repayment of charges and other levies found to be contrary to Community law would be deprived of any effect if the incompatibility between a domestic levy and Community law necessarily had the effect of depriving that levy of its character as a charge and divesting of its fiscal nature the legal relationship established, when the charge in question was levied, between the national tax authorities and the parties liable to pay it.'

Comment

In the present case the ECJ clarified its judgment in *Simmenthal*. The Commission argued that a national provision incompatible with EC law should be treated as non-existent and void. The ECJ disagreed. The Court held that inconsistent domestic law should be disregarded but any rights conferred by EC law have to be enforced under domestic procedure. Also the question of classification of the charge is a matter for national law when a domestic charge is found to be contrary to EC law provided the full effect is given to Community law.

R v Secretary of State for Transport, ex parte Factortame Ltd and Others [1990] 2 AC 85 House of Lords

• *Supremacy of EC law – national law subsequent to EC law – Merchant Shipping Act 1988 – absolute endorsement of the principle of supremacy in the UK – no qualifications for application of post-1972 statutes*

Facts

The statutory requirements for registering vessels as British were radically altered by Part II of the Merchant Shipping Act 1988 and the Merchant Shipping (Registration of Fishing Vessels) Regulations 1988. Vessels which were previously registered as British under the 1984 statute required re-registration under the 1988 Act.

Ninety-five vessels owned by Community nationals failed to satisfy one or more of the conditions for registration under s14(1) of the Act and therefore failed to qualify as British vessels because they were managed or controlled from Spain or by Spanish nationals, or by reason of the proportion of the beneficial ownership of the shares in the applicant companies which was in Spanish hands.

The applicants sought judicial review of the relevant provisions of the Act on the ground that these provisions were in breach of EC law by depriving the applicants of enforceable Community rights. The Divisional Court of the Queen's Bench Division decided to request a preliminary ruling from the ECJ on the substantive question of Community law in order to enable it to determine the application. On a motion by the applicants for interim relief, the Divisional Court ordered that, pending final judgment of the case, the operation of the contested parts of the statute was to be disapplied and that the Secretary of State should be restrained from enforcing any rights under the legislation.

The Court of Appeal, on appeal from the Secretary of State, set aside the order made by the Divisional Court for interim relief. The applicants appealed the matter to the House of Lords.

Held

The House of Lords held that the remedy was not available under English law but in the light of the case law of the ECJ on interim measures a reference would be made to the ECJ under art 177 EC Treaty [art 234 EC] in respect of the award of interim protection.

Judgment

Lord Bridge:

'By virtue of s2(4) of the 1972 Act, Part II of the 1988 Act is to be construed and take effect subject to directly enforceable Community rights and those rights are, by s2(1) of the Act of 1972, to be "recognised and available in law, and ... enforced. allowed and followed accordingl y ...". This has precisely the same effect as if a section were incorporated in Part II of the Act of 1988 which in terms enacted that the provisions with respect to registration of British fishing vessels were to be without prejudice to directly enforceable Community rights of nationals of any Member State of the EEC. Thus it is common ground that, in so far as the applicants succeed before the ECJ in obtaining a ruling in support of the Community rights which they claim, those rights will prevail over the restrictions imposed on registration of British vessels by Part II of the Act of 1988 and the Divisional Court will, in the final determination of the application for judicial review, be obliged to make appropriate declarations to give effect to those rights.

... I turn finally to consider the submission made on behalf of the appellants that, irrespective of the position under national law, there is an overriding principle of Community law which imposes an obligation on the national court to secure effective interim protection of rights having direct effect under Community law where a seriously arguable claim is advanced to be entitled to such rights and where the rights claimed will in substance be rendered nugatory or will be irremediably impaired if not effectively protected during any interim period which must elapse pending determination of a dispute as to the existence of those rights. The basic propositions of Community law on which the appellants rely in support of this submission may be quite shortly summarised. Directly enforceable Community rights are part of the legal heritage of every citizen of a Member State of the EEC. They arise from the Treaty of Rome itself and not from any judgment of the ECJ declaring their existence. Such rights are automatically available and must be given unrestricted retroactive effect. The persons entitled to the enjoyment of such rights are entitled to direct and immediate protection against possible infringement of them. The duty to provide such protection rests with the national court. The remedy to be provided against infringement must be effective, not merely symbolic or illusory. The rules of national law which render the exercise of directly enforceable Community rights excessively difficult or virtually impossible must be overridden.

Mr Vaughan, in a most impressive argument presented in opening this appeal, traced the progressive development of these principles of the jurisprudence of the ECJ through long series of reported decisions on which he relies. I must confess that at the conclusion of his argument I was strongly inclined to the view that, if English law could provide no effective remedy to secure the interim protection of the rights claimed by the appellants, it was nevertheless our duty under Community law to devise such a remedy. But the Solicitor General, in his equally impressive reply, and in his careful and thorough analysis of the case law, has persuaded me that none of the authorities on which Mr Vaughan relies can properly be treated as determinative of the difficult question, which arises for the first time in the instant case, of providing interim protection of putative and disputed rights in Community law before their existence has been established. This is because the relevant decisions of the ECJ, from which the propositions of Community law asserted by Mr Vaughan are derived, were all made by reference to rights which the ECJ was itself then affirming or by reference to the protection of rights the existence of which had already been established by previous decisions of the ECJ.'

Comment

The House of Lords endorsed the principle of supremacy of Community law. The House of Lords held that if the applicants succeeded in their application before the ECJ, their rights protected under Community law would prevail over the restrictions imposed by the 1988 Act. However, the House of Lord made a reference to the ECJ regarding the obligation of the national court to provide an effective interlocutory remedy to protect rights having direct effect under Community law. This was a separate reference from one that had already been made by the Divisional Court.

R v Secretary of State for Transport, ex parte Factortame Ltd and Others Case C–213/89 [1990] ECR I–2433; [1990] 3 CMLR 867 European Court of Justice

• *Supremacy of EC law – conflict between EC law and UK statute – granting of interim relief in the form of the suspension of the statute*

Facts

The House of Lords referred to the ECJ the question of whether or not Community law provides interim protection of rights under Community law in the event of the existence of inconsistent national legislation.

Held

The ECJ held that Community law required that a national court which, in a case before it involving a question of Community law, considered that the sole obstacle which precluded it from granting interim relief was a rule of national law should set aside that rule. As a result, the 1988 Act should be suspended pending the final judgment on its validity.

Judgment

'It is clear from the information before the Court, and in particular from the judgment making reference ... that the preliminary question raised by the House of Lords seeks essentially to ascertain whether a national court which, in a case before it concerning Community law, considers that the sole obstacle which precludes it from granting interim relief is a rule of national law, must disapply that rule.

For the purpose of replying to that question, it is necessary to point out that in its judgment in *Amministrazione delle Finanze dello Stato* v *Simmenthal SpA* [1978] ECR 629 the Court held that directly applicable rules of Community law "must be fully and uniformly applied in all Member States from the date of their entry into force and for so long as they continue in force" and that "in accordance with the principle of precedence of Community law, the relationship between provisions of the Treaty and directly applicable measures of the institutions on the one hand and the national law of the Member States on the other is such that those provisions and measures ... by their entry into force render automatically inapplicable any conflicting provision ... of national law".

In accordance with the case law of the Court, it is for the national court, in application of the principle of co-operation laid down in art 5 of the [EC] Treaty, to ensure the legal protection which persons derive from the direct effect of provisions of Community law.

The Court has also held that any provision of a national legal system and any legislative, administrative or judicial practice which might impair the effectiveness of Community law by withholding from the national court having jurisdiction to apply such law the power to do everything necessary at the moment of its application to set aside national legislative provisions which might prevent, even temporarily, Community rules from having full force and effect are incompatible with those requirements, which are the very essence of Community law.

It must be added that the full effectiveness of Community law would be just as much impaired if a rule of national law could prevent a court seised of a dispute governed by Community law from granting interim relief in order to ensure the full effectiveness of the judgment to be given on the existence of the rights claimed under Community law. It follows that a court which in those circumstances would grant interim relief, if it were not for a rule of national law, is obliged to set aside that rule.

That interpretation is reinforced by the

system established by art 177 of the [EC] Treaty whose effectiveness would be impaired if a national court, having stayed proceedings pending the reply by the Court of Justice to the question referred to it for a preliminary ruling, were not able to grant interim relief until it delivered its judgment following the reply given by the Court of Justice.'

Comment

There should be no difficulties with the recognition of supremacy of Community law in the United Kingdom since when a State accedes to the Communities it must accept the "acquis communautaires". At the time of accession of the United Kingdom, the principle of supremacy was already well rooted in Community law. Furthermore, s2(4) of the European Communities Act 1972 provides that 'any enactment passed or to be passed ... shall be construed and have effect subject to the foregoing provisions of this section'. As a result, all legislative acts enacted subsequent to the European Communities Act 1972 are subject to Community law and thus any conflict between Community law and national subsequent legislation should be resolved in favour of the former on the grounds of supremacy of EC law. For many years , however, the judiciary tried to reconcile the irreconcilable: the principal of supremacy of EC law with Dicey's model of parliamentary sovereignty according to which there is no limit to the legislative power of Parliament subject to the exception that Parliament cannot limit its own powers for the future. It means that no legislation enacted by Parliament is irreversible. The present case confirmed the inevitable.

Their lordships accepted the decision of the ECJ gracefully. Lord Bridge said:

'If the supremacy within the European Community of Community law over national law of Member States was not always inherent in the EEC Treaty it was certainly well-established in the jurisprudence of the European Court of Justice long before the United Kingdom joined the Community. Thus, whatever limitation of its

sovereignty Parliament accepted when it enacted the European Communities Act 1972 it was entirely voluntary. Under the terms of the Act of 1972 it has always been clear that it was the duty of a United Kingdom court, when delivering final judgment, to override any rule of national law found to be in conflict with any directly enforceable rule of Community law' (*Factortame (No 2)*).

Direct applicability and direct effect

Treaty Articles

Defrenne v Sabena (No 2) Case 43/75 [1976] ECR 455; [1976] 2 CMLR 98 European Court of Justice

• *Direct horizontal effect of EC Treaty – art 119 EC Treaty [art 141 EC] – direct and indirect discrimination – limitation ratione temporis of the judgment*

Facts

Miss Defrenne was employed as an air hostess by a Belgian airline company, SABENA. She claimed for loss she sustained in terms of pay she received as compared with male cabin stewards doing the same work. The Court de Travail referred to the ECJ under art 177 EC Treaty [art 234 EC] the question whether she could rely on art 119 EC Treaty [art 141 EC] which prohibits all discrimination between men and women workers and thus requires that they receive equal pay for performing the same task in the same establishment or service.

Held

The ECJ held that in her case it was not difficult to apply art 119 EC Treaty [art 141 EC] as the facts clearly showed that she was discriminated against. It stated that the prohibition on discrimination between men and women applies not only to the action of public authorities, but also extends to all agreements which are intended to regulate paid labour collectively, as contracts between individuals. However, in cases of discrimination which could not be easily identified, implementation measures based on art 119 EC Treaty [art 141 EC] may be necessary.

Judgment

'[*Direct horizontal effect of art 119 EC Treaty*]
The question of the direct effect of art 119 must be considered in the light of the nature of the principle of equal pay, the aim of this provision and its place in the scheme of the Treaty.

Article 119 pursues a double aim.

First, in the light of the different stages of the development of social legislation in the various Member States, the aim of art 119 is to avoid a situation in which undertakings established in States which have actually implemented the principle of equal pay suffer a competitive disadvantage in intra-Community competition as compared with undertakings established in States which have not yet eliminated discrimination against women workers as regards pay.

Secondly, this provision forms part of the social objectives of the Community, which is not merely an economic union, but is at the same time intended, by common action, to ensure social progress and seek the constant improvement of the living and working conditions of their peoples, as is emphasised by the preamble to the Treaty.

... This double aim, which is at once economic and social, shows that the principle of equal pay forms part of the foundations of the Community.

Furthermore, this explains why the Treaty has provided for the complete implementation of this principle by the end of the first stage of the transitional period.

Therefore, in interpreting this provision, it is impossible to base any argument on the dilatoriness and resistance which have delayed the actual implementation of this basic principle in certain Member States.

... Under the terms of the first paragraph of art 119, the Member States are bound to ensure and maintain "the application of the principle that men and women should receive equal pay for equal work".

The second and third paragraphs of the same article add a certain number of details concerning the concepts of pay and work referred to in the first paragraph.

For the purposes of the implementation of these provisions a distinction must be drawn within the whole area of application of art 119 between, first, direct and overt discrimination which may be identified solely with the aid of the criteria based on equal work and equal pay referred to by the article in question and, secondly, indirect and disguised discrimination which can only be identified by reference to more explicit implementing provisions of a Community or national character.

... Among the forms of direct discrimination which may be identified solely by reference to the criteria laid down by art 119 must be included in particular those which have their origin in legislative provisions or in collective labour agreements and which may be detected on the basis of a purely legal analysis of the situation.

This applies even more in cases where men and women receive unequal pay for equal work carried out in the same establishment or service, whether public or private.

... In such situation, at least, art 119 is directly applicable and may thus give rise to individual rights which the courts must protect.

[*Temporal effect of the judgment*]
The governments of Ireland and the United Kingdom have drawn the Court's attention to the possible economic consequences of attributing direct effect to the provisions of art 119, on the ground that such a decision might, in many branches of economic life, result in the introduction of claims dating back to the time at which such effect came into existence.

In view of the large number of people concerned such claims, which undertakings could not have foreseen, might seriously affect the financial situation of such undertakings and even drive some of them to bankruptcy.

... Therefore, the direct effect of art 119 cannot be relied on in order to support claims concerning pay periods prior to the date of this judgment, except as regards those workers who have already brought legal proceedings or made an equivalent claim.'

Comment

This case has established that some provisions of the Treaty may produce horizontal direct effect.

The case law of the ECJ has gradually elucidated which provisions of the Treaty have both direct vertical and horizontal effect. These are: art 119 EC Treaty [art 141 EC], articles relating to competition policy (arts 85 and 86 EC Treaty [arts 81 and 82 EC]), articles concerning the free movement of workers and self-employed (arts 48, 52, 59 and 60 EC Treaty [arts 39, 43, 49 and 50 EC]), and art 6 EC Treaty [art 12 EC] which prohibits discrimination based on nationality,

In addition, art 30 EC Treaty [art 28 EC] which provides for the free movement of goods can be relied upon by an individual against another individual in proceedings before national courts (*Dansk Supermarket A/S* v *A/S Imerco* Case 58/80 [1981] ECR 181).

Preliminary rulings have retroactive effect, that is they apply from the entry into force of the provision in question. For that reason in some cases the ECJ decided to take into consideration the fact that ex tunc effect may cause serious problems in respect of bona fides legal relationships established before the preliminary ruling was delivered and therefore restricted its temporal effects (see *Salumi* Cases 66, 127 and 128/79 [1980] ECR 1258; *Denkavit Italiana* Case 61/79 [1980] ECR 1205; *Blaizot et al* v *University of Liège* Case 24/86 [1988] ECR 379; *Barber* v *Guardian Royal Exchange Assurance Group* Case C–262/88 [1990] ECR I–889; *Société Bautiaa*

Cases C–197 and 252/94 [1996] ECR I–505). Only the ECJ may limit it ex nunc and only in the case in which the ruling was given, not in any subsequent cases. In the present case the ECJ decided to limit ex tunc the temporal effect of its ruling.

Lütticke (Alfons) GmbH v *Hauptzollamt Saarlouis* Case 57/65 [1966] ECR 205 European Court of Justice

• *Direct effect of EC Treaty – requirement of a clear and unconditional obligation imposed on Member States – art 95 EC Treaty [art 90 EC] – discriminatory taxation*

Facts

Lütticke imported whole milk powder from Luxembourg on which German customs levied duty and a turnover tax. Lütticke claimed that the imported product should be exempt from turnover tax as domestic natural milk and wholemilk powder were exempt from the turnover tax. The Finangericht des Saarlands referred the ECJ under art 177 EC Treaty [art 234 EC] to ascertain whether art 95 EC Treaty [art 90 EC], which prohibits the imposition of such tax, has direct effect and thus confers rights upon individuals which a national court must protect.

Held

The ECJ held that art 95 EC Treaty [art 90 EC] was directly effective. The Court stated that this provision contained a general rule which imposed a clear and unconditional obligation on the Member State to refrain from adopting national measures introducing discriminatory internal taxation. The obligation is not qualified by any condition, or subject to the requirement of legislative intervention on the part of the Community institutions. Therefore, art 95 EC Treaty [art 90 EC] being directly effective created rights for individuals to which the national courts must give effect.

Judgment

'The first paragraph of art 95 contains a pro-hibition against discrimination, constituting a clear and unconditional obligation. With the exception of the third paragraph this obligation is not qualified by any condition, or subject, in its implementation or effects, to the taking of any measures either by the institutions of the Community or by the Member States. This prohibition is there-fore complete, legally perfect and conse-quently capable of producing direct effects on the legal relationships between the Member States and persons within their jurisdiction. The fact that this article describes the Member States as being subject to the obligation of non-discrimina-tion does not imply that individuals cannot benefit from it.

With regard to third paragraph of art 95, it indeed imposes an obligation on the Member States to "repeal" or "amend" any provisions which conflict with the rules set out in the preceding paragraphs. The said obligation however leaves no discretion to the Member States with regard to the date by which these obligations must be carried out, that is to say, before 1 January 1962. After this date it is sufficient for the national court to find, should the case arise, that the measures implementing the contested national rules of law were adopted after 1 January 1962, in order to be able to apply the first paragraph directly in any event. Thus the provisions of the third paragraph prevent the application of the general rule only with regard to implementing measures adopted before 1 January 1962, and founded upon provisions existing when the Treaty entered into force.

In the oral and written observations which have been submitted in the course of the proceedings, three governments have relied on art 97 in order to support a different inter-pretation of art 95.

In empowering Member States which levy a turnover tax calculated on a cumula-tive multi-stage tax system to establish average rates for products or groups of prod-ucts, the said article constitutes a special rule for adopting art 95 and this rule is, by its nature, incapable of creating direct effect on the relationship between the Member States and persons subject to their jurisdic-tion. This situation is peculiar to art 97, and can in no circumstances influence the inter-pretation of art 95.

It follows from foregoing that, notwith-standing the exception in the third paragraph for provisions existing when the Treaty entered into force until 1 January 1962, the prohibition contained in art 95 produces direct effects and creates individual rights of which national courts must take account.'

Comment

The ECJ in *Van Gend en Loos* (below) held that direct effect of the Treaty's provisions is not automatic since they must be clear and precise. The question whether other provi-sions of EC Treaty could produce direct effect was confirmed in the present case in respect of art 95 EC Treaty [art 90 EC].

Van Gend en Loos v *Netherlands*
Case 26/62 [1963] ECR 1; [1963] CMLR 105 European Court of Justice

• *Direct effect of EC Treaty – conditions for direct effect – customs duty – art 12 EC Treaty [art 25 EC] – jurisdiction of the ECJ*

Facts

In 1960 Van Gend imported from West Germany into The Netherlands the chemical product, unreaformaldehyde. In December 1959 The Netherlands enacted legislation which modified the Benelux tariff system and which brought into effect the Brussels Convention on Nomenclature unifying the classification of goods for custom purposes. Under the new nomenclature Van Gend's product was reclassified. It resulted in an increase in the duty payable on unreaformaldehyde to 8 per cent on an ad valorem basis as compared to 3 per cent payable previously under Dutch law. On the

14 January 1958 the EEC Treaty came into force. Its art 12 [art 25 EC] provided that:

'Member States shall refrain from introducing between themselves any new custom duties on imports or exports or any charge having equivalent effect, and from increasing those which they already apply in their trade with each other'

Van Gend challenged the increase as contrary to art 12 EC Treaty [art 25 EC]. When its claim was rejected by the customs inspector it appealed to the Dutch Tariecommissie (customs court) in Amsterdam. Under art 177 EC Treaty [art 234 EC] the customs court submitted two questions to the ECJ: first, whether art 12 EC Treaty [art 25 EC] could create rights for individuals as claimed by Van Gend; and, second, provided the answer to the first question was affirmative, whether the modification in custom duties was prohibited by art 12 EC Treaty [art 25 EC].

The governments of Belgium, West Germany and The Netherlands submitted additional memoranda to the ECJ claiming that art 12 EC Treaty [art 25 EC] created obligations for Member States and not rights for individuals. As a result, if a breach of EC law occurred the proceedings should solely be based on arts 169 and 170 EC Treaty [arts 226 and 227 EC].

Held

The ECJ held that art 12 EC Treaty [art 25 EC] should be interpreted as producing direct effects and creating individual rights which national courts must protect.

Judgment

'To ascertain whether the provisions of an international treaty extend so far in their effects it is necessary to consider the spirit, the general scheme and the wording of those provisions.

The objective of the Treaty, which is to establish a Common Market, the functioning of which is of direct concern to interested parties in the Community, implies that this Treaty is more than an agreement which merely creates mutual obligations between the contracting States. This view is confirmed by the preamble to the Treaty which refers not only to governments but to people. It is also confirmed more specifically by the establishment of institutions endowed with sovereign rights, the exercise of which affects Member States and also their citizens. Furthermore, it must be noted that the nationals of the States brought together in the Community are called upon to co-operate in the functioning of this Community through the intermediary of the European Parliament and the Economic and Social Committee.

In addition the task assigned to the Court of Justice under art 177, the object of which is to secure uniform interpretation of that Treaty by national courts and tribunals, confirms that the States have acknowledged that Community law has an authority which can be invoked by their nationals before those courts and tribunals.

The conclusion to be drawn from this is that the Community constitutes a new legal order of international law for the benefit of which the States have limited their sovereign rights, albeit within limited fields, and the subjects of which comprise not only Member States but also their nationals. Independently of the legislation of Member States. Community law therefore not only imposes legislation on individuals but is also intended to confer upon them rights which become part of their legal heritage. These rights arise not only where they are expressly granted by the Treaty, but also by reason of obligations which the Treaty imposes in a clearly defined way upon individuals as well as upon the Member States and upon the institutions of the Community.

With regard to the general scheme of the Treaty as it relates to customs duties and charges having equivalent effect it must be emphasised that art 9, which bases the Community upon a customs union, includes as essential provision the prohibition of these customs duties and charges. This provision is found at the beginning of the part of the Treaty which defines the "Foundations of the Community". It is applied and explained in art 12.

The wording of art 12 contains a clear and unconditional prohibition which is not a positive but a negative obligation. This obligation, moreover, is not qualified by any reservation on the part of States which would make its implementation conditional upon a positive legislative measure enacted under national law. The very nature of this prohibition makes it ideally adopted to produce direct effects in the legal relationship between Member States and their subjects.

The implementation of art 12 does not require any legislative intervention on the part of the States. The fact that under this article it is the Member States who are made the subject of the negative obligation does not imply that their nationals cannot benefit from this obligation.

In addition the argument based on arts 169 and 170 of the Treaty put forward by the three governments which have submitted observations to the Court in their statements of case is misconceived. The fact that these articles of the Treaty enable the Commission and the Member States to bring before the Court a State which has not fulfilled its obligations does not mean that individuals cannot plead these obligations, should the occasion arise, before a national court, any more than the fact that the Treaty placed at the disposal of the Commission ways of ensuring that obligations imposed upon those subject to the Treaty are observed, precludes the possibility, in actions between individuals before a national court, of pleading infringements of these obligations.

A restriction of the guarantees against an infringement of art 12 by Member States to the procedures under art 169 and 170 EC Treaty [arts 226 and 227 EC] would remove all direct legal protection of the individual rights of their nationals. There is the risk that recourse to the procedure under thee Articles would be ineffective if it were to occur after the implementation of a national decision taken contrary to the provisions of the Treaty.

The vigilance of individuals concerned to protect their rights amounts to an effective supervision in addition to the supervision entrusted by arts 169 and 170 to the dili-gence of the Commission and of the Member States.

It follows from the foregoing considerations that, according to the spirit, the general scheme and the wording of the Treaty, art 12 must be interpreted as producing direct effects and creating individual rights which national courts must protect.'

Comment

In the present case the ECJ delivered one of the most important decisions from a point of view of development of Community law. The ECJ held Community law directly effective and thus creating rights and obligations for EC nationals enforceable before national courts.

The ECJ based its decision on a systematic and teleological interpretation of art 12 EC Treaty [art 25 EC]. The Court invoked a number of arguments in support of its decision. It stated that direct effect confirms the peculiar nature of Community law. First, the objectives of the Treaty imply that the Treaty itself is 'more that an agreement which created mutual obligations between the contracting States'. Second, it stems from the Treaty's preamble, which refers not only to the Member States but also to its people as well as the institutional system, that Community law affects both the Member States and their citizens. Third, the Court invoked an argument drawn from art 177 EC Treaty [art 234 EC] that the Member States 'have acknowledged that Community law has an authority which can be invoked by their nationals before those courts and tribunals'. From all these arguments the ECJ inferred that Community law 'independently of the legislation of Member States ... not only imposes obligations on individuals but is also intended to confer upon them rights which become part of their legal heritage'. In addition, direct effect of Community law ensures its effectiveness since the vigilance of individuals concerned to protect their rights amounts to an effective supervision in addition to the supervision entrusted by arts 169 and 170 EC Treaty [arts 226 and 227 EC] to the diligence of the Commission and of the Member States.

In the present case the ECJ established three conditions for a provision of the Treaty to produce direct effect. That provision must be clear, unconditional and self-executing, that is, no further implementing measures are necessary on the part of a Member State or Community institutions.

EC directives

Foster and Others v British Gas plc
Case C–188/89 [1990] ECR I–3313; [1990] 3 CMLR 833 European Court of Justice

• *Direct effect – EC directives – emanation of the State – private corporations – degree of control exercised by the government over the activities of the corporation – Directive 76/207 – discrimination in retirement age between men and women*

Facts
Ms Foster and a number of other female employees were dismissed by the British Gas Corporation, an entity succeeded by British Gas plc, which latter company acquired the rights and liabilities of the former company. The plaintiffs were required to retire at the age of 60, but male employees were not required to retire until they attained the age of 65. An action was raised on the ground that British Gas plc had infringed art 5(1) of Council Directive 76/207 (1976) which had not been incorporated into United Kingdom domestic law.

The House of Lords referred to the ECJ the question whether British Gas plc could be considered an emanation of the State to which the doctrine of the direct effect of unimplemented directives would apply.

Held
The ECJ held that the degree of State control over British Gas plc implied that it was an emanation of the State and the principle of vertical direct effect was applicable.

Judgment
'Before considering the question referred by the House of Lords, it must first be observed as a preliminary point that the United Kingdom has submitted that it is not a matter for the Court of Justice but for the national courts to determine, in the context of the national legal system, whether the provisions of a directive may be relied upon against a body such as the British Gas Corporation.

The question what effects measures adopted by Community institutions have and in particular whether those measures may be relied on against certain categories of persons necessarily involves interpretation of the Articles of the Treaty concerning measures adopted by the institutions and the Community measure in issue.

It follows that the Court of Justice has jurisdiction in proceedings for a preliminary ruling to determine the categories of persons against whom the provisions of a directive may be relied on. It is for the national courts, on the other hand, to decide whether a party before them falls within one of the categories so defined.

As the Court consistently held (see Case 8/81 *Becker (Ursula)* v *Finanzamt Münster-Innenstadt* [1982] ECR 53), where the Community authorities have, by means of a directive, placed Member States under a duty to adopt a certain course of action, the effectiveness of such a measure would be diminished if persons were prevented from relying upon it in proceedings before a court and national courts were prevented from taking into consideration as an element of Community law. Consequently, a Member State which has not adopted the implementing measures required by the directive within the prescribed period may not plead, as against individuals, its own failure to perform the obligations which the directive entails. Thus, wherever the provisions of a directive appear, as far as their subject matter is concerned, to be unconditional and sufficiently precise, those provisions may, in the absence of implementing measures adopted within the prescribed period, be relied upon as against any national provision which is incompatible with the directive or in so far as the provisions define rights which individuals are able to assert against the State.

The Court further held in the *Marshall* case [*Marshall* v *Southampton and South-West Hampshire Area Health Authority (Teaching) (No 1)* Case 152/84 [1986] ECR 723] that where a person is able to rely on a directive as against the State he may do so regardless of the capacity in which the latter is acting, whether as employer or as public authority. In either case it is necessary to prevent the State from taking advantage of its own failure to comply with Community law.

On the basis of those considerations, the Court has held in a series of cases that unconditional and sufficiently precise provisions of a directive could be relied on against organisations or bodies which were subject to the authority or control of the State or had special powers beyond those which result from the normal rules applicable to relations between individuals.

The Court has accordingly held that provisions of a directive could be relied on against tax authorities, local or regional authorities, constitutionally independent authorities responsible for the maintenance of public order and safety, and public authorities providing public health services.

It follows from the foregoing that a body, whatever its legal form, which has been made responsible, pursuant to a measure adopted by the State, for providing a public service under the control of the State and has for that purpose special powers beyond those which result from the normal rules applicable in relations between individuals, is included in any event among the bodies against which the provisions of a directive capable of having direct effect may be relied upon.

With regard to art 5(1) of Directive 76/207 it should be observed that in *Marshall* the Court held that that provision was unconditional and sufficiently precise to be relied on by an individual and to be applied by the national courts.

The answer to the question referred by the House of Lords must therefore be that art 5(1) of Council Directive 76/207 may be relied upon in a claim for damages against a body, whatever its legal form, which has been responsible, pursuant to a measure adopted by the State, for providing a public service under the control of that State and has for that purpose special powers beyond those which result from the normal rules applicable in relations between individuals.'

Comment

In the present case the ECJ elucidated the concept of a State and gave to it a wide interpretation. The ECJ provided a definition of a body which is an emanation of a State. It is a body:

'... whatever its legal form, which has been made responsible pursuant to a measure adopted by a public authority, for providing a public service under the control of that authority and has for that purpose special powers beyond those which result from the normal rules applicable in relations between individuals.'

It results from this definition that three criteria should be satisfied in order to consider an organisation as an emanation of the State. First, it must be made responsible for providing a public service; second, it must provide that service under the control of the State; and, third, it must have special powers, beyond those normally applicable in relations between individuals, to provide that service.

Marshall v *Southampton and South-West Hampshire Area Health Authority (Teaching) (No 1)* Case 152/84 [1986] ECR 723 European Court of Justice

• *Direct vertical effect of EC directives – concept of a State – equal treatment – Directive 76/207/EEC – British Sex Discrimination Act 1975 – discrimination in retirement age between men and women*

Facts

Miss Marshall was an employee of Southampton and South-West Hampshire Area Health Authority (AHA) which maintained a policy of compulsory retirement for women over the age of 60 and men over the age of 65, with extensions in exceptional circumstances. Miss Marshall was dismissed at 62 on the ground that she had exceeded the normal retirement age for women. Miss Marshall wished to remain in employment. She argued that the British Sex Discrimination Act 1975, which excluded from its scope of application provision in relation to death and retirement, was contrary to Council Directive 76/207 on Equal Treatment. The UK had adopted this Directive but had not amended the 1975 Act believing that discrimination in retirement ages was allowed. The Court of Appeal asked the ECJ under art 177 EC Treaty [art 234 EC] whether the dismissal of Miss Marshall was unlawful and whether she was entitled in national courts to rely upon Directive 76/207.

Held

The ECJ held that the policy of the AHA was contrary to the terms of directive 76/207/EEC. The ECJ refused to give horizontal direct effect to EC directives but stated that the AHA was a public body regardless of the capacity in which it was acting, that is public authority or employer. The Court agreed with the argument submitted by the United Kingdom that the possibility of relying on provisions of the Directive against the respondent qua organ of the State would give rise to an arbitrary and unfair distinction between the rights of State employees and those of private employees. The ECJ added that such a distinction would have been avoided if the Member State concerned had correctly implemented the Directive into national law.

Judgment

'It is necessary to consider whether art 5(1) of Directive No 76/207 may be relied upon by an individual before national courts and tribunals.

The appellant and the Commission consider that the question must be answered in the affirmative. They contend in particular, with regard to arts 2(1) and 5(1) of Directive 76/207, that those provisions are sufficently clear to enable national courts to apply them without legislative intervention by the Member States, at least so far as overt discrimination is concerned.

In support of that view, the appellant points out that directives are capable of conferring rights on individuals which may be relied upon directly before the courts of the Member States; national courts are obliged by virtue of the binding nature of a directive, in conjunction with art 5 of the [EC] Treaty, to give effect to the provisions of directives where possible, in particular when construing or applying relevant provisions of national law (Case 14/83 *Von Colson and Kamann* v *Land Nordrhein-Westfalen* [1984] ECR 1891; [1986] 2 CMLR 430). Where there is any inconsistency between national law and Community law which cannot be removed by means of such a construction, the appellant submits that a national court is obliged to declare that the provision of national law is inconsistent with the directive is inapplicable.

The Commission is of the opinion that the provisions of art 5(1) of Directive No 76/207 are sufficiently clear and unconditional to be relied upon before a national court. They may therefore be set up against s6(4) of the Sex Discrimination Act, which, according to the decisions of the Court of Appeal, has been extended to the question of compulsory retirement and has therefore become ineffective to prevent dismissal based upon the difference in retirement ages for men and for women.

The respondent and the United Kingdom propose, conversely, that the second question should be answered in the negative. They admit that a directive may, in certain circumstances, have direct effect as against a Member State in so far as the latter may not rely on its failure to perform its obligations under the directive. However, they maintain that a directive can never impose obligations directly on individuals and that it can only have direct effect against a Member State qua public authority and not against a Member State qua employer. As an employer a State is no different from a provate employer. It would not therefore be proper to put persons employed by the State in a better position than those who are employed by a provate employer.

With regard to the legal position of the respondent's employees the United Kingdom states that they are in the same position as the employees of a private employer. Although according to United Kingdom constitutional law the health authorities, created by the National Health Service Act 1977, as amended by the Health Services Act 1980 and other legislation, are Crown bodies and their employees are Crown servants, nevertheless the administration of the National Health Service by the health authorities is regarded as being separate from the government's central administration and its employees are not regarded as civil servants.

Finally, both the respondent and the United Kingdom take the view that the provisions of Directive No76/207 are neither unconditional nor suffciently clear and precise to give rise to direct effect. The directives provides for a number of possible exceptions, the details of which are to be laid down by the Member States. Furthermore, the wording of art 5 is quite imprecise and requires the adoption of measures for its implementation.

It is necessary to recall that, according to a long line of decisions of the Court (in particular its judgment in Case 8/81 *Becker (Ursula)* v *Finanzamt Münster-Innenstadt* [1982] ECR 53; [1982] 1 CMLR 499), wherever the provisions of a directive appear, as far as their subject matter is concerned, to be unconditional and sufficiently precise, those provisions may be relied upon by an individual against the State where that State fails to implement the directive in national law by the end of the period prescribed or where it fails to implement the directive correctly.

This view is based on the consideration that it would be incompatible with the binding nature which art 189 confers on the directive to hold as a matter of principle that the obligation imposed thereby cannot be relied on by those concerned. From that the Court deduced that a Member State which has not adopted the implementing measures required by the directive within the prescibed period may not plead, as against individuals, its own failure to perform the obligations which the directive entails.

With regard to the argument that a directive may not be relied upon against an individual, it must be emphasised that according to art 189 of the [EC] Treaty the binding nature of a directive, which constitutes the basis for the possibility of relying on the directive before a national court, exist only in relation to "each Member State to which it is addressed". It follows that a directive may not of itself impose obligations on an individual and that a provision of a directive may not be relied upon as such against such a person. It must therefore be examined whether, in this case, the respondent must be regarded as having acted as an individual.

In that respect it must be pointed out that where a person involved in legal proceedings is able to rely on a directive as against the State he may do so regardless of the capacity in which the latter is acting, whether employer or public authority. In either case it is necessary to prevent the State from taking advantage of its own failure to comply with Community law.

It is for the national court to apply those considerations to the circumstances of each case; the Court of Appeal has, however, stated in the order for reference that the respondent, Southampton and South-West Hampshire Area Health Authority (Teaching), is a public authority.

The argument submitted by the United Kingdom that the possibility of relying on provisions of the directive against the respondent qua organ of the State would give rise to an arbitrary and unfair distinction between the rights of State employees and those of private employees does not justify any other conclusion. Such a distinction may easily be avoided if the Member State concerned has correctly implementd the directive in national law.

Finally, with regard to the question whether the provision contained in art 5(1) of Directive No 76/207, which implements the principle of equality of treatment set out in art 2(1) of the directive, may be considered, as far as its contents are concerned, to be unconditional and suficiently precise to be relied upon by an individual as against the State, it must be stated that the provision. taken by itself, prohibits any discrimination on grounds of sex with regard to working conditions, including the conditions governing dismissal, in a general manner and in unequivocal terms. The provision is therefore sufficiently precise to be relied on by an individual and to be applied by the national courts.

It is necessary to consider next whether the prohibition of discrimination laid down by the directive may be regarded as unconditional, in the light of the exceptions contained therein and of the fact that according to art 5(2) thereof the Member States are to take the measures necessary to ensure the application of the principal of equality of treatment in the context of national law.

With regard, in the first place, to the reservation contained in art 1(2) of Directive No 76/207 concerning the application of the principle of equality of treatment in matters of social security, it must be observed that, although the reservation limits the scope of the directive ratione materiae, it does not lay down any condition on the application of that principle in its field of operation and in particular in relation to art 5 of the directive. Similarly, the exceptions to Directive No 76/207 provided for in art 2 thereof are not relevant to this case.

It follows that art 5 of Directive No 76/207 does not confer on the Member States the right to limit the application of the principle of equality of treatment in its field of operation or to subject it to conditions and that that provision is sufficiently precise and unconditional to be capable of being relied upon by an individual before a national court in order to avoid the applica-

tion of any national provision which does not conform to art 5(1).

Consequently, the answer to the second question must be that art 5(1) of Council Directive No 76/207 of 9 February 1976, which prohibits any discrimination on grounds of sex with regard to working conditions, including the conditions governing dismissal, may be relied upon as against a State authority acting in its capacity as employer, in order to avoid the application of any national provision which does not conform to art 5(1).'

Comment

In the present case the ECJ refused to confer on EC directives direct horizontal effect. Therefore, the ECJ restricted the application of the doctrine of the direct effect of EC directives by finding that the terms of unimplemented directives could only be relied upon against a State authority acting as an employer. In order to attenuate this restriction the ECJ extended the concept of a State. The obvious question that arises is what bodies should be considered as being an emanation of the State. In general, the answer is simple. The dichotomy of public/private body is well recognised under national laws of all Member States. Nevertheless, the ECJ in order to maximise the effect of EC directives has introduced an autonomous Community meaning of public body.

Pubblico Ministero v *Ratti* Case 148/78 [1979] ECR 1629; [1980] 1 CMLR 96 European Court of Justice

• *Directives – non-implemented – direct effect – conditions for direct effect – expiry of the time-limit for implementation – non-application of pre-existing national law where EC law harmonising measures introduced less rigorous standards*

Facts

Council directives were passed in 1973 and 1977 on the labelling and packaging of solvents and toxic substances respectively. Italy maintained even stricter requirements and failed to implement these directives into national law. Ratti was selling solvents and varnishes. He fixed labels to certain dangerous substances in conformity with Directive 73/173 and Directive 77/128 but contrary to Italian legislation of 1963. He was prosecuted by Italian authorities for breach of Italian legislation. Directive 73/173 was not implemented in Italy although the time-limit prescribed for its implementation elapsed on 8 December 1974. Also Directive 77/128 was not transposed into Italian law but the time-limit for its implementation had not yet expired. The Milan court asked the ECJ under art 177 EC Treaty [art 234 EC] which set of rules should be applied, national law or Directives 73/173 and 77/128.

Held

The ECJ held that if the provisions of an EC directive are sufficiently precise and unconditional, although not implemented within the prescribed period, an individual may rely upon them. However, if the time-limit for implementation into national law had not been reached at the relevant time, the obligation was not directly effective.

Judgment

'[T]he settled case law of the Court, last reaffirmed by the judgment of the Court in Case 51/76 *Nederlandse Ondernemingen* [1977] ECR 113, lays down that, whilst under art 189 regulations are directly applicable and, consequently, by their nature capable of producing direct effects, that does not mean that other categories of acts covered by that article can never produce similar effects.

It would be incompatible with the binding effect which art 189 ascribes to directives to exclude on principle the possibility of the obligations imposed by them being relied on by persons concerned.

Particularly in cases in which the Community authorities have, by means of directive, placed Member States under a

duty to adopt a certain course of action, the effectiveness of such act would be weakened if persons concerned were prevented from relying on it in legal proceedings and national courts prevented from taking it into consideration as an element of Community law.

Consequently a Member State which has not adopted the implementing measures required by the directive in the prescribed periods may not rely, as against individuals, on its own failure to perform the obligations which the directive entails.

It follows that a national court requested by a person who has complied with the provisions of a directive not to apply a national provision incompatible with the directive not incorporated into the internal legal order of a defaulting Member State, must uphold the request if the obligation in question is unconditional and sufficently precise.

Therefore the answer to the first question must be that after the expiration of the period fixed for the implementaion of a directive a Member State may not apply its internal law – even if it is provided with penal sanctions – which has not yet been adopted in compliance with the directive, to a person who has complied with the requirements of the directive.

In the second question the national court asks, essentially, whether, in incorporating the provisions of the directive on solvents into its internal legal order, the State to which it is addressed may prescribe "obligations and limitations which are more precise and detailed than, or at all events different from, those set out in the directive", requiring in particular information not required by the directive to be affixed to the containers.

The combined effect of arts 3 to 8 of Directive 73/173 is that only solvents which "comply with the provisions of this directive and the annex thereto" may be placed on the market and that Member States are not entitled to maintain, parallel with the rules laid down by the said directive for imports, different rules for the domestic market.

Thus it is a consequence of the system introduced by Directive 73/173 that a

Member State may not introduce into its national legislation conditions which are more restrictive than those laid down in the directive in question, or which are even more detailed or in any event different, as regards the classification, packaging and labelling of solvents, and that this prohibition on the imposition of restrictions not provided for applies both to the direct marketing of the products on the home market and to imported products.

The second question submitted by the national court must be answered in that way.'

Comment

In order to curtail non-implementation of EC directives by the Member States within a specific time-limit, usually laid down in the measures themselves, the ECJ held in the present case that after the expiration of the period fixed for the implementation of a directive a Member State may not apply its internal law which is not in conformity with Community law to a person who has complied with the requirements of the directive. A logical corollary to this principle is that a Member State which has failed to transpose an EC directive within the prescribed time-limit cannot rely on an unimplemented directive in proceedings against individuals.

Van Duyn v *Home Office* Case 41/74 [1974] ECR 1337 European Court of Justice

• *Direct vertical effect of EC directives – Directive 64/221/EEC – free movement of workers – art 48 EC Treaty [art 39 EC] – public policy exception*

Facts

Miss Van Duyn, a Dutch national, arrived at Gatwick Airport on 9 May 1973. She intended to work as a secretary at the British headquarters of the Church of Scientology of California. British immigration authorities refused her leave to enter on the grounds of public policy. Although it was not unlawful to work for the Church of Scientology, the government of the United Kingdom warned foreigners that the effect of the Church's activities were harmful to the mental health of those involved. Miss Van Duyn challenged the decision of the immigration authorities on two grounds: the basis of art 48 EC Treaty [art 39 EC] which grants workers the right to free movement between Member States subject to its para 3 which imposes limitations on grounds of public policy, public security or public health; and on the basis of art 3(1) of Directive 64/221 which further implements art 48(3) EC Treaty [art 39(3) EC] and which provides that measures taken by Member States regarding public policy must be 'based exclusively on the personal conduct of the individual concerned'. She claimed that art 3(1) of Directive 64/221 was directly effective and that the refusal to allow her to enter the UK was not based on her conduct but on the general policy of the British government towards the Church of Scientology.

For the first time an English court referred to the ECJ under art 177 EC Treaty [art 234 EC]. The High Court asked the question whether both art 48 EC Treaty [art 39 EC] and the Directive were directly effective.

Held

The ECJ held that both art 48 EC Treaty [art 39 EC] and the Directive produce direct effect. In particular, the ECJ held that given the nature, general scheme and wording of art 3(1) of Directive 64/221 its effectiveness would be greater if individuals were entitled to invoke it in national courts. Therefore, based on the principle of effect utile the ECJ decided that art 3(1) of Directive 64/221 was directly effective. The United Kingdom was entitled to rely on the public policy exception to refuse admission to Miss Van Duyn.

Judgment

'[*First question*]
By the first question, the Court is asked to say whether art 48 of the [EC] Treaty is

directly applicable so as to confer on individuals rights enforceable by them in the courts of a Member State.

It is provided, in art 48(1) and (2), that freedom of movement for workers shall be secured by the end of the transitional period and that such freedom shall entail "the abolition of any discrimination based on nationality between workers of Member States as regards employment, remuneration and other conditions of work and employment".

These provisions impose on Member States a precise obligation which does not require the adoption of any further measure on the part either of the Community institutions or of the Member States and which leaves them, in relation to its implementation, no discretionary power.

Paragraph (3), which defines the rights implied by the principle of freedom of movement for workers, subjects them to limitations justified on grounds of public policy, public security or public heath. The application of these limitations is, however, subject to judicial control, so that a Member State's right to invoke the limitations does not prevent the provisions of art 48, which enshrine the principle of freedom of movement for workers, from conferring on individuals rights which are enforceable by them and which the national courts must protect.

The reply to the first question must therefore be in the affirmative.

[Second question]
The second question asks the Court to say whether Council Directive 64/221 of 25 February 1964 on the co-ordination of special measures concerning the movement and residence of foreign nationals which are justified on grounds of public policy, public security or public health is directly applicable so as to confer on individuals rights enforceable by them in courts of a Member State.

It emerges from the order making the reference that the only provision of the Directive which is relevant is that contained in art 3(1) which provides that "measures taken on grounds of public policy or public security shall be based exclusively on the personal conduct of the individual concerned".

The United Kingdom observes that, since art 189 of the Treaty distinguishes between the effects ascribed to regulations, directives and decisions, it must therefore be presumed that the Council in issuing a directive rather than making a regulation, must have intended that the directive should have an effect other than that of a regulation and accordingly that the former should not be directly applicable.

If, however, by virtue of the provisions of art 189, regulations are directly applicable and, consequently, may by their very nature have direct effects, it does not follow from this that other categories of acts mentioned in that art can never have similar effects. It would be incompatible with the binding effect attributed to a directive by art 189 to exclude, in principle, the possibility that the obligation which it imposes may be invoked by those concerned. In particular, where the Community authorities have, by directive, imposed on Member States the obligation to pursue a particular course of conduct, the useful effect of such an act would be weakened if individuals were prevented from relying on it before their national courts and if the latter were prevented from taking it into consideration as an element of Community law. Article 177, which empowers national courts to refer to the Court questions concerning the validity and interpretation of all acts of the Community institutions, without distinction, implies furthermore that these acts may be invoked by individuals in the national courts. It is necessary to examine, in every case, whether the nature, general scheme and wording of the provision in question are capable of having direct effects on the relations between Member States and individuals.

By providing that measures taken on grounds of public policy shall be based exclusively on the personal conduct of the individual concerned, art 3(1) of Directive 64/221 is intended to limit the discretionary power which national laws generally confer on the authorities responsible for the entry and expulsion of foreign nationals. First, the provision lays down an obligation which is not subject to any exception or condition and which, by its very nature, does not require the intervention of any act on the part either of the institutions of the Community or of Member State. Secondly, because Member States are thereby obliged, in implementing a clause which derogates from one of the fundamental principles of the Treaty in favour of individuals, not to take account of factors extraneous to personal conduct, legal certainty for the persons concerned requires that they should be able to rely on this obligation even though it has been laid down in a legislative act which has no automatic direct effect in its entirety.

If the meaning and exact scope of the provision raise questions of interpretation, these questions can be resolved by the courts, taking into account also the procedure under art 177 of the Treaty.

Accordingly, in reply to the second question, art 3(1) of Council Directive 64/221 of 25 February 1964 confers on individuals rights which are enforceable by them in the courts of a Member State and which the national courts must protect.'

Comment

The ECJ for the first time expressly recognised the direct effect of an EC directive.

The general principle is that EC directives should be correctly implemented into national law so that individuals can rely on their provisions before national courts through the national implementing measures. There should be no need to verify whether a provision of an EC directive satisfies the three criteria for direct effect, that is, it must be clear and precise, unconditional and self-executing. In this way, an individual may secure rights conferred by EC directives in the manner envisaged by art 189 EC Treaty [art 249 EC]. Therefore, the question of direct effect does not arise since the correct transposition of provisions of EC directives means that they are part of national law. The

question whether an EC directive has been correctly implemented into national law concerns, in reality, the conformity of national law with EC law and not the question of direct effect. Thus, any provision of an EC directive transposed into national law may be invoked in any dispute (including a dispute between individuals) in order to verify whether national authorities have implemented it in accordance with requirements specified in the directive (*Nederlandse Ondernemingen* Case 51/76 [1977] ECR 113 at 127). Direct effect of EC directive becomes an issue only if the implementation measures adopted by a Member State are incompatible with its provisions (*Enka BV* v *Inspecteur der Invoerrechten en Accijnzen Arnhem* Case 38/77 [1977] ECR 2203; *Fratelli Costanzo SpA* v *Commune di Milano* Case 103/88 [1989] ECR 1839) or insufficient (*Rutili* v *Minister for the Interior* Case 36/75 [1975] ECR 1219) or (as in *Pubblico Ministero* v *Ratti* Case 148/78) not implemented within the prescribed time-limit.

Indirect effect

Marleasing SA v *La Comercial Internacional de Alimentacion SA*
Case C–106/89 [1990] ECR I–4135; [1992] 1 CMLR 305 European Court of Justice

• *EC directives – horizontal direct effect – interpretation of national law in conformity with EC law – arts 5 and 189 EC Treaty [arts 10 and 249 EC] – company law – Directive 68/151 – grounds for annulment of a company – lack of cause – lack of consideration*

Facts

A Spanish company was formed, allegedly to defraud the creditors of one of its founders. The company took over the assets of the individuals setting it up, and for legal purposes this process put the assets of those individuals beyond the reach of their creditors. Certain creditors sought to have the 'founders contract', which is one way of setting up a company in Spanish law, voided for lack of consideration or, in the alternative, on the ground that it was a sham transaction vitiated by the lack of a lawful cause.

The defendants argued that under art 11 of the EC First Company Directive 68/151, which provided an exhaustive list of the grounds on which the nullity of a company may be declared, lack of consideration or lack of lawful cause was not mentioned. Directive 68/151 was not implemented in Spain although the prescribed time-limit for its implementation had elapsed. The Spanish court asked the ECJ under art 177 EC Treaty [art 234 EC] proceedings whether art 11 of Directive 68/151 was directly effective and whether it prevented a declaration of nullity on grounds other than enumerated in that provision.

Held
The ECJ confirmed that EC directives could not produce horizontal direct effect, thus the defendants could not rely on art 11 in proceedings against another individual. Also art 11 of Directive 68/151 exhaustively listed the grounds of nullity and did not include the grounds on which Marleasing relied. Nevertheless, the ECJ held that, based on its judgment in *Von Colson*, a Spanish court was obliged 'so far as was possible' to interpret national law, whether it pre-dated or post-dated the Directive, in the light of its terms – meaning that a Spanish court had to interpret Spanish law in such a way as to disregard provisions of the Spanish Civil Code which pre-dated Directive 68/151. Therefore, the formation of the company could not be declared null or void for lack of consideration or lack of lawful cause.

Judgment
'With regard to the question whether an

individual may rely on the directive against a national law, it should be observed that, as the Court has consistently held, a directive may not of itself impose obligations on an individual and, consequently, a provision of a directive may not be relied upon as such against such a person.

However, it is apparent from the documents before the Court that the national court seeks in substance to ascertain whether a national court hearing a case which falls within the scope of Directive 68/151 is required to interpret its national law in the light of the wording and purpose of that directive in order to preclude a declaration of nullity of a public limited company on a ground other than those listed in art 11 of the Directive.

In order to reply to that question, it should be observed that, as the Court pointed out in *Von Colson and Kamann v Land Nordrhein-Westfalen* [1984] ECR 1891, the Member State's obligation arising from a directive to achieve the result envisaged by the directive and their duty under art 5 [EC] to take all appropriate measures, whether general or particular, to ensure the fulfilment of that obligation, is binding on all the authorities of Member States including, for matters within their jurisdiction, the courts. It follows that, in applying national law, whether the provisions in question were adopted before or after the directive, the national court called upon to interpet it is required to do so, so far as possible, in the light of the wording and the purpose of the directive in order to achieve the result pursued by the latter and thereby comply with the third paragraph of art 189 [EC].

It follows that the requirement that national law must be interpreted in conformity with art 11 of Directive 68/151 precludes the interpretation of provisions of national law relating to public limited companies in such a manner that the nullity of a public limited company may be ordered on grounds other than those exhaustively listed in art 11 of the directive in question.

With regard to the interpretation given to art 11 of the Directive, in particular art 11(2)(b), it should be observed that that provision prohibits the laws of the Member States from providing for a judicial declaration of nullity on grounds other than those exhaustively listed in the Directive, amongst which is the ground that the objects of the company are unlawful or contrary to public policy.

According to the Commission, the expression "objects of the comapny" must be interpreted as referring exclusively to the objects of the company as described in the instrument of incorporation or the articles od assiciation. It follows, in the Commission's view, that a declaration of nullity of a company cannot be made on the basis of the activity pursued by it, for instance defrauding the founder's creditors.

That argument must be upheld. As is clear from the preamble to Directive 65/151, its purpose was to limit the cases in which nullity can arise and the retroactive effect of a declaration of nullity in order to ensure "certainty in the law as regards relations between the company and third parties, and also between members". Furthermore, the protection of third parties "must be ensured by provisions which restrict to the greatest possible extent the grounds on which obligations entered into in the name of the company are not valid". It follows, therefore, that each ground of nullity provided in art 11 of the Directive must be interpreted strictly. In those circumstances the words "objects of the company" must be understood as referring to the objects of the company as described in the instrument of incorporation or the articles of association.

The answer to the question submitted must therefore be that a national court hearing a case which falls within the scope of Directive 68/151 is required to interpret its national law in the light of the wording and purpose of that Directive in order to preclude a declaration of nullity of a public limited company on a ground other than those listed in art 11 of the Directive.'

Comment

Marleasing is a very controversial case. On the one hand, the ECJ stated that the obliga-

tion to interpret national law in conformity with EC law is demanded only 'as far as possible', on the other hand it did not require a national judge to interpret a national provision in the light of the Directive. It simply strikes down a conflicting national provision which was never intended to implement Directive 68/151.

Von Colson and Kamann v Land Nordrhein-Westfalen Case 14/83 [1984] ECR 1891 and *Harz v Deutsche Tradax GmbH* Case 79/83 [1984] ECR 1921 European Court of Justice

• *EC directives – interpretation of national law in conformity with EC law – arts 5 and 189 of EC Treaty [arts 10 and 249 EC] – Directive 76/207 – sex discrimination – insufficient national remedy*

Facts

Both Von Colson and Harz were females discriminated against on grounds of gender when applying for a job. Von Colson was in the public service when she applied for the post of prison social worker and Harz was in the private sector when she applied to join a training programme with a commercial company. Under German law implementing Council Directive 76/207 they were entitled to receive only nominal damages, being reimbursement of their travel expenses. They claimed that the implementation was contrary to art 6 of Directive 76/207 which provided that:

'Member States shall introduced into their national legal systems such measures as are necessary to enable all persons who consider themselves wronged by failure to apply to them the principle of equal treatment ... to pursue their claims by judicial process after possible recourse to other competent authorities.'

Both applicants argued that they should be offered the post applied for or receive substantial damages. The German labour court referred under art 177 EC Treaty [art 234 EC] to ECJ the questions whether art 6 of Directive 76/207 was directly effective and whether under that Directive Member States were required to provide for particular sanctions or other legal consequences in cases of discrimination on grounds of sex against a person seeking employment.

Held

The ECJ avoided the question of direct effect of art 6 of Directive 76/207 and instead concentrated on the interpretation of national law in conformity with EC law. It held that national law must be interpreted in such a way as to achieve the result required by the Directive regardless of whether the defendant was the State or a private party.

Judgment

'[This part of the judgment is identical in both cases]

... the Member States' obligation arising from a directive to achieve the result envisaged by the directive and their duty under art 5 of the Treaty to take all appropriate measures, whether general or particular, to ensure the fulfilment of that obligation, is binding on all authorities of Member States including, for matters within their jurisdiction, the courts. It follows that, in applying the national law and in particular the provisions of a national law specifically introduced in order to implement Directive No 76/207, national courts are required to interpret their national law in the light of the wording and the purpose of the Directive in order to achieve the result referred to in the third paragraph of art 189.

On the other hand, as the above considerations show, the Directive does not include any unconditional and sufficiently precise obligation as regards sanctions for discrimination which, in the absence of implementing measures adopted in good time, may be relied on by individuals in order to obtain specific compensation under the Directive, where that is not provided for or permitted under national law.

It should, however, be pointed out to the national court that although Directive No 76/207/EEC, for the purpose of imposing sanctions for the breach of the prohibition of discrimination, leaves the Member States free to choose between the different solutions suitable for achieving its objective, it nevertheless requires that if a Member State chooses to penalise breaches of that prohibition by the award of compensation, then in order to ensure that it is effective and that it has a deterrent effect, that compensation must in any event be adequate in relation to the damage sustained and must therefore amount to more than purely nominal compensation such as, for example, the reimbursement only of the expense incurred in connection with the application. It is for the national court to interpret and apply the legislation adopted for the implementation of the Directive in conformity with the requirements of Community law, in so far as it is given discretion to do so under national law.'

Comment

In *Von Colson* and *Harz* the ECJ provided a new solution to the problem of lessening the vertical/horizontal public/private dichotomy regarding EC directives. The ECJ held that national judges are required to interpret national law in the light of the text and objectives of Community law, in the present cases it was an EC directive. This solution is based on art 5 EC Treaty [art 10 EC] which applies to all national bodies, including national courts which have a duty to ensure that national law conforms with Community law and thus the requirement of the principle of effect utile is satisfied, that is, rights vested in individuals by Community law are protected by national courts.

The principle of interpretation of national law in conformity with EC law constitutes a logical consequence of the supremacy of EC law and applies in relation to all Community law irrespective of whether or not a provision of EC law is directly effective. National law whether anterior or subsequent must conform to Community law.

In *Von Colson* and *Harz* the interpretation of national law in conformity with the Directive resulted in providing an efficient remedy to the applicants tantamount to conferring on art 6 of Directive 76/207 horizontal direct effect. The German labour court found that it had power to award damages to both plaintiffs not exceeding six months' gross salary.

Webb v EMO Air Cargo (UK) Ltd (No 2) [1995] 4 All ER 577 House of Lords

• *EC directives – interpretation of national law in conformity with EC law – Directive 76/207 – unlawful dismissal – pregnancy – ss1(1)(a) and 5(3) of the Sex Discrimination Act 1975*

Facts

Ms Webb was offered a temporary job to replace her colleague who was taking maternity leave. Before the commencement of her employment Mrs Webb discovered that she was pregnant and as a result she was dismissed. She argued that her dismissal was unlawful under Directive 76/207 which prohibits discrimination based on sex. The House of Lords, called to interpret the Sex Discrimination Act 1975 which implemented Directive 76/207 asked, the ECJ under art 177 EC Treaty [art 234 EC] proceedings whether Ms Webb's dismissal was contrary to Directive 76/207.

Held

The ECJ held that Ms Webb's dismissal was in breach of Directive 76/207.

Judgment

Lord Keith of Kinkel (at p582 a–h):

'The provisions of the 1975 Act which your Lordships must endeavour to construe, so as to accord if at all possible with the ruling of the European Court, are ss1(1)(a) and 5(3).

Section 1(1)(a) provides:

"A person discriminates against a woman in any circumstances relevant for the purposes of any provisions of this Act if – (a) on the ground of her sex he treats her less favourably than he treats or would treat a man ..."

Section 5(3) provides:

"A comparison of the cases of persons of different sex and martial status under section 1(1) or 3(1) must be such that the relevant circumstances in the one case are the same or not materially different, in the other."

The reasoning in my speech in the earlier proceedings was to the effect that the relevant circumstances which existed in the present case, and which should be taken to be present in the case of the hypothetical man, was unavailability for work at the time when the worker was particularly required, and that the reason for the unavailability was not a relevant circumstance (see [1994] 4 All ER 929 at 933–935; [1993] 1 WLR 49 at 53–55). So it was not relevant that the reason for the woman's unavailability was pregnancy, a condition which could not be present in a man.

The ruling of the European Court proceeds on an interpretation of the broad principles dealt with in arts 2(1) and 5(1) of Directive 76/207. Sections 1(1)(a) and 5(3) of the 1975 Act set out a more precise test of unlawful discrimination, and the problem is how to fit the terms of that test into the ruling. It seems to me that the only way of doing so is to hold that, in a case where a woman is engaged for an indefinite period, the fact that the reason why she will be temporarily unavailable for work at a time when to her knowledge her services will be particularly required is pregnancy is a circumstance relevant to her case, being a circumstance which could not be present in the case of the hypothetical man. It does not necessarily follow that pregnancy would be a relevant circumstance in the situation where the woman is denied employment for a fixed period in the future during the whole of which her pregnancy would make her unavailable for work, nor in the situation where after engagement for such a period the discovery of her pregnancy leads to cancellation of the engagement.

My Lords, for these reasons I would allow the appeal and remit the case to the industrial tribunal to assess compensation.'

Comment

The House of Lords clearly accepted the decision of the ECJ in *Marleasing*, that is, that national legislation pre-dating Community law must be interpreted in conformity with the latter.

In order to interpret the Sex Discrimination Act 1975 as required by Directive 76/207 the House of Lords construed the s5(3) of the 1975 Act concept of 'relevant circumstances' as meaning in the case of Ms Webb her unavailability for work due to pregnancy and not as previously stated her unavailability to work (*Webb* v *EMO Air Cargo (UK) Ltd* [1992] 4 All ER 929 House of Lords). The House of Lords held that a male employee could not be dismissed on those grounds and thus Ms Webb's dismissal was discriminatory.

Limitations on indirect effect

Criminal Proceedings against Kolpinghuis Nijmegen BV Case 80/86 [1989] 2 CMLR 18 European Court of Justice

- *EC directives – non-implementation – right of State authorities to rely on non-implemented directives – criminal proceedings, interpretation of national law in conformity with EC law – Directive 80/777/EEC*

Facts

Directive 80/777/EEC on the approximation of the laws of the Member States relating to the exploitation and marketing of natural waters had not been implemented in The Netherlands within the prescribed time-limit.

After its implementation period elapsed, but before the entry into force of national implementing measures, criminal proceedings were brought against Kolpinghuis Nijmengen for non-compliance of its beverage (intended for trade and human consumption which was called 'mineral water' but which consisted of tap water and carbon dioxide) with art 2 of the Dutch inspection regulation of the municipality of Nijmengen which prohibited the marketing of waters 'of unsound composition' as natural mineral waters. The problem with the Dutch regulation was that it did not define the expression 'unsound composition' although Directive 80/777/EEC contained specific provisions as to the composition of natural mineral water. The Dutch public prosecutor (the Officier van Justitie) argued that the Directive in question should have guided the national court in the interpretation of a national law which predated the Directive, since from the end of the transposition period the Directive had the force of law in The Netherlands.

Held

The ECJ held that a Member State in order to impose criminal liability on individuals could not rely on its own failure to fulfil an obligation arising out of the Treaty. This decision was based on the well established principle that EC directives can never impose direct obligations on individuals since they are addressed to Member States and therefore individuals may only be bound by the legislation or regulations which a Member State to which the directive is addressed is obliged to adopt.

Judgment

'[*The obligation to interpret national law in conformity with EC law*]
As the Court stated in its judgment of 10 April 1984 in Case 14/83 *Von Colson and Kamann* v *Land Nordrhein-Westfalen* [1984] ECR 1891, the Member States' obligation arising from a directive to achieve the result envisaged by the directive and their duty under art 5 of the Treaty to take all

appropriate measures, whether general or particular, to ensure the fulfilment of that obligation, is binding on all authorities of Member States including, for matters within their jurisdiction, the courts. It follows that, in applying the national law and in particular the provisions of a national law specifically introduced in order to implement the directive, national courts are required to interpret their national law in the light of the wording and the purpose of the directive in order to achieve the result referred to in the third paragraph of art 189 of the Treaty.

However, that obligation on the national court to refer to the content of the directive when interpreting the relevant rules of its national law is limited by the general principles of law which form part of Community law and in particular the principles of legal certainty and non-retroactivity. Thus the Court ruled in its judgment of 11 June 1987 in Case 14/86 *Pretore di Salo* v *X* [1987] ECR 2545 that a directive cannot, of itself and independently of a national law adopted by a Member State for its implementation, have the effect of determining or aggravating the liability in criminal law of persons who act in contravention of the provisions of that directive.

[A Member State cannot base proceedings on an unimplemented directive when it failed to implement it within the prescribed time-limit]
[A]ccording to the established case law of the Court whenever the provisions of a directive appear, as far as their subject matter is concerned, to be unconditional and sufficiently precise, those provisions may be relied upon by an individual against the State where that State fails to implement the directive into national law by the end of the period prescribed or where it fails to implement the directive correctly.

That view is based on the consideration that it would be incompatible with the binding nature which art 189 confers on the directive to hold as a matter of principle that the obligation imposed thereby cannot be relied on by those concerned. From that the Court deduced that a Member State which has not adopted the implementing measures required by the directive within the prescribed period may not plead, as against individuals, its own failure to perform the obligations which the directive entails.'

Comment

In the present case the ECJ defined the limit of a national court's obligation to interpret national law in conformity with EC law. The ECJ held that the uniform interpretation of Community law must be qualified in criminal proceedings where the effect of interpreting national legislation in the light of the Directive would be to impose criminal liability in circumstances where such liability would not arise under the national legislation taken alone. In the present case the ECJ stated that the obligation for a national judge to make reference to the terms of the Directive, when he interprets relevant provisions of national law, is limited by general principles of Community law and especially by the principles of legal certainty and non-retroactivity. This was further explained in *Criminal Proceedings against X* Joined Cases C–74 and 129/95 [1996] ECR I–6609 in which the ECJ held that:

'... the obligation on the national court to refer to the content of the Directive when interpreting the relevant rules of its national law is not unlimited, particularly where such interpretation would have the effect, on the basis of the Directive and independently of legislation adopted for its interpretation, of determining or aggravating the liability in criminal law of persons who act in contravention of its provisions' (Ibid, para 24).

The ECJ explained that the principle of legality in relation to crime and punishment and especially the principle of legal certainty, its corollary, precludes bringing criminal proceedings in respect of conduct not clearly defined as culpable by law. In support of its decision the ECJ referred to the general principles of law which result from the common constitutional tradition of the Member States and art 7 of the European Convention on Human Rights.

Wagner Miret v *Fondo de Garantia Salarial* Case C–334/92 [1995] 2 CMLR 49 European Court of Justice

• *Directives – horizontal direct effect – interpretation of national law in conformity with EC law – arts 5 and 189 EC Treaty [arts 10 and 249 EC] – Directive 80/987/EEC – State liability*

Facts

Wagner Miret was employed as a senior manager in a Spanish company that became insolvent. Under Directive 80/897 Member States were required to set up a fund compensating employees in the case of insolvency of their employer. Spain established such a fund but it did not apply to senior management staff. The referring court asked whether higher management staff were entitled, by virtue of Directive 80/897, to request payment of unpaid salary from the guarantee body established by national law for the other categories of employee or, if this was not the case, whether they were entitled to base their claims on the principle of State liability in tort for incorrect implementation of Directive 80/897.

Held

The ECJ held that Directive 80/897 was not precise enough to produce direct effect and that Spanish law clearly limited access to the fund. Spanish law could not be interpreted in such a way as to include senior management staff within a group of people to be compensated from that fund. As a result, the duty to interpret national law in conformity with Community law was not absolute so as to require interpretation of national law contra legem but only 'so far as possible'. However, Wagner Miret was not left without remedy as he could bring proceedings against Spain for incorrect implementation of Directive 80/897 as a result of which he suffered damage.

Judgment

'It should first be observed that Spain has

established no guarantee institution other than the Fondo de Garantia Salarial.

Secondly, in its judgment of 19 November 1991 (Case C–6 and 9/90) *Francovich and Bonifaci* v *Italian Republic* [1991] ECR I–5357), the Court held that under art 5 of the directive on the insolvency of employers, the Member States have a broad discretion with regard to the organisation, operation and financing of the guarantee institutions. The Court concluded that even though the provisions of the directive are sufficiently precise and unconditional as regards the determination of the persons entitled to the guarantee and as regards the content of that guarantee, those elements are not sufficient to enable individuals to rely, as against the State, on those provisions, before the national courts.

With regard, more particularly, to the problem raised by the national court, it should be pointed out that the directive on the insolvency of employers does not oblige the Member States to set up a single guarantee institution for all categories of employee, and consequently to bring higher management staff within the ambit of the guarantee institution established for the other categories of employee. Article 3(1) leaves it to the Member States to adopt the measures necessary to ensure that guarantee institutions guarantee payment of employees' outstanding claims.

From the discretion thus given to the Member States it must therefore be concluded that higher management staff cannot rely on the directive in order to request the payment of amounts owing by way of salary from the guarantee institution established for the other categories of employee.

Thirdly, it should be borne in mind that when it interprets and applies national law, every national court must presume that the State had the intention of nullifying entirely the obligations arising from the directive concerned. As the Court held in *Marleasing SA* v *La Commercial Internacional de Alimentacion SA* Case C–106/89, in applying national law, whether the provision in question was adopted before or after the directive, the national court called upon to interpret it is required to do so, as far as possible, in the light of the wording and the purpose of the directive in order to achieve the result pursued by the latter and thereby comply with the third paragraph of art 189 of the Treaty.

The principle of interpretation in conformity with directives must be followed in particular where a national court considers, as in the present case, that the pre-existing provisions of its national law satisfy the requirements of the directive concerned.

It would appear from the order for reference that the national provisions cannot be interpreted in a way which conforms with the directive on the insolvency of employers and therefore do not permit higher management staff to obtain the benefit of the guarantees for which it provides. If that is the case, it follows from the *Francovich* judgment, cited above, that the Member State concerned is obliged to make good the loss and damage sustained as a result of the failure to implement the directive in their respect.'

Comment

In the present case the ECJ limited the scope of *Marleasing*. National courts are under a duty to take into consideration all national law, whether adopted before or after the directive, concerning the matter in question in order to determine whether national legislation can be interpreted in the light of the wording and the purpose of the directive. The interpretation contra legem is required 'as far as possible'.

9　Free Movement of Persons

European citizenship

Criminal Proceedings against Bickel and Franz Case C–274/96 [1998] ECR I–7637 European Court of Justice

• *Citizenship of the European Union – free movement of persons – non-discrimination on the ground of nationality – language rules applicable to criminal proceedings*

Facts
Italian authorities commenced criminal proceedings against Mr Bickel, an Austrian national, who drove his lorry at Castelbello in the Trentino-Aldo Adige region of Italy under the influence of alcohol and Mr Franz, a German national, who, while visiting the same region of Italy, was found by a customs inspection in possession of a type of knife that is prohibited in Italy. Both offenders made a declaration before the District Magistrate of Bolzano that they had no knowledge of Italian and requested that the proceedings were conducted in German on the basis that the German-speaking citizens of the province of Bolzano were permitted to use German in relations with the judicial and administrative authorities located in that province or entrusted with responsibility at regional level. The referring court asked the ECJ whether the situation of both offenders was within the scope of EC Treaty and, if so, whether the right conferred on the German-speaking minority living in the province of Bolzano should be extended to nationals from other German-speaking Member States travelling or staying in that area.

Held
The ECJ held that the right conferred by national rules upon its linguistic minority was within the scope of the EC Treaty. It stated that the principle of non-discrimination embodied in art 6 EC Treaty [art 12 EC] precludes national rules which, in respect of a particular language (other than the principal language of the Member State concerned), confer on citizens whose language is that particular language and who are resident in a defined area the right to require that criminal proceedings be conducted in that language, without conferring the same right on nationals of other Member States travelling or staying in that area, whose language is the same.

Judgment
'Situations governed by Community law include those covered by the freedom to provide services, the right to which is laid down in art 59 of the Treaty. The Court has consistently held that this right includes the freedom for the recipients of services to go to another Member State in order to receive a service there. Article 59 therefore covers all nationals of Member States who, independently of other freedoms guaranteed by the Treaty, visit another Member State where they intend or are likely to receive services. Such persons (and they include both Mr Bickel and Mr Franz) are free to visit and move around within the host State.

In that regard, the exercise of the right to move and reside freely in another Member State is enhanced if the citizens of the Union are able to use a given language to communicate with the administrative and judicial authorities of a State on the same footing as its nationals. Consequently, persons such as Mr Bickel and Mr Franz, in exercising that right in another Member State, are in principle entitled, pursuant to art 6 of the Treaty, to treatment no less favourable than that accorded to nationals of the host State so far as concerns the use of languages which are spoken there.

In the submission of Mr Bickel and Mr Franz, if any discrimination contrary to art 6 of the Treaty is to be avoided, the right to have proceedings conducted in German must be extended to all citizens of the Union, since it is already available to nationals of one of the Member States.

The documents before the Court show that the German-speaking nationals of other Member States, particularly Germany and Austria (such as Mr Bickel and Mr Franz) who travel or stay in the province of Bolzano cannot require criminal proceedings to be conducted in German despite the fact that the national rules provide that the German language is to have the same status as Italian.

In those circumstances, it appears that German-speaking nationals of other Member States travelling or staying in the province of Bolzano are at a disadvantage by comparison with Italian nationals resident there whose language is German ...

... The Italian government's contention that the aim of those rules is to protect the ethno-cultural minority residing in the province in question does not constitute a valid justification in this context. Of course, the protection of such a minority may constitute a legitimate aim. It does not appear, however, from the documents before the Court that that aim would be undermined if the rules in issue were extended to cover German-speaking nationals of other Member States exercising their right to freedom of movement.'

Comment

The ECJ confirmed that although the rules of criminal law and criminal procedure are within the competence of a Member State, that competence cannot be exercised contrary to fundamental principles of Community law – in particular the principle of equality of treatment as stated in art 6 EC Treaty [art 12 EC]. The ECJ based its reasoning on art 8 EC Treaty [art 17 EC] rather than on the principle of non-discrimination on the ground of nationality as the Court wished to emphasise the equality of treatment among the citizens of the EU. From this perspective, the reference to the citizenship of the EU permitted the ECJ to compare German-speaking nationals of the province of Bolzano with German-speaking nationals from other Member States. The ECJ considered that the latter when travelling or staying in that province were disadvantaged in comparison to the former. Therefore, the requirement of residence in the province of Bolzano as a condition for benefiting from a special linguistic regime was neither justified on the ground of objective criteria not related to nationality nor proportional to the aim of Italian rules intended to protect the ethno-cultural German-speaking minority residing in the province of Bolzano. The decision of the ECJ in the present case confirms that the Court pays special attention to the protection of rights and facilities of individuals in linguistic matters (see *Criminal Proceedings against Mutsch* Case 137/84 [1985] ECR 2681).

Criminal Proceedings against Wijsenbeek Case C–378/97 [1999] ECR I–6207 European Court of Justice

• *Freedom of movement for persons – right of citizens of the EU to move and reside freely – border controls – national legislation requiring persons coming from another Member State to present a passport*

Facts

Mr Wijsenbeek, a Dutch national, refused to present and hand over his passport to the national police officer in charge of border controls at Rotterdam Airport when he entered The Netherlands on 17 December 1993. He was ordered by the Kantonrechter to pay a fine of HFL 65 and to serve one day's imprisonment for breach of The Netherlands' legislation requiring Dutch nationals, when entering The Netherlands, to present to officials responsible for border controls travel and identity papers in their possession and to establish by any other means their Dutch nationality. Mr Wijsenbeek appealed from the decision of the Kantonrechter and the appellate court referred a question to the ECJ regarding the compatibility of the Dutch legislation with Community law.

Held

The ECJ held, at the time of the events in question, neither art 14 nor art 18 EC precluded a Member State from requiring a person, whether or not a citizen of the European Union, under threat of criminal penalties, to establish his nationality on his entry into the territory of that Member State upon crossing an internal frontier of the Community. However, the penalties provided for by national legislation must satisfy two conditions: they must be comparable to those which apply to similar infringements of national law, and they must not be so disproportionate as to create an obstacle to the free movement of persons. In this context, the term of imprisonment would appear disproportionate.

Judgment

'The Court observes that the first paragraph of art 7a of the Treaty [now, after amendment, art 14 EC] provides that the Community is to adopt measures with the aim of progressively establishing the internal market before 31 December 1992, in accordance with the provisions of the Treaty cited in that provision. Under the second paragraph of art 7a, the internal market is to comprise an area without internal frontiers in which the free movement of goods, persons, services and capital is ensured in accordance with the provisions of the Treaty.

That Article cannot be interpreted as meaning that, in the absence of measures adopted by the Council before 31 December 1992 requiring the Member States to abolish controls of persons at the internal frontiers of the Community, that obligation automatically arises from expiry of that period. As the Advocate-General points out in point 77 of his Opinion, such an obligation presupposes harmonisation of the laws of the Member States governing the crossing of the external borders of the Community, immigration, the grant of visas, asylum and the exchange of information on those questions (see, to this effect, as regards social security, *Baglieri* [*INPS* v *Baglieri* Case C–297/92 [1993] ECR 5211] paras 16 and 17).

Moreover, art 8a(1) of the Treaty [now, after amendment, art 18 EC] confers the right to move and reside freely in the territory of the Member States on citizens of the Union, subject to the limitations and conditions laid down in the Treaty and by the measures adopted to give it effect. According to art 8a(2) of the Treaty, the Council may adopt provisions with a view to facilitating the exercise of those rights.

However, as the Commission has rightly pointed out, as long as Community provisions on controls at the external borders of the Community, which also imply common or harmonised rules on, in particular, conditions of access, visas and asylum, have not been adopted, the exercise of those rights presupposes that the person concerned is able to establish that he or she has the nationality of a Member State.

At the time of the events in question in the main proceedings, there were no common rules or harmonised laws of the Member States on, in particular, controls at external frontiers and immigration, visa and asylum policy. Consequently, even if, under art 7a or art 8a of the Treaty, nationals of the Member States did have an unconditional right to move freely within the territory of the Member States, the Member States retained the right to carry out identity checks at the internal frontiers of the Community, requiring persons to present a valid identity card or passport, as provided for by Directives 68/360, 73/148, 90/364, 90/365 and 93/96, in order to be able to establish whether the person concerned is a national of a Member State, thus having the right to move freely within the territory of the Member States, or a national of a non-Member country, not having that right.

In the absence of Community rules governing the matter, the Member States remain competent to impose penalties for breach of such an obligation, provided that the penalties applicable are comparable to those which apply to similar national infringements. However, Member States may not lay down a penalty so disproportionate as to create an obstacle to the free movement of persons, such as a term of imprisonment (see, in particular, Case C–265/88 *Messner* [1989] ECR 4209, para 14, and Case C–193/94 *Criminal Proceedings against Skanavi and Chryssanthakopoulos* [1996] ECR I–929, para 36). The same considerations apply as regards breach of the obligation to present an identity card or a passport upon entry into the territory of a Member State.

The answer to be given to the questions submitted must therefore be that, as Community law stood at the time of the events in question, neither art 7a nor art 8a of the Treaty precluded a Member State from requiring a person, whether or not a citizen of the European Union, under threat of criminal penalties, to establish his nationality upon his entry into the territory of that Member State by an internal frontier of the Community, provided that the penalties applicable are comparable to those which apply to similar national infringements and are not disproportionate, thus creating an obstacle to the free movement of persons.'

Comment

Member States are entitled to carry out passport controls at internal Community borders in order to establish the nationality of the person concerned. In this respect the ECJ examined art 14 EC regarding the establishment of the common market on 1 January 1993, an area without internal frontiers in which, inter alia, the free movement of persons is ensured in accordance with the EC Treaty, and art 18 EC under which citizens of the EU have the right to move and reside freely within the EU territory subject to limitations and conditions laid down in the EC Treaty and to measures adopted to give it effect. The ECJ held that art 14 could not be construed as meaning that the obligation to ensure the free movement of persons automatically arose on 1 January 1993 since such an obligation presupposed harmonisation of the Member States' laws governing the crossing of the external borders of the EC, immigration, the grant of visas etc. Furthermore, as long as Community provisions concerning these issues have not been adopted, the exercise of the rights in art 16(1) EC presupposes that a person concerned is required to establish that he has the nationality of a Member State. At the time of the events in the present case there were no such common rules. Consequently, even if citizens of the EU had an unconditional right under arts 14 and 18 EC, the Member States retained the right to carry out identity checks at the internal frontiers of the EU in order to establish whether the person concerned was a national of a Member State.

In the absence of Community rules in this area, the Member States are entitled to impose penalties for refusal to hand over a passport by an EU citizen, provided that the penalties are comparable to those applicable to similar infringements of national law and proportionate. In this case, a term of imprisonment was disproportionate and as such constituted an obstacle to the free movement of persons.

***Sala (Maria Martinez) v Freistaat Bayern* Case C–85/96 [1998] ECR I–2691 European Court of Justice**

• *Citizenship of the European Union – principle of non-discrimination on the ground of nationality – free movement of persons – definition of 'worker' – art 4 of*

Regulation 1408/71 – child-raising allowance – definition of family benefit – art 7(2) of Regulation 1612/68 – definition of social advantage – requirement of possession of a residence permit or authorisation

Facts

The German authorities of the Freistaat Bayern (State of Bavaria) refused to grant a child-raising allowance for a child of Mrs Martinez Sala, a Spanish national who had resided in Germany for many years. The basis of residence was: first, a residence permit (until May 1984); second, documents specifying that she had applied for an extension of her residence permit; third, a residence permit issued on 19 April 1994 and expiring on 18 April 1995; and fourth, a one-year extension (to 18 April 1996) of the residence permit which expired on 18 April 1995. Mrs Martinez Sala was born in 1956 and came to Germany in 1968. Between 1976 and 1986 she had various jobs and was in employment again from 12 September to 24 October 1989. After that she received social assistance from the German authorities. When she applied for child-raising allowance in January 1993 she did not have a residence permit. Her application was refused on the grounds that she was neither a German national nor in possession of a residence entitlement/residence permit. She challenged that decision before a German court which referred to the ECJ for a preliminary ruling on four questions, concerning:

1. whether a national of one Member State who resides in another Member State, where he is employed and receives social assistance has the status of worker;
2. whether a child-raising allowance is considered as a family benefit within the meaning of art 4(1)(h) of Regulation 1408/71; or
3. as a social advantage within the scope of art 7(2) of Regulation 1612/68;
4. whether it is necessary for a national of other Member States to produce a formal

residence permit in order to receive a child-raising benefit in a host Member State.

Held

The ECJ held that Community law precludes a Member State from requiring nationals of other Member States authorised to reside in its territory to produce a formal residence permit in order to receive a child-raising allowance, whereas that Member State's own nationals are only required to be permanently or ordinarily resident in that Member State. The ECJ also stated that a benefit such as the child-raising allowance is considered as a family benefit within the meaning of art 4(1) of Regulation 1408/71, and as a social advantage within the meaning of art 7(2) of Regulation 1612/68. The ECJ left to a national court the decision as to whether a person such as the appellant should be considered as a worker within the meaning of art 48 EC Treaty [art 39 EC].

Judgment

'[*The first question*]
In the present case the referring court has not furnished sufficient information to enable the Court to determine whether a person in the position of the appellant in the main proceedings is a worker within the meaning of art 48 of the Treaty and Regulation No 1612/68, by reason, for example, of the fact that she is seeking employment. It is for the national court to undertake that investigation.

[*The second and third questions*]
In its judgment of 10 October 1996 in *Hoever and Zachow* v *Land Nordrhein-Westfalen* Cases C–245 and 312/94 [1996] ECR I–4895 the Court has already held that a benefit such as the child-raising allowance provided for by the BErzGG [the Federal Law on the Grant of Child-raising Allowance and Parental Leave], which is automatically granted to persons fulfilling certain objective criteria, without any individual and discretionary assessment of per-

sonal needs, and which is intended to meet family expenses, must be treated as a family benefit within the meaning of art 4(1)(h) of Regulation No 1408/71.

The child-raising allowance in question here is an advantage granted, inter alia, to workers who work part-time. It is therefore a social advantage within the meaning of art 7(2) of Regulation No 1612/68.

[The fourth question]
Whilst Community law does not prevent a Member State from requiring nationals of other Member States lawfully resident in its territory to carry at all times a document certifying their right of residence, if an identical obligation is imposed upon its own nationals as regards their identity cards, the same is not necessarily the case where a Member State requires nationals of other Member States, in order to receive a child-raising allowance, to be in possession of a residence permit for the issue of which the administration is responsible.

For the purposes of recognition of the right of residence, a residence permit can only have declaratory and probative force. However, the case-file shows that, for the purposes of the grant of the benefit in question, possession of a residence permit is constitutive of the right to the benefit.

Consequently, for a Member State to require a national of another Member State who wishes to receive a benefit such as the allowance in question to produce a document which is constitutive of the right to the benefit and which is issued by its own authorities, when its own nationals are not required to produce any document of that kind, amounts to unequal treatment.

In the sphere of application of the Treaty and in the absence of any justification, such unequal treatment constitutes discrimination prohibited by art 6 of the EC Treaty.

The German government, while accepting that the condition imposed by the BErzGG constituted unequal treatment within the meaning of art 6 of the Treaty, argued that the facts of the case being considered in the main proceedings did not fall within either the scope ratione materiae or the scope ratione personae of the Treaty so that the appellant in the main proceedings could not rely on art 6.

As regards the scope ratione materiae of the Treaty, reference should be made to the replies given to the first, second and third questions, according to which the child-raising allowance in question in the main proceedings indisputably falls within the scope ratione materiae of Community law.

As regards its scope ratione personae, if the referring court were to conclude that, in view of the criteria provided in reply to the first preliminary question, the appellant in the proceedings before it has the status of worker within the meaning of art 48 of the Treaty and of Regulation No 1612/68 or of employed person within the meaning of Regulation No 1408/71, the unequal treatment in question would be incompatible with arts 48 and 51 of the Treaty.

Should this not be the case, the Commission submits that, in any event, since 1 November 1993 when the Treaty on European Union came into force, the appellant in the main proceedings has a right of residence under art 8a of the EC Treaty, which provides that: "Every citizen of the Union shall have the right to move and reside freely within the territory of the Member States, subject to the limitations and conditions laid down in this Treaty and by the measures adopted to give it effect."

According to art 8(1) of the EC Treaty, every person holding the nationality of a Member State is to be a citizen of the Union.

As a national of a Member State lawfully residing in the territory of another Member State, the appellant in the main proceedings comes within the scope ratione personae of the provisions of the Treaty on European citizenship.

Article 8(2) of the Treaty attaches to the status of citizen of the Union the rights and duties laid down by the Treaty, including the right, laid down in art 6 of the Treaty, not to suffer discrimination on grounds of nationality within the scope of application ratione materiae of the Treaty.

It follows that a citizen of the European Union, such as the appellant in the main proceedings, lawfully resident in the territory of the host Member State, can rely on art 6 of the Treaty in all situations which fall within the scope ratione materiae of Community law, including the situation where that Member State delays or refuses to grant to that claimant a benefit that is provided to all persons lawfully resident in the territory of that State on the ground that the claimant is not in possession of a document which nationals of that same State are not required to have and the issue of which may be delayed or refused by the authorities of that State.'

Comment

In the present case the ECJ, for the first time, invoked the concept of citizenship of the European Union embodied in art 8 EC Treaty. [art 17 EC] It stated that a national of a Member State lawfully residing in the territory of another Member State may rely on art 8(2) EC Treaty [art 17(2) EC] in all situations within the scope of application ratione materiae of Community law. The ECJ made reference to art 8(2) EC Treaty [art 17(2) EC] in response to the argument submitted by the German authorities that Mrs Marinez Sala was not a worker within the meaning of art 48 EC Treaty [art 39 EC] and therefore outside the scope of application of art 6 EC Treaty [art 12 EC]. The ECJ replied that even if she was not a worker (and that is to be determined by the German court) she is a citizen of the European Union and as such is entitled to move and to reside freely within the territories of the Member States as well as not to be subject to discrimination based on nationality prohibited by art 6 EC Treaty [art 12 EC]. Two important implications of the present decisions of the ECJ are that, first, art 8(2) EC Treaty [art 17(2) EC] is directly effective and, second, the scope of application of the principle of non-discrimination on the grounds of nationality embodied in art 6 EC Treaty [art 12 EC] has been considerably extended via the application of art 8(2) EC Treaty [art 17(2) EC].

In relation to other issues referred by the

German court, the ECJ confirmed its prior solutions, that a child-raising allowance is in principle a family benefit (see *Hoever and Zachow* v *Land Nordrhein-Westfalen* Cases C–245 and 312/94 [1996] ECR I–4895) within the meaning of art 4(1) of Regulation 1408/71, although this benefit is also a social advantage within the meaning of art 7(2) of Regulation 1612/68 as it is related to the contract of employment even on a part-time basis. Community law has already recognised the possibility of a double qualifications for certain benefits in *EC Commission* v *Luxembourg* Case C–111/91 [1993] ECR I–817.

The question of a residence permit was answered by the ECJ in conformity with its previous case law. A Member State may impose upon nationals from other Member States residing in its territory the requirement of carrying at all times a document certifying their right of residence if an identical obligation is imposed upon its own nationals (confirmed in *EC Commission* v *Germany* Case C–24/97 [1998] ECR I–2133). Such a document can only have declaratory and probative force (*Royer* Case 48/75 [1976] ECR 497).

The free movement of workers

CPM Meeusen v *Hoofddirectie van de Informatie Beheer Groep* Case C–337/97 [1999] ECR I–3289
European Court of Justice

• *Concept of worker – Regulation 1612/68 – social benefit – study finance – discrimination on the ground of nationality – residence requirement – freedom of establishment*

Facts

Miss Meeusen, a Belgian national and resident at the material time, commenced her study in August 1993 at the provincial Higher Technical Institute for Chemistry in Antwerp, which was, for the purposes of the financing of studies, regarded as a Dutch institution of higher education (Law on the Financing of Studies – Wet op de Studienfinanciering). Both her parents were Belgian nationals, resident in Belgium. Her father was the director and sole shareholder of a company established in The Netherlands. Her mother was employed there by that company two days a week. When Miss Meeusen applied to the relevant Dutch authorities for a study grant her application was ultimately rejected on the ground that she did not reside in the State of her parents' employment. Miss Meeusen appealed. She argued that the right to have her study financed could not be subject to the requirement that she live or reside in the territory of the Member State where her parents are employed, any more than it could be related to nationality.

Held

The ECJ held that a person who is related by marriage to the director and sole shareholder of the company for which she pursues an effective and genuine activity may be classified as a 'worker' within the meaning of art 39 EC.

In respect of the right of a dependant child of a national of one Member State who pursues an activity as an employed person in another Member State while maintaining his residence in the State of which he is a national, the child can rely on the principle of equal treatment in order to claim the social benefit under art 7(2) of Regulation 1612/68 regarding study finance under the same conditions as are applicable to children of nationals of the State of employment, and in particular without any further requirement as to the child's place of residence. Also, the dependant child of a self-employed person who pursues an activity in another Member State while maintaining his residence in the State of which he is a national is entitled to study finance without any further requirement as to his place of residence.

Judgment

'[*Question 1(a)*]

By this question the national court seeks to ascertain, in substance, whether the fact that a person is related by marriage to the director and sole shareholder of the company for which he pursues his activity precludes that person from being classified as a "worker" within the meaning of art 48 of the Treaty and of Regulation No 1612/68.

The Court has consistently held that the concept of "worker", within the meaning of the abovementioned provisions, has a specific Community meaning and must not be interpreted narrowly. Any person who pursues activities which are effective and genuine, to the exclusion of activities on such a small scale as to be regarded as purely marginal and ancillary, must be regarded as a "worker". The essential feature of an employment relationship is, according to that case law, that for a certain period of time a person performs services for and under the direction of another person in return for which he receives remuneration (see, in particular, Case 66/85 *Lawrie-Blum* v *Land Baden-Württemberg* [1986] ECR 2121, paras 16 and 17; and Case C–85/96 *Sala (Maria Martinez)* v *Freistaat Bayern* [1998] ECR I–2691, para 32).

The fact that that person is related by marriage to the director and sole owner of the undertaking is not, of itself, such as to affect that classification.

The Court did indeed hold, in Case C–107/94 *Asscher* v *Staatssecretaris van Financiën* [1996] ECR I–3089, para 26, that the director of a company of which he is the sole shareholder is not carrying out his activity in the context of a relationship of subordination, and so he is not to be regarded as a "worker' within the meaning of art 48 of the Treaty. However, that result cannot be automatically transposed to his spouse. The personal and property relations between spouses which result from marriage do not rule out the existence, in the context of the organisation of an undertaking, of a relationship of subordination characteristic of an employment relationship.

The existence of a relationship of subordination is a matter which it is for the national court to verify.

The answer to question 1(a) must therefore be that the fact that a person is related by marriage to the director and sole shareholder of the company for which he pursues an effective and genuine activity does not preclude that person from being classified as a "worker" within the meaning of art 48 of the Treaty and of Regulation No 1612/68, so long as he pursues his activity in the context of a relationship of subordination.

[Question 1(b) and (c)]

By these questions, which it is appropriate to examine together, the national court seeks to ascertain, in substance, whether the dependent child of a national of one Member State who pursues an activity as an employed person in another Member State while maintaining his residence in the State of which he is a national can rely on art 7(2) of Regulation No 1612/68 in order to obtain study finance under the same conditions as are applicable to children of nationals of the State of employment, and in particular without any further requirement as to the child's place of residence.

As is clear from *Bernini* [*Bernini* v *Minister van Onderwijs en Wetenschappen* Case C–3/90 [1992] ECR I–1071], para 25, study finance awarded by a Member State to children of workers constitutes for a migrant worker a social advantage within the meaning of art 7(2) of Regulation No 1612/68 where the worker continues to support the child.

The Netherlands and German governments submit that that rule cannot be extended to cover the case of a frontier worker. The equality of treatment provided for in art 7(2) of Regulation No 1612/68 aims, as is evident from the fifth recital in its preamble, only to facilitate the mobility of workers and the integration of the migrant worker and his family in the host State. The granting by the host State, for the child of a worker resident with his family in another Member State, of finance for the pursuit of studies abroad does not come within that

context. A residence requirement, as imposed by the national legislation at issue in the main proceedings, is thus objectively justified and proportionate to the objective pursued by Regulation No 1612/68.

As the Court held in Case C–57/96 *Meints* v *Minister van Landbouw, Natuurbeheer en Visserij* [1997] ECR I–6689, para 50, that argument disregards the wording of Regulation No 1612/68. It is expressly stated in the fourth recital in the preamble to that Regulation that the right of free movement must be enjoyed "without discrimination by permanent, seasonal and frontier workers and by those who pursue their activities for the purpose of providing services" and art 7 of the Regulation refers, without reservation, to a "worker who is a national of a Member State". The Court deduced from that and ruled, in *Meints*, that a Member State may not make the grant of a social advantage within the meaning of art 7 of the Regulation dependent on the condition that the beneficiaries be resident within its territory.

It should also be added that the Court has consistently held that the principle of equal treatment laid down in art 7 of Regulation No 1612/68 is also intended to prevent discrimination to the detriment of descendants dependent on the worker (see Case 94/84 *ONEM* v *Deak* [1985] ECR 1873, para 22). Those descendants can thus rely on art 7(2) in order to obtain study finance under the same conditions as are applicable to children of national workers (*Bernini*, para 28).

It follows that, in a situation where national legislation, such as that in point in the main proceedings, does not impose any residence requirement on the children of national workers for the financing of their studies, such a requirement must be regarded as discriminatory if it is imposed on the children of workers who are nationals of other Member States.

Such a requirement would operate to the detriment of, in particular, migrant workers who, by definition, are resident in a Member State where, as a general rule, the members of their family are also resident.

In the light of the foregoing, the answer to

the questions referred must be that the dependent child of a national of one Member State who pursues an activity as an employed person in another Member State while maintaining his residence in the State of which he is a national can rely on art 7(2) of Regulation No 1612/68 in order to obtain study finance under the same conditions as are applicable to children of nationals of the State of employment, and in particular without any further requirement as to the child's place of residence.

[*The second question*]

By this question, the national court seeks to ascertain, in substance, whether the dependent child of a national of one Member State who pursues an activity as a self-employed person in another Member State while maintaining his residence in the State of which he is a national can obtain study finance under the same conditions as are applicable to children of nationals of the State of establishment, and in particular without any further requirement as to the child's place of residence.

In that regard, it should be observed that art 52 of the Treaty confers on nationals of one Member State who wish to pursue activities as self-employed persons in another Member State the benefit of the same treatment as the host State's own nationals and prohibits any discrimination based on nationality which hinders the taking up or pursuit of such activities. As the Court held in Case C–111/91 *EC Commission v Luxembourg* [1993] ECR I–817, para 17, that prohibition covers not only specific rules on the pursuit of occupational activities, but also, as emerges from the General Programme for the abolition of restrictions on the freedom of establishment (OJ, English Special Edition, Second Series (IX), p7), any measure which, pursuant to any provision laid down by law, regulation or administrative action in a Member State, or as the result of the application of such a provision, or of administrative practices, hinders nationals of other Member States in their pursuit of activities as self-employed persons by treating nationals of other

Member States differently from nationals of the country concerned.

That prohibition thus applies to the imposition of a residence requirement in respect of the grant of a social advantage where it has been established that that requirement is discriminatory in nature (*EC Commission v Luxembourg*, cited above, para 18).

The principle of equal treatment thus laid down is also intended to prevent discrimination to the detriment of descendants who are dependent on a self-employed worker. It precludes, therefore, the imposition of a residence requirement such as that provided for in the national legislation concerned which, as stated in para 23 of this judgment, must be regarded as discriminatory.

In the light of the foregoing, the answer to the second question must be that the dependent child of a national of one Member State who pursues an activity as a self-employed person in another Member State while maintaining his residence in the State of which he is a national can obtain study finance under the same conditions as are applicable to children of nationals of the State of establishment, and in particular without any further requirement as to the child's place of residence.'

Comment

The first question examined by the ECJ was whether Miss Meeusen's mother can be regarded as a worker within the meaning of art 39 EC and Regulation 1612/68. In this respect, the ECJ held that the concept of 'worker' has a Community meaning and must be interpreted broadly: *Levin v Staatssecretaris van Justitie* Case 53/81 [1982] ECR 1053. That concept must be defined in accordance with objective criteria which distinguish the employment relationship by reference to the rights and duties of the persons concerned. The essential feature of an employment relationship, however, is that for a certain period of time a person performs services for and under the direction of another person in return for which he receives remuneration: *Lawrie-Blum* Case 66/85 [1986] ECR 2121. These conditions are satisfied in the present case, and the fact that a person is related by marriage to the director and sole owner of the undertaking does not affect the classification of that person as a worker. The ECJ held that the personal and property relations between spouses resulting from marriage do not exclude, in the context of the organisation of an undertaking, the existence of a relationship of subordination which is characteristic of an employment relationship. However, the ECJ emphasised that the concept of a 'worker' cannot be extended to include a director of a company of which he is the sole shareholder, as that person is not carrying out his activity in the context of a relationship of subordination: *Asscher* v *Staatssecretaris van Financiën* Case C–107/94 [1996] ECR I–3089. Therefore, Miss Meeusen's father cannot be regarded as a 'worker' within the meaning of art 39 EC Treaty. His situation should be assessed in the context of the freedom of establishment and art 43 EC.

In respect of Miss Meeusen's entitlement to a study grant, she can claim it on the double basis, that is, her mother as a 'worker' can rely on art 7(2) of Regulation 1612/68 and her father as a self-employed person can invoke the principle of non-discrimination in the context of freedom of establishment. It had previously been decided by the ECJ that a study grant is regarded as a social advantage within the meaning of art 7(2) of Regulation 1612/68: *Bernini* Case C–3/90 [1992] ECR I–1071. As a result, a dependant child is entitled to obtain study finance under the same conditions as are applicable to children of national workers.

The requirement of residence is unjustified both under the Community provisions concerning the free movement of persons and those regarding the freedom of establishment. In the context of the free movement of workers the ECJ held in *Meints* v *Minister van Landbouw* Case C–57/96 [1997] ECR I–6689 that Regulation 1612/68 requires that the right of free movement should be enjoyed without discrimination by permanent, seasonal and frontier workers and by those who pursue their

activities for the purpose of providing services, and that a Member State is not permitted to make the grant of a social advantage conditional upon the beneficiary's residence within its territory. The principle of non-discrimination applies to descendants dependant on the worker. In the context of the freedom of establishment, the principle of non-discrimination requires that a national of one Member State who pursues activities as a self-employed person in another Member State should benefit from the same treatment as the host State's own nationals. In *EC Commission* v *Luxembourg* Case C–111/91 [1993] ECR I–817 the ECJ held that the prohibition of discrimination in the context of the freedom of establishment covers not only specific rules on the pursuit of professional activities, but also encompasses any measure which, pursuant to any provision laid down by law, regulation or administrative action in a Member State or resulting from their application, hinders nationals of other Member States in their pursuit of activities as self-employed persons by treating nationals of other Member States differently from its own nationals. The imposition of a residence requirement is discriminatory in nature.

Kaba (Arden) v *Secretary of State for the Home Department* Case C–356/98 [2000] ECR I–2623 European Court of Justice

• *Regulation 1612/68 – spouses – right to obtain indefinite leave to remain in the UK – social advantage – discrimination*

Facts
Mr Kaba, a Yugoslav national, arrived in the United Kingdom on 5 August 1991. His application for leave to enter the UK for one month as a visitor was refused but he did not leave the country. In February 1992 he applied for asylum. However, he did not need it as on 4 May 1994 he married Virginie Michonneau, a French national who worked and lived in the

UK with periods of stay in France. After their marriage the couple lived together.

In November 1994 Ms Michonneau obtained a five-year UK residence permit valid until 2 November 1999. Her husband was granted leave to remain in the UK for the same period, being a spouse of an EU national.

On 23 January 1996 Mr Kaba applied for indefinite leave to remain in the UK. This was refused under para 255 of the Immigration Rules because his wife had not been resident in the UK for the requisite period of four years. Paragraph 255 of the Immigration Rules requires a period of four years' residence in the UK before an application for indefinite leave to remain in the UK may be made and considered. Mr Kaba appealed against the decision to the Immigration Adjudicator. He argued that the Immigration Rules were discriminatory as they favoured spouses of persons 'present and settled' in the UK and foreign spouses of British nationals (para 287 of the Immigration Rules), both of which could apply for indefinite leave to remain in the UK after one year's residence there, as compared to persons like himself and his wife.

The Immigration Adjudicator considered that the above situation was similar to that in *Netherlands* v *Reed* Case 59/85 [1986] ECR 1283, in which the ECJ held that the ability for an EC migrant worker to obtain a residence permit for his cohabitee was a social advantage within the meaning of art 7(2) of Regulation 1612/68.

In the above circumstances the Immigration Adjudicator asked the ECJ for a preliminary ruling on whether or not paras 255 and 287 of the Immigration Rules were in breach of EC law.

Held

The ECJ held that paras 255 and 287 of the Immigration Rules are not in breach of EC law.

Therefore, legislation of a Member State which requires spouses of migrant workers who are nationals of other Member States to have resided in the territory of that Member State for four years before they become entitled to apply for indefinite leave to remain and to have their applications considered, but which requires residence of only 12 months for the spouses of persons who are settled in that territory, does not constitute discrimination contrary to art 7(2) of Regulation 1612/68.

Judgment

'The aim of Regulation No 1612/68, namely freedom of movement for workers, requires, for such freedom to be guaranteed in compliance with the principles of liberty and dignity, the best possible conditions for the integration of the Community worker's family in the society of the host country (Case C–308/89 *Carmina Di Leo* v *Land Berlin* [1990] ECR I–4185, para 13).

To that end, art 10(1) of that Regulation provides inter alia that a spouse, of whatever nationality, is entitled to install himself with a worker who is a national of one Member State and who is employed in the territory of another Member State.

A spouse who is not a national of a Member State is entitled, under art 4(4) of Directive 68/360, to be issued with a residence document having the same validity as that issued to the worker on whom he is dependent.

It follows that the Community rules confer on the spouses of migrant workers who are nationals of other Member States a right of residence co-extensive with that accorded to those workers.

In this case, however, the appellant in the main proceedings, in seeking indefinite leave to remain in the United Kingdom, is applying, in his capacity as the spouse of a migrant worker, for a more extensive right of residence than that conferred on the migrant worker herself.

Even if such a right constitutes a social advantage within the meaning of art 7(2) of Regulation No 1612/68, the question still arises whether legislation of a Member State which requires spouses of migrant workers who are nationals of other Member States to have resided in the territory of that Member State for four years before they become entitled to apply for indefinite leave to remain and to have their applications considered, but which requires residence of only 12 months for the spouses of persons who are present and settled in that territory, constitutes discrimination contrary to that provision of Community law.

Paragraphs 255 and 287 of the Immigration Rules provide that the period of residence in the United Kingdom prescribed for obtaining leave to reside there indefinitely is shorter for the spouses of persons present and settled in the United Kingdom than for persons who are nationals of Member States and members of their families who are not present and settled. Persons who are ordinarily resident in the United Kingdom are regarded as being present and settled in the United Kingdom and they are not subject to any restriction on the period for which they may remain there.

The Court has consistently held that the equal treatment rule laid down in art 48 of the Treaty and in art 7 of Regulation No 1612/68 prohibits not only overt discrimination by reason of nationality but also all covert forms of discrimination which, by the application of other distinguishing criteria, lead in fact to the same result.

It must be conceded that, where rules make the grant of an advantage subject to the requirement that the beneficiary be present and settled in national territory, that condition is more easily met by national workers than by workers who are nationals of other Member States.

The United Kingdom government considers, however, that the situation of a spouse of a national of a Member State exercising rights conferred on him by the Treaty is not comparable to that of a spouse of a person who is settled in the United Kingdom.

As Community law stands at present, the right of nationals of a Member State to reside in another Member State is not unconditional. That situation derives, first, from the provisions on the free movement of

persons contained in Title III of Part Three of the EC Treaty and the secondary legislation adopted to give them effect and, second, from the provisions of Part Two of the EC Treaty, and more particularly art 8a of the EC Treaty (now, after amendment, art 18 EC), which, whilst granting citizens of the Union the right to move and reside freely within the Member States, expressly refers to the limitations and conditions laid down in the Treaty and by the measures adopted to give it effect.

Accordingly, the Member States are entitled to rely on any objective difference there may be between their own nationals and those of other Member States when they lay down the conditions under which leave to remain indefinitely in their territory is to be granted to the spouses of such persons.

More particularly, the Member States are entitled to require the spouses of persons who do not themselves enjoy an unconditional right of residence to be resident for a longer period than that required for the spouses of persons who already enjoy such a right, before granting the same right to them.

Once leave to remain indefinitely has been granted no condition can be imposed on the person to whom such leave has been granted, and therefore the authorities of the host Member State must be able, when the application is made, to require the applicant to have established sufficiently enduring links with that State. Such links may result, in particular, from the fact that the spouse has been granted indefinite leave to remain in the national territory or that the person applying has already been resident for a considerable period.

Furthermore, migrant workers who are nationals of other Member States may themselves acquire the status of a person present and settled in the United Kingdom, so that their spouses will then qualify to be granted indefinite leave to remain after only 12 months' residence pursuant to para 287 of the Immigration Rules.

For the foregoing reasons and without there being any need to rule whether leave to remain indefinitely in national territory constitutes a social advantage within the meaning of art 7(2) of Regulation No 1612/68, the answer to be given to the national court must be that legislation of a Member State which requires spouses of migrant workers who are nationals of other Member States to have resided in the territory of that Member State for four years before they become entitled to apply for indefinite leave to remain and to have their applications considered, but which requires residence of only 12 months for the spouses of persons who are present and settled in that territory and are not subject to any restriction on the period for which they may remain there, does not constitute discrimination contrary to art 7(2) of Regulation No 1612/68.'

Comment

The decision of the ECJ is surprising in that it justifies an obstacle to the free movement of workers rather than abolishing the existing restrictions imposed by national laws in this area. The reasoning of the ECJ is very interesting in respect of the principle of non-discrimination. The Court examined para 287 of the Immigration Rules which provides that spouses of persons 'present and settled' in the UK and foreign spouses of British nationals are entitled to apply for leave to reside indefinitely in the UK after one year's residence, and therefore that period is much shorter for them than that for EC nationals who are not considered 'present and settled'. Persons who are ordinarily resident in the UK are considered as being 'present and settled'. No time-limit is imposed on their residence in the UK. Upon examination the ECJ stated that under art 39 EC and art 7 of Regulation 1612/68 all discrimination, direct and indirect, is prohibited in respect of EC migrant workers. Therefore, it would seem that paras 255 and 287 of the Immigration Rules were indirectly discriminatory: *Meints* v *Minister van Landbouw, Natuurbeheer en Vissenj* Case C–57/96 [1997] ECR I–6689. Indeed, the requirement laid down in the Immigration Rules is more easily met by national workers

than by EC migrant workers. This is not, however, the conclusion which the ECJ reached. The argument submitted by the UK government that the situation of a spouse of an EC national is not comparable to that of a spouse of a person who is settled in the UK was accepted by the ECJ. The Court stated that:

'... the Member States are entitled to rely on any objective difference there may be between their own nationals and those of other Member States when they lay down the conditions under which leave to remain indefinitely in their territory is to be granted to the spouses of such persons.'

The ECJ emphasised that leave to remain indefinitely imposes no restrictions on the period for which its beneficiary may remain in the UK, because the applicant has established sufficiently enduring links with that State. Such a link may be evidenced by the fact that a foreign national is a spouse of a British national or a spouse of a person 'present and settled' in the UK, or when a person has already resided in the UK for four years. Furthermore, it is always possible for EC nationals to become ordinary residents in the UK, that is to acquire the status of persons 'present and settled' in the UK, in which circumstances a spouse of an EC national will qualify to be granted indefinite leave to remain after only one year's residence in the UK.

Lawrie-Blum v Land Baden-Württenberg Case 66/85 [1986] ECR 2121 European Court of Justice

• *Freedom of movement of workers – definition of a worker – discrimination based on nationality – employment in public service – art 48(4) EC Treaty [art 39(4) EC]*

Facts

Deborah Lawrie-Blum, a British national, was, after successfully passing her examination for the profession of teacher, refused admission to the period of probationary service which had to be completed in order to become a teacher in Germany. During the probationary period a trainee teacher is considered as a civil servant and receives remuneration for conducting classes. Under the German law of Länder Baden-Württenberg only German nationals were admitted to probationary service. Deborah Lawrie-Blum challenged the decision of the German authorities on the basis of art 6 EC Treaty and art 48(2) EC Treaty [art 12 EC and art 39(2) EC]. The Länder authorities contended that a trainee teacher is not a 'worker' within the meaning of art 48 EC Treaty [art 39 EC] and that the probationary service should be regarded as employment in the public service within the meaning of art 48(4) EC Treaty [art 39(4) EC].

Held
The ECJ held that a trainee teacher who, under the direction and supervision of the school authorities, is undergoing a period of service in preparation for the teaching profession during which he provides services by conducting classes and receives remuneration must be considered as a 'worker' under art 48(1) EC Treaty [art 39(1) EC] irrespective of the legal nature of the employment relationship. The ECJ stated that a trainee teacher cannot be regarded as employed in the public service within the meaning of art 48(4) EC Treaty [art 39(4) EC].

Judgment
'[*The concept of a "worker" under art 48(1) EC Treaty*]
Since freedom of movement for workers constitutes one of the fundamental principles of the Community, the term "worker" in art 48 may not be interpreted differently according to the law of each Member State but has a Community meaning. Since it defines the scope of that fundamental freedom, the Community concept of a "worker" must be interpreted broadly (judgment of 23 March 1982 in *Levin* v

Staatssecretaris van Justitie Case 53/81 [1982] ECR 1053).
That concept must be defined in accordance with objective criteria which distinguish the employment relationship by reference to the rights and duties of the persons concerned. The essential feature of an employment relationship, however, is that for a certain period of time a person performs services for and under the direction of another person in return for which he receives remuneration.
In the present case it is clear that during the entire period of preparatory service the trainee teacher is under the direction and supervision of the school to which he is assigned. It is the school that determines the services to be performed by him and his working hours and it is the school's instructions that he must carry out and its rules that he must observe. During a substantial part of the preparatory service he is required to give lessons to the school's pupils and thus provides a service of some economic value to the school. The amounts which he receives may be regarded as remuneration for the services provided and for the duties involved in completing the period of preparatory service. Consequently the three criteria for the existence of an employment relationship are fulfilled in this case ...
The fact that trainee teachers give lessons for only a few hours a week and are paid remuneration below the starting salary of a qualified teacher does not prevent them from being regarded as workers. In its judgment in *Levin*, cited above, the Court held that the expression "worker" and "activity as an employed person" must be understood as including persons who, because they are not employed full time, receive pay lower than that for full-time employment provided that the activities performed are effective and genuine. The latter requirement is not called into question in this case.
Consequently the reply to the first part of the question must be that a trainee teacher who under the direction and supervision of the school authorities is undergoing a period of service in preparation for the teaching profession during which he provides ser-

vices by giving lessons and receives remuneration must be regarded as a worker within the meaning of art 48(1) of the EEC Treaty irrespective of the legal nature of the employment relationship.

[*The concept of "employment in the public service" under art 48(4) EC Treaty*]

... access to certain posts may be limited by reason of the fact that in a given Member State person appointed to such posts have the status of civil servants. To make the application of art 48(4) dependant on the legal nature of the relationship between the employee and the administration would enable the Member States to determine at will the post covered by the exception laid down in that provision.

As the Court has already stated in its judgment of 17 December 1980 in *EC Commission* v *Belgium (Re State Employees)* Case 149/79 [1980] ECR 3881 and of 26 May in *EC Commission* v *Belgium (No 2)* Case 149/79 [1982] ECR 1845, "employment in the public service" within the meaning of art 48(4), which is excluded from the ambit of art 48(1), (2) and (3), must be understood as meaning those posts which involve direct or indirect participation in the exercise of powers conferred by public law and in the discharge of functions whose purpose is to safeguard the general interest of the State or of other public authorities and which therefore require a special relationship of allegiance to the State on the part of persons occupying them and reciprocity of rights and duties which form the foundation of the bond of nationality. The posts excluded are confined to those which, having regard to the tasks and responsibilities involved, are apt to display the characteristics of the specific activities of the public service in the sphere described above.

Those very strict conditions are not fulfilled in the case of a trainee teacher, even if he does in fact take the decisions described by the Länder Baden-Württenberg.

Consequently, the reply to the second part of the question must be that the period of preparatory service for the teaching profession cannot be regarded as employment in the public service within the meaning of art 48(4) to which nationals of other Member States may be denied access.'

Comment

The ECJ established an autonomous Community definition of a worker. A 'worker' within the meaning of art 48 EC Treaty [art 39 EC] is a person who performs services of some economic value for and under the direction of another person, in return for which she/he receives remuneration.

In the present case the ECJ provided a Community meaning in respect of the notion of 'employment in the public service' contained in art 48(4) EC Treaty [art 39(4) EC]. Two elements are necessary in order to invoke the exception embodied in art 48(4) EC Treaty [art 39(4) EC]: the post in question must involve both the exercise of power conferred by public law and the safeguarding of the general interest of the State. As with any exception to a general rule the ECJ restrictively interpreted the notion of 'employment in the public service'. The Member States have tried unsuccessfully to challenge the restrictive approach of the ECJ in a number of cases (see *EC Commission* v *Belgium (No 2)* Case 149/79 [1982] ECR 1845; *EC Commission* v *Italy* Case 225/85 [1986] ECR 2625).

Österreichischer Gewerkschaftsbund, Gewerkschaft Öffentlicher Dienst v *Austria* Case C–195/98 [2000] ECR I–10497 European Court of Justice

• *Free movement of workers – equal treatment – work in public administration – remuneration – seniority – part of career spent abroad – indirect discrimination*

Facts

Under Austrian law there are two categories of workers in federal public administration. The first category comprises civil servants (Beamte) appointed by administrative act and not under contract, whose employment is guaranteed for life and whose status is governed by specific laws. The second category consists of contractual employees engaged on the basis of a private law employment contract. Their status is governed by the Austrian Federal Law on Contractual Public Servants 1948 (VBG). Under VBG periods of employment spent in Austria are treated differently from those spent in other Member States for the purposes of determining the pay of contractual teachers and teaching assistants. The periods of employment spent in other Member States are taken into account with the approval of the competent authorities. Such approval is only given if employment in other Member States is 'of special importance for the successful deployment of the contractual employee'. If approval is not given only 50 per cent of the periods of employment in other Member States are taken into account if the employment relationship commenced on or before 30 April 1995. If it commenced after that date, they are taken into account as regards half of their duration and provided they do not exceed a total of three years.

The Gewerkschaftsbund (a union representing, inter alia, public sector employees) argued that VBG was in breach of art 39 EC and art 7 of Regulation 1612/68.

Held
The ECJ held that VBG was incompatible with art 39 EC and art 7 of Regulation 1612/68. The ECJ stated that a Member State must take into account, in calculating the pay of contractual teachers and teaching assistants, periods of employment in certain institutions in other Member States where these institutions are comparable to Austrian institutions listed in VBG. Such periods must be taken into account without any temporal limitation.

Judgment
'[*Question 2*]
By its second question, the national court is

essentially asking whether art 48 of the Treaty or art 7(1) and (4) of the Regulation preclude a national rule such as para 26 of the VBG concerning the account to be taken of previous periods of service for the purposes of determining the pay of contractual teachers and teaching assistants, under which the requirements which apply to periods spent in other Member States are stricter than those applicable to periods spent in comparable institutions of the Member State concerned.

In order to determine the advancement and hence the pay scale of a contractual employee of the public administration, para 26 of the VBG provides for previous periods of employment in the service of an Austrian public authority or a teaching establishment in Austria to be taken into account. However, periods of employment spent in a Member State other than the Republic of Austria are taken into account in full only where it is in the public interest to do so and with the consent of the competent authorities.

It is first necessary to consider the argument of the Republic of Austria that contractual teachers and teaching assistants fall within the definition of "employment in the public service" within the meaning of art 48(4) of the Treaty.

The derogation in art 48(4) of the Treaty, according to which the provisions on freedom of movement for workers are not to apply to "employment in the public service", concerns only access for nationals of other Member States to certain posts in the civil service (Case C–248/96 *Grahame and Hollanders* v *Bestuur van de Nieuwe Algemene Bedrijfsvereniging* [1997] ECR I–6407, para 32, and Case C–15/96 *Schöning-Kougebetopoulou* v *Freie und Hansestadt Hamburg* [1998] ECR I–47, para 13). It is settled case law that it does not apply to the activities of teachers and teaching assistants (Case 66/85 *Lawrie-Blum* [1986] ECR 2121, para 28; Case C–4/91 *Bleis* v *Ministère de l'Education Nationale* [1991] ECR I–5627, para 7; and Case C–473/93 *EC Commission* v *Luxembourg* [1996] ECR I–3207, para 33).

In any event, the case in the main proceedings does not concern the rules for access to "employment in the public service", but simply the determination of the seniority of contractual teachers or teaching assistants for the purposes of calculating their pay. Once a Member State has admitted workers who are nationals of other Member States into its public administration, art 48(4) of the Treaty cannot justify discriminatory measures against them with regard to remuneration or other conditions of employment (see, inter alia, Case 152/73 *Sotgiu* v *Deutsche Bundespost* [1974] ECR 153, para 4).

It follows that art 48(4) does not apply to the facts of the case in the main proceedings. It must therefore be considered whether a rule such as para 26 of the VBG might breach the principle of non-discrimination laid down in art 48 of the Treaty and art 7(1) and (4) of the Regulation.

According to the settled case law of the Court, art 48 of the Treaty prohibits not only overt discrimination by reason of nationality but also all covert forms of discrimination which, by the application of other distinguishing criteria, lead in fact to the same result (see, inter alia, Case C–419/92 *Scholz* v *Opera Universitaria di Cagliari and Cinza Porcedda* [1994] ECR I–505, para 7, and Case C–237/94 *O'Flynn* v *Adjudication Officer* [1996] ECR I–2617, para 17).

A provision of national law must be regarded as indirectly discriminatory if it is intrinsically liable to affect migrant workers more than national workers and there is a consequent risk that it will place the former at a particular disadvantage and if it is not justified by objective considerations independent of the nationality of the workers concerned, and proportionate to the legitimate aim pursued by that law (see, *O'Flynn*, cited above, paras 19 and 20).

The Court has already held that national rules under which previous periods of employment in the public service of another Member State may not be taken into consideration constituted unjustified indirect discrimination and contravened art 48(2) of the Treaty (see *Scholz*, cited above, para 11, *Schöning-Kougebetopoulou*, cited above,

para 23; and Case C–187/96 *EC Commission* v *Greece* [1998] ECR I–1095, para 21).

It is true that, unlike the national rules at issue in the cases cited in the last paragraph, para 26 of the VBG does not preclude account being taken of previous periods of employment spent in other Member States.

However, such periods are taken into account in full only if the public interest requires it and with the consent of the competent authorities. That consent is granted only if those periods are "of special importance for the successful deployment" of the contractual teacher or teaching assistant. No such condition is imposed in order for periods of employment spent in Austria to be taken into account.

It follows that para 26 of the VBG imposes stricter conditions in respect of periods of employment spent in a Member State other than the Republic of Austria, to the detriment of migrant workers who have spent part of their career in another Member State. That paragraph is liable, therefore, to breach the principle of non-discrimination enshrined in art 48 of the Treaty and art 7(1) and (4) of the Regulation.

The Austrian government, however, contends that the restrictions on freedom of movement are justified by overriding reasons of public interest and are consistent with the principle of proportionality.

In that regard, it argues that the principle of homogeneity laid down in the second sentence of para 21(1) of the Austrian constitution ensures the free movement of public service employees on Austrian territory. That freedom of movement would be impeded if transfer from one service to another were made financially unattractive. Moreover, the pay scheme for the staff concerned was intended to reward their loyalty. However, the same scheme could not be extended to cover periods of employment spent in other Member States since, at the current stage of the integration process, the public services of the Member States are not interconnected to the same extent as Austrian local authorities and have very different characteristics.

It must first be observed that the objective of staff mobility within the Austrian public administration does not require a discriminatory restriction on the mobility of migrant workers.

Next, the differences between the public services in Austria and those in the other Member States cannot justify a difference in the conditions under which previous periods of service are taken into account. In particular, such differences cannot explain why the periods spent in a Member State other than Austria have to be of special importance for the deployment of the person concerned, a condition which is not imposed in respect of periods of employment spent in Austria.

Finally, as regards the argument concerning the objective of rewarding the loyalty of the staff concerned, given the large number of employers covered by para 26(2) of the VBG, the pay scheme is intended to allow the greatest possible mobility within a group of legally distinct employers and not to reward the loyalty of an employee to a particular employer.

It follows from the foregoing that para 26 of the VBG is not in any event proportionate to the objective the Austrian government claims it is intended to achieve.

The answer to the second question must therefore be that art 48 of the EC Treaty and art 7(1) and (4) of the Regulation preclude a national rule such as para 26 of the VBG concerning the account to be taken of previous periods of service for the purposes of determining the pay of contractual teachers and teaching assistants, where the requirements which apply to periods spent in other Member States are stricter than those applicable to periods spent in comparable institutions of the Member State concerned.

[Question 3]
By its third question, the national court is essentially asking whether, a Member State which is obliged to take into account, in calculating the pay of contractual teachers and teaching assistants, periods of employment in certain institutions in other Member States comparable to the Austrian institutions listed in para 26(2) of the VBG, must

take such periods into account without temporal limitation.

The purpose of the question is to determine whether periods of employment spent by such staff before the accession of the Republic of Austria to the European Union must be taken into account.

It is important to note that the case in the main proceedings does not concern the recognition of rights under Community law allegedly acquired before the accession of the Republic of Austria, but concerns the current discriminatory treatment of migrant workers.

The Act concerning the conditions of accession of the Republic of Austria, the Republic of Finland and the Kingdom of Sweden and the adjustments to the Treaties on which the European Union is founded (OJ 1994 C241 p21, and OJ 1995 L1, p1) contains no transitional provisions concerning the application of art 48 of the Treaty and art 7(1) of the Regulation. Those provisions must be considered to be immediately applicable and binding as regards the Republic of Austria as of the date of its accession to the European Union, that is to say 1 January 1995. Since that date, they can be relied on by migrant workers from the Member States. In the absence of transitional provisions, previous periods of employment must necessarily be taken into account.

The answer to the third question must therefore be that where a Member State is obliged to take into account, in calculating the pay of contractual teachers and teaching assistants, periods of employment in certain institutions in other Member States comparable to the Austrian institutions listed in para 26(2) of the VBG, such periods must be taken into account without any temporal limitation.'

Comment

In this case two important items were examined by the ECJ:

1. national rules indirectly discriminating against EC migrant workers employed in public administration;

2. the application of art 39 EC to situations existing before the accession of Austria to the EU in the absence of transitional provisions.

On the first issue, the ECJ rejected the argument submitted by the Austrian authorities that contractual teachers and teaching assistants fall within the definition of 'employment in the public services' within the meaning of art 39(4) EC. In this respect the ECJ held, first, that its previous case law clearly established that teachers and teaching assistants are not to be considered as employed in the public service (*Lawrie-Blum* v *Land Baden-Württenburg* Case 66/85 [1986] ECR 2121, *Bleis* Case C–4/91 [1991] ECR I–5627 and *EC Commission* v *Luxembourg* Case C–473/93 [1996] ECR I–3210) and, second, that art 39(4) EC was not relevant to the matter at issue, as it concerns access for nationals of other Member States to certain posts in the civil service: *Grahame and Hollanders* v *Bestuur van de Nieuwe Algemene Bedrijfsverening* Case C–248/96 [1997] ECR I–6407; *Schöning-Kougebetopoulou* v *Freie und Hansestadt Hamburg* Case C–15/96 [1998] ECR I–47. The case under consideration concerned the determination of the seniority of contractual teachers or teaching assistants for the purpose of calculating their pay, that is their actual conditions of work and not the rules for access to 'employment in the public service'. Indeed, once an EC migrant worker is admitted to employment in the public administration of a host Member State he must be treated without any discrimination with regard to remuneration or other conditions of employment: *Sotgiu* v *Deutsche Bundespost* Case 152/73 [1974] ECR 153.

In the light of the previous case law of the ECJ (especially *EC Commission* v *Greece* Case C–187/96 [1998] ECR I–1095; *Scholtz* Case 419/92 [1994] ECR I–505) the Court not surprisingly found Austrian legislation indirectly discriminatory, that is intrinsically liable to affect migrant workers more than national workers and therefore creating a risk

that migrant workers would be treated less favourably than national workers: *Biehl* v *Administration des Contributions du Grand-Duché de Luxembourg* Case C–175/88 [1990] ECR I–1779. However, a national rule which is indirectly discriminatory may be justified by overriding reasons of public interest, provided it is proportional to the objective pursued. In this respect the Austrian authorities pointed out that the VBG did not preclude account being taken of previous periods of employment spent in other Member States. In response, the ECJ stated that under the VGB such periods of employment in another Member State were taken into account in full only if the public interest required it and subject to consent being given by the competent Austrian authorities. No such conditions were imposed in respect of periods of employment in Austria. Consequently, the VGB was indirectly discriminatory and therefore in breach of art 39 EC and art 7(1) of the Regulation.

The Austrian authorities argued that the VGB was justified by overriding reasons of public interest and was in conformity with the principle of proportionality. The overriding reasons of public interest, that is an objective justification for the restriction on freedom of movement, provided by the Austrian government was the necessity to ensure staff mobility within the Austrian public administration. They argued that the freedom of movement of Austrian public servants would be impeded if transfer from one service to another were made financially unattractive. Furthermore, the pay scheme was designed to reward loyalty. Also, it could not be extended to cover periods of employment spent in other Member States because of the peculiarity of Austrian public services.

The ECJ rejected these arguments. The Court held that the objective of staff mobility within the Austrian public administration could not be justified by a discriminatory restriction on the mobility of EC migrant workers. The VBG was not intended to reward the loyalty of the staff, since the pay scheme aimed at promoting the greatest possible mobility within a group of legally distinct employees and not at rewarding the loyalty of an employee to a particular employer. Also, differences between the public services in Austria and those in other Member States could not justify a difference in the treatment of previous periods of service in other Member States, taking into account that some of them were regarded as being of special importance for the deployment of the worker. Such a condition was not imposed in respect of periods of employment spent in Austria.

The restrictions on freedom of movement of workers imposed by the VGB were unjustified and disproportionate to the objective pursued by it.

On the second issue the referring court asked the ECJ whether periods of employment spent by contractual teachers and teaching assistants in certain institutions in other Member States similar to Austrian institutions listed in the VBG before the accession of Austria to the EU must be taken into account in calculating their pay. This was a hypothetical question, as the main proceedings concerned the discriminatory treatment of EC migrant workers and not the recognition of rights under EC law acquired before the accession of Austria to the EU. The ECJ decided to answer the question. The Court held that since the Act of Accession contained no transitional provisions concerning the application of art 39 EC and art 7(1) of the Regulation, those provisions must be considered as applicable and binding from the date of accession of Austria to the EU, that is from 1 January 1995. Consequently, previous periods of employment must necessarily be taken into account for the purposes of determining the pay of contractual teachers and teaching assistants without any temporal limitation.

R v Immigration Appeal Tribunal and Surinder Singh, ex parte Secretary of State for the Home Department Case C–370/90 [1992] 3 CMLR 335 European Court of Justice

• *Free movement of workers – family members' rights – non-EC spouse – divorce – deportation*

Facts

Mr Singh, an Indian national, married a British citizen in the United Kingdom in 1982. The couple then left the UK to work in Germany for three years where both obtained employment. They subsequently returned to the UK to start a private business. However, at no time during this period did Mr Singh acquire British nationality.

Decree nisi of divorce was made against Mr Singh in July 1987 and the date of expiry of his temporary leave to stay in the UK, which had been periodically extended during his marriage, was brought forward to September of that year. After the expiry of his temporary leave, Mr Singh remained in the UK without permission and, in December 1988, the Secretary of State for the Home Department issued a deportation order against him. In February 1989, after the deportation proceedings had commenced, decree absolute was pronounced in the divorce hearing.

The issue of deportation came before the Immigration Appeal Tribunal, before decree absolute had been pronounced, which held that Mr Singh was entitled to remain in the UK on the ground that he had Community rights, as a spouse of a British citizen, under the principles of the free movement of persons and the right of establishment.

The Secretary of State applied to the High Court for judicial review of this decision and that court referred the question of Mr Singh's right to remain in the UK under Community law to the ECJ for a preliminary ruling.

Held

Where a national of one Member State travels to another for the purpose of obtaining employment the whole gambit of Community rights under the principle of the free movement of workers is activated. These rights are contained not only in art 48 EC Treaty [art 39 EC] but also in secondary legislation including Regulation 1612/68, Directive 68/360 and Directive 73/148.

These measures confer rights on both the worker and his or her spouse and family. In particular, even a non-EC spouse is entitled to such rights as the relevant legislation makes no distinction between EC national spouses and non-EC national spouses.

If these rights have been activated, an individual may rely on the rights stemming from the principle of free movement when returning to his or her own country. This includes the right to be accompanied by a non-EC spouse under the same conditions as other migrant workers.

Once inside the home country, the Community national has the right to establish a business under art 52 EC Treaty [art 43 EC] and the non-EC spouse is entitled to enjoy at least the same rights in this respect as would be available under Community law on entering and residing in another Member State.

The Court did not rule whether Mr Singh was entitled to remain in the UK after the decree absolute but confined its decision to the interpretation of the rights of Mr Singh during the period before then, since proceedings were commenced before the date of decree absolute.

Judgment

'The provisions of the Council regulations and directives on freedom of movement within the Community for employed and self-employed persons, in particular art 10 of Regulation 1612/68, arts 1 and 4 of Directive 68/360 and arts 1(c) and 4 of Directive 73/148, provide that the Member States must grant the spouse and children of such a person rights of residence equivalent to that granted to the person himself.

A national of a Member State might be deterred from leaving his country of origin in order to pursue an activity as an employed or self-employed person as envisaged by the Treaty in the territory of another Member State if, on returning to the Member State of which he is a national in order to pursue an activity there as an employed or self-employed person, the conditions of his entry and residence were not at least equivalent to those which he would enjoy under the Treaty or secondary law in the territory of another Member State.

He would in particular be deterred from so doing if his spouse and children were not also permitted to enter and reside in the territory of his Member State of origin under conditions at least equivalent to those granted them by Community law in the territory of another Member State.

It follows that a national of a Member State who has gone to another Member State in order to work there as an employed person pursuant to art 48 [EC] and returns to establish himself in order to pursue an activity as a self-employed person in the territory of the Member State of which he is a national has the right, under art 52 [EC] Treaty, to be accompanied in the territory of the latter State by his spouse, a national of a non-Member country, under the same conditions as are laid down by Regulation 1612/68, Directive 68/360 or Directive 73/148.

Admittedly, as the United Kingdom submits, a national of a Member State enters and resides in the territory of that State by virtue of the rights attendant upon his nationality and not by virtue of those conferred on him by Community law. In particular, as is provided, moreover, by art 3 of the Fourth Protocol to the European Convention on Human Rights, a State may not expel one of its own nationals or deny him entry to its territory.

However, this case is concerned not with a right under national law but with the rights of movement and establishment granted to a Community national by arts 48 and 52 [EC] Treaty. These rights cannot be fully effective if such a person may be deterred from exercising them by obstacles raised in his or her country of origin to the entry and residence of his or her spouse. Accordingly, when a Community national who has availed himself or herself of those rights returns to his or her country of origin, his or her spouse must enjoy at least the same rights of entry and residence as would be granted to him or her under Community law if his or her spouse chose to enter and reside in another Member State. Nevertheless, arts 48 and 52 [EC] do not prevent Member States from applying to foreign spouses of their own nationals rules on entry and residence more favourable than those provided for by Community law ...'

Comment

So far the ECJ has not decided on the right of residence of a divorced spouse who is a non-EC national and who was married to an EC national. In the present case the deportation proceedings had been instituted before the decree nisi of divorce was made. Therefore, it is still uncertain to what extent Community law will assist a divorced non-EC national in securing his right of permanent residence, in particular in the light of the principle set up in *Morson and Jhanjan* v *Netherlands* Cases 35 and 36/82 [1982] ECR 3723 that Community law does not apply to 'wholly internal situations'. In this case two Dutch nationals working and residing in The Netherlands wanted to bring their mothers of Surinamese nationality to reside with them in The Netherlands. Under Dutch law they were not permitted to do so and the ECJ held that Community law did not apply to their situation as there was no link connecting it with EC law.

It is submitted that both the above situations should be resolved on the basis of art 8 of the European Convention on Human Rights taking into account that fundamental principles of human rights are part of Community law. In this respect the European Court of Human Rights in *Berrehab* (21 June 1988, series A no 138, pp15 and 16) held that the

expulsion of a divorced husband whose child remained in Belgium was contrary to art 8 the ECHR. The European Court of Human Rights did not grant an automatic right of residence to a divorced spouse but took into consideration the degree of contact between the divorced parent and the child. This solution is also in line which the ECJ judgment in *Kus* v *Landeshaupt Stadt Wiesbaden* Case C–237/91 [1992] ECR I–6781 in which it was decided that a Turkish national who married an EC national (and on that basis was granted the right of residence in a Member State) was allowed to reside after his divorce on two grounds: first, he was lawfully working in that Member State and, second, on the basis of certain provisions of the EEC-Turkey Association Agreement. In this case the ECJ held that the divorce did not affect the legality of his continuing residence.

The State v *Jean Noël Royer* Case 48/75 [1976] ECR 497; [1976] 2 CMLR 619 European Court of Justice

• *Free movement of workers – art 48(3) EC Treaty [art 39(3) EC] – direct effect – art 1 Regulation 1612/68 – art 4 Directive 68/360 – expulsion – public policy*

Facts

Royer was a French national who had been convicted of minor offences and prosecuted for a number of armed robberies but never convicted. His wife was also a French national, but worked in Liège in Belgium. He visited his wife in Belgium, but omitted to comply with the administrative formalities upon entry into the country. He was subsequently convicted of illegal entry and residence in Belgium and left the country.

Some time later, Royer returned to Belgium, but again failed to comply with the necessary administrative formalities. He was served with a ministerial decree of expulsion which alleged that his presence was a danger to public policy in Belgium. As a defence,

Royer invoked art 48 EC Treaty [art 39 EC], and the related Community directives, to establish that he was entitled to enter and remain in Belgium as a worker.

Held

The ECJ gave direct effect to art 48 EC Treaty [art 39 EC] and relied on the directives implementing the right of workers and their families to reside in other Member States to reject the need for a permit in order to acquire residency in other Member States. In addition, the failure of a Community national to comply with the administrative formalities upon entry into another Member State did not justify expulsion.

Judgment

'[*Referring to the rights granted by arts 48, 52 and 59 of the Treaty*]
These provisions, which may be construed as prohibiting Member States from setting up restrictions or obstacles to the entry into and residence in their territory of nationals of other Member State, have the effect of conferring rights directly on all persons falling within the ambit of the above-mentioned articles, as later given closer articulation by regulations or directives implementing the Treaty.

This interpretation has been recognised by all the measures of secondary law adopted for the purpose of implementing the above-mentioned provisions of the Treaty.

Thus art 1 of Regulation 1612/68 provides that any national of a Member State, shall, irrespective of his place of residence, have "the right to take up activity as an employed person and to pursue such activity within the territory of another Member State" and art 10 of the same regulation extends the "right to instal themselves" to the members of the family of such a national.

Article 4 of Directive 68/360 provides that "Member State shall grant the right of residence in their territory" to the persons referred to and further states that as "proof" of this right an individual residence permit shall be issued.

Further the preamble to Directive 73/148 states that freedom of establishment can be fully attained only "if a right of permanent residence is granted to the persons who are to enjoy freedom of establishment" and that freedom to provide services entails that persons providing and receiving services should have "the right of residence for the time during which the services are being provided".

These provisions show that the legislative authorities of the Community were aware that, while not creating new rights in favour of persons protected by Community law, the regulation and directives concerned determined the scope and detailed rules for the exercise of rights conferred directly by the Treaty.

... (a) It follows from the foregoing that the right of nationals of a Member State to enter the territory of another Member State and reside there for the purposes intended by the Treaty – in particular to look for or pursue an occupation or activities as employed or self-employed persons, or to rejoin their spouse or family – is a right conferred directly by the Treaty, or, as the case may be, by the provisions adopted for its implementation.

It must therefore be concluded that the right is acquired independently of the issue of a residence permit by the competent authority of a Member State.

The grant of this permit is therefore to be regarded not as a measure giving rise to rights but as a measure by a Member State serving to prove the individual position of a national of another Member State with regard to provisions of Community law.

(b) Article 4(1) and (2) of Directive 68/360 provides, without prejudice to art 10 thereof, that Member States shall "grant" the right of residence in their territory to persons who are able to produce the documents listed in the directive and that "proof" of the right of residence shall be constituted by issue of a special residence permit.

The above-mentioned provisions of the directive are intended to determine details regulating the exercise of rights conferred directly by the Treaty.

It follows, therefore, that the right of residence must be granted by the authorities of the Member States to any person falling within the categories set out in art 1 of the Directive and who is able to prove, by producing the documents specified in art 4(3), that he falls within one of these categories.

The answer to the question put should therefore be that art 4 of Directive 68/360 entails an obligation for Member States to issue a residence permit to any person who provides proof, by means of the appropriate documents, that he belongs to one of the categories set out in art 1 of the directive.

(c) The logical consequence of the foregoing is that the mere failure by a national of a Member State to complete the legal formalities concerninng access, movement and residence of aliens does not justify a decision ordering expulsion.'

Comment

The ECJ held that the right to entry and residence is granted directly by art 48 EC Treaty [art 39 EC] and is therefore independent from the question of a residence permit. The latter has only declaratory and probatory force. Consequently, a failure to comply with formalities regarding entry and residence cannot justify a decision ordering expulsion from the territory of a host Member State or temporary imprisonment. In respect of sanctions that a Member State may impose on nationals from other Member States for failure to comply with administrative requirements regarding entry and residence such sanctions are subject to the principle of proportionality. Any national measures which are disproportionate to the objectives of the Treaty in the area of free movement of persons will be struck out by the ECJ as contrary to Community law.

In the present case the ECJ held that art 48(3) EC Treaty [art 39(3) EC] encompasses the right to enter in search of work although it did not fix any time-limit for such a search. It seems that a six-months' period can be considered as a reasonable time for the purpose of seeking employment. This was implied from the ECJ decision in *R* v *Immigration Appeal Tribunal, ex parte Antonissen* Case C–292/89 [1991] ECR I–745 in which the ECJ accepted that if after a six-month stay in a host Member State for the purpose of seeking employment, an EC migrant had failed to find employment a deportation order could be issued, unless the migrant provided evidence that he was actively seeking employment and had a genuine chance of being employed.

10 Freedom of Establishment and Services

Right of establishment

Centros Ltd v Erhvervs-og Selskabsstyrelsen Case C–212/97 [1999] ECR I–1459 European Court of Justice

- *Freedom of establishment – arts 56 and 58 EC Treaty [arts 46 and 48 EC] – establishment of a branch by a company not carrying on any actual business – circumvention of national law – refusal to register – fraud – free movement of workers – art 52 EC Treaty [art 43 EC]*

Facts

In May 1992 Mrs Bryde, a Danish national, registered her company Centros in the UK, taking advantage of the UK law which did not impose any requirement on limited liability companies as to the paying-up of a minimum share capital.

During the summer of 1992 Mrs Bryde requested the Danish Trade and Companies Board to register a branch of Centros in Denmark. The Board refused on the grounds that Centros had never traded since its formation and that Mrs Bryde was, in fact, seeking to establish in Denmark not a branch but a principal establishment by circumventing Danish rules concerning the paying-up of minimum capital fixed at DKK 200,000.

Centros challenged the decision of the Danish Trade and Companies Board.

Held

The ECJ held that it was contrary to arts 52 and 58 of the EC Treaty [arts 43 and 48 EC] for a Member State to refuse on the above-mentioned grounds to register a branch of a company formed in accordance with the law of another Member State in which it had its registered office but in which the company itself was not engaged in any business activities.

Judgment

'By its question, the national court is in substance asking whether it is contrary to arts 52 and 58 of the Treaty for a Member State to refuse to register a branch of a company formed in accordance with the legislation of another Member State in which it has its registered office but where it does not carry on any business when the purpose of the branch is to enable the company concerned to carry on its entire business in the State in which that branch is to be set up, while avoiding the formation of a company in that State, thus evading application of the rules governing the formation of companies which are, in that State, more restrictive so far as minimum paid-up share capital is concerned.

According to the Court, a situation in which a company formed in accordance with the law of a Member State in which it has its registered office desires to set up a branch in another Member State falls within the scope of Community law. In that regard, it is immaterial that the company was formed in the first Member State only for the purpose of establishing itself in the second, where its main, or indeed entire, business is to be conducted.

The fact that Mrs and Mrs Bryde formed the company Centros in the United Kingdom for the purpose of avoiding

Danish legislation requiring that a minimum amount of share capital be paid up does not, however, mean that the formation by that British company of a branch in Denmark is not covered by freedom of establishment for the purposes of art 52 and 58 of the Treaty. The question of the application of those articles of the Treaty is different from the question whether or not a Member State may adopt measures in order to prevent attempts by certain of its nationals to evade domestic legislation by having recourse to the possibilities offered by the Treaty.

Where it is the practice of a Member State, in certain circumstances, to refuse to register a branch of a company having its registered office in another Member State, the result is that companies formed in accordance with the law of that other Member State are prevented from exercising the freedom of establishment conferred on them by arts 52 and 58 of the Treaty.

Consequently, that practice constitutes an obstacle to the exercise of the freedoms guaranteed by those provisions.

A Member State is entitled to take measures designed to prevent certain of its nationals from attempting, under cover of the rights created by the Treaty, improperly to circumvent their national legislation or to prevent individuals from improperly or fraudulently taking advantage of provisions of Community law.

However, the national courts must nevertheless assess such conduct in the light of the objectives pursued by those provisions.

In the present case, the provisions of national law, application of which the parties concerned have sought to avoid, are rules governing the formation of companies and not rules concerning the carrying on of certain trades, professions or businesses. The provisions of the Treaty on freedom of establishment are intended specifically to enable companies formed in accordance with the law of a Member State and having their registered office, central administration or principal place of business within the Community to pursue activities in other Member States through an agency, branch or subsidiary.

That being so, the fact that a national of a Member State who wishes to set up a company chooses to form it in the Member State whose rules of company law seem to him the least restrictive and to set up branches in other Member States cannot, in itself, constitute an abuse of the right of establishment. The right to form a company in accordance with the law of a Member State and to set up branches in other Member States is inherent in the exercise, in a single market, of the freedom of establishment guaranteed by the Treaty.

In this connection, the fact that company law is not completely harmonised in the Community is of little consequence. Moreover, it is always open to the Council, on the basis of the powers conferred upon it by art 54(3)(g) of the EC Treaty, to achieve complete harmonisation.

The fact that a company does not conduct any business in the Member State in which it has its registered office and pursues its activities only in the Member State where its branch is established is not sufficient to prove the existence of abuse or fraudulent conduct which would entitle the latter Member State to deny that company the benefit of the provisions of Community law relating to the right of establishment.

Accordingly, the refusal of a Member State to register a branch of a company formed in accordance with the law of another Member State in which it has its registered office on the grounds that the branch is intended to enable the company to carry on all its economic activity in the host State, with the result that the secondary establishment escapes national rules on the provision for and the paying-up of a minimum capital, is incompatible with arts 52 and 58 of the Treaty, in so far as it prevents any exercise of the right freely to set up a secondary establishment which arts 52 and 58 are specifically intended to guarantee.

The national measures liable to hinder or make less attractive the exercise of fundamental freedoms guaranteed by the Treaty must fulfill four conditions: they must be applied in a non-discriminatory manner;

they must be justified by imperative requirements in the general interest; they must be suitable for securing the attainment of the objective which they pursue; and they must not go beyond what is necessary in order to attain it.

Those conditions are not fulfilled in the case in the main proceedings. First, the practice in question is not such as to attain the objective of protecting creditors which it purports to pursue since, if the company concerned had conducted business in the United Kingdom, its branch would have been registered in Denmark, even though Danish creditors might have been equally exposed to risk.

Second, it is possible to adopt measures which are less restrictive, or which interfere less with fundamental freedoms, by, for example, making it possible in law for public creditors to obtain the necessary guarantees.

Lastly, the fact that a Member State may not refuse to register a branch of a company formed in accordance with the law of another Member State in which it has its registered office does not preclude that first State from adopting any appropriate measure for preventing or penalising fraud, either in relation to the company itself, if need be in cooperation with the Member State in which it was formed, or in relation to its members, where it has been established that they are in fact attempting, by means of the formation of the company, to evade their obligations towards private or public creditors established on the territory of a Member State concerned. In any event, combating fraud cannot justify a practice of refusing to register a branch of a company which has its registered office in another Member State.'

Comment

The ECJ confirmed its liberal approach towards the freedom of establishment by stating that national rules regarding the prevention of fraud cannot justify restrictions which impair the freedom of establishment of companies. In its advisory opinion, Advocate-General La Pergola suggested that in the light of the evolution of the Community the freedom of establishment should be approached in the same manner as the free movement of goods, that is, the principles of *Cassis de Dijon* should apply. The echo of his suggestion can be found in the statement of the ECJ that only 'imperative requirements' in the general interest may justify national measures hindering the exercise of the right to freely set up a branch in other Member States.

The ECJ did not 'look behind the veil' of a company, it applied the provisions relating to the right of establishment. Therefore, the fact that Mrs Bryde was taking advantage of more lenient company law in the UK permitting her to avoid paying the capital required by Danish law for the establishment of the company, and that the main purpose of establishing her company in the UK was to open a branch in Denmark which actually was intended to be a principal establishment, did not constitute an abuse of right of establishment. The decision in the present case in not surprising taking into account that the ECJ in previous cases applied a restrictive approach to national measures intended to fight fraud which imposed restrictions on the freedom of establishment (*EC Commission* v *France* Case 270/83 [1986] ECR 273 in which the right of establishment was exercised in order to benefit from tax advantages in another Member State; and *Segers* v *Bestuur van de Bedrifsvereniging voor bank-en verzekeringswezen* Case C–79/85 [1986] ECR 2375 concerning social security benefits).

The only danger of this approach is that it might create the so-called 'Delaware 'effect within the EU. Under the 'Delaware' effect many states in the USA have introduced very lenient rules in respect of the formation of companies (in particular in relation to the protection of creditors) in order to attract new companies. In the context of the EU it will be necessary to harmonise national laws of the Member States in this area in order to prevent some Member States from introducing new legislation aimed at attracting businesses from other Member States but at the cost of weaker protection for creditors.

EC Commission v Luxembourg (Re Access to the Medical Profession)
Case C–351/90 [1992] 3 CMLR 124
European Court of Justice

• *Freedom of establishment for medical profession – arts 48 and 52 EC Treaty [arts 39 and 43 EC] – prohibition on maintaining multiple practices in different Member States – national measures amounted to discrimination – no justification for national measures*

Facts
Under Luxembourg law, doctors, dentists and veterinary surgeons with practices in other Member States were prohibited from practising in Luxembourg without the express permission of the Luxembourg authorities. However, this prohibition did not apply to members of these professions from Luxembourg.

The Commission brought proceedings against Luxembourg on the grounds that the requirement to obtain express permission was in breach of arts 48 and 52 EC Treaty [arts 39 and 43 EC] as it discriminated between nationals and non-nationals.

Held
The ECJ held that Luxembourg was in breach of its obligations under arts 48 and 52 EC Treaty [arts 39 and 43 EC] by requiring nationals of Member States to obtain a special permission before practising in Luxembourg. Any derogations from the terms of these articles must be justified on objective grounds and must not be unduly harsh or restrictive. In the circumstances of the present case, the restrictions were considered to be too restrictive and therefore unjustified.

Judgment
'It should be observed that the so-called single-practice rule for doctors, dentists and veterinary surgeons has the effect of restricting the freedom of movement of workers and the right of establishment which are guaranteed by arts 48 and 52 [EC].

In accordance with the Court's settled case law, the right of establishment includes freedom to set up and maintain, subject to observance of the professional rules of conduct, more than one place of work within the Community.

This is just as true where a person who is employed or self-employed and established in one Member State wishes to work in another Member State, irrespective of whether he proposes to do so as an employed or self-employed person.

As the Court pointed out in *EC Commission v France* [1986] ECR 1425, with regard to the medical and dental professions, the professional rules of conduct which must be observed are those which reflect a concern to ensure that individuals enjoy the most effective and complete health protection possible. The rules governing the profession of veterinary surgeon likewise have the same objective of health.

However, it follows from the same judgment that those rules, in so far as they have the effect of restricting the right of establishment and freedom of movement of workers, are compatible with the Treaty only if the restrictions they entail are actually justified by general obligations inherent in good professional practice and if the restrictions are imposed without distinction on nationals of the Member State in question and those of other Member States. In this connection the Court found that this was not the case where the restrictions were likely to create discrimination against practitioners established in other Member States or obstacles to entering the profession which go beyond what is necessary to attain the above-mentioned objectives.

On this point it must be said that the single-practice rule, which the Luxembourg government describes as essential for continuity of patient care, is applied more strictly to doctors and dentists practising in other Member States than to those working in

Luxembourg. In effect, s16, sentence 2 of the Act permits an exception to the single-practice rule only in favour of persons practising in Luxembourg.

In this connection the Luxembourg government contends that the exception can be extended by ministerial decisions, in special cases, to persons established in other Member States.

This argument cannot succeed. Firstly, s16 of the Act refers only to practitioners established in Luxembourg. Secondly, observance of the principles of equal treatment which find expression in arts 48 and 52 [EC] should not depend on the unilateral will of national authorities.

Accordingly it must be said that, although the legal position is clear in the sense that arts 48 and 52 [EC] are directly applicable in the Member States, nevertheless the continued existence of s16 of the Act in question gives rise to an ambiguous de facto situation by keeping the individuals concerned in a state of uncertainty with regard to their rights under Community law.

It should be added that a general prohibition on practitioners established or employed in another Member State from working from an establishment in Luxembourg is unduly restrictive.

On this point the Luxembourg government argues that the single practice rule is objectively justified on grounds of public health and public policy, and by the general interest. It adds that the relationship between practitioner and patient is inherently personal and requires continuity of attendance by the practitioner at his surgery or place of employment in order to provide continuous care, and that the emergency service would be disorganised if practitioners with more than one place of work were involved.

These arguments likewise cannot succeed.

Firstly, there is no need for a practitioner, whether a general practitioner, dentist or veterinary surgeon, or even a specialist, to be close to the patient or client continuously. Secondly, the single-practice rule does not necessarily ensure that the same practitioner is continuously available if, for example, he

has to be elsewhere, works part-time or belongs to a group practice. Finally, continuity of patient care and efficient organisation of the emergency service can be secured by less restrictive means, such as requirements for minimum attendance or arrangements to provide substitutes.

These considerations show that the prohibition is too absolute and too general to be justified by the need to provide continuity of patient care.

Therefore, it must be found that, by preventing medical practitioners, dentists and veterinary surgeons established in another Member State or working as employed persons there from establishing themselves in Luxembourg or working there as employed persons while retaining their practice or employment in the other Member State, the Grand Duchy of Luxembourg has failed to fulfill its obligations under arts 48 and 52 [EC].'

Comment

National rules imposing restrictions on the right of establishment must fulfill four criteria in order to be justified. They must apply without distinction to nationals and non-nationals, they must be justified by imperative requirements in the general interest, they must be suitable for the attainment of the objective which they pursue, and they must not go beyond what is necessary to attain that objective. In the present case, these criteria were not fulfilled.

Erpelding (Jeff) v *Ministre de la Santé* Case C–16/99 [2000] ECR I–6821 European Court of Justice

• *Freedom of establishment – Directive 93/16/EEC – interpretation of its arts 10 and 19 – use of the title of specialist doctor in the host Member State by a doctor who has obtained in another Member State a qualification not included, as regards that State, on the list in art 7 of the Directive – preliminary ruling*

Facts

Dr Erpelding obtained his medical qualification in Austria in 1985. This was recognised in 1986 by the Luxembourg Ministry of Education. In 1991 Dr Erpelding was authorised by the professional organisation of Austrian doctors to practise medicine as a specialist in internal medicine. This qualification was also recognised by the Luxembourg Ministry of Health which authorised him to practise as a specialist in internal medicine. Two years later (the doctor having acquired an additional specialisation) the Austrian organisation of doctors awarded Dr Erpelding the diploma of a specialist in internal medicine, cardiology practice (Teilgebiet Kardiologie). The Luxembourg Ministry of Health authorised Dr Erpelding to use, in addition to his professional title of specialist in internal medicine, his academic title relating to his new specialisation but in the language of the State in which the specialisation had been obtained. In 1997 Dr Erpelding decided to abandon the professional title of 'specialist in internal medicine' and to use the title of 'specialist in cardiology'. This became the main issue in his dispute with the Luxembourg Ministry of Health, which refused to authorise the use on the ground that cardiology did not constitute a specialist field recognised by the Austrian authorities. The Luxembourg Ministry of Health stated that they could only recognise diplomas as worded in the original language. Dr Erpelding challenged the decision.

Held

The ECJ held that the right to use the title which is in use in the host Member State is a necessary corollary of the mutual recognition of diplomas, but only on condition that such a title satisfies the minimum requirements for recognition. However, a host Member State retains the right to authorise the use of the title in a language other than that of the Member State of origin or Member State from which the person concerned comes.

Judgment

'By its first question the national court asks, in essence, whether a doctor who has obtained in another Member State a diploma in specialised medicine which does not appear on the list of specialist training courses in art 7 of Directive 93/16 may rely on art 19 of that Directive to use the corresponding professional title of specialist in the host State.

Directive 93/16 establishes a system of automatic and compulsory mutual recognition for the diplomas, certificates and other evidence of formal qualifications in medicine and specialised medicine awarded to nationals of the Member States by those States, in accordance with arts 3, 5 and 7 of the Directive.

This system of automatic compulsory recognition would be incomplete and its effectiveness would be seriously undermined if its beneficiaries were not entitled to use the professional title of doctor or specialist doctor, as the case may be, in the host Member State. Without the right to use those titles in that State, the beneficiaries of the system of mutual recognition would be deprived of the possibility of making their professional qualifications known in the relevant circles in the same way and under the same conditions as Community nationals who had obtained such a title in the host Member State.

The right to use the title of doctor or specialist doctor in the host Member State, in the language of that State and in accordance with its nomenclature, is thus a necessary corollary of the mutual recognition of diplomas, certificates and other evidence of formal qualifications established by Directive 93/16.

However, that applies only if the title of doctor or specialist doctor satisfies the minimum conditions required for this automatic and compulsory mutual recognition. It is thus fully consistent with that system of mutual recognition that art 19 of Directive 93/16 entitles Community nationals to use the professional title of doctor or specialist doctor only if they fulfil the conditions laid down in the first and second paragraphs of that provision.

The answer to be given to the first question must therefore be that a doctor who has obtained in another Member State a diploma in specialised medicine which does not appear on the list of specialist training courses in art 7 of Directive 93/16 may not rely on art 19 of that Directive to use the corresponding professional title of specialist in the host State.

[*The second question*]

The national court considers that art 10 of Directive 93/16 may be construed in two different ways. The first interpretation is that the provision does no more than ensure that the beneficiaries of the system of mutual recognition of diplomas established by the Directive have the right to use their academic titles in the language of the Member State of origin or Member State from which they come. The second interpretation is that the provision, while acknowledging that the beneficiaries of the system have that right, precludes any possibility of the host Member State authorising use of the equivalent title in the language and according to the nomenclature of that State.

Directive 93/16 regulates the right of the beneficiaries of the system of mutual recognition of diplomas established by the Directive to use, first, their professional title of doctor or specialist doctor and, second, their academic titles in the host Member State.

Since any restriction on the use in the host Member State of an academic title obtained in another Member State is liable to render that title less attractive and hence to hamper the exercise of fundamental freedoms guaranteed by the Treaty, it must comply with the requirements of the Treaty (see Case C–19/92 *Kraus* v *Land Baden-Württemberg* [1993] ECR I–1663, para 32). Community legislation, including art 10 of Directive 93/16 which is the subject of the national court's question, must likewise be interpreted in the light of those requirements.

The first sentence of art 10(1) substantially repeats the ninth recital in the preamble to the Directive, which states that, since a directive on the mutual recognition of diplomas does not necessarily imply equivalence in the training covered by such diplomas, the use of the academic title should be authorised only in the language of the Member State of origin or of the Member State from which the person comes.

The first sentence of art 10(1) of Directive 93/16 should therefore be interpreted as referring only to the right of beneficiaries of the system of mutual recognition of diplomas established by the Directive to use their academic title, and if appropriate its abbreviation, in the language of the Member State of origin or the Member State from which they come. However, neither the wording of that provision nor the structure of Directive 93/16 indicates that the host Member State may not authorise the use in its territory of the academic title or an equivalent title in a language other than that of the Member State of origin or Member State from which the person concerned comes.

The answer to be given to the second question must therefore be that the first sentence of art 10(1) of Directive 93/16 is to be interpreted as referring only to the right of beneficiaries of the system of mutual recognition of diplomas established by the Directive to use their academic title, and if appropriate its abbreviation, in the language of the Member State of origin or the Member State from which they come. This does not affect the right of the host Member State to authorise the use in its territory of the academic title or an equivalent title in a language other than that of the Member State of origin or Member State from which the person concerned comes.'

Comment

The main issue in the above case was the interpretation of arts 10 and 19 of Directive 93/16/EEC aimed at facilitating the free movement of doctors and the mutual recognition of their diplomas, certificates and other evidence of formal qualifications. Dr

Erpelding's specialisation was not included in the list of specialist training courses contained in art 7 of the Directive. The issue was therefore whether by virtue of art 19 of the Directive the applicant could obtain authorisation to use an equivalent professional title in the host Member State, taking into account the fact that a Member State in which such qualification had been obtained did not recognise cardiology as a specialist field. The ECJ made the right to use the title in the host Member State conditional. Although the use of a title obtained in another Member State, in the language and in conformity with the nomenclature of a host Member State, constitutes a necessary corollary of the mutual recognition of diplomas, it is nevertheless applicable 'only if the title of doctor or specialised doctor satisfies the minimum conditions required for its automatic and compulsory recognition'. In the above case this condition was not satisfied. The particular specialisation obtained by Dr Erpelding was not included on the list of specialist training courses contained in art 7 of the Directive. Consequently Dr Erpelding was not entitled to rely on art 19 of the Directive to use the corresponding professional title of specialist in the host Member State.

Article 10 of the Directive provides that beneficiaries of the system of mutual recognition of diplomas are entitled to use their academic titles in the language of the Member State of origin or Member State from which they come. In respect of art 10 of the Directive the issue was whether this provision precluded a host Member State from authorising use of the equivalent title in its language and according to its nomenclature. The ECJ held that a host Member State may authorise the use in its territory of the academic title or an equivalent title in a language other than that of the Member State of origin or Member State from which the person concerned comes.

Grand Duchy of Luxembourg v *European Parliament and Council of the European Union* Case C–168/98 [2000] ECR I–9131
European Court of Justice

• *Freedom of establishment – mutual recognition of diplomas – harmonisation – Directive 98/5/EC – practice, on a permanent basis, of the profession of lawyer in a Member State other than that in which the qualification was acquired – action for annulment – principle of non-discrimination – obligation to state reasons*

Facts
On 16 February 1998 the European Parliament and the Council adopted Directive 98/5/EC on the right of establishment of lawyers who have obtained professional qualifications in the home Member State and wish to practise their profession on a permanent basis in any other Member State. The deadline for its implementation was set at 14 March 2000 and it has been implemented in the UK.

The Grand Duchy of Luxembourg brought an action for annulment of Directive 98/5/EC arguing, inter alia, that the Directive infringed art 43(2) EC.

Held
The ECJ rejected the action brought by the Grand Duchy of Luxembourg and thus confirmed the validity of Directive 98/5/EC.

Judgment
'The Grand Duchy of Luxembourg argues that the second paragraph of art 52 of the Treaty establishes a principle that a migrant self-employed worker is to be treated in the same way as his national counterpart. That national treatment rule means that equal treatment, or non-discrimination, must be measured by reference to the legislation of the host Member State and not to that of the home Member State, or Member State of

origin, of the migrant self-employed worker. Further, the right of establishment may not be granted in breach of overriding principles governing the self-employed professions, common to the laws of the various Member States.

The applicant claims that, while harmonisation may justify dispensing with any assessment of knowledge of international law, Community law and the law of the Member State of origin, no such dispensation can be contemplated as regards the law of the host Member State. The knowledge to be acquired in the field of national law, unlike the knowledge imparted in other training contexts, is not identical or even broadly the same from one Member State to another. Moreover, the special characteristics of knowledge of national law are recognised by Directive 89/48.

The Grand Duchy of Luxembourg points out that art 52 of the Treaty constitutes a particular expression of the general principle of equal treatment.

In its submission, by abolishing all requirement of prior training in the law of the host Member State and by permitting migrant lawyers to practise that law, Directive 98/5 unjustifiably discriminates between nationals and migrants which is unjustified and contrary to art 52 of the Treaty, which does not authorise the Community legislature to abolish a requirement of prior training in a directive which does not purport to harmonise training conditions.

The applicant adds that at the same time Directive 98/5 ignores the essential difference which exists, and must continue to exist, between establishment and provision of services, in so far as Council Directive 77/249/EEC of 22 March 1977 to facilitate the effective exercise by lawyers of freedom to provide services (OJ 1977 L78, p17) itself permits lawyers providing services to practise the law of the host Member State without having to show any knowledge of that law.

The Parliament and the Council, supported by the interveners, deny the existence of any reverse discrimination. They submit that lawyers practising under their home-country professional title and lawyers practising under the professional title of the host Member State are in different situations, the first being subject to several restrictions on the pursuit of their activity. In any event, it is no part of the function of art 52 of the Treaty to prescribe limits on the process of liberalising access to self-employed activity.

In response to those arguments, it must be stated that the prohibition of discrimination laid down in art 52 of the Treaty is only the specific expression of the general principle of equality which, as one of the fundamental principles of Community law, must be respected by the Community legislature and which requires that comparable situations should not be treated differently unless such difference in treatment is objectively justified (see, to this effect, Case C–27/95 *Woodspring District Council* v *Bakers of Nailsea Ltd* [1997] ECR I–1847, para 17).

In this case, it must be concluded that the Community legislature has not infringed that principle, since the situation of a migrant lawyer practising under his home-country title and the situation of a lawyer practising under the professional title of the host Member State are not comparable.

Whereas the latter may undertake all the activities open or reserved to the profession of lawyer by the host Member State, the former may be forbidden to pursue certain activities and, with regard to the representation or defence of clients in legal proceedings, may be subject to certain obligations.

Thus, art 5(2) of Directive 98/5 permits, subject to certain conditions, the host Member State to exclude lawyers practising under a home-country professional title from the activity of preparing deeds for obtaining title to administer the estates of deceased persons or for creating or transferring interests in land.

Similarly, the first subparagraph of art 5(3) allows the host Member State, in certain circumstances, to require lawyers practising under their home-country professional title to work in conjunction with either a lawyer practising under the professional title of that State before the judicial authority in question or with an "avoué" practising before it. The second subparagraph of that Article authorises the Member States to lay down specific rules for access to supreme courts, such as the use of specialist lawyers.

In addition, under art 4(1) of Directive 98/5, a lawyer practising in a host Member State under his home-country professional title is required to do so under that title, which "must be expressed ... in an intelligible manner and in such a way as to avoid confusion with the professional title of the host Member State".

The complaint of discrimination against lawyers practising under the professional title of the host Member State is therefore unfounded. In consequence, the first part of the first plea must be rejected.

[*The second part*]
The Grand Duchy of Luxembourg asserts that it has challenged the validity of Directive 98/5 in the interests of consumers and in the interest of the proper administration of justice. According to the case law of the Court, the application of professional rules to lawyers, in particular those relating to organisation, qualifications, professional ethics, supervision and liability, provides ultimate consumers of legal services and the sound administration of justice with the necessary guarantees of integrity and experience (Case C–3/95 *Reisebüro Broede* v *Sandker* [1996] ECR I–6511, para 38). By abolishing all requirement of training in the law of the host Member State, Directive 98/5 prejudices the public interest, in particular the protection of consumers, pursued by the various Member States in requiring, for access to and practice of the profession of lawyer, a legally prescribed qualification. In this connection, the applicant argues that to accept that training may be acquired in practice necessarily implies that practice precedes training. In addition, to claim that a lawyer practising under his home-country professional title will not practise the national law of the host Member State

which he does not know is to disregard the imperative requirements which militate against running such a risk; the quantitative likelihood of such a risk should not have any bearing on the determination that it is unacceptable.

The Parliament and Council, supported by the interveners, submit that Directive 98/5 takes into account overriding public interest grounds, in particular those of consumer protection, in arts 4, 5, 6 and 7. The Parliament and the United Kingdom point out that, under the rules of professional conduct, lawyers are in any event obliged not to handle cases when they know or ought to know that those cases fall outside their competence and that any breach of that rule constitutes a disciplinary offence.

In that regard, the Court observes that, in the absence of coordination at Community level, the Member States may, subject to certain conditions, impose national measures pursuing a legitimate aim compatible with the Treaty and justified on overriding public interest grounds, which include the protection of consumers. They may thus, in certain circumstances, adopt or maintain measures constituting a barrier to freedom of movement. Article 57(2) of the Treaty authorises the Community to eliminate obstacles of that kind in order to make it easier for persons to take up and pursue activities as self-employed persons. When adopting measures to that end, the Community legislature is to have regard to the public interest pursued by the various Member States and to adopt a level of protection for that interest which seems acceptable in the Community (see, to that effect, Case C–233/94 *Germany* v *EC Parliament and EC Council* [1997] ECR I–2405, paras 16 and 17). It enjoys a measure of discretion for the purposes of its assessment of the acceptable level of protection.

In this instance it is clear that several of the provisions of Directive 98/5 lay down rules intended to protect consumers and to ensure the proper administration of justice.

Thus, art 4 provides that a lawyer practising under his home-country professional title is required to do so under that title, so that consumers are informed that the professional to whom they entrust the defence of their interests has not obtained his qualification in the host Member State and that his initial training did not necessarily cover the host Member State's national law.

As has already been pointed out, art 5(2) and (3) authorise the host Member State, subject to certain conditions, to forbid migrant lawyers to undertake certain activities and to impose certain obligations on them in connection with the representation or defence of a client in legal proceedings.

Article 6(1) makes a lawyer practising under his home-country professional title subject not only to the rules of professional conduct applicable in his home Member State but also to the same rules of professional conduct as lawyers practising under the professional title of the host Member State in respect of all the activities which he pursues in its territory.

Article 6(3) authorises the host Member State to require a lawyer practising under his home-country professional title either to take out professional indemnity insurance or to become a member of a professional guarantee fund in accordance with the rules which that State lays down for professional activities pursued in its territory, unless he is covered by insurance taken out or a guarantee provided in accordance with the rules of his home Member State, without prejudice to the possibility of requiring additional insurance or an additional guarantee to be contracted where the equivalence is only partial.

Under art 7(1), where a lawyer practising under his home-country professional title fails to fulfil the obligations in force in the host Member State, the rules of procedure, penalties and remedies provided for in that State are to apply.

Article 7(2) and (3) imposes, in disciplinary matters, obligations of reciprocal information and cooperation between the competent authority of the home Member State and that of the host Member State.

Article 7(4) further provides that the competent authority in the home Member State shall decide what action to take, under its own procedural and substantive rules, in the light of a decision of the competent authority in the host Member State concerning a lawyer practising under his home-country professional title.

Last, art 7(5) provides that the temporary or permanent withdrawal by the competent authority in the home Member State of the authorisation to practise the profession shall automatically lead to the lawyer concerned being temporarily or permanently prohibited from practising under his home-country professional title in the host Member State.

Furthermore, it should be noted that, quite apart from the applicable rules of professional liability, the rules of professional conduct applicable to lawyers generally entail, like art 3.1.3 of the Code of Professional Conduct adopted by the Council of the Bars and Law Societies of the European Union (CCBE), an obligation, breach of which may incur disciplinary sanctions, not to handle matters which the professionals concerned know or ought to know they are not competent to handle.

It would therefore seem that the Community legislature, with a view to making it easier for a particular class of migrant lawyers to exercise the fundamental freedom of establishment, has chosen, in preference to a system of a priori testing of qualification in the national law of the host Member State, a plan of action combining consumer information, restrictions on the extent to which or the detailed rules under which certain activities of the profession may be practised, a number of applicable rules of professional conduct, compulsory insurance, as well as a system of discipline involving both the competent authorities of the home Member State and the host State. The legislature has not abolished the requirement that the lawyer concerned should know the national law applicable in the cases he handles, but has simply released him from the obligation to prove that knowledge in advance. It has thus allowed, in some circumstances, gradual assimilation of knowledge through practice, that assimilation being made easier by experience of other laws gained in the home Member

State. It was also able to take account of the dissuasive effect of the system of discipline and the rules of professional liability.

In making such a choice of the method and level of consumer protection and of ensuring the proper administration of justice, the Community legislature has not overstepped the limits of its discretion.

In consequence, the second part of the first plea must also be rejected.'

Comment

The most interesting aspect of the above case concerns the plea put forward by Luxembourg which submitted that Directive 98/5/EC introduces reverse discrimination contrary to art 43(2) EC, prejudices the interests of consumers and jeopardises the proper administration of justice. In respect of reverse discrimination, Luxembourg emphasised the fact that the principle of non-discrimination requires that a migrant EC lawyer should be treated in the same manner as his national counterpart. Luxembourg claimed that this was not the case under the Directive, taking into account the fact that a migrant EC lawyer is allowed to practise the law of the host Member State without any prior training in that law. Whilst dispensation as to the assessment of knowledge of international law, EC law or the home Member State's law is justifiable, national law of a host Member State and its peculiarity, as compared to national law of a home Member State, requires that a migrant EC lawyer must show that he possesses some knowledge of the law of a host Member State. This approach is, according to Luxembourg, also justified on the ground that there is a fundamental difference between the provision of legal services and the right of establishment for EC lawyers. The ECJ answered that the principle of non-discrimination requires that comparable situations must not be treated differently unless such difference in treatment is objectively justified: *Germany* v *EC Council* Case C–280/93 [1994] ECR I–4973 and *Woodspring District Council* v *Bakers of Nailsea Ltd* Case C–27/95 [1997] ECR I–1847. The situations of a migrant EC

lawyer and his host State counterpart are not comparable because a national lawyer is entitled to undertake all the activities open or reserved to the profession, whilst Directive 98/5/EC imposes important limitations on a migrant EC lawyer, such as the necessity to practise under the title of his home State, and, at the discretion of a host Member State, he may be excluded from carrying out certain activities referred to in art 5(2) of the Directive (ie the preparation of deeds, the administration of estates of deceased persons or the creation or transfer of interests in land if such activities are reserved to non-lawyers in a host Member State). Also art 5(3) of the Directive requires him to work in conjunction with a lawyer practising under the professional title of a host State in certain circumstances.

The ECJ also rejected the plea of Luxembourg based on the protection of consumers and the proper administration of justice. In particular, Luxembourg argued that the abolition of all requirements of prior training in the law of the host Member State for a migrant EC lawyer prejudices the interests of consumers. In this respect the most powerful argument is embodied in art 4(1) of the Directive which provides that a migrant lawyer must practise in a host Member State under his home State professional title which 'must be expressed ... in an intelligible manner and in such a way as to avoid confusion with the professional title of the host Member State'. Consequently, consumers are informed that his qualification has been obtained in another Member State. The ECJ emphasised that when a measure is adopted by the Community legislature the public interests pursued by the various Member States are duly taken into consideration in order to adopt a level of protection for those interests which seem acceptable in the Community: *Germany* v *EC Parliament and EC Council* Case C–233/94 [1997] ECR I–2405. In respect of the Directive the ECJ pointed out that it contains numerous safeguards aimed at ensuring the protection of consumers and the proper administration of justice, such as the application of rules of professional conduct of both the home Member State and the host Member State. This entails that a migrant EC lawyer is obliged not to handle cases when he knows, or ought to know, that they fall outside his competence and that any breach of that rule constitutes a disciplinary offence. Other safeguards include compulsory insurance and the system of discipline involving both the competent authorities of the home Member State and the host Member State. The ECJ held that the Directive did not abolish the requirement that a migrant EC lawyer must know the national law of a host Member State in the cases he handles but:

> '... has simply released him from the obligation to prove that knowledge in advance. It has thus allowed, in some circumstances, gradual assimilation of knowledge through practice, that assimilation being made easier by experience of other laws gained in the home Member State.'

Hocsman (Hugo Fernando) v *Ministre de l'Emploi et de la Solidarite* Case C–238/98 [2000] 3 CMLR 1025 European Court of Justice

• *Right of establishment – Directive 93/16/EEC – Community national holding an Argentinian diploma recognised by the authorities of a Member State as equivalent in that State to a university degree in medicine and surgery – obligations of another Member State with respect to an application to practise medicine on its territory – preliminary ruling*

Facts
Doctor Hocsman, a national of Argentina, had acquired Spanish nationality before being naturalised in France in 1998. He obtained his qualification as a medical doctor in Argentina in 1976, which was recognised by a Spanish university as being equivalent to a Spanish qualification and on the basis of which he

practised medicine in Spain and was trained as a specialist in urology. In 1982 he was awarded the qualification of specialist in urology by the University of Barcelona. Upon the acquisition of Spanish nationality in 1986 Dr Hocsman obtained authorisation to practise as a specialist in urology in Spain, where he worked for some years. In 1990 Dr Hocsman moved to France where he held posts as assistant or associate specialising in urology in a number of French hospitals. In 1998 he obtained French nationality. In 1997 the French Minister for Employment and Solidarity refused to grant Dr Hocsman authorisation to practise medicine in France on the ground that the Argentinian diploma did not entitled him to practise in France. Dr Hocsman challenged the decision refusing to recognise his original Argentinian medical qualification. The referring court ask the ECJ whether an equivalence accorded by one Member State should be recognised in another Member State and in particular whether a specialised training acquired in another Member State is included in the scope of a directive concerning the mutual recognition of diplomas.

Held
The ECJ held that art 43 EC requires that, in situations not regulated by a directive on mutual recognition of diplomas, when a Community national applies for authorisation to practise a profession, access to which depends, under national law, on the possession of a diploma or professional qualification, or on periods of practical experience, the competent authorities of the Member State concerned must take into consideration all the diplomas, certificates and other evidence of formal qualifications of the person concerned and his relevant experience, by comparing the specialised knowledge and abilities certified by those diplomas and that experience with the knowledge and qualifications required by the national rules.

Judgment
> 'Dr Hocsman sees a contradiction in the fact that he has lawfully worked for some years

as a specialist in urology in various hospitals in France, while at the same time his application to be registered with the Ordre National des Médecins has been rejected. In reliance on the Court's case law on art 52 of the Treaty, in particular Case C–340/89 *Vlassopoulou* v *Ministerium für Justiz, Bundes-und Europaangelegenheiten Baden-Württemburg* [1991] ECR I–2357 and Case C–319/92 *Haim* v *Kassenzahnärztliche Vereinigung Nordrhein* [1994] ECR I–425, he submits that the French authorities' refusal to recognise his Argentine diploma in medicine is contrary to both the spirit and the letter of that Article.

In *Vlassopoulou*, para 16, the Court held that art 52 of the Treaty must be interpreted as meaning that a Member State to which an application is made for authorisation to practise a profession to which access, under national law, depends on the possession of a diploma or professional qualification must take into consideration the diplomas, certificates and other evidence of qualifications which the person concerned has acquired in order to practise that profession in another Member State, by comparing the specialised knowledge and abilities certified by those diplomas with the knowledge and qualifications required by the national rules.

Applying the same principle, the Court held in *Haim*, para 28, that in order to verify whether a training period requirement prescribed by the national rules is satisfied the competent national authorities must take into account the professional experience of the person concerned, including that which he has acquired in another Member State.

Since those decisions have been confirmed on several occasions (see, as the most recent authority, Case C–234/97 *Fernández de Bobadilla* v *Museo Nacional del Prado* [1999] ECR I–4773, paras 29 to 31), it is settled that the authorities of a Member State to whom an application has been made by a Community national for authorisation to practise a profession access to which depends, under national law, on the possession of a diploma or professional qualification, or on periods of practical experience, must take into consideration all

the diplomas, certificates and other evidence of formal qualifications of the person concerned and his relevant experience, by comparing the specialised knowledge and abilities so certified and that experience with the knowledge and qualifications required by the national rules.

It must be observed that those judgments are merely the expression in individual cases of a principle which is inherent in the fundamental freedoms of the Treaty.

The Spanish and Italian governments, supported at the hearing by the French government, submit that this principle does not apply to the present case. Where there is a directive on mutual recognition of diplomas, such as Directive 93/16, and the qualification held by the person concerned does not satisfy the requirements of that directive, he may not rely directly on the Treaty provisions on fundamental Community freedoms.

Those governments consider that art 57(3) of the Treaty makes the freedom of movement of those practising the medical and allied and pharmaceutical professions subject to conditions specified in secondary legislation, and conclude that those persons may exercise that right only in accordance with the procedure and conditions laid down by the secondary legislation, that is, as regards the main proceedings, in the context of Directive 93/16.

They observe that the Court's case law on the point concerned professions such as that of lawyer (at issue in *Vlassopoulou*) or estate agent (see Case C–104/91 *Colegio Nacional de Agentes de la Propiedad Inmobiliaria* v *Aguirre Borrell and Others* [1992] ECR I–3003) which at the time when those judgments were delivered were not the subject of any directive on the coordination or mutual recognition of diplomas. Those cases are therefore of no relevance to the freedom of movement of doctors, which is regulated exhaustively by Directive 93/16 as regards the determination of those who are entitled to that freedom and those who are not.

They state that the purpose of the restriction for the medical and allied and pharmaceutical professions introduced by art 57(3) of the Treaty is to guarantee a high level of health protection, which is one of the objectives expressly given to the Community by art 3(o) of the EC Treaty (now, after amendment, art 3(1)(p) EC). Attainment of that objective would be compromised if it were accepted that the medical or allied professions could be practised without complying with the conditions laid down by the relevant directives.

The Finnish and United Kingdom governments and the Commission, on the other hand, consider that the obligations concerning mutual recognition of diplomas imposed on Member States by art 52 of the Treaty subsist whether or not there is a Community directive in this field. The Commission observes that it would be paradoxical if the existence of a directive aimed at mutual recognition of diplomas had the effect of restricting freedom of establishment by depriving Community nationals whose diplomas did not satisfy the requirements of that directive of the possibility of relying on the principle stated in paras 23 and 24 above, when they would certainly have been able to do so in the absence of such a directive.

In view of those observations, the scope of the principle stated in paras 23 and 24 above should be clarified.

While that principle was indeed applied in cases concerning professions for the practice of which there were no harmonisation or coordination measures in existence at the time, its legal ambit cannot be reduced as a result of the adoption of directives on mutual recognition of diplomas.

The object of such directives is, as appears from art 57(1) of the Treaty, to make it easier for persons to take up and pursue activities as self-employed persons, and hence to make the existing possibilities of taking up those activities easier for nationals of other Member States. In that context the Court has held that, if the freedom of establishment provided for by art 52 can be ensured in a Member State either under the laws and regulations in force or by virtue of the practices of the public administration or professional associations, a person subject to Community law cannot be denied the practical benefit of that freedom solely because, for a particular profession, the directives provided for by art 57 of the Treaty have not yet been adopted (see Case 71/76 *Thieffry* v *Conseil de l'Ordre des Avocats à la Cour de Paris* [1977] ECR 765, para 17).

The function of directives which lay down common rules and criteria for mutual recognition of diplomas is thus to introduce a system in which Member States are obliged to accept the equivalence of certain diplomas and cannot require the persons concerned to comply with requirements other than those laid down by the relevant directives.

Such mutual recognition of those diplomas makes it superfluous, where the requirements such as those set out in Directive 93/16 are satisfied, to recognise them under the principle referred to in paras 23 and 24 above. However, that principle retains a certain relevance in situations not covered by such directives, as in Dr Hocsman's case.

In such a situation, as stated in para 23 above, the authorities of a Member State to whom an application has been made by a Community national for authorisation to practise a profession access to which depends, under national law, on the possession of a diploma or professional qualification, or on periods of practical experience, must take into consideration all the diplomas, certificates and other evidence of formal qualifications of the person concerned and his relevant experience, by comparing the specialised knowledge and abilities so certified and that experience with the knowledge and qualifications required by the national rules.

If that comparative examination of diplomas and professional experience results in the finding that the knowledge and qualifications certified by the diploma awarded abroad correspond to those required by the national provisions, the competent authorities of the host Member State must recognise that diploma, and if appropriate also the professional experience, as fulfilling the requirements laid down by its national provisions. If, on the other hand, the comparison reveals that the knowledge and qualifications correspond only partially, those authorities are entitled to require the person concerned to show that he has acquired the knowledge and qualifications not attested (see, to that effect, *Vlassopoulou*, paras 19 and 20, and *Fernández de Bobadilla*, paras 32 and 33).

The main proceedings concern a doctor whose diploma in basic medicine from Argentina was recognised in a Member State as equivalent to the national diploma, thus allowing him to pursue specialist studies in urology in that State and obtain there a diploma of specialist in urology which, according to the documents before the Court, would have been recognised under Community law as equivalent in all the Member States if the basic diploma had also been awarded in a Member State.

Dr Hocsman then also lawfully practised for several years in the host Member State precisely the medical specialisation which he wishes to practise there in future in a self-employed capacity, for which he must be registered with the professional medical association of the host Member State, and must therefore possess a diploma in basic medicine awarded by the competent national authorities or recognised as equivalent to that diploma.

It is for the national court, or if appropriate the competent national authorities, to assess in the light of all the evidence in the case and the above considerations, whether Dr Hocsman's diploma is to be accepted as equivalent to the corresponding French diploma. In particular, it will have to be considered whether recognition in Spain of Dr Hocsman's diploma from Argentina as equivalent to the Spanish university degree in medicine and surgery was given on the basis of criteria comparable to those intended, in the context of Directive 93/16, to ensure that Member States may rely on the quality of the diplomas in medicine awarded by the other Member States.

Accordingly, the answer to be given to the national court's question must be that art 52 of the Treaty is to be interpreted as meaning that where, in a situation not regulated by a directive on mutual recognition of diplomas, a Community national applies for authorisation to practise a profession access to which depends, under national law, on the possession of a diploma or professional qualification, or on periods of practical experience, the competent authorities of the Member State concerned must take into consideration all the diplomas, certificates and other evidence of formal qualifications of the person concerned and his relevant experience, by comparing the specialised knowledge and abilities certified by those diplomas and that experience with the knowledge and qualifications required by the national rules.'

Comment

In the above case the ECJ provided interesting clarifications in respect of the situation when EC nationals obtain their qualification in a non-Member State, exercise their right of establishment in a host Member State and subsequently seek to practise in another Member State. This matter was previously examined by the ECJ in *Tawil-Albertini* v *Ministre des Affaires Sociales* Case C–154/93 [1994] ECR I–451 and in *Haim* Case C–319/92 [1994] ECR I–425.

In the present case the ECJ stated that the adoption of directives aimed at mutual recognition of diplomas did not challenge the principles established in the previous case law of the ECJ. As the Commission rightly pointed out, it would be paradoxical if the existence of secondary legislation (ie directives on mutual recognition of diplomas) had the effect of restricting freedom of establishment and thus depriving EC nationals, whose diplomas did not satisfy the requirements of a relevant directive, of the possibility of relying directly on art 43 EC. Indeed, in such a situation the person concerned would have been able to have his diplomas recognised in the absence of a directive! The ECJ stated that the objective of directives aimed at mutual recognition of diplomas is to make it easier for persons to take up and pursue activities as self-employed persons. Consequently, if the requirements for recognition set out in such directives are satisfied, a Member State is obliged to accept the equivalence of certain diplomas. In other words the recognition is automatic. However, if the requirements are not fulfilled, art 43 EC retains its importance. In such situations, the authorities of a host Member State must take into consideration all the diplomas, certificates and other relevant experience, and compare the specialised knowledge and abilities so certified, and that experience, with the knowledge and qualifications required by the national rules.

Although the final decision as to the recognition of Dr Hocsman's Argentinian diploma was left to the referring court, the ECJ pointed out that his Spanish diploma of specialist in urology would have been recognised under Community law as equivalent in all Member States if the basic diploma had also been awarded in a Member State, and that Dr Hocsman had lawfully practised for several years in France the medical specialisation which he wished to continue to practise there.

Reyners (Jean) v *Belgium* Case 2/74 [1974] ECR 631; [1974] 2 CMLR 305 European Court of Justice

- *Freedom of establishment – art 52 EC Treaty [art 43 EC] – national restrictions based on nationality preventing foreign nationals practising law – discrimination contrary to arts 6 and 52 EC Treaty [arts 12 and 43 EC] – direct effect of art 52 EC Treaty [art 43 EC] – need for professional qualification – art 55 EC Treaty [art 45 EC] – advocates do not exercise official authority*

Facts

Jean Reyners, a Dutch national born and bred in Belgium, a holder of the Belgian doctorate in law (docteur en droit), sat the necessary examinations to become an advocate in Belgium. The Belgian legislation provided that only Belgian nationals could be called to the Belgian Bar. Reyners challenged the compatibility of this legislation with art 52 EC Treaty [art 43 EC]. The Belgian Conseil d'Etat referred the matter to the ECJ under the preliminary ruling procedure. During these proceedings, the Belgian Bar and the government of Luxembourg submitted that the profession of advocate was excluded from art 52 EC Treaty [art 43 EC] as its activities were connected with the exercise of official authority within the meaning of art 55 EC Treaty [art 45 EC]. In Belgium an advocate may be called upon to sit as a judge in certain cases, and a judge exercises official authority.

Held

The rule established in art 52 EC Treaty [art 43 EC] had to be interpreted in the light of the whole scheme of the EC Treaty, including art 6 EC Treaty [art 12 EC] which prohibits any discrimination on the grounds of nationality. The ECJ held that art 52 EC Treaty [art 43 EC] was directly effective. The Court stated that the exception to freedom of establishment contained in art 55 EC Treaty [art 45 EC] did not apply to the profession of advocate as it was restricted to activities which involved a direct and specific connection with the exercise of official authority.

Judgment

'[*On the interpretation of art 52 EC Treaty*] The rule on equal treatment with nationals is one of the fundamental legal provisions of the Community.

As a reference to a set of legislative provisions effectively applied by the country of establishment to its own nationals, this rule is, by its essence, capable of being directly invoked by nationals of all the other Member States.

In laying down that freedom of establishment shall be attained at the end of the transitional period, art 52 thus imposes an obligation to attain a precise result, the fulfilment of which had to made easier by, but not made dependent on, the implementation of a programme of progressive measures.

The fact that this progression has not been adhered to leaves the obligation itself intact beyond the end of the period provided for its fulfilment.

This interpretation is in accordance with art 8(7) of the Treaty, according to which the expiry of the transitional period shall constitute the latest date by which all the rules laid down must enter into force and all the measures required for establishing the Common Market must be implemented.

It is not possible to invoke against such an effect the fact that the Council has failed to issue the directives provided for by arts 54 and 57 or the fact that certain of the directives actually issued have not fully attained the objective of non-discrimination required by art 52.

After the expiry of the transitional period the directives provided for by the Chapter on the right of establishment have become superfluous with regard to implementing the rule on nationality, since this is henceforth sanctioned by the Treaty itself with direct effect.

These directives have however not lost all interest since they preserve an important scope in the field of measures intended to make easier the effective exercise of the right of freedom of establishment.

It is therefore to reply to the question raised that, since the end of the transitional period, art 52 of the Treaty is a directly applicable provision despite the absence in a particular sphere of the directives prescribed by arts 54(2) and 57(1) of the Treaty.

[*On the interpretation of art 55 EC Treaty*]
The Conseil d'Etat has also requested a definition of what is meant in the first paragraph of art 55 by "activities which in that State are connected, even occasionally, with the exercise of official authority".

... Professional activities involving contacts, even regular and organic, with the courts, including even compulsory co-operation in their functioning, do not constitute, as such, connection with the exercise of official authority.

The most typical activities of the profes-

sion of avocat, in particular, such as consultation and legal assistance and also representation and the defence of parties in court, even when the intervention or assistance of the avocat is compulsory or is a legal monopoly, cannot be considered as connected with the exercise of judicial authority.

The exercise of these activities leaves the discretion of judicial authority and the free exercise of judicial power intact.

It is therefore right to reply to the question raised that the exception to freedom of establishment provided for by the first paragraph of art 55 must be restricted to those activities referred to in art 52 which in themselves involve a direct and specific connection with the exercise of official authority.

In any case it is not possible to give this description, in the context of a profession such as that of avocat, to activities such as consultation and legal assistance or the representation and defence of parties in court, even if the performance of these activities is compulsory or there is a legal monopoly in respect of it.'

Comment

In the present case the ECJ held that art 52 EC Treaty [art 43 EC] was directly effective and the fact that this provision stated that the restrictions on the freedom of establishment 'shall be abolished by progressive stages in the course of the transitional period' did not affect the rights of nationals of one Member State wishing to establish themselves in another Member State to enjoy immediate protection. The ECJ held that art 52 EC Treaty [art 43 EC] imposed an obligation to attain a precise result which was not conditional upon the implementation of a programme of progressive measures. The latter would only facilitate the attainment of the prescribed result.

The ECJ also stated that the legal profession is within the scope of art 52 EC Treaty [art 43 EC] and therefore the exception to freedom of establishment based on art 55 EC Treaty [art 45 EC] can not be invoked (the situation is uncertain in respect of the notariat of the Member States of continental Europe).

Thieffry v Conseil de l'Ordre des Avocats à la Cour de Paris Case 71/76 [1977] ECR 765; [1977] 2 CMLR 373 European Court of Justice

• *Free movement of lawyers – art 52 of EC Treaty [art 43 EC] – discrimination on the grounds of nationality – art 57 of EC Treaty [art 47 EC] – recognition of professional qualification – national practice or legislation – admission to professional bodies*

Facts

Jean Thieffry, a Belgian advocate and a holder of a Belgian diploma of Doctor of Laws which was recognised by a French University as equivalent to the French licentiate's degree of law, applied for admission to the training stage required for an advocate at the Paris Bar. He satisfied the condition for admission to the training stage as he sat and successfully passed the French examination for the Certificat d'Aptitude à la Profession d'Avocat (Qualifying Certificate for the Profession of Advocate). The Paris Bar refused to call him to the bar. The refusal was justified on the ground that he 'offers no French diploma evidencing a licentiate's degree or a doctor's degree'. He challenged the decision of the Paris Bar Council before the French Court of Appeal (Cour d'Appel) which referred to the ECJ a question concerning the interpretation of art 57 EC Treaty [art 47 EC], which relates to the mutual recognition of evidence of professional qualifications for the purpose of access to activities as self-employed persons, with regard, in particular, to admission to exercise the profession of advocate.

Held

The ECJ held that national authorities, including national professional bodies such as the Paris Bar Council, have a duty to ensure that national practices and legislation are compatible which the objectives of the Treaty. Even

in the absence of Community measures adopted under art 57 EC Treaty [art 47 EC] for a particular profession, by virtue of art 52 EC Treaty [art 43 EC] a person cannot be denied the practical benefit of the freedom of establishment on the ground that national legislation providing for the recognition of equivalence of diplomas limits such recognition to university purposes, in particular in circumstances when the applicant had also obtained a professional qualifying certificate in accordance with legislation of the State of establishment.

Judgment

'... if the freedom of establishment provided for by art 52 can be ensured in a Member State either under the provisions of laws and regulations in force, or by virtue of the practices of the public service or of professional bodies, a person subject to Community law cannot be denied the practical benefit of that freedom solely by virtue of the fact that, for a particular profession, the directives provided for by art 57 of the Treaty have not yet been adopted.

Since the practical enjoyment of freedom of establishment can thus in certain circumstances depend upon national practice or legislation, it is incumbent upon the competent public authorities – including legally recognised professional bodies – to ensure that such practice or legislation [is] applied in accordance with the objective defined by the provisions of the Treaty relating to freedom of establishment.

In particular, there is an unjustified restriction on that freedom where, in a Member State, admission to a particular profession is refused to a person covered by the Treaty who holds a diploma which has been recognised as an equivalent qualification by the competent authority of the country of establishment and who furthermore has fulfilled the specific conditions regarding professional training in force in that country, solely by reason of the fact that the person concerned does not possess the national diploma corresponding to the diploma which he holds and which has been recognised as an equivalent qualification.

The national court specifically referred to the effect of a recognition of equivalence "by the university authority of the country of establishment", and in the course of the proceedings the question has been raised whether a distinction should be drawn, as regards the equivalence of diplomas, between university recognition, granted with a view to permitting the pursuit of certain studies, and a recognition having "civil effect", granted with a view to permitting the pursuit of professional activity.

It emerges from the information supplied in this connection by the Commission and the governments which took part in the proceedings that the distinction between the academic effect and the civil effect of the recognition of foreign diplomas is acknowledged, in various forms, in the legislation and practice of several Member States.

Since the distinction falls within the ambit of the national law of the different States, it is for the national authorities to assess the consequences thereof, taking account, however, of the objectives of Community law.

In this connection it is important that, in each Member State, the recognition of evidence of a professional qualification for the purposes of establishment may be accepted to the full extent compatible with the observance of the professional requirements mentioned above.

Consequently, it is for the competent national authorities, taking account of the requirements of Community law set out above, to make such assessments of the facts as will enable them to judge whether a recognition granted by a university authority can, in addition to its academic effect, constitute valid evidence of a professional qualification.

The fact that a national legislation provides for recognition of equivalence only for university purposes does not of itself justify the refusal to recognise such equivalence as evidence of a professional qualification.

This is particularly so when a diploma

recognised for university purposes is supplemented by a professional qualifying certificate obtained according to the legislation of the country of establishment.

In these circumstances, the answer to the question referred to the Court should be that when a national of one Member State desirous of exercising a professional activity such as the profession of advocate in another Member State has obtained a diploma in his country of origin which has been recognised as an equivalent qualification by the competent authority under the legislation of the country of establishment and which has thus enabled him to sit and pass the special qualifying examination for the profession in question, the act of demanding the national diploma prescribed by the legislation of the country of establishment constitutes, even in the absence of the directives provided for in art 57, a restriction incompatible with the freedom of establishment guaranteed by art 52 of the Treaty.'

Comment

In the context of the present case it is interesting to note that at last in 1998 the European Parliament and the Council adopted Directive 98/5/EC on the right of establishment for lawyers who have obtained professional qualifications in the home Member State and wish to practise their profession on a permanent basis in any other Member State. The deadline for its implementation expired on 11 March 2000. The Directive has been implemented in the UK. (Directive 98/5/EC was challenged by Luxembourg: see *Grand Duchy of Luxembourg* v *European Parliament and Council of the European Union* Case C–168/98 [2000] ECR I–9131.)

The free movement of services

Freedom to provide services

Criminal Proceedings against Jean-Claude Arblade and Arblade & Fils SARL and Bernard Leloup, Serge Leloup, Solfrage SARL Joined Cases C–369 and 376/96 [1999] ECR I–8453 European Court of Justice

• *Temporary deployment of workers for the purpose of performing a contract – arts 49 and 50 EC – 'public order legislation' subject to EC law – social protection of temporarily deployed workers – application of the most favourable social legislation of a host Member State to such workers – additional obligations of a social and administrative nature*

Facts
Under Belgian legislation, construction undertakings, irrespective of their place of establishment, carrying out work in Belgium are required to pay their workers the minimum remuneration, to pay 'timbres-intermpéries' and 'timbre-fidelité' contributions to each worker, to draw up and keep various social documents and to produce these documents at the request of the competent Belgian authorities.

Arblade and Leloup, two French construction undertakings, carried out construction works in Belgium. During the period between 1991 and 1993 they deployed workers on Belgian sites. When checks were carried out on the sites in 1993 the competent Belgian authorities requested the production of various social documents from the French undertakings. Both undertakings refused on the grounds that they had complied with all the French legislation and that the obligations imposed by the Belgian legislation were in breach of arts 49 and 50 EC. Criminal prosecutions were commenced against the French

undertakings. The Huy Criminal Court (the Tribunal Correctionnel de Huy) referred to the ECJ for a preliminary ruling regarding the compatibility of various social obligations provided by the Belgian legislation with arts 49 and 50 EC.

Held
The ECJ held that arts 49 and 50 EC do not preclude the imposition by a Member State on an undertaking established in another Member State, and temporarily carrying out work in the first Member State, of an obligation to pay the workers deployed by it the minimum remuneration as required by the legislation of the first Member State, provided that the provisions in question are sufficiently precise and accessible and that they do not render it impossible or excessively difficult in practice for such an employer to determine the obligations with which he is required to comply.

However, additional obligations of a social and administrative nature which are imposed by a host Member State's legislation are justified only where workers temporarily deployed there do not enjoy equivalent social protection in their home Member State and where such an obligation is imposed on all providers of services within the territory of the host Member State.

The obligation to keep social and labour documents can only be imposed if an undertaking is not already subject, in the Member State in which it is established, to obligations which are comparable, in terms of their objectives of safeguarding the interests of workers, to those imposed by the legislation of the host Member State, and which relate to the same workers and the same type of activity.

Judgment
'[*The questions referred*]
It is common ground, first, that Arblade and Leloup, who are established in France, moved, within the meaning of arts 59 and 60 of the Treaty, to another Member State, namely Belgium, in order to carry on activities of a temporary nature there and,

second, that their activities are not wholly or principally directed towards the latter State with a view to avoiding the rules which would apply to them if they were established within its territory.

It is settled case law that art 59 of the Treaty requires not only the elimination of all discrimination on grounds of nationality against providers of services who are established in another Member State but also the abolition of any restriction, even if it applies without distinction to national providers of services and to those of other Member States, which is liable to prohibit, impede or render less advantageous the activities of a provider of services established in another Member State where he lawfully provides similar services (see Case C–76/90 *Säger* v *Dennemeyer* [1991] ECR I–4221, para 12, Case C–43/93 *Van der Elst* v *Office des Migrations Internationales* [1994] ECR I–3803, para 14, Case C–272/94 *Criminal Proceedings against Guiot* [1996] ECR I–1905, para 10, Case C–3/95 *Reisebüro Broede* v *Sandker* [1996] ECR I–6511, para 25, and Case C–222/95 *Parodi* v *Banque H Albert de Bary* [1997] ECR I–3899, para 18).

Even if there is no harmonisation in the field, the freedom to provide services, as one of the fundamental principles of the Treaty, may be restricted only by rules justified by overriding requirements relating to the public interest and applicable to all persons and undertakings operating in the territory of the State where the service is provided, in so far as that interest is not safeguarded by the rules to which the provider of such a service is subject in the Member State where he is established (see, in particular, Case 279/80 *Webb* v *Air Cargo (UK) Ltd* [1981] ECR 3305, para 17, Case C–180/89 *EC Commission* v *Italy* [1991] ECR I–709, para 17, Case C–198/89 *EC Commission* v *Greece* [1991] ECR I–727, para 18, *Säger*, cited above, para 15, *Van der Elst*, cited above, para 16, and *Guiot*, cited above, para 11).

The application of national rules to providers of services established in other Member States must be appropriate for

securing the attainment of the objective which they pursue and must not go beyond what is necessary in order to attain it (see, in particular, *Säger*, para 15, Case C–19/92 *Kraus* v *Land Baden-Württemberg* [1993] ECR I–1663, para 32, Case C–55/94 *Gebhard* v *Consiglio dell'Ordine degli Avvocati e Procuratori di Milano* [1995] ECR I–4165, para 37, and *Guiot*, cited above, paras 11 and 13).

The overriding reasons relating to the public interest which have been acknowledged by the Court include the protection of workers (see *Webb*, cited above, para 19, Joined Cases 62/81 and 63/81 *Seco* v *EVI* [1982] ECR 223, para 14, and Case C–113/89 *Rush Portuguesa* v *Office National d'Immigration* [1990] ECR I–1417, para 18), and in particular the social protection of workers in the construction industry (*Guiot*, para 16).

By contrast, considerations of a purely administrative nature cannot justify derogation by a Member State from the rules of Community law, especially where the derogation in question amounts to preventing or restricting the exercise of one of the fundamental freedoms of Community law (see, in particular, Case C–18/95 *Terhoeve* v *Inspecteur van de Balastigdienst Particulieren/Ondernemingen Buitenland* [1999] ECR I–345, para 45).

However, overriding reasons relating to the public interest which justify the substantive provisions of a set of rules may also justify the control measures needed to ensure compliance with them (see, to that effect, *Rush Portuguesa*, cited above, para 18).

It is therefore necessary to consider, in turn, whether the requirements imposed by national rules such as those at issue in the main proceedings have a restrictive effect on freedom to provide services, and, if so, whether, in the sector under consideration, such restrictions on freedom to provide services are justified by overriding reasons relating to the public interest. If they are, it is necessary, in addition, to establish whether that interest is already protected by the rules of the Member State in which the service provider is established and whether the same result can be achieved by less restrictive rules (see, in particular, *Säger*, para 15, *Kraus*, cited above, para 32, *Gebhard*, cited above, para 37, *Guiot*, cited above, para 13, and *Reisebüro Broede*, cited above, para 28).

It is appropriate in that context to examine the various obligations mentioned in the questions referred, in the following order:
– payment of the minimum remuneration,
– payment of contributions to the "timbres-intempéries" and "timbres-fidélité" schemes and the drawing-up of individual records,
– the keeping of social documents, and
– the retention of social documents.

[*Payment of the minimum remuneration*]
As regards the obligation on an employer providing services to pay his workers the minimum remuneration fixed by a collective labour agreement applying in the host Member State to the activities carried on, it must be recalled that Community law does not preclude Member States from extending their legislation, or collective labour agreements entered into by both sides of industry, relating to minimum wages, to any person who is employed, even temporarily, within their territory, regardless of the country in which the employer is established, and, moreover, that Community law does not prohibit Member States from enforcing those rules by appropriate means (*Seco*, cited above, para 14, *Rush Portuguesa*, para 18, and *Guiot*, para 12).

It follows that the provisions of a Member State's legislation or collective labour agreements which guarantee minimum wages may in principle be applied to employers providing services within the territory of that State, regardless of the country in which the employer is established.

However, in order for infringement of the provisions in question to justify the criminal prosecution of an employer established in another Member State, those provisions must be sufficiently precise and accessible that they do not render it impossible or excessively difficult in practice for such an employer to determine the obligations with

which he is required to comply. It is for the competent authority – in the present case, the Belgian Social Law Inspectorate – when laying an information before the criminal courts, to state unequivocally the obligations with which the employer is accused of having failed to comply.

Thus, it is for the national court to determine, in the light of those considerations, which of the relevant provisions of its national law are applicable to an employer established in another Member State and, where appropriate, the amount of the minimum wage prescribed by them.

The Belgian and Austrian governments consider that the advantages guaranteed to workers by the "timbres-intempéries" and "timbres-fidélité" schemes, as provided for by the CLA of 28 April 1988, constitute part of the minimum annual income of a construction worker within the meaning of the Belgian legislation.

However, it is apparent from the documents before the Court, first, that it was only Arblade that was prosecuted for failure to pay its workers the minimum wage provided for by the CLA of 28 March 1991 and, second, that art 4(1) of the CLA of 28 April 1988 fixes the contribution payable in respect of "timbres-intempéries" and "timbres-fidélité" on the basis of 100 per cent of the worker's gross remuneration. Since the amount due under the "timbres-intempéries" and "timbres-fidélité" schemes is calculated by reference to the gross minimum wage, it cannot form an integral part of that wage.

In those circumstances, it would appear – though this is a point for the national court to confirm – that the advantages guaranteed to workers by the "timbres-intempéries" and "timbres-fidélité" schemes cannot constitute an element to be taken into account when determining the minimum wage which Arblade is accused of having failed to pay.

[*Payment of the contribution to the "timbres-intempéries" and "timbres-fidélité" schemes and the drawing-up of individual records*]
As regards the obligation to pay employers'

contributions to the Belgian "timbres-intempéries" and "timbres-fidélité" schemes, it is apparent from the judgment of the national court, and in particular from the wording of the first question referred in each of the two cases, that Arblade and Leloup are already subject, in the Member State in which they are established, to obligations which, while not identical, are at least comparable as regards their objective, and which relate to the same workers and the same periods of activity.

The Belgian government submits that the referring court has not determined the existence of such obligations in the Member State of establishment. However, the Court is bound to accept the national court's finding that the undertaking providing the services is already subject, in the Member State in which it is established, to obligations which, because of their objective, are comparable.

National rules which require an employer, as a provider of services within the meaning of the Treaty, to pay employers' contributions to the host Member State's fund, in addition to those which he has already paid to the fund of the Member State in which he is established, constitute a restriction on freedom to provide services. Such an obligation gives rise to additional expenses and administrative and economic burdens for undertakings established in another Member State, with the result that such undertakings are not on an equal footing, from the standpoint of competition, with employers established in the host Member State, and may thus be deterred from providing services in the host Member State.

It must be acknowledged that the public interest relating to the social protection of workers in the construction industry and the monitoring of compliance with the relevant rules may constitute an overriding requirement justifying the imposition on an employer established in another Member State who provides services in the host Member State of obligations capable of constituting restrictions on freedom to provide services. However, that is not the case where the workers employed by the employer in question are temporarily engaged in carrying out works in the host Member State and enjoy the same protection, or essentially similar protection, by virtue of the obligations to which the employer is already subject in the Member State in which he is established.

Moreover, an obligation requiring a provider of services to pay employers' contributions to the host Member State's fund cannot be justified where those contributions confer no social advantage on the workers in question (*Seco*, para 15).

It is therefore for the national court to establish, first, whether the contributions payable in the host Member State give rise to any social advantage for the workers concerned and, second, whether, in the Member State of establishment, those workers enjoy, by virtue of the contributions already paid by the employer in that State, protection which is essentially similar to that afforded by the rules of the Member State in which the services are provided.

Only if the employer's contributions to the host Member State's fund confer on workers an advantage capable of providing them with real additional protection which they would not otherwise enjoy will it be possible to justify the payment of the contributions in question, and, even then, those contributions will be justifiable only if they are payable by all providers of services operating within the national territory in the industry concerned.

Lastly, it is clear that the obligation under the Belgian legislation to issue an individual record to each worker is inextricably linked to the obligation to pay the "timbres-intempéries" and "timbres-fidélité" contributions provided for in the CLA of 28 April 1988. If an undertaking is already subject, in the Member State in which it is established, to obligations which are essentially similar, by reason of their objective, to those imposed under the "timbres-intempéries" and "timbres-fidélité" schemes, and which relate to the same workers and the same periods of activity, that undertaking is only obliged to issue its workers with the equivalent documents which it is required to issue pursuant to the legislation of the Member State in which it is established. If the system applying in the latter State did not provide for the issue of documents to employees, the undertaking in question would be required only to justify to the authorities of the host Member State that it is up to date with the payment of the contributions required under the rules of the Member State of establishment, by producing the documents prescribed for that purpose by those rules.

[*The principle of keeping social and labour documents*]

As regards the obligation to draw up labour regulations and to keep a special staff register and an individual account for each worker, it is likewise apparent from the judgment of the national court, and in particular from the wording of the first question referred in each of the two cases, that Arblade and Leloup are already subject, in the Member State in which they are established, to obligations which, while not identical, are at least comparable as regards their objective, and which relate to the same workers and the same periods of activity.

As stated in para 49 of this judgment, and despite the objections raised by the Belgian government, the Court is bound to base its ruling on the facts as stated by the national court.

An obligation of the kind imposed by the Belgian legislation, requiring certain additional documents to be drawn up and kept in the host Member State, gives rise to additional expenses and administrative and economic burdens for undertakings established in another Member State, with the result that such undertakings are not on an equal footing, from the standpoint of competition, with employers established in the host Member State.

Consequently, the imposition of such an obligation constitutes a restriction on freedom to provide services within the meaning of art 59 of the Treaty.

Such a restriction is justifiable only if it is necessary in order to safeguard, effectively and by appropriate means, the overriding public interest which the social protection of workers represents.

The effective protection of workers in the construction industry, particularly as regards health and safety matters and working hours, may require that certain documents are kept on site, or at least in an accessible and clearly identified place in the territory of the host Member State, so that they are available to the authorities of that State responsible for carrying out checks, particularly where there exists no organised system for cooperation or exchanges of information between Member States as provided for in art 4 of Directive 96/71.

Furthermore, in the absence of an organised system for cooperation or exchanges of information of the kind referred to in the preceding paragraph, the obligation to draw up and keep on site, or at least in an accessible and clearly identified place in the territory of the host Member State, certain of the documents required by the rules of that State may constitute the only appropriate means of control, having regard to the objective pursued by those rules.

The items of information respectively required by the rules of the Member State of establishment and by those of the host Member State concerning, in particular, the employer, the worker, working conditions and remuneration may differ to such an extent that the monitoring required under the rules of the host Member State cannot be carried out on the basis of documents kept in accordance with the rules of the Member State of establishment.

On the other hand, the mere fact that there are certain differences of form or content cannot justify the keeping of two sets of documents, one of which conforms to the rules of the Member State of establishment and the other to those of the host Member State, if the information provided, as a whole, by the documents required under the rules of the Member State of establishment is adequate to enable the controls needed in the host Member State to be carried out.

Consequently, the authorities and, if need be, the courts of the host Member State must verify in turn, before demanding that social or labour documents complying with their own rules be drawn up and kept in the territory of that State, that the social protection for workers which may justify those requirements is not sufficiently safeguarded by the production, within a reasonable time, of originals or copies of the documents kept in the Member State of establishment or, failing that, by keeping the originals or copies of those documents available on site or in an accessible and clearly identified place in the territory of the host Member State.

Where the authorities or courts of the host Member State find, as has the court making the reference in the two cases, that, as regards the keeping of social or labour documents such as labour regulations, a special staff register and an individual account for each employee, the employer is subject, in the Member State in which it is established, to obligations which are comparable as regards their objective, and which relate to the same workers and the same periods of activity, the production of the social and labour documents kept by the employer in accordance with the rules of the Member State of establishment must be regarded as sufficient to ensure the social protection of workers; consequently, the employer concerned should not be required to draw up documents in accordance with the rules of the host Member State.

In the context of the kind of verification referred to in para 65 of this judgment, it is necessary to have regard to the Community directives providing for coordination or a minimum degree of harmonisation in respect of the information necessary for the protection of workers.

First, Council Directive 91/533/EEC of 14 October 1991 on an employer's obligation to inform employees of the conditions applicable to the contract or employment relationship (OJ 1991 L288, p32) is designed, according to the second recital in its preamble, to provide employees with improved protection against possible infringements of their rights and to create greater transparency on the labour market. That Directive lists certain essential elements of the contract or employment relationship, including, where appropriate,

those rendered necessary on account of the worker concerned being deployed in another country, which the employer is required to bring to the notice of the worker. According to art 7, that Directive does not affect Member States' prerogative to apply or to introduce laws, regulations or administrative provisions which are more favourable to employees or to encourage or permit the application of agreements which are more favourable to employees.

Second, art 10 of Council Directive 89/391/EEC of 12 June 1989 on the introduction of measures to encourage improvements in the safety and health of workers at work (OJ 1989 L183, p1) provides, in particular, that workers are to receive certain information concerning risks to their safety and health.

In the context of such verification, the national authorities of the host Member State may additionally, in so far as they are not themselves in possession of it, require the provider of services to communicate the information held by him concerning the obligations to which he is subject in the Member State in which he is established.

[The detailed rules regarding the keeping and retention of social documents]
The provisions of Belgian law laying down the detailed rules regarding the keeping and retention of documents by an employer established in another Member State are made up of three parts. First, where the employer employs workers to work in Belgium, social documents must be kept either at one of the workplaces or at the residential address in Belgium of a natural person who is to keep those documents as the employer's agent or servant.

Second, where the employer ceases to employ workers in Belgium, the originals or copies of the social documents must be retained for five years at the address in Belgium of the agent or servant in question.

Finally, the national authorities must be notified in advance of the identity of the agent or servant, whether that person is designated to keep the documents or to retain them.

For the reasons set out in paras 61 to 63 of this judgment, the need for effective control by the authorities of the host Member State may justify the imposition on an employer established in another Member State who provides services in the host Member State of the obligation to keep certain documents available for inspection by the national authorities on site or, at least, in an accessible and clearly identified place in the territory of the host Member State.

It is for the national court to establish, having regard to the principle of proportionality, which documents are covered by such an obligation.

Where, as in the present case, there is an obligation to keep available and retain certain documents at the address of a natural person residing in the host Member State, who is to keep them as the agent or servant of the employer by whom he has been designated, even after the employer has ceased to employ workers in that State, it is not sufficient, for the purposes of justifying such a restriction of freedom to provide services, that the presence of such documents within the territory of the host Member State may make it generally easier for the authorities of that State to perform their supervisory task. It must also be shown that those authorities cannot carry out their supervisory task effectively unless the undertaking has, in that Member State, an agent or servant designated to retain the documents in question (see, to that effect, Case 205/84 *EC Commission v Germany* [1986] ECR 3755, para 54).

In any event, the obligations to retain social documents within the territory of the host Member State for a period of five years and to retain them at the address of a natural person, as opposed to a legal person, cannot be justified.

Monitoring of compliance with rules concerning the social protection of workers in the construction industry can be achieved by less restrictive measures. As the Advocate-General observes in point 88 of his Opinion, where an employer established in another Member State ceases to employ workers in Belgium, the originals or copies of the social documents comprising the staff register and the individual accounts, or of the equivalent documents which the undertaking is required to draw up under the legislation of the Member State of establishment, may be sent to the national authorities, who may check them and, if necessary, retain them.

For the rest, it should be noted that the organised system for cooperation and exchanges of information between Member States, as provided for in art 4 of Directive 96/71, will shortly render superfluous the retention of the documents in the host Member State after the employer has ceased to employ workers there.'

Comment

The important aspect of the present case is that the most favourable social legislation should be applied to workers temporarily carrying out work in another Member State. In respect of the requirement imposed on an employer providing services to pay his workers the minimum remunaration in the Member State where they provide services, the ECJ held that a Member State is entitled under EC law to impose the payment of the minimum remuneration to any person who provides services within its territory, irrespective of the place of establishment of his employer, as well as to enforce those rules by appropriate means: *Rush Portuguesa* v *Office National d'Immigration* Case C–113/89 [1990] ECR I–1417 and *Criminal Proceedings against Guiot* Case C–272/94 [1996] ECR I–1905. The application of that obligation is subject to review by the national courts. However, criminal prosecutions against an employer may only be commenced in so far as the national rules imposing this obligation are sufficiently precise and accessible, and thus it would not be impossible, or would be excessively difficult in practice, for such an employer to comply with it. In respect of other social contributions which a host Member State may impose on an employer, as a provider of services, to pay to that Member State's fund, in addition to those which he has already paid to the fund of the Member State of his establishment, the ECJ held that the employer's contributions are justified only if they afford workers a real social advantage, additional to that which they already enjoyed in the home Member State, and that these contributions are payable by all providers of services operating within the territory of the host Member State in the industry concerned.

Josef Corsten Case C–58/98 [2000] ECR I–7919 European Court of Justice

• *Provision of services – Directive 64/427/EEC – national rules requiring foreign skilled trade undertakings to be entered on the trade register – the principle of proportionality*

Facts

The German Workplace Inspectorate imposed an administrative fine of DM 2,000 on Mr Corsten, a self-employed architect, for breach of the German legislation against black market work, because he employed an undertaking established in The Netherlands to lay composition floors in Germany. The Dutch undertaking was lawfully established in The Netherlands but was not entered on the Skilled Traders Register in Germany. Under German legislation the procedure for obtaining authorisation to pursue skilled activities in Germany, and for being entered on the trade register, was long, complicated and entailed compulsory membership of the Chamber of Skilled Trades involving payment of the related subscription.

The activities carried out by the Dutch undertaking were within the scope of application of Directive 64/427 EEC which provides for a system of mutual recognition of occupational experience acquired in the Member State of origin, and is applicable to both the right of establishment and the right to provide services in another Member State.

Mr Corsten challenged the fine before the Amstsgricht Heinsberg (AH). The AH asked

the ECJ to determine whether the German rules were compatible with Community law on freedom to provide services.

Held

The ECJ held that art 49 EC and art 4 of Directive 64/427/EEC preclude any national rules of a Member State which make the carrying out on its territory of skilled trade work by providers of services established in other Member States subject to an authorisation procedure, which procedure is likely to delay or complicate the exercise of the right to freedom to provide services in a situation where examination of the conditions governing access to the activities concerned has been carried out in a Member State of establishment and it has there been established that those conditions are satisfied. The ECJ also held that any requirement of entry on the trade register of the host Member State, assuming it is justified, should neither give rise to additional administrative expense nor entail compulsory payment of subscriptions to the Chamber of Trades.

Judgment

'Given the nature of the activities at issue in the main proceedings, it is therefore necessary to consider whether the requirement of entry on the register and the administrative procedure relating to it are compatible with the principle of freedom to provide services and do not compromise the effectiveness of Directive 64/427, and of art 4 thereof in particular.

It is settled case law that art 59 of the Treaty requires not only the elimination of all discrimination on grounds of nationality against providers of services who are established in another Member State but also the abolition of any restriction, even if it applies to national providers of services and to those of other Member States alike, which is liable to prohibit, impede or render less advantageous the activities of a provider of services established in another Member State where he lawfully provides similar services (see Case C–76/90 *Säger* v *Dennemeyer* [1991]

ECR I–4221, para 12; Case C–43/93 *Van der Elst* v *Office des Migrations Internationales* [1994] ECR I–3803, para 14; Case C–272/94 *Criminal Proceedings against Guiot* [1996] ECR I–1905, para 10; Case C–3/95 *Reisebüro Broede* v *Sandker* [1996] ECR I–6511, para 25; Case C–222/95 *Parodi* v *Banque H Albert de Bary* [1997] ECR I–3899, para 18).

In that respect, the requirement imposed on an undertaking established in one Member State which wishes, as a provider of a service, to carry on a skilled trade activity in another Member State to be entered on the latter's trades register constitutes a restriction within the meaning of art 59 of the Treaty.

It is also settled case law that, even if there is no harmonisation in the field, such a restriction on the fundamental principle of freedom to provide services can be based only on rules justified by overriding requirements relating to the public interest and applicable to all persons and undertakings operating in the territory of the State where the service is provided, in so far as that interest is not safeguarded by the rules to which the provider of such a service is subject in the Member State where he is established ...

The German government states that the entire qualification system for skilled tradesmen, which is based on the requirement of a "Meisterprüfung" certificate and compulsory membership of the Chamber of Skilled Trades, is aimed at maintaining the level of service and occupational skills in the skilled trades sector. Such interests constitute overriding requirements relating to the public interest and would not be safeguarded by the provisions of the Member State in which the provider of a service is established.

Kreis Heinsberg claims that the register fulfils the purpose of a public register containing information on skilled tradesmen working in an independent capacity within the area of the Chamber of Skilled Trades concerned. Thus the register is intended to enable the authorities and the public to know which undertakings have obtained authorisation to carry on skilled trade activities in an independent capacity within the area of the Chamber of Skilled Trades concerned and accordingly to entrust skilled trade services to providers who are able to supply services of quality.

It must be acknowledged, as the Commission pointed out, that the objective of guaranteeing the quality of skilled trade work and of protecting those who have commissioned such work is an overriding requirement relating to the public interest capable of justifying a restriction on freedom to provide services.

However, in accordance with the principle of proportionality, the application of national rules to providers of services established in other Member States must be appropriate for securing attainment of the objective which they pursue and must not go beyond what is necessary in order to attain it ...

Rules such as the national rules at issue in the main proceedings, even though they apply regardless of the nationality of the providers of services and appear apt to ensure attainment of objectives which all seek to maintain the quality of the services provided, go beyond what is necessary to attain such objectives.

The examination prior to the grant of exceptional authorisation to be entered on the register can be one of form alone, since it must be confined to ascertaining whether the conditions laid down in art 3 of Directive 64/427 are met. It follows from art 4 thereof that, when conducting that examination, the authorities of the host Member State are in principle bound by the findings concerning the activities which have been pursued by the provider of services concerned and their duration, as contained in the certificate issued by the State from which the provider comes. At the stage when he is entered on the register no additional examination is carried out.

The reasons for the requirement of entry on the register being purely of an administrative nature, such considerations cannot justify derogation by a Member State from the rules of Community law, especially where the derogation in question amounts to preventing or restricting the exercise of one of the fundamental freedoms of Community law (see, in particular, Case C–18/95 *Terhoeve* v *Inspecteur van de Belastingdienst Particulieren/ Ondernemingen Buitenland* [1999] ECR I–345).

As the Austrian government rightly noted, a Member State may not make the provision of services in its territory subject to compliance with all the conditions required for establishment and thereby deprive of all practical effectiveness the provisions of the Treaty whose object is, precisely, to guarantee the freedom to provide services (see *Säger*, cited above, para 13).

In the main proceedings, the national law of the host Member State makes no distinction, as regards undertakings of other Member States wishing to provide skilled trade services in the host State, between those who are established only in the Member State from which they come and those who are also established, within the meaning of art 52 of the Treaty, in the host Member State. Those two categories of undertaking are subject in the same way to the requirement of entry on the register before they can carry out skilled trade work in the host Member State.

Even if the requirement of entry on that register, entailing compulsory membership of the Chamber of Skilled Trades for the undertakings concerned and therefore payment of the related subscription, could be justified in the case of establishment in the host Member State, which is not the situation in the main proceedings, the same is not true for undertakings which intend to provide services in the host Member State only on an occasional basis, indeed perhaps only once.

The latter are liable to be dissuaded from going ahead with their plans if, because of the compulsory requirement that they be entered on the register, the authorisation procedure is made lengthier and more expensive, so that the profit anticipated, at least for small contracts, is no longer economically worthwhile. For those undertakings, therefore, the freedom to provide ser-

vices, a fundamental principle of the Treaty, and likewise Directive 64/427 are liable to become ineffective.

In consequence, the authorisation procedure instituted by the host Member State should neither delay nor complicate exercise of the right of persons established in another Member State to provide their services on the territory of the first State where examination of the conditions governing access to the activities concerned has been carried out and it has been established that those conditions are satisfied.

Moreover, any requirement of entry on the trades register of the host Member State, assuming it was justified, should neither give rise to additional administrative expense nor entail compulsory payment of subscriptions to the Chamber of Trades.

In view of all the foregoing considerations, the reply to the question referred to the Court must be that art 59 of the Treaty and art 4 of Directive 64/427 preclude rules of a Member State which make the carrying out on its territory of skilled trade work by providers of services established in other Member States subject to an authorisation procedure which is likely to delay or complicate exercise of the right to freedom to provide services, where examination of the conditions governing access to the activities concerned has been carried out and it has been established that those conditions are satisfied. Furthermore, any requirement of entry on the trades register of the host Member State, assuming it was justified, should neither give rise to additional administrative expense nor entail compulsory payment of subscriptions to the Chamber of Trades.'

Comment

It is important to note that the requirement of entry on the trade register may be justified in respect of undertakings exercising their right of establishment in another Member State, but not those which wish to provide services in another Member State. Such a requirement may dissuade the providers of services from exercising the freedom conferred upon them by virtue of art 49 EC and call into question the effectiveness of Directive 64/427, especially if the authorisation procedure is lengthier and more expensive than the amount of the anticipated profit.

Läärä and Others v *Kihlakunnansyyttäjä and Others*
Case C–124/97 [1999] ECR I–6067
European Court of Justice

• *Freedom to provide services – art 59 EC – national legislation which reserves gaming and the operation of gaming machines to a single public law association – an obstacle to freedom to provide services – justified by public interest – preliminary ruling*

Facts
Under Finnish legislation, a single public body has been granted rights to organise lotteries and betting, to manage casinos and to operate slot machines. Funds collected by that body have been used to finance non-profit-making causes. The public body consists of 96 organisations operating in the areas of health and social activities. It is called RAY.

In 1996 the English company CMS entered into a contract with the Finnish company TAS, under which TAS was given the exclusive right to instal and operate in Finland slot machines for a commission representing a percentage of the profits made from their use. CMS had manufactured the slot machines, delivered them to Finland and remained their owner.

Criminal proceedings were brought against Markku Läärä, the chairman of TAS, for operating slot machines in Finland without licence and contrary to the above-mentioned Finnish gaming legislation. He argued that the Finnish legislation was contrary to Community law, in particular in breach of EC rules on freedom to provide services.

The Finnish Court of Appeal (Vaasan Hovioikeus) referred to the ECJ a preliminary question on the compatibility of the Finnish gaming legislation with Community law.

Held
The ECJ held that national legislation granting to a single body exclusive rights to operate slot machines was not in breach of Community law on the freedom to provide services, in view of the public interest objectives which justified it.

Judgment
'... as the Court held in *Schindler* [*Commissioners of Customs and Excise* v *Schindler* Case C–275/92 [1994] ECR I–1039] in relation to the organisation of lotteries, the provisions of the Treaty relating to freedom to provide services apply to activities which enable users, in return for payment, to participate in gaming. Consequently, such activities fall within the scope of art 59 of the Treaty, since at least one of the service providers is established in a Member State other than that in which the service is offered.

As the referring court points out, national legislation on slot machines such as the Finnish legislation prohibits any person other than the licensed public body from running the operation of the machines in question; it therefore involves no discrimination on grounds of nationality and applies without distinction to operators who might be interested in that activity, whether they are established in Finland or in another Member State.

However, such legislation constitutes an impediment to freedom to provide services in that it directly or indirectly prevents operators in other Member States from themselves making slot machines available to the public with a view to their use in return for payment.

It is therefore necessary to examine whether that obstacle to freedom to provide services can be permitted pursuant to the derogations expressly provided for by the Treaty, or whether it may be justified, in accordance with the Court's case law, by overriding reasons relating to the public interest.

In that regard, arts 55 (now art 45 EC) and 56 of the EC Treaty, which are applicable pursuant to art 66 of the EC Treaty (now art 55 EC), permit restrictions which are justified by virtue of a connection, even on an occasional basis, with the exercise of official authority or on grounds of public policy, public security or public health. Furthermore, it is clear from the Court's case law (see, to that effect, Case C–288/89 *Stichting Collectieve Antennevoorziening Gouda* v *Commissariaat voor de Media* [1991] ECR I–4007, paras 13 to 15) that obstacles to freedom to provide services arising from national measures which are applicable without distinction are permissible only if those measures are justified by overriding reasons relating to the public interest, are such as to guarantee the achievement of the intended aim and do not go beyond what is necessary in order to achieve it.

According to the information contained in the order for reference and in the observations of the Finnish government, the legislation at issue in the main proceedings responds to the concern to limit exploitation of the human passion for gambling, to avoid the risk of crime and fraud to which the activities concerned give rise and to authorise those activities only with a view to the collection of funds for charity or for other benevolent purposes.

As the Court acknowledged in para 58 of the *Schindler* judgment, those considerations must be taken together. They concern the protection of the recipients of the service and, more generally, of consumers, as well as the maintenance of order in society. The Court has already held that those objectives are amongst those which may be regarded as overriding reasons relating to the public interest (see Joined Cases 110/78 and 111/78 *Ministère Public* v *Van Wesemael* [1979] ECR 35, para 28; Case 220/83 *EC Commission* v *France* [1986] ECR 3663, para 20; and Case 15/78 *Société Générale Alsacienne de Banques SA* v *Koestler* [1978] ECR 1971, para 5). However, it is still necessary, as stated in para 31 of this judgment, that measures based on such grounds guarantee the achievement of the intended aims and do not go beyond that which is necessary in order to achieve them.

As noted in para 21 of this judgment, the Finnish legislation differs in particular from the legislation at issue in *Schindler* in that it does not prohibit the use of slot machines but reserves the running of them to a licensed public body.

However, the power to determine the extent of the protection to be afforded by a Member State on its territory with regard to lotteries and other forms of gambling forms part of the national authorities' power of assessment, recognised by the Court in para 61 of the *Schindler* judgment. It is for those authorities to assess whether it is necessary, in the context of the aim pursued, totally or partially to prohibit activities of that kind or merely to restrict them and, to that end, to establish control mechanisms, which may be more or less strict.

In those circumstances, the mere fact that a Member State has opted for a system of protection which differs from that adopted by another Member State cannot affect the assessment of the need for, and proportionality of, the provisions enacted to that end. Those provisions must be assessed solely by reference to the objectives pursued by the national authorities of the Member State concerned and the level of protection which they are intended to provide.

Contrary to the arguments advanced by the appellants in the main proceedings, the fact that the games in issue are not totally prohibited is not enough to show that the national legislation is not in reality intended to achieve the public interest objectives at which it is purportedly aimed, which must be considered as a whole. Limited authorisation of such games on an exclusive basis, which has the advantage of confining the desire to gamble and the exploitation of gambling within controlled channels, of preventing the risk of fraud or crime in the context of such exploitation, and of using the resulting profits for public interest purposes, likewise falls within the ambit of those objectives.

The position is not affected by the fact that the various establishments in which the slot machines are installed receive from the licensed public body a proportion of the takings.

The question whether, in order to achieve those objectives, it would be preferable, rather than granting an exclusive operating right to the licensed public body, to adopt regulations imposing the necessary code of conduct on the operators concerned is a matter to be assessed by the Member States, subject however to the proviso that the choice made in that regard must not be disproportionate to the aim pursued.

On that point, it is apparent, particularly from the rules on slot machines, that the RAY, which is the sole body holding a licence to run the operation of those machines, is a public law association the activities of which are carried on under the control of the State and which is required, as noted in para 5 of this judgment, to pay over to the State the amount of the net distributable proceeds received from the operation of the slot machines.

It is true that the sums thus received by the State for public interest purposes could equally be obtained by other means, such as taxation of the activities of the various operators authorised to pursue them within the framework of rules of a non-exclusive nature; however, the obligation imposed on the licensed public body, requiring it to pay over the proceeds of its operations, constitutes a measure which, given the risk of crime and fraud, is certainly more effective in ensuring that strict limits are set to the lucrative nature of such activities.

In those circumstances, in conferring exclusive rights on a single public body, the provisions of the Finnish legislation on the operation of slot machines do not appear to be disproportionate, in so far as they affect freedom to provide services, to the objectives they pursue.'

Comment

The ECJ held that the Finnish gambling legislation was not discriminatory on the ground of nationality, as it applied without distinction to all economic operators irrespective of the Member State of their establishment. However, it constituted an obstacle to freedom to provide services, taking into account that it prevented, directly and indirectly, operators from other Member States from making slot machines available to the public with a view to their use in return for payment.

The reasoning of the ECJ in the present case followed the established pattern. National rules imposing restrictions on the freedom to provide services must fulfil four criteria in order to be justified. They must apply without distinction to nationals and non-nationals, they must be justified by imperative requirements in the general interest, they must be suitable for the attainment of the objective being pursued, and they must not go beyond what is necessary to attain that objective.

In *Commissioners of Customs and Excise v Schindler* Case C–275/92 [1994] QB 610; [1994] ECR I–1039, involving the operation of lotteries, the ECJ held that Member States enjoyed a large measure of discretion in matters relating to such activities. Thus, it was for Member States to assess whether it was necessary to restrict or even prohibit the activities concerned, taking into consideration their social and cultural characteristics, in order to maintain order in society. This large discretion was confirmed in the present case. In this respect, the ECJ held that:

'The objectives of the Finnish legislation, to limit exploitation of the human passion for gambling, to avoid the risk of crime and fraud, and to authorise gaming activities only in order to collect funds for charitable purposes, concerned the protection of consumers and the maintenance of order in society, and were to be regarded as overriding reasons relating to public interest.'

In this context, it is not surprising that the ECJ held that the solution adopted by Finland, that is to grant to a single public body exclusive rights to operate slot machines and to use funds collected by RAY for charitable purposes, were not disproportionate to the objective pursued.

Van Binsbergen v *Bestuur van de Bedrijfsvereniging voor de Metaalnijverheid* Case 33/74 [1974] ECR 1299; [1973] 1 CMLR 298 European Court of Justice

• *Freedom to supply services – arts 59 and 60 EC Treaty [arts 49 and 50 EC]– requirement of permanent residence in a host Member State – rules of conduct and professional ethics*

Facts

Van Binsbergen was represented before the Dutch social security court by Kortmann, a Dutch national. During the proceedings Kortmann, a legal adviser and representative in social security matters, moved from The Netherlands to Belgium and from there he corresponded with the Dutch court. He was informed by the court registrar that only persons established in The Netherlands were permitted to represent their clients before the Dutch social security court and as a permanent resident of Belgium he could no longer act for Van Binsbergen. Kortmann challenged this provision of the relevant Netherlands statute on procedure in social security matters as incompatible with art 59 EC Treaty [art 49 EC].

Held

The ECJ held that arts 59 and 60 EC Treaty [arts 49 and 50 EC] were directly effective. The Court stated that those provisions must be interpreted as meaning that the national law of a Member State cannot, by imposing a requirement as to habitual residence within that State, deny persons established in another Member State the right to provide services, where the provision of such services is not subject to any special condition under the national law applicable.

However, the ECJ held that a residence requirement would be compatible with arts 59 and 60 EC Treaty [arts 49 and 50 EC] if it were objectively justified by the need to ensure observance of professional rules of conduct, provided such rules are non-discriminatory, objectively justified and proportionate.

Judgment

'[*Professional rules of conduct*]
... The question put by the national court therefore seeks to determine whether the requirement that legal representatives be permanently established within the territory of the State where the service is to be provided can be reconciled with the prohibition, under arts 59 and 60, on all restrictions on freedom to provide services within the Community.

The restrictions to be abolished pursuant to arts 59 and 60 include all requirements imposed on the person providing the service by reason in particular of his nationality or the fact that he does not habitually reside in the State where the service is provided, which do not apply to persons established within the national territory or which may prevent or otherwise obstruct the activities of the person providing the service.

In particular, a requirement that the person providing the service must be habitually resident within the territory of the State where the service is to be provided may, according to the circumstances, have the result of depriving art 59 of all useful effect, in view of the fact that the precise object of that Article is to abolish restrictions on freedom to provide services imposed on persons who are not established in the State where the service is to be provided.

However, taking into account the particular nature of the services to be provided, specific requirements imposed on the person providing the service cannot be considered incompatible with the Treaty where they have as their purpose the application of professional rules justified by the general good – in particular rules relating to organisation, qualifications, professional ethics, supervision and liability – which are binding upon any person established in the State in which the service is provided, where the person providing the service would escape from the ambit of those rules by being established in another Member State.

Likewise, a Member State cannot be denied the right to take measures to prevent the exercise by a person providing services whose activity is entirely or principally directed towards its territory of the freedom guaranteed by art 59 for the purpose of avoiding the professional rules of conduct which would be applicable to him if he were established within that State; such a situation may be subject to judicial control under the provisions of the chapter relating to the right of establishment and not of that on the provision of service.

In accordance with these principles, the requirement that persons whose functions are to assist the administration of justice must be permanently established for professional purposes within the jurisdiction of certain courts or tribunals cannot be considered incompatible with the provisions of art 59 and 60, where such requirement is objectively justified by the need to ensure observance of professional rules of conduct connected, in particular, with the administration of justice and with respect for professional ethics.

That cannot, however, be the case when the provision of certain services in a Member State is not subject to any sort of qualification or professional regulation and when the requirement of habitual residence is fixed by reference to the territory of the State in question.

In relation to a professional activity the exercise of which is similarly unrestricted within the territory of a particular Member State, the requirement of residence within that State constitutes a restriction which is incompatible with arts 59 and 60 of the Treaty if the administration of justice can satisfactorily be ensured by measures which are less restrictive, such as the choosing of an address for service.

It must therefore be stated in reply to the question put to the Court that the first paragraph of art 59 and the third paragraph of art 60 of the [EC] Treaty must be interpreted

as meaning that the national law of a Member State cannot, by imposing a requirement as to habitual residence within that State, deny persons established in another Member State the right to provide services, where the provision of services is not subject to any special condition under the national law applicable ...

[*Direct effect of arts 59 and 60 EC Treaty*]
... as regards at least the specific requirement of nationality or of residence, arts 59 and 60 impose well-defined obligations, the fulfilment of which by the Member States cannot be delayed or jeopardised by the absence of powers which were to be adopted in pursuance of powers conferred under arts 63 and 66.

Accordingly, the reply should be that the first paragraph of art 59 and the third paragraph of art 60 have direct effect and may therefore be relied on before national courts, at least in so far as they seek to abolish any discrimination against a person providing a service by reason of his nationality or the fact that he resides in a Member State other than that in which the service is provided.'

Comment

The ECJ held that arts 59 and 60 EC Treaty [arts 49 and 50 EC] are directly effective. The Court emphasised that both provisions are subject to the principle of non-discrimination based on the ground of nationality. However, the concept of the free movement of services goes beyond mere discrimination as it covers disproportionate and unjustified restrictions. National restrictions should be assessed in the light of these three criteria, that is they should be non-discriminatory, proportional and objectively justified. In the present case, the requirement of permanent residence applied without discrimination to nationals and non-nationals; it is objectively justified by the general good, that is, by the need to ensure observance of professional rules of conduct especially connected with the administration of justice and with respect for professional ethics. In respect to the third criterion the ECJ held that the requirement of permanent residence would, in the present case, be disproportionate as the objective of the proper administration of justice can be achieved by less restrictive measures such as the choosing of an address in the Member State in which the service is provided. This test has clear parallels with the *Cassis de Dijon* case, although the ECJ has refused to adopt a Keck case limitation to the freedom to provide services (*Alpine Investments BV* v *Minister van Financiën* Case C–384/93 [1995] ECR I–1141).

It is also interesting to note that the present case concerned a Dutch national who provided services in The Netherlands acting for a Dutch client before a Dutch court. The fact that he was established in Belgium brought the case within the scope of Community law. Therefore, in some cases EC law protects nationals of a Member State against their own State!

Freedom to receive services

BSM Geraets-Smits v *Stichting Ziekenfonds VGZ; HTM Peerbooms* v *Stichting CZ Groep Zorgverzekeringen* Case C–157/99 [2001] ECR I–5473

• *Freedom to provide services – arts 49 and 50 EC – social security – sickness insurance – hospital treatment incurred in another Member State – prior authorisation – criteria – justification*

Facts

Mrs Geraets-Smits and Mr Peerbooms, both nationals of The Netherlands, received medical treatment respectively in Germany and in Austria without prior authorisation from their Netherlands-based sickness insurance fund.

Mrs Geraets-Smits suffered from Parkinson's disease. She went to Germany for specific multidisciplinary treatment of her disease consisting, inter alia, of determining the best possible medical treatment, physiotherapy, ergotherapy and socio-psychology, based on a symptom-by-symptom basis. Her request for reimbursement of the medical costs incurred was refused by her sickness insurance fund on the ground that the methods used in Germany were not regarded as normal treatment within the professional circles concerned, and even if they were regarded as normal the costs were not necessary as satisfactory and adequate medical treatment was available in The Netherlands. An expert witness appointed by the referring court confirmed that there was no clinical or scientific evidence that the treatment she received in Germany was more appropriate than that available in The Netherlands. Consequently, there was no medical justification for the treatment she received in Germany.

Mr Peerbooms fell into a coma following a road accident. He was first taken to a hospital in The Netherlands and later transferred to a hospital in Austria, which provided a special therapy using neurostimulation. This kind of treatment was used in The Netherlands only in two medical centres and in respect of patients below the age of 25. In The Netherlands Mr Peerbooms did not qualify for the treatment since he was born in 1961. Mr Peerbooms came out of the coma in a hospital in Austria and was transferred to a clinic in The Netherlands to continue his rehabilitation. When he sought reimbursement of the treatment costs incurred in Austria, his insurer in The Netherlands refused on the ground that the treatment he received in Austria, due to its experimental nature and the absence of scientific evidence of its effectiveness, was not regarded as normal within the professional circles concerned and, even if it had been regarded as normal, satisfactory and adequate treatment was available without undue delay in The Netherlands. Mr Peerbooms's neurologists requested, on two occasions, that his insurer pay the costs of the treatment in Austria. Furthermore, the neurologist appointed as an expert witness by the referring court submitted a report stating that appropriate and adequate treatment, such as that provided to Mr Peerbooms in Austria, was not available in The Netherlands owing to his age, and that he would not have been able to receive adequate therapy in any hospital in The Netherlands.

Under The Netherlands social security legislation, a patient can receive medical treatment, either in The Netherlands or abroad, at an establishment which has not entered into agreement with his sickness insurance fund only after obtaining prior authorisation. Such an authorisation is granted if two conditions are satisfied.

1. The proposed treatment must be among the benefits for which the sickness insurance scheme of the first Member State assumes responsibility, which means that the treatment must be considered as 'normal in the professional circles concerned'.
2. The treatment in another Member State must be necessary in the sense that adequate care cannot be provided without undue delay in the first Member State.

In both cases the referring court asked the ECJ to decide whether national legislation, which made the reimbursement of the costs of medical treatment in another Member State subject to prior authorisation by the sickness insurance fund with which the insured person was registered, was compatible with arts 49 and 50 EC.

Held

The ECJ held that The Netherlands legislation is question was compatible with arts 49 and 50 EC provided that:

1. the requirement that the treatment must be regarded as 'normal' is construed to the effect that authorisation cannot be refused on the ground that the treatment is not normal where it appears that the treatment concerned is sufficiently tried and tested by international medical science; and
2. the authorisation can only be refused on the ground of lack of medical necessity if

the same or equally effective treatment can be obtained without undue delay at an establishment having a contractual arrangement with the insured person's sickness insurance fund.

Judgment

'It is settled case law that medical activities fall within the scope of art 60 of the Treaty, there being no need to distinguish in that regard between care provided in a hospital environment and care provided outside such an environment (see Joined Cases 286/82 and 26/83 *Luisi and Carbone* [1984] ECR 377, para 16; *Society for the Protection of Unborn Children (Ireland) Ltd* v *Grogan* [Case C–159/90 [1991] ECR I–4685], para 18, concerning advertising for clinics involved in the deliberate termination of pregnancies; and *Kohll* [*Kohll* v *Union des Caisses de Matadie* Case C–158/96 [1998] ECR I–1931], paras 29 and 51).

It is also settled case law that the special nature of certain services does not remove them from the ambit of the fundamental principle of freedom of movement (Case 279/80 *Webb* [1981] ECR 3305, para 10, and *Kohll*, para 20), so that the fact that the national rules at issue in the main proceedings are social security rules cannot exclude application of arts 59 and 60 of the Treaty (*Kohll*, para 21).

With regard more particularly to the argument that hospital services provided in the context of a sickness insurance scheme providing benefits in kind, such as that governed by the ZFW, should not be classified as services within the meaning of art 60 of the Treaty, it should be noted that, far from falling under such a scheme, the medical treatment at issue in the main proceedings, which was provided in Member States other than those in which the persons concerned were insured, did lead to the establishments providing the treatment being paid directly by the patients. It must be accepted that a medical service provided in one Member State and paid for by the patient should not cease to fall within the scope of the freedom to provide services guaranteed by the Treaty merely because reimbursement of the costs of the treatment involved is applied for under another Member State's sickness insurance legislation which is essentially of the type which provides for benefits in kind.

Furthermore, the fact that hospital medical treatment is financed directly by the sickness insurance funds on the basis of agreements and pre-set scales of fees is not in any event such as to remove such treatment from the sphere of services within the meaning of art 60 of the Treaty.

First, it should be borne in mind that art 60 of the Treaty does not require that the service be paid for by those for whom it is performed (Case 352/85 *Bond van Adverteerders* v *Netherlands* [1988] ECR 2085, para 16, and Joined Cases C–51/96 and C–191/97 *Deliège* [2000] ECR I–2549, para 56).

Second, art 60 of the Treaty states that it applies to services normally provided for remuneration and it has been held that, for the purposes of that provision, the essential characteristic of remuneration lies in the fact that it constitutes consideration for the service in question (*Belgian State* v *Humbel* [Case 263/86 [1998] ECR 5365], para 17). In the present cases, the payments made by the sickness insurance funds under the contractual arrangements provided for by the ZFW, albeit set at a flat rate, are indeed the consideration for the hospital services and unquestionably represent remuneration for the hospital which receives them and which is engaged in an activity of an economic character.

Since the provisions of services at issue in the main proceedings do fall within the scope of the freedom to provide services within the meaning of arts 59 and 60 of the Treaty, it is necessary to consider whether the rules at issue in the main proceedings place restrictions on that freedom and, if so, whether those restrictions can be objectively justified ...

[The prior authorisation requirement]
As regards the prior authorisation requirement to which the ZFW subjects the assumption of the costs of treatment pro-

vided in another Member State by a non-contracted care provider, the Court accepts, as all the governments which have submitted observations have argued, that, by comparison with medical services provided by practitioners in their surgeries or at the patient's home, medical services provided in a hospital take place within an infrastructure with, undoubtedly, certain very distinct characteristics. It is thus well known that the number of hospitals, their geographical distribution, the mode of their organisation and the equipment with which they are provided, and even the nature of the medical services which they are able to offer, are all matters for which planning must be possible.

As may be seen, in particular, from the contracting system involved in the main proceedings, this kind of planning therefore broadly meets a variety of concerns.

For one thing, it seeks to achieve the aim of ensuring that there is sufficient and permanent access to a balanced range of high-quality hospital treatment in the State concerned.

For another thing, it assists in meeting a desire to control costs and to prevent, as far as possible, any wastage of financial, technical and human resources. Such wastage is all the more damaging because it is generally recognised that the hospital care sector generates considerable costs and must satisfy increasing needs, while the financial resources which may be made available for health care are not unlimited, whatever the mode of funding applied.

From both those perspectives, a requirement that the assumption of costs, under a national social security system, of hospital treatment provided in another Member State must be subject to prior authorisation appears to be a measure which is both necessary and reasonable ...

[The condition that the proposed treatment be "normal"]
... In the present two cases, it is clear from the arguments submitted to the national court, reflected in part (b) of the first preliminary question, and from the observa-

tions submitted to the Court that the expression "normal in the professional circles concerned" is open to a number of interpretations, depending, in particular, on whether it is considered that regard should be had to what is considered normal only in Netherlands medical circles, which, to judge by the order for reference, seems to be the interpretation favoured by the national court (see para 23 above) or, on the other hand, to what is considered normal according to the state of international medical science and medical standards generally accepted at international level ...

To allow only treatment habitually carried out on national territory and scientific views prevailing in national medical circles to determine what is or is not normal will not offer those guarantees and will make it likely that Netherlands providers of treatment will always be preferred in practice.

If, on the other hand, the condition that treatment must be regarded as "normal" is extended in such a way that, where treatment is sufficiently tried and tested by international medical science, the authorisation sought under the ZFW cannot be refused on that ground, such a condition, which is objective and applies without distinction to treatment provided in The Netherlands and to treatment provided abroad, is justifiable in view of the need to maintain an adequate, balanced and permanent supply of hospital care on national territory and to ensure the financial stability of the sickness insurance system, so that the restriction of the freedom to provide services of hospitals situated in other Member States which might result from the application of that condition does not infringe art 59 of the Treaty.

Further, where, as in the present case, a Member State decides that medical or hospital treatment must be sufficiently tried and tested before its cost will be assumed under its social security system, the national authorities called on to decide, for authorisation purposes, whether hospital treatment provided in another Member States satisfies that criterion must take into consideration all the relevant available information, including, in particular, existing scientific

literature and studies, the authorised opinions of specialists and the fact that the proposed treatment is covered or not covered by the sickness insurance system of the Member State in which the treatment is provided.

[*The condition concerning the necessity of the proposed treatment*]

... it can be concluded that the condition concerning the necessity of the treatment, laid down by the rules at issue in the main proceedings, can be justified under art 59 of the Treaty, provided that the condition is construed to the effect that authorisation to receive treatment in another Member State may be refused on that ground only if the same or equally effective treatment can be obtained without undue delay from an establishment with which the insured person's sickness insurance fund has contractual arrangements.

Furthermore, in order to determine whether equally effective treatment can be obtained without undue delay from an establishment having contractual arrangements with the insured person's fund, the national authorities are required to have regard to all the circumstances of each specific case and to take due account not only of the patient's medical condition at the time when authorisation is sought but also of his past record.

Such a condition can allow an adequate, balanced and permanent supply of high-quality hospital treatment to be maintained on the national territory and the financial stability of the sickness insurance system to be assured.

Were large numbers of insured persons to decide to be treated in other Member States even when the hospitals having contractual arrangements with their sickness insurance funds offer adequate identical or equivalent treatment, the consequent outflow of patients would be liable to put at risk the very principle of having contractual arrangements with hospitals and, consequently, undermine all the planning and rationalisation carried out in this vital sector in an effort to avoid the phenomena of hospital overcapacity, imbalance in the supply of hospital medical care and logistical and financial wastage.

However, once it is clear that treatment covered by the national insurance system cannot be provided by a contracted establishment, it is not acceptable that national hospitals not having any contractual arrangements with the insured person's sickness insurance fund be given priority over hospitals in other Member States. Once such treatment is ex hypothesi provided outside the planning framework established by the ZFW, such priority would exceed what is necessary for meeting the overriding requirements referred to in para 105 above.'

Comment

The ECJ provided three important clarifications in the above cases: first, the Court confirmed that medical activities fall within the scope of art 50 EC; second, it held that a system of prior authorisation required under national law constitutes an obstacle to freedom to provide services; and third, it explained the circumstances under which such a system may be justified under Community law.

Cowan v *Trésor Public* Case 186/87 [1989] ECR 195; [1990] 2 CMLR 613 European Court of Justice

• *Freedom to provide services includes freedom to receive services – discrimination on the ground of nationality – art 6 EC Treaty [art 12 EC] – assault on tourist – criminal compensation*

Facts

A British national, Ian Cowan, was violently assaulted outside a Metro station in Paris. The perpetrators of the offence were never apprehended. Mr Cowan applied to the Commission d'Indeminsation des Victims d'Infraction, the French equivalent of the Criminal Injuries Compensation Board, for compensation for his injuries. The French Code of Criminal Procedure allows compensation to be paid to

victims of assaults if physical injury has been sustained and compensation cannot be sought from another source. However, the same Code of Criminal Procedure restricted the payment of compensation to French nationals and holders of French residence permits. On this grounds Mr Cowan's application for compensation was refused by the French Treasury.

Mr Cowen challenged this decision relying on art 6 EC Treaty [art 12 EC]. He argued that art 6 EC Treaty [art 12 EC] prohibited discrimination based on nationality and that such discrimination prevented tourists from going freely to other Member States to receive services.

Held

The ECJ held that the freedom to provide services also entailed the right to receive services. Since the right to receive services was embodied in the EC Treaty, it was subject to the prohibition of discrimination on the grounds of nationality as prescribed by art 6 EC Treaty [art 12 EC]. Laws and regulations which prevent the exercise of this right were declared to be incompatible with Community law and, in the circumstances of this case, the requirement of French nationality or a French residence permit, in order to claim compensation for criminal injuries constituted unjustifiable discrimination.

Judgment

'Under art [6] of the [EC] Treaty the prohibition of discrimination applies "within the scope of application of this Treaty" and "without prejudice to any special provisions contained therein". This latter expression refers particularly to other provisions of the Treaty in which the application of the general principle set out in that article is given concrete form in respect of specific situations. Examples of that are the provisions concerning free movement of workers, the right of establishment and the freedom to provide services.

On that last point, in its judgment of 31 January 1984 in Joined Cases 286/82 and 26/83 (*Luisi and Carbone* v *Ministero del*

Tesoro [1984] ECR 377), the Court held that the freedom to provide services includes the freedom for the recipient of the services to go to another Member State in order to receive a service there, without being obstructed by restrictions, and that tourists, among others, must be regarded as recipients of services.

When Community law guarantees a natural person the freedom to go to another Member State the protection of that person from harm in the Member State in question, on the same basis as that of nationals and persons residing there, is a corollary of that freedom of movement. It follows that the prohibition of discrimination is applicable to recipients of services within the meaning of the Treaty as regards protection against the risk of assault and the right to obtain financial compensation provided for by national law when the risk materialises. The fact that the compensation at issue is financed by the Public Treasury cannot alter the rules regarding the protection of the rights guaranteed by the Treaty.

In the light of all the foregoing the answer to the question submitted must be that the prohibition of discrimination laid down in particular in art [6] of the EC Treaty must be interpreted as meaning that in respect of persons whose freedom to travel to a Member State, in particular as recipients of services, is guaranteed by Community law that State may not make the award of State compensation for harm caused in that State to the victim of an assault resulting in physical injury subject to the condition that he holds a residence permit or be a national of the country which has entered into a reciprocal agreement with that Member State.'

Comment

The ECJ held that the freedom to provide services included the freedom to receive services and that tourists were within the scope of art 59 EC Treaty [art 49 EC] as recipients of services. In the present case the ECJ, by virtue of the prohibition of discrimination contained in art 6 EC Treaty [art 12 EC], extended the category of persons protected under Community law. The combined effect of arts 59 and 6 EC Treaty [arts 49 and 12 EC] permitted Cowan to act against the French State.

11 Derogating from Free Movement for Workers, Establishment and Services

Bonsignore v Oberstadtdirector of the City of Cologne Case 67/74 [1975] ECR 297 European Court of Justice

• *Free movement of persons – limitation on ground of public policy – arts 3(1) of Directive 64/221/EEC – deportation – general preventive measure*

Facts

An Italian national permanently residing in Germany, Carmelo Bonsignore, shot his brother by accident. The weapon he used was a pistol he had illegally acquired. He was fined for this offence but no punishment was imposed for the accidental killing of his brother. The German authorities ordered his deportation for 'reasons of a general preventive nature' based on 'the deterrent effect which the deportation of an alien found in illegal possession of a firearm would have in immigration circles having regard to the resurgence of violence in the large urban cities'. The German court referred to the ECJ a question whether art 3 of Directive 64/221/EEC prohibits deportation for reasons of a general preventive nature when it is clear that the individual concerned would not commit further offences.

Held

The ECJ held that art 3(1) and (2) of Directive 64/221/EEC prevents the deportation of a national of a Member State if such deportation is ordered for the purpose of deterring other aliens as a general preventive measure.

Judgment

'According to art 3(1) and (2) of Directive No 64/221 "measures taken on grounds of public policy or of public security shall be based exclusively on the personal conduct of the individual concerned" and "previous criminal convictions shall not in themselves constitute grounds for the taking of such measures".

These provisions must be interpreted in the light of the objectives of the directive which seeks in particular to co-ordinate the measures justified on grounds of public policy and for maintenance of public security envisaged by arts 48 and 56 of the Treaty, in order to reconcile the application of these measures with the basic principle of the free movement of persons within the Community and the elimination of all discrimination, in the application of the Treaty, between the nationals of the State in question and those of the other Member States.

With this view, art 3 of the Directive provides that measures adopted on grounds of public policy and for the maintenance of public security against the nationals of Member States of the Community cannot be justified on grounds extraneous to the individual case, as is shown in particular by the requirement set out in para (1) that "only" the "personal conduct" of those affected by the measures is to be regarded as determinative.

As departures from the rules concerning

the free movement of persons constitute exceptions which must be strictly construed, the concept of "personal conduct" expresses the requirement that a deportation order may only be made for breaches of the peace and public security which might be committed by the individual affected.

The reply to the question referred should therefore be that art 3(1) and (2) of Directive No 64/221 prevents the deportation of a national of a Member State if such deportation is ordered for the purpose of deterring other aliens, that is, if it is based, in the words of the national court, on reasons of a "general preventive nature".'

Comment

The ECJ held that any departure from the rule concerning free movement of persons must be strictly interpreted. A Member State should base the decision on deportation solely on the requirements embodied in art 3(1) of Directive 64/221, that is taking into account exclusively the personal conduct of the individual concerned. Future behaviour is only relevant in so far as there are clear indications that the individual would commit further offences. In *R* v *Bouchereau* Case 30/77 [1977] ECR 1999 the ECJ held that a likelihood of re-offending may be found in past conduct, although previous criminal convictions do not in themselves constitute grounds for taking measures on the basis of public policy or public security. The Court stated that it is possible that past conduct alone may constitute such a threat to the requirements of public policy when the individual concerned has a 'propensity to act in the same way in the future' as he did in the past.

Criminal Proceedings against Calfa
Case C–348/96 [1999] ECR I–11
European Court of Justice

• *Freedom to provide service – free movement of persons – public policy – prohibited drugs – exclusion for life from a Member State's territory – personal conduct in the light of art 3(1) of Directive 64/221/EEC*

Facts
Donatella Calfa, an Italian national, went for holidays to Crete where she was convicted of the possession and use of prohibited drugs. She was sentenced by a Greek court to three months' imprisonment and expulsion for life from Greek territory. Under Greek penal law, foreign nationals convicted of certain drug offences were automatically subject to an expulsion order for life unless for some compelling reasons, particularly family matters, their continued residence in Greece was allowed. Donatella Calfa challenged the expulsion order as contrary to a number of provisions of the EC Treaty, especially arts 48, 52 and 59 EC Treaty [arts 39, 43 and 49 EC], as well as Council Directive 64/221/EEC of 25 February 1964 on the Co-ordination of Special Measures Concerning the Movement and Residence of Foreign Nationals which Are Justified on Grounds of Public Policy, Public Security or Public Health.

Held
The ECJ held that arts 48, 52 and 59 EC Treaty [arts 39, 43 and 49 EC] and art 3(1) of Directive 64/21/EEC precluded legislation which (with certain exceptions, in particular where they were family reasons) required a Member State's courts to order expulsion for life from its territory of nationals of other Member States found guilty on that territory of the offences of obtaining and being in possession of drugs for their own personal use.

Judgment
'Although in principle criminal legislation is a matter for which the Member States are responsible, the Court has consistently held that Community law sets certain limits to their power, and such legislation may not restrict the fundamental freedoms guaranteed by Community law.

In the present case, the penalty of expulsion for life from the territory, which is applicable to the nationals of other Member States in the event of conviction for obtaining and being in possession of drugs for their own use, clearly constitutes an obstacle to the freedom to provide services. This would also be true for the other fundamental freedoms.

Article 56 permits Member States to adopt, with respect to nationals of other Member States, and in particular on the grounds of public policy, measures which they cannot apply to their own nationals, inasmuch as they have no authority to expel the latter from the territory or to deny them access thereto.

The concept of public policy may be relied upon in the event of a genuine and sufficiently serious threat to the requirements of public policy affecting one of the fundamental interests of society.

In this respect, it must be accepted that a Member State may consider that the use of drugs constitutes a danger for society such as to justify special measures against foreign nationals who contravene its laws on drugs, in order to maintain public order.

However, as the Court has repeatedly stated, the public policy exception, like all derogations from a fundamental principle of the Treaty, must be interpreted restrictively.

In that regard, Directive 64/221 sets certain limits on the right of Member States to expel foreign nationals on the grounds of public policy and states that measures taken on grounds of public policy or of public security that have the effect of restricting the residence of a national of another Member State must be based exclusively on the personal conduct of the individual concerned. In addition, previous criminal convictions cannot in themselves constitute grounds for the taking of such measures. It follows that the existence of a previous criminal conviction can, therefore, only be taken into account in so far as the circumstances which gave rise to that conviction are evidence of personal conduct constituting a present threat to the requirements of public policy.

In the present case, the legislation at issue in the main proceedings requires nationals of other Member States found guilty, on the national territory in which that legislation applies, of an offence under the drugs laws, to be expelled for life from that territory, unless compelling reasons, in particular family reasons, justify their continued residence in the country. The penalty can be revoked only by a decision taken at the discretion of the Minister for Justice after a period of three years.

Therefore, expulsion for life automatically follows a criminal conviction, without any account being taken of the personal conduct of the offender or of the danger which that person represents for the requirements of public policy.

It follows that the conditions for the application of the public policy exception provided for in Directive 64/221, as interpreted by the Court of Justice, are not fulfilled and that the public policy exception cannot be successfully relied upon.'

Comment

The ECJ held that Donatella Calfa, as a tourist, was a recipient of services in another Member State and as such within the scope of application of art 59 EC Treaty [art 49 EC] (see *Cowan* v *Trésor Public* Case 186/87 [1989] ECR 195). The ECJ emphasised that although national legislation in criminal matters is within the competence of a Member State the requirements of EC law set limitations on Member States' powers. Such legislation should not limit the fundamental freedoms guaranteed by Community law. The ECJ held that the expulsion for life from a territory of a Member State was an obstacle to the freedom to receive services under art 59 EC Treaty [art 49 EC] as well as the freedom of establishment under art 52 EC Treaty [art 43 EC] and the free movement of workers contained in art 48 EC Treaty [art 39 EC]. In those circumstances it was necessary to examine whether the expulsion order could be justified under art 56 EC Treaty [art 46 EC] and art 3(1) of Directive 64/221 on the ground of public policy. The ECJ emphasised that the exception to the free movement of persons should be interpreted restrictively and decided that the expulsion order could not be justified on the ground of public policy since the Greek legislation provided for an automatic expulsion for life following a criminal conviction without taking into account the personal conduct of the offender or whether that conduct created a genuine and sufficiently serious threat affecting one of the fundamental interests of society (see *Bouchereau* Case 30/77 [1977] ECR 1999).

R v Secretary of State for the Home Department, ex parte Shingara and Radiom Joined Cases C-65 and 111/95 [1997] ECR I–3341 European Court of Justice

• *Derogations from the freedom of movement based on public policy – public security – right of entry – legal remedies – arts 8 and 9 of Directive 64/221/EEC*

Facts

In separate proceedings for judicial review each applicant was refused leave to enter the United Kingdom. Mr Shingara, a holder of French citizenship, was refused entry to the UK in 1991 on the grounds of public policy and public security. The notice refusing him entry specified that the Secretary of State had personally decided that it would be contrary to the interests of public policy and public security to admit him to the UK and that under s15(3) of the Immigration Act 1971 he was not entitled to appeal against this decision. In 1993 Mr Shingara was admitted to the UK on the basis of his French identity card but seven days later was arrested in Birmingham and detained as an illegal entrant and duly returned to France. The Secretary of State indicated that the deportation decision was based on the fact that Mr Shingara was promoting Sikh terrorism. On that occasion he was granted leave to apply for judicial review, but in fact did not apply.

Mr Radiom, a holder of Iranian and Irish

nationality, who by some legal means obtained an indefinite residence permit for the UK in 1983, worked in the UK for the Iranian consular services from 1983 to 1989. Following the severing of diplomatic relations between the UK and the Islamic Republic of Iran in 1989 Mr Radiom was asked by the Home Office to leave the UK within seven days, after which time, if he stayed within the country, he would be detained and deported on the grounds of public security. He decided to voluntarily leave the UK but subsequently submitted an application to the Home Office for a residence permit claiming that as an EC national he was entitled to work in the UK. The application was refused and Mr Radiom was informed by the Secretary of State that it was considered that his presence in the UK would still pose a threat to public security since he was a supporter of violence against dissidents as advocated by the Iranian government. He was also refused a right of appeal against this decision notwithstanding the fact that he was an EC national.

Both applicants argued that the United Kingdom law refusing them the opportunity of an appeal against the decision of the Secretary of State to deny them entry to the UK on the grounds of public policy and public security was contrary to Community law, in particular arts 8 and 9 of Directive 64/221/EEC. They both applied for judicial review of Home Office decisions.

Held

The ECJ held that English law was in conformity with arts 8 and 9 of Directive 64/221/EEC.

In respect of art 8 of the Directive (which requires that a Member State provide the same remedies for nationals of other Member States as those available to its own nationals in respect of decisions concerning entry, renewal of residence permit or expulsion), the ECJ held that art 8 did not impose on a Member State an obligation to introduce specific appeal provisions against such decisions. It is sufficient that there is a general system of judicial review available to nationals from other

Member States under the same conditions as to nationals of that Member State

The ECJ held that the three situations mentioned in art 9(1) (that is, 'where there is no right of appeal to a court of law, or where such appeal may be only in respect of the decisions, or where the appeal cannot have suspensory effect') in which a Member State has an obligation to delay the implementation of a decision to refuse the renewal of residence permit or the expulsion of the holder of such permit until a competent authority of the host country gives an opinion, constitute the conditions under which rights provided for in art 9(2) are to be exercised. Under art 9(2) in the event of a refusal to issue a first residence permit, or a decision ordering expulsion before the issue of such a permit, a national of another Member State is entitled to ask an independent authority to review such a decision.

The ECJ held that a national of a Member State who had been refused entry into another Member State on the grounds of public policy, public security or public order but did not appeal against the decision had a right of appeal against a second decision preventing him from entering or remaining in that Member State within a reasonable time of it having been made although he did not appeal against the first decision.

Judgment

'[*First and second questions*]
The first part of the first question asks in substance whether, on a proper construction of art 8 of the Directive, where under the national legislation of a Member State (i) remedies are available in respect of acts of the administration generally and (ii) different remedies are available in respect of decisions concerning entry by nationals of the State concerned, the obligation imposed on the Member State by that provision is satisfied if nationals of other Member States enjoy the same remedies as those available against acts of the administration generally in that Member State.

The Court notes that art 8 does not govern

the ways in which remedies are to be made available, for instance by stipulating the courts from which such remedies may be sought, such details being dependent upon the organisation of the courts in each Member State.

However, the obligation to grant the person concerned the same legal remedies in respect of any decision concerning entry, or refusing the issue or renewal of a residence permit, or ordering expulsion from the territory as are available to nationals in respect of acts of the administration, means that a Member State cannot, without being in breach of the obligation imposed by art 8, organise, for persons covered by the directive, legal remedies governed by special procedures affording lesser safeguards than those pertaining to remedies available to nationals in respect of acts of the administration.

As regards the main proceedings here, the national legislation provides for remedies in respect of acts of the administration generally and another kind of remedy in respect of decisions concerning entry of nationals of the Member State concerned. In addition, the order for reference states that the latter remedy is also available to non-nationals regarding entry, with the exception, however, of refusals of entry on grounds of the public good.

The reservations contained in arts 48 and 56 of the EC Treaty permit Member States to adopt, with respect to the nationals of other Member States and on the grounds specified in those provisions, in particular grounds justified by the requirements of public policy, measures which they cannot apply to their own nationals, inasmuch as they have no authority to expel the latter from the national territory or to deny them access thereto.

It follows that the remedies available to nationals of other Member States in the circumstances defined by the Directive cannot be assessed by reference to the remedies available to nationals concerning the right of entry.

The two situations are indeed in no way comparable: whereas in the case of nationals the right of entry is a consequence of the status of national, so that there can be no margin of discretion for the State as regards the exercise of that right, the special circumstances which may justify reliance on the concept of public policy as against nationals of other Member States may vary over time and from one country to another, and it is therefore necessary to allow the competent national authorities a margin of discretion.

In the light of that reply it is not necessary to answer either the second part of the first question or the second question.

[*Third question*]

The third question asks whether, on a proper construction of art 9 of the Directive, the three hypotheses mentioned in art 9(1) (namely "where there is no right of appeal to a court of law, or where such appeal may be only in respect of the legal validity of the decision, or where the appeal cannot have suspensory effect") apply equally as regards art 9(2), that is to say, where the decision challenged is a refusal to issue a first residence permit or a decision ordering expulsion before the issue of such a permit.

The provisions of art 9 of the Directive complement those of art 8. Their purpose is to provide minimum procedural guarantees for persons affected by one of the measures referred to in the three cases defined in art 9(1). Where the right of appeal is restricted to the legality of the decision, the purpose of the intervention of the competent authority referred to in art 9(1) is to enable an exhaustive examination of all the facts and circumstances, including the expediency of the proposed measure, to be carried out before the decision is finally taken.

If art 9(2) of the Directive were to be interpreted as meaning that the addressee of a decision refusing to issue a first residence permit or a decision ordering expulsion before the issue of such a permit was entitled to obtain an opinion from the competent authority mentioned in art 9(1) in circumstances other than those defined in that paragraph, he would be entitled to do so even where the remedies available entailed a

review of the substance and an exhaustive examination of all the facts and circumstances. Such an interpretation would not be in accordance with the purpose of the provisions, since the procedure of referral for consideration and an opinion provided for in art 9 is intended to mitigate the effect of deficiencies in the remedies referred to in art 8 of the Directive.

[*Fourth and fifth questions*]

The fourth and fifth questions ask in substance whether a national of a Member State who has been refused entry into another Member State for reasons of public order or public security has a right of appeal in respect of measures adopted subsequently which prevent his entering that State, even if the first decision has not been the subject of an appeal or an opinion.

A Community national expelled from a Member State may apply for a fresh residence permit, and, if that application is made after a reasonable time, it must be examined by the competent administrative authority in that State, which must take into account, in particular, the arguments put forward to establish that there has been a material change in the circumstances which justified the first decision ordering expulsion.

Decisions prohibiting entry into a Member State of a national of another Member State constitute derogations from the fundamental principle of freedom of movement. Consequently, such a decision cannot be of unlimited duration. A Community national against whom such a prohibition has been issued must therefore be entitled to apply to have his situation re-examined if he considers that the circumstances which justified prohibiting him from entering the country no longer exist.

When a fresh application has been made for entry or a residence permit, after a reasonable time has elapsed since the preceding decision, the person concerned is entitled to a new decision, which may be the subject of an appeal on the basis of art 8 and, where appropriate, art 9 of the Directive.'

Comment

Directive 64/221/EEC regulates the application of the three derogations from the right to freedom of movement conferred on EC nationals by Community law. Those derogations based on the grounds of public policy, public security and public health, as exceptions to the provisions of the EC Treaty, must be interpreted restrictively. No Community definition is provided in respect of those three derogations. The Directive only describes the situations in which a Member State may prevent an EC national from exercising his right to enter the territory of another Member State on the grounds of public policy, public security and public order. Consequently, the Directive permits a Member State a certain discretion in the application of those derogations, provided its exercise is within the limits of the EC Treaty. Furthermore, Directive 64/221/EEC provides procedural safeguards for EC nationals from other Member States seeking to enforce their rights of entry and residence in a Member State. Articles 8 and 9 of Directive 64/221/EEC establish requirements for remedies against immigration decisions excluding an EC national from the territory of a host Member State.

The main issue under art 8 of the Directive was that a decision made by the Secretary of State under s13 of the Immigration Act 1970, which excluded an EC national from that State's territory on the grounds of 'public good', was not subject to appeal although it remained subject to judicial review as does any act of administration. The ECJ emphasised that the requirements of art 8 of the Directive are satisfied if EC nationals from other Member State have the same legal remedies as are available to nationals of a host State, in the present cases consisting of general judicial review provisions.

Article 9 of Directive 64/221/EEC poses a problem of interpretation. Under art 9(1) of the Directive a decision refusing renewal of a residence permit or ordering the expulsion of the holder of a residence permit from the territory of a host State should be suspended (save in cases of urgency) until an opinion has been obtained from a competent authority of the host State different from that which has taken the challenged decision. Before that competent authority the applicant must have a right of defence and of assistance and representation in three situations: 'where there is no right of appeal to a court of law, where such an appeal may be only in respect of validity of the decision, or where the appeal cannot have suspensory effect'. Article 9(2) of the Directive concerns a decision in respect of a refusal to issue a first residence permit or a decision ordering expulsion before the issue of such a permit, but does not indicate the conditions precedent to the exercise of that right. The ECJ held that the right of appeal against decisions enumerated in art 9(2) applies in the three situations mentioned in art 9(1). This interpretation is consistent with the objective of art 9 of the Directive which intends to mitigate the effect of deficiencies in the remedies referred to in art 8 of the Directive.

The ECJ held that where an EC national is refused entry into the territory of another Member State on the grounds of public security, and does not challenge this decision, and later applies for a residence permit, and a new decision confirming the previous one is issued against him, he has a right of appeal within a reasonable time against a second decision, notwithstanding the fact that he did not appeal against the first.

R v *Secretary of State for the Home Department, ex parte Yiadom* Case C–357/98 [2000] ECR I–9265 European Court of Justice

• *Freedom of movement of persons – derogation based on public policy – decisions concerning entry of EC nationals – temporary admission – judicial safeguards – legal remedies, arts 8 and 9 of Directive 64/221/EEC – preliminary ruling*

Facts

A Dutch national of Ghanaian origin, Ms Nana Yaa Konadu Yiadom, was temporarily allowed entry to the United Kingdom pending the investigation of her case by the competent authorities. She arrived in the UK on 7 August 1995 accompanied by another woman, whom she falsely claimed to be her daughter. The UK authorities sent the other woman to Ghana. On 3 March 1996 the Secretary of State refused Ms Yiadom leave to enter the UK on the ground that she had facilitated the illegal entry of others and that there was a likelihood that she would do so again in the future. Ms Yiadom challenged that decision, initially before the High Court where her application for judicial review was dismissed, and then before the Court of Appeal. She argued, first, that there was no sufficient evidence for restricting her right to freedom of movement on the ground of public policy and, second, that by virtue of arts 8 and 9 of Directive 64/221/EEC she was entitled to a right of appeal to the adjudicator whilst she was physically present in the UK (an in-country right of appeal) and not merely the right of appeal granted by national law where the person concerned is no longer in the country (an out-of-country appeal). The Court of Appeal agreed with the Secretary of State as to the reasons for refusal of leave to enter the UK, but referred a number of questions to the ECJ regarding the second matter raised by Ms Yiadom.

Held

The ECJ held that arts 8 and 9 of Directive 64/221/EEC must be interpreted as meaning that a decision adopted by the authorities of a Member State refusing an EC national, not in possession of a residence permit, leave to enter its territory cannot be classified as a 'decision concerning entry' within the meaning of art 8 where the person concerned had been temporarily admitted to the territory of that Member State, pending a decision following the enquiries required for the investigation of her case, and as a result resided for almost seven months in that territory before

that decision was notified to her. For that reason such an EC national must be entitled to the procedural safeguards referred to in art 9 of Directive 64/222/EEC.

The fact that an EC national was granted permission to take up employment pending the investigation of her case by the competent authorities, and the fact that several months elapsed between her arrival in the territory of the Member State and the decision refusing entry, cannot have any bearing on the classification of that decision under Directive 64/221/EEC.

Judgment

'Article 8a of the EC Treaty (now, after amendment, art 18 EC) provides that every citizen of the Union is to have the right to move and reside freely within the territory of the Member States, subject to the limitations and conditions laid down in the Treaty and by measures adopted to give it effect.

The Court has consistently held that the principle of freedom of movement of persons must be given a broad interpretation.

In the same way, provisions protecting Community nationals who exercise that fundamental freedom must be interpreted in their favour.

It should also be recalled that the need for uniform application of Community law and the principle of equality require that the terms of a provision of Community law which makes no express reference to the law of the Member States for the purpose of determining its meaning and scope must normally be given an autonomous and uniform interpretation throughout the Community; that interpretation must take into account the context of the provision and the purpose of the legislation in question (Case 327/82 *Ekro* v *Produktschap voor Vee en Vlees* [1984] ECR 107, para 11; and Case C–287/98 *State of the Grand Duchy of Luxembourg* v *Linster and Others* [2000] ECR I–6917, para 43).

The purpose of arts 8 and 9 of the Directive is to define the minimum procedural safeguards to which Community nationals are entitled when they rely on freedom of movement in relation to the situation in which they find themselves.

Article 8 of the Directive requires Member States to provide for Member State nationals the same legal remedies in respect of a decision concerning entry, or refusing the issue or renewal of a residence permit, or ordering expulsion from the territory, as are available to nationals of the State concerned in respect of acts of the administration.

The provisions of art 9 of the Directive complement those of art 8. Their purpose is to provide minimum procedural safeguards for persons affected by one of the measures referred to in the three cases mentioned in art 9(1), namely where there is no right of appeal to a court of law, or where such appeal lies only in respect of the legal validity of the decision, or where the appeal cannot have suspensory effect.

The Court held that those three cases must be taken into account in relation both to measures referred to in art 9(1) of the Directive and to those mentioned in art 9(2) thereof.

Accordingly, art 9(1) of the Directive provides that, in those cases, a decision refusing renewal of a residence permit or ordering the expulsion of the holder of a residence permit from the territory may not be taken, save in cases of urgency, until an opinion has been obtained from a competent authority of the host Member State before which the person concerned enjoys such rights of defence and of assistance or representation as the domestic law of that country provides for.

Article 9(2) of the Directive provides that, in the same cases, any decision refusing the issue of a first residence permit or ordering expulsion of the person concerned before the issue of the permit must, where that person so requests, be referred for consideration to a competent authority before which the person concerned is to be entitled to submit his defence in person, except where this would be contrary to the interests of national security.

By contrast, art 9 of the Directive does not lay down any particular requirement in relation to legal remedies in respect of decisions refusing entry to the territory. A Community national who is the subject of such a decision is therefore granted only the same legal remedies in respect of that decision as are available to nationals of the State concerned in respect of acts of the administration.

The limited nature of the procedural safeguards laid down in favour of the national who challenges a decision refusing entry may be explained by the fact that, as a rule, the person against whom such a decision is made is not physically present in the territory of a Member State and it is, therefore, materially impossible for him to submit his defence in person before the competent authority.

The Court has, moreover, interpreted art 8 of the Directive as meaning that there may not be inferred from that provision an obligation for the Member States to permit a foreign national to remain in their territory for the duration of the proceedings, so long as he is able nevertheless to obtain a fair hearing and to present his defence in full (Case 98/79 *Pecastaing* v *Belgium* [1980] ECR 691, para 13).

The main proceedings concern a Community national who was temporarily admitted to the territory of the Member State many months previously and was therefore physically present there when the competent national authorities notified her of a decision prohibiting her from entering that territory for the purposes of national law.

By reason of a legal fiction under national law, according to which the national who is physically present in the territory of the host Member State is regarded as not yet having been the subject of a decision concerning entry, that national does not qualify for the procedural safeguards granted under art 9 of the Directive to nationals regarded as lawfully present in the territory who are the subject of a decision refusing the issue or renewal of a residence permit, or ordering expulsion from the territory.

In the light of the principles for interpreting the Directive which are set out in paras

24 to 26 above, it must be held that the measure determining the situation of such a national cannot be classified as a "decision concerning entry" within the meaning of the Directive, but that the national must be entitled to the procedural safeguards laid down in art 9 of the Directive.

It should be added that, in the main proceedings, almost seven months elapsed between the physical admission to the territory and the decision refusing entry.

It is of course understandable that a Member State should take the time necessary to carry out an administrative investigation of a Community national's situation before taking a decision refusing her leave to enter its territory.

However, if that State has accepted the physical presence of that national in its territory for a period which is manifestly longer than is required for such an investigation, it can also accept that national's presence during the time needed for him to exercise the rights of appeal referred to in art 9 of the Directive.

All that must be taken into account is the time which elapsed between the physical entry into the territory and the competent authority's decision refusing admission, since the time which elapsed as a result of bringing legal proceedings having a suspensory effect and the grant of permission to take up employment pending the determination of those proceedings are not relevant for the purpose of determining the nature of that decision and its classification under the Directive (see, to that effect, Case C–192/89 *Sevince* v *Staatssecretaris van Justitie* [1990] ECR I–3461, para 31).

The answer to the questions referred must therefore be that arts 8 and 9 of the Directive must be interpreted as meaning that a decision adopted by the authorities of a Member State refusing a Community national, not in possession of a residence permit, leave to enter its territory cannot be classified as a "decision concerning entry" within the meaning of art 8 thereof in a case such as that at issue in the main proceedings where the person concerned was temporarily admitted to the territory of that Member State, pending a decision following the enquiries required for the investigation of her case, and therefore resided for almost seven months in that territory before that decision was notified to her, since such a national must be entitled to the procedural safeguards referred to in art 9 of the Directive.

The time which elapsed after the competent authority's decision as a result, first, of the suspensory effect of legal proceedings and, second, of the grant of permission to take up employment pending the determination of those proceedings, cannot have any bearing on the classification of that decision under the Directive.'

Comment

The ECJ took a realistic approach to the interpretation of arts 8 and 9 of Directive 64/221/EEC. The Court repeated that the principle of freedom of movement must be interpreted broadly (*R* v *Immigration Appeal Tribunal, ex parte Antonissen* Case C–292/89 [1991] ECR I–745, *EC Commission* v *Belgium* Case C–344/95 [1997] ECR I–1036) whilst all exceptions to the principle must be given a strict interpretation: *Van Duyn* v *Home Office* Case 41/74 [1974] ECR 1337; *Bonsignore* v *Oberstadtdirector of the City of Cologne* Case 67/74 [1975] ECR 297. The ECJ explained the purpose of both arts 8 and 9 of the Directive.

Article 9 complements art 8 but it does not apply to legal remedies in respect of decisions refusing entry to the territory. The limited protection provided by art 8 of the Directive is explained by the fact that, normally, an EC national against whom a decision refusing entry is made is not physically present in the territory of a Member State, and therefore it is in practice impossible for him to submit his defence in person before the competent authority. In addition, under art 8 of the Directive a Member State is not obliged to temporarily admit an EC national to the territory for the duration of the proceedings aimed at determining whether or not such a person should be granted leave of entry: *Pecastaing* v *Belgian State* Case 98/79 [1980] ECR 691. Nevertheless, in the case of Ms Yiadom the situation was peculiar in the sense that, by reason of a legal fiction under national law, she was deemed not to have entered the territory, although she was physically present there, when the competent national authorities notified her of a decision prohibiting her from entering that territory. The ECJ rejected the legal fiction existing under national law. The Court held that although a decision concerning Ms Yiadom was within the scope of art 8 of the Directive, as it concerned a decision regarding entry, she was entitled to the procedural safeguards laid down in art 9 of the Directive. This conclusion was especially justified, taking into account that almost seven months had elapsed between her physical admission and the decision refusing her entry. In this respect the ECJ held that:

'... if [a] State has accepted the physical presence of [an EC] national in its territory for a period which is manifestly longer than is required for such an investigation, it can also accept that national's presence during the time needed for him to exercise the rights of appeal referred to in art 9 of the Directive.'

The ECJ emphasised that in the classification of a decision (that is, whether it was within the scope of art 8 or 9 of the Directive), the time which elapsed after the competent authority's decision as a result, first, of the suspensory effect of legal proceedings and, second, of the grant of permission to take up employment pending the determination of those proceedings, could not have any bearing on such a classification.

Rutili v *Minister for the Interior* Case 36/75 [1975] ECR 1219; [1976] 1 CMLR 140 European Court of Justice

• *Free movement of workers – art 48(3) EC Treaty [art 39(3) EC] – residence permit – restriction on entry and residence within a Member State – public policy*

Facts
Rutili was an Italian national who resided in France and, between 1967 and 1968, he actively participated in political and trade union activities. The French authorities grew increasingly concerned with his activities, and issued a deportation order. This was subsequently altered to a restriction order requiring him to remain in certain provinces of France. In particular, the order prohibited him from residing in the province in which he was habitually resident and in which his family resided.

The plaintiff challenged the legality of these measures on the ground that they interfered with his right of freedom of movement. The question was referred to the ECJ for a preliminary ruling.

Held
The ECJ interpreted the right of a Member State to limit the free movement of workers on the ground of public policy and concluded that this right must be construed strictly. In particular, a Member State cannot, in the case of a national of another Member State, impose prohibitions on residence which are territorially limited except in circumstances where such prohibitions may be imposed on its own nationals.

Judgment
'[*Justification of measures adopted on grounds of public policy from the point of view of substantive law*]
By virtue of the reservation contained in art 48(3), Member States continue to be, in principle, free to determine the requirements of public policy in the light of their national needs.

Nevertheless, the concept of public policy must, in the Community context and where, in particular, it is used as a justification for derogating from the fundamental principles of equality of treatment and freedom of movement for workers, be interpreted strictly, so that its scope cannot be determined unilaterally by each Member State without being subject to control by the institutions of the Community.

Accordingly, restrictions cannot be imposed on the right of a national of any Member State to enter the territory of another Member State, to stay there and to move within it unless his presence or conduct constitutes a genuine and sufficiently serious threat to public policy.

In this connection art 3 of Directive 64/221 imposes on Member States the duty to base their decision on the individual circumstances of any person under the protection of Community law and not on general considerations.

[*The justifiaction for, in particular, a prohibition on residence in part of the national territory*]

The questions put by the Tribunal Administratif were raised in connection with a measure prohibiting residence in a limited part of the national territory.

In reply to a question from the Court, the government of the French Republic stated that such measures may be taken in the case of its own nationals either, in the case of certain criminal convictions, as an additional penalty, or following the declaration of a state of emergency.

The provisions enabling certain areas of the national territory to be prohibited to foreign nationals are, however, based on legislative instruments specifically concerning them.

In this connection, the government of the French Republic draws attention to art 4 of the Council Directive 64/220 of 25 February 1964 on the abolition of restrictions on movement and residence within the Community for nationals of Member States with regard to establishment and the provision of services.

Right of entry into the territory of Member States and the right to stay there and to move freely within it is defined in the Treaty by reference to the whole territory of these States and not by reference to its internal subdivisions.

The reservation contained in art 48(3) concerning the protection of public policy has the same scope as the rights the exercise of which may, under that paragraph, be subject to limitations.

It follows that prohibitions on residence under the reservation inserted to this effect in art 48(3) may be imposed only in respect of the whole of the national territory.

On the other hand, in the case of partial prohibitions on residence, limited to certain areasof the territory, persons covered by Community law must, under art [6] of the Treaty and within the field of application of that provision, be treated on a footing of equality with the nationals of the Member State concerned.

It follows that a Member State cannot, in the case of a national of another Member State covered by the provisions of the Treaty, impose prohibitions on residence which are territorially limited exept in circumstances where such prohibitions may be imposed on its own nationals.'

Comment

In the present case the ECJ clarified the scope of art 48(3) EC Treaty [art 39(3) EC] which provides for an exception to the free movement of workers based on the grounds of public policy, public security and public health. The ECJ stated that the exception must be interpreted restrictively so as not to undermine the fundamental principle of the free movement of workers.

The interesting aspect of the present case is that a Member State may only impose partial prohibitions on residence, that is restrict the residence of an EC migrant worker to certain areas of its territory if such a restriction may be imposed on its own nationals. If a Member State has no power to restrict the residence of its own nationals to a specific area then it has only two options in relation to an EC migrant worker: to refuse his entry or to permit him to reside in the whole of the national territory.

As to restrictions on admission to or residence within a Member State for nationals of other Member States based on types of activities they intend to carry on once admitted and which are lawful when conducted by host State nationals, the ECJ did confirm its previous decision in *Van Duyn* v *Home Office* Case 41/74. The ECJ reversed its position in *Adoui and Cornvaille* v *Belgian State* Joined Cases 115 and 116/81 [1982] ECR 1665 in which the Court held that a Member State may only justify such restrictions on the admission to or residence within its territory of nationals of another Member State if it adopted, with respect to the same conduct on the part of its own nationals, repressive measures or other genuine and effective measure intended to combat such conduct.

12 Equal Treatment for Women and Men

Abdoulaye and Others v Régie Nationale des Usines Renault SA
Case C–218/98 [1999] ECR I–5723
European Court of Justice

- *Social policy – men and women – equal pay for men and women – art 141 EC – indirect discrimination – Directives 75/117/EEC and 76/207/EEC – collective agreement providing for an allowance for pregnant women taking maternity leave*

Facts
Under a social benefit agreement for Renault workers, a female worker when taking maternity leave was entitled to receive a payment of FF 7,500. This was in addition to her normal salary. Male workers were not entitled to this kind of payment. A number of male workers challenged this payment on the ground that is was in breach of the principle of equal pay for men and women, since it only applied to a pregnant woman and not to the father of the child. The applicants argued that whilst certain instances of discrimination, such as maternity leave, were justified, taking into account that they were related to the physiological characteristics of one sex, it was different in the case of the challenged payment since, although the birth of a child concerned only women alone from a strictly physiological point of view, it was a social event which concerned the whole family, including the father. Therefore, to deny him the same allowance would amount to unlawful discrimination.

Held
The ECJ held that the allowance in question is not contrary to EC law where that allowance is designed to offset the occupational disadvantages which arise for pregnant women as a result of their being away from work.

Judgment
'Article 119 of the Treaty lays down the principle of equal pay for men and women for the same work. That provision is clarified by art 1 of Directive 75/117.

According to the case law of the Court, the definition contained in the second paragraph of art 119 of the Treaty makes clear that the term "pay" used in the abovementioned provisions includes all consideration which workers receive directly or indirectly from their employers in respect of their employment. The legal nature of such consideration is not important for the purposes of the application of art 119 of the Treaty provided that it is granted in respect of employment.

Consideration classified as pay includes, inter alia, consideration paid by the employer by virtue of legislative provisions and under a contract of employment whose purpose is to ensure that workers receive income even where, in certain cases specified by the legislature, they are not performing any work provided for in their contracts of employment.

Since the benefit paid by an employer to a female employee when she goes on maternity leave, such as the payment in question in the main proceedings, is based on the employment relationship, it constitutes pay within the meaning of art 119 of the Treaty and Directive 75/117.

While such a payment is not made periodically and is not indexed on salary, its characteristics do not, contrary to what Renault contends, alter its nature of pay within the meaning of art 119 of the Treaty (see Case 12/81 *Garland* v *British Rail Engineering* [1982] ECR 359, para 9).

According to the case law of the Court, the principle of equal pay, like the general principle of non-discrimination of which it is a particular expression, presupposes that male and female workers whom it covers are in comparable situations (see *Gillespie* v *Northern Ireland Health and Social Services Board* [Case C–342/93 [1996] ECR I–475], paras 16 to 18).

The compatibility with art 119 of the Treaty of a payment such as that in question in the main proceedings thus depends on the question whether, with regard to that payment, female workers are in a situation comparable to that of male workers.

In its answer to a question put by the Court, Renault mentioned several occupational disadvantages, inherent in maternity leave, which arise for female workers as a result of being away from work.

First of all, a woman on maternity leave may not be proposed for promotion. On her return, her period of service will be reduced by the length of her absence; second, a pregnant woman may not claim performance-related salary increases; third, a female worker may not take part in training; lastly, since new technology is constantly changing the nature of jobs, the adaptation of a female worker returning from maternity leave becomes complicated.

As the United Kingdom government and the Commission rightly point out, art 119 of the Treaty does not preclude the making of a payment such as that in question in the main proceedings exclusively to female workers since it is designed to offset the occupational disadvantages, such as those mentioned by Renault. In this case, male and female workers are, in their view, in different situations, which excludes any breach of the principle of equal pay laid down in art 119 of the Treaty.

It is for the national court to determine whether this is the case.'

Comment

The ECJ held that such a payment constitutes pay within the meaning of art 141 EC as it is based on the employment relationship. However, its compatibility with art 141 EC depends on the question of whether female workers are in a situation comparable to that of male workers. In this respect Renault invoked a number of arguments which demonstrated that the situation of Renault's male workers was not comparable, as women on maternity leave suffer several occupational disadvantages, such as not being proposed for promotion, not being entitled to performance-related salary increases, not taking part in training etc. Therefore, the granting of such an allowance exclusively to female workers was designed to offset those occupational disadvantages. In such a case the situation of male workers and female workers is different, which excludes any breach of the principle of equal pay laid down in art 141 EC.

However, it is for the national court to determine whether the allowance in question is designed to offset the occupational disadvantages arising for female workers as a result of them being away from work.

Boyle (Margaret) and Others v Equal Opportunities Commission
Case C–411/96 [1998] 3 CMLR 1133
European Court of Justice

• *Social policy – sex discrimination – equal pay and equal treatment for men and women – maternity leave – rights of pregnant women in respect of sick leave – annual leave – accrual of pension rights – obligation to repay maternity pay received*

Facts

Margaret Boyle and five other applicants

brought proceedings before the Industrial Tribunal against their employer, the Equal Opportunities Commission, for a declaration that some provisions of the maternity scheme applied to them by their employer were contrary to Community law in so far as they discriminated against female employees. In particular the following clauses of the maternity scheme were called into question.

First, a clause which makes the payment, during the period of maternity leave, of pay higher than the statutory payment but requires repayment of the difference if the worker fails to return to work after childbirth.

Second, a clause requiring an employee who has expressed her intention to commence her maternity leave during the six weeks preceding the expected confinement, and is on sick leave with a pregnancy-related illness immediately before that date and gives birth during the period of sick leave, to bring forward the date on which her paid maternity leave commences, either to the beginning of the six weeks preceding the expected week of childbirth or to the beginning of the period of sick leave, whichever is later.

Third, a clause prohibiting a woman from taking sick leave during the minimum period of 14 weeks' maternity leave to which a female worker is entitled pursuant to art 8 of Directive 92/85, or any supplementary period of maternity leave granted to her by the employer, unless she elects to return to work and thus terminates her maternity leave.

Fourth, a clause limiting the period during which annual leave accrues to the minimum period of 14 weeks' maternity leave to which female workers are entitled under the Directive.

Fifth, a clause limiting, in the context of an occupational scheme wholly financed by the employer, the accrual of pension rights during maternity leave to the period during which the woman receives the pay provided for by that employment contract or national legislation.

Held

The ECJ held that only the clause that pro-

hibits a woman from taking sick leave during the minimum period of 14 weeks' maternity leave and the clause limiting, in the context of an occupational scheme wholly financed by the employer, the accrual of pension rights during the period of maternity leave to the period during which the woman receives the pay provided for by her employment contract or national legislation were in breach of Community law.

Judgment

'[*The first question*]
In that respect, it should be noted that it was in view of the risk that the provisions relating to maternity leave would be ineffective if rights connected with the employment contract were not maintained, that the Community legislature provided that "maintenance of a payment to, and/or entitlement to an adequate allowance" for workers to whom the Directive applies must be ensured in the case of the maternity leave.

The concept of allowance to which that provision refers ... includes all income received by the worker during her maternity leave which is not paid to her by her employer pursuant to the employment relationship.

In this respect, the provisions of the Directive are intended to ensure that, during her maternity leave, the worker receives an income at least equivalent to the sickness allowance provided for by national social security legislation in the event of a break in her activities on health grounds.

Female workers must be guaranteed an income of that level during their maternity leave, irrespective of whether it is paid in the form of an allowance, pay or a combination of the two.

However, the Directive is not intended to guarantee her any higher income which the employer may have undertaken to pay her, under the employment contract, should she be on sick leave.

It follows that a clause in an employment contract according to which a worker who does not return to work after childbirth is required to repay the difference between the pay received by her during her maternity leave and the statutory payments to which she was entitled in respect of maternity leave is compatible with Directive 92/85 in so far as the level of those payments is not lower than the income which the worker concerned would receive, under the relevant national social security legislation, in the event of a break in her activities on grounds connected with her state of health.

A clause in an employment contract which makes the application of a more favourable set of rules than that prescribed by national legislation conditional on the pregnant woman, unlike any worker on sick leave, returning to work after childbirth, failing which she must repay the contractual maternity pay in so far as it exceeds the level of the statutory payments in respect of that leave, therefore does not constitute discrimination on grounds of sex.

[*The second question*]
… In that respect, art 8 of Directive 92/85 leaves it open to the Member States to determine the date on which maternity leave is to commence.

National legislation may therefore, as here, provide that the period of maternity leave commences with the date notified by the person concerned to her employer as the date on which she intends to commence her period of absence, or the first day after the beginning of the sixth week preceding the expected week of childbirth during which the employee is wholly or partly absent because of pregnancy, should that day fall on an earlier date.

The clause to which the second question relates merely reflects the choice made in such national legislation.

[*The third question*]
… In that respect, although the Member States are required to take the necessary measures to ensure that workers are entitled to a period of maternity leave of at least 14 weeks, those workers may waive that right, with the exception of the two weeks compulsory maternity leave which, in the United Kingdom, commence on the day on which the child is born.

In contrast, if a woman becomes ill during the period of maternity leave referred to by Directive 92/85 and places herself under the sick leave arrangements, and that sick leave ends before the expiry of the period of maternity leave, she cannot be deprived of the right to continued enjoyment, after that date, of the maternity leave provided for by the aforementioned provision until the expiry of the minimum period of 14 weeks, that period being calculated from the date on which the maternity leave commenced.

The third question need be examined only in so far as the clause of the employment contract referred to therein applies to the supplementary period of maternity leave granted by the employer to female workers.

In that respect, the principle of non-discrimination laid down by the equal treatment directive does not require a woman to be able to exercise simultaneously both the right to supplementary maternity leave granted to her by the employer and the right to sick leave.

Consequently, in order for a woman on maternity leave to qualify for sick leave, she may be required to terminate the period of supplementary maternity leave granted to her by the employer.

[*The fourth question*]
… It should be noted that substantially more women than men take periods of unpaid leave during their career because they take supplementary maternity leave, so that, in practice, the clause at issue applies to a greater percentage of women than men.

However, the fact that such a clause applies more frequently to women results from the exercise of the right to unpaid maternity leave granted to them by their employers in addition to the period of protection guaranteed by Directive 92/85.

The supplementary unpaid maternity leave constitutes a special advantage, over and above the protection provided for by Directive 92/85 and is available only to women, so that the fact that annual leave ceases to accrue during that period of leave cannot amount to less favourable treatment of women.

[*The fifth question*]

... The accrual of pension rights in the context of an occupational scheme wholly financed by the employer constitutes one of the rights connected with the employment contracts of the workers.

Such rights must, in accordance with Directive 92/85, be ensured during the period of maternity leave of at least 14 weeks to which female workers are entitled.

Although, in accordance with Directive 92/85, it is open to Member States to make entitlement to pay or the adequate allowance conditional upon the worker concerned fulfilling the conditions of eligibility for such benefits laid down under national legislation, no such possibility exists in respect of rights connected with the employment contract.

The accrual of pension rights under an occupational scheme during the period of maternity leave referred to by Directive 92/85 cannot therefore be made conditional upon the woman's receiving the pay provided for by her employment contract or SMP [statutory maternity pay] during that period.'

Comment

In the present case the ECJ defined some aspects of the financial arrangements and other rights to which women are entitled during the period of maternity leave.

Brown v Rentokil Case C–394/96 [1998] ECR I–4185; [1998] 2 CMLR 1049 European Court of Justice

• *Social policy – sex discrimination – Directive 76/207/EEC – equal treatment for men and women – pregnant woman – dismissal – absences due to illness con nected to pregnancy*

Facts

Mary Brown worked for Rentokil as a driver. Rentokil's contract of employment contained a clause stipulating that if an employee was absent from work due to illness for more than 26 weeks continuously, the employee would be dismissed. In August 1990 Mary Brown informed her employer that she was pregnant. Shortly afterwards, she suffered from health problems connected with her pregnancy. From 16 August 1990 she submitted a succession of four-week medical certificates mentioning various pregnancy-related disorders. She did not return to work. In accordance with her contract she was informed by a letter of 30 January 1991 that she would be dismissed on 8 February 1991. Mary Brown was therefore dismissed while pregnant. Her child was born on 22 March 1991. She challenged her dismissal, as contrary to Community law, before the Industrial Tribunal which rejected her application. She appealed to the House of Lords, which referred two questions on the interpretation of Directive 76/207/EEC, namely its arts 2(1) and 5(1) regarding the implementation of the principle of equal treatment for men and woman in relation to employment, vocational training and working conditions, to the ECJ for a preliminary ruling.

Held

The ECJ held that Community law precludes dismissal of a woman at any time during her pregnancy for absences due to incapacity for work caused by illness resulting from her pregnancy, even if the dismissal was based on a contractual provision permitting the employer to dismiss an employee, regardless of gender, after a certain number of weeks of continuous absence.

Judgment

'According to settled case law of the Court of Justice, the dismissal of a female worker on account of pregnancy, or essentially on account of pregnancy, can affect only women and therefore constitutes direct discrimination on grounds of sex.

It is clear from the documents before the Court that the question concerns the dismissal of a female worker during her pregnancy as a result of absences through incapacity for work arising from her pregnant condition. As Rentokil points out, the cause of Mrs Brown's dismissal lies in the fact that she was ill during her pregnancy to such an extent that she was unfit for work for 26 weeks. It is common ground that her illness was attributable to her pregnancy.

However, dismissal of a woman during pregnancy cannot be based on her inability, as a result of her condition, to perform the duties which she is contractually bound to carry out. If such an interpretation were adopted, the protection afforded by Community law to a woman during pregnancy would be available only to pregnant women who were able to comply with the conditions of their employment contracts, with the result that the provisions of Directive 76/207 would be rendered ineffective.

Although pregnancy is not in any way comparable to a pathological condition, the fact remains, that pregnancy is a period during which disorders and complications may arise compelling a woman to undergo strict medical supervision and, in some cases, to rest absolutely for all or part of her pregnancy. Those disorders and complications, which may cause incapacity for work, form part of the risks inherent in the condition of pregnancy and are thus a specific feature of that condition.

In its judgment in Case C–179/88 *Handels-og Kontorfunktionaerernes Forbund i Danmark* v *Dansk Arbejdsgiverforening* [1990] ECR I–3979, the Court concluded that, during the maternity leave accorded to her under national law, a woman is protected against dismissal on the grounds of her absence.

If such protection against dismissal must be afforded to women during maternity leave, the principle of non-discrimination, for its part, requires similar protection throughout the period of pregnancy. Finally, dismissal of a female worker during pregnancy for absences due to incapacity for work resulting from her pregnancy is linked

to the occurrence of risks inherent in pregnancy and must therefore be regarded as essentially based on the fact of pregnancy. Such a dismissal can affect only women and therefore constitutes direct discrimination on grounds of sex.

It follows that arts 2(1) and 5(1) of the Directive preclude dismissal of a female worker at any time during her pregnancy for absences due to incapacity for work caused by an illness resulting from that pregnancy.

It is clear from all the foregoing considerations that, contrary to the Court's ruling in Case C–400/95 *Larsson* v *Føtex Supermarked* [1997] ECR I–2757, where a woman is absent owing to illness resulting from pregnancy or childbirth, and that illness arose during pregnancy and persisted during and after maternity leave, her absence not only during maternity leave but also during the period extending from the start of her pregnancy to the start of her maternity leave cannot be taken into account for computation of the period justifying her dismissal under national law. As to her absence after maternity leave, this may be taken into account under the same conditions as a man's absence, of the same duration, through incapacity for work.'

Comment

In the present case the ECJ extended the scope of protection for pregnant female workers. It held that the principle of non-discrimination prohibits their dismissed at any time during their pregnancy if the dismissal is based on absences due to incapacity for work caused by an illness resulting from their pregnancy. A contractual provision which permits the employer to dismiss any worker, regardless of gender, after a stipulated number of weeks of continuous absence affects a female and a male worker differently. In the case of a pregnant female worker the application of such a contractual provision amounts to direct sex discrimination if her absence is caused by pregnancy-related illness.

Handels-og Kontorfunktionaerernes Forbund v *Fællesforeningen for Danmarks Brugsforeninger* Case C–66/96 [1998] ECR I–7327
European Court of Justice

• *Social policy – art 119 EC Treaty [art 141 EC] – equal treatment for men and women – Directive 76/207/EEC – remuneration – working conditions for a pregnant woman – Directive 92/85/EEC*

Facts
A group of Danish female employees brought proceedings against their respective employers in relation to maintenance of their wages during absences from work connected with their pregnancy. All applicants (whose pregnancy followed an abnormal course during the three months preceding the expected date of confinement) challenged Danish law as contrary to Community law. The contested Danish law provided that in the event of incapacity for work, or legitimate impediment for a particular reason linked with the pregnancy, arising before the three months' period prior the confinement, the employee was not entitled to receive her wages but would receive benefits in accordance with the Law on Benefits and Danish Administrative Instruction No 191 of 27 October 1994, which benefits did not equal the full pay. The Danish court referred to the ECJ a number of question relating to the contested Danish law which law made a distinction between incapacity for work on grounds of pregnancy/confinement and on grounds of illness. The ECJ placed those questions in three groups relating to the conformity of Danish law with Community law in the following situations.

First, Danish law stipulates that for a maximum of five weeks' absence over a period beginning not earlier than three months before the confinement and ending not later than three months after the confinement, the employee is entitled to receive half pay from her employer whilst in the event of incapacity

for work on grounds of illness a worker is in principle entitled to receive full pay from his or her employer.

Second, Danish law provides that a pregnant woman is not entitled to receive pay from her employer where, before the beginning of her maternity leave, she is absent from work due to routine pregnancy-related inconveniences or mere medical recommendation where there is no risk to the unborn child or any actual pathological condition, while any worker who is unfit for work on the ground of illness is entitled to full pay from his/her employer.

Third, Danish law provides that an employer when he considers that he cannot provide work for a woman who is pregnant although not unfit for work, may send her home without paying her full wages.

Held
The ECJ held Danish law in breach of Community law when it stipulated that a pregnant woman who, before the beginning of her maternity leave, was unfit for work due to a pathological condition connected with her pregnancy, as attested by a medical certificate, was not entitled to receive full pay from her employer but only benefits paid by a local authority when, in the event of incapacity for work on grounds of illness, as attested by a medical certificate, a worker was entitled to receive full pay from his/her employer. The Court stated that it was lawful for national law to provide that a pregnant woman was not entitled to receive her pay from her employer where, before the beginning of her maternity leave, she is absent from work by reason either of routine pregnancy-related inconveniences, when there is in fact no incapacity for work, or of medical recommendation intended to protect the unborn child but not based on an actual pathological condition or on any special risks for the unborn child, while any worker who is unfit for work on the grounds of illness is in principle entitled to full pay from his/her employer. The Court held that it was contrary to Community law for national legislation to

provide that an employer could send home a woman who was pregnant although not unfit for work, without paying her salary in full, when he considers that he cannot provide work for her.

Judgment

'[*The first situation*]
In this case, it is clear from the case file that all workers are in principle entitled, under the legislation at issue in the main proceedings, to continue to be paid in full in the event of incapacity for work.

Thus, the fact that a woman is deprived, before the beginning of her maternity leave, of her full pay when her incapacity for work is the result of a pathological condition connected with the pregnancy must be regarded as treatment based essentially on the pregnancy and thus as discriminatory.

It follows that the application of legislative provisions such as those at issue in the main proceedings involves discrimination against women, in breach of art 119 of the Treaty and of Directive 75/117.

[*The second situation*]
The next point is that the pay received by a worker while on sick leave constitutes pay within the meaning of art 119 of the Treaty.

In contrast to the [first situation] outlined by the national court, the pregnant woman is absent from her work before the beginning of her maternity leave not because of a pathological condition or of any special risks for the unborn child giving rise to an incapacity for work attested by a medical certificate but by reason either of routine pregnancy-related inconveniences or of mere medical recommendation, without there being any incapacity for work in either of those two situations.

Consequently, the fact that the employee forfeits some, or even all, of her salary by reason of such absences which are not based on an incapacity for work cannot be regarded as treatment based essentially on the pregnancy but rather as based on the choice made by the employee not to work.

[*The third situation*]
By reserving to Member States the right to retain or introduce provisions which are intended to protect women in connection with "pregnancy and maternity", Directive 76/207 recognises the legitimacy, in terms of the principle of equal treatment, of protecting a woman's biological condition during and after pregnancy.

However, legislation such as that at issue in the main proceedings cannot fall within the scope of that provision.

It appears from the order for reference that the Danish legislation is aimed not so much at protecting the pregnant woman's biological condition as at preserving the interests of her employer. Given the nature of the employment, the employer may impose requirements with regard to the employee's working capacity which justify her ceasing work at a date prior to the three-month period preceding the confinement.

Directive 92/85 sets up an assessment and information procedure in respect of activities liable to involve a risk to safety or health or an effect on workers who are pregnant or breastfeeding. That procedure can lead to the employer making a temporary adjustment in working conditions and/or working hours or, if such an adjustment is not feasible, a move to another job. It is only when such a move is also not feasible that the worker is granted leave in accordance with national legislation or national practice for the whole of the period necessary to protect her safety or health.

That legislation such as that at issue does not satisfy the substantive and formal conditions laid down in Directive 92/85 for granting the worker leave from her duties since, first, the reason for giving leave to the employee is based on the interest of the employer and, secondly, that decision can be taken by the employer without first examining the possibility of adjusting the employee's working conditions and/or working hours or even the possibility of moving her to another job.'

Comment

It is interesting to note that the ECJ confirmed the right of an employer to forfeit some or even all of the salary of a pregnant worker who is absent from work before her maternity leave not because of a pathological condition or any special risk for the unborn child but for reasons either of routine pregnancy-related inconveniences or of mere medical recommendation, without there being any incapacity for work in either of those two situations. In such a case it is her choice not to work. Although this distinction is well justified as it protects the employer against possible abuses of the rights conferred upon pregnant workers by Community law, in practice its usefulness is limited. It is very difficult to distinguish between routine-related inconveniences and more serious medical problems resulting from pregnancy.

Grant v South West Trains Ltd Case C–249/96 [1998] ECR I–621; [1998] 1 CMLR 993 European Court of Justice

• *Sex discrimination – sexual orientation – art 119 EC Treaty [art 141 EC] – discrimination based on sexual orientation not equivalent to discrimination between the sexes – homosexuality outside the scope of equal pay legislation*

Facts

A British woman employed by the rail operator South West Trains Ltd challenged the decision of her employer who refused free travel and travel concessions on its network for her lesbian partner. Such benefits are granted to an employee's spouse, or to a partner of the opposite sex of an employee, provided there has been a meaningful relationship between them for at least two years. The plaintiff argued that the restrictions regarding 'opposite sex' were contrary to art 119 EC Treaty [art 141 EC] as supplemented by Directive 75/117 on Equal Pay since travel concessions amounted to pay.

Held

The ECJ held that discrimination in employment based on sexual orientation is outside the scope of application of the EC Treaty.

Judgment

'First, it should be observed that the regulations of the undertaking in which Ms Grant works provide for travel concessions for the worker, for the worker's "spouse", that is, the person to whom he or she is married and from whom he or she is not legally separated, or the person of the opposite sex with whom he or she has had a "meaningful" relationship for at least two years, and for the children, dependent members of the family, and surviving spouse of the worker.

The refusal to allow Ms Grant the concessions is based on the fact that she does not satisfy the conditions prescribed in those regulations, more particularly on the fact that she does not live with a "spouse" or a person of the opposite sex with whom she has had a "meaningful" relationship for at least two years.

That condition, the effect of which is that the worker must live in a stable relationship with a person of the opposite sex in order to benefit from the travel concessions, is, like the other alternative conditions prescribed in the undertaking's regulations, applied regardless of the sex of the worker concerned. Thus travel concessions are refused to a male worker if he is living with a person of the same sex, just as they are to a female worker if she is living with a person of the same sex.

Since the condition imposed by the undertaking's regulations applies in the same way to female and male workers, it cannot be regarded as constituting discrimination directly based on sex.

Second, the Court must consider whether, with respect to the application of a condition such as that in issue in the main proceedings, persons who have a stable relationship with a partner of the same sex are in the same situation as those who are married or have a stable relationship outside marriage with a partner of the opposite sex.

While the European Parliament, as Ms Grant observes, has indeed declared that it deplores all forms of discrimination based on an individual's sexual orientation, it is nevertheless the case that the Community has not as yet adopted rules providing for such equivalence.

As for the laws of the Member States, while in some of them cohabitation by two persons of the same sex is treated as equivalent to marriage, although not completely, in most of them it is treated as equivalent to a stable heterosexual relationship outside marriage only with respect to a limited number of rights, or else is not recognised in any particular way.

The European Commission of Human Rights for its part considers that despite the modern evolution of attitudes towards homosexuality, stable homosexual relationships do not fall within the scope of the right to respect for family life under art 8 of the Convention and that national provisions which, for the purpose of protecting the family, accord more favourable treatment to married persons and persons of opposite sex living together as man and wife than to persons of the same sex in a stable relationship are not contrary to art 14 of the Convention, which prohibits inter alia discrimination on the ground of sex.

In another context, the European Court of Human Rights has interpreted art 12 of the Convention as applying only to the traditional marriage between two persons of opposite biological sex.

It follows that, in the present state of the law within the Community, stable relationships between two persons of the same sex are not regarded as equivalent to marriages or stable relationships outside marriage between persons of opposite sex. Consequently, an employer is not required by Community law to treat the situation of a person who has a stable relationship with a partner of the same sex as equivalent to that of a person who is married to or has a stable relationship outside marriage with a partner of the opposite sex.

In those circumstances, it is for the legis-lature alone to adopt, if appropriate, measures which may affect that position.

Finally, Ms Grant submits that it follows from *P v S* [*P v S and Cornwall County Council* Case C–13/94 [1996] ECR I–2143] that differences of treatment based on sexual orientation are included in the "discrimination based on sex" prohibited by art 119 of the Treaty.

The Court stated that the provisions of the directive prohibiting discrimination between men and women were simply the expression, in their limited field of application, of the principle of equality, which is one of the fundamental principles of Community law. It considered that that circumstance argued against a restrictive interpretation of the scope of those provisions and in favour of applying them to discrimination based on the worker's gender reassignment.

The Court considered that such discrimination was in fact based, essentially if not exclusively, on the sex of the person concerned. That reasoning, which leads to the conclusion that such discrimination is to be prohibited just as is discrimination based on the fact that a person belongs to a particular sex, is limited to the case of a worker's gender reassignment and does not therefore apply to differences of treatment based on a person's sexual orientation ...'

Comment

The ECJ did not follow the opinion of the Advocate-General although it was widely expected that the ECJ would include discrimination based on sexual orientation within the scope of the EC Treaty. The ECJ decided that the employers were neither in breach of art 119 EC Treaty [art 141 EC] nor of Directive 75/117 on Equal Pay and that they had not indirectly discriminated against the plaintiff.

The ECJ held that art 119 EC Treaty [art 141 EC] applies only if men and women are treated differently. In this present case there was no discrimination based on sex as the same rule applied to female and male workers.

The ECJ refused to recognise stable homosexual relationships as equivalent to stable heterosexual relationships and dismissed the argument based on indirect discrimination accepted in *Cornwall* Case C–13/94 [1996] ECR I–2143 in which the ECJ held that the dismissal of a worker on the ground of that worker's sex change constituted unlawful discrimination. The ECJ refused to extend this decision to the present case. Also, the ECJ refused to take into consideration art 28 of the United Nations' Covenant on International Civil and Political Rights 1966 which states that sexual orientation forms an element of sex. Although international instruments such as the Covenant on International Civil and Political Rights 1966 contains international human rights principles they are not part of EC law and therefore outside its material scope of application.

The decision of the ECJ in *Grant* should be assessed in the light of art 13 EC which requires the Council to adopt, by unanimity, measures removing all forms of discrimination, including discrimination based on sexual orientation. Therefore, the matter is only settled temporarily and the Treaty of Amsterdam will certainly call into question the present position. Nevertheless, Community measures in this area will be difficult to adopt taking into account the divergencies existing in treatment of homosexual relationships under national laws of the Member States.

Kalanke v Freie Hansestadt Bremen
Case C–450/93 [1995] ECR I–3051
European Court of Justice

- *Discrimination based on sex on promotion – art 119 EC Treaty [art 141 EC] – Directive 76/207/EEC – equally qualified male and female – compatibility of affirmative schemes – prohibited when implemented too restrictively*

Facts
The city of Bremen, in Germany, enacted a law which promoted positive discrimination in

the appointment of staff to certain public positions. The aim of the legislation was to increase the number of female staff in these positions. In essence, where two employees or job applicants had the same qualifications or the same levels of experience, the female employees were to be appointed to the post.

The applicant was a candidate for a post in the city's parks department. At the final selection both he and a female candidate were interviewed. The interview panel found the two candidates to have approximately the same qualifications and levels of experience. In the circumstances, they appointed the female applicant in compliance with the terms of law.

The applicant brought proceedings in a German court which referred a question to the ECJ seeking clarification of the compatibility of positive discrimination with art 119 EC Treaty [art 141 EC] and Community measures introducing equal pay between genders.

Held
The ECJ held that Community law precludes a Member State from introducing legislation discriminating in favour of female employees. National rules which guarantee women absolute and unconditional priority for appointments or promotion exceed the objective of equal opportunities between genders which is the objective of Community law in this area. The challenged legislation was too excessive in its structure and had the direct effect of unconditionally discriminating against men.

Judgment
'Paragraph 4 of the Landesgleichstellungsgesetz of 20 November 1990 (Bremen Law on Equal Treatment for Men and Women in the Public Service, hereinafter "the LGG") provides:

"Appointment, assignment to an official post and promotion
(1) In the case of an appointment (including establishment as a civil servant or judge) which is not made for training pur-

poses, women who have the same qualifications as men applying for the same post are to be given priority in sectors where they are under-represented ...

(2) There is under-representation if women do not make up at least half of the staff in the individual pay, remuneration and salary brackets in the relevant group within a department ..."

The national court asks, essentially, whether art 2(1) and (4) of the Directive precludes national rules such as these in the present case which, where candidates of different sexes shortlisted for promotion are equally qualified, automatically give priority to women in sectors where they are under-represented, under-representation being deemed to exist when women do not make up at least half of the staff in the individual pay brackets in the relevant group or in the function levels provided for in the organisation chart ...

A national rule that, where men and women who are candidates for the same promotion are equally qualified, women are automatically to be given priority in sectors where they are under-represented, involves discrimination on grounds of sex.

It must, however, be considered whether such a national rule is permissible under art 2(4), which provides that the Directive "shall be without prejudice to measures to promote equal opportunities for men and women, particularly by removing existing inequalities which affect women's opportunities" ...

[A]s a derogation from an individual right laid down in Directive, art 2(4) must be interpreted strictly.

National rules which guarantee women absolute and unconditional priority for appointment or promotion go beyond promoting equal opportunities and overstep the limits of the exception in art 2(4) of the Directive.

Furthermore, in so far as it seeks to achieve equal representation of men and women in all grades and levels within a department, such a system substitutes for equality of opportunity as envisaged in art 2(4) the result which is only to be arrived at by providing such equality of opportunity.

The answer to the national court's question must therefore be that art 2(1) and (4) of the Directive preclude national rules such as those in the present case which, where candidates of different sexes shortlisted for promotion are equally qualified, automatically give priority to women in sectors where they are under-represented, under-representation being deemed to exist where women do not make up at least half of the staff in the individual brackets in the relevant personnel group or in the function levels provided for in the organisation chart.'

Comment

In the present case a national rule giving automatic priority to women candidates over equally qualified male candidates for the same promotion in a work sector in which there are fewer women than men was declared by the ECJ to be in breach of art 2(4) of Directive 76/207. The ECJ held that the discretion granted to Member States under art 2(4) of Directive 76/207 must be exercised within the confines laid down by that Directive and being a derogation from an individual right must be interpreted strictly (*Johnston* v *Chief Constable of the Royal Ulster Constabulary* Case 222/84 [1986] ECR 1651). Consequently, national law giving women absolute and unconditional priority for promotion went beyond promoting equal opportunities and overstepped the limit of exception provided for in art 2(4) of Directive 76/207.

Levez (BS) v *Jennings (TH) (Harlow Pools) Ltd* Case C–326/96 [1999] 2 CMLR 363 European Court of Justice

• *Social policy – men and women – equal pay – art 119 EC Treaty [art 141 EC] – Directive 75/117/EEC – remedies for breach of the prohibition on discrimination – pay arrears – domestic legislation placing a two-year limit on awards for the period prior to the institution of proceedings – similar domestic actions*

Facts

In February 1991 Mrs Levez was employed at a salary of £10,000 per annum as the manager of a betting shop owned by Jennings. In December 1991 she was appointed at a salary of £ 10,800 per annum as the manager of another betting shop belonging to Jennings. She replaced a man who was subject to the same contract terms and performed the same job but was paid £11,400 per annum. At the time of her appointment, she was told by Mr Jennings that her salary was the same as the salary paid to her predecessor. Her salary reached £ 11,400 in April 1992. When Mrs Levez was leaving her employment with Jennings in March 1993 she discovered that until her rise in April 1992 she was paid less then her male predecessor. In September 1993 Mrs Levez brought proceedings before the industrial tribunal under the Equal Pay Act 1970 against Mr Jennings claiming breach of the deemed equality clause implied into her contract by the Equal Pay Act 1970 under which she would be entitled to a salary of £11,400 from February 1991. She also claimed payment of the corresponding salary arrears. Mr Jennings argued that she was not entitled, in proceedings brought for breach of an equality clause, to be awarded any payment by way of arrears of remuneration or damages in respect of a time earlier than two years before the date on which the proceedings had been instituted. The tribunal dismissed her application as time-barred and held that it had no power to extend the time-limit. Mrs Levez appealed claiming that a two-year time limit was contrary to Community law. The referring court asked the ECJ whether the national limitation period was contrary to EC law and whether the fact that Mrs Levez had available to her an alternative cause of action (that is breach of contract and deceit in the county court for which the time-limit is six years) justified a two-year limitation period for claims under the Equal Pay Act 1970.

Held

The ECJ held that Community law precludes the application of a rule of national law which limits an employee's entitlement to arrears of remuneration or damages for breach of the principle of equal pay to a period of two years prior to the date on which the proceedings were instituted, there being no possibility of extending that period, where the delay in bringing a claim is attributable to the fact that the employer deliberately misrepresented to the employee the level of remuneration received by persons of the opposite sex performing like work. That was so even where another remedy was available, if that remedy entailed procedural rules or other conditions less favourable than those applicable to similar domestic actions.

Judgment

'[*The first question*]
The first point to note is that, according to established case law, in the absence of Community rules governing the matter it is for the domestic legal system of each Member State to designate the courts and tribunals having jurisdiction and to lay down the detailed procedural rules governing actions for safeguarding rights which individuals derive from Community law, provided, however, that such rules are not less favourable than those governing similar domestic actions (the principle of equivalence) and do not render virtually impossible or excessively difficult the exercise of rights conferred by Community law (the principle of effectiveness).

The Court has thus recognised that it is compatible with Community law for national rules to prescribe, in the interests of legal certainty, reasonable limitation periods for bringing proceedings.

Consequently, a national rule under which entitlement to arrears of remuneration is restricted to the two years preceding the date on which the proceedings were instituted is not in itself open to criticism.

However, with respect to the main proceedings, it is clear from the order for reference that Jennings misinformed Mrs Levez in stating that her male predecessor had been paid a salary of £10,800, which accordingly was the amount to which her salary was increased with effect from 30 December 1991. It was not until April 1992 that her salary was increased to £11,400.

It is clear, therefore, that it was because of that inaccurate or, indeed, deliberately misleading information provided by the employer that Mrs Levez was in no position to realise that, even after December 1991, she had been the victim of sex discrimination.

As regards the period preceding December 1991, it was not until April 1993 that Mrs Levez discovered the extent of the discrimination against her.

Where an employer provides an employee with inaccurate information as to the level of remuneration received by employees of the opposite sex performing like work, the employee so informed has no way of determining whether he is being discriminated against or, if so, to what extent. Consequently, by relying on the rule at issue in that situation, the employer would be able to deprive his employee of the means provided for by the Directive of enforcing the principle of equal pay before the courts.

In short, to allow an employer to rely on a national rule such as the rule at issue would, in the circumstances of the case before the national court, be manifestly incompatible with the principle of effectiveness referred to above. Application of the rule at issue is likely, in the circumstances of the present case, to make it virtually impossible or excessively difficult to obtain arrears of remuneration in respect of sex discrimination. It is plain that the ultimate effect of this rule would be to facilitate the breach of Community law by an employer whose deceit caused the employee's delay in bringing proceedings for enforcement of the principle of equal pay.

[*The second question*]
The second question should be construed as seeking to ascertain whether Community law precludes the application of the rule at issue even when another remedy is available but, compared with other domestic actions which may be regarded as similar, is likely to entail procedural rules or other conditions which are less favourable.

In view of the explanations given by the United Kingdom government, it must be held that, where an employee can rely on the rights derived from art 119 of the Treaty and the Directive before another court, the rule at issue does not compromise the principle of effectiveness. It remains to be determined whether, in the circumstances of the case before the national court, proceedings such as those which may be brought before the county court comply with the principle of equivalence.

In principle, it is for the national courts to ascertain whether the procedural rules intended to ensure that the rights derived by individuals from Community law are safeguarded under national law comply with the principle of equivalence.

In order to determine whether the principle of equivalence has been complied with in the present case, the national court which alone has direct knowledge of the procedural rules governing actions in the field of employment law must consider both the purpose and the essential characteristics of allegedly similar domestic actions.

It is necessary to consider the possibilities contemplated by the order for reference. It is there suggested that claims similar to those based on the Act may include those linked to breach of a contract of employment, to discrimination in terms of pay on grounds of race, to unlawful deductions from wages or to sex discrimination in matters other than pay.

If it transpires that a claim under the Act which is brought before the county court is similar to one or more of the forms of action listed by the national court, it would remain for that court to determine whether the first-mentioned form of action is governed by procedural rules or other requirements which are less favourable.

On that point, it is appropriate to consider whether, in order fully to assert rights conferred by Community law before the county court, an employee in circumstances such as those of Mrs Levez will incur additional costs and delay by comparison with a claimant who, because he is relying on what may be regarded as a similar right under domestic law, may bring an action before the Industrial Tribunal, which is simpler and, in principle, less costly.'

Comment
In the present case the ECJ applied the principle of equivalence and the principle of effectiveness to national procedural rules for enforcing Community law in the area of equal pay. The ECJ held that domestic limitation periods which comply with those principles are permissible. As a result the two-year time-limit was not open to criticism as it is consistent with EC law. Nevertheless its application to the present circumstances was contrary to Community law since there had been misrepresentation by the employer, the claim submitted by Mrs Levez was time-barred, and the national court had no jurisdiction to extend the two-year limitation period. Consequently, the rule in question was in breach of both principles. In relation to the second question, the ECJ left to the national court the task of assessing whether an alternative cause of action, for breach of contract and deceit, in the county court with a six-year time-limit complies with the principle of equivalence. In this respect, the ECJ enumerated factors, such as additional costs and delays incurred by the applicant, that should be taken into consideration by a national court in deciding whether or not an action brought before a county court is less favourable than an action brought before an Industrial Tribunal.

Magorrian and Cunningham v Eastern Health and Social Services Board and Department of Health and Social Services Case C–246/96 [1997] ECR I–7153 European Court of Justice

• *Article 119 EC Treaty [art 141 EC] – Protocol 2 annexed to the Treaty on European Union – equal pay for male and female – part-time workers – occupational social security pension scheme – additional pension benefits – its exclusion of part-time workers – backdating of the claims under art 119 EC Treaty [art 141 EC] – national procedural time-limits contrary to Community law*

Facts
Two British women were employed as nurses in the public sector in Northern Ireland. At the beginning of their careers they worked as full-time nurses, Mrs M for nine years and Mrs C for 18 years. At that time they were considered as mental health officers (MHO). Later, and until their retirement, they both worked on a part-time basis – Mrs M from 1979 to 1992, thus accumulating the equivalent of 11 years' full-time pensionable service, and Mrs C from 1980 to 1994 thus accumulating the equivalent of over 11 years' full-time pensionable service. Both (as part-time workers) were no longer considered as MHOs. The change of status had two important consequences. First, an MHO was entitled to retire at 55 rather than 60 and every year served after 20 years' service or after reaching the age of 50 counted as double for pension purposes. Second, the employer was party to a voluntary contributory contracted-out pension scheme which was open to part-time workers provided that they worked the minimum hours. When they retired they obtained their basic pensions but were deprived of some additional benefits which they would have received had they worked full-time throughout their careers as MHOs. Before their retirement both brought proceedings against their employer under art 119 EC Treaty [art 141 EC]. They argued that they were discriminated against in respect of their pay on the ground of sex by reason of their period of part-time work being discounted in the calculation of their pensions. According to s2(5) of the Equal Pay (Northern Ireland) Act 1970 any compensation awarded for breach of the equal pay rules in that Act is

to be limited to two years immediately before the date on which the proceedings were commenced. Substan-tive provisions of the Equal Pay (Northern Ireland) Act 1970 are identical to the UK Equal Pay Act 1970.

In this context three questions arose: first, whether both claimants were discriminated against on the ground of sex contrary to art 119 EC Treaty [art 141 EC]; second, whether the two years' cut-off in s2(5) of the Equal Pay (Northern Ireland) Act 1970 could be enforced; and, third, in the event that this rule was invalid it was necessary to determine the date to which the claims could be backdated. The industrial tribunal in Northern Ireland had no problem in finding that both claimants were discriminated against in respect of their pay in breach of art 119 EC Treaty [art 141 EC] and that there was indirect discrimination on the ground of sex given that more women than men worked part-time and thus did not qualify for MHO status. However, the two remaining issues were referred to the ECJ under art 177 EC Treaty [art 234 EC].

Held
The ECJ held that both claimants were entitled to additional benefits.

Judgment
'[*First question*]
In *Defrenne*, the Court held that the principle of equal pay under art 119 may be relied on before national courts and that those courts have a duty to ensure the protection of the rights which that provision vests in individuals. However, the Court also stated that judgment, that important considerations of legal certainty affecting all the interests involved, both public and private, meant that the direct effect of art 119 could not be relied on in order to support claims concerning pay periods prior to the date of that judgment, 8 April 1976, except as regards workers who had already brought legal proceedings or made an equivalent claim.

Although those principles were upheld in the judgment in *Barber* in relation to "contracted-out" occupational pension schemes,

the Court also stated that overriding considerations of legal certainty precluded reliance being placed on the direct effect of art 119 of the Treaty in order to claim entitlement to a pension with effect from a date prior to delivery of the judgment in that case, except in the case of persons who had in the meantime taken steps to safeguard their rights.

However, in *Vroege* and *Fisscher* [*Vroege v NCIV Institut voor Volkhuisvesting BV and Stichting Pensioenfonds NCIV* Case C–57/93 [1994] ECR I–4541; *Fisscher v Voorhuis Hengelo BV and Stichting Bedrijfspenioenfonds voor de Detailhandel* Case C–128/93 [1994] ECR I–4583] the Court took the view that the limitation of the effects in time of the *Barber* judgment concerned only those kinds of discrimination which, owing to the transitional derogations for which Community law provided and which were capable of being applied to occupational pensions, employers and pension schemes could reasonably have considered to be permissible.

As the judgment in *Bilka* [*Bilka-Kaufhaus GmbH v Karin Weber von Hartz* Case 170/84 [1986] ECR 1607] included no limitation of its effects in time, the direct effect of art 119 may be relied on, as from 8 April 1976, the date of the judgment in *Defrenne*, in which that article was first held to have direct effect, in order retroactively to claim equal treatment in relation to the right to join an occupational pension scheme.

As regards the right to receive benefits additional to a retirement pension under an occupational scheme such as that involved in the main proceedings, the Court finds that, even if the persons concerned have always been entitled to a retirement pension under the Superannuation Scheme, nevertheless they were not fully admitted to that contributory scheme. Solely on account of the fact that they worked part-time, they were specifically excluded from MHO status which gives access to a special scheme under the Superannuation Scheme.

It is sufficient to recall in this regard that … the Court stated that membership of a scheme would be of no interest to employees if it did not confer entitlement to the benefits provided by the scheme in question. In a situation such as that involved in that case, the Court took the view that entitlement to a retirement pension under an occupational scheme was indissolubly linked to the right to join such a scheme.

The same is true where the discrimination suffered by part-time workers stems from discrimination concerning access to a special scheme which confers entitlement to additional benefits.

[*Question 2*]

By its second question the national court is asking essentially whether Community law precludes the application to a claim based on art 119 of the Treaty of a national rule under which entitlement, in the event of a successful claim, is limited to a period which starts to run from a point in time two years prior to commencement of proceedings in connection with the claim.

As far as this issue is concerned, it must be stated that application of a procedural rule such as regulation 12 of the Occupational Pensions Regulations whereby, in proceedings concerning access to membership of occupational pension schemes, the right to be admitted to a scheme may have effect from a date no earlier than two years before the institution of proceedings would deprive the applicants in the main proceedings of the additional benefits under the scheme to which they are entitled to be affiliated, since those benefits could be calculated only by reference to periods of service completed by them as from 1990, that is to say two years prior to commencement of proceedings by them.

However, it should be noted that, in such a case, the claim is not for the retroactive award of certain additional benefits but for recognition of entitlement to full membership of an occupational scheme through acquisition of MHO status which confers entitlement to the additional benefits.

Whereas the rules at issue in *Johnston* v *Chief Constable of the Royal Ulster Constabulary* [Case 222/84 [1986] ECR 1651] merely limited the period, prior to commencement of proceedings, in respect of which backdated benefits could be obtained, the rule at issue in the main proceedings in this case prevents the entire record of service completed by those concerned after 8 April 1976 until 1990 from being taken into account for the purposes of calculating the additional benefits which would be payable even after the date of the claim.

Consequently, a rule such as that before the national court in this case is such as to render any action by individuals relying on Community law impossible in practice.

Moreover, the effect of that national rule is to limit in time the direct effect of art 119 of the Treaty in cases in which no such limitation has been laid down either in the Court's case law or in Protocol No 2 annexed to the Treaty on European Union.'

Comment

The complexity of the solution imposed by the ECJ in respect of temporal effects of art 119 EC Treaty [art 141 EC] has engendered many disputes. In the present case the same uncertainty emerges from the questions as to what dates should any backdating of the claim be calculated – the date indicated in *Defrenne* v *Sabena* Case 43/75, that is 8 April 1976, or the date of the judgment as in *Barber* v *Guardian Royal Exchange Assurance Group* Case C–262/88, that is 17 May 1990?

The ECJ held that the date applicable in the present case was that indicated in the case of *Defrenne* (8 April 1976) and therefore for both claimants the pensionable employment commenced on that date. The ECJ explained that considerations for the limitation of the temporal effect of art 119 EC Treaty [art 141 EC] were no longer applicable since 'there was no reason to suppose that those concerned could have been mistaken as to the applicability of art 119 EC Treaty [art 141 EC]'. The ECJ emphasised that in this case access to the status of MHO which conferred certain benefits to the claimants under their pension scheme was at issue and not the amount of pension payable to them.

The question of validity of s2(5) of the

Equal Pay (Northern Ireland) Act 1970 was then examined by the ECJ. The ECJ invoked the principles of effectiveness and equivalence in order to determine whether national procedural rules were in conformity with EC law. In the present case they were in breach of those principles. The ECJ emphasised that even though both claimants were successful in their action, national procedural rules would deprive them of the benefit of art 119 EC Treaty [art 141 EC]. For that reason, s2(5) of the Equal Pay (Northern Ireland) Act 1970 is incompatible with Community law as it renders the enforcement of rights conferred by Community law impossible in practice.

This solution has important financial implications. Part-time female employees of health services who have been deprived of additional benefits from the occupational pension scheme will welcome the decision in the present case while the Treasury, no doubt, will be less pleased!

Marschall v *Land Nordrhein-Westfalen* Case C–409/95 [1997] ECR I–6363; [1998] 1 CMLR 547 European Court of Justice

• *Discrimination based on sex in promotion – equally qualified male and female candidates – priority for female candidates – saving clause*

Facts

Hellmut Marschall, a tenured teacher (teacher qualified for teaching in first-grade secondary school and so employed) for the Länder of North Rhine-Westphalia applied for a higher grade post. He was informed by the District Authorities that they intended to appoint a female candidate to that position. When Marschall challenged the decision, the District Authorities replied that the female candidate must necessarily be promoted as according to their official assessment both candidates were equally qualified but there were fewer women than men at the level of the relevant post. The

preference of a female candidate was based on art 25(5), para 2 of the German Law on Civil Servants of the Land which states that:

'Where, in the sector of the authority responsible for promotion, there are fewer women than men in the particular higher grade post in the career bracket, women are to be given priority for promotion in the event of equal suitability, competence and professional performance, unless reasons specific to an individual (male) candidate tilt the balance in his favour.'

Marschall brought proceedings before a German Administrative court. The latter referred to the ECJ for a preliminary ruling on the interpretation of art 2(1) and 2(4) of Directive 76/207.

Held

The ECJ held that where there are fewer women than men in a particular level of seniority, and the male and female candidates for a post at that level were equally qualified in terms of suitability, competence and performance, it is permissible for national law to provide that the woman is to be appointed unless there are reasons specific to the male candidate which tilt the balance in his favour.

Judgment

'... unlike the provision in question in *Kalanke* [*Kalanke* v *Freie Hansestadt Bremen* Case C–450/93 [1995] ECR I–3051], the provision in question in this case contains a clause ("Öffnungsklausel", hereinafter "saving clause") to the effect that women are not to be given priority if reasons specific to an individual male candidate tilt the balance in his favour.

It is therefore necessary to consider whether a national rule containing such a clause is designed to promote equality of opportunity between men and women within the meaning of art 2(4) of the Directive.

Article 2(4) is specifically and exclusively designed to authorise measures which, although discriminatory in appearance, are in fact intended to eliminate or reduce actual instances of inequality which may exist in the reality of social life.

It thus authorises national measures relating to access to employment, including promotion, which gives a specific advantage to women with a view to improving their ability to compete on the labour market and to pursue a career on an equal footing with men.

It appears that even where male and female candidates are equally qualified, male candidates tend to be promoted in preference to female candidates particularly because of prejudices and stereotypes concerning the role and capacities of women in working life and the fear, for example, that women will interrupt their careers more frequently, that owing to household and family duties they will be less flexible in their working hours, or that they will be absent from work more frequently because of pregnancy, childbirth and breastfeeding.

For those reasons, the mere fact that male candidates are equally qualified does not mean that they have the same chances.

It follows that a national rule in terms of which, subject to the application of the saving clause, female candidates for promotion who are equally as qualified as the male candidates are to be treated preferentially in sectors where they are under-represented may fall within the scope of art 2(4) if such a rule may counteract the prejudicial effects on female candidates of the attitudes and behaviour described above and thus reduce actual instances of inequality which may exist in the real world.'

Comment

Advocate-General Jacobs recommended the same solution as in *Kalanke* Case C–450/93, that is, that the German law in question was contrary to art 2(4) of Directive 76/207 although it contained a 'saving clause' providing that women are not to be given priority in promotion if reasons specific to a male candidate tilt the balance in his favour. The ECJ disagreed. The Court held that for many reasons, especially because of prejudices and stereo-

types relating to the role and capacity of women in working life, there is a tendency to promote male candidates to the disadvantage of female candidates and that 'the mere fact that a male candidate and a female candidate are equally qualified does not mean that they have the same chances'. However, in this particular instance, the saving clause was sufficient to fall within the scope of art 2(4) of Directive 76/207 provided it is strictly interpreted as an exception to the general rule. As a result, the German law in question is in conformity with the Community law since it does not confer automatic and unconditional priority to female candidates and since it provides that male candidates who are as equally qualified as female candidates will be subject to an objective assessment which will take into consideration all criteria specific to both female and male candidates and will override the priority given to female candidates where one or more of those criteria tilt the balance in favour of the male candidate, and that those criteria are not such as to discriminate against the female candidates.

This solution seems fair: while encouraging the promotion of women candidates it ensures equal opportunities for both sexes. It also softens the decision of the ECJ in *Kalanke* which has been strongly criticised especially by Northern European Member States which are already more committed to combat the prejudicial effects on women in employment. It is interesting to note that art 13 EC, which prohibits any discrimination, may change the approach of the ECJ towards national measures which appear discriminatory even though they intend to reduce or eliminate actual inequality between men and women.

Schnorbus v *Land Hessen* Case C–79/99 [2000] ECR I–10997 European Court of Justice

• *Equal treatment for men and women – Directive 76/207/EEC – indirect discrimination – rules on access to practical legal training in the Land of Hesse – military or civilian service – preliminary ruling*

Facts

Both the law of Germany and that of the Land of Hesse provide that a post in the judicial service or in the higher civil service can be obtained by a person who, after successfully passing the First State Examination in Law, has undergone practical legal training and has then passed the Second State Examination. Julia Schnorbus passed the First State Examination but was refused access to practical legal training on the ground that the number of applications exceeded the number of available training places, and therefore it was necessary to make a selection in accordance with the Law on Legal Training (JAG), by virtue of which applicants who completed compulsory military or civilian service were immediately admitted without having satisfied any further requirements whilst other applicants, both male and female, might be deferred for up to 12 months. Julia Schnorbus claimed that the selection procedure discriminated against women, since only men were required to do compulsory military or civilian service. The referring court asked the ECJ a number of questions, inter alia:

1. whether or not the national provisions governing admission to the practical legal training were within the scope of Directive 76/207/EEC on the implementation of the principle of equal treatment for men and women as regards access to employment, vocational training and promotion, and working conditions;
2. whether or not the national provisions in question constituted direct or indirect discrimination based on sex;
3. whether or not the national provisions in question could be justified under art 2(4) of Directive 76/207/EEC solely on the ground that they counterbalanced disadvantages not faced by women who were not required to do compulsory military or civilian service.

Held

The ECJ held that the national provisions in question were within the scope of Directive 76/207/EEC. Those provisions indirectly discriminated on the ground of sex but were justified by objective reasons and prompted solely by a desire to counterbalance to some extent the delay resulting from the undergoing of compulsory military or civilian service by men.

Judgment

'[*The first question*]

By its first question, the national court essentially asks whether national provisions such as those at issue in the main proceedings, in so far as they govern the dates of admission to practical legal training, fall within the scope of the Directive.

Land Hessen proposes that this question be answered in the negative. According to it, the provisions at issue concern only the waiting period prior to admission to the practical legal training guaranteed by law, and do not include any element which would justify application of the Directive.

The Commission contends that no distinction should be made between access to the practical training as such and the waiting period prior to admission to that training. Since practical legal training constitutes both a period of training and employment, the provisions governing the conditions of access to that practical training, including the temporal aspects, fall within the scope of the directive.

It is sufficient to note in this regard that the provisions at issue govern the circumstances in which the admission of applicants to practical legal training may or may not be delayed because there are not enough places. Since that practical training constitutes a period of training and a necessary prerequisite of access to employment in the judicial service or the higher civil service, such a delay may affect the development of the career of the persons concerned. Such provisions therefore fall within the scope of the Directive, which applies to employment in the public service (see Case 248/83 *EC Commission* v *Germany* [1985] ECR 1459, para 16, and Case C–1/95 *Gerster* v *Freistaat Bayern* [1997] ECR I–5253, para 18).

The answer to the first question must therefore be that national provisions governing the date of admission to the practical training which is a necessary prerequisite of access to employment in the civil service fall within the scope of the Directive.

[*The second question*]

By its second question, the national court asks whether national provisions such as those at issue in the main proceedings, in so far as they result in preferential admission to practical legal training for male applicants who have completed compulsory military or civilian service, constitute direct discrimination on grounds of sex.

Land Hessen and the Commission propose that this question be answered in the negative. In particular, they take the view that the persons favoured by the rules at issue are favoured not on the basis of the sex of the applicant but because of disadvantages arising from a deferment, which may be suffered by men and women alike.

As was noted in para 13 of this judgment, para 14a of the JAG provides for a number of circumstances which may be taken into account for priority access to practical legal training. They include the completion of compulsory military or civilian service. In such a case, the benefit of the priority envisaged by the abovementioned provisions cannot be regarded as being directly based on the sex of the persons concerned.

According to the criteria established by the case law of the Court, only provisions which apply differently according to the sex of the persons concerned can be regarded as constituting discrimination directly based on sex (see, in particular, Case C–249/96 *Grant* v *South West Trains Ltd* [1998] ECR I–621, para 28).

The answer to the second question must therefore be that national provisions such as those at issue in the main proceedings do not constitute discrimination directly based on sex.

[*The third question*]

By its third question, the national court asks whether national provisions such as those at issue in the main proceedings, in so far as they result in preferential admission to practical legal training for male applicants who have completed compulsory military or civilian service, constitute indirect discrimination on grounds of sex.

Land Hessen proposes that the answer be in the negative. In particular, it argues that the determination of hardship cases as envisaged by the provisions at issue is based on criteria unconnected with the sex of the persons concerned and that the statistics relied on by the national court, which relate to only one admission date, are not significant.

The Commission contends that those statistics, according to which the percentage of female applicants who were admitted as hardship cases to practical training commencing in March 1998 was considerably lower than that of male applicants, even though women accounted for approximately 60 per cent of the total number of applications, reveal indirect discrimination within the meaning of the case law of the Court.

However, it is not necessary in this case to analyse the specific consequences of the application of the JAG. It is sufficient to note that, by giving priority to applicants who have completed compulsory military or civilian service, the provisions at issue themselves are evidence of indirect discrimination since, under the relevant national legislation, women are not required to do military or civilian service and therefore cannot benefit from the priority accorded by the abovementioned provisions of the JAG to applications in circumstances regarded as cases of hardship.

The answer to the third question must therefore be that national provisions such as those at issue in the main proceedings constitute indirect discrimination based on sex.

[*The fourth, fifth, sixth and seventh questions*]

By these questions, which must be examined together, the national court essentially asks whether justification of the rules at issue on the basis of art 2(4) of the Directive is precluded because those rules automatically result in preferential admission for men, towards whom, according to the national court, that provision is not directed, or whether, on the contrary, it must be accepted because those rules counterbalance disadvantages not faced by women.

Land Hessen is of the opinion that the exceptional admission provided for by the rules at issue is by no means automatic, since it involves a specific examination of the circumstances of each applicant. Moreover, those rules are justified solely on the ground that they are intended to counterbalance disadvantages not faced by women, since the latter are not required to do national service.

After pointing out that the measures envisaged in art 2(4) of the Directive may apply equally to men and to women, the Commission submits that the rules at issue are justified in so far as they seek to reduce the inequality suffered by men as a result of the obligation to do military or civilian service.

As was noted in para 38 of this judgment, a measure giving priority to persons who have completed compulsory military or civilian service is evidence of indirect discrimination in favour of men, who alone are subject by law to such an obligation.

However, it is clear that the provision at issue, which takes account of the delay experienced in the progress of their education by applicants who have been required to do military or civilian service, is objective in nature and prompted solely by the desire to counterbalance to some extent the effects of that delay.

In such circumstances, the provision at issue cannot be regarded as contrary to the principle of equal treatment for men and women.

Furthermore, as the Commission points out, the advantage conferred on the persons concerned, whose enjoyment of priority may operate to the detriment of other applicants only for a maximum of 12 months,

does not seem disproportionate, since the delay they have suffered on account of the activities referred to is at least equal to that period.

The answer to the abovementioned questions must therefore be that the Directive does not preclude national provisions such as those at issue in the main proceedings, in so far as such provisions are justified by objective reasons and prompted solely by a desire to counterbalance to some extent the delay resulting from the completion of compulsory military or civilian service.'

Comment

In the above case the national provisions provided for a number of circumstances to be taken into consideration in assessing priority access to practical legal training, inter alia, the undergoing of compulsory military or civilian service. Consequently, the benefit of priority was not directly based on the sex of the persons concerned. Nevertheless, the challenged national provisions were indirectly discriminatory, since women were not required to do military or civilian service and therefore were precluded from benefiting from the priority accorded by the provisions at issue. However, the ECJ found that the challenged provision could be justified on the basis of art 2(4) of the Directive. In this respect the Court held that:

'... it is clear that the provision at issue, which takes account of the delay experienced in the progress of their education by applicants who have been required to do military or civilian service, is objective in nature and prompted solely by the desire to counterbalance to some extent the effects of that delay.'

Furthermore, the provision was not disproportionate, since it only delayed the admission of applicants other then those who had undergone compulsory or civilian service for a maximum period of 12 months, and at the same time, to some extent, compensated for the inequality suffered by men required to do military or civilian service.

Sirdar v *The Army Board and Secretary of State for Defence* Case C–273/97 [1999] 3 CMLR 559 European Court of Justice

• *Principle of equal treatment – marine commando units – exclusion of women – the Sex Discrimination Act 1975 – art 224 EC – Directive 76/207/EEC*

Facts

Mrs Sirdar had served in the British Army since 1983 and as a chef since 1990 in a commando regiment of the Royal Artillery. In 1994 she was made redundant as a result of the reduction of defence costs. She applied for a transfer to the Royal Marines, who had a shortage of chefs. Her application was rejected on the ground that the Royal Marines do not admit women, as their presence is incompatible with the requirement of 'interoperability', that is the need for every Marine, irrespective of his specialisation, to be capable to fight in a commando unit. Mrs Sirdar argued that she had been the victim of discrimination based on sex. The Industrial Tribunal referred a number of questions to the ECJ relating to the principle of equal treatment between men and women as regards access to employment in the armed forces.

Held

The ECJ held that national rules regarding access to employment, vocational training and working conditions in the armed forces for the purpose of ensuring combat effectiveness are within the scope of Community law. However, the exclusion of women from service in special combat units, such as the Royal Marines, may be justified by reason of the nature of the activities in question and the context in which they are carried out.

Judgment

'[*The first and second questions*]
By its first two questions, the national tribunal is asking whether decisions taken by Member States with regard to access to employment, vocational training and working conditions in the armed forces for the purpose of ensuring combat effectiveness, particularly with regard to marine commando units, fall outside the scope of Community law.

Mrs Sirdar submits that the Court's answer should be in the negative. She argues that there is no provision which specifically excludes the armed forces from the scope of the Treaty and that no such general exclusion can be inferred from the specific derogations provided for different reasons by the Treaty or the Directive.

The French, Portuguese and United Kingdom governments submit, on the contrary, that decisions concerning the organisation and administration of the armed forces, particularly those taken for the purpose of ensuring combat effectiveness in preparation for war, fall outside the scope of the Treaty. Those governments rely primarily on general considerations derived from the objectives of the Treaty or on specific provisions thereof, such as art 48(4) (now, after amendment, art 39(4) EC) and art 224.

The Commission takes the view that decisions relating to the organisation and administration of the armed forces are not excluded from the scope of the Treaty but may come within the derogation set out in art 224 thereof.

It is for the Member States, which have to adopt appropriate measures to ensure their internal and external security, to take decisions on the organisation of their armed forces. It does not follow, however, that such decisions must fall entirely outside the scope of Community law.

As the Court has already held, the only Articles in which the Treaty provides for derogations applicable in situations which may affect public security are arts 36, 48, 56, 223 (now, after amendment, arts 30 EC, 39 EC, 46 EC and 296 EC) and 224, which deal with exceptional and clearly defined cases. It is not possible to infer from those Articles that there is inherent in the Treaty a general exception covering all measures taken for reasons of public security. To recognise the existence of such an exception, regardless of the specific requirements laid down by the Treaty, might impair the binding nature of Community law and its uniform application (see, to that effect, Case 222/84 *Johnston* v *Chief Constable of the Royal Ulster Constabulary* [1986] ECR 1651, para 26).

The concept of public security, within the meaning of the Treaty Articles cited in the preceding paragraph, covers both a Member State's internal security, as in the main proceedings in *Johnston*, and its external security (in this connection, see Case C–367/89 *Criminal Proceedings against Richardt and 'Les Accessoires Scientifiques'* [1991] ECR I–4621, para 22, and Case C–83/94 *Criminal Proceedings against Leifer and Others* [1995] ECR I–3231, para 26).

Furthermore, some of the derogations provided for by the Treaty concern only the rules relating to the free movement of goods, persons and services, and not the social provisions of the Treaty, of which the principle of equal treatment of men and women on which Mrs Sirdar relies forms part. In accordance with settled case law, this principle is of general application and the Directive applies to employment in the public service (Case 248/83 *EC Commission* v *Germany* [1985] ECR 1459, para 16, and Case C–1/95 *Gerster* v *Freistaat Bayern* [1997] ECR I–5253, para 18).

It follows that application of the principle of equal treatment for men and women is not subject to any general reservation as regards measures for the organisation of the armed forces taken on grounds of the protection of public security, apart from the possible application of art 224 of the Treaty, which concerns a wholly exceptional situation and is the subject matter of the third and fourth questions (*Johnston*, para 27).

The answer to the first and second questions must therefore be that decisions taken by Member States in regard to access to employment, vocational training and working conditions in the armed forces for the purpose of ensuring combat effectiveness do not fall altogether outside the scope of Community law.

[*The fifth and sixth questions*]

By these questions, which should be examined before the third and fourth questions, the national tribunal asks whether, and if so under what conditions, the exclusion of women from service in combat units such as the Royal Marines may be justified under art 2(2) of the Directive.

Mrs Sirdar and the Commission, as well as, by way of alternative argument, the governments which have submitted observations, take the view that the justification provided for such an exclusion must be assessed by reference to the criteria which the Court set out in *Johnston*, ensuring in particular compliance with the principle of proportionality. The United Kingdom government, however, takes the view that judicial review in this area is necessarily limited and must confine itself to the question of whether the national authorities could reasonably have formed the view that the policy in issue was necessary and appropriate.

Under art 2(2) of the Directive, Member States have the option of excluding from the scope of that Directive occupational activities for which, by reason of their nature or the context in which they are carried out, sex constitutes a determining factor; it must be noted, however, that, as a derogation from an individual right laid down in the Directive, that provision must be interpreted strictly (*Johnston*, para 36).

The Court has thus recognised, for example, that sex may be a determining factor for posts such as those of prison warders and head prison warders (Case 318/86 *EC Commission* v *France* [1988] ECR 3559, paras 11 to 18), or for certain activities such as policing activities where there are serious internal disturbances (*Johnston*, para 37).

A Member State may restrict such activities and the relevant professional training to men or to women, as appropriate. In such a case, as is clear from art 9(2) of the Directive, Member States have a duty to assess periodically the activities concerned in order to decide whether, in the light of social developments, the derogation from the general scheme of the Directive may still be maintained (*Johnston*, para 37).

In determining the scope of any derogation from an individual right such as the equal treatment of men and women, the principle of proportionality, one of the general principles of Community law, must also be observed, as the Court pointed out in para 38 of *Johnston*. That principle requires that derogations remain within the limits of what is appropriate and necessary in order to achieve the aim in view and requires the principle of equal treatment to be reconciled as far as possible with the requirements of public security which determine the context in which the activities in question are to be performed.

However, depending on the circumstances, national authorities have a certain degree of discretion when adopting measures which they consider to be necessary in order to guarantee public security in a Member State (*Leifer*, para 35).

The question is therefore whether, in the circumstances of the present case, the measures taken by the national authorities, in the exercise of the discretion which they are recognised to enjoy, do in fact have the purpose of guaranteeing public security and whether they are appropriate and necessary to achieve that aim.

As pointed out in para 7 of this judgment, the reason given for refusing to employ the applicant in the main proceedings as a chef with the Royal Marines is the total exclusion of women from that unit by reason of the "interoperability" rule established for the purpose of ensuring combat effectiveness.

It is clear from the documents in the case that, according to the findings already made by the national court, the organisation of the Royal Marines differs fundamentally from that of other units in the British armed forces, of which they are the "point of the arrow head". They are a small force and are intended to be the first line of attack. It has been established that, within this corps, chefs are indeed also required to serve as front-line commandos, that all members of the corps are engaged and trained for that purpose, and that there are no exceptions to this rule at the time of recruitment.

In such circumstances, the competent authorities were entitled, in the exercise of their discretion as to whether to maintain the exclusion in question in the light of social developments, and without abusing the principle of proportionality, to come to the view that the specific conditions for deployment of the assault units of which the Royal Marines are composed, and in particular the rule of interoperability to which they are subject, justified their composition remaining exclusively male.'

Comment

In the above case the ECJ considered that the UK was justified in maintaining the exclusively male composition of the Royal Marines. The ECJ held that the national authority was entitled, while exercising their discretion, to decide that 'the specific conditions for deployment of the assault units of which the Royal Marines are composed, and in particular the rules of interoperability to which they are subject, justified their composition remaining exclusively male'. Therefore, sex was a determining factor for service in the Royal Marines and the exclusion of women was justified under art 2(2) of Directive 76/207/EEC. This exclusion was also necessary and appropriate to guarantee public security.

13 The External Trading Relations of the European Community and the Customs Union

The elimination of customs duties and charges having equivalent effect

EC Commission v Belgium (Re Storage Charges) Case 132/82 [1983] ECR 1649; [1983] 3 CMLR 600 European Court of Justice

• *Free movement of goods – customs duties – arts 9 and 12 EC Treaty [arts 23 and 25 EC] – charges having equivalent effect – concept – consideration for service rendered – criteria – storage charges levied on goods presented at public warehouses in the interior of a Member State – permissibility limits*

Facts
The Belgian authorities introduced a system whereby goods in Community transit could undergo customs clearance either at the border or in assigned warehouses within Belgium. If customs clearance in a warehouse was selected, the customs authorities imposed charges on the goods in respect of storage costs.

The Commission took exception to the levying of these costs, alleging that they were charges having an equivalent effect to customs duties and as such were prohibited under arts 9, 12, 13 and 16 EC Treaty [arts 23 and 25 EC: arts 13 and 16 EC Treaty are repealed]. The Commission brought proceedings against Belgium before the ECJ.

Held
The ECJ held that charges which are assessed as part of the process of customs clearance on Community goods, or goods in free circulation within the Community, constitute charges having equivalent effect if they are imposed solely in connection with the completion of customs formalities.

Judgment
'The prohibition of charges having an effect equivalent to customs duties, laid down in provisions of the Treaty, is justified on the ground that pecuniary charges imposed by reason or on the occasion of the crossing of a frontier represent an obstacle to the free movement of goods.

It is in the light of those principles that the question whether the disputed storage charges may be classified as charges having an effect equivalent to customs duties must be assessed. It should therefore be noted, in the first place, that the placing of imported goods in temporary storage in the special stores of public warehouses represents a service rendered to traders. A decision to deposit the goods there can indeed be taken only at the request of the trader and then ensures their storage without payment of duties, until the trader has decided how they are to be dealt with.

However, it appears ... that the storage charges are payable equally when the goods are presented at the public warehouse solely for the completion of customs formalities, even though they have been exempted from storage and the importer has not requested that they be put in temporary storage.

Admittedly the Belgian government claims that even in that case a service is rendered to the importer.

It is always open to the latter to avoid payment to the disputed charges by choosing to have his goods cleared through customs at the frontier, where such procedure is free. Moreover, by using a public warehouse, the importer is entitled to have the goods declared through customs near the places for which his products are bound and he is therefore relieved of the necessity of himself either having at his own disposal premises suitable for their clearance or having recourse to private premises, the use of which is more expensive than that of the public warehouses. It is therefore legitimate, in the Belgian government's view, to impose a charge commensurate with that service.

That argument cannot be accepted. Whilst it is true that the use of a public warehouse in the interior of the country offers certain advantages to importers it seems clear first of all that such advantages are linked solely with the completion of customs formalities which, whatever the place, is always compulsory. It should moreover be noted that such advantages result from the scheme of Community transit … in order to increase the fluidity of the movement of goods and to facilitate transport within the Community. There can therefore be no question of levying any charges for customs clearance facilities accorder in the interest of the Common Market.

It follows from the foregoing, that when payment of storage charges is demanded solely in connection with the completion of customs formalities, it cannot be regarded as the consideration for a service actually rendered to the importer.

Consequently, it must be declared that, by levying storage charges on goods which originate in a Member State or are in free circulation, and which are imported into Belgium, and presented merely for the completion of customs formalities at a special store, the Kingdom of Belgium failed to fulfil its obligations under arts 9 and 12 of the [EC] Treaty.'

Comment

It has been well established that any pecuniary charge, however small and whatever its designation and mode of application, which is imposed unilaterally on goods by reason of the fact that they cross a frontier and which is not a custom duty in the strict sense, is considered as a charge having equivalent effect to a custom duty and as such is prohibited under Community law as contrary to the free movement of goods (*EC Commission* v *Italy (Re Statistical Levy)* Case 24/68 [1969] ECR 193). The only justification for such a charge is when it is levied for a service actually rendered to the importer provided its amount is commensurate with that service (*Germany* v *EC Commission* Cases 52 and 55/65 [1966] ECR 159; *Rewe-Zentralfinanz GmbH* v *Direktor der Landwirtschaftskammer Westfalen-Lippe* Case 39/73 [1973] ECR 1039). In the present case the ECJ held that when a charge results from the storage of goods in connection with the completion of customs formalities carried out inland it would be in breach of art 13(2) EC Treaty [repealed].

EC Commission v *Germany (Re Animals Inspection Fees)* Case 18/87 [1990] 1 CMLR 561 European Court of Justice

• *Articles 9 and 12 EC Treaty [arts 23 and 25 EC] – charges having equivalent effect to customs duties – veterinary inspection – Directive 81/389 – charges for inspection of animals for health reasons – charges must not exceed the value of the service*

Facts

Measures were brought into effect throughout the European Community by Council Directive 81/389 which permitted Member States to carry out veterinary inspections on live animals transported into or through their national territories. Certain German provinces, known as 'Länder', charged fees for the cost of conducting those inspections. The charges imposed were justified, according to the German government, to cover the actual costs incurred in maintaining the inspection facilities,

The Commission argued that these charges amounted to charges having an equivalent effect to customs duties and could not be justified under the Directive. Accordingly, the Commission brought an action against Germany before the ECJ.

Held

The ECJ held that the fees did not exceed the actual costs incurred as a consequence of the inspections. The inspections themselves were prescribed by Community law and had the objective of promoting the free movement of goods. Hence, imposing charges genuinely incurred for such services did not amount to charges having equivalent effect to customs duties.

Judgment

'It should be observed in the first place that, as the Court has held on a number of occasions, the justification for the prohibition of customs duties and any charges having an equivalent effect lies in the fact that any pecuniary charge, however small, imposed on goods by reason of the fact that they cross a frontier, constitutes an obstacle to the movement of goods which is aggravated by the resulting administrative formalities. It follows that any pecuniary charge, whatever its designation and mode of application, which is imposed unilaterally on goods by reason of the fact that they cross a frontier and is not a customs duty in the strict sense constitutes a charge having an equivalent effect to a customs duty within the meaning of arts 9, 12, 13, and 16 of the Treaty.

However, the Court has also held that such a charge escapes that classification if it relates to a general system of internal dues applied systematically and in accordance with the same criteria to domestic products and imported products alike (Case 132/78 *Denkavit* v *France* [1979] 3 CMLR 605), if

it constitutes payment for a service in fact rendered to the economic operator of a sum in proportion to the service (Case 158/82 *EC Commission* v *Denmark* [1983] ECR 3573; [1984] 3 CMLR 658), or again, subject to certain conditions, if it attaches to inspections carried out to fulfil obligations impose by Community law (Case 4/76 *Bauhuis* v *Netherlands* [1977] ECR 5).

The contested fee, which is payable in importation and transit, cannot be regarded as relating to a general system of internal dues. Nor does it constitute payment for a service rendered to the operator, because this condition is satisfied only if the operator in question obtains a definite specific benefit (see Case 24/68 *EC Commission* v *Italy* [1969] ECR 193; [1971] CMLR 611), which is not the case if the inspection serves to guarantee, in the public interest, the health and life of animals in international transport (see Case 314/82 *EC Commission* v *Belgium* [1984] ECR 1543; [1985] 3 CMLR 134).

Since the contested fee was charged in connection with inspections carried out pursuant to a Community provision, it should be noted that according to the case law of the Court (*Bauhuis*, cited above; *EC Commission* v *Netherlands* [1977] ECR 1355; [1978] 3 CMLR 630; Case 1/83 *IFG* v *Freistaat Bayern* [1984] ECR 349; [1985] 1 CMLR 453) such fees may not be classified as charges having an effect equivalent to a customs duty if the following conditions are satisfied:

a) they do not exceed the actual costs of the inspections in connection with which they are charged;

b) the inspections in question are obligatory and uniform for all the products concerned in the Community;

c) they are prescribed by Community law in the general interest of the Community;

d) they promote the free movement of goods, in particular by neutralising obstacles which could arise from unilateral measures of inspection adopted in accordance with art 36 of the Treaty.

In this instance these conditions are satisfied by the contested fee. In the first place it has not been contested that it does not exceed the real cost of the inspections in connection with which it is charged.

Moreover, all the Member States of transit and destination are required, under, inter alia, art 2(1) of Directive 81/389, cited above, to carry out the veterinary inspections in question when animals are brought into their territories, and therefore the inspections are obligatory and uniform for all the animals concerned in the Community.

Those inspections are prescribed by Directive 81/389, which establishes the measures necessary for the implementation of Council Directive 77/489 on the protection of animals during international transport, with a view to the protection of live animals, an objective which is pursued in the general interest of the Community and not a specific interest of individual States.

Finally, it appears from the preambles to the two above-mentioned Directives that they intended to harmonise the laws of the Member States regarding the protection of animals in international transport in order to eliminate technical barriers resulting from disparities in the national laws (see third, fourth and fifth recitals in the preamble to Directive 77/489 and third recital in the preamble to Directive 81/389).

In addition, failing such harmonisation, each Member State was entitled to maintain or introduce, under the conditions laid down in art 36 of the Treaty, measures restricting trade which were justified on grounds of the protection of the health and life of animals. It follows that the standardisation of the inspections in question is such as to promote the free movement of goods.

The Commission has claimed, however, that the contested fee is to be regarded as a charge having equivalent effect to a customs duty because, in so far as fees of this type have not been harmonised, such harmonisation, moreover, being unattainable in practice – their negative effect on the free movement of goods could not be compensated or, consequently, justified by the positive effects of the Community standardisation of inspections.

In this respect, it should be noted that since the fee in question is intended solely as the financially and economically justified compensation for an obligation imposed in equal measure on all the Member States by Community law, it cannot be regarded as equivalent to a customs duty; nor, consequently, can it fall within the ambit of the prohibition laid down in arts 9 and 12 of the Treaty.

The negative effects which such a fee may have on the free movement of goods in the Community can be eliminated only by virtue of Community provisions providing for the harmonisation of fees, or imposing the obligation on the Member States to bear the costs entailed in the inspections or, finally, establishing that the costs in question are to be paid out of the Community budget.

It follows from the foregoing that the Commission's application must be dismissed.'

Comment

The ECJ held that charges imposed in relation to health inspections required by Community law are not to be regarded as having equivalent effect to custom duties. In the present case the ECJ established strict conditions under which fees charged in connection with inspections prescribed by Community law are not to be considered as charges having an effect equivalent to a custom duty.

Kapniki Michailidis AE v Idryma Koinonikon Asfaliseon (IKA) Cases C–441 and 442/98 [2000] ECR I–7145 European Court of Justice

• *Charges having equivalent effect to customs duties – tobacco exports – levy imposed for the benefit of a social fund – refund of charges levied in breach of Community law – unjust enrichment – burden of proof – preliminary ruling*

Facts

Michaïlidis was a Greek law public limited company carrying on business in the tobacco sector. Michaïlidis brought proceedings against the IKA for the refund of charges paid by it on the export of tobacco from Greece to Member States and non-Member States between 1990 and 1995. The charges were in fact (under different guises) imposed unilaterally on both domestic tobacco products being exported and on domestic tobacco products intended for the domestic market, and were credited to the IKA for the benefit of the Tobacco Workers' Pension Branch. Michaïlidis argued that the charges were incompatible with Community law as being charges having equivalent effect to customs duties on exports. The IKA, a Greek social security institution which paid pensions and lump-sum compensation to insured persons and pensioners of the Tobacco Workers' Insurance Funds, claimed that the charges levied were in fact a tax imposed on domestic tobacco products irrespective of whether or not exported, in accordance with the objective criteria and within the framework of the Greek general system of taxation. In addition, the Greek referring court asked a number of questions concerning the refund of charges levied in breach of Community law.

Held

The ECJ held that a charge on exported tobacco products, which is not levied either on the same tobacco products when they are sold on the domestic market or on those imported from another Member State, cannot escape, by reason of its social objective, classification as a charge having equivalent effect to a customs duty on exports. Such a charge may, however, be classified as a tax under art 90 EC provided that the alleged comparable charge levied on domestic products is applied at the same rate, at the same marketing stage and on the basis of a chargeable event which is identical to that giving rise to a charge on exports.

In respect of the questions concerning the refund of unlawful charges, the ECJ held that although Community law does not preclude a Member State from refusing repayment of charges levied in breach of its provisions where it is established that repayment would entail unjust enrichment, it does preclude any presumption or rule of evidence intended to shift to the trader concerned the burden of proving that the charges unduly paid have not been passed on to other persons, and any rule intended to prevent him from adducing evidence in order to refute any allegation that the charges have been passed on.

Judgment

'[*The first question*]
By its first question, the national court is asking essentially whether an ad valorem charge on exported tobacco products, which is not imposed on the same products when they are distributed in the domestic market or imported from another Member State, may, because of its social objective, escape classification as a charge having an effect equivalent to a customs duty on exports which is incompatible with arts 9, 12 and 16 of the Treaty.

It follows from the general and absolute nature of the prohibition of all customs duties applicable to goods moving between Member States that customs duties are prohibited regardless of the purpose for which they were introduced and the destination of the revenue from them (see, inter alia, Joined Cases 2/69 and 3/69 *Sociaal Fonds voor de Diamantarbeiders* v *Brachfeld and Chougol Diamond Co* [1969] ECR 211, para 13).

As the Court has frequently held, any pecuniary charge, however small and whatever its designation and mode of application, which is imposed unilaterally on domestic or foreign goods by reason of the fact that they cross a frontier, and which is not a customs duty in the strict sense, constitutes a charge having equivalent effect within the meaning of arts 9, 12 and 16 of the Treaty, even if it is not imposed for the benefit of the State (see *Sociaal Fonds voor de Diamantarbeiders* v *Brachfeld and*

Chougol Diamond Co, para 18; Case 158/82 *EC Commission* v *Denmark* [1983] ECR 3573, para 18; Case C–426/92 *Germany* v *Deutsches Milch-Kontor* [1994] ECR I–2757, para 50; and Case C–347/95 *Fazenda Pública* v *Ucal* [1997] ECR I–4911, para 18).

In addition, although Community law does not detract from the powers of the Member States to organise their social security systems, they must nevertheless comply with Community law when exercising those powers (see, to that effect, Case C–120/95 *Decker* v *Caisse de Maladie des Employés Privés* [1998] ECR I–1831, paras 21 and 23).

It follows that neither the social purpose for which the disputed charge was introduced nor the fact that its proceeds are paid to the IKA can prevent the charge from being classified as a charge having equivalent effect to a customs duty for the purposes of arts 9, 12 and 16 of the Treaty.

The Greek government and the IKA claim, however, that the disputed charge cannot be classified as a charge having equivalent effect to a customs duty given that it constitutes a revenue of a social character and that it is levied not only on exported tobacco but also on tobacco for domestic consumption. Therefore, the disputed charge is an integral part of a general system of internal taxation and is consistent with Community law by virtue of art 95 of the EC Treaty (now, after amendment, art 90 EC).

In that regard, it should be observed that, according to the case law of the Court, a charge such as the disputed charge escapes classification as a charge having equivalent effect to a customs duty if it relates to a general system of internal dues applied systematically and in accordance with the same criteria to domestic products and imported or exported products alike (see, in particular, Case 132/78 *Denkavit* v *France* [1979] ECR 1923, para 7).

Even though it appears from the question referred that the national court considers that the disputed charge is imposed only on exported tobacco products, the submissions of the Greek government and the IKA should nevertheless be taken into account and consideration should be given to the conditions in which the charge might be capable of falling within the scope of art 95 of the Treaty.

Although it falls to the national court to assess, on the basis of an examination of the scope of the domestic provisions referred to by the Greek government and the IKA, whether the relevant conditions are satisfied, the Court of Justice has jurisdiction to provide the national court with all the guidance of interpretation which will enable it to carry out such an assessment for the purposes of deciding the case before it.

In that regard, it should be noted, first, that it is settled case law that the essential feature of a charge having an effect equivalent to a customs duty which distinguishes it from an internal tax is that the former is borne solely by a product which crosses a frontier, as such, whilst the latter is borne by imported, exported and domestic products (see, to that effect, Case 90/79 *EC Commission* v *France* [1981] ECR 283, para 13; and Case C–109/98 *CRT France International* v *Directeur Régional des Impôts de Bourgogne* [1999] ECR I–2237, para 11).

Secondly, in order to relate to a general system of internal taxation, the charge to which the exported tobacco product is subject must impose the same duty on both domestic products and identical exported products at the same marketing stage and the chargeable event triggering the duty must also be identical in the case of both products. It is therefore not sufficient that the objective of the charge imposed on the exported products is to compensate for a charge imposed on similar domestic products – or which has been imposed on those products or a product from which they are derived – at a production or marketing stage prior to that at which the exported products are taxed. To exempt a charge levied at the frontier from being classified as a charge having equivalent effect when it is not imposed on similar national products or is imposed on them at different marketing stages, because that charge aims to compensate for a domestic fiscal charge applying to the same products, would make the prohibition on charges having an effect equivalent to customs duties empty and meaningless (see, to that effect, *Denkavit* v *France*, para 8).

Therefore, a charge such as the disputed charge, which is levied at the frontier when the export operation takes place, is deemed to be a charge having equivalent effect to a customs duty, unless the allegedly comparable charge levied on national products is applied at the same rate, at the same marketing stage and on the basis of an identical chargeable event.

In that regard, although it is for the national court alone to determine the exact effect of the national legislative provisions at issue in the main proceedings, it should be pointed out, as the Advocate-General has done in points 28 to 32 of his Opinion, that the Greek government and the IKA have not succeeded in removing serious doubts as to whether the allegedly comparable charge levied on domestic products, as described by the Greek government, is applied at the same rate, at the same marketing stage and on the basis of a chargeable event identical to that giving rise to the disputed charge.

Therefore, the answer to be given to the first question must be that an ad valorem charge on exported tobacco products, which is not levied either on the same tobacco products when they are sold on the domestic market or on those imported from another Member State, cannot escape, by reason of its social objective, classification as a charge having equivalent effect to a customs duty on exports that is incompatible with arts 9, 12 and 16 of the Treaty, unless the allegedly comparable charge levied on domestic products is applied at the same rate, at the same marketing stage and on the basis of a chargeable event which is identical to that giving rise to the disputed charge.

[The second question]

By its second question, the national court asks, in substance, (i) whether Community law allows a Member State to refuse to refund charges levied in breach of Community law when it has been established that the refund would involve unjust enrichment and (ii) how proof of unjust enrichment may be established.

Michaïlidis submits that it should not have to bear the burden of proof. The Commission, which supports Michaïlidis on this point, observes that, according to the case law of the Court, there is no presumption that taxes have been passed on to third parties and that it is not for the taxable person to prove the contrary.

By contrast, the IKA and the Greek government contend (i) that a Member State is entitled to refuse to refund a charge levied in breach of Community law if it is established that that would give rise to unjust enrichment and (ii) that inasmuch as Michaïlidis has failed to show that the levying of the disputed charge caused an increase in the price of the products and a reduction in the volume of sales, it must be inferred that refunding the charge entails unjust enrichment. Therefore, the IKA and the Greek government maintain that the competent authorities are not obliged to refund the disputed charge to the plaintiff in the main proceedings.

As a preliminary point, it is apparent from well established case law that the right to a refund of charges levied in a Member State in breach of rules of Community law is the consequence of, and complement to, the rights conferred on individuals by the Community provisions prohibiting charges having an effect equivalent to customs duties. The Member State is therefore obliged in principle to repay charges levied in breach of Community law (Case 199/82 *Amministrazione delle Finanze dello Stato* v *San Giorgio* [1983] ECR 3595, para 12; and, most recently, Case C–343/96 *Dilexport* v *Amministrazione delle Finanze dello Stato* [1999] ECR I–579, para 23).

As regards the first part of the second question, it is settled case law that the protection of rights guaranteed in the matter by Community law does not require an order for the recovery of charges improperly levied to be granted in conditions which would involve the unjust enrichment of those entitled (see, in particular, Case 68/79 *Just* v *Danish Ministry for Fiscal Affairs* [1980] ECR 501, para 26).

It is therefore for the national courts to determine, in the light of the facts of each case, whether the burden of the charge has been transferred in whole or in part by the trader to other persons and, if so, whether reimbursement to the trader would amount to unjust enrichment (see, inter alia, Joined Cases C–192/95 to C–218/95 *Comateb and Others* v *Directeur Général des Douanes et Droits Indirects* [1997] ECR I–165, para 23).

However, a Member State may resist repayment to the trader of a charge levied in breach of Community law only where it is established that the charge has been borne in its entirety by someone other than the trader and that reimbursement of the latter would constitute unjust enrichment. It follows that if the burden of the charge has been passed on only in part, it is for the national authorities to repay the trader the amount not passed on (*Comateb*, paras 27 and 28).

Furthermore, even where it is established that the burden of the charge has been passed on in whole or in part to third parties, repayment to the trader of the amount thus passed on does not necessarily entail his unjust enrichment (*Comateb*, para 29).

The Court has already observed on several occasions that it would be compatible with the principles of Community law for courts before which claims for repayment were brought to take into consideration the damage which the trader concerned might have suffered because measures such as the disputed charge had the effect of restricting the volume of exports (*Just*, para 26; and *Comateb*, para 30).

As regards the second part of the second question, it should be borne in mind that any rules of evidence which have the effect of making it virtually impossible or excessively difficult to secure repayment of charges levied in breach of Community law are incompatible with Community law. That is so particularly in the case of presumptions or rules of evidence intended to place upon the taxpayer the burden of establishing that the charges unduly paid have not been passed on to other persons or of special limitations concerning the form of the evidence to be adduced, such as the exclusion of any kind of evidence other than documentary evidence (*San Giorgio*, cited above, para 14).

In that regard, Community law precludes a Member State from making repayment of customs duties and taxes contrary to Community law subject to a condition, such as the requirement that such duties or taxes have not been passed on to third parties, which the plaintiff must show he has satisfied (*Dilexport*, para 54).

Therefore, if under national law it were for Michaïlidis to show, as the IKA and the Greek government maintain should be the case, that the disputed charge caused an increase in the price of the products and a reduction in the volume of exports, the provisions in question would have to be considered contrary to Community law (see, to that effect, *Dilexport*, para 52).

As regards proof as to whether the disputed charge has been passed on to third parties, Michaïlidis asserts that the question at issue in the main proceedings is whether the national court should base its findings solely on the documents provided by the competent authorities, which Michaïlidis had been obliged to submit to them for the purposes of paying the disputed charge, or whether it should also take into account the documents exchanged with the undertakings with which Michaïlidis entered into contracts.

Although the question of whether a tax has been passed on is a question of fact falling within the jurisdiction of the national court and although it is for that court alone to evaluate the evidence to that effect, the rules of evidence must not have the effect of making it virtually impossible or excessively difficult to secure repayment of a charge levied in breach of Community law.

It follows that, if the national court were confined to evaluating the evidence adduced by the competent authorities and were not able to take account of evidence submitted to it by the trader concerned in order to show that, notwithstanding the authorities' allegations to the contrary, the charge has not actually been passed on, or at least not entirely, the provisions in question would have to be considered contrary to Community law, given that the taxpayer must always be in a position to enforce the rights conferred on him by Community law.

Therefore the answer to the second question must be that, although Community law does not preclude a Member State from refusing repayment of charges levied in breach of its provisions where it is established that repayment would entail unjust enrichment, it does preclude any presumption or rule of evidence intended to shift to the trader concerned the burden of proving that the charges unduly paid have not been passed on to other persons and to prevent him from adducing evidence in order to refute any allegation that the charges have been passed on.'

Comment

In the past the approach of the ECJ to charges which were imposed exclusively on domestic goods was different from that concerning imported products. It is, indeed, unusual for a Member State to discriminate against goods produced domestically and thus afford preferential treatment to imported goods. Such reverse discrimination was examined by the ECJ in *Apple and Pear Development Council v K J Lewis* Case 222/82 [1983] ECR 4083 and *Irish Creamery Milk Suppliers' Association v Ireland* Cases 36 and 71/80 [1981] ECR 735.

In the current case the ECJ applied exactly the same approach to charges imposed exclusively on domestic products, irrespective of whether they are intended for export or for domestic market, as to charges imposed on imported products. The ECJ held that:

'... it follows from the general and absolute nature of the prohibition of all customs duties applicable to goods moving between Member States that customs duties are prohibited.'

The ECJ reiterated the case law in this area. If a charge is imposed by reason of the fact that goods cross a frontier, which is very likely in the current case because the charge was imposed on domestic tobacco products when they crossed the Greek frontier, the charge would have equivalent effect to a customs duty and as such would be in breach of arts 23 and 25 EC. However, the IKA and the Greek government argued that the charge escaped classification as a charge having equivalent effect to a customs duty because it was in fact a tax within the meaning of art 90 EC. In this respect the ECJ left it to the referring court to decide whether this was the case, but specified that before such a conclusion could be reached by the referring court it would be necessary for the disputed charge to relate to a general system of internal dues. In order to be so classified:

'... the charge to which exported tobacco products is subject must impose the same duty on both domestic products and identical exported products at the same marketing stage and the chargeable event triggering the duty must also be identical in the case of both products.'

It seems that in the above case the disputed charge would not satisfy these criteria. Nevertheless this question is to be determined by the referring court.

Also, the ECJ reiterated the general principles concerning the refund of charges levied in breach of Community law: *Amministrazione delle Finanze dello Stato v San Giorgio* Case 199/82 [1983] ECR 3595; *Dilexport v Amministrazione delle Finanze dello Stato* Case C–343/96 [1999] ECR I–579. However, the ECJ provided interesting clarifications in respect of national rules of evidence in this area. First, if under Greek law, as the Greek government stated, it was for Michaïlidis to prove that the disputed charge caused an increase in the price of the product and a reduction in the volume of exports, then Greek law is contrary to EC law: see *Dilexport*. Second, the ECJ held that:

'... if the national court were confined to evaluating the evidence adduced by the competent authorities and were not able to take account of evidence submitted to it by the trader concerned in order to show that, notwithstanding the authorities' allegations to the contrary, the charge has not actually been passed on, or at least not entirely, the provisions in question would have to be considered contrary to Community law, *given that the taxpayer must always be in a position to enforce the rights conferred on him by Community law.*' (author's italics)

Article 90 EC

EC Commission v Hellenic Republic
Case C–375/95 [1997] ECR I–5981
European Court of Justice

• *Failure to fulfil obligation – breach of art 95 EC Treaty [art 90 EC] – prohibition of discriminatory internal taxation – 'similar products' under art 95 EC Treaty [art 90 EC] – objective justification for indirect taxation based on the protection of the environment*

Facts
The Commission brought proceedings against the Hellenic Republic for introducing and maintaining in force the following national rules contrary to art 95 EC Treaty [art 90 EC].

Article 1 of Greek Law 363/1976, as amended by Law No 1676/1986, relating to a special consumer tax applicable to imported used cars under which in the assessment of their taxable value only a 5 per cent reduction of the price of equivalent new cars was permitted for each year of age of the used cars and the maximum reduction was fixed at 20 per cent of the value of equivalent new cars.

Article 3(1) of Law No 363/1976, which was replaced by art 2(7) of Law 2187/1994, concerning the determination of the taxable value of cars in order to levy the flat-rate added special duty which contained no reduction for used cars.

Article 1 of Law No 1858/1989, as amended many times, regarding the reduction of a special consumer tax for anti-pollution technology cars applied only to new cars and not to imported used cars with the same technology.

The Commission stated that the Greek government was in breach of art 95 EC Treaty [art 90 EC] since the above-mentioned legislation created a system of internal taxation which indirectly discriminated against used cars imported from the other Member States in comparison with cars bought in Greece.

The Greek government rejected the arguments of the Commission.

Held
The ECJ held that national rules for calculating special consumer tax and flat-rate added duty in order to determine the taxable value of imported used cars were in breach of art 95 EC Treaty [art 90 EC]. Also, national rules granting tax advantages (reducing the special consumer tax, which applied only to new anti-pollution technology cars and not to imported second-hand cars with the same technology) cannot be objectively justified under art 95 EC Treaty [art 90 EC]. As a result the ECJ held that the Hellenic Republic had failed to fulfil its obligations under art 95 EC Treaty [art 90 EC].

The ECJ dismissed a complaint regarding the incompatibility of the old version of the rules regarding payment of the flat-rate added special duty contained in art 3(1) of Greek Law No 363/1976 on the basis that the Commission's reasoned opinion and the application submitted to the ECJ under art 169 EC Treaty [art 226 EC] must be based on identical grounds of complaint. However, it is not necessary that they are completely identical; it is sufficient so long as the essence of the complaint remains intact. For that reason, a complaint concerning a new version of the above mentioned legislation was declared admissible.

Judgment
'[*The first ground of complaint*]
Under its first ground of complaint, the

Commission questions the compatibility with art 95 of the Treaty of the rules for calculating the basis of assessment to the special consumer tax for imported used cars inasmuch as they determine the taxable value of those cars by reducing the price of equivalent new cars by 5 per cent for each year of age of the vehicles in question, the maximum reduction allowed as a rule being 20 per cent.

The Greek government contends, primarily, that the Commission's comparison of the treatment of imported used cars and that of used cars bought in Greece is of no relevance on the ground that the latter have already borne the special consumer tax when new.

It should first of all be noted that the special consumer tax does not apply to domestic used-car transactions because it is charged only once, when the vehicle is first purchased within the country, and part of it remains incorporated in the value of those cars.

It is common ground that imported used cars and those bought locally constitute similar or competing products and art 95 therefore applies to the special consumer tax charged on the importation of used cars.

It follows that the Commission was correct in comparing, for the purpose of verifying compliance with art 95, the amount of the special consumer tax borne by imported used cars with the residual portion of the tax still incorporated in vehicles put into circulation in Greece when new before being resold in that country.

In the present case it is not disputed that as a result of the detailed rules for determining the taxable value of imported used cars, the special consumer tax on those vehicles, whatever their condition, is reduced for each year of use by only 5 per cent of the total of the tax charged on a new vehicle, and that reduction cannot as a rule be more than 20 per cent of the total of that tax, however old the vehicle in question may be. At the same time, the residual portion of the special consumer tax incorporated in the value of a used car bought in Greece decreases proportionately as the vehicle depreciates.

It should be noted that, in general, the annual depreciation in the value of cars is considerably more than 5 per cent, that depreciation is not linear, especially in the first years when it is much more marked than subsequently, and, finally, that vehicles continue to depreciate more than four years after being put into circulation.

It follows that the special consumer tax on imported used cars is usually higher than the proportion of the tax still incorporated in the value of used cars already registered and purchased on the Greek market.

Consequently, the Commission's first ground of complaint must be upheld.

[The second ground of complaint]
Under its second ground of complaint the Commission submits that the detailed rules for calculating the flat-rate added special duty on imported used cars are incompatible with art 95 of the Treaty.

According to settled case law, an application under art 169 of the Treaty is circumscribed by the pre-litigation procedure provided for by that article and, consequently, the Commission's reasoned opinion and the application must be based on identical grounds of complaint.

The Court did, however, make it clear that requirement could not go so far as to make it necessary that, irrespective of the circumstances, the national provisions mentioned in the reasoned opinion and in the application should be completely identical. Where a change in the legislation occurred between those two phases of the procedure, it is sufficient that the system established by the legislation contested in the pre-litigation procedure has as a whole been maintained by the new measures which were adopted by the Member State after the issue of the reasoned opinion and have been challenged in the application.

That is exactly the case with respect to the Greek legislation on the flat-rate added special duty after the amendments introduced in 1994. Accordingly, the Commission's second ground of complaint, in so far as it relates to the new version of that duty, must be declared admissible.

As to the substance, it is sufficient to point

out that since Law No 2187/1994 was adopted the detailed rules for determining the taxable value of imported used cars for the purposes of levying the flat-rate added special duty have been similar to those in force for the special consumer tax.

Thus they also give rise to discriminatory taxation of those vehicles.

In the circumstances, the Commission's second ground of complaint must be upheld in so far as it relates to the detailed rules for calculating the flat-rate special added duty on imported used cars as it has been structured since 1994.

[The third ground of complaint]
Under its third ground of complaint, the Commission charges the Hellenic Republic with excluding, in all events, imported used cars from the benefit of the reduced rates of special consumer tax applicable to anti-pollution technology cars.

It is not disputed that a Member State cannot, without offending against the prohibition on discrimination laid down in art 95 of the Treaty, confer tax advantages on less polluting cars while refusing those advantages to cars from the other Member States which nevertheless satisfy the same criteria as the domestic cars which do benefit from them.

In those circumstances the Commission's third ground of complaint must be upheld.'

Comment

In the present case the ECJ clarified an important procedural aspect of proceedings under art 169 EC Treaty [art 226 EC] concerning the need for the grounds of complaint and legal arguments to be identically set out in the letter of formal notice, the reasoned opinion and the application for declaration of violation of EC law. The ECJ decided to examine this question *ex* officio. The ECJ stated that the formal requirements could not be so strict as to impose upon the Commission the duty to commence the proceedings ab novo in circumstances where the legislation challenged in the pre-litigation procedure has, as a whole, been maintained by new legislation adopted by the Member State after the issue of the reasoned opinion.

As to the substance the ECJ examined the concept of 'similar products' under art 95 EC Treaty [art 90 EC] for the purposes of a tax comparison. Imported used cars and used cars bought locally constituted similar or competing products within the meaning of art 95 EC Treaty [art 90 EC].

The ECJ analysed factors indicating indirect discrimination of imported products. In this respect, it has been well settled that art 95 EC Treaty [art 90 EC] encompasses not only national taxation systems that discriminate according to the origin of goods but also any tax which on its face discriminates on the basis of other factors and results in placing imported products at a disadvantage compared with domestic products (*Humblot* v *Directeur des Services Fiscaux* Case 112/84 [1985] ECR 1367; *Sequela* v *Administration des Impôts* Case 76/87 [1988] ECR 2397). Consequently, not only the rate of direct and indirect internal taxation on domestic and imported products but also the basis of assessment and rules regarding the imposition of the tax are important in determining whether there is a breach of art 95 EC Treaty [art 90 EC]. In this case it is clear that the rules for calculating the basis of assessment of the special consumer tax were discriminatory.

The ECJ rejected the justification for indirect discrimination of imported goods based on the protection of environment. The ECJ recognises that some tax arrangements which differentiate between domestic and imported products are lawful, despite their indirectly discriminatory effect against imported products, provided they are objectively justifiable, that is based on factors unconnected with the nationality (irrespective of origin of the products, see *EC Commission* v *Italy* Case 200/85 [1986] ECR 3953, and *Haahr Petroleum Ltd* v *Albenra Havn* Case C–90/94 [1997] ECR I–4085). In this case, the ECJ rejected the defence based on the protection of the environment since the benefit of the reduced rates of special consumer tax could not be objectively justified as it did not apply to used imported cars which satisfied the same technical criteria as new cars.

14 The Prohibition on Quantitative Restrictions and Equivalent Measures

Articles 28 and 29 EC

Commission of the European Communities Supported by the United Kingdom v French Republic
[2002] 1 CMLR 627 European Court of Justice

- *Article 226 EC – failure of a Member State to fulfill its obligations – refusal of the French government to lift the ban on British beef and veal – breach of arts 10 and 28 EC*

Facts

On 27 March 1996 the Commission imposed a complete ban on exports of all kinds of bovine products from the United Kingdom to other Member States and third countries. This decision was adopted following the discovery of a probable link between a form of Creutzfeldt-Jakob disease in humans and bovine spongiform encephalopathy (BSE), the latter of which, at that time, was widespread throughout the UK. Under the decision the Commission was monitoring the situation in the UK and was to decide whether or not to lift the ban. From June 1998 the Commission and the Council adopted a number of decisions gradually lifting the ban, first in respect of certain meat and meat products from bovine animals slaughtered in Northern Ireland, subject to the strict conditions of a scheme based on the certification of herds (the Export Certified Herds Scheme, hereinafter the

ECHS), and then authorising exports of bovine products from the UK under a scheme based on the animal's date of birth (the Date-Based Export Scheme, hereinafter the DBES). The DBES was defined in Commission Decision 98/692/EC adopted on 25 November 1998. The objective of the DBES was to ensure the identification and traceability of animals; therefore, only animals born after 1 August 1996 (the date the ban was imposed), whose origin and all movements after birth were either recorded in the animal's official passport or on an official computerised identification tracing system, were eligible to be exported. The DBES was considered sufficient to ensure that the animal concerned did not originate from any stock of animals infected with BSE and had not developed, or was not suspected of contracting, BSE.

The export of bovine products from the UK was to be resumed on 1 August 1999 (by virtue of Commission Decision 99/514/EC).

The French authorities refused to implement the relevant decisions lifting the ban, although they authorised the transit of beef and veal originating from the UK. The Commission wrote a letter to the French government urging it to comply with the relevant decisions. In response the French government submitted a report prepared by the French Food Safety Agency claiming that there was no sufficient scientific evidence guaranteeing the safety of products subject to the DBES, in particular:

1. there was a possibility that the infection of cattle could come from a third source,

and not only from two sources already known, namely feed and maternal transmission;

2. the eligibility criteria set out under the DBES were not sufficient, taking into account the incubation period of BSE; and

3. the reliability of the DBES put in place depended on the reliability of the system of identification and tracing of animals. Under the DBES traceability of certain products was not guaranteed.

The French authorities requested that the above report be examined by the Scientific Steering Committee (the SSC) set up by Commission Decision 97/404/EC. The SSC, after examining the French report, decided that the measures adopted by the UK made the risk to humans of being infected by meat and other products subject to the DBES comparable to that in the other Member States. Nevertheless, the French authorities still refused to lift the ban. Subsequently, the Commission, the French and the UK governments started negotiations aimed at resolving the crises. An agreement of understanding was concluded between them on 24 November 1999 under which the French authorities declared that they were satisfied with the clarifications provided by the UK authorities and the Commission in respect of traceability of the products in question in the UK and the on-the-spot controls in the UK. Despite this agreement the French authorities maintained the ban.

On 4 January 2000 the Commission brought an action under art 226 EC for a declaration that, by refusing to adopt necessary measures, France had failed to fulfil its obligations under arts 28 EC and 10 EC.

Held

The ECJ declared that the French Republic, by refusing to adopt the measures necessary to comply with Council Decision 98/256/EC of 16 March 1998, as amended by Commission Decision 98/692/EC of 25 November 1998 and Commission Decision 99/514/EC of 23 July 1999, and in particular by refusing to

permit the marketing in its territory after 30 December 1999 of products subject to the DBES which were correctly marked or labelled, had failed to fulfil its obligations under those two Decisions. However, the ECJ held that the above Community Decisions were unclear and dismissed the remainder of the application. Consequently, the Court ordered the costs of proceedings to be shared between France and the Commission.

Judgment

'[*Lack of traceability of products subject to the DBES*]

The French government essentially argues that traceability of products subject to the DBES was one of the fundamental conditions of that scheme but that, when exports of British meat resumed, such traceability did not exist beyond United Kingdom cutting plants. At the meetings of the Standing Veterinary Committee of 23 and 24 November and 6 December 1999, the other Member States announced their decision not to implement the provisions of Decision 98/256 as amended and the Commission abandoned the idea of requiring them to do so. The French government was not aware of those matters until after the time-limit had expired for bringing an action for annulment of Decision 99/514 setting the date for the resumption of exports under the DBES, a fact justifying its challenge to the legality of that Decision in the present action.

Given the lack of harmonisation regarding labelling and traceability, the French government contends that it was entitled to rely on art 30 EC in order to prevent the import of products subject to the DBES. Its reaction was consistent with the principle of proportionality because it did not prevent transit of those products through its territory. It submits that the Commission adopts too formalistic a position by requiring notification of a protective measure making express reference to the protective clauses in Directives 89/662 and 90/425. First, negotiations were in progress. Secondly, it is apparent from the account of the facts in the judgment in

Case C–477/98 *Eurostock Meat Marketing Ltd* v *Department of Agriculture for Northern Ireland* [2000] ECR I–10695, at para 24, that the Commission showed more concern for another Member State which had made a notification error. Pleading the circumstances of the case and in particular the fact that it was France that drew the Commission's attention to the problems posed by traceability, the French government claims that it has complied with its obligation to cooperate in good faith under art 10 EC.

The Commission acknowledges first of all that traceability was one of the fundamental conditions of the DBES. However, traceability was adequately provided for by the Community legislation in force at the material time. It was, moreover, improved by Regulation (EC) No 1760/00 of the European Parliament and of the Council of 17 July 2000 establishing a system for the identification and registration of bovine animals and regarding the labelling of beef and beef products and repealing Regulation No 820/97 (OJ 2000 L204, p1).

The Commission then submits that the French Republic cannot put the legality of Decision 99/514 in issue or plead as a defence the failure of the other Member States to fulfil their obligations. In any event, the failure of the other Member States to comply with their obligations regarding traceability affected only triangular trade, that is to say cases where products from the United Kingdom pass through another Member State before arriving in France. By contrast, where products were correctly labelled on leaving United Kingdom cutting plants, the French government could not rely on the lack of traceability in its own territory to prevent direct imports of those products from the United Kingdom.

Finally, the Commission disputes that art 30 EC may be relied on since the decisions at issue achieved full harmonisation and Directives 89/662 and 90/425 set out the procedure for applying the protective clauses.

As to those arguments, it should be noted at the outset that traceability of products subject to the DBES was a fundamental condition for the proper operation of that scheme, in order to protect public health.

As is clear from the 13th recital in the preamble to Decision 98/692 and point 7 of Annex III to Decision 98/256 as amended, it was essential for products subject to the DBES to be traceable up to the point of sale in order to enable a consignment to be recalled, in particular if it were to become apparent that an animal was ineligible under the DBES.

However, the evidence submitted to the Court shows that such traceability was not fully guaranteed by the Community legislation existing at the time of adoption of Decision 99/514, in particular so far as concerns meat and products subject to the DBES which had been cut, processed or rewrapped.

The Commission acknowledged the existence of that legislative lacuna, since point 5 of the protocol of understanding stated that, at the time of signature of that document, traceability was not very transparent or rapid.

In order to remedy that problem, point 5 of the protocol of understanding provided that consignments under the DBES directly dispatched to France could be subject to specific identification laid down under French legislation and allowing for transparent traceability in a way which, if necessary, would permit recall as quickly as possible.

As for triangular trade, the interpretative declaration of the Commission set out in Annex II to the protocol of understanding provided that each Member State was to take binding measures to ensure that all meat and meat-based products dispatched from the United Kingdom under the ECHS or DBES were marked or labelled with a distinct mark and remained so where the meat or meat-based products were cut, processed or rewrapped on its territory. Point 5 of the protocol of understanding stated, however, that, if appropriate, the system of traceability should be improved through an agreement based on "mutual assistance between Member States".

It is apparent from the report of the meeting of the Standing Veterinary Committee of 6 December 1999 that, at that meeting, the representatives of most of the Member States stated that they did not intend to use a distinct mark for United Kingdom meat. They were nevertheless in favour of harmonisation of labelling at Community level.

When the Commission reminded the veterinary authorities of the Member States, by letter of 16 October 2000, that, in accordance with the 13th recital in the preamble to Decision 98/692 and point 4 of Annex III to Decision 98/256 as amended, they could be required, if need be, to take measures at the place of destination and that the recall of meat or meat-based products would be facilitated if the Member States adopted specific marking which remained even when the meat or meat-based products were cut, processed or rewrapped, certain Member States expressed the view in reply that the Community legislation was sufficient or that additional marking could not be introduced without amending the Community rules.

Regulation No 820/97 which, despite its title, merely contained provisions regulating the power of the Member States to impose a labelling system was to remain in force until 31 December 1999. It provided in art 19(1) that "a compulsory beef-labelling system shall be introduced which shall be obligatory in all Member States from 1 January 2000 onwards". As the Court has recorded in its judgment delivered today in Case C–93/00 *Parliament* v *Council* [2001] ECR I–0000, at paras 8 and 10, it was, however, not until 13 October 1999 that the Commission presented to the European Parliament and the Council two proposals for regulations, the first designed to establish a compulsory labelling system with effect from 1 January 2003 and the second temporarily to prolong the validity of Regulation No 820/97.

On 21 December 1999 the Council adopted Regulation (EC) No 2772/99 providing for the general rules for a compulsory beef labelling system (OJ 1999 L334,

p1). Since it corresponded to the Commission's second proposal, its effect was, however, only to maintain in force the voluntary labelling system.

It was not until 17 July 2000 that the European Parliament and the Council, by Regulation No 1760/00, established a complete compulsory tracing and labelling system. However that regulation, as stated in the second paragraph of art 25, is applicable only to meat from cattle slaughtered on or after 1 September 2000.

Accordingly, at the time of adoption of Decision 99/514, that is to say 23 July 1999, there was no binding legislation enabling the DBES to be implemented in compliance with the conditions imposed by it concerning traceability. It was thus for the Member States to adopt, on their own initiative, appropriate measures for organising a system of specific marking and tracing of products subject to the DBES.

It is in the light of those circumstances that the subject matter of the failure to fulfil obligations and the defence put forward by the French Republic should be assessed.

The arguments relating to lack of traceability relied on by the French government by way of defence are apposite in so far as they concern products subject to the DBES which have been cut, processed or rewrapped in another Member State and subsequently exported to France without the affixing of a distinct mark in order, in particular, to enable consignments to be recalled.

The Commission has not, however, established that the French government would have prevented the import of all beef and veal or all meat-based products from other Member States not bearing the distinct mark of products subject to the DBES on the ground that certain consignments of meat or of cut, processed or rewrapped products could include beef, veal or products of United Kingdom origin which would not be identifiable as such.

It follows that the application for a finding of failure to fulfil obligations must be dismissed in so far as it concerns that category of products.

So far as concerns products subject to the DBES which are correctly marked or labelled, whether coming directly from the United Kingdom or from another Member State, the French government has not put forward a ground of defence capable of justifying the failure to implement Decisions 98/256 as amended and 99/514.

It is settled case law that a Member State may not plead provisions, practices or circumstances existing in its internal legal system in order to justify a failure to comply with its obligations under Community law (Case C–217/88 *EC Commission* v *Germany* [1990] ECR I–2879, para 26).

Furthermore, a Member State which encounters temporarily insuperable difficulties preventing it from complying with its obligations under Community law may plead force majeure only for the period necessary in order to resolve those difficulties (see, to that effect, Case 101/84 *EC Commission* v *Italy* [1985] ECR 2629, para 16).

In the present case, the French government has not referred to specific difficulties which would have prevented it from adopting, at the very least after expiry of the period allowed for complying with the reasoned opinion, the legislation necessary in order to ensure the traceability of any products subject to the DBES which are cut, processed or rewrapped on its own territory.

It should be noted that traceability requirements for meat and meat-based products originating from the United Kingdom were not established by Decision 99/514, but had existed since 1 June 1998 under the ECHS, set up by Decision 98/256. Furthermore, Decision 98/692 made clear the importance of traceability for the proper operation of the DBES.

It is true that there were difficulties in interpreting and consequently in implementing Decision 98/256 as amended, since the requirements imposed on all the Member States were neither clear nor precise. Exports of products subject to the DBES were to commence at a time when there was no compulsory Community system providing a means of ensuring that those products could be traced. The protocol of understanding seems to permit the French government to make arrangements for tracing products dispatched directly to France, whereas the Commission specifies, in the interpretative declaration annexed to that protocol, the obligations imposed on the Member States while retaining the possibility of improving if necessary the working of the system by an agreement negotiated between the Member States. It is also apparent from the documents relating to the positions adopted by the national veterinary authorities that certain Member States took the view that national legislation was not needed or that only Community harmonisation would enable the required traceability to be achieved.

However, the French Republic was fully informed by the protocol of understanding concluded on 24 November 1999 of the extent of its obligations under Decisions 98/256 as amended and 99/514 as regards the traceability of meat and meat-based products from the United Kingdom dispatched directly to French territory. The same is true of correctly marked or labelled meat and meat-based products originating from the United Kingdom but coming from another Member State.

Since the French Republic had to have a reasonable period for implementing Decisions 98/256 as amended and 99/514, as interpreted and clarified by the protocol of understanding, it must be held that the infringement consisting of a failure to implement those Decisions is proved only from expiry of the period allowed for complying with the reasoned opinion, that is to say after 30 December 1999.'

Comment

The decision of the ECJ is not surprising. It was widely expected that the ECJ would confirm that France was in breach of its obligations arising out of the EC Treaty.

The proper course of action for the French authorities would seem to have been to carry out inspections in respect of meat and other products subject to the DBES coming from the

UK, to refuse any consignments from other Member States not satisfying the requirement for traceability and to urge the Commission to improve the rules on traceability, in particular to establish a compulsory tracing and labelling system of products subject to the DBES in all Member States. This was not the course taken by the French authorities. First, it seems that the French authorities did not prevent the import of beef and veal or other meat-based products from other Member States not bearing the distinct mark of products subject to the DBES, although there was a strong possibility that certain consignments of meat could include beef, veal or other products of UK origin processed or rewrapped in other Member States. Second, it seems strange that the French authorities did not bring in due time appropriate proceedings for reviewing the legality of Council Decision 98/256 or subsequent decisions adopted by the Community institutions relating to the DBES or the lifting of the ban, which were obviously unclear and did not ensure the traceability of products subject to the DBES up to the point of sale.

Criminal Proceedings against Guimont Case C–448/98 [2000] ECR I–10663 European Court of Justice

• *Measures having equivalent effect to a quantitative restriction – purely internal situation – reverse discrimination – manufacture and marketing of Emmenthal cheese without rind – preliminary ruling*

Facts
On 6 January 1998 Mr Guimont, the technical manager of the 'Laiterie d'Argis', was ordered by the Directorate for Competition, Consumer Affairs and Prevention of Fraud of the Department of Vaucluse to pay a fine of FF 260 for holding for sale, selling or offering Emmenthal cheese without rind contrary to the French law which expressly required that cheese bearing the designation

'Emmenthal' must have, inter alia, 'a hard, dry rind, of a colour between golden yellow and light brown'. When Mr Guimont refused to pay the fine, criminal proceedings were brought against him before the Tribunal de Police (the local criminal court) of Belley. Mr Guimont argued that the French legislation was in breach of art 28 EC. The Tribunal de Police asked the ECJ to answer whether or not this was the case.

Held
The ECJ held that art 28 EC precludes a Member State from applying to Emmenthal cheese imported from another Member State, where it is lawfully produced and marketed, a national rule prohibiting the marketing of that cheese without rind under the designation 'Emmenthal' in that Member State.

Judgment
'Second, it is necessary to examine the argument of the French government that art 30 of the Treaty [art 28 EC] does not apply to a case such as that at issue in the main proceedings.

On the one hand, the French government argues that the inapplicability of art 30 follows from the simple fact that the rule which Mr Guimont is accused of infringing is not, in practice, applied to imported products. It maintains that that rule was designed to create obligations solely for national producers and does not therefore concern intra-Community trade in any way. In its submission, the case law of the Court of Justice, and particularly the judgment in Case 98/86 *Criminal Proceedings against Mathot* [1987] ECR 809, paras 8 and 9, demonstrates that art 30 of the Treaty is designed to protect only intra-Community trade.

In response to that argument, it should be observed that art 30 of the Treaty covers any measure of the Member States which is capable, directly or indirectly, actually or potentially, of hindering intra-Community trade (Case 8/74 *Procureur du Roi* v *Dassonville* [1974] ECR 837, para 5). However, that Article is not designed to ensure that goods of national origin enjoy the same treatment as imported goods in every case, and a difference in treatment as between goods which is not capable of restricting imports or of prejudicing the marketing of imported goods does not fall within the prohibition contained in that Article (*Mathot*, paras 7 and 8).

However, as regards the national rule at issue in the main proceedings, the French government does not deny that, according to its wording, it is applicable without distinction to both French and imported products.

This argument of the French government cannot therefore be accepted. The mere fact that a rule is not applied to imported products in practice does not exclude the possibility of it having effects which indirectly or potentially hinder intra-Community trade (see Case C–184/96 *EC Commission* v *France* [1998] ECR I–6197, para 17).

On the other hand, the French government, supported on this point by the Danish government, argues that, in the particular case before the national court, the rule at issue does not constitute a hindrance, even an indirect or a potential hindrance, to intra-Community trade within the meaning of the Court's case law. According to those governments, the facts underlying the reference to the Court relate to a purely internal situation, the accused being of French nationality and the product in question being manufactured entirely in French territory.

Mr Guimont, the German, Netherlands and Austrian governments and the Commission argue that, according to the Court's case law, art 30 cannot be considered inapplicable simply because all the facts of the specific case before the national court are confined to a single Member State (Joined Cases C–321/94 to C–324/94 *Criminal Proceedings against Pistre and Others* [1997] ECR I–2343, para 44).

In regard to that argument, it should be noted that the *Pistre* judgment concerned a situation where the national rule in question was not applicable without distinction but created direct discrimination against goods imported from other Member States.

As for a rule such as that at issue in the main proceedings, which, according to its wording, applies without distinction to national and imported products and is designed to impose certain production conditions on producers in order to permit them to market their products under a certain designation, it is clear from the Court's case law that such a rule falls under art 30 of the Treaty only in so far as it applies to situations that are linked to the importation of goods in intra-Community trade (Case 286/81 *Criminal Proceedings against Oosthoek's Uitgeversmaatschappij* [1982] ECR 4575, para 9; *Mathot*, paras 3 and 7 to 9).

However, that finding does not mean that there is no need to reply to the question referred to the Court for a preliminary ruling in this case. In principle, it is for the national courts alone to determine, having regard to the particular features of each case, both the need for a preliminary ruling in order to enable them to give their judgment and the relevance of the questions which they refer to the Court. A reference for a preliminary ruling from a national court may be rejected only if it is quite obvious that the interpretation of Community law sought by that court bears no relation to the actual nature of the case or the subject matter of the main action (Case C–281/98 *Angonese* v *Cassa di Risparmio di Bolzano* [2000] ECR I–4139, para 18).

In this case, it is not obvious that the interpretation of Community law requested is not necessary for the national court. Such a reply might be useful to it if its national law were to require, in proceedings such as those in this case, that a national producer must be allowed to enjoy the same rights as those which a producer of another Member State would derive from Community law in the same situation.

In those circumstances, it needs to be examined whether a national rule such as that at issue in the main proceedings might, in so far as applied to imported products, constitute a measure having equivalent effect to a quantitative restriction contrary to art 30 of the Treaty.

[*The interpretation of art 30 of the Treaty*]
As a preliminary observation, it should be noted that, as is undisputed in these proceedings, a national rule such as that at issue in the main proceedings constitutes a measure having equivalent effect to a quantitative restriction on imports within the meaning of art 30 of the Treaty, in so far as it is applied to imported products.

National legislation which subjects goods from other Member States, where they are lawfully manufactured and marketed, to certain conditions in order to be able to use the generic designation commonly used for that product, and which thus in certain cases requires producers to use designations which are unknown to, or less highly regarded by, consumers, does not, it is true, absolutely preclude the importation into the Member State concerned of products originating in other Member States. It is, however, likely to make their marketing more difficult and thus impede trade between Member States (Case 298/87 *Proceedings for Compulsory Reconstruction against Smanor SA* [1988] ECR 4489, para 12).

As for the question whether such a rule may still be in conformity with Community law, it should be remembered that, according to the Court's case law, national rules adopted in the absence of common or harmonised rules and applicable without distinction to national products and to products imported from other Member States may be compatible with the Treaty in so far as they are necessary in order to satisfy overriding requirements relating, inter alia, to fair trading and consumer protection (Case C–39/90 *Denkavit* v *Land Baden-Württemberg* [1991] ECR I–3069, para 18), where they are proportionate to the objective pursued and that objective is not capable of being achieved by measures which are less restrictive of intra-Community trade (Case C–368/95 *Familiapress* v *Bauer Verlag* [1997] ECR I–3689, para 19).

In this context, it is necessary to refer, as the Commission has done, to Council Directive 79/112/EEC of 18 December 1978 on the approximation of the laws of the Member States relating to the labelling, presentation and advertising of foodstuffs for sale to the ultimate consumer (OJ 1979 L33, p1), as amended by Council Directive 89/395/EEC of 14 June 1989 (OJ 1989 L186, p17), which, at the time of the facts at issue in the main proceedings, provided in art 5(1):

"The name under which a foodstuff is sold shall be the name laid down by whatever laws, regulations or administrative provisions apply to the foodstuff in question or, in the absence of any such name, the name customary in the Member State where the product is sold to the ultimate consumer and to mass caterers, or a description of the foodstuff and, if necessary, of its use, that is sufficiently precise to inform the purchaser of its true nature and to enable it to be distinguished from products with which it could be confused."

Whilst that provision demonstrates the importance of a correct use of foodstuff designations for the protection of consumers, it does not authorise Member States to adopt in the matter of designations rules which restrict the importation of goods lawfully manufactured and marketed in another Member State where those rules are not proportionate to that purpose or where that protection could have been achieved by measures less restrictive of intra-Community trade.

It is true that, according to the case law of the Court, Member States may, for the purpose of ensuring fair trading and the protection of consumers, require the persons concerned to alter the description of a foodstuff where a product offered for sale under a particular name is so different, in terms of its composition or production, from the products generally understood as falling within that description within the Community that it cannot be regarded as falling within the same category (Case C–366/98 *Criminal Proceedings against Geffroy* [2000] ECR I–0000, para 22).

However, where the difference is of minor importance, appropriate labelling should be sufficient to provide the purchaser or consumer with the necessary information (*Geffroy*, para 23).

In the case at issue in the main proceedings, it should be noted that, according to the Codex alimentarius referred to in para 10 of this judgment, which provides indications allowing the characteristics of the product concerned to be defined, a cheese manufactured without rind may be given the name "Emmenthal" since it is made from ingredients and in accordance with a method of manufacture identical to those used for Emmenthal with rind, save for a difference in treatment at the maturing stage. Moreover, it is undisputed that such an "Emmenthal" cheese variant is lawfully manufactured and marketed in Member States other than the French Republic.

Therefore, even if the difference in the maturing method between Emmenthal with rind and Emmenthal without rind were capable of constituting a factor likely to mislead consumers, it would be sufficient, whilst maintaining the designation "Emmenthal", for that designation to be accompanied by appropriate information concerning that difference.

In those circumstances, the absence of rind cannot be regarded as a characteristic justifying refusal of the use of the "Emmenthal" designation for goods from other Member States where they are lawfully manufactured and marketed under that designation.

The answer to the question referred for a preliminary ruling must therefore be that art 30 of the Treaty precludes a Member State from applying to products imported from another Member State, where they are lawfully produced and marketed, a national rule prohibiting the marketing of a cheese without rind under the designation "Emmenthal" in that Member State.'

Comment

The answer of the ECJ was simple. The ECJ applied the *Dassonville* formula (*Procureur du Roi* v *Dassonville* Case 8/74 [1974] ECR 837) in order to determine whether or not the

French legislation constituted a measure having an equivalent effect to a quantitative restriction. The ECJ answered in the affirmative. What is surprising is that the ECJ applied it in the context of a case concerning a purely internal situation.

Consequently, the ECJ should have declined to answer the referred question, but it had decided that:

'Such a reply might be useful to it [the referring court] if its national law were to require, in proceedings such as those in this case, that a national producer must be allowed to enjoy the same rights as those which a producer of another Member State would derive from Community law in the same situation.'

This is certainly a new solution which drastically changes the approach of the ECJ to cases of reverse discrimination. It seems that the ECJ is asking national courts to sanction national rules indistinctly applicable which discriminate domestic products as compared to products imported from another Member State. However, this solution is only possible if a national court is able to find a national rule allowing it to do so. In the above quotation the ECJ went on to give an example of such a national rule: the principle of equal treatment of domestic and imported products.

Criminal Proceedings against Keck and Mithouard Joined Cases C–267 and 268/91 [1993] ECR I–6097 European Court of Justice

• *Free movement of goods – measures having equivalent effect – concept – obstacles resulting from national provisions regulating selling arrangements not discriminatory – prohibition of resale at a loss – inapplicability of art 30 EC Treaty [art 28 EC]*

Facts

The French authorities commenced criminal proceedings against Keck and Mithouard for selling goods at a price lower than their actual price (resale at a loss) which was in breach of French law of 1963, as amended in 1986, although that law did not ban sales at loss by the manufacturers. Both offenders argued that the law in question was contrary to fundamental freedoms under the EC Treaty: free movement of goods, persons, services and capital as well as in breach of EC competition law. The French court referred to the ECJ.

Held

The ECJ dismissed all arguments but one based on the free movement of goods. The ECJ held that French law concerned the selling arrangement and as such was outside the scope of art 30 EC Treaty [art 28 EC].

Judgment

'By virtue of art 30, quantitative restrictions on imports and all measures having equivalent effect are prohibited between Member States. The Court has consistently held that any measure which is capable of directly or indirectly, actually or potentially, hindering intra-Community trade constitutes a measure having equivalent effect to a quantitative restriction.

It is not the purpose of national legislation imposing a general prohibition on resale at a loss to regulate trade in goods between Member States.

Such legislation may, admittedly, restrict the volume of sales, and hence the volume of sales of products from other Member States, in so far as it deprives traders of a method of sales promotion. But the question remains whether such a possibility is sufficient to characterise the legislation in question as a measure having equivalent effect to a quantitative restriction on imports.

In view of the increasing tendency of traders to invoke art 30 of the Treaty as a means of challenging any rules whose effect is to limit their commercial freedom even where such rules are not aimed at products from other Member States, the Court considers it necessary to re-examine and clarify its case law on this matter.

In 'Cassis de Dijon' (*Rewe-Zentrale AG v Bundesmonopolverwaltung für Branntwein (Cassis De Dijon)* Case 120/78 [1979] ECR 649) it was held that, in the absence of harmonisation of legislation, measures of equivalent effect prohibited by art 30 include obstacles to the free movement of goods where they are the consequence of applying rules that lay down requirements to be met by such goods (such as requirements as to designation, form, size, weight, composition, presentation, labelling, packaging) to goods from other Member States where they are lawfully manufactured and marketed, even if those rules apply without distinction to all products unless their application can be justified by a public-interest objective taking precedence over the free movement of goods.

However, contrary to what has previously been decided, the application to products from other Member States of national provisions restricting or prohibiting certain selling arrangements is not such as to hinder directly or indirectly, actually or potentially, trade between Member States within the meaning of the *Dassonville* judgment (Case 8/74 [1974] ECR 837), provided that those provisions apply to all affected traders operating within the national territory and provided that they affect in the same manner in law and in fact, the marketing of domestic products and of those from other Member States.

Where those conditions are fulfilled, the application of such rules to the sale of products from another Member State meeting the requirements laid down by that State is not by nature such as to prevent their access to the market or to impede access any more than it impedes the access of domestic products. Such rules therefore fall outside the scope of art 30 of the Treaty.'

Comment

The ECJ set new limits on art 30 EC Treaty [art 28 EC]. It re-examined and clarified its case law on the scope of art 30 EC Treaty [art 28 EC] and, at the same time departed from its earlier decision in *Dassonville* by stating that the *Dassonville* formula did not apply to selling arrangements if national rules prima facie contrary to art 30 EC Treaty [art 28 EC] affect all traders operating within the national territory and provided they affect in the same manner, in law and fact, the marketing of both domestic and imported products, even though they may have some impact on the overall volume of sales. The main point made by the ECJ in the present case is a distinction between national rules which relate to the goods themselves and which are within the scope of art 30 EC Treaty [art 28 EC] and national rules relating to the selling agreements which fall outside the ambit of art 30 EC Treaty [art 28 EC] provided that the two conditions are satisfied: national rules must apply to all traders operating within the national territory and they must affect in the same manner, in law and fact, the marketing of domestic products and of those from other Member States. The main question is how to determine whether a particular national rule concerns the nature of the product itself or the selling arrangements for that product. In this respect there is still a lot of confusion.

EC Commission v *France* Case C–265/95 [1997] ECR I–6959 European Court of Justice

• *Free movement of goods – a Member State's responsibility for private block-ades – obligations of the Member States under arts 30 and 5 EC Treaty [arts 28 and 10 EC]*

Facts

The Commission brought proceedings under art 169 EC Treaty [art 226 EC] against France for failure to take all necessary and propor-tionate measures to prevent the free movement of fruit and vegetables from being obstructed by actions of private individuals. France had failed to fulfil its obligations under arts 30 and 5 EC Treaty [arts 28 and 10 EC], as well as its obligations flowing from the common

organisation of the markets in agricultural products. For a decade the Commission received complaints regarding the passivity of the French government in face of acts of violence and vandalism such as: interception of lorries transporting agricultural products from other Member States and destruction of their loads; threats against French supermar-kets, wholesalers and retailers dealing with those products; and damage to such products when on display in shops, etc, committed by French farmers. The Commission supported by the governments of Spain and the UK stated that on a number of occasions French authorities showed unjustifiable leniency vis-à-vis the French farmers, for example by not prosecuting the perpetrators of such acts when their identity was known to the police since often the incidents were filmed by television cameras and the demonstrators' faces were not covered. Furthermore, the French police were often not present on the spot, although the French authorities had been warned of the imminence of demonstrations or they did not interfere, as happened in June 1995 when Spanish lorries transporting strawberries were attacked by French farmers at the same place within a period of two weeks and the police who were present took no protective action. The government of France rejected the argu-ments submitted by the Commission as unjus-tified.

Held

The ECJ held that France was in breach of its obligations under art 30 EC Treaty [art 28 EC], in conjunction with art 5 EC Treaty [art 10 EC], and under the common organisation of the markets in agricultural products for failing to take all necessary and proportionate measures in order to prevent its citizens from interfering with the free movement of fruit and vegetables.

Judgment

'It should be stressed from the outset that the free movement of goods is one of the fundamental principles of the Treaty.

That fundamental principle is implemented by art 30 et seq of the Treaty.

That provision, taken in its context, must be understood as being intended to eliminate all barriers, whether direct or indirect, actual or potential, to flows of imports in intra-Community trade.

As an indispensable instrument for the realisation of a market without internal frontiers, art 30 therefore does not prohibit solely measures emanating from the State which, in themselves, create restrictions on trade between Member States. It also applies where a Member State abstains from adopting the measures required in order to deal with obstacles to the free movement of goods which are not caused by the State.

Article 30 therefore requires the Member States not merely themselves to abstain from adopting measures or engaging in conduct liable to constitute an obstacle to trade but also, when read with art 5 of the Treaty, to take all necessary and appropriate measures to ensure that fundamental freedom is respected on their territory.

In the latter context, the Member States, which retain exclusive competence as regards the maintenance of public order and the safeguarding of internal security, unquestionably enjoy a margin of discretion in determining what measures are most appropriate to eliminate barriers to the importation of products in a given situation.

However, it falls to the Court to verify, in cases brought before it, whether the Member State concerned has adopted appropriate measures for ensuring the free movement of goods.

As regards the present case, the facts which gave rise to the action brought by the Commission against the French Republic for failure to fulfil obligations are not in dispute.

It is therefore necessary to consider whether in the present case the French government complied with its obligations under art 30, in conjunction with art 5, of the Treaty, by adopting adequate and appropriate measures to deal with actions by private individuals which create obstacles to the free movement of certain agricultural products.

It should be stressed that the Commission's written pleadings show that the incidents to which it objects in the present proceedings have taken place regularly for more than ten years.

Moreover, in the present case the Commission reminded the French government on numerous occasions that Community law imposes an obligation to ensure de facto compliance with the principle of the free movement of goods by eliminating all restrictions on the freedom to trade in agricultural products from other Member States.

In the present case the French authorities therefore had ample time to adopt the measures necessary to ensure compliance with their obligations under Community law.

Since 1993 acts of violence and vandalism have not been directed solely at the means of transport of agricultural products but have extended to the wholesale and retail sector for those products.

Further serious incidents of the same type also occurred in 1996 and 1997.

Moreover, it is not denied that when such incidents occurred the French police were either not present on the spot, despite the fact that in certain cases the competent authorities had been warned of the imminence of demonstrations by farmers, or did not intervene, even where they far outnumbered the perpetrators of the disturbances.

As regards the numerous acts of vandalism committed between April and August 1993, the French authorities have been able to cite only a single case of criminal prosecution.

In the light of all the foregoing factors, the Court, while not discounting the difficulties faced by the competent authorities in dealing with situations of the type in question in this case, cannot but find that, having regard to the frequency and seriousness of the incidents cited by the Commission, the measures adopted by the French government were manifestly inadequate to ensure freedom of intra-Community trade in agricultural products on its territory by preventing and effectively dissuading the perpetrators of the offences in question from committing and repeating them.

Although it is not impossible that the threat of serious disruption to public order may, in appropriate cases, justify non-intervention by the police, that argument can, on any view, be put forward only with respect to a specific incident and not, as in this case, in a general way covering all the incidents cited by the Commission.

As regards the fact that the French Republic has assumed responsibility for the losses caused to the victims, this cannot be put forward as an argument by the French government in order to escape its obligations under Community law.

Nor is it possible to accept the arguments based on the very difficult socio-economic context of the French market in fruit and vegetables after the accession of the Kingdom of Spain.

It is settled case law that economic grounds can never serve as justification for barriers prohibited by art 30 of the Treaty.

Having regard to all the foregoing considerations, it must be concluded that in the present case the French government has manifestly and persistently abstained from adopting appropriate and adequate measures to put an end to the acts of vandalism which jeopardise the free movement on its territory of certain agricultural products originating in other Member States and to prevent the recurrence of such acts.'

Comment

This is one of the landmark decisions of the ECJ. Article 30 EC Treaty [art 28 EC] has been used by the ECJ as a principal tool for the removal of all barriers to the free movement of goods. Its scope of application has been gradually extended in order to respond to the development of the Community and its changing economic objectives. However, its remarkable evolution has not yet been completed. This has been confirmed by the ECJ in the present case. Article 30 EC Treaty [art 28 EC] is addressed to the Member States and concerns measures taken by them. The expression 'measures taken by the Member States' has been broadly interpreted to include measures taken by any public body (whether legislative, executive or judicial) as well as any semi-public body (*Apple and Pear Development Council* v *K J Lewis Ltd* Case 222/82 [1984] 3 CMLR 733) or a professional body which exercises regulatory and disciplinary powers conferred upon it by statutory instrument (*R* v *Royal Pharmaceutical Society of Great Britain, ex parte Association of Pharmaceutical Importers* Cases 266 and 267/87 [1989] ECR 1295) and even private companies when carrying out activities contrary to art 30 EC Treaty [art 28 EC] supported financially or otherwise by a Member State (*EC Commission* v *Ireland (Re Buy Irish Campaign)* Case 249/81 [1982] ECR 4005). It has always been accepted that the prohibition contained in art 30 EC Treaty [art 28 EC] concerns some activity, or some action taken by the Member State not passivity or inaction. The ECJ has decided otherwise. The ECJ inferred from the requirements imposed by art 3(c) EC Treaty [art 6 EC] and art 7a EC Treaty [art 14 EC], which are implemented in art 30 EC Treaty [art 28 EC], that the latter is also applicable where a Member State abstains from adopting the measures required in order to deal with obstacles to the free movement of goods which are not caused by the State.

Abstention constitutes a hindrance to the free movement of goods and is just as likely to obstruct intra-Community trade as a positive act. However, art 30 EC Treaty [art 28 EC] in itself is not sufficient to engage the responsibility of a Member State for acts committed by its citizens, but is so when read in the light of art 5 EC Treaty [art 10 EC] which requires the Member States not merely themselves to abstain from adopting measures or engaging in conduct liable to constitute an obstacle to trade but also to take all necessary and appropriate measures to ensure that fundamental freedom regarding the free movement of goods is respected on their territory.

Notwithstanding the fact that the ECJ recognises that a Member State has exclusive competences in relation to the maintenance of public order and the safeguard of internal security, it assesses the exercise of that competence by a Member State in the light of art

30 EC Treaty [art 28 EC]! As a result, the ECJ states that the French authorities failed to fulfil their obligations under the Treaty on two counts: first, they did not take necessary preventive and penal measures; and, second, the frequency and seriousness of the incidents taking into account the passivity of the French authorities not only made the importation of goods into France more difficult but also created a climate of insecurity which adversely affected the entire inter-Community trade.

The decision of the ECJ has far-reaching implications. It means that, a Member State may be liable under art 30 EC Treaty [art 28 EC] linked with art 5 EC Treaty [art 10 EC] if it does not prevent or adequately punish conduct of its economic operators which is capable of hindering the free movement of goods. Therefore, a Member State is forced to intervene in situations where, for example, private individuals decide to promote national products or otherwise obstruct inter-Community trade.

The ECJ rejected the three defences put forward by the French government.

Konsumentombudsmannen (KO) v Gourmet International Products AB (GIP) Case C–405/98 [2001] ECR I–1795 European Court of Justice

• *Free movement of goods – arts 28 and 30 EC – Swedish legislation on the advertising of alcohol beverages – selling arrangements – measures having an effect equivalent to a quantitative restriction – freedom to provide services – arts 46 and 40 EC*

Facts
Swedish legislation providing for a total ban on the advertisement on radio, television and in periodicals and other publications of alcoholic beverages containing more than 2.25 per cent of alcohol by volume, but allowing such advertisement in the specialist press (that is

the press addressed to manufacturers and restaurateurs, and publications distributed solely at the point of sale of such beverages) was challenged by Gourmet International Products AB (GIP), a Swedish publisher of a magazine entitled *Gourmet*, as being in breach of EC law, inter alia, of art 28 EC.

GIP published in *Gourmet* three pages of advertisements for alcoholic beverages, one for red wine and two for whisky. These pages did not appear in the edition sold in shops but in the edition addressed to the subscribers, 90 per cent of whom were manufacturers and retailers and 10 per cent of whom were private individuals. The Swedish Consumer Ombudsman applied to the Stockholm District Court for an injunction restraining GIP from placing advertisements for alcoholic beverages in magazines and for a fine in the event of failure to comply. The Stockholm District Court referred to the ECJ the question of whether national rules imposing an absolute prohibition on certain advertisements might be regarded as measures having equivalent effect to a quantitative restriction and, if so, whether or not they might be justified under art 30 EC.

Held
The ECJ held that arts 28 and 30 and arts 46 and 49 EC do not preclude a prohibition on the advertisement of alcoholic beverages such as laid down in the challenged Swedish legislation unless it is apparent that, in the circumstances of law and fact which characterise the situation in the Member State concerned, the protection of public health against the harmful effects of alcohol can be ensured by measures having less effect on intra-Community trade.

Judgment
'[*Free movement of goods*]
By the questions referred to the Court, which can be considered together, the national court is asking essentially, first, whether the provisions of the Treaty on the free movement of goods preclude a prohibition on advertisements for alcoholic beverages such as that laid down in art 2 of the Alkoholreklamlagen.

The Consumer Ombudsman and the intervening governments accept that the prohibition on advertising in Sweden affects sales of alcoholic beverages there, including those imported from other Member States, since the specific purpose of the Swedish legislation is to reduce the consumption of alcohol.

However, observing that the Court held in para 16 of its judgment in Joined Cases C–267/91 and C–268/91 *Keck and Mithouard* [1993] ECR I–6097 that national provisions restricting or prohibiting certain selling arrangements are not liable to hinder intra-Community trade, so long as they apply to all relevant traders operating within the national territory and so long as they affect in the same manner, in law and in fact, the marketing of domestic products and of those from other Member States, the Consumer Ombudsman and the intervening governments contend that the prohibition on advertising in issue in the main proceedings does not constitute an obstacle to trade between Member States, since it satisfies the criteria laid down by the Court in that judgment.

GIP contends that an outright prohibition such as that at issue in the main proceedings does not satisfy those criteria. It argues that such a prohibition is, in particular, liable to have a greater effect on imported goods than on those produced in the Member State concerned.

Although the Commission takes the view that the decision as to whether, on the facts of the case, the prohibition does or does not constitute an obstacle to intra-Community trade is a matter for the national court, the Commission expresses similar doubts as to the application in the present case of the criteria referred to in para 15 above.

It should be pointed out that, according to para 17 of its judgment in *Keck and Mithouard*, if national provisions restricting or prohibiting certain selling arrangements are to avoid being caught by art 30 of the Treaty, they must not be of such a kind as to prevent access to the market by products from another Member State or to impede access any more than they impede the access of domestic products.

The Court has also held, in para 42 of its judgment in Joined Cases C–34/95 to C–36/95 *Konsumentombudsmannen (KO)* v *De Agostini* [1998] 1 CMLR 32, that it cannot be excluded that an outright prohibition, applying in one Member State, of a type of promotion for a product which is lawfully sold there might have a greater impact on products from other Member States.

It is apparent that a prohibition on advertising such as that at issue in the main proceedings not only prohibits a form of marketing a product but in reality prohibits producers and importers from directing any advertising messages at consumers, with a few insignificant exceptions.

Even without its being necessary to carry out a precise analysis of the facts characteristic of the Swedish situation, which it is for the national court to do, the Court is able to conclude that, in the case of products like alcoholic beverages, the consumption of which is linked to traditional social practices and to local habits and customs, a prohibition of all advertising directed at consumers in the form of advertisements in the press, on the radio and on television, the direct mailing of unsolicited material or the placing of posters on the public highway is liable to impede access to the market by products from other Member States more than it impedes access by domestic products, with which consumers are instantly more familiar.

The information provided by the Consumer Ombudsman and the Swedish government concerning the relative increase in Sweden in the consumption of wine and whisky, which are mainly imported, in comparison with other products such as vodka, which is mainly of Swedish origin, does not alter that conclusion. First, it cannot be precluded that, in the absence of the legislation at issue in the main proceedings, the change indicated would have been greater; second, that information takes into account only some alcoholic beverages and ignores, in particular, beer consumption.

Furthermore, although publications containing advertisements may be distributed at points of sale, Systembolaget AB, the company wholly owned by the Swedish State which has a monopoly of retail sales in Sweden, in fact only distributes its own magazine at those points of sale.

Last, Swedish legislation does not prohibit "editorial advertising", that is to say, the promotion, in articles forming part of the editorial content of the publication, of products in relation to which the insertion of direct advertisements is prohibited. The Commission correctly observes that, for various, principally cultural, reasons, domestic producers have easier access to that means of advertising than their competitors established in other Member States. That circumstance is liable to increase the imbalance inherent in the absolute prohibition on direct advertising.

A prohibition on advertising such as that at issue in the main proceedings must therefore be regarded as affecting the marketing of products from other Member States more heavily than the marketing of domestic products and as therefore constituting an obstacle to trade between Member States caught by art 30 of the Treaty.

However, such an obstacle may be justified by the protection of public health, a general interest ground recognised by art 36 of the Treaty.

In that regard, it is accepted that rules restricting the advertising of alcoholic beverages in order to combat alcohol abuse reflects public health concerns (Case 152/78 *EC Commission* v *France* [1980] ECR 2299, para 17, and Joined Cases C–1/90 and C–176/90 *Aragonesa de Publicidad Exterior and Publivía* v *Departmento di Sanidad y Sequiridad Social de la Generalitat de Cataluña* [1991] ECR I–4151, para 15).

In order for public health concerns to be capable of justifying an obstacle to trade such as that inherent in the prohibition on advertising at issue in the main proceedings, the measure concerned must also be proportionate to the objective to be achieved and must not constitute either a means of arbitrary discrimination or a disguised restriction on trade between Member States.

The Consumer Ombudsman and the intervening governments claim that the derogation provided for in art 36 of the Treaty can cover the prohibition on advertising at issue in the main proceedings. The Consumer Ombudsman and the Swedish government emphasise in particular that the prohibition is not absolute and does not prevent members of the public from obtaining information, if they wish, in particular in restaurants, on the Internet, in an "editorial context" or by asking the producer or importer to send advertising material. Furthermore, the Swedish government observes that the Court of Justice has acknowledged that, in the present state of Community law, Member States are at liberty, within the limits set by the Treaty, to decide on the degree of protection which they wish to afford to public health and on the way in which that protection is to be achieved (*Aragonesa de Publicidad Exterior and Publivía*, cited above, para 16). The Swedish government maintains that the legislation at issue in the main proceedings constitutes an essential component of its alcohol policy.

GIP claims that the outright prohibition on advertising laid down by the legislation at issue in the main proceedings is disproportionate, since the protection sought could be obtained by prohibitions of a more limited nature, concerning, for example, certain public places or the press aimed at children and adolescents. It must be borne in mind that the Swedish policy on alcoholism is already catered for by the existence of the monopoly on retail sales, by the prohibition on sales to persons under the age of 20 years and by information campaigns.

The Commission submits that the decision as to whether the prohibition on advertising at issue in the main proceedings is or is not proportionate is a matter for the national court. However, it also states that the prohibition does not appear to be particularly effective, owing in particular to the existence of "editorial" publicity and the abundance of indirect advertising on the Internet, and that requirements as to the form of advertising, such as the obligation to exercise moderation already found in the Alkoholreklamlagen, may suffice to protect the interest in question.

It should be pointed out, first, that there is no evidence before the Court to suggest that the public health grounds on which the Swedish authorities rely have been diverted from their purpose and used in such a way as to discriminate against goods originating in other Member States or to protect certain national products indirectly (Case 34/79 *R v Henn and Darby* [1979] ECR 3795, para 21, and *Aragonesa de Publicidad Exterior and Publivía*, cited above, para 20).

Second, the decision as to whether the prohibition on advertising at issue in the main proceedings is proportionate, and in particular as to whether the objective sought might be achieved by less extensive prohibitions or restrictions or by prohibitions or restrictions having less effect on intra-Community trade, calls for an analysis of the circumstances of law and of fact which characterise the situation in the Member State concerned, which the national court is in a better position than the Court of Justice to carry out.

The answer to the question must therefore be that, as regards the free movement of goods, arts 30 and 36 of the Treaty do not preclude a prohibition on the advertising of alcoholic beverages such as that laid down in art 2 of the Alkoholreklamlagen, unless it is apparent that, in the circumstances of law and of fact which characterise the situation in the Member State concerned, the protection of public health against the harmful effects of alcohol can be ensured by measures having less effect on intra-Community trade.'

Comment

In the above case the ECJ refined its post-*Keck* (see above) approach to national measures prohibiting or severely restricting advertisement. In the first cases after *Keck* the ECJ decided that national measures relating to advertisement, being selling arrangements, were outside the scope of art 28 EC, without carrying out any examination as to whether,

and to what extent, they had, in fact, affected imported products or prevented their access to the market in a Member State. The ECJ assumed that such measures had the same effect on imported products as on domestic products. For example in *Hünermund v Landesapothekerkammer Baden-Württenburg* Case C–292/92 [1993] ECR I–6787 and *Leclerc-Siplec v TFI Publicité SA and MG Publicité SA* Case 412/93 [1995] ECR I–179 the ECJ provided neither any clarification as to the meaning of selling arrangements, nor any guidance as to the criteria for the application of *Keck* which, if applied, would in practice allow the verification of whether national measures affected in the same manner (in fact or in law) the marketing of imported products and of domestic products and the degree of impediment that national rules imposing an outright ban on advertisement represented for imported products in terms of their access to the market in a Member State. In fact, an approach has subsequently, gradually evolved. In Joined Cases C–34/95 to C–36/95 *Konsumentombudsmannen (KO) v De Agostini* [1998] 1 CMLR 32 the ECJ held that national measures imposing an outright ban on advertisement might have a greater impact on products from other Member States, but stated that the matter, whether or not this was the case, had to be decided by the referring court.

In the above case, the ECJ went further. The Court acknowledged that advertisement plays an important role in the marketing of imported products and is essential in the launching of new products. Without advertising it would be extremely difficult for a manufacturer established in one Member State to penetrate the market in another Member State, since his products are unknown to prospective consumers. National measures prohibiting or severely restricting advertisement, especially in respect of new products, tend to protect domestic manufacturers, to crystallize existing patterns of consumption and to restrict access to the market of goods from other Member States. This new, more realistic approach by the ECJ means that national rules prohibiting or severely restricting advertisement are not automatically excluded from the scope of art 28 EC but must be assessed in the context of their effect on imported goods. If they affect the marketing of imported products more heavily than the marketing of domestic products, which will always occur in respect of new imported products since only by means of advertising can consumers be induced to buy them, they will constitute measures having equivalent effect to a quantitative restriction. This new approach also challenges the relevance of *Keck*. Indeed, whether one applies the *Dassonville* formula or the principle of *Keck* as explained by the ECJ in the above case, the final result in the same. The more things change, the more they stay the same!

Procureur du Roi v *Dassonville* Case 8/74 [1974] ECR 837; [1974] 2 CMLR 436 European Court of Justice

• *Article 30 EC Treaty [art 28 EC] – measures having equivalent effect to a quantitative restriction – prohibition – trading rules capable of hindering trade – designation of origin of a product – Scotch whisky – admissibility of protective measures – conditions*

Facts

A trader imported Scotch whisky into Belgium. The whisky had been purchased from a French distributor and had been in circulation in France. However, the Belgian authorities required a certificate of origin which could only be obtained from British customs, and which had to be made out in the name of the importers, before the goods could be legally imported into Belgium. As the certificate of origin could not be obtained for the consignment, the defendants went ahead with the transaction. They were charged by the Belgian authorities with the criminal offence of importing goods without the requisite certificate of origin.

The defendants claimed that the requirement of a certificate of origin in these circumstances was tantamount to a measure having an effect equivalent to a quantitative restriction and therefore was prohibited by art 30 EC Treaty [art 28 EC]. The Belgian court referred to the ECJ for a preliminary ruling on this question.

Held

The ECJ defined the concept of a measure having an equivalent effect to a quantitative restriction on imports and decided that the Belgian legislation fell into this classification. Consequently, the requirement of a certificate of origin, which is less easily obtainable by importers of an authentic product than importers of a product in free circulation, constitutes a prohibited measure of equivalent effect to a quantitative restriction.

Judgment

'It emerges from the file and from the oral proceedings that a trader, wishing to import into Belgium Scotch whisky which is already in free circulation in France, can obtain such a certificate only with great difficulty, unlike the importer who imports directly from the producer country.

All trading rules enacted by Member States which are capable of hindering directly or indirectly, actually or potentially, intra-Community trade are to be considered as measures having an effect equivalent to quantitative restrictions.

In the absence of a Community system guaranteeing for consumers the authenticity of a product's designation of origin, if a Member State takes measures to prevent unfair practices in this connection, it is however subject to the condition that these measures should be reasonable and that the means of proof required should not act as a hindrance to trade between Member States and should, in consequence, be accessible to all Community nationals.

Even without having to examine whether or not such measures are covered by art 36, they must not, in any case, by virtue of the principle expressed in the second sentence of that Article, constitute a means of arbitrary discrimination or a disguised restriction on trade between Member States. That may be the case with formalities, required by a Member State for the purpose of proving the origin of a product, which only direct importers are really in a position to satisfy without facing serious difficulties.

Consequently, the requirement by a Member State of a certificate of authenticity which is less easily obtainable by importers of an authentic product which has been put into free circulation in a regular manner in another Member State than by importers of the same product coming directly from the country of origin constitutes a measure having an effect equivalent to a quantitative restriction as prohibited by the Treaty.'

Comment

This is one of the leading cases on the free movement of goods. The ECJ held that: 'All trading rules enacted by Member States which are capable of hindering directly or indirectly, actually or potentially, intra-Community trade are to be considered as measures having an effect equivalent to quantitative restrictions.' This is know as the *Dassonville* formula. This formula includes both distinctly applicable measures affecting imports and indistinctly applicable measures affecting imported and domestic products. The formula is very broad, the effect of the measure, including its potential effect (*EC Commission* v *Ireland (Re 'Buy Irish' Campaign)* Case 249/81 [1982] ECR 4005) is decisive in determining whether it should be considered as a measure having an equivalent effect to a quantitative restriction. Discriminatory intent is not required.

R v *Royal Pharmaceutical Society of Great Britain, ex parte Association of Pharmaceutical Importers* Cases 266 and 267/87 [1989] ECR 1295 European Court of Justice

• *Free movement of goods – rules enacted by professional bodies – statutory author-*

ity of such bodies – professional and ethical rules – contrary to art 30 EC Treaty [art 28 EC] – measures having equivalent effect to a quantitative restriction

Facts

The Pharmaceutical Society of Great Britain is a professional body established to enforce rules of ethics for pharmacists throughout the United Kingdom. This organisation convenes periodic meetings of a committee which has statutory authority to impose disciplinary measures on pharmacists found to have violated these professional rules of ethics.

The Society enacted rules which prohibited a pharmacist from substituting one product for another with the same therapeutic effect, but bearing a different trade mark, when doctors refer to a particular brand of medication. Pharmacists were therefore required to dispense particular brand name products when these were specified in prescription. This rule was challenged as being a measure having an equivalent effect to a quantitative restriction as prohibited by art 30 EC Treaty [art 28 EC].

Held

Rules prescribed by regulatory agencies and professional bodies established under statutory authority may constitute measures having an equivalent effect to a quantitative restriction within the meaning of art 30 EC Treaty [art 28 EC] even though the rules were not enacted by a national legislative body.

Judgment

'Before the question whether the measures at issue fall under the prohibition in art 30 of the Treaty or whether they are justified under art 36 of the Treaty is considered, the point raised by the national court's third question, which is whether a measure adopted by a professional body such as the Pharmaceutical Society of Great Britain may come within the scope of the said articles, should be resolved.

According to the documents before the Court, the Society, which was incorporated by Royal Charter in 1843 and whose existence is also recognised in United Kingdom legislation, is the sole professional body for pharmacy. It maintains the Register in which all pharmacists must be enrolled in order to carry on their business. As can be seen from the order for reference, it adopts rules of ethics applicable to pharmacists. Finally, United Kingdom legislation has established a disciplinary committee within the Society which may impose disciplinary sanctions on a pharmacist for professional misconduct; those sanctions may even involve his removal from the Register. An appeal lies to the High Court decisions of that committee.

It should be stated that measures adopted by a professional body on which national legislation has conferred powers of that nature may, if they are capable of affecting trade between Member States, constitute "measures" within the meaning of art 30 of the Treaty.

The reply to the third question should therefore be that measures adopted by a professional body, such as the Pharmaceutical Society of Great Britain, which lays down rules of ethics applicable to the members of the profession and has a committee upon which national legislation has conferred disciplinary powers that could involve removal from the register of person authorised to exercise the profession, may constitute "measures" within the meaning of art 30 of the [EC] Treaty.'

Comment

In the present case the ECJ held that art 30 EC Treaty [art 28 EC] applies not only to rules enacted by the Member States but also encompasses rules adopted by a professional body such as the Royal Pharmaceutical Society for Great Britain which exercises regulatory and disciplinary powers conferred upon it by statutory instrument. The ECJ stated that professional and ethical rules adopted by the society which required pharmacists to supply, under a prescription, only a particular brand name

drug, may constitute measures having equivalent effect to a quantitative restriction in breach of art 30 EC Treaty [art 28 EC]. However, in the present case the measures were justified under art 36 EC Treaty [art 30 EC].

Rewe-Zentrale AG v Bundes-monopolverwaltung für Branntwein (*Cassis de Dijon*) Case 120/78 [1979] ECR 649; [1979] 3 CMLR 337 European Court of Justice

• *Free movement of goods – art 30 EC Treaty [art 28 EC] – mandatory requirements – legitimate objectives of such requirements – proportionality – rule of reason – rule of recognition*

Facts

German legislation governing the marketing of alcoholic beverages set a minimum alcohol strength of 25 per cent per litre for certain categories of alcoholic products. This regulation prevented an importer from marketing Cassis de Dijon, a French liqueur with an alcohol strength of between 15–20 per cent, into Germany.

The German government invoked human health and consumer protection concerns as the justification for the prohibition. The importer challenged the German legislation in the German court which referred the matter to the ECJ for a preliminary ruling.

Held

The ECJ held that the requirement was tantamount to a measure equivalent to a quantitative restriction and as such was prohibited by art 30 EC Treaty [art 28 EC]. Although the Court recognised that certain measures may be necessary for the protection of public health, the effectiveness of fiscal supervision, the fairness of commercial transactions and the defence of the consumer, this particular measure could not be justified on these grounds.

Judgment

'In the absence of common rules relating to the protection and marketing of alcohol – a proposal for a regulation submitted to the Council by the Commission on 7 December 1976 (OJ C309 p2) not yet having received the Council's approval – it is for the Member States to regulate all matters relating to the production and marketing of alcohol and alcoholic beverages on their own territory.

Obstacles to movement within the Community resulting from disparities between the national laws relating to the marketing of the products in question must be accepted in so far as those provisions may be recognised as being necessary in order to satisfy mandatory requirements relating in particular to the effectiveness of fiscal supervision, the protection of public health, the fairness of commercial transactions and the defence of the consumer.

The government of the Federal Republic of Germany, intervening in the proceedings, put forward various arguments which, in its view, justify the application of provisions relating to the minimum alcohol content of alcoholic beverages, adducing considerations relating on the one hand to the protection of public health and on the other to the protection of the consumer against unfair commercial practices.

As regards the protection of public health the German government states that the purpose of the fixing of minimum alcohol contents by national legislation is to avoid the proliferation of alcoholic beverages on the national market, in particular alcoholoc beverages with a low alcohol content since, in its view, such products may more easily induce a tolerance towards alcohol than more highly alcoholic beverages.

Such considerations are not decisive since the consumer can obtain on the market an extremely wide range of weakly or moderately alcoholic products and furthermore a large proportion of alcoholic beverages with a high alcohol content freely sold on the German market is generally in a diluted form.

The German government also claims that the fixing of a lower limit for the alcohol content of certain liqueurs is designed to protect the consumer against unfair practices on the part of producers and distributors of alcoholic beverages.

This argument is based on the consideration that the lowering of the alcohol content secures a competitive advantage in relation to beverages with a higher alcohol content, since alcohol constitutes by far the most expensive constituent of beverages by reason of the high rate of tax to which it is subject.

Furthermore, according to the German government, to allow alcoholic products into free circulation wherever, as regards their alcohol content, they comply with the rules laid down in the country of production would have the effect of imposing as a common standard within the Community the lowest alcohol content permitted in any of the Member States, and even of rendering any requirements in this field inoperative since a lower limit of this nature is foreign to the rules of several Member States.

As the Commission rightly observed, the fixing of limits in relation to the alcohol content of beverages may lead to the standardisation of products placed on the market and of their designations, in the interests of a greater transparency of commercial transactions and offers for sale to the public.

However, this line of argument cannot be taken so far as to regard the mandatory fixing of minimum alcohol contents as being as essential guarantee of the fairness of commercial transactions, since it is a simple matter to ensure that suitable information is conveyed to the purchaser by requiring the display of an indication of origin and of the alcohol content on the packaging of products.

It is clear from the foregoing that the requirements relating to the minimum alcohol content of alcoholic beverages do not serve a purpose which is in the general interest and such as to take precedence over the requirements of the free movement of goods, which constitutes one of the fundamental rules of the Community.

In practice, the principle effect of requirements of this nature is to promote alcoholic beverages having a high alcohol content by excluding from the national market products of other Member States which do not answer that description.

It therefore appears that the unilateral requirement imposed by the rules of a member States of a minimum alcohol content for the purposes of the sale of alcoholic beverages constitutes an obstacle to trade which is incompatible with the provisions of art 30 of the Treaty.

There is therefore no valid reason why, provided that they have been lawfully produced and marketed in one of the Member States, alcoholic beverages should not be introduced into any other Member State; the sale of such products may not be subject to a legal prohibition on the marketing of beverages with an alcohol content lower than the limit set by the national rules.

Consequently, the first question should be answered to the effect that the concept of "measures having an effect equivalent to quantitative restrictions on imports" contained in art 30 of the Treaty is to be understood to mean that the fixing of a minimum alcohol content for alcoholic beverages intended for human consumption by the legislation of a Member State also falls within the prohibition laid down in that provision where the importation of alcoholoc beverages lawfully produced and marketed in another Member State is concerned.'

Comment

This is one of the leading cases in the area of free movement of goods. In it the ECJ established two fundamental rules in respect of indistinctly applicable measures:

1. the rule of reason according to which, in the absence of common rules, obstacles to the free movement of goods resulting from disparities between national laws relating to the marketing of the products in question must be accepted in so far as those provisions may be recognised as necessary in order to satisfy mandatory requirements relating in particular to the effectiveness of

fiscal supervision, the protection of public health, the fairness of commercial transactions and the defence of the consumer;

2. the rule of recognition which provides that there is no valid reason why goods which have been produced and marketed in one Member State should not be introduced into any other Member State.

The decision in the present case displaced the previous assumption that art 30 EC Treaty [art 28 EC] did not apply to a national measure unless it could be shown that the measure discriminated between imports and domestic products or between different forms of intra-Community trade.

Under the first rule, certain measures which are within the *Dassonville* formula will not infringe art 30 EC Treaty [art 28 EC] provided they are necessary to protect a mandatory requirement enumerated in the first rule. The list of mandatory requirements is not exhaustive. The ECJ may add additional justifications if necessary.

Under the second rule there is a presumption that goods which have been lawfully marketed in one Member State will comply with mandatory requirements of the State into which they are being imported. For that reason a national rule must not only pursue a legitimate objective but must be necessary and proportionate for the attainment of that objective.

Snellers Auto's BV v Algemeen Directeur van de Dienst Wegverkeer
Case C–314/98 [2000] 3 CMLR 1275
European Court of Justice

• *Free movement of goods – art 28 EC – measures having an effect equivalent to a quantitative restriction on imports – imperative requirements – route safety, protection of the environment – parallel imports – first authorisation of a vehicle for use on the public highway – determination of the date – Directives 83/189/EC and 94/10/EC – technical standards and regulations*

Facts

The question regarding the determination of the date on which an imported vehicle was first authorised for use on the public highway was at the centre of the controversy. In this case Snellers, a Dutch car dealer who was not an official dealer of the BMW AG distribution network, but marketed vehicles in The Netherlands imported through parallel channels, bought a BMW vehicle in Germany which was described in the sales invoice as new; the odometer reading of 800km was explained to be due to the fact that it had been delivered by road from the factory to the dealer. The seller, Autohaus Werner Pelster GmbH, was a German official dealer in BMW cars who had registered the car in Germany on 6 August 1996.

On 15 August 1996 Snellers took the vehicle to the Dutch Road Traffic Office (DRTO) for inspection and registration purposes. During the inspection Snellers was handed a form which stated, under the heading concerning the date of first authorisation for use on the public highway, the word 'new'.

On 10 January 1997 the DRTO issued a registration certificate which stated that the date of first authorisation for use on the public highway was 6 August 1996. Snellers challenged the decision, arguing that the Dutch regulations concerning the rules relating to the determination of the date on which the vehicle was first authorised for use and which entered into force on 1 January 1995 were contrary to EC law, in particular Directive 83/189/EC as amended by Directive 94/10/EC. Snellers also argued that the Dutch regulations were in breach of art 28 EC as they constituted a measure equivalent in effect to a quantitative restriction. When Snellers' complaint was rejected by the DRTO, Snellers brought proceedings against the DRTO before a Dutch District Court, which agreed with Snellers. The DRTO brought an appeal before a Dutch Administrative Appeals Division Court, which referred to the ECJ a number of questions, in particular:

1. whether the Dutch regulations constituted

a measure having an effect equivalent to a quantitative restriction on imports within the meaning of art 28 EC and, if so, whether it might be justified by considerations relating to road safety and/or the protection of the environment.

Held

The ECJ held that the Dutch regulations constituted a measure having an effect equivalent to a quantitative restriction on imports within the meaning of art 28 EC but might be justified by imperative requirements such as road safety or/and the protection of the environment if it could be shown that the resulting restriction was necessary to ensure road safety and/or the protection of the environment, and that the restriction was not disproportionate to those objectives, in the sense that no other, less restrictive measures were available.

Judgment

'[*Fourth question*]
By its fourth question, the national court is essentially asking whether national rules which provide that the date on which an imported vehicle was first authorised for use on the public highway is to be fixed at the date on which its registration certificate is issued only where the vehicle has not been registered for more than two days in another Member State ("the contested condition") constitute a measure having an effect equivalent to a quantitative restriction on imports within the meaning of art 30 of the Treaty [art 28 EC].

The national court observes that the regulation draws no formal distinction between official importers and parallel importers, but that its practical effect is to place parallel importers at a disadvantage by comparison with official importers.

Snellers claims that the regulation constitutes a measure having an effect equivalent to a quantitative restriction on imports within the meaning of art 30 of the Treaty. It observes that in practice it is virtually impossible for parallel importers to obtain supplies of unregistered vehicles from approved dealers in other Member States, since vehicle manufacturers and suppliers generally prohibit their approved dealers from selling unregistered vehicles. Snellers further contends that as a result of the regulation it is only able to sell vehicles at a lower price than it paid for them, although it informs purchasers that the vehicles in question are new and unused. Purchasers take into account the price they might receive if they resold the vehicles in question as used vehicles. In The Netherlands, that price is essentially determined by the date of first authorisation shown on The Netherlands' registration certificate. When a vehicle is resold there is no documentary proof of whether the vehicle was a new, unused vehicle when the certificate was issued, since that fact is not indicated on the certificate. It is precisely because the vehicle would realise a lower resale price that Netherlands' purchasers do not purchase such vehicles, or do not purchase them at the same price.

The Netherlands government maintains that the way in which the date of first authorisation for use on the public highway is determined in The Netherlands does not constitute a measure having an effect equivalent to a quantitative restriction on imports within the meaning of art 30 of the Treaty. It follows from the regulation that where application is made in The Netherlands for a registration certificate for a vehicle which has already been authorised for use on the public highway on a previous date, in principle it is the latter date which is entered on the registration certificate as the date of first authorisation for use on the public highway. In that regard, no distinction is made according to the place where such authorisation was first granted. Any obstacles which parallel importers may encounter are the result of the constraints which manufacturers impose on their approved distributors.

The Austrian government and the Commission maintain that a national rule such as the regulation has the effect that the parallel distribution channel is placed at a disadvantage by comparison with the official network and can therefore be regarded as a measure having an effect equivalent to a quantitative restriction on imports within the meaning of art 30 of the Treaty.

In that regard, it must be pointed out that, even though the regulation draws no formal distinction between official importers and parallel importers, in practice it places parallel importers at a disadvantage in that they must comply with strict requirements which are difficult to satisfy in order to obtain registration certificates on which the date on which the vehicle was first authorised to use the public highway is shown as the date on which the certificate was issued. The regulation thus does not have the same effect on the marketing of vehicles imported by approved distributors and the marketing of vehicles imported via parallel channels by non-approved distributors.

The fact that the difficulties which parallel importers experience in complying with the contested condition may be caused by problems which they encounter in obtaining from approved dealers in other Member States vehicles registered on a date which enables them to comply with that condition, as The Netherlands' government has observed, does not mean that that condition does not constitute an obstacle to the free movement of goods for the purposes of art 30 of the Treaty.

Therefore the answer to the fourth question must be that national rules which provide that the date on which an imported vehicle was first authorised for use on the public highway is to be fixed at the date on which its registration certificate was issued only where the vehicle has not been registered for more than two days in another Member State constitute a measure having an effect equivalent to a quantitative restriction on imports for the purposes of art 30 of the Treaty.

[Fifth and sixth questions]
By its fifth and sixth questions, the national court is essentially asking whether, in spite of having restrictive effects on the free movement of goods, national rules such as the regulation may be justified by considerations relating to road safety and/or protec-

tion of the environment and, if so, whether such a restriction is proportionate to the objectives pursued.

In that context, the national court asks whether the answer to that question is affected by the fact that a parallel importer may agree with his supplier in the Member State of export that, after the registration certificate has been issued in that State, the supplier is to seek suspension of the authorisation thus granted and is to have that suspension lifted when the parallel importer applies for registration in the Member State of import.

Snellers contends that considerations of road safety and/or protection of the environment cannot justify the contested condition. Furthermore, if such an obstacle to trade were to be regarded as justified, it could not be considered proportionate to the objective pursued if it prevented the vehicle from being shown to be new.

The Netherlands' government claims that the contested condition is justified by considerations of road safety and protection of the environment. The interests which the regulation seeks to protect in determining the date on which the vehicle is first authorised for use on the highway are such that it is only to a very limited extent that exceptions to the rule that that date is to be determined in accordance with the true situation can be allowed. Were that not so, the aims pursued would not be achieved, or would not be sufficiently achieved. The regulation provides for one exception to the rule that it is the date on which the first registration is issued that is decisive, and such relaxation of the rule cannot be granted unless strict conditions apply.

The French government contends that the protection of health and the environment by means of rules to control vehicles and polluting gas emissions from those vehicles may justify the regulation. As regards the proportionality of the measure, the French government contends that the geographical situation of The Netherlands is such that it is possible, within a radius of 2,500km and within a period of two days, to purchase and import a vehicle, in parallel to the official network, from any of the Member States.

The Commission maintains that road safety may be regarded as a ground which justifies a restriction on the free movement of goods. The older a vehicle is and the more it has been used, the more important it is to ensure that it still satisfies basic safety requirements. However, the national rule must be necessary and proportionate to the objective pursued, which is not the case here. The fact that a vehicle has been registered for more than two days in another Member State is no indication of its age or of the extent to which it has been used.

In that regard, it should be pointed out that it follows from settled case law that restrictions on the free movement of goods within the meaning of art 30 of the Treaty may be justified by imperative requirements such as road safety (see Case C–55/93 *Criminal Proceedings against Van Schaik* [1994] ECR I–4837) and protection of the environment (see Case C–341/95 *Bettati v Safety Hi-Tech Srl* [1998] ECR I–4355, para 62), and that it cannot be precluded that national rules which define criteria for the determination of the date on which a vehicle was first authorised for use on the public highway, such as the regulation, may be justified. It is for the national court to ascertain whether that is actually so in the case before it.

If, having done so, the national court finds that such a rule is justified by considerations relating to road safety and/or protection of the environment, it still remains, according to a consistent line of decisions (see the judgment in *Bettati*, cited above, paras 63 and 64), to be ascertained whether the restriction on the free movement of goods arising under the contested condition specifically for parallel importers is necessary to ensure road safety and/or protection of the environment and whether that restriction is not disproportionate to its objectives, particularly in the sense that no other, less restrictive, measures are available.

In that regard, as the Commission has observed, the fact that a vehicle has been registered in another Member State for more than two days does not provide any information as to its age or the extent to which it has been used, and, furthermore, the technical inspection makes it possible, at least to a certain degree, to establish the vehicle's technical condition and to ascertain the truth of the seller's declaration that the vehicle is new and unused.

Furthermore, the possibility that the parallel importer and his supplier may reach agreements in terms such as those referred to in para 50 of this judgment may be taken into account for the purpose of determining whether or not the contested condition is proportionate to its objective. In order that such a factor may be taken into account, however, there must be a real possibility that the parallel importer can conclude such an agreement.

It is for the national court to ascertain, in the light of the foregoing considerations, whether in the present case the contested condition is actually necessary to ensure road safety and/or protection of the environment, and whether the resulting restriction is not disproportionate to those objectives, particularly in the sense that no other, less restrictive, measures are available.

Having regard to the foregoing, the answer to the fifth and sixth questions must be that national rules such as the regulation may, in spite of their restrictive effects on the free movement of goods, be justified by imperative requirements such as road safety and/or protection of the environment if it can be shown that the resulting restriction is necessary to ensure road safety and/or protection of the environment and that the restriction is not disproportionate to those objectives, particularly in the sense that no other, less restrictive, measures are available.'

Comment

The first interesting point in the commented case was that the ECJ held that national rules (such as the contested regulation which provided that the date on which an imported vehicle was first authorised for use on the public highway is to be fixed at the date on which its registration certificate is issued only where the vehicle has not been registered for

more than two days in another Member State) constitute a measure having an effect equivalent to a quantitative restriction on imports in breach of art 28 EC. Although the contested legislation made no distinction between official importers and parallel importers it, nevertheless, placed the latter at a disadvantage for a number of reasons.

1. First, the obligation to register is almost always imposed on official dealers by the manufacturers. Therefore, it is virtually impossible for parallel importers to obtain supplies of unregistered vehicles.
2. Second, unauthorised dealers are forced to sell new, unused vehicles at lower prices than are authorised dealers, thereby reducing the value of the vehicles. In Snellers' case, new, unused vehicles would be registered as 1996 vehicles and not as 1997 vehicles (Snellers wanted the date to be 19 January 1997).
3. Third, parallel importers, as the ECJ stated:

   '... must comply with strict requirements, which are difficult to satisfy, in order to obtain registration certificates on which the date on which the vehicle was first authorised to use the public highway is shown as the date on which the certificate was issued. The [contested] regulation thus does not have the same effect on the marketing of vehicles imported by approved distributors and the marketing of vehicles imported via parallel channels by non-approved distributors.'

The second interesting aspect of the above case is that the ECJ, for the first time, held that obstacles to the free movement of goods may be justified by considerations relating to road safety. As a result the ECJ recognised a new imperative requirement capable of justifying national rules restricting the free movement of goods within the Community. Thus, the non-exhaustive list of mandatory requirements provided by the ECJ in *Cassis de Dijon* has been extended once again.

In this context it is noteworthy to mention

that road safety was already considered as an imperative requirement of a general nature capable of justifying national rules restricting the freedom to provide services in *Van Schaik* Case C–55/93 [1994] ECR I–4837. However, the ECJ left to the referring court the task of ascertaining whether the contested regulation may actually be justified by imperative requirements such as road safety and/or the protection of the environment.

Article 30 EC

Conegate Limited v *HM Customs and Excise* Case 121/85 [1986] ECR 1007; [1986] 1 CMLR 739 European Court of Justice

• *Free movement of goods – art 36 EC Treaty [art 30 EC] – protection of public morality – abolishment of double morality standards*

Facts
A British company set up businesss importing inflatable dolls from Germany into the United Kingdom. A number of consignment of the products were seized by Customs officials on the ground that the dolls were 'indecent and obscene', and accordingly subject to the prohibition on imports contained in the Customs Consolidation Act 1876. Although national rules prohibited the importation of these dolls, no regulation prevented their manufacture in the United Kingdom.

The company brought an action for recovery of the dolls. In particular, it was alleged that the prohibition order contravened art 30 EC Treaty [art 28 EC], and was accordingly a measure having an effect equivalent to a quantitative restriction. In reply, the British authorities claimed that the measures were justified under art 36 EC Treaty [art 30 EC] in order to protect public morality.

Held
The ECJ held that the United Kingdom could not rely on art 36 EC Treaty [art 30 EC] to prohibit the importation of products, when no internal provisions had been enacted to prevent the manufacture and distribution of the offending products within the United Kingdom. To allow a Member State to prevent the importation of particular goods, while simultaniously allowing nationals to manufacture such products, would amount to discrimination on the ground of nationality.

Judgment
'The Court would observe that the first question raises, in the first place, the general problem of whether a prohibition on the importation of certain goods may be justified on grounds of public morality where the legislation of the Member State concerned contains no prohibition on the manufacture or marketing of the same products within the national territory.

So far as that problem is concerned, it must be borne in mind that according to art 36 of the [EC] Treaty the provisions relating to the free movement of goods within the Community do not preclude prohibitions on imports justified "on grounds of public morality". As the Court held in its judgment of 14 December 1979, cited above [*R* v *Henn and Darby* Case 34/79 [1979] ECR 3795], in principle it is for each Member State to determine in accordance with its own scale of values and in the form selected by it the requirements of public morality in its territory.

However, although Community law leaves the Member States free to make their own assessment of the indecent or obscene character of certain articles, it must be pointed out that the fact that goods cause offence cannot be regarded as sufficiently serious to justify restrictions on the free movement of goods where the Member State concerned does not adopt, with respect to the same goods manufactured or marketed within its territory, penal measures or other serious and effective measures intended to prevent the distribution of such goods in its territory.

It follows that a Member State may not rely on grounds of public morality in order to prohibit the importation of goods from other Member States when its legislation contains no prohibition on the manufacture or marketing of the same goods on its territory.

It is not for the Court, within the framework of the powers conferred upon it by art 177 of the [EC] Treaty, to consider whether, and to what extent, the United Kingdom legislation contains such a prohibition. However, the question whether or not such a prohibition exists in a State comprised of different constituent parts which have their own legislation, can be resolved by taking into consideration all the relevant legislation. Although it is not necessary, for the purpose of the application of the above mentioned rule, that the manufacture and marketing of the products whose importation has been prohibited should be prohibited in the territory of all the constituent parts, it must at least be possible to conclude from the applicable rules, taken as a whole, that their purpose is, in substance, to prohibit the manufacture and marketing of those products.

In this instance, in the actual wording of its first question the High Court took care to define the substance of the national legislation the compatibility of which with Community law is a question which it proposes to determine. Thus it refers to rules in the importing Member State under which the goods in question may be manufactured freely and marketed subject only to certain restrictions, which it sets out explicitely, namely as absolute prohibition on the transmission of such goods by post, a restriction on their public display and, in certain areas of the Member State concerned, a system of licensing of premises for the sale of those goods to customers aged 18 years and over. Such restrictions cannot however be regarded as equivalent in substance to a prohibition on manufacture and marketing.

At the hearing, the United Kingdom again stressed the fact that at present no articles comparable to those imported by Conegate are manufactured on United Kingdom territory, but that fact, which does not exclude the posssibility of manufacturing such articles and which, moreover, was not referred to by the High Court, is not such as to lead to a different assessment of the situation.

In reply to the first question it must therefore be stated that a Member State may not rely on grounds of public morality within the meaning of art 36 of the Treaty in order to prohibit the importation of certain goods on the grounds that they are indecent or obscene, where the same goods may be manufactured freely on its territory and marketed on its territory subject to an absolute prohibition on their transmisssion by post, a restriction on their public display and, in certain regions, a system of licensing of premises for the sale of those goods to customers aged 18 and over.

That conclusion does not preclude the authorities of the Member State concerned from applying to those goods, once imported, the same restrictions on marketing which are applied to similar products manufactured and marketed within the country.'

Comment

In the light of the objective of completion of the common market, the ECJ decided to abolish double morality standards. In the present case the ECJ held that the United Kingdom could not rely on art 36 EC Treaty [art 30 EC] to prohibit the importation of inflatable sex dolls and other erotic materials, when no internal provisions had been enacted to prevent the manufacture and distribution of the offending products within the United Kingdom. To allow a Member State to prevent the importation of particular goods, while simultaneously allowing nationals to manufacture such products, would amount to discrimination based on nationality.

Criminal Proceedings against Bluhme (Brown Bees of Laesø) Case C–67/97 [1998] ECR I–8033
European Court of Justice

- *Free movement of goods – application of art 30 EC Treaty [art 28 EC] to different parts of the territory of a Member State – prohibition of quantitative restrictions and measures having equivalent effect between Member States – derogations under art 36 EC Treaty [art 30 EC] – de minimis justification – protection of the health and life of animals – bees of the subspecies apis mellifera mellifera (Laesø brown bees)*

Facts
Criminal proceedings were instituted against Ditlev Bluhme for breach of Danish law prohibiting the keeping on the island of Laesø bees other than those of the subspecies *Apis mellifera mellifera* (brown bees of Laesø). Mr Bluhme argued that the prohibition constituted a measure having equivalent effect to a quantitative restriction and as such was contrary to art 30 EC Treaty [art 28 EC], whilst the Dutch authorities claimed that such legislation, even if in breach of art 30 EC Treaty [art 28 EC], was justified on the ground of the protection of the health and life of animals.

Held
The ECJ held that the Danish legislation prohibiting the keeping on the island of Laesø of any species of bee other than the subspecies Apis mellifera mellifera constituted a measure having an equivalent effect to a quantitative restriction within the meaning of art 30 EC Treaty [art 28 EC] but it was justified under art 36 EC Treaty [art 30 EC] on the ground of the protection of the health and life of animals.

Judgment
'In so far as art 6 of the [Danish legislation] at issue in the main proceedings involves a general prohibition on the importation onto Laesø and neighbouring islands of living bees and reproductive material for domestic bees, it also prohibits their importation from other Member States, so that it is capable of hindering intra-Community trade. It therefore constitutes a measure having an effect equivalent to a quantitative restriction.

It follows that a legislative measure prohibiting the keeping on an island such as Laesø of any species of bee other than the subspecies Apis mellifera mellifera (Læsø brown bee) constitutes a measure having an effect equivalent to a quantitative restriction within the meaning of art 30 of the Treaty.

[*Justification for legislation such as that at issue in the main proceedings*]

… Measures to preserve an indigenous animal population with distinct characteristics contribute to the maintenance of biodiversity by ensuring the survival of the population concerned. By so doing, they are aimed at protecting the life of those animals and are capable of being justified under art 36 of the Treaty.

From the point of view of such conservation of biodiversity, it is immaterial whether the object of protection is a separate subspecies, a distinct strain within any given species or merely a local colony, so long as the populations in question have characteristics distinguishing them from others and are therefore judged worthy of protection either to shelter them from a risk of extinction that is more or less imminent, or, even in the absence of such risk, on account of a scientific or other interest in preserving the pure population at the location concerned.

As for the threat of the disappearance of the Laesø brown bee, it is undoubtedly genuine in the event of mating with golden bees by reason of the recessive nature of the genes of the brown bee. The establishment by the national legislation of a protection area within which the keeping of bees other than Læsø brown bees is prohibited, for the purpose of ensuring the survival of the latter, therefore constitutes an appropriate measure in relation to the aim pursued.'

Comment

It is interesting to note that this case confirms the confusion created by *Criminal Proceedings against Keck and Mithouard* Cases C–267 and 268/93. Indeed, the arguments submitted by the Danish government intended to exclude the application of art 30 EC Treaty [art 28 EC] rather than justifying national legislation on the ground of art 36 EC Treaty [art 30 EC], in particular the protection of the health and life of animals. The ECJ did not examine the arguments submitted by the Danish government (supported by the Italian and Norwegian governments – the latter is permitted to submit written observations by virtue of of art 20 of the Statute of the ECJ as being a Member State of the EEA) probably because they were either patently wrong or contrary to the well established case law relating to art 30 EC Treaty [art 28 EC]. The argument that Danish legislation was applicable to a part of the territory was dismissed by the ECJ without any reference to *Aragonesa de Publicidad* v *Departamento di Sanidad y Sequiridad Social de la Generalitat de Cataluna* Cases C–1 and 171/90 [1991] ECR I–4165 or *Ligur Carni* Cases C–277, 318 and 319/91 [1993] ECR I–6621. The argument based on the de minimis rule was not discussed by the ECJ probably because it has been well established that art 30 EC Treaty [art 28 EC] applies to all obstacles to the free movement of goods without taking into account the extent to which they affect trade between Member States (see *Pranti* Case 16/83 [1984] ECR 1299). The argument based on the dichotomy introduced by *Keck and Mithouard* was dealt with in a particularly disappointing manner. In this respect the ECJ stated that the legislation in question focused on intrinsic characteristics of bees and therefore was not concerned with the modality of sale. Finally, the ECJ failed to fully explain the relationship between national measures and the protection of the health and life of animals within the meaning of art 36 EC Treaty [art 30 EC]. This approach would be welcomed, taking into account that in prior cases in this area the justifications based on the protection of the health and life of animals were made in the context of the prevention of propagation of animal diseases (*EC Commission* v *Germany* Case C–131/93 [1994] ECR I–3303) or the prevention of unnecessary suffering by animals (*R* v *Ministry of Agriculture, Fisheries and Food, ex parte Compassion in World Farming Ltd* Case C–1/96 [1998] 2 CMLR 661). In the present case the ECJ stated that such national measures 'contribute to the maintenance of biodiversity' and 'by so doing, they are aimed at protecting the life of those animals and are capable of being justified under art 36 EC Treaty [art 30 EC]'. The relationship between the maintenance of biodiversity and the protection of environment, which is outside the scope of art 36 EC Treaty [art 30 EC] should have been more clearly explained by the ECJ, taking into account that the ECJ has always emphasised that exceptions to art 30 EC Treaty [art 28 EC] must be strictly interpreted.

Criminal Proceedings against Heinonen Case C–394/97 [1999] ECR I–3599 European Court of Justice

• *Goods contained in traveller's personal luggage – travellers arriving from non-Member States – duty-free allowances – prohibition on imports linked to minimum period spent abroad – Council Regulation 918/83/EEC – Council Directive 69/169/EEC*

Facts

Under a Finnish decree on alcoholic drinks and spirits a resident of Finland who arrives in the country otherwise than by air transport from outside the European Economic Area, and whose journey has lasted for 20 hours at most, is not entitled to import any alcoholic drinks. Mr Heinonen, a resident in Finland, sailed from Finland to Tallin in Estonia and back in less than 20 hours. After his short trip, a routine customs check revealed that Mr Heinonen was in possession of 19 0.33 litre cans of beer. The customs authorities issued a notice ordering him to pay a fine for smuggling beer and ordering his beer to be confiscated. Mr Heinonen challenged that notice on the ground that his conduct was not liable to criminal penalties, as he was entitled under Community law to import freely at least the quantity of beer in question.

The Helsinki District Court asked the ECJ whether the Finnish decree was in conformity with Council Regulation 918/83 of 28 March 1983 which eliminated differences in the field of exemptions from customs duties for goods contained in the personal luggage of travellers coming from non-Member States (which complements Directive 69/169/EEC on exemptions from turnover tax and excise duty on imports in international travel).

Held

The ECJ held that the Finnish decree was in conformity with Community law.

Judgment

'[*The first question*]

By its first question, the national court is asking, essentially, whether national legislation prohibiting or restricting imports of certain goods by travellers arriving from non-Member countries on grounds of public morality, public policy, public security or protection of health and life of humans is contrary to Regulation No 918/83 and Directive 69/169.

As stated in the fourth recital in its preamble, the objective of Regulation No 918/83 is, in accordance with the requirements of the Customs Union, to eliminate differences in the field of exemptions from customs duties. More specifically, the objective of arts 45 to 49 is to simplify the clearance through customs of goods contained in the personal luggage of travellers coming from non-Member countries (Case 158/80 *Rewe* v *Hauptzollamt Kiel* [1981] ECR 1805, para 11), and thus to facilitate passenger traffic.

The purpose of Directive 69/169, as its

title suggests, is to harmonise exemptions from turnover tax and excise duty on imports in international travel. As is clear from the recitals in its preamble and from those in the preambles to the directives subsequently amending it, the aim is to liberalise the system of taxes on imports in travel in order to facilitate such travel.

The ninth recital in its preamble states, however, that Regulation No 918/83 does not preclude the application by Member States of import or export prohibitions or restrictions which are justified on grounds of public morality, public policy or public security, protection of health and life of humans, that it to say, grounds which, even in the context of intra-Community trade, are capable of justifying restrictions on the free movement of goods in accordance with art 36 of the EC Treaty (now, after amendment, art 30 EC).

The same interpretation must apply as regards Directive 69/169 which, like Regulation No 918/83, is limited to providing for a system of exemptions applicable to goods whose importation is not otherwise prohibited on one of the grounds set out in the preceding paragraph of this judgment.

It should be noted, in this connection, that both art 24(2)(a)(i) of Regulation No 3285/94 and art 19(2)(a)(i) of Regulation No 519/94 expressly provide that those Regulations are not to preclude the adoption or application by Member States of prohibitions, quantitative restrictions or surveillance measures on grounds of public morality, public policy, public security or the protection of health and life of humans.

It follows that, while Regulation No 918/83 and Directive 69/169 are intended to define the customs and tax rules applicable to imports of a non-commercial nature by travellers from non-Member countries, it is not the objective of that harmonising legislation to govern specifically the protection of the public policy interest requirements referred to in art 24(2)(a)(i) of Regulation No 3285/94 and art 19(2)(a)(i) of Regulation No 519/94, with the result that the Member States retain their competence to adopt the necessary measures to protect those requirements.

The answer to be given to the first question must therefore be that national legislation prohibiting or restricting imports of certain goods by travellers arriving from non-Member countries on grounds of public morality, public policy, public security or protection of health and life of humans is not contrary to Regulation No 918/83 and Directive 69/169.

[The second question]
By its second question the national court is asking, essentially, whether the circumstances described in para 18 of this judgment can be such as to justify a restriction on imports of alcoholic drinks by travellers arriving from third countries.

It must first of all be pointed out that economic considerations, such as the last two circumstances mentioned in para 18 of this judgment, are not included among the reasons which, according to art 24(2)(a)(i) of Regulation No 3285/94 and art 19(2)(a)(i) of Regulation No 519/94, may justify a restriction on imports of products from non-Member countries (see, by analogy, with respect to art 36 of the Treaty, Case 95/81 *EC Commission v Italy* [1982] 2187, para 27).

By contrast, maintenance of public order and protection of internal security are among the first group of interests referred to in art 24(2)(a)(1) of Regulation No 3285/94 and art 19(2)(a)(i) of Regulation No 519/94. The same is true of protection of health and life of humans, to which the campaign against alcoholism makes a contribution.

In those circumstances, the answer to be given to the second question must be that national legislation restricting imports of alcoholic drinks by travellers arriving from non-Member countries in order to maintain public order is not, in principle, contrary to Regulation No 918/83 or Directive 69/169.

[The third question]
By its third question, the national court is asking, essentially, whether national legislation restricting imports of alcoholic drinks,

including drinks with a low alcohol content, by travellers arriving from third countries on the basis of the duration of the journey, with a view to combating disturbances of public order connected with the consumption of alcohol is contrary to Regulation No 918/83 and Directive 69/169.

In order to clarify the meaning of that question, it should be borne in mind that, with regard to art 30 of the EC Treaty (now, after amendment, art 28 EC) and art 36 of the Treaty, the Court has stated that, while it is for the Member States to decide at what level they wish to protect the interests referred to in art 36 of the Treaty and how that level is to be attained, they may however do so only within the limits set by the Treaty and, in particular, in compliance with the principle of proportionality ...

As the Advocate-General has noted at point 28 of his Opinion, the point at issue here is therefore whether the measure adopted by the Finnish legislature is proportionate to the objective pursued.

However, while the objective pursued by arts 30 and 36 of the Treaty is to guarantee respect of the fundamental freedom which is the free movement of goods in the internal market, the objective of the Community customs and tax provisions at issue in the main proceedings is more restricted in that it is intended to facilitate passenger travel from non-Member countries in conformity with the requirements of the customs union.

The question whether or not the legislation in question in the main proceedings is appropriate and necessary must be considered in the light of those considerations.

As regards the question of its appropriateness, that legislation introduces only a limited derogation from the Community system of customs and tax reliefs applicable to travellers, since it covers only one specific category of goods, alcoholic drinks. That derogation is further limited by the fact that it relates only to journeys which satisfy precise criteria, namely journeys by land or sea lasting less than 20 hours.

Those limitations correspond to the typical circumstances singled out by the Finnish authorities as being the chief source of the social and health problems with which they were faced. The Finnish government has, moreover, stated that it was possible to detect an improvement in the situation as soon as the legislation at issue in the main proceedings was implemented. Those factors are such that it may properly be inferred from them that the legislation in question is appropriate.

With regard to the need for legislation such as that applicable in the main proceedings, the Commission claimed that, by establishing stricter checks on the movement of travellers, the Finnish authorities could have made better use of the opportunities offered by the Community legislation, such as strict application of the concept of "imports of a non-commercial nature", a reduction in the reliefs granted to frontier workers and crews of means of transport and refusing travellers making a purely token journey to another country any relief at all. The Finnish government replied that recourse to those options would have provided only an inadequate response to the problems it had to resolve. In addition, such recourse would have required material resources, particularly in the computer field, which were either not, or at least not immediately, available, whilst the authorities had to confront serious disturbances of public order connected with a sharp rise in the consumption of alcohol.

It should be pointed out that the Member States, which retain exclusive competence as regards the maintenance of public order and the safeguarding of internal security (Case C–265/95 *EC Commission v France* [1997] ECR I-6959, para 33), enjoy a margin of discretion in determining, according to particular social circumstances and to the importance attached by those States to a legitimate objective under Community law, such as the campaign against various forms of criminality linked to the consumption of alcohol, the measures which are likely to achieve concrete results.

In the circumstances described in para 18 of this judgment, the introduction of a restriction on imports of alcoholic drinks by travellers arriving from non-Member countries would seem to be a necessary measure, since the alternatives proposed by the Commission do not appear to be effective enough to attain the objective pursued.

Accordingly, the answer to be given to the third question must be that national legislation restricting imports by travellers arriving from third countries of alcoholic drinks, on the basis of the duration of the journey, with a view to combating disturbances of public order connected with the consumption of alcohol, is not contrary to Regulation No 918/83 or Directive 69/169.'

Comment

The ECJ held that both Regulation 918/83 and Directive 69/169 allow a Member State to adopt or apply prohibitions, quantitative restrictions or surveillance measures on grounds of public morality, public policy, public security or the protection of health and life of humans. Accordingly, a Member State is entitled to impose restrictions on imports of alcoholic drinks by travellers arriving from outside the EU: *Criminal Proceedings against Franzén* Case C–189/95 [1997] ECR I–5909. In the present case Finland invoked the exception based on maintenance of public order and the protection of internal security. However, the ECJ emphasised that national measures have to satisfy the requirements of art 28 EC, that is they must be necessary and proportionate. This applies even though the objectives of the Community measures in the present case were not to ensure the free movement of goods but to facilitate passenger traffic. Indeed, the objective of Regulation 918/83 is to simplify the clearance through customs of goods contained in the personal luggage of travellers coming from non-Member States, whilst the purpose of Directive 69/169 is to liberalise the system of taxes on imports in international travel. The ECJ stated that the different context in which the requirements of necessity and proportionality are to be applied should be taken into account by a national court which examines national measures.

The ECJ accepted the arguments of the Finnish government as to the necessity of national measures. In respect of proportionality the ECJ stated that in the area of maintenance of public order and the protection of internal security, Member States are solely competent to decide what measures are necessary to attain the objective pursued. They enjoy a large measure of discretion. It is submitted that the ECJ should have taken into consideration the Commission's proposal as to alternatives to restrictions on imports of alcoholic drinks by travellers arriving from non-Member States. Indeed, according to the ECJ decision in the present case, Member States enjoy total freedom as to the choice of national measures. This could permit a total ban on importation of alcoholic drinks by travellers arriving from non-Member States!

The protection of industrial and commercial property

Bayerische Motorenwerke AG (BMW) and BMW Netherland BV v Ronald Karel Deenik Case C–63/97 [1999] 1 CMLR 1099 European Court of Justice

• *Trade mark – infringement – arts 5–7 of Directive 89/104/EEC – unauthorised use of the BMW trade mark in advertisements for a garage business*

Facts
A German car manufacturer BMW and its Dutch branch BMW Netherlands brought an action against Mr Deenik, an independent owner of a garage specialising in the sale of second-hand BMW cars and repairs and maintenance of BMW cars, for using the BMW mark in advertisements of his business. The Hoge Raad (the Supreme Court of The Netherlands) considered that some of the advertisements might be unlawful as suggesting that Mr Deenik's business was affiliated to the trade-mark proprietor's distribution

network, whilst other uses of the trade mark such as 'repairs and maintenance of BMW' 'BMW specialist' did not constitute infringement of that mark. The Hoge Raad referred to the ECJ five questions concerning the interpretation of arts 5–7 of Directive 89/104/EEC for a preliminary ruling.

Held
The ECJ held that arts 5–7 of Directive 89/104/EEC prevent the proprietor of a trade mark from prohibiting a third party from using the mark for informing the public that he carries out the repair and maintenance work of goods protected by that mark and put on the market under that mark by the proprietor or with his consent, or that he has specialised or is a specialist in the sale or repair of such goods. However, a reseller is not permitted to use the mark to lead the public to believe that his business is affiliated to the trade mark proprietor's distribution network or that there is a special relationship between the two undertakings. The Court stated that the use of a trade mark, without the authorisation of its owner, for advertisement purposes such as described in the present case is within the scope of art 5 of Directive 89/104/EEC.

Judgment
'The Hoge Raad is asking the Court to interpret arts 5–7 of the Directive so that it can decide whether use of the BMW mark in advertisements such as "Repairs and maintenance of BMWs", "BMW specialist" or "Specialised in BMWs" constitutes infringement of that mark.

It should be borne in mind that arts 6 and 7 of the directive contain rules limiting the right of the proprietor of a trade mark, under art 5, to prohibit a third party from using his mark. In this connection, art 6 provides, inter alia, that the proprietor of a trade mark may not prohibit a third party from using the mark where it is necessary to indicate the intended purpose of a product, provided that he uses it in accordance with honest practices in industrial or commercial matters. Article 7 provides that the proprietor is not entitled to prohibit the use of a trade mark in relation to goods which have been put on the market in the Community under that trade mark by the proprietor or with his consent, unless there exist legitimate reasons for him to oppose further commercialisation of the goods.

[*Questions 2 and 3*]
Whether the use of a trade mark, without the proprietor's authorisation, in order to inform the public that another undertaking carries out repairs and maintenance of goods covered by that trade mark or that it has specialised, or is a specialist, in such goods constitutes a use of that mark for the purposes of one of the provisions of art 5 of the Directive.

[*Questions 4 and 5*]
The national court is in substance asking whether arts 5–7 of the Directive entitle the proprietor of a trade mark to prevent another person from using that mark for the purpose of informing the public that he carries out the repair and maintenance of goods covered by a trade mark and put on the market under that mark by the proprietor or with his consent, or that he has specialised or is a specialist in the sale or the repair and maintenance of such goods.

The Court is asked to rule, in particular, on the question whether the trade mark proprietor may prevent such use only where the advertiser creates the impression that his undertaking is affiliated to the trade mark proprietor's distribution network, or whether he may also prevent such use where, because of the manner in which the trade mark is used in the advertisements, there is a good chance that the public might be given the impression that the advertiser is using the trade mark in that regard to an appreciable extent for the purpose of advertising his own business as such, by creating a specific suggestion of quality.

That question must be considered, first, in relation to the advertisements for the sale of second-hand cars and, second, in relation to the advertisements for the repair and maintenance of cars.

[*The advertisements for the sale of second-hand BMW cars*]
Article 7 of the Directive for the proprietor of the BMW mark to prohibit the use of its mark by another person for the purpose of informing the public that he has specialised or is a specialist in the sale of second-hand BMW cars, provided that the advertising concerns cars which have been put on the Community market under that mark by the proprietor or with its consent and that the way in which the mark is used in that advertising does not constitute a legitimate reason, within the meaning of art 7(2), for the proprietor's opposition.

The fact that the trade mark is used in a reseller's advertising in such a way that it may give rise to the impression that there is a commercial connection between the reseller and the trade mark proprietor, and in particular that the reseller's business is affiliated to the trade mark proprietor's distribution network or that there is a special relationship between the two undertakings, may constitute a legitimate reason within the meaning of art 7(2) of the Directive.

If there is no risk that the public will be led to believe that there is a commercial connection between the reseller and the trade mark proprietor, the mere fact that the reseller derives an advantage from using the trade mark in that advertisements for the sale of goods covered by the mark, which are in other respects honest and fair, lend an aura of quality to his own business does not constitute a legitimate reason within the meaning of art 7(2) of the Directive.

It is sufficient to state that a reseller who sells second-hand BMW cars and who genuinely has specialised or is a specialist in the sale of those vehicles cannot in practice communicate such information to his customers without using the BMW mark. In consequence, such an informative use of the BMW mark is necessary to guarantee the right of resale under art 7 of the Directive and does not take unfair advantage of the distinctive character or repute of that trade mark.

[*The advertisements relating to repair and maintenance of BMW cars*]

So far as those advertisements are concerned, it is still necessary to consider whether use of the trade mark may be legitimate in the light of the rule laid down in art 6(1)(c) of the Directive, that the proprietor may not prohibit a third party from using the trade mark to indicate the intended purpose of a product or service, in particular as accessories or spare parts, provided that the use is necessary to indicate that purpose and is in accordance with honest practices in industrial or commercial matters.

If an independent trader carries out the maintenance and repair of BMW cars or is in fact a specialist in that field, that fact cannot in practice be communicated to his customers without using the BMW mark.'

Comment

In relation to art 5 of Directive 89/104/EEC the ECJ held that both the sale of second-hand BMW cars and the services such as repair and maintenance of BMW cars were within the scope of art 5 of the Directive. In order to determine whether the use of a trade mark is lawful for advertisement purposes the Court distinguished between the sale of goods covered by that trade mark and their repair and maintenance. In the first case, the ECJ confirmed its decision in *Parfums Christian Dior* Case C–337/95 (see below), that is that a reseller is entitled to make use of the trade mark to bring to the public's attention their further commercialisation, although the owner of a trade mark may stop a reseller from using his trade marks if advertisement damages the reputation of the trade marks. If the reseller advertises the goods covered by a trade mark in a manner customary to the resellers sector of trade, the owner of a trade mark may invoke art 7(2) of Directive 89/104/EEC to prohibit the use of its mark by a reseller in special circumstances. It occurs when a reseller advertises in such a manner as to induce the public to believe that there is a commercial connection between the two undertakings. This kind of advertisement is dishonest, unfair and harms legitimate interests of the trade mark

owner. However, if there is no risk that the public will have the impression that there is a commercial connection between the two undertakings, the reseller may derive advantage from using the trade mark in the advertisement, in particular to enhance the quality of his business.

In respect of the advertisement for repair and maintenance of BMW cars, the rule of the 'exhaustion of rights' does not apply as there is no further commercialisation of goods. In this context art 6(1)(c) of the Directive lays down the conditions for using a trade mark. A third party is entitled to use the trade mark to indicated the intended purpose of products or services, in particular as accessories or spare parts, provided that the use is necessary to indicate that purpose. In this context, the use of a trade mark is lawful provided there is no risk that the public will be induced to believe that there is a commercial link between the two undertakings.

Parfums Christian Dior SA and Parfums Christian Dior BV v *Evora BV* Case C–337/95 [1997] ECR I–6013; [1998] 1 CMLR 234
European Court of Justice

• *Trade marks and the free movement of goods – meaning of 'exhaustion of rights' in relation to the further commercialisation of the protected goods by a nonauthorised reseller – interpretation of arts 5–7 of the First Directive 89/104/EEC on the approximation of the laws of the Member States relating to trade marks*

Facts

The French company Parfums Christian Dior SA (Dior France) and the Dutch company Parfums Christian Dior BV (Dior Netherlands) brought an action against the Dutch company Evora, which operates a chain of chemists' shops under the name of its subsidiary Kruidvat, for infringement of Dior trade marks and copyrights and applied for an order to stop Evora from advertising Dior products in a manner which damaged the luxurious image of Dior products. In a Christmas promotion in 1993 Kruidvat advertised some Dior products. Advertising leaflets of Evora depicted packaging and bottles of some Dior products which, according to the judgment of the referring court, related clearly and directly to the good offered for sale. The advertisement itself was carried out in a manner customary to retailers in this market sector. Kruidvat was neither a distributor of Dior France nor of Dior Netherlands. Dior products sold by the Kruidvat shops were supplied by Evora which obtained them by means of parallel imports.

The President of the Rechbank (lower court) granted Dior's application. On appeal by Evora against that order the Regional Court of Amsterdam set it aside. Dior appealed against that judgment to the Hoge Raad. The Supreme Court of The Netherlands (Hoge Raad) decided that the question of interpretation of the Uniform Benelux Law on Trade Marks should be dealt with by the Benelux Court and the questions on Community law should be referred to the ECJ. In this context the Hoge Raad referred to the ECJ the following questions.

1. Is the Benelux Court or the referring court to be regarded as the court or tribunal against whose decisions there is no judicial remedy under national law and therefore obliged to refer under art 177(3) EC Treaty?
2. On the interpretation of arts 5–7 of Directive 89/104/EEC and, in particular, whether a reseller is entitled to make use of the trade mark to bring to the public's attention the further commercialisation of goods when those trade-marked goods have been previously put on the Community market by or with the consent of the proprietor of the trade mark.
3. The application of the 'exhaustion of rights' rule in the light of art 7(2) of the Directive.
4. The rights of the owner of a trade mark or holder of copyright vis-à-vis a reseller in the context of the free movement of goods.

Held

The ECJ held that under arts 5 and 7 of Directive 89/104 when the owner of the trade mark, either directly or by the grant of licences to a third party, has put trade-marked goods on the Community market a reseller is entitled both to resell those goods and to make use of the trade mark in order to bring to the public's attention the further commercialisation of those goods. However, the owner of a trade mark may by virtue of art 7(2) of the Directive oppose the use of the trade mark for the further commercialisation of protected goods by a non-authorised reseller but only if it is established in the light of the specific circumstances of the case that the use of the trade mark for this purpose seriously damages the reputation of the trade mark.

Similarly, in the context of the free movement of goods, the owner of a trade mark or holder of copyright cannot prevent a reseller who habitually markets, in ways customary in the reseller's sector of trade, articles of the same kind as the protected goods, but not necessarily of the same quality, from using a trade mark or a copyright for the purpose of advertisement of protected goods unless it is established, taking into account the circumstances of a particular case, that the use of those goods for that purpose seriously damages their reputation.

Judgment

'[The first question]
By its first question, the Hoge Raad asks whether, in a case where a question relating to the interpretation of the Directive is raised in proceedings in one of the Benelux Member States concerning the interpretation of the Uniform Benelux Law on Trade Marks, it is the highest national court or the Benelux Court which is the national court against whose decisions there is no judicial remedy under national law and which is therefore obliged under the third paragraph of art 177 of the Treaty to make a reference to the Court of Justice.

First of all, it appears that the question submitted by the Hoge Raad is based, quite rightly, on the premises that a court such as the Benelux Court is a court which may submit questions to this Court for a preliminary ruling.

There is no good reason why such a court, common to a number of Member States, should not be able to submit questions to this Court, in the same way as courts or tribunals of any of those Member States.

In this regard, particular account must be taken of the fact that the Benelux Court has the task of ensuring that the legal rules common to the three Benelux States are applied uniformly and of the fact that the procedure before it is a step in the proceedings before the national courts leading to definitive interpretations of common Benelux legal rules.

To allow a court, like the Benelux Court, faced with the task of interpreting Community rules in the performance of its function, to follow the procedure provided for by art 177 of the Treaty would therefore serve the purpose of that provision, which is to ensure the uniform interpretation of Community law.

Next, as regards the question whether a court like the Benelux Court may be under an obligation to refer a question to the Court of Justice, it is to be remembered that, according to the third paragraph of art 177 of the Treaty, where a question of Community law is raised in a case pending before a court or tribunal of a Member State against whose decisions there is no judicial remedy under national law, that court or tribunal must bring the matter before the Court of Justice.

In these circumstances, in so far as no appeal lies against decisions of a court like the Benelux Court, which gives definitive rulings on questions of interpretation of uniform Benelux law, such a court may be obliged to make a reference to this Court under the third paragraph of art 177 where a question relating to the interpretation of the Directive is raised before it.

As regards, further, the question whether the Hoge Raad may be obliged to refer questions to this Court, there is no question that such a national supreme court, against

whose decisions likewise no appeal lies under national law, may not give judgment without first making a reference to this Court under the third paragraph of art 177 of the Treaty when a question relating to the interpretation of Community law is raised before it.

However, it does not necessarily follow that, in a situation such as that described by the Hoge Raad, both courts are actually obliged to make a reference to this Court.

If, prior to making a reference to the Benelux Court, a court like the Hoge Raad has made use of its power to submit the question raised to the Court of Justice, the authority of the interpretation given by the latter may remove from a court like the Benelux Court its obligation to submit a question in substantially the same terms before giving its judgment. Conversely, if no reference has been made to the Court of Justice by a court like the Hoge Raad, a court like the Benelux Court must submit the question to the Court of Justice, whose ruling may then remove from the Hoge Raad the obligation to submit a question in substantially the same terms before giving its judgment.

[The second question]

By its second question, the Hoge Raad asks in substance whether, on a proper interpretation of arts 5–7 of the Directive, when trade-marked goods have been put on the Community market by or with the consent of the proprietor of the trade mark, a reseller, besides being free to resell those goods, is also free to make use of the trade mark to bring to the public's attention the further commercialisation of those goods.

If the right to prohibit the use of his trade mark in relation to goods, conferred on the proprietor of a trade mark under art 5 of the Directive, is exhausted once the goods have been put on the market by himself or with his consent, the same applies as regards the right to use the trade mark for the purpose of bringing to the public's attention the further commercialisation of those goods.

It follows from the case law of the Court that art 7 of the Directive is to be interpreted in the light of the rules of the Treaty relating to the free movement of goods, in particular art 36 and that the purpose of the "exhaustion of rights" rule is to prevent owners of trade marks from being allowed to partition national markets and thus facilitate the maintenance of price differences which may exist between Member States.

Even if the right to make use of a trade mark in order to attract attention to further commercialisation were not exhausted in the same way as the right of resale, the latter would be made considerably more difficult and the purpose of the "exhaustion of rights" rule laid down in art 7 would thus be undermined.

[*The third question*]

According to art 7(2) of the Directive, the "exhaustion of rights" rule laid down in para (1) is not applicable where there are legitimate reasons for the proprietor to oppose further commercialisation of trade-marked goods, especially where the condition of the goods is changed or impaired after they have been put on the market.

It follows that, where a reseller makes use of a trade mark in order to bring the public's attention to further commercialisation of trade-marked goods, a balance must be struck between the legitimate interest of the trade mark owner in being protected against resellers using his trade mark for advertising in a manner which could damage the reputation of the trade mark and the reseller's legitimate interest in being able to resell the goods in question by using advertising methods which are customary in his sector of trade.

As regards the instant case, which concerns prestigious, luxury goods, the reseller must not act unfairly in relation to the legitimate interests of the trade mark owner. He must therefore endeavour to prevent his advertising from affecting the value of the trade mark by detracting from the allure and prestigious image of the goods in question and from their aura of luxury.

For example, such serious damage to the reputation of the trade mark could occur if, in an advertising leaflet distributed by him,

the reseller did not take care to avoid putting the trade mark in a context which might seriously detract from the image which the trade mark owner has succeeded in creating around his trade mark.

[*The fourth question*]

By its ... question the Hoge Raad asks in substance whether arts 30 and 36 of the Treaty preclude the owner of a trade mark or holder of copyright relating to the bottles and packaging which he uses for his goods from preventing a reseller, by invoking the trade mark right or copyright, from advertising the further commercialisation of those goods in a manner customary to retail traders in the relevant sector. It asks, further, whether this is also the case where the reseller, as a result of the manner in which he uses the trade mark in his advertising material, damages the luxurious and prestigious image of the trade mark, or where the publication or reproduction of the trade mark takes place in circumstances liable to cause damage to the person entitled to the copyright.

Contrary to Dior's contention, the national court is quite right in considering that a prohibition such as that envisaged in the main proceedings may constitute a measure having an effect equivalent to a quantitative restriction, in principle prohibited by art 30. In this regard, it is enough that, according to the judgment referring the questions for a preliminary ruling, the main proceedings concern goods which the reseller has procured through parallel imports and that a prohibition of advertising such as that sought in the main proceedings would render commercialisation, and consequently access to the market for those goods, appreciably more difficult.

As regards the question relating to trade mark rights, it is to be remembered that, according to the case law of the Court, art 36 of the Treaty and art 7 of the Directive are to be interpreted in the same way.

As regards the part of the ... question relating to copyright, it is to be remembered that, according to the case law of the Court, the grounds of protection of industrial and commercial property referred to in art 36 include the protection conferred by copyright.

Literary and artistic works may be the subject of commercial exploitation, whether by way of public performance or by way of the reproduction and marketing of the recordings made of them, and the two essential rights of the author, namely the exclusive right of performance and the exclusive right of reproduction, are not called in question by the rules of the Treaty.

It is also clear from the case law that, while the commercial exploitation of copyright is a source of remuneration for the copyright owner, it also constitutes a form of control on marketing exercisable by the owner and that, from this point of view, commercial exploitation of copyright raises the same issues as that of any other industrial or commercial property.

Having regard to that case law – there being no need to consider the question whether copyright and trade mark rights may be relied on simultaneously in respect of the same product – it is sufficient to hold that, in circumstances such as those in point in the main proceedings, the protection conferred by copyright as regards the reproduction of protected works in a reseller's advertising may not, in any event, be broader than that which is conferred on a trade mark owner in the same circumstances.'

Comment

The most important question in this case concerned the meaning of the 'exhaustion of rights' in relation to trade marks and copyrights in the situation where a non-authorised reseller, who has obtained protected goods by means of parallel import, proceeds to their further commercialisation, particularly by using trade marks and copyrights to advertise those goods.

The ECJ held that a proper interpretation of arts 5–7 requires that when trade-marked goods have been put on the Community market by or with the consent of the owner of the trade mark, a reseller is entitled not only to resell those goods but also to make use of

the trade mark to bring to the public's attention their further commercialisation. Although the rights to make use of a trade mark by the reseller for advertisement purposes are not exhausted in the same way as the right to their resale, the latter would be more difficult if further commercialisation of those goods is not covered by the concept of the 'exhaustion of rights'.

However, the ECJ held that in some circumstances the owner of a trade mark may stop a reseller from advertising the further commercialisation of goods. The legitimate interests of the trade-mark owner must be protected, especially when a reseller is using his trade marks for advertising in a manner which could damage the reputation of the trade marks. In this respect the ECJ emphasised that by virtue of art 7(2) of Directive 89/104 the trade-mark owner may prevent the reputation of his trade mark from being damaged by a reseller. This solution is not new (see for example *Bristol-Myers Squibb* v *Paranova A/S* Cases C–427, 429 and 436/93 [1996] ECR I–3457). However, the ECJ has not particularised the conditions in which the trade-mark owner may control a non-authorised reseller advertising the further commercialisation of protected goods under Community law. The ECJ based its conclusions on art 7(2) of Directive 89/104 and limited its reasoning to the present case. According to the ECJ in order to strike a balance between the legitimate interests of the trade-mark owner regarding the image of luxury which he has created around his trade mark and the right of a reseller to commercialise the protected goods by using advertising methods which are customary in his sector of trade, the reseller must endeavour to prevent his advertising from affecting the value of the trade mark by detracting from the allure and prestigious image of the goods in question and from their aura of luxury. This requirement is particularly difficult to satisfy, taking into account the fact that the reseller is not an authorised distributor of Dior products.

This may lead to surprising results under

national law. In many Member States, for example in France, a non-authorised distributor is obliged not to follow too closely the methods of sale and advertisement put in place by the trade mark owner in relation to his network of exclusive distributors. Furthermore, this solution is particularly troublesome for manufacturers and exclusive distributors of luxury perfumes as it places them is a precarious situation. Community competition law has gradually determined the legal framework for agreements between manufacturers and exclusive distributors of perfumes (*Yves Saint-Laurent et Givenchy* Cases T–19 and 88/92 [1996] ECR II–1851, 1931 and 1961). However, now under the free movement of goods (as interpreted in this case), the ECJ introduces insecurity since it permits non-authorised distributors to advertise and to further commercialise the protected goods. The obvious consequence for the authorised distributors is that they may loose their customers.

The ECJ held that in the context of the free movement of goods (that is under arts 30 and 36 EC Treaty [arts 28 and 30 EC]) the owner of the trade mark or holder of copyright is precluded in relation to bottles and packaging from preventing the reseller from advertising the further commercialisation of those goods in a manner customary to the reseller sector of trade unless it is established in the light of the specific circumstances of the case that the use of those goods for that purpose damages their reputation. The ECJ held that the restriction imposed upon a reseller regarding the advertisement of protected goods may constitute a quantitative restriction contrary to art 30 EC Treaty [art 28 EC] since it would render commercialisation and consequent access to the market for those goods more difficult. As a result, arts 36 EC Treaty [art 30 EC] and 7 of Directive 89/104 should be interpreted in the same way.

The ECJ transposes its solution in respect to trade marks to copyright. This solution is surprising since under Community law trade marks and copyrights are treated differently in the context of the 'exhaustion of rights'. In relation to copyright Community law has always made distinction between those rights which by their nature may be 'exhausted', for instance the right of parallel imports once literary and artistic works have been put into circulation in a Member State (*Musik-Vertrieb* v *GEMA* Joined Cases 55/80 and 57/80 [1981] ECR 147), and those which cannot be 'exhausted', such as the right to hire video cassettes in *Warner Brothers Inc* v *Christiansen* Case 158/86 [1988] ECR 2605, and see also *Coditel SA* v *Ciné Vog Films* Case 62/79 [1980] ECR 881. Also, a draft directive on copyright submitted on 10 December 1997 favours a more generous approach to copyright protection in the Community and proposes important limitations on the exhaustion principle. This is not the case with trade marks in respect of which Community law does not impose restrictions on the concept of the 'exhaustion of rights'. Therefore, it seems that copyrights and trade marks should not be treated in the same way. This is not the approach of the ECJ.

The ECJ held that the Benelux Court is within the scope of art 177(3) EC Treaty [art 234 EC]. The ECJ has also explained the circumstances in which both courts – the Hoge Raad and the Benelux Court – are obliged to make a referral. Subject to the *CILFIT* guidelines, the Benelux Court and the Hoge Raad, as courts of last resort, are obliged to refer to the ECJ. In the case of the Hoge Raad, the Supreme Court of The Netherlands if, prior to making a reference to the Benelux Court on matters of interpretation of the Benelux Treaties, it refers to the ECJ, the Benelux Court has to accept a preliminary ruling of the ECJ and is not obliged to submit to the ECJ a question in substantially the same terms before deciding the matter. However, the Benelux Court is obliged to refer to the ECJ if the Hoge Raad decides not to ask for a preliminary ruling.

SABEL BV v *Puma AG, Rudolf Dassler Sport* Case C–151/95 [1998] 1 CMLR 445 European Court of Justice

• *Trade marks and the free movement of goods – Directive 89/104 on approximation of laws relating to trade marks – conditions of validity of registration of trade marks – risk of confusion – likelihood of association*

Facts

Puma AG, a German company, brought proceedings against a Dutch company, SABEL BV, opposing the registration of a trade mark, under the international registration system of the Madrid Arrangement, by SABEL in Germany on the basis that ideas conveyed by the pictorial elements of the mark consisting of the name of SABEL and the representation of a running leopard conflicted with Puma's trade mark of a running puma. Both companies sold similar goods, that is leather and imitation leather products. The German Supreme Court, the Bundesgerichtshof, referred to the ECJ for a preliminary ruling a question on the interpretation of art 4(1)(b) of First Council Directive 89/104. This sets out the additional grounds on which registration of a trade mark may be refused or a registered mark declared invalid if, due to similarity or identity of an earlier registered trade mark with the trade mark to be registered (or already registered but later than the first trade mark) there is a likelihood of confusion of both trade marks on the part of the public, which includes the likelihood of association between the two marks. The German court asked the ECJ to clarify the meaning of the criterion 'likelihood of confusion ... which includes the likelihood of association with the earlier trade mark'.

Held

The ECJ held that the criterion of the 'likelihood of confusion ... which includes the likelihood of association with the earlier trade mark' contained in art 4(1)(b) of Directive 89/104 is to be interpreted as meaning that the mere association which the public might make between two trade marks resulting from a similarity of their semantic content does not constitute in itself a sufficient ground for concluding that there is a likelihood of confusion within the meaning of that provision. Consequently, the registration of a mark cannot be opposed on the ground that there is a similarity between it and another mark unless it is established that there is genuine and properly substantiated likelihood of confusion about the origin of the products or services in question, which should be assessed globally, taking into account all factors relevant to the circumstances of the case.

Judgment

'In its question the Bundesgerichtshof is essentially asking whether the criterion of the "likelihood of confusion ... which includes the likelihood of association with the earlier trade mark" contained in art 4(1) of the Directive is to be interpreted as meaning that the mere association which the public might make between the two marks as a result of a resemblance in their semantic content, is a sufficient ground for concluding that there exists a likelihood of confusion within the meaning of that provision, taking into account that one of those marks is composed of a combination of a word and a picture, whilst the other, consisting merely of a picture, is registered for identical and similar goods, and is not especially well known to the public.

Article 4(1)(b) of the Directive, which sets out the additional grounds on which registration may be refused or a registered mark declared invalid in the event of conflict with earlier marks, provides that a trade mark conflicts with an earlier trade mark if, because of the identity or similarity of both the trade marks and the goods or services covered, there exists a likelihood of confusion on the part of the public, which includes the likelihood of association between the two marks.

... In that connection, it is to be remembered that art 4(1)(b) of the Directive is designed to apply only if, by reason of the identity or similarity both of the marks and of the goods or services which they designate, "their exists a likelihood of confusion on the part of the public, which includes the likelihood of association with the earlier trade mark". It follows from that wording that the concept of likelihood of association is not an alternative to that of likelihood of confusion, but serves to define its scope. The terms of the provision itself exclude its application where there is no likelihood of confusion on the part of the public.

In that respect, it is clear from the tenth recital in the preamble to the Directive that the appreciation of the likelihood of confusion "depends on numerous elements and, in particular, on the recognition of the trade mark on the market, of the association which can be made with the used or registered sign, of the degree of similarity between the goods or services identified". The likelihood of confusion must therefore be appreciated globally, taking into account all factors relevant to the circumstances of the case.

The global appreciation of the visual, aural or conceptual similarity of the marks in question, must be based on the overall impression given by the marks, bearing in mind, in particular, their distinctive and dominant components.

In that perspective, the more distinctive the earlier mark, the greater will be the likelihood of confusion. It is therefore not impossible that the conceptual similarity resulting from the fact that two marks use images with analogous semantic content may give rise to a likelihood of confusion where the earlier mark has a particularly distinctive character, either per se or because of the reputation it enjoys with the public.

However. in circumstances such as those in point in the main proceedings, where the earlier mark is not especially well known to the public and consists of an image with little imaginative content, the mere fact that the two marks are conceptually similar is not sufficient to give rise to a likelihood of confusion.'

Comment

The ECJ held that the likelihood of confusion between the two trade marks depends upon the distinctiveness of the earlier mark either per se or because of the reputation its enjoys with the public. As a result, the criterion of 'likelihood of confusion which includes the likelihood of association with an earlier mark' means that the mere association which the consumers might make between two trade mark with analogous semantic content does not constitute in itself a sufficient ground for concluding that there is a likelihood of confusion.

The decision of the ECJ in the present case is in line with the objective of abolishing obstacles to the free movement of goods but at odds with its earlier decisions. For example in *SA CNL Sucal NV* v *Hag GF AG (Hag II)* Case C–10/89 [1990] ECR I–3711 the holder was allowed to rely on his trade mark to exclude products made by a third party but bearing a trade mark with a common origin to his, in a manner that would partition the common market. The likelihood of confusion between both products was an essential factor in deciding the case. In this respect the ECJ held that:

'To determine the exact effect of this exclusive right which is granted to the owner of the mark, it is necessary to take account of the essential function of the mark, which is to give the consumer or final user a guarantee of the identity of the origin of the marked product by enabling him to distinguish, without any possible confusion, that product from others of a different provenance.'

This approach was confirmed and intensified in *IHT Internationale Heiztechnik GmbH* v *Ideal Standard GmbH* Case C–9/93 [1994] ECR I–2789. The change of approach by the ECJ should be viewed in the light of considerable unification of intellectual property law by the Community. Furthermore, the change in attitude of the ECJ can be explained by the requirements of both the internal and the international market. In the context of the internal market the monopolistic tendencies of non-origin association is contrary to the free movement of goods and free competition. As to the international aspect this was discussed by Advocate-General Jacobs who placed Directive 89/104 and particularly the concept of confusion against the background of the Paris Convention for the Protection of Industrial Property of 20 March 1883 (as revised) and the GATT/TRIPs Agreement under which this concept is considered as the foundation for trade-mark protection.

Sebago Inc v *GB–Unic SA* Case C–173/98 [1999] ECR I–4103; [1999] 2 CMLR 1317 European Court of Justice

• *Trade marks – exhaustion of rights – art 7(1) of Directive 89/104 – concept of consent*

Facts

Sebago Inc (a company incorporated in the USA) the proprietor of two trade marks in the name of 'Docksides' and three trade marks in the name of 'Sebago' all registered in the Benelux countries for shoes, and Ancienne Maison Dubois et Fils SA, an exclusive distributor in the Benelux countries of shoes bearing Sebago's trade marks, brought joint proceedings against GB-Unic SA for infringement of Sebago's trade mark rights by the marketing of shoes in the Community without Sebago's consent. GB-Unic SA advertised and sold in its Maxi-GB hypermarkets in Belgium 2,561 pairs of 'Docksides' Sebago shoes manufactured in El Salvador, which it purchased from a Belgian company specialising in parallel importation. Sebago did not contest the fact that the shoes so sold were genuine Sebago shoes.

Held

The ECJ held that art 7(1) of Directive 89/104 was to be interpreted as meaning that, first, the rights conferred by the trade mark were exhausted only if the product had been put on

the market in the EEA (European Economic Area), second, this provision did not leave it open to the Member States to provide in their domestic legislation for exhaustion of the rights conferred by the trade mark in respect of products put on the market in non-Member States, and third, the concept of consent within the meaning of art 7(1) of Directive 89/104 is that it must relate to each individual item of the product in respect of which exhaustion is pleaded.

Judgment

'In its judgment of 16 July 1998 in Case C–355/96 *Silhouette International Schmied* v *Hartlauer* [1998] ECR I-4799, which was delivered after the national court made its order for reference in the present case, the Court held that national rules providing for exhaustion of trade-mark rights in respect of products put on the market outside the European Economic Area ("the EEA") under that mark by the proprietor or with his consent are contrary to art 7(1) of the Directive, as amended by the EEA Agreement.

The parties to the main proceedings, the French government and the Commission take the view that the Court answered the first three questions in *Silhouette*, so that it is necessary to answer only the last two.

As to those last two questions, Sebago, Maison Dubois, the French government and the Commission contend that the consent of the trade mark proprietor to the marketing in the EEA of one batch of goods does not exhaust the rights conferred by the trade mark as regards the marketing of other batches of his goods even if they are identical.

GB-Unic considers, on the other hand, that art 7 of the Directive does not require that the consent relate to the actual goods involved in the parallel import. It bases its argument, in particular, on the concept of the essential function of the trade mark, which, according to the case law of the Court, is to guarantee to the consumer the identity of the product's origin, the object being to enable him to distinguish that product without any risk of confusion from those of different origin. However, according to GB-Unic, that function does not imply that the proprietor has the right to prohibit the importation of genuine goods. It would thus be wrong to argue that art 7 of the Directive refers only to the consent of the proprietor to the marketing of imported individual items of original goods. GB-Unic thus takes the view that there is consent within the meaning of art 7 of the Directive if the consent relates to the type of goods in question.

The Court finds, first, that the interveners in the present case are correct in submitting that the answer to the first three questions referred has already been given by the Court in *Silhouette*. The Court held, in paras 18 and 26 of that judgment, that, according to the text of art 7 of the Directive itself, rights conferred by the mark are exhausted only if the products have been put on the market in the Community (in the EEA since the EEA Agreement entered into force) and that the Directive does not leave it open to the Member States to provide in their domestic law for exhaustion of the rights conferred by the trade mark in respect of products put on the market in non-Member countries.

Next, it should be noted that, by its last two questions, the national court is asking essentially whether there is consent within the meaning of art 7 of the Directive where the trade mark proprietor has consented to the marketing in the EEA of goods which are identical or similar to those in respect of which exhaustion is claimed or if, on the other hand, consent must relate to each individual item of the product in respect of which exhaustion is claimed.

The text of art 7(1) of the Directive does not give a direct answer to that question. Nevertheless, the rights conferred by the trade mark are exhausted only in respect of the individual items of the product which have been put on the market with the proprietor's consent in the territory there defined. The proprietor may continue to prohibit the use of the mark in pursuance of the right conferred on him by the Directive in regard to individual items of that product which

have been put on the market in that territory without his consent.

That is the interpretation of art 7(1) that the Court has already adopted. Thus, the Court has already held that the purpose of that provision is to make possible the further marketing of an individual item of a product bearing a trade mark that has been put on the market with the consent of the trade mark proprietor and to prevent him from opposing such marketing (Case C–337/95 *Parfums Christian Dior SA and Parfums Christian Dior BV* v *Evora* [1997] ECR I–6013, paras 37 and 38, and Case C–63/97 *BMW* v *Deenik* [1999] ECR I–905, para 57). That interpretation is, moreover, confirmed by art 7(2) of the Directive which, in its reference to the "further commercialisation" of goods, shows that the principle of exhaustion concerns only specific goods which have first been put on the market with the consent of the trade mark proprietor.

Furthermore, in adopting art 7 of the Directive, which limits exhaustion of the right conferred by the trade mark to cases where the goods bearing the mark have been put on the market in the Community (in the EEA since the EEA Agreement entered into force), the Community legislature has made it clear that putting such goods on the market outside that territory does not exhaust the proprietor's right to oppose the importation of those goods without his consent and thereby to control the initial marketing in the Community (in the EEA since the EEA Agreement entered into force) of goods bearing the mark. That protection would be devoid of substance if, for there to be exhaustion within the meaning of art 7, it were sufficient for the trade mark proprietor to have consented to the putting on the market in that territory of goods which were identical or similar to those in respect of which exhaustion is claimed.'

Comment

The ECJ cofirmed its judgment in *Silhouette International* Case C–355/96 ([1998 ECR I–4799) in respect of the principle of international exhaustion. The ECJ held that national rules providing for exhaustion of trade mark rights in respect of products put on the market outside the EEA under that mark by the proprietor or with his consent were contrary to art 7(1) of Directive 89/104.

The interesting aspect of the present case is that the ECJ clarified the meaning of consent under art 7(1) of Directive 89/104. The ECJ restrictively interpreted the conditions under which the trade mark owner's consent is deemed to have been given for the purposes of the exhaustion of his trade mark rights. Such consent must relate to each individual item of the product in respect of which exhaustion is pleaded. Therefore, the consent of Sebago to the marketing in the EEA of one batch of shoes bearing the mark does not exhaust its trade mark rights in relation to the marketing of other batches of identical or similar shoes bearing the same mark, the marketing of which in the EEA Sebago has not consented to. This means that a particular product sold by, or with consent of, the trade mark proprietor within the EEA could be resold freely within the territory of the EEA under the exhaustion principle, although a particular product sold by, or with the consent of, the trade mark proprietor outside the EEA could not then be simiralrly resold freely within the EEA even if the trade mark proprietor authorises sale within the EEA of an identical product.

15 Article 81 EC

Bayer AG v Commission of the European Communities Case T–41/96 [2001] CMLR 4 Court of First Instance

• *Article 81(1) EC – parallel imports – meaning of agreement between undertakings – proof of the existence of an agreement – pharmaceutical products*

Facts

Bayer AG (one of the most important chemical and pharmaceutical groups in Europe which has subsidiaries in all the Member States) brought proceedings before the CFI challenging Commission Decision 96/478/EC in the case of *Adalat* (OJ L201 (1996)) in which Bayer was found to be in breach of art 81(1) EC.

Under the trade mark 'Adalat' or 'Adalate' Bayer AG had manufactured and marketed a range of medicinal preparations designed to treat cardio-vascular disease. In a number of Member States the price for 'Adalat' was directly determined by the national health authorities. Between 1989 and 1993 in France and Spain the price was 40 per cent lower than the price in the United Kingdom. The price difference had encouraged parallel imports of 'Adalat' from France and Spain to the UK. According to Bayer, sales of 'Adalat' by its British subsidiary fell by almost half between 1989 and 1993. In order to recover the lost profit, Bayer AG decided to cease fulfilling all of the increasingly large orders placed by wholesalers in Spain and France with its Spanish and French subsidiaries. Some French and Spanish wholesalers complained to the Commission. Following its investigations the Commission found that Bayer AG was in breach of art 81(1) EC. The Commission

decided that the prohibition on the export to other Member States of 'Adalat' from France and Spain agreed between Bayer France and its wholesalers since 1991, and between Bayer Spain and its wholesalers since 1989, constituted a breach of art 81(1) EC. Bayer AG argued that the Commission went too far in its interpretation of the concept of an agreement within the meaning of art 81(1) EC and that in fact Bayer AG's unilateral conduct was outside the scope of that Article.

Held

The CFI annulled Decision 96/478/EC.

Judgment

'[*The concept of an agreement within the meaning of art 85(1) of the Treaty*]
The case law shows that, where a decision on the part of a manufacturer constitutes unilateral conduct of the undertaking, that decision escapes the prohibition in art 85(1) of the Treaty.

It is also clear from the case law in that in order for there to be an agreement within the meaning of art 85(1) of the Treaty it is sufficient that the undertakings in question should have expressed their joint intention to conduct themselves on the market in a specific way.

As regards the form in which that common intention is expressed, it is sufficient for a stipulation to be the expression of the parties' intention to behave on the market in accordance with its terms, without its having to constitute a valid and binding contract under national law.

It follows that the concept of an agreement within the meaning of art 85(1) of the Treaty, as interpreted by the case law, centres around the existence of a concurrence of wills between at least two parties, the form in which it is manifested being unimportant so long as it constitutes the faithful expression of the parties' intention.

In certain circumstances, measures adopted or imposed in an apparently unilateral manner by a manufacturer in the context of his continuing relations with his distributors have been regarded as constituting an agreement within the meaning of art 85(1) of the Treaty.

That case law shows that a distinction should be drawn between cases in which an undertaking has adopted a genuinely unilateral measure, and thus without the express or implied participation of another undertaking, and those in which the unilateral character of the measure is merely apparent. Whilst the former do not fall within art 85(1) of the Treaty, the latter must be regarded as revealing an agreement between undertakings and may therefore fall within the scope of that Article. That is the case, in particular, with practices and measures in restraint of competition which, though apparently adopted unilaterally by the manufacturer in the context of its contractual relations with its dealers, nevertheless receive at least the tacit acquiescence of those dealers.

It is also clear from that case law that the Commission cannot hold that apparently unilateral conduct on the part of a manufacturer, adopted in the context of the contractual relations which he maintains with his dealers, in reality forms the basis of an agreement between undertakings within the meaning of art 85(1) of the Treaty if it does not establish the existence of an acquiescence by the other partners, express or implied, in the attitude adopted by the manufacturer.

[*The application of the concept of an agreement in this case*]
In this case, in the absence of direct documentary evidence of the conclusion of an agreement between the parties concerning the limitation or reduction of exports, the Commission has held that the concurrence of wills underlying that agreement is clear from the conduct of the applicant and the wholesalers referred to in the Decision respectively.

Thus, in the Decision, the Commission states (recital 155) that "Bayer France and Bayer Spain have committed an infringement of art 85(1)" of the Treaty and that the conditions for applying that Article were met because those subsidiaries imposed "an export ban as part of their continuous commercial relations with their customers". It then states (recital 156) that "analysis of the conduct engaged in by Bayer France and Bayer Spain vis-à-vis their wholesalers shows that Bayer France and Bayer Spain have imposed an export ban in their commercial relations with their wholesalers" and presents it as an established fact (recital 176) that the wholesalers adopted "an implicit acquiescence in the export ban".

Where, therefore, the Commission refers in the Decision to the "export ban", it views it as a unilateral demand which has formed the subject matter of an agreement between the applicant and the wholesalers. If the Commission concluded that an agreement existed contrary to art 85(1) of the Treaty, it did so because it considered it established that the applicant sought and obtained an agreement with its wholesalers in Spain and France, the purpose of which was to prevent or limit parallel imports.

The applicant acknowledges having introduced a unilateral policy designed to reduce parallel imports. However, it denies having planned and imposed an export ban. In that regard, it denies ever having had discussions with the wholesalers, let alone making an agreement with them, in order to prevent them from exporting or to limit them in the export of the quantities delivered. Moreover, it states that the wholesalers did not adhere in any way to its unilateral policy and had no wish to do so.

In those circumstances, in order to determine whether the Commission has established to the requisite legal standard the existence of a concurrence of wills between the parties concerning the limitation of parallel exports, it is necessary to consider whether, as the applicant maintains, the

Commission wrongly assessed the respective intentions of Bayer and the wholesalers.

[Preliminary observations]
… The applicant acknowledges in this case that it adopted and unilaterally implemented a new supply policy designed to make it more difficult for wholesalers to carry out parallel exports. According to case law, as has already been noted, apparently unilateral conduct on the part of a manufacturer, adopted in the context of the contractual relations which it maintains with his dealers, may in reality form the basis of an agreement between undertakings within the meaning of art 85(1) of the Treaty, if express or implied acquiescence by the other contracting parties in the attitude adopted by the manufacturer is established.

The Commission claims that, in order to establish its policy of restricting supplies, the applicant counted on the acquiescence of the wholesalers.

Therefore, in the circumstances of this case, it is necessary to consider whether the Commission has proved to the requisite legal standard the express or implied adherence of the wholesalers to the unilateral policy of preventing parallel imports adopted by Bayer.

[Proof of the wholesalers' "implicit acquiescence"]
The Commission maintains in recital 176 of the Decision that the wholesalers' conduct reflected an "implicit acquiescence in the export ban", and describes that conduct in more detail in recitals 181 to 185. It arrives at that conclusion in the light of a series of facts which it considers to be established.

First, the Commission notes (recital 180), on the one hand, that the wholesalers were aware of the existence of the export ban, a factor, it claims, which had been decisive in the *Sandoz* case [*Sandoz Prodotti Farmaceutici SpA v EC Commission* Case C–277/87 [1990] ECR I–45] and in the light of which the mere "fact that they did not react to the export ban suggested that they accepted it and that the necessary evidence substantiating the existence of an agreement" was present, and, on the other hand,

that, as in *Sandoz*, the export ban formed part of continuous commercial relations between Bayer France or Bayer Spain and their respective wholesalers.

Secondly, the Commission states (recital 180) that, in this case, as a further element in addition to those held to be relevant in *Sandoz*, "the conduct of the wholesalers shows that they have not only understood that an export ban applies to the goods supplied, but also that they have aligned their conduct on this ban".

The Commission contends that that "alignment of the wholesalers" conduct on the requirements imposed by Bayer France and Bayer Spain is established by the finding that, once they had understood the real intentions of Bayer France and Bayer Spain, the wholesalers demonstrated, "at least in appearance, their acceptance … of their supplier's export ban in their commercial relations with the supplier" (recital 181). They adapted themselves to the requirement of Bayer France and Bayer Spain, as is proved by the various systems they put in place in order to obtain supplies, particularly the system of spreading orders intended for export among the various agencies and the orders with small wholesalers (recital 182).

According to the Decision (recitals 183 and 184), the wholesalers "compl[ied] with the national 'quotas' imposed by their supplier, negotiating as far as they could to increase them to the maximum, thus bowing to the strict application of and compliance with the figures regarded by Bayer France and Bayer Spain as normal for the supplying of the domestic market". That attitude shows, the Commission claims, that the wholesalers "were aware of the real motives of Bayer France and Bayer Spain and of the tactics deployed by the two companies to thwart parallel exports: they adapted to the system established by their supplier so as to comply with its requirements".

It should, however, be borne in mind, first, that, as has been held, the Commission has not sufficiently established in law that Bayer adopted a systematic policy of monitoring the final destination of the packets of Adalat supplied, that it applied a policy of threats and penalties against wholesalers who had exported them, that, therefore, Bayer France and Bayer Spain imposed an export ban on their respective wholesalers, or, finally, that supplies were made conditional on compliance with the alleged export ban.

Second, there is nothing in the documents before the Court to show that Bayer France or Bayer Spain required any particular form of conduct on the part of the wholesalers concerning the final destination of the packets of Adalat supplied or compliance with a certain manner of placing orders, its policy having consisted simply in limiting supplies unilaterally by determining in advance the quantities to be supplied, using traditional needs as the basis.

Finally, the Commission has not established that the applicant made any attempt to obtain the agreement or acquiescence of the wholesalers to the implementation of its policy. It has not even claimed that Bayer sought to get the wholesalers to change their way of formulating orders.

It follows that the statements contained in recitals 181 to 185 of the Decision, on the basis of which the Commission considers that the wholesalers aligned their conduct in accordance with the alleged export ban, fail on factual grounds, because they are based on factual circumstances that have not been established.

Since, in this case, the Commission does not have any document referring expressly to an agreement between Bayer and its wholesalers concerning exports for the purpose of establishing a concurrence of wills, it claims to have followed the case law approach consisting of examining the actual conduct of the wholesalers in order to determine the existence of their acquiescence. Thus, the Commission states in recital 180 of the Decision: "In the present case, ... the conduct of the wholesalers shows that they have not only understood that an export ban applies to the goods supplied, but also that they have aligned their conduct on this ban". By contrast, the applicant maintains that it is precisely their conduct which is the best proof that there was no concurrence of wills.

In the circumstances of this case, it therefore needs to be determined whether, having regard to the actual conduct of the wholesalers following the adoption by the applicant of its new policy of restricting supplies, the Commission could legitimately conclude that they acquiesced in that policy.

[*The conduct of the French wholesalers*]

As a preliminary point, it should be borne in mind that recital 96 of the Decision, in which the Commission gives a general description of the way in which the three French wholesalers organised themselves in order to try to obtain supplies, states:

> "The three wholesalers adopted the same method: they stopped placing orders for export and made arrangements to increase the orders which were officially intended for the French market.
>
> Bayer France accepts as normal an increase or decrease of 10 per cent in domestic requirements. The wholesalers have a number of local agencies situated throughout France which normally provide supplies at local level.
>
> The domestic orders placed by each of the agencies increased, with no indication being given to Bayer France of their destination. The aim was to induce Bayer France to believe that domestic demand had increased, by spreading it over the different agencies. The amounts which were in fact intended for export were then rechannelled within each wholesaler's organisation so that they could be exported."

Recitals 97 to 101 of the Decision, which are devoted to setting out the strategy put in place by the wholesaler CERP Rouen in order to circumvent Bayer's policy of restricting supplies, reproduce several letters exchanged between October 1991 and January 1992 between CERP Rouen's central purchasing department and the directors of the group's local agencies in order to obtain the extra packets of Adalat needed by the Boulogne agency, which had responsibility within the group for exporting to the United Kingdom. However, contrary to what the Commission claims, the passages of those documents are not capable of proving that that wholesaler agreed to cease exporting, reduce its orders or limit its exports, or that it tried to give Bayer the impression that it was going to do so. The only illustration they provide is that of the reaction of an undertaking in trying to continue its export activities as far as possible. There is no direct mention or evidence of an intention to support Bayer's policy of preventing exports, of which the wholesaler was perfectly aware, as is indicated in recital 94 of the Decision.

Examination of the documents referred to in recitals 102 and 103 of the Decision, concerning the cases of CERP Lorraine and OCP, merely confirms that finding. Moreover, recital 102 shows that, despite the difficulties raised by Bayer's attitude, CERP Lorraine succeeded in obtaining significant quantities for export. That recital contains an extract from an internal CERP Lorraine report, in which the author states:

"Although I do not see a favourable solution in the short term concerning supplies from Bayer (we have managed to obtain minimal quantities of product through the agencies), I think that the budget should be attainable at the end of the financial year."

The documents reproduced in recitals 105, 106 and 107 go in the opposite direction to the Commission's argument, because they show that the CERP Lorraine and CERP Rouen wholesalers did not genuinely adapt their orders to the new policy of restricting supplies put in place by Bayer. They show that Bayer are "blocking supplies of Adalat" ordered by CERP Lorraine (recital 105), that CERP Rouen's demand at the beginning of 1992 amounted to "up to 50,000 packets a month" but that it was able to supply "only 7,000 packets" to meet that demand, and that OCP had sent Bayer an initial order projection of 50,000 packets per month for February and March 1992, but that it was supplied with only 15,000 packets in February and 5,000 packets in March (recitals 91 and 107).

It follows that the passages reproduced in recitals 96 to 107 of the Decision are not capable of supporting the argument that the French wholesalers expressly or impliedly agreed to the policy put in place by Bayer. Those passages do not refer to any predisposition to adhere in any way to Bayer's policy of preventing parallel exports. On the contrary, they bear witness to the fact that those wholesalers adopted a line of conduct demonstrating a firm and persistent intention to react against a policy that was fundamentally contrary to their interests.

[*The conduct of the Spanish wholesalers*]
Nor, in relation to the Spanish wholesalers, do recitals 113 to 130 of the Decision contain anything capable of supporting the argument of tacit acquiescence put forward by the Commission.

On the contrary, recitals 115, 118, 119 and 120 contradict such an argument. Those recitals show, first, that Bayer Spain constantly maintained its policy of restricting supplies to the level of traditional needs and, second, that the wholesalers were very annoyed by the losses caused by the impossibility of obtaining the quantities necessary to respond to orders from their British customers. Particular note should be taken of recital 115, which reproduces passages from documents exchanged between CERP Rouen and its Spanish subsidiary Commercial Genové:

"Every week I want a copy of the order forms for Adalat and ... sent to the laboratories and the delivery notes corresponding to those orders. I am trying to present a watertight case against the labs ... With regard to your fax today concerning ... and Bayer laboratories, I give you my word that I am doing my utmost to obtain supplies greater than our requirements. The laboratories are refusing to listen to any arguments. They know that the quantities they supply to us are easily enough to cover the needs of the Spanish market."

Similarly, the quotations contained in recital 118 – "they do not supply as much as we need. We have only stock for our market" – and in recital 119 – "Bayer does not deliver to us the quantities we order" – demonstrate that, contrary to what the Commission alleges, the wholesalers did not adapt their ordering policy to the new situation and continued to order quantities greater than their traditional needs.

It is necessary to examine the case of each of the Spanish wholesalers concerned by the Decision.

As regards Cofares, the main wholesaler in Spain, the Decision states in recital 121 that the proof of its acquiescence is to be found in the statement made by the managers of that undertaking during an investigation by the Commission at its premises. The managing director of Cofares is said to have stated that "Cofares' export activity account[ed] for a very small proportion of its total invoicing because of the difficulties posed by certain laboratories (including Bayer) to orders for export", and that, in his capacity as director with responsibility for purchasing, "when Bayer set an Adalat quota for Cofares that was initially clearly insufficient to cover the requirements of its domestic market ... [he] warned them of a possible complaint because of such restrictions. Since then, Bayer ha[d] supplied Cofares with sufficient quantities to meet national consumption of the product in question".

Contrary to what the Commission claims, it cannot be deduced from that document that "Cofares complied with Bayer Spain's requirement that it confine itself to its domestic market".

The first sentence, to the effect that the negligible extent of exports in relation to turnover was due to the difficulties caused by certain laboratories in supplying products for export, does not in itself constitute direct evidence of an agreement between that wholesaler and Bayer Spain that the packets of Adalat received should not be exported. The fact that the exports were negligible cannot lead to the conclusion that they did not exist or that they had ceased. On the contrary, that statement may demonstrate that, at least in part, Cofares continued to export. The fact that, unlike the situation as regards the other wholesalers, the Decision does not show that Cofares set up a strategy

for circumventing Bayer's policy does not reverse the burden of proving its acquiescence in Bayer's new policy, which still rests with the Commission. Since this was the largest wholesaler in Spain, with 20.6 per cent of the market (according to recital 112 of the Decision), the Commission could not legitimately consider that the statement reproduced in recital 121 proves that Cofares complied with Bayer Spain's requirement that it confine itself to its domestic market without verifying whether Cofares had a strong export tradition and without considering the possibility that, quite simply, Cofares had decided to view exports only as a very subsidiary possibility; such a decision might have been the most reasonable one to take given the difficulty of obtaining additional quantities of products in relation to habitual needs. That is so a fortiori in view of the lack of any reference in the Decision to the relative importance of Adalat in the overall sales of Cofares.

Moreover, that statement by the managing director of Cofares, rather than being evidence of alleged adherence to an alleged export ban, calls for the finding that Bayer's policy of restricting supplies, together with the difficulties raised by other laboratories, had led that wholesaler to consider exporting only once appropriate supply of the domestic market was assured. That interpretation seems more plausible than that of the Commission, bearing in mind, in particular, the fact that wholesalers are required to ensure the distribution of products on the national market in an appropriate and stable manner, and that this case concerns the premier national wholesaler.

According to recital 137 of the Decision, the figures for export sales between 1989 and 1993, supplied by Cofares at the Commission's request, show that export sales "remained at a minimum level" and that proves that "Cofares accepted the regime imposed by Bayer Spain and confined itself strictly to the Spanish domestic market".

However, examination of those figures reveals rather the contrary, because, even if it constitutes a minimal percentage of

Cofares' sales as a whole, the percentage corresponding to exports of Adalat only rises in the course of the years, in an irregular but constant fashion, as is demonstrated by the fact that the smallest percentage of the five years under consideration is precisely that of the first year, namely 1989. Finally, it should be added that it was hard for the Commission to come to the above conclusion without knowing the figures for the years before 1989, that is to say the period immediately prior to the establishment by Bayer Spain of its policy of restricting supplies. Without that information it is impossible to determine whether Cofares modified its tendency to export that product following the introduction of that policy by Bayer.

As regards the passage, contained in the statement, concerning the discussions between the managing director of Cofares and Bayer Spain, it needs to be considered whether, in the absence of any direct or indirect reference to the freedom to export the quantities received, the fact that the parties agreed to increase the supply quantities initially assigned by Bayer to that wholesaler in order to ensure that its national needs were met demonstrates acquiescence by the wholesaler in the applicant's policy designed to make parallel exports difficult. Recital 143 of the Decision contains a passage of a document which, although it was not directly relied on by the Commission in the context of this question, must be referred to because it is an internal memorandum of Bayer Spain which also refers to the quota which Bayer initially conceded to Cofares to cover its needs on the national market.

That internal memorandum shows that Bayer Spain and Cofares discussed minimum supply quantities to enable that wholesaler to meet its growth and penetration needs on the national market and that they reached an agreement on the figures corresponding to those needs. It appears to be undisputed that Bayer Spain assured Cofares that the supplies would, at least, correspond to those quantities. It is also clear that Bayer Spain was ready to envisage

revision of the reduced supply levels initially adopted if problems in supplying the national market appeared, bearing in mind its legal and moral obligation to ensure appropriate distribution of its products on the Spanish market.

However, nothing in that internal memorandum refers to the slightest restriction on the freedom of Cofares to assign products received after the conversations on the level of national needs to exports. The Commission therefore has no basis for arguing that Cofares was supplied only after assuring Bayer that the supplies were intended solely for the internal market. Finally, it should be noted that, during the bargaining, Bayer Spain claimed that Spanish pharmacies not supplied by the wholesalers were supplied directly by the manufacturer. That fact, instead of indicating that the wholesalers were prevented or penalised by Bayer when they decided to export those products even at the cost of abandoning parts of the national market, seems rather to demonstrate that they were covered in that respect by the manufacturer.

In those circumstances, the conclusion must be that neither the document referred to by recital 143 of the Decision nor the statement by the managing director of Cofares reproduced in recital 121 of the Decision may be construed as proving either the alleged "requirement" by Bayer Spain that the wholesaler should stay in the domestic market or any acceptance of that requirement on the part of Cofares.

The Decision then goes on to describe (recital 122) how the Spanish wholesaler Hefame established a system for obtaining packets of Adalat for export. It sets out in detail a standard agreement headed "Cooperation Agreement for External Markets" which Hefame concluded with several small wholesalers in order to obtain larger quantities of medicinal products that it was profitable to export, including Adalat. However, there is nothing in that document to show that Hefame's conduct had been favourable to any idea of acquiescing in Bayer's new policy.

As regards the Spanish subsidiaries of

CERP Rouen, the description of the conduct of Commercial Genové, Hufasa and Disdasa, contained in recitals 125 to 129 of the Decision, confirms the lack of proof of any concurrence of wills or acquiescence in the policy of preventing parallel exports.

The Commission itself says in recital 126 of the Decision:

"Documents were found on the premises of Commercial Genové showing that CERP Rouen used its Spanish subsidiaries, Commercial Genové, Hufasa and Disdasa, to meet British demand. CERP Rouen thus acted as an international group and made use of all its scope both in France and in Spain for obtaining supplies of the necessary quantities for its British customers. Under this system, the Spanish subsidiaries were used in the same way as the French regional agencies: they were asked to make a plausible increase in their orders for the Spanish market, and the amounts thus obtained were supplied to British customers on behalf of CERP Rouen."

The Decision then refers to the wholesaler Hufasa (recital 127), citing a record of a meeting between Hufasa and Bayer Spain which is alleged to demonstrate that Hufasa fully accepted Bayer Spain's arguments, namely that it had to concentrate on domestic sales. In that regard, the Commission relies on the following quotation in particular:

"... we had reached an agreement with Bayer to maintain higher supplies of Adalat, it was better not to submit figures that would not be accepted as possible for Hufasa and which revealed our interest in exporting significant amounts."

That record shows that a conversation took place between a representative of Hufasa and managers of Bayer Spain, during which the Bayer managers refused to supply the quantities requested because they accounted for 50 per cent of the domestic market and were much higher than those of other firms in the same area; that the Hufasa representative reacted by arguing that his company needed larger quantities of Adalat on the

ground, in particular, that the estimate of needs for the domestic market had been made on the basis of needs recorded in an untypical year in which Hufasa had suffered a crisis that was reflected in the abnormally low level of Adalat purchases; and that, following those conversations, Bayer undertook to revise the supply limit figures and increase them to the level of those of another, unidentified, wholesaler.

That record clearly shows that the true intentions and the actual conduct of the Spanish subsidiaries of the CERP Rouen group could not be further removed from any intention to comply with, or align themselves upon, Bayer's policy of preventing parallel imports. It is sufficient in that regard to cite the part of that document which follows the passage cited above and to read it in the context of the group strategy adopted by CERP Rouen:

"I took the view that it was more important to obtain a quantity of Adalat for export with very plausible figures rather than to maintain a very high level of orders which would not be supplied. The important thing was actual receipts rather than the order. That is no doubt why ... orders less than forecast."

Moreover, whilst it is true that the record reproduced shows that that company bargained hard with Bayer Spain to secure its acknowledgement that its traditional domestic needs were higher and that they should be satisfied, that fact cannot serve to support the Commission's statement that "Hufasa completely accepted Bayer Spain's arguments, namely that it had to concentrate on domestic sales".

Finally, although the Hufasa manager refers in that record to "an agreement with Bayer to maintain higher supplies of Adalat", which Hufasa is said to have concluded with Bayer Spain, it is clear from the literal content of that statement and its context that the parties limited themselves to negotiating the exact determination of the quantities which the wholesaler traditionally requested, that being the criterion in accordance with which the applicant had decided to adjust its new supply policy, and the upward revision of the figures for national needs and, therefore, the quantities to which Hufasa was to be entitled pursuant to that criterion. Since the sentence "[T]his led them to believe that a substantial proportion of the product was intended for export" was only a subjective assessment on the part of the Hufasa manager, it cannot be regarded as demonstrating an intention on the part of Bayer to deal with the question of exports or the actual destinations of the products supplied. Moreover, it is not in any event capable of contradicting the general sense of the record, which merely reflects the difficulties which Bayer was encountering in implementing its new policy of reducing supplies and in which, what is more, there is nothing capable of establishing that Bayer Spain and Hufasa concluded an agreement to limit or to prevent in any way parallel exports of the packets of Adalat supplied. The absence of any concurrence of wills in relation to exports is corroborated, moreover, by the text of this recital in the Decision itself, where the Commission states:

> "However, the record is explicit; the pressure put on Bayer Spain on the basis of domestic-market arguments was merely a means used by Hufasa to obtain the amounts intended for export."

Recitals 128 and 129 of the Decision set out the content of a letter from CERP Rouen to its subsidiaries and of a letter sent to CERP Rouen by its subsidiary Commercial Genové, also concerning the mechanism put in place by that group to try to obtain more products of the applicant in Spain and underlining the difficulty in obtaining extra packets of Adalat. The Commission cannot rely on these documents either in order to establish that the subsidiaries of CERP Rouen in Spain wished to adhere in any way whatsoever to Bayer Spain's new policy designed to limit parallel exports of the products supplied.

Examination of the attitude and actual conduct of the wholesalers shows that the Commission has no foundation for claim-ing that they aligned themselves on the applicant's policy designed to reduce parallel imports.

The argument based on the fact that the wholesalers concerned had reduced their orders to a given level in order to give Bayer the impression that they were complying with its declared intention thereby to cover only the needs of their traditional market, and that they acted in that way in order to avoid penalties, must be rejected, because the Commission has failed to prove that the applicant demanded or negotiated the adoption of any particular line of conduct on the part of the wholesalers concerning the destination for export of the packets of Adalat which it had supplied, and that it penalised the exporting wholesalers or threatened to do so.

For the same reasons, the Commission cannot claim that the reduction in orders could be understood by Bayer only as a sign that the wholesalers had accepted its requirements, or maintain that it is because they satisfied Bayer's requirements that they had to procure extra quantities destined for export from wholesalers who were not "suspect" in Bayer's eyes and whose higher orders were therefore fulfilled without difficulty.

Moreover, it is obvious from the recitals of the Decision examined above that the wholesalers continued to try to obtain packets of Adalat for export and persisted in that line of activity, even if, for that purpose, they considered it more productive to use different systems to obtain supplies, namely the system of distributing orders intended for export among the various agencies on the one hand, and that of placing orders indirectly through small wholesalers on the other. In those circumstances, the fact that the wholesalers changed their policy on orders and established various systems for breaking them down or diversifying them, by placing them through indirect means, cannot be construed as evidence of their intention to satisfy Bayer or as a response to any request from Bayer. On the contrary, that fact could be regarded as demonstrating the firm intention on the part of the wholesalers to continue carrying on parallel exports of Adalat.

In the absence of evidence of any requirement on the part of the applicant as to the conduct of the wholesalers concerning exports of the packets of Adalat supplied, the fact that they adopted measures to obtain extra quantities can be construed only as a negation of their alleged acquiescence. For the same reasons, the Court must also reject the Commission's argument that, in the circumstances of the case, it is normal that certain wholesalers should have tried to obtain extra supplies by circuitous means since they had to undertake to Bayer not to export and thus to order reduced quantities, not capable of being exported.

Nor, finally, has the Commission proved that the wholesalers wished to pursue Bayer's objectives or wished to make Bayer believe that they did. On the contrary, the documents examined above demonstrate that the wholesalers adopted a line of conduct designed to circumvent Bayer's new policy of restricting supplies to the level of traditional orders.

The Commission was therefore wrong in holding that the actual conduct of the wholesalers constitutes sufficient proof in law of their acquiescence in the applicant's policy designed to prevent parallel imports.'

Comment

The above case will become one of the leading cases on art 81(1) EC, in particular in respect of the meaning of an agreement under that Article. The difference between an agreement within the meaning of art 81(1) EC and the unilateral conduct of an undertaking is vital for the application of art 81(1) EC.

Agreements have been defined as consensual arrangements between undertakings irrespective of whether or not they are formally binding contracts, and as involving the acceptance of an obligation irrespective of whether or not the obligation is legally binding. For an agreement to be caught by art 81(1) EC it is sufficient that the undertakings concerned should have expressed their joint intention to conduct themselves on the market in a spe-

cific way: *ACF Chemiefarma NV v Commission* Case 41/69 [1970] ECR 661; *Van Landewyck and Others v Commission* Joined Cases 209 and 218/78 [1980] ECR 3125. The prohibited conduct must be co-ordinated bilaterally or multilaterally. Unilateral conduct of an undertaking is outside the scope of art 81(1) EC: *AEG Telefunken AG v EC Commisssion* Case 107/82 [1983] ECR 3151; *Dunlop Slazenger International v Commission* Case T–43/92 [1994] ECR II–441. In the case under consideration the CFI emphasised that an undertaking must adopt genuinely unilateral conduct, without the express or implied participation of another undertaking, in order to escape the prohibition contained in art 81(1) EC.

However, when a unilateral measure is merely apparent it will fall within the scope of art 81(1) EC. Therefore, a unilateral act of an undertaking which forms in fact part of the general framework of commercial relationships between other undertakings involved may be considered as an agreement within the meaning of art 81(1) EC (see *AEG Telefunken AG v EC Commission* Case 107/82 [1983] ECR 3151).

In the present case the CFI and the Commission interpreted the concept of an agreement within the meaning of art 81(1) EC differently. The CFI took into consideration two elements: the intention of Bayer to impose an export ban and the intention of the wholesalers to adhere to Bayer's policy designed to reduce parallel imports.

The CFI rejected the main argument of the Commission as to the existence of an agreement. The Commission argued that, to prove the existence of an agreement, it was sufficient to find that the parties maintained their commercial relations. In this respect the CFI held:

'The proof of an agreement between undertakings within the meaning of art 81(1) must be founded upon the direct or indirect finding of the existence of the subjective element that characterises the very concept of an agreement, that is to say a concurrence of wills between economic operators on the implementation of a policy, the pursuit of an objective, or the adoption of a given line of conduct on the market, irrespective of the manner in which the parties' intention to behave on the market in accordance with the terms of that agreement is expressed. The Commission misjudged that concept of the concurrence of wills in holding that the continuation of commercial relations with the manufacturer when it adopts a new policy, which it implements unilaterally, amounts to acquiescence by the wholesalers in that policy, although their de facto conduct is clearly contrary to that policy.'

Consten and Grundig v *Commission* Cases 56 and 58/64 [1966] ECR 299; [1966] CMLR 418 European Court of Justice

• *Article 85(1) EC Treaty [art 81(1) EC] – exclusive distributorship agreements – vertical restraints – absolute territorial protection – effect on trade between Member States – restriction on competition – extent of prohibition in art 85(1) EC Treaty [art 81(1) EC]*

Facts

Grundig, a large German manufacturer of electrical equipment, entered into an agreement with a French distributor, Consten, according to which Consten was appointed as Grundig's exclusive agent in France, Corsica and the Saar region. The distribution agreement contained terms which, inter alia, allowed Consten to employ the Grundig trade mark 'GINT' and emblem in its promotions. On the basis of this authority, Consten registered the Grundig trade mark in France. A French competitor imported a number of Grundig products from Germany and attempted to sell these in the French market. Consten raised an action for infringement of a trade mark against this rival, relying on the earlier registration of the trade mark. The Commission objected to these proceedings and commenced an investigation into the

functioning of the exclusive distribution agreement.

The Commission found that the agreement was contrary to art 85(1) EC Treaty [art 81(1) EC], being an agreement which had the object of distorting competition within the Community by restricting trade. The plaintiffs brought an action in the ECJ contesting these findings.

Held

The ECJ severed the offending clauses of the agreement and declared them void under art 85(2) EC Treaty [art 81(2) EC]. In respect of the agreement, the only clauses which were prohibited under art 85 EC Treaty [art 81 EC] were those giving absolute territorial protection The ECJ annulled the decision of the Commission in so far as it declared void all clauses of the agreement.

Judgment

'[*Vertical agreements*]
The applicants submit that the prohibition in art 85(1) applies only to so-called horizontal agreements. The Italian government submits furthermore that sole distributorship contracts do not constitute "agreements between undertakings" within the meaning of that provision, since the parties are not on a footing of equality. With regard to these contracts, freedom of competition may only be protected by virtue of art 86 of the Treaty.

Neither the wording of art 85 nor that of art 86 gives any ground for holding that distinct areas of application are to be assigned to each of the two articles according to the level in the economy at which the contracting parties operate. Article 85 refers in a general way to all agreements which distort competition within the Common Market and does not lay down any distinction between those agreements based on whether they are made between competitors operating at the same level in the economic process or between non-competing persons operating at a different level. In principle, no distinction can be made where the Treaty does not make any distinction.

Furthermore, the possible application of art 85 to a sole distributorship contract cannot be excluded merely because the grantor and the concessionaire are not competitors inter se and not on a footing of equality. Competition may be distorted within the meaning of art 85(1) not only by agreements which limit it as between the parties, but also by agreements which prevent or restrict the competition which might take place between one of them and third parties. For this purpose, it is irrelevant whether the parties to the agreement are or are not on a footing of equality as regards their position and function in the economy. This applies all the more, since, by such an agreement, the parties might seek, by preventing or limiting the competition of third parties in respect of the products, to create or guarantee for their benefit an unjustified advantage at the expense of the consumer or user, contrary to the general aims of art 85.'

Comment

This is the first case concerning exclusive distribution agreements and the first judgment of the ECJ on appeal from the decision of the Commission. It is also the first case in which the ECJ held that art 85(1) EC Treaty [art 81(1) EC] applies not only to undertakings at horizontal level but also to undertakings at vertical level, that is between undertakings which do not compete with each other as they operate at different levels of the market. The ECJ restrictively interpreted art 85 EC Treaty [art 81 EC]. It held that the agreement intended to isolate the French market for Grundig products and therefore partition the common market along national lines which in itself distorted competition in the common market. For that reason, without examining other factors, such as economic data, the correctness of criteria which the Commission had applied in order to compare the French market with the German market, etc, the ECJ held that the agreement was in breach of art 85(1) EC Treaty [art 81(1) EC] and upheld the Commission's position in this matter.

Courage Ltd v Bernard Crehan and Bernard Crehan v Courage Ltd and Others Case C–453/99 [2001] ECR I–6297 European Court of Justice

• *Article 81(1) and (2) EC – beer tie – leasing of public houses –restrictive agreement – right to damages of a party to the contract*

Facts

In 1990, Courage, a brewery holding a 19 per cent share of the United Kingdom market in sales of beer, and Grand Metropolitan plc, a company with a range of catering and hotel interests, agreed to merge the ownership of their leased public houses (pubs). The undertakings concerned created a new company, Inntrepreneur Estates Ltd (hereinafter IEL), to which they transferred their pubs. Courage and Grand Metropolitan plc held an equal number of shares in IEL. Courage and IEL concluded an agreement under which all IEL public house tenants were to buy their requirement of beer exclusively from Courage at the prices specified by Courage (referred to here as a 'beer tie' agreement).

The relationship between IEL and its tenants was regulated by a standard form lease agreement under which some conditions, such as the level of rent, were negotiable whilst others, such as the exclusive purchase obligation (beer tie), were not negotiable between the parties. The Commission granted to the standard form lease agreement an exemption under art 81(3) EC.

In 1991, Mr Crehan entered into two 20-year leases with IEL containing a beer tie clause requiring him to purchase a minimum quantity of beer from Courage. In 1993, Courage brought proceedings against Mr Crehan for recovery of the sum of UK £15,266 for unpaid deliveries of beer. Mr Crehan refused to pay on the ground that the agreement between him and IEL was in breach of art 81(1) EC. Mr Crehan argued that Courage sold its beers to independant tenants of pubs not leased by IEL at substantially lower prices than those applicable to the pubs leased by IEL, and therefore reduced the profitability of tied tenants and drove many of them out of business. Mr Crehan also counterclaimed for damages for breach of EC law. Courage argued that Mr Crehan was prevented from claiming damages as he was a party to an agreement in breach of art 81(1) EC. Only a non-party who was harmed was entitled to claim damages arising out of a breach of art 81(1) EC.

The Court of Appeal referred to the ECJ the following questions.

1. Is art 81(1) to be interpreted as meaning that a party to a prohibited tied house agreement may rely upon that Article to seek relief from the courts from the other contracting party?
2. If so, is the party claiming relief entitled to recover damages alleged to arise as a result of his adherence to the clause in the agreement which is prohibited under art 81(1) EC?
3. Should a rule of national law, whereby a court must prevent a person from pleading or relying on his own illegal actions as a necessary step to the recovery of damages, be allowed as consistent with Community law?
4. If the answer to (3) above is that, in some circumstances, such a rule may be inconsistent with Community law, what circumstances should the national court take into consideration?

Held

The ECJ held that a party to an agreement prohibited under art 81(1) EC could rely on the breach of that provision to obtain relief from the other contracting party.

A national rule under which a party to an agreement, which is in breach of art 81(1) EC, is barred from claiming damages for loss caused by performance of that contract on the sole ground that the claimant is a party to that contract is contrary to art 81 EC.

However, Community law does not preclude a rule of national law from denying a

party who is found to bear significant responsibility for the distortion of competition the right to obtain damages from the other contracting party.

Judgment

'[*The questions*]
By its first, second and third questions, which should be considered together, the referring court is asking essentially whether a party to a contract liable to restrict or distort competition within the meaning of art 85 of the Treaty [art 81 EC] can rely on the breach of that provision before a national court to obtain relief from the other contracting party. In particular, it asks whether that party can obtain compensation for loss which he alleges to result from his being subject to a contractual clause contrary to art 85 and whether, therefore, Community law precludes a rule of national law which denies a person the right to rely on his own illegal actions to obtain damages.

If Community law precludes a national rule of that sort, the national court wishes to know, by its fourth question, what factors must be taken into consideration in assessing the merits of such a claim for damages.

It should be borne in mind, first of all, that the Treaty has created its own legal order, which is integrated into the legal systems of the Member States and which their courts are bound to apply. The subjects of that legal order are not only the Member States but also their nationals. Just as it imposes burdens on individuals, Community law is also intended to give rise to rights which become part of their legal assets. Those rights arise not only where they are expressly granted by the Treaty but also by virtue of obligations which the Treaty imposes in a clearly defined manner both on individuals and on the Member States and the Community institutions.

Secondly, according to art 3(g) of the EC Treaty (now, after amendment, art 3(1)(g) EC), art 85 of the Treaty constitutes a fundamental provision which is essential for the accomplishment of the tasks entrusted to the

Community and, in particular, for the functioning of the internal market.

Indeed, the importance of such a provision led the framers of the Treaty to provide expressly, in art 85(2) of the Treaty, that any agreements or decisions prohibited pursuant to that Article are to be automatically void.

That principle of automatic nullity can be relied on by anyone, and the courts are bound by it once the conditions for the application of art 85(1) are met and so long as the agreement concerned does not justify the grant of an exemption under art 85(3) of the Treaty. Since the nullity referred to in art 85(2) is absolute, an agreement which is null and void by virtue of this provision has no effect as between the contracting parties and cannot be set up against third parties. Moreover, it is capable of having a bearing on all the effects, either past or future, of the agreement or decision concerned.

Thirdly, it should be borne in mind that the Court has held that art 85(1) of the Treaty and art 86 of the EC Treaty (now art 82 EC) produce direct effects in relations between individuals and create rights for the individuals concerned which the national courts must safeguard.

It follows from the foregoing considerations that any individual can rely on a breach of art 85(1) of the Treaty before a national court even where he is a party to a contract that is liable to restrict or distort competition within the meaning of that provision.

As regards the possibility of seeking compensation for loss caused by a contract or by conduct liable to restrict or distort competition, it should be remembered from the outset that, in accordance with settled case law, the national courts whose task it is to apply the provisions of Community law in areas within their jurisdiction must ensure that those rules take full effect and must protect the rights which they confer on individuals.

The full effectiveness of art 85 of the Treaty and, in particular, the practical effect of the prohibition laid down in art 85(1) would be put at risk if it were not open to any individual to claim damages for loss caused to him by a contract or by conduct liable to restrict or distort competition.

Indeed, the existence of such a right strengthens the working of the Community competition rules and discourages agreements or practices, which are frequently covert, which are liable to restrict or distort competition. From that point of view, actions for damages before the national courts can make a significant contribution to the maintenance of effective competition in the Community.

There should not therefore be any absolute bar to such an action being brought by a party to a contract which would be held to violate the competition rules.

However, in the absence of Community rules governing the matter, it is for the domestic legal system of each Member State to designate the courts and tribunals having jurisdiction and to lay down the detailed procedural rules governing actions for safeguarding rights which individuals derive directly from Community law, provided that such rules are not less favourable than those governing similar domestic actions (principle of equivalence) and that they do not render practically impossible or excessively difficult the exercise of rights conferred by Community law (principle of effectiveness) (see Case C–261/95 *Palmisani* v *Istituto Nazionale della Previdenza Sociale (INPS)* [1997] ECR I–4025, para 27).

In that regard, the Court has held that Community law does not prevent national courts from taking steps to ensure that the protection of the rights guaranteed by Community law does not entail the unjust enrichment of those who enjoy them (see, in particular, Case 238/78 *Ireks-Arkady GmbH* v *EC Council and EC Commission* [1979] ECR 2955, para 14, Case 68/79 *Just* [1980] ECR 501, para 26, and Joined Cases C–441/98 and C–442/98 *Michaïlidis AE* v *Idryma Koinonikan Asfaliseon (IKA)* [2000] ECR I–7145, para 31).

Similarly, provided that the principles of equivalence and effectiveness are respected (see *Palmisani*, cited above, para 27), Community law does not preclude national law from denying a party who is found to bear significant responsibility for the distortion of competition the right to obtain damages from the other contracting party. Under a principle which is recognised in most of the legal systems of the Member States and which the Court has applied in the past (see Case 39/72 *EC Commission v Italy* [1973] ECR 101, para 10), a litigant should not profit from his own unlawful conduct, where this is proven.

In that regard, the matters to be taken into account by the competent national court include the economic and legal context in which the parties find themselves and, as the United Kingdom government rightly points out, the respective bargaining power and conduct of the two parties to the contract.

In particular, it is for the national court to ascertain whether the party who claims to have suffered loss through concluding a contract that is liable to restrict or distort competition found himself in a markedly weaker position than the other party, such as seriously to compromise or even eliminate his freedom to negotiate the terms of the contract and his capacity to avoid the loss or reduce its extent, in particular by availing himself in good time of all the legal remedies available to him.

Referring to the judgments in Case 23/67 *Brasserie de Haecht v Wilkin* [1967] ECR 127 and Case C–234/89 *Delimitis v Henninger Bräu AG* [1991] ECR I–935, paras 14 to 26, the Commission and the United Kingdom government also rightly point out that a contract might prove to be contrary to art 85(1) of the Treaty for the sole reason that it is part of a network of similar contracts which have a cumulative effect on competition. In such a case, the party contracting with the person controlling the network cannot bear significant responsibility for the breach of art 85, particularly where in practice the terms of the contract were imposed on him by the party controlling the network.

Contrary to the submission of Courage, making a distinction as to the extent of the parties' liability does not conflict with the case law of the Court to the effect that it does not matter, for the purposes of the application of art 85 of the Treaty, whether the parties to an agreement are on an equal footing as regards their economic position and function (see inter alia Joined Cases 56/64 and 58/64 *Consten and Grundig v Commission* [1966] ECR 299). That case law concerns the conditions for application of art 85 of the Treaty while the questions put before the Court in the present case concern certain consequences in civil law of a breach of that provision.'

Comment

The main issue in the above case was that under English law a party to an illegal agreement is prevented from claiming damages from the other contracting party (*Tinsley v Milligan* [1994] 1 AC 340). This rule applies even when a party to an illegal contract is not responsible for the illegality. This situation was confirmed by the Court of Appeal in a previous case concerning beer ties (*Gibbs Mew plc v Gemmell* [1998] EuLR 588) in which the Court of Appeal decided not to refer the matter to the ECJ as it considered that art 81(1) EC was intended to protect third parties, whether competitors or consumers, and not parties to an agreement which was in breach of that provision. The Court of Appeal stated that the parties to such an agreement were the cause, not the victims, of the restriction of competition. However, in the present case the Court of Appeal decided to seek a ruling from the ECJ on that point, as it took into consideration the decision of the Supreme Court of the United States of America in *Perma Life Mufflers Inc v International Parts Corporation* 392 US 134 (1968) where it was held that a party to an anti-competitive agreement who was in an economically weaker position was entitled to claim damages from the other party. Therefore, under US competition law an 'innocent' party (for example, a party who is in an economically weaker position) may sue the other party for damages. Consequently, the Court of Appeal was uncertain whether or not Community law conferred similar protection on an innocent party to a contract liable to restrict or distort competition.

The decision of the ECJ in the present case has far-reaching consequences. The ECJ noted the following points.

1. Even a party to a contract that is liable to restrict or distort competition within the meaning of art 81(1) EC is entitled to rely on breach of that Article before a national court. His participation in an unlawful contract does not deprive him of his right to bring an action.
2. A party to a contract which is liable to restrict or distort competition cannot be deprived of his right to seek compensation from the other party for loss caused by such a contract on the sole ground that he is a party to an unlawful contract. Only the fact that such a party bears significant responsibility for the distortion of competition may deprive him of the right to obtain damages.
3. In order to determine whether a party bears significant responsibility for the distortion of competition, and therefore to assess the merits of a claim for damages, a national court must take into account the economic and legal context in which the parties find themselves and their respective bargaining power and conduct.

The decision of the ECJ in the present case means that a party to an anti-competitive agreement will now be entitled to recover damages from the other party in circumstances where he is not significantly responsible for the distortion of competition, irrespective of whether the claim is made under EC law or under the UK Competition Act 1998. Indeed, courts in the UK must ensure that national law is applied in conformity with EC competition law.

The decision of the ECJ in the present case is in line which US anti-trust law. It also protects a weaker party, who is often forced to enter into an agreement contrary to art 81(1) EC. Now, a weaker party is entitled both to damages and to a restitutory remedy in respect of sums already paid under the agreement. In this context a party with a greater bargaining power will gain nothing by forcing a weaker

party to accept an agreement contrary to art 81(1) EC. As the ECJ stated, the right conferred on a weaker party to seek compensation from the other party to an agreement will contribute to the maintenance of effective competition in the Community.

Furthermore, the decision of the ECJ in the present case may also influence English contract law, under which a party to an illegal contract is automatically prevented from claiming damages under that contract.

Imperial Chemical Industries Ltd v *Commission (Dyestuffs)* Case 48/69 [1972] ECR 619 European Court of Justice

• *Article 85(1) EC Treaty [art 81(1) EC] – agreements – decisions and concerted practices – parallel behaviour – oligopoly – exchange of information*

Facts
ICI was one of a number of undertakings which manufactured aniline dyestuffs. The leading producers of aniline dyestuffs increased their prices almost simultaneously on three occasion: in 1964 by 10 per cent; in 1965 by 10–15 per cent; and in 1967 by 8 per cent. The Commission decided that these three general and uniform increases in prices indicated that there had been a concerted practice between the undertakings concerned contrary to art 85(1) EC Treaty [art 81(1) EC] and imposed fines on them. ICI challenged the Commission's decision on the grounds that the price increase merely reflected parallel behaviour in an oligopolistic market and did not result from concerted practices.

Held
The ECJ dismissed the application of ICI.

Judgment
'[*The concept of a concerted practice*]
Article 85 draws a distinction between the concept of "concerted practices" and that of

"agreements between undertakings" or a "decision by associations of undertakings"; the object is to bring within the prohibition of that Article a form of co-ordination between undertakings which, without having reached the stage where an agreement properly so-called has been concluded, knowingly substitutes practical co-operation between them for the risks of competition.

By its very nature, then, a concerted practice does not have all the elements of a contract but may inter alia arise out of co-ordination which becomes apparent from the behaviour of the participants.

Although parallel behaviour may not by itself be identified with a concerted practice, it may however amount to strong evidence of such a practice if it leads to conditions of competition which do not correspond to the normal conditions of the market, having regard to the nature of the products, the size and number of the undertakings, and the volume of the said market.

This is especially the case if the parallel conduct is such as to enable those concerned to attempt to stabilise prices at a level different from that to which competition would have led, and to consolidate positions to the detriment of effective freedom of movement of the products in the Common Market and of the freedom of consumers to choose their suppliers.

Therefore the question whether there was a concerted action in this case can only be correctly determined if the evidence upon which the contested decision is based is considered, not in isolation, but as a whole, account being taken of the specific features of the market in the products in question.

... The general and uniform increase on those different markets can only be explained by a common intention on the part of those undertakings, first, to adjust the level of prices and the situation resulting from competition in the form of discounts, and secondly, to avoid the risk, which is inherent in any price increase, of changing the conditions of competition.

... Although every producer is free to change his prices, taking into account in so

doing the present or foreseeable conduct of his competition, nevertheless it is contrary to the rules on competition contained in the Treaty for a producer to co-operate with his competitors, in a way whatsoever, in order to determine a co-ordinated course of action resulting to a price increase and to ensure its success by prior elimination of all uncertainty as to each other's conduct regarding the essential elements of that action, such as the amount, subject matter, date and place of the increase.

... In these circumstances and taking into account the nature of the market in the products in question, the conduct of the applicant, in conjunction with other undertakings against which proceedings have been taken, was designed to replace the risks of competition and the hazards of competitors' spontaneous reactions by co-operation constituting a concerted practice prohibited by art 85(1) of the Treaty.'

Comment

Concerted practices are most difficult to evidence. In the present case the ECJ defined a concept of concerted practice which with some modifications introduced in *Suiker Unie* v *Commission* Cases 40–48, 50, 54–56, 111, 113 and 114/73 [1976] 1 CMLR 295 can be described as a form of co-ordination between undertakings which, without having been taken to the stage where an agreement properly so-called exists, knowingly substitutes practical co-operation between them for the risks of competition. In the situation of an oligopolistic market, in which the market in dominated by a small number of large concerns, it is extremely difficult to establish collusive practices as it is expected that when one producer changes its prices others will follow. Therefore, it is difficult to distinguish between parallel behaviour and a concerted practice. The case law of the ECJ indicates that the distinction is made on the basis of an external observation of the market. Parallelism in prices can often be explained by the structure of the market. In the *Wood Pulp* cases the ECJ emphasised that inference cannot be made unless it is the only plausible explanation of the observed conduct of undertakings and decided that the oligopolistic tendencies of the market in wood pulp explained the behaviour of the undertaking concerned. However, in the present case the ECJ held that the market in the products in question was not oligopolistic.

Sarrio SA v *EC Commission* Case T–334/94 [1998] ECR II–1727; [1998] 5 CMLR 195 Court of First Instance

• *Article 85(1) EC Treaty [art 81(1) EC] – participation in concerted practices – liability established by participating in meetings with anti-competitive object – price agreement – market sharing – exchange of information, definition of cartel – not necessary to participate in all elements of infringement where collusion part of overall plan – aggravating circumstances – concealment of a cartel – right to defence – fines*

Facts

The decision of the Commission of 13 July 1994 in so-called 'cartonboard' cases in which 19 suppliers of cartonboard were found in breach of art 85(1) EC Treaty [art 81(1) EC] as they operated a price-fixing and market sharing cartel was challenged by 17 of them, including Sarrio. The Commission had found that the undertakings concerned fixed prices for cartonboard through committees set up under the auspices of the Product Group Paperboard (PGP), their trade association. In this respect a number of structures were set up comprising the President's Working Group (PWG) that took general decisions concerning the timing and level of price increases by producers and which submitted reports to the President's Conference (PC), the latter bringing together managing directors and managers of the undertaking twice a year. In 1987 the undertakings set up the Joint Marketing

Committee (JMC) which essentially defined the mode of price policy decided by PWG, country-by-country, and for the major customers in order to achieve a system of equivalent prices in Europe. The Commission also discovered that there was a systematic exchange of information between the cartonboard suppliers operated by a secretarial company, Fides, registered in Switzerland which collated all reports on orders, production, sales and capacity utilisations by the undertakings concerned and sent back to them aggregated data. On appeal the undertakings submitted similar arguments concerning: the proof of their participation in an agreement prohibited under art 85(1) EC Treaty [art 81(1) EC], the infringement of their right of defence in the Commission's proceedings, and the fining policy of the Commission. Taking into account the outcome of the case, as well as the similarity of arguments presented by the parties, only Sarrio's appeal is examined. Sarrio argued that it had not participated in any agreement either to set prices (as it charged different prices for each transaction) or to fix the market shares and outputs of the participants. Sarrio also argued that the fines imposed by the Commission were unjustified and that its right to defence in the proceedings was infringed as the Commission submitted as evidence a document not notified to them and consequently they had no opportunity to make comment on it.

Held

The CFI confirmed the Commission decision in *Sarrio.*

Judgment

'[*Error committed by the Commission in considering that there was one overall infringement and that Sarrió was responsible for it as a whole*]
First of all, the Commission found that the applicant had infringed art 85(1) of the Treaty by participating, from mid-1986 until at least April 1991, in an agreement and a concerted practice which started in mid-

1986 and which consisted of several separate constituent elements.

According to the second paragraph of point 116 of the Decision, the "whole gravamen of the infringement lies in the combination of the producers over several years in a joint unlawful enterprise pursuant to a common design". That view of the infringement is also expressed in point 128 of the Decision: "It would however be artificial to subdivide what is clearly a continuing common enterprise having one and the same overall objective into several discrete infringements."

Consequently, even though the Commission did not expressly use the concept of a "single infringement" in the Decision, it implicitly referred to that concept, as is shown by the reference to para 260 of the judgment of this Court in *Imperial Chemical Industries Ltd* v *Commission*.

Furthermore, the Commission's repeated use of the word "cartel" to cover the various kinds of anti-competitive conduct which it found expresses a comprehensive view of the infringements of art 85(1) of the Treaty. As is clear, in fact, from point 117 of the Decision, the Commission's view is as follows:

"The proper approach in a case such as the present one is to demonstrate the existence, operation and salient features of the cartel as a whole and then to determine (a) whether there is credible and persuasive proof to link each individual producer to the common scheme and (b) for what period each producer participated."

It adds:

"The Commission ... is not required to compartmentalise the various constituent elements of the infringement by identifying each separate occasion during the duration of the cartel on which a consensus was reached on one or another matter or each individual example of collusive behaviour and the[n] exonerating from involvement on that occasion or in that particular manifestation of the cartel any producer not implicated on that occasion by direct evidence."

It also states (in point 118): "There is ample

direct evidence to prove the adherence of each suspected participant to the infringement", without distinguishing between the constituent elements of the overall infringement.

Thus, the single infringement, as conceived by the Commission, is bound up with "the cartel as a whole" or "the overall cartel" and is characterised by a continuous course of action adopted by a number of undertakings pursuing a common unlawful objective. That view of a single infringement gives rise to the system of proof set out in point 117 of the Decision and to unitary responsibility, in the sense that any undertaking "linked" to the overall cartel is held responsible for it whatever the constituent elements in which it is proved to have participated.

In order to be entitled to hold each addressee of a decision, such as the present decision, responsible for an overall cartel during a given period, the Commission must demonstrate that each undertaking concerned either consented to the adoption of an overall plan comprising the constituent elements of the cartel or that it participated directly in all those elements during that period. An undertaking may also be held responsible for an overall cartel even though it is shown that it participated directly only in one or some of the constituent elements of that cartel, if it is shown that it knew, or must have known, that the collusion in which it participated was part of an overall plan and that the overall plan included all the constituent elements of the cartel.

Where that is the case, the fact that the undertaking concerned did not participate directly in all the constituent elements of the overall cartel cannot relieve it of responsibility for the infringement of art 85(1) of the Treaty. Such a circumstance may nevertheless be taken into account when assessing the seriousness of the infringement which it is found to have committed.

In the present case, it is apparent from the Decision that the infringement found in art 1 consisted of collusion on three matters which were different but which pursued a common objective. Those three types of collusion must be regarded as the constituent elements of the overall cartel. According to that article, each of the undertakings mentioned infringed art 85(1) of the Treaty by participating in an agreement and concerted practice by which the undertakings: (a) agreed regular price increases for each grade of the product in each national currency and planned and implemented those increases; (b) reached an understanding on maintaining the market shares of the major producers at constant levels, subject to modification from time to time; and (c) increasingly, from early 1990, took concerted measures to control the supply of the product in the Community in order to ensure the implementation of the concerted price rises.

Despite its view that there was a "single" infringement, the Commission explains in the Decision that:

> "... [t]he 'core' documents which prove the existence of the overall cartel or individual manifestations thereof often identify participants by name, and there is also a vast body of further documentary evidence showing the role of each producer in the cartel and the extent of its involvement" (point 118, first paragraph, of the Decision).

The Court must therefore consider, in the light of the foregoing considerations, whether the Commission has proved the applicant's participation in the cartel, as found in art 1 of the Decision.

As has already been held the Commission has proved that, as an undertaking which took part in the meetings of the PWG from its establishment, the applicant participated, from mid-1986, in collusion on prices and, from the end of 1987, in collusion on market shares and in collusion on downtime, that is to say, in the three constituent elements of the infringement found in art 1 of the Decision. It was therefore fully entitled to decide to hold the applicant responsible for an infringement consisting of those three types of collusion pursuing the same objective.

So the Commission did not place on the applicant responsibility for the conduct of other producers and did not hold it responsible on the sole basis of its participation in the PG Paperboard.

[The application for annulment of art 2 of the Decision]

It will be recalled that art 2 of the Decision provides as follows:

> "The undertakings named in art 1 shall forthwith bring the said infringement to an end, if they have not already done so. They shall henceforth refrain in relation to their cartonboard activities from any agreement or concerted practice which may have the same or a similar object or effect, including any exchange of commercial information:
>
> (a) by which the participants are directly or indirectly informed of the production, sales, order backlog, machine utilisation rates, selling prices, costs or marketing plans of other individual producers; or
>
> (b) by which, even if no individual information is disclosed, a common industry response to economic conditions as regards price or the control of production is promoted, facilitated or encouraged; or
>
> (c) by which they might be able to monitor adherence to or compliance with any express or tacit agreement regarding prices or market sharing in the Community.
>
> Any scheme for the exchange of general information to which they subscribe, such as the Fides system or its successor, shall be so conducted as to exclude not only any information from which the behaviour of individual producers can be identified but also any data concerning the present state of the order inflow and backlog, the forecast utilisation rate of production capacity (in both cases, even if aggregated) or the production capacity of each machine.
>
> Any such exchange system shall be limited to the collection and dissemination in aggregated form of production and sales statistics which cannot be used to promote or facilitate common industry behaviour.
>
> The undertakings are also required to abstain from any exchange of information

of competitive significance in addition to such permitted exchange and from any meetings or other contact in order to discuss the significance of the information exchanged or the possible or likely reaction of the industry or of individual producers to that information.

A period of three months from the date of the communication of this Decision shall be allowed for the necessary modifications to be made to any system of information exchange."

As is apparent from point 165 of the Decision, art 2 was adopted in accordance with art 3(1) of Regulation No 17. By virtue of that provision, where the Commission finds that there is an infringement, inter alia, of art 85 of the Treaty, it may require the undertakings concerned to bring the infringement to an end.

It is settled law that art 3(1) of Regulation No 17 may be applied so as to include an order directed at bringing an end to certain acts, practices or situations which have been found to be unlawful.

Moreover, since art 3(1) of Regulation No 17 is to be applied according to the nature of the infringement found, the Commission has the power to specify the extent of the obligations on the undertakings concerned in order to bring an infringement to an end. Such obligations on the part of the undertakings may not, however, exceed what is appropriate and necessary to attain the objective sought, namely to restore compliance with the rules infringed.

In the present case, in order to verify whether, as the applicant claims, the scope of the direction in art 2 of the Decision is too wide, it is necessary to consider the extent of the various prohibitions it places on the undertakings.

The prohibition in the second sentence of the first paragraph of art 2, requiring the undertakings to refrain in future from any agreement or concerted practice which may have an effect which is the same as, or similar to, those of the infringements found in art 1 of the Decision, is aimed solely at preventing the undertakings from repeating the behaviour found to be unlawful.

Consequently, in adopting such directions, the Commission has not exceeded the powers conferred on it by art 3 of Regulation No 17.

The provisions of subparas (a), (b) and (c) of the first paragraph of art 2 are directed more specifically at prohibiting future exchange of commercial information.

The direction in subpara (a) of the first paragraph of art 2, which prohibits any future exchange of commercial information by which the participants directly or indirectly obtain individual information on competitors, presupposes a finding by the Commission in the Decision that an information e exchange of such a nature is unlawful under art 85(1) of the Treaty.

It should be noted that art 1 of the Decision does not state that the exchange of individual commercial information in itself constitutes an infringement of art 85(1) of the Treaty.

It states more generally that the undertakings infringed that article of the Treaty by participating in an agreement and concerted practice whereby the undertakings, inter alia, "exchanged commercial information on deliveries, prices, plant standstills, order backlogs and machine utilisation rates in support of the above measures".

However, since the operative part of a decision must be interpreted in the light of the statement of reasons for it, it should be noted that the second paragraph of point 134 of the Decision states:

"The exchanging by producers of normally confidential and sensitive individual commercial information in meetings of the PG Paperboard (mainly the JMC) on order backlog, machine closures and production rates was patently anti-competitive, being intended to ensure that the conditions for implementing agreed price initiatives were as propitious as possible."

Consequently, as the Commission duly found in the Decision that the exchange of individual commercial information in itself constituted an infringement of art 85(1) of the Treaty, the future prohibition of such an exchange of information satisfies the conditions for the application of art 3(1) of Regulation No 17.

The prohibitions relating to the exchanges of commercial information referred to in subparas (b) and (c) of the first paragraph of art 2 of the Decision must be considered in the light of the second, third and fourth paragraphs of that Article, which support what is expressed in those subparagraphs. It is in this context that it is necessary to determine whether, and if so to what extent, the Commission considered the exchanges in question to be illegal, since the extent of the obligations on the undertakings must be restricted to that which is necessary in order to bring their conduct into line with what is lawful under art 85(1) of the Treaty.

The Decision must be interpreted as meaning that the Commission considered the Fides system to be contrary to art 85(1) of the Treaty in that it underpinned the cartel (point 134, third paragraph, of the Decision). Such an interpretation is borne out by the wording of art 1 of the Decision, from which it is apparent that the commercial information was exchanged between the undertakings "in support of the ... measures" considered to be contrary to art 85(1) of the Treaty.

The scope of the future prohibitions set out in subparas (b) and (c) of the first paragraph of art 2 of the Decision must be assessed in the light of that interpretation by the Commission of the compatibility, in the present case, of the Fides system with art 85 of the Treaty.

In that regard, first, the prohibitions in question are not restricted to exchanges of individual commercial information, but relate also to certain aggregated statistical data (art 2, first paragraph, (b), and second paragraph, of the Decision). Second, subparas (b) and (c) of the first paragraph of art 2 prohibit the exchange of certain statistical information in order to prevent the establishment of a possible support for future anti-competitive conduct.

Such a prohibition exceeds what is necessary in order to bring the conduct in question into line with what is lawful because it seeks to prevent the exchange of purely statistical information which is not in, or

capable of being put into, the form of individual information on the ground that the information exchanged might be used for anti-competitive purposes. First, it is not apparent from the Decision that the Commission considered the exchange of statistical data to be in itself an infringement of art 85(1) of the Treaty. Second, the mere fact that a system for the exchange of statistical information might be used for anti-competitive purposes does not make it contrary to art 85(1) of the Treaty, since in such circumstances it is necessary to establish its actual anti-competitive effect. It follows that the Commission's argument that art 2 of the Decision is purely declaratory in nature is unfounded.

Consequently, the first to fourth paragraphs of art 2 of the Decision must be annulled, save and except as regards the following passages:

"The undertakings named in art 1 shall forthwith bring the said infringement to an end, if they have not already done so. They shall henceforth refrain in relation to their cartonboard activities from any agreement or concerted practice which may have the same or a similar object or effect, including any exchange of commercial information:

(a) by which the participants are directly or indirectly informed of the production, sales, order backlog, machine utilisation rates, selling prices, costs or marketing plans of other individual producers.

Any scheme for the exchange of general information to which they subscribe, such as the Fides system or its successor, shall be so conducted as to exclude any information from which the behaviour of individual producers can be identified."

[The claim for annulment or reduction of the amount of the fine]

[Error of appraisal by the Commission in that it considered that the cartel "was largely successful in achieving its objectives" and infringement of the obligation to state reasons in that regard]
According to the seventh indent of point 168

of the Decision, the Commission determined the general level of fines by taking
into account, inter alia, the fact that the
cartel "was largely successful in achieving
its objectives". It is common ground that
this consideration refers to the effects on the
market of the infringement found in art 1 of
the Decision.

In order to review the Commission's
appraisal of the effects of the infringement,
the Court considers that it suffices to consider the appraisal of the effects of the collusion on prices. First, it is apparent from the
Decision that the finding concerning the
large measure of success in achieving objectives is essentially based on the effects of
collusion on prices. While those effects are
considered in points 100 to 102, 115, and
135 to 137 of the Decision, the question
whether the collusion on market shares and
collusion on downtime affected the market
was, by contrast, not specifically examined
in it.

Second, consideration of the effects of the
collusion on prices also makes it possible, in
any event, to assess whether the objective of
the collusion on downtime was achieved, as
the aim of that collusion was to prevent the
concerted price initiatives from being undermined by an excess of supply.

Third, as regards collusion on market
shares, the Commission does not submit that
the objective of the undertakings which participated in the meetings of the PWG was an
absolute freezing of their market shares.
According to the second paragraph of point
60 of the Decision, the agreement on market
shares was not static "but was subject to
periodic adjustment and re-negotiation". In
view of that point, the fact that the
Commission took the view that the cartel
was largely successful in achieving its
objectives without specifically examining in
the Decision the success of that collusion
on market shares is not therefore open to
objection.

As regards collusion on prices, the
Commission appraised the general effects of
this collusion. Consequently, even assuming
that the individual data supplied by the
applicant show, as it claims, that the effects

of collusion on prices were, in its case, less
significant than those found on the
European cartonboard market taken as a
whole, such individual data cannot in themselves suffice to call into question the
Commission's assessment.

It is apparent from the Decision, as the
Commission confirmed at the hearing, that a
distinction was drawn between three types
of effects. Moreover, the Commission relied
on the fact that the price initiatives were
considered by the producers themselves to
have been an overall success.'

Comment

In the 'cartonboard' cases the CFI clearly
defined the conditions under which an undertaking may be held responsible for an overall
cartel. Sarrio argued that it had participated
only in some, not all, aspects of the agreement.
The CFI held that it was possible for a
member of a cartel to be held liable for the
overall cartel once it has become aware of the
overall plan of the cartel, although its limited
participation may constitute a mitigating
factor in relation to the fine imposed by the
Commission.

The CFI rejected the argument that
although Sarrio had participated in an agreement which co-ordinated price changes it had
applied its own prices to each individual transaction. The CFI held that the agreement had
impact on transaction prices as it provided the
bases for price negotiation in each transaction
and that Sarrio infringed art 85(1) EC Treaty
[art 81(1) EC] solely by participating in the
agreement. The CFI followed the same line of
reasoning while rejecting Sarrio's argument
concerning no implementation of the agreement. The CFI stated that a serious anti-competitive intent is contrary to art 85(1) EC
Treaty [art 81(1) EC] whether or not the
agreement was in fact implemented.

In relation to the fine imposed by the
Commission, the CFI confirmed the
Commission decision. It stated that the cartel
had been successful in co-ordinating prices,
and that even though there were variations in
prices, all prices were based on announced

prices and that market shares had been regulated although not absolutely frozen. The CFI also approved the increase in fines based on the fact that the undertakings tried to conceal the operation of the cartel. Sarrio argued that secrecy was essential for the operation of a cartel. The Commission and the CFI disagreed, especially in the light of the fact that there were no minutes or other internal or external memos of the meetings of the JMC.

Völk v *Etablissements Vervaecke Sprl* Case 5/69 [1969] ECR 295
European Court of Justice

• *Article 85(1) EC Treaty [art 81(1) EC] – exclusive distribution agreement – absolute territorial protection – effect on inter-State trade – the de minimis rule*

Facts
Völk, a small undertaking manufacturing washing machines, concluded an exclusive distribution agreement with Vervaecke, a Dutch distributor. Völk's share of the market in washing machines was less than 1 per cent. When a dispute arose between the parties, a Dutch court referred to the ECJ a question whether art 85(1) EC Treaty [art 81(1) EC] should apply taking into account the small share of the market held by Völk.

Held
The ECJ held that even an exclusive distributorship agreement ensuring absolute territorial protection was outside the scope of art 85(1) EC Treaty [art 81(1) EC] as the effects produced on trade between Member States were not appreciable.

Judgment
'If an agreement is to be capable of affecting trade between Member States it must be possible to foresee with a sufficient degree of probability on the basis of set of objective factors of law or of fact that the agreement in question may have an influence, direct or indirect, actual or potential, on the pattern of trade between Member States in such a way that it might hinder the attainment of the objectives of a single market between States. Moreover the prohibition in art 85(1) is applicable only if the agreement in question also has as its object or effect the prevention, restriction or distortion of competition within the Common Market. Those conditions must be understood by reference to the actual circumstances of the agreement. Consequently an agreements falls outside the prohibition in art 85 when it has only an insignificant effect on the markets, taking into account the weak position which the persons concerned have on the market of the product in question. Thus an exclusive dealing agreement even with absolute territorial protection may, having regard to the weak position of the persons concerned on the market in the product in question in the area covered by the absolute protection, escape the prohibition laid down in art 85(1).'

Comment
In the present case the ECJ established the de minimis rule under which some agreements prima facie in breach of art 85 (1) EC Treaty [art 81(1) EC] are, nevertheless, outside its scope of application where the market share of the parties is minimal so their agreement has no effect on intra-Community trade. The manufacturer's share of the market (0.6 per cent) was considered by the ECJ as insignificant and the agreement itself concerned only 600 units.

In order to help businesses to assess whether the de minimis rule applies to their agreement the Commission has published a Notice on Agreements of Minor Importance, which was revised (OJ C373 9.12.1997 pp13–15) in 1997.

The Notice is not binding but very useful for undertakings since if their agreement falls below the fixed thresholds they can proceed and do not have to notify it to the Commission. The Commission states in its Notice that no infringement proceedings will be commenced in respect of any such agreement, and if the parties mistakenly, but in good faith, fail to notify their agreement, believing that it is within the scope of the Notice, the Commission will not impose fines on them. If the parties are uncertain whether or not their agreement is excluded from art 85(1) EC Treaty [art 81(1) EC] they should notify it to the Commission in the usual way. Horizontal agreements which are within the scope of the de minimus rule but have as their object price-fixing, restriction of production or sales or market sharing being per se contrary to art 85(1) EC Treaty [art 81(1) EC] are excluded from the scope of the Notice. Although the Commission in general will not commence proceedings in respect of such agreements, unless the interests of the Community require it, they should be notified to the Commission. Similar treatment is applied to vertical agreements which are (by their nature) in breach of art 85(1) EC Treaty [art 81(1) EC], that is those which either fix resale prices or confer territorial protection upon the participating undertakings or third undertakings.

The Notice distinguishes between three types of agreement.

1. Horizontal agreements. In the case of undertakings operating at the same level of production or marketing a threshold is fixed at 5 per cent, ie the aggregate market shares held by participating undertakings in any of the relevant market must not exceed 5 per cent.
2. Vertical agreements. Agreements between undertakings operating at different economic level in the distribution process are within the scope of the Notice if the aggregate market shares of participating undertakings do not exceed in any of the relevant market a threshold of 10 per cent.
3. Mixed agreements. In a mixed horizontal/vertical agreement (or in the event that the classification of an agreement is difficult) a threshold of 5 per cent is applicable.

The Commission will consider agreements, whether horizontal, vertical or mixed, as protected by the Notice if they exceed the fixed threshold by no more that one-tenth in relation to market shares over two successive financial years.

16 Article 82 EC – Abuse of a Dominant Position

AKZO Chemie BV v *Commission*
Case C–62/86 [1991] ECR I–3359; [1993] 5 CMLR 197 European Court of Justice

• *Article 86 EC Treaty [art 82 EC] – relevant market share – relevant product market – relevant geographical market – determination of dominant position – predatory pricing*

Facts
Benzoyl peroxide is a chemical that can be used for bleaching flour and as a catalyst in plastic manufacture. Engineering and Chemical Supplies Ltd (ECS), an English undertaking producing benzoyl peroxide, which had mainly operated in the flour additive sector, decided to expand its sales into the larger plastics sector in the United Kingdom and Ireland. The plastic sector was dominated by AKZO, a producer of organic peroxides including benzoyl peroxide (one of the main organic peroxides) which was also present in the flour additive sector. When one of the largest customers of AKZO in the plastics sector became a customer of ECS, AKZO threatened to reduce prices in the UK flour sector. ECS complained to the Commission. The Commission ordered interim measures under which AKZO's branch in the UK was to stay within the profit levels prior to ECS's expansion to the plastics sector. The Commission found a memo prepared by one of the AKZO's directors stating that the ECS managing director was informed that 'aggressive commercial action would be taken on the milling side unless he refrained from selling his products to the plastics industry'.

The Commission found that AKZO abused its dominant position in the market for organic peroxides by engaging in predatory pricing in order to eliminate ECS. AKZO challenged the methodology employed by the Commission in assessing the existence of a dominant position, in particular in the determination of the relevant product market and the geographical market, and claimed that its prices were not abusive as they always included an element of profit.

Held
The allegations of AKZO were rejected. The ECJ upheld the Commission's assessment of the relevant product market and relevant geographical market.

Judgment
'[*Identification of the relevant product market*]
In the decision it is primarily the organic peroxide market (including benzoyl peroxide used in the plastic industry) that is held to be the relevant market, because that was the market from which AKZO sought in the long-term to exclude ECS. Alternatively, according to the decision, the abuse took place in the flour additives market in the United Kingdom and Ireland.

It must be determined, firstly, whether the Commission was right to define the relevant market as the organic peroxides market.

AKZO disputes this definition in view of the subject matter of the decision, which relates solely to its allegedly unlawful behaviour in the flour additive sector. It points out in this respect that in *Commercial Solvents Corporation* v *Commission* [1974] ECR 223, the Court held that the market in which the effects of the abuse appear is "irrelevant as regards the determination of the relevant market to be considered for the purpose of a finding that a dominant position exists".

That argument must be examined in the light of the particular circumstances of this case.

In that respect it must be observed that benzoyl peroxide, one of the main organic peroxides used in the manufacture of plastics, is also one of the main additives for flour because of its use as a bleaching agent for flour in the United Kingdom and Ireland.

Secondly, it should be pointed out that before 1979 ECS operated solely in the flour additive sector. It was only in the course of that year that it decided to extend its activities to the plastics sector. Consequently, when the dispute arose, ECS had only an extremely small share in that sector.

Moreover, it is not disputed that the plastic sector was more important to AKZO than the flour additives sector, since it had much higher turnover in that sector.

AKZO therefore applied price reductions in a sector (that of flour additives) which was vital to ECS but only of limited importance to itself. Furthermore, AKZO was able to set off any losses that it incurred in the flour additives sector against profits from its activity in the plastic sector, a possibility not available to ECS.

Finally, according to statements made by a manager of AKZO, which will be considered when the complaint relating to the threats is examined, AKZO did not adopt its behaviour in order to strengthen its position in the flour additive sector, but to preserve its position in the plastic sector by preventing ECS from extending its activities to that sector.

The Commission was in those circumstances justified in regarding the organic peroxides market as the relevant market, even though the abusive behaviour alleged was intended to damage ECS's main business activity in a different market.

[*Predatory pricing*]
... Prices below average variable costs (that is to say, those which vary depending on the

quantities produced) by means of which a dominant undertaking seeks to eliminate a competitor must be regarded as abusive. A dominant undertaking has no interest in applying such prices except that of eliminating competitors so as to enable it subsequently to raise its prices by taking advantage of its monopolistic position, since each sale generates a loss, namely the total amount of the fixed costs (that is to say, those which remain constant regardless of the quantities produced) and, at least, part of the variable costs relating to the unit produced.

Moreover, prices below average total costs, that is to say, fixed costs plus variable costs, but above average variable costs must be regarded as abusive if they are determined as part of a plan for eliminating a competitor. Such prices can drive from the market undertakings which are perhaps as efficient as the dominant undertaking but which, because of their smaller resources, are incapable of withstanding the competition waged against them.'

Comment

The divergencies between the Commission and the undertaking under investigation in the determination of the relevant product market followed a not unusual pattern, bearing in mind that undertakings always seek a broad interpretation and the Commission always seeks the opposite. The narrower the definition of a product market the greater the market share of any one undertaking. In the present case, the ECJ defined the relevant product market not by reference to demand and supply substitutability but focused on AKZO's behaviour in relation to the flour additives market. The practices of AKZO in that market, which practices were allegedly abusive, would not be financially viable if AKZO was not in a dominant position. Therefore, by its action AKZO defined the relevant product market.

In respect of predatory prices, in the present case the Commission based its conclusion that AKZO applied predatory prices on an internal memorandum and the desire of AKZO to eliminate the expansion of ECS to the plastics market. There is neither a Community definition of predatory pricing nor a recognised test under EC law for determining what prices should be considered as such. In *Tetra Pak Rausing SA* v *Commission (No 2)* Case C–333/94P [1997] 4 CMLR 662 the ECJ stated that prices which were considerably lower than average variable cost are per se predatory and in such a case no proof of intention to eliminate competitors was necessary. However, if there is over-capacity or over-supply in the relevant product market, or if there is a restructuring of the market, an undertaking applying such prices would be able to escape the prohibition contained in art 86 EC Treaty [art 82 EC].

Hilti AG v *Commission* Case T–30/89 [1991] ECR II–1439; [1992] 4 CMLR 16 Court of First Instance

• *Article 86 EC Treaty [art 82 EC] – relevant product market – substitutability of different component products*

Facts
Hilti manufactured nail guns and the nails and cartridge strips for such equipment. After an investigation by the Commission Hilti was found to have abused its dominant position within the EC market for each of these products, namely the market in nail guns, the market in cartridge strips and the market in nails.

The Commission stated that Hilti abused its position, inter alia, by pursuing a policy of supplying cartridge strips to certain end users or distributors only when such cartridge strips were purchased with the necessary complement of nails ('tying' of cartridge strips and nails), by blocking the sale of competitors' nails by a policy of reducing discounts for orders of cartridges without nails (the reduction of discounts was based essentially on the fact that the customer was purchasing nails from Hilti's competitors), by exercising pres-

sure on independent distributors (mainly in The Netherlands) not to fulfil certain export orders (notably to the UK), by refusing to supply cartridges to independent nail manufactures (mainly to the undertakings that complained to the Commission), etc.

Hilti challenged the Commission's definition of the relevant product market. Hilti argued that these three markets must be regarded as constituting a single indivisible market because each of the products could not be used by consumers without the others.

Held
The CFI upheld the decision of the Commission. The CFI stated that the Commission was correct in identifying three separate product markets because all the products could be manufactured separately and could be purchased by consumers without them having to buy the other products. The relevant product market was therefore the three distinct product markets and the relevant geographical market was the Community as a whole.

Judgment
'[*The relevant geographical market*]
The documents before the Court show that there are large price differences for Hilti products between the Member States and that transport costs for nails are low.

Those two factors make parallel trading highly likely between the national markets of the Community. It must therefore be concluded that the Commission was right in taking the view that the relevant geographical market in this case is the Community as a whole.

The applicant's argument on this point must therefore be rejected.

[*The relevant product market*]
… In order to determine … whether Hilti, as a supplier of nail guns and of consumables designed for them, enjoys such power over the relevant product market as to give it a dominant position within the meaning of art 86, the first question to be answered is

whether the relevant market in the market for all construction fastening systems or whether the relevant markets are for power-actuated fastening (PAF) tools and the consumables designed for them, namely cartridge strips and nails.

The Court takes the view that nail guns, cartridge strips and nails constitute three specific markets. Since cartridge strips and nails are specifically manufactured, and purchased by users, for a single brand of gun, it must be concluded that there are separate markets for Hilti-compatible strips and nails, as the Commission found in its decision.

With particular regard to the nails whose use in Hilti is essential element of the dispute, it is common ground that since the 1960s there have been independent producers, including the interveners, making nails for use in nail guns. Some of those producers are specialised and produce only nails, and indeed some make only nails designed for Hilti tools. That fact in itself is sound evidence that there is a specific market for Hilti-compatible nails.

Hilti's contention that guns, cartridge strips and nails should be regarded as forming an indivisible whole, a "powder-actuated fastening system" is in practice tantamount to permitting producers of nail guns to exclude the use of consumables other than their own branded products in their tools. However, in the absence of general and binding statements or rules, any independent producer is quite free, as far as Community competition law is concerned, to manufacture consumables intended for use in equipment manufactured by others, unless in doing so it infringes a patent or some other industrial or intellectual property right.

Even on the assumption that, as the applicant has argued, components of different makes cannot be interchanged without the system characteristics being influenced, the solution should lie in the adoption of appropriate laws and regulations, not in unilateral measures taken by nail gun producers which have the effect of preventing independent producers from pursuing the bulk of their business.

Hilti's argument that PAF tools and consumables form part of the market in PAF systems for the construction industry generally cannot be accepted either. The Court finds the PAF systems differ from other fastening systems in several important respects. The specific features of PAF systems, set out in para 62 of the Decision, are such as to make them the obvious choice in a number of cases. It is evident from the documents before the Court that in many cases there is no realistic alternative either for a qualified operator carrying out a job on site or for a technician instructed to select the fastening methods to be used in a given situation.

The Court considers that the Commission's description of those features in its decision is sufficiently clear and convincing to provide solid legal justification for the conclusions drawn from it.

Those findings leave no real doubt as to the existence, in practice, of a variety of situations, some of which inherently favour the use of a PAF system whilst others favour one or more other fastening systems. As the Commission notes, the fact that several different fastening methods have each continued for long periods to account for an important share of total demand for fastening systems shows that there is only a relatively low degree of substitutability between them.

In such circumstances the Commission was entitled to base its conclusions on arguments which took account of the qualitative characteristics of the products at issue.

[Factors indicating dominance]
The Commission has proved that Hilti holds a market share of around 70 per cent to 80 per cent in the relevant market for nails. That figure was supplied to the Commission by Hilti following a request by the Commission for information pursuant to art 11 of Regulation No 17. As the Commission has rightly emphasised, Hilti was therefore obliged to supply information which, to the best of its knowledge, was as accurate as possible. Hilti's subsequent assertion that the figure were unsound is not corroborated by any evidence or by any examples

showing them to be unreliable. The argument of the applicant must therefore be rejected.

... With particular reference to market shares, the Court of Justice has held ... that very large shares are in themselves, and save in exceptional circumstances, evidence of a dominant position.

In this case it is established that Hilti holds a share of between 70 per cent and 80 per cent in the relevant market. Such a share is, in itself, a clear indication of the existence of a dominant position in the relevant market ...'

Comment

In the context of the present case it should be noted that the Commission published its Notice on the Definition of the Relevant Market for the Purposes of Community Competition Law (OJ C37 1997 p5) based on the then existing practices of both the Commission and the ECJ.

The Notice identifies three main factors of competitive constraints to which undertakings are subject and which identify the relevant market: demand substitutability, supply substitutability and potential competition. In relation to demand and supply substitutability the Notice provides examples in order to illustrate the reasoning of the Commission. Thus, to assess the demand substitutability a hypothetical situation is examined in which a small (up to 10 per cent) and permanent price increase is applied: if the existence of other products within the geographical markets would make the price rise unprofitable due to loss of sales, those products are part of the market since in those circumstances the consumer would substitute one product for another.

The supply substitutability is determined by reference to the ability of competitors to switch their resources to manufacture a product which has been subject to a small and permanent price rise without significant increase in cost and risk for such an undertaking. If switching the production involves major investment, or risks then there is no

supply substitutability for the product in question. The Notice suggests that the third constraint, the impact of potential competition, is not applied when determining markets but in a later stage when the relevant market has been defined in order to assess whether the presence of potential competition might influence the market strength in relation to the undertaking concerned.

According to the Notice a product market: 'comprises all those products and/or services which are regarded as interchangeable or substitutable by the consumer by reason of the products' characteristics, their prices and their intended use'.

In order to establish whether there are possible relevant markets the Commission will take into consideration the following evidence:

1. evidence of substitution in the recent past such as price changes and introduction of new products on the market;
2. views of customers and competitors in relation to the effect on the product market of a small and permanent price increase;
3. consumer preference which may be assessed conducting surveys among consumers and retailers. Also information gathered by the undertaking concerned may be useful;
4. costs and obstacles involved in switching demand to potential substitutes;
5. the category of consumers and price discrimination which is important where there is a clearly defined group of consumers.

In relation to a geographical market the Notice states that it 'comprises the area in which the undertakings concerned are involved in the supply and demand of products or services, in which the conditions of competition are sufficiently homogenous and which can be distinguished from neighbouring areas because the conditions of competition are appreciably different in those areas'.

Criteria very similar to those regarding a relevant product market are to be applied in order to identify a geographical market, although not all of them will be relevant in any one case. The heads of evidence are: past evidence of diversion of orders to other areas; basic demand characteristics, ie whether there are local preferences based on brand, language, culture and the need for a local presence; views of customers and retailers; current geographical pattern of purchase; trade flow pattern of shipment when ascertaining actual geographical pattern in the context of a large number of customers; and barriers and cost associated with switching orders to companies situated in other areas.

The Commission also provides a useful note on the range of evidence which it examines in each case for market definition purposes. It includes information forwarded by the undertakings under inquiry, by competitors, by customers and by trade associations. Visits and inspections are also part of the evidence-gathering procedure. Furthermore, the Notice specifies that in the determination of market share both volume sales and value sales are to be taken into consideration.

Irish Sugar plc v *Commission* Case T–228/97 [1999] ECR II–2969; [2000] All ER (EC) 198 Court of First Instance

• *Article 82 EC – dominant position – abuses – concept of joint dominant position – fine*

Facts

Irish Sugar, a company incorporated under Irish law in 1933 by the Irish government, was the sole processor of sugar beet in Ireland and Northern Ireland. On the accession of Ireland to the Community, Irish Sugar was allocated the entire sugar quota for Ireland. Heavy losses suffered by Irish Sugar in the first half of the 1980s forced the Irish government to reform the industry. A rationalisation scheme was implemented which resulted in the gradual improvement of Irish Sugar's profitability. In April 1991 Irish Sugar was priva-

tised. The mechanism for reducing the State's holding in Irish Sugar included the incorporation of a new holding company, Greencore plc, which acquired Irish Sugar.

Irish Sugar as a main supplier of sugar in Ireland held more than 90 per cent of the market share between 1985 and 1995. Imports of sugar came mainly from France through ASI, an Irish company established in Ireland. The very high cost of transport prevented competitors from other Member States from importing sugar to Ireland. From 1990 onwards the only domestic competitor to Irish Sugar on the retail market was an organisation named Round Tower.

In 1993 four Irish food packers, including Gem Pack and Burcom (both packers of Irish Sugar and sugar imported by ASI) and ASI (using imported French sugar), launched 1 kg white granulated sugar brands. In response to ASI launching its own brand of retail sugar, ASI's distributor Allied Distribution Merchants (ADM) was approached by Sugar Limited (SDL) who offered to buy the ASI brand sugar. This was accepted by ADM. Furthermore, a chain of supermarkets selling the ASI brand were approached by SDL and a deal was struck to swap ASI brand sugar for the Irish Sugar brand. Irish Sugar was informed by SDL of the product swap. A year later all competitors of Irish Sugar on the retail sugar market withdrew or ceased to trade. In 1994 Irish Sugar launched its own brand of 1 kg retail sugar, distribution of which in Ireland was carried out by SDL and in Northern Ireland by SDL's distributor McKinney. McKinney was set up in 1976, and 51 per cent of the company was owned by SDL. In 1989 SDL increased its shareholding in McKinney to 60 per cent. Until February 1990 Irish Sugar held 51 per cent of the equity of SDL's parent company, Sugar Distributors Holding (SDH). The managing director of Irish Sugar and a number of other Irish Sugar directors were on the boards of SDH and SDL. In February 1990 Irish Sugar acquired all the remaining shares in SDH and thereby became the sole owner of SDL.

The Commission investigated the commercialisation of sugar in Ireland in the period from 1985 onwards. The Commission stated that Irish Sugar was in breach of art 82 EC as it:

1. took measures to restrict the opportunities for transportation available to its competitors, especially in respect of ASI sugar imported from France, by threatening the main shipping company with the removal of all Irish Sugar business if they continued to carry French sugar. Irish Sugar was successful as the shipping companies agreed not to carry French sugar;
2. swapped its own sugar for ASI sugar; and
3. sought to eliminate competition from the EU. In respect of the UK, Irish Sugar applied selective rebates (including border rebates) and in respect of other Member States it granted sugar export rebates according to the Member State to which export was made, and to certain customers.

The Commission decided that Irish Sugar and SDL jointly held a dominant position on the sugar market between 1985 and February 1990.

Irish Sugar contested the Commission's decision, arguing that the links with SDL guaranteed the independence of the board of SDH/SDL. Furthermore, it argued that the concept of joint dominance could not apply to vertical relationships (SDL was its distributor) but only to horizontal relationships, and that the novelty of the concept of abuse of a joint dominant position had the effect that it had not yet any practical implementation.

Held
The CFI held that Irish Sugar and SDL held a joint dominant position on the sugar market in Ireland and were in breach of art 82 EC.

Judgment
'[*The finding of a joint dominant position*]
The applicant denies that it held a joint dominant position together with SDL between 1985 and February 1990.

In that regard, it sets out the historical background of its relations with SDH, which at that time held all the shares in SDL. It emphasises that, even though it held 51 per cent of the shares in SDH before acquiring all of them in February 1990, it did not control the management of that company. Since 1982, responsibilities had been allocated for practical purposes between it and its sales subsidiaries in such a way that it was responsible for technical services and marketing, including consumer promotions and rebates, while its sales subsidiaries were responsible for the operation and funding of sales, trade promotions, merchandising and distribution of the products. Contrary to what the Commission alleges in the contested Decision (point 30), however, that arrangement did not deprive SDL of the right to trade in competing products. It refers in that respect to transactions by SDL which until 1991 involved, through McKinney's, the purchase and sale in Northern Ireland of sugar from a British supplier. The applicant states, moreover, that its responsibilities under that arrangement were the subject of a management services agreement pursuant to which SDL paid the applicant management charges between 1982 and 1989, the amount of which varied each year and was calculated by the financial director of SDL. It adds that, in practice, the pricing of sugar was essentially a matter for SDL. In order to confirm the autonomy of SDL's management, the applicant also cites extracts from a report drawn up by two experts appointed by the High Court in 1992 and from a report drawn up by Arthur Andersen.

The applicant also asserts that since its economic ties with SDH did not have the effect of uniting the two undertakings they were not capable of supporting a finding of a joint dominant position in the retail and industrial markets in granulated sugar in Ireland. It criticises the Commission for using in the contested Decision (point 112) a false criterion, the parallel interests of the two companies vis-à-vis third parties, in order to find that they held a joint dominant position. It also claims that the reference to the judgment in Joined Cases T–68/89, T–77/89 and T–78/89 *SIV and Others* v *EC Commission* [1992] ECR II–1403, para 358, is not logical.

The applicant maintains that its links with SDH guaranteed the independence of the board and management of the latter. The test used in the case law to determine the existence of a joint dominant position held by linked undertakings is the adoption of the same conduct on the relevant market (Case C–393/92 *Almelo* v *Energiebedrijf Ijsselmij* [1994] ECR I–1477, para 42, and Joined Cases T–24/93, T–25/93, T–26/93 and T–28/93 *Compagnie Maritime Belge Transports and Others* v *EC Commission* [1996] ECR II–1201, paras 62 to 68). Adopting the same conduct on the market represents more than mere parallel interests, which tends to be the rule in a producer – trader relationship, and the more so in a situation of structural oversupply, as in this case. The applicant also points out that in the statement of objections the Commission did not address the issue of whether the relationship between the two undertakings led them to adopt the same conduct on the market, since it merely found that there were structural ties between the applicant and SDH/SDL (statement of objections, paras 102, 103 and 104 et seq).

Similarly, the applicant points out that, whilst the absence of competition in a vertical commercial relationship between a producer and a trader may be a salient feature of a collective dominant position, it is not sufficient to establish the existence of such a dominant position. The applicant questions the relevance of the concept of a collective dominant position in a vertical commercial relationship. Furthermore, all the collective dominant position cases decided by the Community judicature so far concerned horizontal commercial relationships. In its reply the applicant adds that a vertical commercial relationship is characterised by the absence of competition.

The applicant also criticises the allegedly collective nature of most of the abuses committed in the context of the joint dominance alleged. In that regard, it points out that

although the Commission finds that the product swap operations were exclusively arranged by SDL (point 48 of the contested Decision) and that the applicant was only informed of these on 18 July 1988 (point 52), it none the less considers that this amounted to abusive exploitation of a joint dominant position. It accuses the Commission of "recycling" certain facts in the contested Decision by using them to establish both the existence of a joint dominant position (point 112) and abusive exploitation of that joint dominant position (points 117, 127 and 128), contrary to the principle laid down in the case law in that regard (*Compagnie Maritime Belge Transports*, para 67). That "recycling" exercise is said also to amount to an infringement of the applicant's rights of defence, and therefore of art 4 of Regulation No 99/63, since the fact that the applicant financed the rebates allowed by SDL, as distinct from granting them, was not considered to constitute an abuse in the statement of objections.

It is obvious, first, that although the applicant disputes the collective nature of the dominant position which it is alleged to have held with SDH/SDL on the retail sugar market between 1985 and February 1990, it has not in any way denied in its application that it carried out more than 88 per cent of sales registered on that market for the entire duration of the infringement period (point 159 of the contested Decision). Thus, even if it formally denies having held an individual or joint dominant position on the industrial sugar market (see the examination of the second plea of the principal claim below), it has not raised any specific arguments capable of casting doubt on the assessment that it held a dominant position on the retail sugar market.

Moreover, whilst the applicant castigates as inappropriate the criterion used by the Commission at point 112 of the contested Decision to establish the existence of a joint dominant position, the parties nevertheless agree on a number of the conditions required by the case law to establish the existence of a joint dominant position. They thus maintain that, according to the case law, two independent economic entities may hold a joint dominant position on a market (*SIV*, para 358, cited in point 112 of the contested Decision). They also consider that there must be close links between the two entities, and that those links must be such as to be capable of leading to the adoption of the same conduct and policy on the market in question. In that respect, both parties cite the judgments in *Almelo* and *Compagnie Maritime Belge Transports*.

Their analysis of the state of the case law on this question must be accepted. Following its earlier case law and the case law of the Court of First Instance (*Almelo*, para 42; Case C–96/94 *Centro Servizi Spediporto* v *Spedizioni Marittima del Golfo* [1995] ECR I–2883, paras 32 and 33; Joined Cases C–140/94, C–141/94 and C–142/94 *DIP and Others* v *Comune di Bassano del Grappa* [1995] ECR I–3257, para 26; Case C–70/95 *Sodemare and Others* v *Regione Lombardia* [1997] ECR I–3395, paras 45 and 46; *SIV*, para 358; *Compagnie Maritime Belge Transports*, para 62), the Court of Justice has confirmed that a joint dominant position consists in a number of undertakings being able together, in particular because of factors giving rise to a connection between them, to adopt a common policy on the market and act to a considerable extent independently of their competitors, their customers, and ultimately consumers (Joined Cases C–68/94 and C–30/95 *France and Others* v *EC Commission* [1998] ECR I–1375, para 221).

It is therefore necessary to determine in this case whether, by reason of the factors connecting the applicant and SDL from 1985 to February 1990, they had the power to adopt a common market policy.

The applicant relies on the nature of its relations with SDL up to 1990 to dispute the existence of a joint dominant position. It insists that the two entities were independent, making existence of links of the type claimed by the Commission ipso facto impossible.

In the first place, the applicant's argument is based on the false premiss that the eco-nomic independence of the two entities prevents them from holding a joint dominant position. In fact, the case law relied on by the applicant and referred to in para 46 above shows that the mere independence of the economic entities in question is not suf-ficient to remove the possibility of their holding a joint dominant position.

Secondly, the factors connecting the applicant and SDL identified in the con-tested decision show that between 1985 and February 1990 those two economic entities had the power to adopt a common market policy.

In the contested Decision (point 112), the Commission thus identifies as connecting factors the applicant's shareholding in SDH, its representation on the boards of SDH and SDL, the policy-making structure of the companies and the communication process established to facilitate it, and the direct eco-nomic ties constituted by SDL's commit-ment to obtain its supplies exclusively from the applicant and the applicant's financing of all consumer promotions and rebates offered by SDL to its customers. Details thereof are set out in points 29, 30 and 111 of the contested Decision.

The arguments whereby the applicant seeks to question the reality of those factors are both few in number and largely unfounded. It does not deny, for example, that it held 51 per cent of the shares of SDH, which in turn held all the shares in SDL; that half the board of SDH were its representa-tives; that its chief executive and several of its board members sat on the board of SDL; that from July 1982 to February 1990 it was responsible, on the basis of an allocation of tasks jointly determined in July 1982, for technical services and marketing, commer-cial strategy, consumer promotions and rebates; that SDL carried out the distribution of sugar produced by the applicant in Ireland; that SDL undertook, subject to the availability of supplies, to purchase its sugar requirements only from the applicant and not to become concerned or interested in the purchase, sale, resale or promotion of any products of a like or similar kind to those available from the applicant; that the applicant and SDL were required to communicate to each other certain information concerning marketing, sales, advertising, consumer promotions and financial matters; and, finally, that monthly meetings were held between representatives of SDL and of the applicant.

On the other hand, it claims that SDL's exclusive supply undertaking did not prevent it from trading in competing products, particularly in Northern Ireland through the intermediary of McKinney; that the management charges paid by SDL to the applicant arose from the performance of a contract, the amount varying each year and being calculated by the financial director of SDL (letter of 23 October 1991 addressed to the shareholders of Greencore); that those management charges did not constitute a financing of SDL's commercial policy; that the chairmanship of the monthly meetings between the two undertakings was assumed in turn by a representative of the applicant and a representative of SDL and not exclusively by the chief executive of the applicant's sugar division; and, finally, that the pricing of sugar was essentially a matter for SDL.

Those criticisms are, however, not capable of affecting the probative value of the documents used by the Commission to support its analysis of the relations between the applicant and SDL. To demonstrate that, it is sufficient to examine the extract from the minutes of the SDL board meeting of 1 July 1982 which appears in Annex 3 to the statement of objections:

"*Proposals for Marketing/Sales/Distribution of Irish Sugar*
Currently sugar products are sold into three market areas: home market; Northern Ireland market; UK market.

The overall responsibility for the Irish Sugar industry rests with CSET [the abbreviation of the name under which the applicant was founded by the Irish government in 1933, 'Comhlucht Siúcra Éireann Teoranta'] and the policies of the CSET Board towards the overall interests of CSET are fulfilled by the CSET

Organisation and the subsidiary and Associated Boards to whom certain of these functions have been allocated.

To improve the organisation and eliminate the areas where responsibilities are unclear, it is necessary to:

(a) clarify both the duties of the CSET Sugar Division staff and the SDL sales and distribution roles and the co-responsibilities of areas of mutual interest, with the clear recognition of the parent company position of CSET as a major State company;

(b) clarify the co-operation and communications framework within which the two companies should operate;

(c) clarify the communications framework between the above functions and the production units.

To meet these objectives, it is proposed that SDL would be responsible for sales, trade promotions, merchandising and distribution of all CSET sugar products in the Home and Northern Ireland markets, and that CSET would be responsible for marketing and technical services in these markets. In detail, the duties of the staff in both companies will be broken down as follows.

CSET Responsibilities
(A) Home and Northern Ireland
1. Marketing strategy.
2. Advertising (generic and brand) (subject as outlined under co-responsibilities).
3. Packaging and presentation.
4. Product development.
5. New products.
6. Quality.
7. Dealing with all customer complaints re quality and packaging both received directly and advised by SDL, JC Cole Limited and William McKinney (1975) Limited.
8. Consumer promotions.
9. Technical support (including R&D) and services.
10. Product availability.
11. Rebating as required to ensure that we maximise the optimum levels of both price and volume in the Home and Northern Ireland markets.

(B) UK market
1. Sales
2. Marketing.
3. Distribution.

SDL Responsibilities
1. Operation and funding of sales, trade promotions, merchandising and distribution in respect of CSET sugar products in the South and Northern markets. The above responsibilities divided into the designated areas between SDL, JC Cole Limited and William McKinney (1975) Limited.
2. SDL to be responsible for sales decisions including pricing decisions for all of the three sales and distribution companies above. These decisions to be taken in accordance with policy as laid down by the Chief Executive of the Sugar Division.
3. Sugar Distributors Limited will, subject to availability of supplies, purchase its sugar requirements only from CSET and shall not be concerned or interested in the purchase, sale, resale or promotion of any products which are of a like or similar kind to those available from CSET.
4. SDL and JC Cole Limited to distribute sugar from the factory as designated by CSET. The distribution costs to be borne as part of the sales margin.
5. Invoicing/administration of UK sugar sales at no additional administration costs to CSET.

Co-responsibilities – Covering Areas of Mutual Interest
1. Advising and reviewing of pricing and promotion policies to ensure the maintenance of markets at optimum price and volume levels.
2. Communicating information as necessary to each other on all aspects of sugar marketing, sales, trading, advertising, consumer promotions and financial.
3. Brand and consumer advertising in respect of Northern Ireland in consultation with the Board of William McKinney (1975) Limited.
4. Agreeing market research and any other studies required to update market information.

To ensure that all aspects of sugar trading

as outlined above are effectively communicated between CSET and SDL and that the areas of co-responsibility are properly covered, it is proposed that a monthly meeting should take place to discuss all aspects of sugar trading as outlined above between the CSET Sugar Division and SDL. Those meetings to be attended by:

For CSET: Chief Executive; Sugar Division General Manager; Marketing Area General Manager; Carlow Financial Controller; Sugar Division.

For SDL: Managing Director; Sales Director; Financial Director.
The meetings to be chaired by the Chief Executive of the Sugar Division.
Other persons to attend as required."

Bearing in mind the contents of that document and the matters referred to in the contested Decision, the applicant's claim that SDL traded competing products in Northern Ireland through the intermediary of McKinney does not in any way undermine the Commission's assessment of SDL's exclusive supply clause with the applicant. First, it is a claim not supported by any particular proof. Next, McKinney was not in principle legally bound by SDL's undertaking to the applicant. The same applies to the explanations it put forward in its reply to a written question of the Court, concerning sales of German and French sugar through the intermediary of Trilby Trading Ltd, 51 per cent of whose shares the applicant claims to have acquired in August 1987. Contrary to the applicant's claims, the only examples which it adduces in an attempt to minimise the importance of the exclusive supply clause concluded in 1982, namely McKinney's sales in Northern Ireland and the sales by Trilby Trading Ltd after August 1984, tend rather to demonstrate that SDL remained loyal to its undertaking. The minutes of the SDL board meeting of 1 July 1982 also mention McKinney where that company is concerned. McKinney is not expressly referred to by the exclusive supply clause, as drafted in those minutes. Finally, the example of McKinney concerns Northern Ireland, which is not part of the geographical market at issue in this case.

The applicant's presentation of the financing characteristics of the rebates granted by SDL to its customers is full of contradictions. For example, it acknowledges in the final subparagraph of para 28 of its application that it accepted for its account all rebates granted by SDL, and advertising and promotion costs, only to deny in its reply that it financed rebates granted by SDL. In those circumstances, the Court can only find that the Commission correctly assessed the nature of the financial services organised between the applicant and SDL. The contents of the letter from the chairman of Greencore to shareholders of 23 October 1991 is of no use to the applicant in that respect, since it contains no details as to the actual allocation of roles between the applicant and SDL.

Similarly, the statement that the "monthly communication meetings" between the applicant and SDL were chaired in turn by their respective representatives is not only unsupported by any probative document but is also irrelevant. Little purpose is served by stating who chaired the monthly meetings in turn, their existence alone being sufficient to demonstrate that such meetings constitute a connecting factor within the meaning of the case law (see para 46 above). The Court cannot but note, moreover, that the text of the minutes of the SDL board meeting of 1 July 1982 is quite unequivocal, since it states: "The meetings are to be chaired by the Chief Executive of the Sugar Division".

Nor do the applicant's criticisms concerning the price fixing policy, to the effect that this was essentially a matter for SDL, correspond to the minutes of the SDL board meeting of 1 July 1982, which state, in para 2 of the section dealing with SDL's responsibilities:

"SDL to be responsible for sales decisions including pricing decisions for all of the three sales and distribution companies above. These decisions to be taken in accordance with policy as laid down by the Chief Executive of the Sugar Division."

Once again, moreover, these claims are not supported by any particular item of evidence. The letter from the chairman of Greencore to shareholders of 23 October 1991 makes no mention of the allocation of responsibilities in the fixing of prices.

The Court therefore finds that the applicant has not succeeded in demonstrating that the Commission committed an error of assessment in finding that the connecting factors mentioned in the contested Decision showed that, between 1985 and February 1990, SDL and the applicant had the power to adopt a common market policy (see para 46 above).

Furthermore, other market operators considered that the applicant and SDL formed one and the same economic entity. For example, ASI International Foods (formerly ASI International Trading Ltd), the importer of French sugar to the Irish market ("ASI"), sent a letter to the applicant on 18 July 1988 complaining about its market conduct and that of SDL. The author of that letter, which is addressed to the chief executive of the applicant, states:

"I write to draw your attention to the unfair practices which are the direct creation of your undertaking or of SDL which is controlled by you, as regards our efforts to retail our Eurolux sugar in one kilo packets in Ireland."

The fact that the applicant and SDL are in a vertical commercial relationship does not affect that finding.

First, documents of the applicant show that the two companies were active in the same market from 1985 to 1990, so that there could not have been an exclusively vertical commercial relationship. At para 27 of its application, for example, the applicant reproduces an extract from an agreement between SDH shareholders in 1975, which stipulates that "SDL and the Sugar Company shall continue to trade as independent and competing enterprises ...". Moreover, in its reply to a written question of the Court, the applicant insists that SDL distributed the whole of the applicant's supply on the retail sugar market only as from 1988. It also supplies information showing that on the industrial sugar market SDL and the applicant shared the market with a third undertaking, Harcourt Agency Ltd, until the beginning of the 1980s. However, although it maintains that it was no longer present in the industrial sugar market from 1985 to 1989, it does not supply any evidence in support of that allegation. In those circumstances, the applicant's argument based on the absence of competition between itself and SDL may be rejected at the outset.

Nor does the case law contain anything to support the conclusion that the concept of a joint dominant position is inapplicable to two or more undertakings in a vertical commercial relationship. As the Commission points out, unless one supposes there to be a lacuna in the application of art 86 of the Treaty, it cannot be accepted that undertakings in a vertical relationship, without however being integrated to the extent of constituting one and the same undertaking, should be able abusively to exploit a joint dominant position.

Moreover, since all the factual elements relied on in the contested Decision to demonstrate that the applicant and SDL held a joint dominant position were mentioned in the statement of objections, the applicant cannot now accuse the Commission of not considering the relations between the two undertakings in the light of the same market conduct in the statement of objections. As the Commission emphasises in the discussion concerning the amount of the fine, the applicant was perfectly aware of the nature of its links with SDL and of the use which might be made of them in the market. A memorandum headed "Notes on meeting dealing with SDL held on 21st November 1988 in Head Office" (Annex 3 to the statement of objections) states at para 6:

> "Having 51 per cent of SDL should prevent any action being taken against us under art 85. We would have to use our influential presence in SDL to prevent any breaches of art 86 occurring."

Nor can the applicant derive an argument

from the alleged absence of any collective nature in the abuses of a dominant position found in the contested Decision.

Whilst the existence of a joint dominant position may be deduced from the position which the economic entities concerned together hold on the market in question, the abuse does not necessarily have to be the action of all the undertakings in question. It only has to be capable of being identified as one of the manifestations of such a joint dominant position being held. Therefore, undertakings occupying a joint dominant position may engage in joint or individual abusive conduct. It is enough for that abusive conduct to relate to the exploitation of the joint dominant position which the undertakings hold in the market. In this case, the Commission maintains that the exploitation of that joint dominant position formed part of a continuous overall policy of maintaining and strengthening that position, and that conduct adopted by both SDL and the applicant between 1985 and February 1990 fell within that policy. Point 117 of the contested Decision states:

> "The actions taken by Irish Sugar before 1990 with regard to the transport restriction, by both companies with respect to border rebates, export rebates and the fidelity rebate and by SDL with respect to the product swap and selective pricing, were undertaken from a position of joint dominance."

The Commission was therefore entitled to take the view that the individual conduct of one of the undertakings together holding a joint dominant position constituted the abusive exploitation of that position.

Nor can the applicant complain that there has been "recycling" of certain facts in the contested Decision within the meaning that the case law gives to that concept (*SIV*, para 360; *Compagnie Maritime Belge Transports*, para 67). The Commission has not used the same facts to establish both the existence of a joint dominant position and its abusive exploitation. Thus, even if the applicant's financing of rebates granted by SDL was held by the Commission to be one of the connecting factors between the two entities (see para 51 above), it has not in any way been regarded as an abuse in itself. The abuse consists in having granted certain rebates in the particular circumstances of the market in question at that time. The applicant cannot therefore claim to have established infringement of its defence rights and of art 4 of Regulation No 99/63.

It follows that the third limb of the first plea of the principal claim must be dismissed, as, in consequence, must that plea in its entirety.'

Comment

The CFI held that Irish Sugar and SDL held a joint dominant position in the sugar market in Ireland. The Court stated that the factors connecting both undertakings provided sufficient evidence that they had the power to adopt a common market policy. These factors were: Irish Sugar's shareholding in SDH; its representation on the boards of SDH and SDL; the policy-making structure of the undertakings; the direct economic ties constituted by SDL's commitment to obtain all its sugar requirements from Irish Sugar; the financing of all consumer promotions and related offers by SDL to its customers by Irish Sugar; constant communications between both undertakings regarding all aspects of SDL's activities; and monthly meetings between their representatives.

The CFI confirmed that a joint dominant position can apply to vertical relationships. The Court emphasised that nothing in art 82 EC precludes its application to a vertical relationship. The undertakings concerned were not integrated to such an extent as to constitute one undertaking. The CFI also held that the relationship between the undertakings was not exclusively based on a vertical commercial relationship, as SDL was a competitor in the same market.

In respect of the novelty of the concept, the CFI held, first, that although the prohibited conduct took place before the Commission Decision in *Società Italiana Vetro* v *Commission (Re Italian Flat Glass Suppliers)*

Cases T–68, 77 and 78/89 [1992] 2 CLMR 302, it had been well established that the novelty of a concept should be taken into account when fixing the amount of the fine: *AKZO Chemie BV* v *Commission* Case C–62/82 [1991] ECR I–3359. Second, that even if that concept was not yet fully clarified (as the Commission admitted in its Communication of 10 December 1996: Com (96) 649 final), its Decision in *Società Italiana Vetro* v *Commission (Re Italian Flat Glass Suppliers)* Cases T–68, 77 and 78/89 [1992] 2 CLMR 302, was adopted in December 1988: OJ L33 (1989). Third, that the purpose of the conduct which constituted abuse of the joint dominant position was the protection of a market position and the prevention of sugar imports into Ireland. This type of conduct always constituted an infringement of art 82 EC: *Compagnie Maritime Belge* Cases T–26 and 28/93 [1997] 4 CMLR 273. Finally, both Irish Sugar and SDL were aware of the closeness of their economic links and the possibility of co-ordinating their conduct on the sugar market. As a result, the Commission was right in not taking into account the alleged novelty of the concept as a mitigating circumstance when fixing the fine.

The cumulative application of arts 81(1) and 82 EC will assist the Commission in tackling the problem of oligopolistic markets in which undertakings, without entering into prohibited agreements or concerted practices, adjust their conduct with their competitors in a manner advantageous to both parties. Such conduct may fall into the scope of art 82 EC.

It is important to note that art 82 EC refers to an abuse of a dominant position by one or more undertakings, not to a dominant position held by more than one undertaking.

Oscar Bronner GmbH & Co KG v *Mediaprint Zeitungs-und Eitschriftenverlag GmbH & Co KG*
Case C–7/97 [1998] ECR I–7701
European Court of Justice

• *Article 86 EC Treaty [art 82 EC] –*

abuse of a dominant position – newspaper home-delivery scheme – refusal of an undertaking holding a dominant position to include another undertaking in the scheme

Facts

The Austrian Regional Court in Vienna referred to the ECJ for a preliminary ruling two questions on the interpretation of art 86 EC Treaty [art 82 EC] which had been raised in proceedings between two Austrian undertakings. They were Oscar Bronner, editor, publisher, manufacturer and distributor of the daily newspaper *Der Standard* which in 1994 held 3.6 per cent of circulation and 6 per cent of advertising share of the Austrian daily newspaper market and Mediaprint Zeitungs, publisher of two daily newspapers which in 1994 held 46.8 per cent of the Austrian daily newspaper market in terms of circulation and 42 per cent in terms of advertising revenues. Mediaprint Zeitungs' two newspapers reached 53.3 per cent of the population from the age of 14 in private households and 71 per cent of all newspaper readers. Mediaprint set up a nationwide delivery system consisting of delivering the newspapers directly to subscribers in the early hours of the morning. Oscar Bronner (for financial reasons) was not able to set up a similar system of delivery on its own and had to use postal service for delivery of its newspaper which took place late in the mornings. Brunner sought an order requiring Mediaprint to cease abusing Mediaprint's alleged dominant position in the market by including Bronner's newspaper, *Der Standard*, in its home-delivery service against payment of reasonable remuneration. Mediaprint refused to do so.

Held

The ECJ held that the refusal by a press undertaking which held a very large share of the daily newspaper market in a Member State and operated the only nationwide newspaper home-delivery scheme in that Member State to allow the publisher of a rival newspaper, which by reason of its small circulation was unable either alone or in co-operation with other publishers to set up and operate its own home-delivery scheme in economically reasonable conditions, to have access to that scheme for appropriate remuneration did not constitute abuse of a dominant position within the meaning of art 86 EC Treaty [art 82 EC].

Judgment

'In examining whether an undertaking holds a dominant position within the meaning of art 86 of the Treaty, it is of fundamental importance, as the Court has emphasised many times, to define the market in question and to define the substantial part of the common market in which the undertaking may be able to engage in abuses which hinder effective competition.

As regards the definition of the market at issue in the main proceedings, it is therefore for the national court to determine, inter alia, whether home-delivery schemes constitute a separate market, or whether other methods of distributing daily newspapers, such as sale in shops or at kiosks or delivery by post, are sufficiently interchangeable with them to have to be taken into account also.

The case law indicates that the territory of a Member State over which a dominant position extends is capable of constituting a substantial part of the common market.

Finally, it would need to be determined whether the refusal by the owner of the only nationwide home-delivery scheme in the territory of a Member State, which uses that scheme to distribute its own daily newspapers, to allow the publisher of a rival daily newspaper access to it constitutes an abuse of a dominant position within the meaning of art 86 of the Treaty, on the ground that such refusal deprives that competitor of a means of distribution judged essential for the sale of its newspaper.

It would still be necessary not only that the refusal of the service comprised in home delivery be likely to eliminate all competition in the daily newspaper market on the part of the person requesting the service and that such refusal be incapable of being objectively justified, but also that the service in itself be indispensable to carrying on that person's business, inasmuch as there is no actual or potential substitute in existence for that home-delivery scheme.

That is certainly not the case.

In the first place, it is undisputed that other methods of distributing daily newspapers, such as by post and through sale in shops and at kiosks, even though they may be less advantageous for the distribution of certain newspapers, exist and are used by the publishers of those daily newspapers.

Moreover, it does not appear that there are any technical, legal or even economic obstacles capable of making it impossible, or even unreasonably difficult, for any other publisher of daily newspapers to establish, alone or in cooperation with other publishers, its own nationwide home-delivery scheme and use it to distribute its own daily newspapers.

It should be emphasised in that respect that, in order to demonstrate that the creation of such a system is not a realistic potential alternative and that access to the existing system is therefore indispensable, it is not enough to argue that it is not economically viable by reason of the small circulation of the daily newspaper or newspapers to be distributed.'

Comment

The ECJ distinguished the present case from others where the refusal of a dominant undertaking in a particular sector to supply or to give access to its facilities were considered as an abuse of that position on the market. In particular, in *Commercial Solvents* v *EC Commission* Cases 6 and 7/73 [1974] ECR 223 the refusal of Commercial Solvents, the world's only large-scale producer of raw materials from which the drug ethambutol could be made (and as such holding a dominant position in that sector), to supply raw materials to Zoja, one of the three makers of ethambutol in the EC, was considered as contrary to art 86(1)(d) EC Treaty [art 82(1)(d) EC]. In *Télémarketing* Case 311/84 [1985]

ECR 3261 an undertaking registered in Luxembourg and dominant over the transmission of advertisements to Belgium refused to transmit telemarketing spots unless its own answering services were used was condemned by the ECJ for abusing its dominant position (see also *Independent Television Publications Limited* v *EC Commission* Case T–76/89 [1991] 4 CMLR 745). It seems that the restrictive approach of the ECJ to the refusal of an undertaking enjoying a dominant position to supply or to give access to its facilities has been relaxed.

In the present case the ECJ specifies two conditions under which the refusal of the dominant undertaking cannot be justified: first, if the refusal of participation in the service comprising home delivery would be likely to eliminate all competition in the daily newspaper market; and, second, if there is no actual or potential substitute in existence for that home-delivery scheme. These two conditions were not satisfied in the present case and therefore, the ECJ held that there was no abuse of a dominant position on the part of Mediaprint.

Merger control

Gencor Ltd v *Commission of the European Communities* Case T–102/96 [1999] ECR II–753 Court of First Instance

• *Competition – merger – Regulation 4064/89 – decision declaring a concentration incompatible with the common market – collective dominant position – extraterritorial scope of application of Regulation 4064/89 – principle of public international law – commitments – admissibility of an action for annulment – legal interest in bringing proceedings*

Facts

Gencor Ltd, a company incorporated under South African law operating mainly in the mineral resources and metals industries, held 46.5 per cent of Impala Platinum Holdings (Implats), also a company registered in South Africa, which brought together Gencor's activities in the platinum group metal ('PGM') sector. Lonrho, an English company operating in various sectors such as mining, metals, hotels, agriculture and general trade, held 73 per cent of Eastern Platinum Ltd and Western Platinum Ltd (LPD), both incorporated under South African law which brought together Lonrho's activities in the PGM sector. The remaining 27 per cent of LPD was held by Gencor.

Gencor and Lonrho proposed to acquire joint control of Implats in order to control LPD. As a result of that transaction Implats was to be held as to 32 per cent by Gencor, 32 per cent by Lonrho and 36 per cent by the public. In practical terms, the concentration would eliminate competition between Gencor and Lonrho not only in the PGM sector in South Africa but also in the marketing of PGMs in the Community where Implats and LPD are important suppliers in this sector, which instead of being supplied by three South African companies would have only two suppliers, Implats/LPD and Amplats (the leading worldwide suppliers in the PGM sector).

The proposed concentration was approved on 22 August 1995 by the South African Competition Board.

On 17 November 1995 Gencor and Lonrho jointly notified the Commission of the above agreements. The Commission declared that the concentration was incompatible with the common market and the functioning of the EEA Agreement, because it would have led to the creation of a dominant duopoly position between Amplats and Implats/LPD in the world platinum and rhodium market as a result of which effective competition would have been significantly impeded in the common market.

On 28 June 1996 the applicant brought this action for the annulment of the contested Decision on the grounds that the Commission had no jurisdiction under Regulation 4064/89 since the transaction was carried out outside the Community and, in the alternative, if the Regulation did apply, it was unlawful and therefore inapplicable pursuant to art 184 of the Treaty.

Held

The CFI dismissed the application.

Judgment

'[*Assessment of the territorial scope of the Regulation*]

The Regulation, in accordance with art 1 thereof, applies to all concentrations with a Community dimension, that is to say to all concentrations between undertakings which do not each achieve more than two-thirds of their aggregate Community-wide turnover within one and the same Member State, where the combined aggregate worldwide turnover of those undertakings is more than ECU 5,000 million and the aggregate Community-wide turnover of at least two of them is more than ECU 250 million.

Article 1 does not require that, in order for a concentration to be regarded as having a Community dimension, the undertakings in question must be established in the Community or that the production activities covered by the concentration must be carried out within Community territory.

With regard to the criterion of turnover, it must be stated that the concentration at issue has a Community dimension within the meaning of the Regulation. The undertakings concerned have an aggregate worldwide turnover of more than ECU 10,000 million, above the ECU 5,000 million threshold laid down by the Regulation. Gencor and Lonrho each had a Community-wide turnover of more than ECU 250 million in the latest financial year. Finally, they do not each achieve more than two-thirds of their aggregate Community-wide turnover within one and the same Member State.

The legal bases for the Regulation (namely arts 87 and 235 of the Treaty, as well as arts 3(g) and 85 and 86 thereof) as well as the first to fifth, ninth and eleventh recitals in the preamble to the Regulation, merely point to the need to ensure that competition is not distorted in the common market, in particular by concentrations which result in the creation or strengthening of a dominant position. They in no way exclude from the Regulation's field of application concentrations which, while relating to mining and/or production activities outside the Community, have the effect of creating or strengthening a dominant position as a result of which effective competition in the common market is significantly impeded.

By referring, in general terms, to the concept of substantial operations, the Regulation does not, for the purpose of defining its territorial scope, ascribe greater importance to production operations than to sales operations. On the contrary, by setting quantitative thresholds which are based on the worldwide and Community turnover of the undertakings concerned, it rather ascribes greater importance to sales operations within the common market as a factor linking the concentration to the Community.

[*Compatibility of the contested decision with public international law*]
Application of the Regulation is justified under public international law when it is foreseeable that a proposed concentration will have an immediate and substantial effect in the Community.

The Court of First Instance states that it was in fact foreseeable that the immediate and substantial effect of creating a dominant duopoly position in a world market would also be to impede competition significantly in the Community, an integral part of that market.

In those circumstances, the contested decision is not inconsistent with either the Regulation or the rules of public international law relied on by the applicant.

Secondly, the applicant maintains that the creation or strengthening of a collective dominant position cannot be prohibited under the Regulation.

The question thus arises as to whether the words "which creates or strengthens a dominant position" cover only the creation or strengthening of an individual dominant position or whether they also refer to the creation or strengthening of a collective dominant position, that is to say one held by two or more undertakings.

The reference in the fifteenth recital in the preamble to the Regulation to a 25 per cent threshold for market share cannot justify a restrictive interpretation of the Regulation. Since oligopolistic markets in which one of the jointly dominant undertakings has a market share of less than 25 per cent are relatively rare, that reference cannot remove cases of joint dominance from the scope of the Regulation. It is more common to find oligopolistic markets in which the dominant undertakings hold market shares of more than 25 per cent. Thus, the market structures which encourage oligopolistic conduct most are those in which two, three or four suppliers each hold approximately the same market share.

That threshold is given purely by way of guidance, as is made clear by the fifteenth recital itself, and it is not incorporated in any way in the provisions of the Regulation.

Since the interpretations of the Regulation based on their wording and the history and the scheme of the Regulation do not permit their precise scope to be assessed as regards the type of dominant position concerned, the legislation in question must be interpreted by reference to its purpose.

It follows from the sixth, seventh, tenth and eleventh recitals in the preamble to the Regulation that it, unlike arts 85 and 86 of the Treaty, is intended to apply to all concentrations with a Community dimension in so far as, because of their effect on the structure of competition within the Community, they may prove incompatible with the system of undistorted competition envisaged by the Treaty.

A concentration which creates or strengthens a dominant position on the part of the parties to the concentration with an entity not involved in the concentration is liable to prove incompatible with the system of undistorted competition laid down by the Treaty. Consequently, if it were accepted that only concentrations creating or strengthening a dominant position on the part of the parties to the concentration were covered by the Regulation, its purpose as indicated by the abovementioned recitals would be partially frustrated. The Regulation would thus be deprived of a not insignificant aspect of its effectiveness, without that being necessary from the perspective of the general structure of the Community system of control of concentrations.

According to the Court of First Instance, the Commission was fully entitled to conclude that the concentration would have led to the creation of a dominant duopoly on the part of Amplats and Implats/LPD in the platinum and rhodium market, as a result of which effective competition would have been significantly impeded in the common market within the meaning of art 2 of the Regulation. It also follows that the reasoning in the contested decision fulfils the requirements laid down by art 190 of the Treaty.

Finally, the Court of First Instance considers what type of commitment (in particular, behavioural) may be accepted under the Regulation.

Where the Commission concludes that the concentration is such as to create or strengthen a dominant position, it is required to prohibit it, even if the undertakings concerned by the proposed concentration pledge themselves vis-à-vis the Commission not to abuse that position.

Consequently, the Commission has power to accept only such commitments as are capable of rendering the notified transaction compatible with the common market.

Since the commitments as a whole were not capable of eliminating the impediment to effective competition caused by the concentration, the Commission was justified in rejecting them, even if there were no particular difficulties in verifying whether they had been carried out.'

Comment

The extra-territorial application of EC competition law is in the present case less controversial than in *Ahlström and Others* v *Commission (Re Wood Pulp Cartel)* Cases 89, 104, 114, 116, 117 and 125–129/85 [1994] ECR I–99 as Lonrho is a company incorporated in the UK. Therefore under the principle of nationality the jurisdiction of the EC competition authorities is justified. Juridiction based on nationality is recognised under public international law, while jurisdiction based on the effects doctrine is still contested. From a practical point of view the strict application of the effects doctrine may create international disputes and is likely to disrupt good international relations. For that reason, the courts in the USA since the mid-1970s have imposed important limitations based on international comity (non-binding rules of goodwill and civility, founded on the moral right of each State to receive courtesy from others) on the application of the effects doctrine under which an anti-competitive practice must have direct and substantial effect in the USA, and the court should balance interests involved in order to determine whether or not the extra-territorial jurisdiction should be upheld (especially see *Mannington Mills Inc* v *Congoleum Corp* 595 F 2d 1287 (3d Cir 1979) and *United States* v *Nippon Paper Indust Co* 109 F3d (1st Cir 1997)).

The Commission enjoys a large measure of discretion in relation to the enforcement of arts 85 and 86 EC Treaty [arts 81 and 82 EC] and has used it to avoid international disputes (see Boeing/ McDonnell Douglas 97/816 (1997) OJ L336 p16). This is not the case in relation to merger control under Regulation 4064/89. It seems that once the envisaged merger satisfies the threshold requirements, the Commission must act, or at least assess the proposed merger from the point of view of Community interests.

It is interesting to note that Merger Regulation 4064/89 which was updated on 26 June 1997 by Regulation 1310/97/EC (entered into force on 1 March 1998) was applied to the present case.

The main changes introduced by the 1997 Merger Regulation concern the thresholds triggering its application and the abolition of a distinction between 'co-operative' and 'concentrative' ventures. The basic rule set out in art 1 of the old Merger Regulation remains, that is a concentration has a 'Community dimension' where, first, the combined aggregate worldwide turnover of all undertakings concerned is over EUR 5 billion and, second, the aggregate Community-wide turnover of each of at least two undertakings concerned is more than EUR 250 million unless each of the undertakings concerned achieves more than two-thirds of its aggregate Community-wide turnover within one and the same Member State. The 1997 Regulation introduces a 'one-stop-shop' EU notification procedure for cross-border merger agreements involving at least three Member States and meeting a slightly lower turnover criteria.

In relation to joint-ventures the 97 Regulation abolishes the distinction between 'co-operative' and 'concentrative' ventures and establishes only one category for all of them – the 'full-function' joint ventures. There is one notification procedure for all joint-ventures carried out within the same time-limit as applicable to merger agreements, that is at the maximum five months (one month for the initial examination followed, if necessary, by a four-months' inquiry). As a result, the full-function joint-ventures will obtain a decision from the Commission in a very short period of time as compared with the old rules. Also, under new rules commitments may be made by the undertakings concerned during the first stage of the investigation in order to allay the Commission's reservations on competition grounds.

17 The Enforcement of Competition Rules

Extra-territorial application of Community law

Ahlström and Others v *Commission (Re Wood Pulp Cartel)* Joined Cases 89, 104, 114, 116, 117 and 125–129/85 [1994] ECR I–99 European Court of Justice

• *Extra-territorial application of EC Treaty – effects doctrine – undertakings from third countries – art 85(1) EC Treaty [art 81(1) EC] – concerted price-fixing*

Facts
The Commission found more than 40 suppliers of wood pulp in violation of Community competition law despite the fact that none of these was resident within the European Community. Fines were imposed on 36 of these undertakings for violation of art 85(1) EC Treaty [art 81(1) EC]. A number of these undertakings appealed against the decision to the ECJ. One of their arguments was that EC competition law was not capable of having extra-territorial effect and therefore the fines were unlawful.

Held
The ECJ confirmed the extra-territorial application of EC competition law.

Judgment
'It should be noted that the main sources of supply of wood pulp are outside the Community, in Canada, the United States, Sweden and Finland and that the market therefore has a global dimension. Where wood pulp producers established in those countries sell directly to purchasers established in the Community and engage in price competition in order to win orders from those customers, that constitutes competition within the Common Market.

It follows that where those producers concert on the prices to be charged to their customers in the Community and put that concertation into effect by selling at prices which are actually co-ordinated, they are taking part in concertation which has the object and effect of restricting competition within the Common Market within the meaning of art 85 of the Treaty.

Accordingly, it must be concluded that by applying the competition rules in the Treaty in the circumstances of this case to undertakings whose registered offices are situated outside the Community, the Commission has not made an incorrect assessment of the territorial scope of art 85.

The applicants have submitted that the Decision is incompatible with public international law on the grounds that the application of the competition rules in this case was founded exclusively on the economic repercussions within the Common Market of conduct restricting competition which was adopted outside the Community.

It should be observed that an infringement of art 85, such as the conclusion of an agreement which has had the effect of restricting competition within the Common Market, consists of conduct made up of two elements: the formation of the agreement, decision or concerted practice and the implementation thereof. If the applicability of prohibitions laid down under competition law were made to depend on the place where the agreement, decision or concerted practice was formed, the result would obviously be to give undertakings an easy means of evading these prohibitions. The decisive factor is therefore the place where it is implemented.

The producers in this case implemented their pricing agreement within the Common Market. It is immaterial in that respect whether or not they had recourse to subsidiaries, agents, sub-agents, or branches within the Community in order to make their contacts with purchasers within the Community.

Accordingly, the Community's jurisdiction to apply its competition rules to such conduct is covered by the territoriality principle as universally recognised in public international law.'

Comment

Extra-territorial jurisdiction was developed to respond to the internationalisation of criminal activities at the end of the nineteenth century. It has also found its application in anti-trust cases, especially in the US anti-trust laws and the EC competition rules.

In certain circumstances the exercise of extra-territorial jurisdiction by the EC is justified when the effect of some anti-competitive conduct of foreign undertakings is realised or felt within the territory of the Union. In the present case the ECJ held that activities of undertakings concerned, although situated outside the territory of the EC, were within the scope of application of EC competition rules because implementation of their agreement had effect within the Community. Their concerted practice had intended a direct and substantial effect on trade within the Community through a reduction in competition in terms of price in sales of wood pulp to Community undertakings. As a result, the concerted practice restricted competition within the EC.

The extra-territorial application of EC competition law creates many problems. The investigation of alleged breaches of EC com-

petition rules outside the territory of the Union often necessitates co-operation of competent authorities of a third State. Even more challenging is the actual enforcement outside the territory of Decisions of the Commission and judgments of the ECJ in competition cases because a third State, where the undertaking is located, has no obligation to co-operate or assist the Commission.

Procedural rights and duties

Baustahlgewebe GmbH v Commission of the European Communities Case C–185/95P [1999] 4 CMLR 1203 European Court of Justice

• *Competition – appeal – excessive duration of the procedure before the CFI – art 6 of the European Convention on Human Rights – reasonable satisfaction for the excessive duration of proceedings – access to the file – general principle of Community law – independent assessment of fines by the CFI*

Facts

On 20 October 1989 Baustahlgewebe brought action for annulment of the Commission Decision 89/515/EEC which imposed fines on 14 producers of welded steel mesh for infringement of art 85(1) EC Treaty [art 81(1) EC]. After five years and six months the CFI delivered its decision reducing the fine from ECU 4.4 million to ECU 3 million and partially annulling the Commission Decision. The applicant claimed, inter alia, that the CFI was in breach of the principle that proceedings must be disposed of within a reasonable time as enshrined in art 6 of the European Convention on Human Rights, that the CFI infringed its rights of defence by refusing access to the file, and that a disproportionate fine was imposed upon it.

Held

The ECJ held that the proceedings before the CFI were excessively protracted. For that reason the ECJ partially annulled the Decision of the CFI. The ECJ stated that the excessive duration of proceedings before the CFI had no impact on the outcome of the case and decided that ECU 50,000 constituted fair satisfaction for a procedural irregularity of that kind. The fine imposed on the applicants was reduced to 2,950,000. The right to consult the CFI's file is governed by the EC Statute of the Court of Justice and by the Rules of Proceedings of the Court of First Instance and not by the general principles of Community law. Consequently, the refusal of the CFI was justified by virtue of art 64 of its rules of procedure. The ECJ held that the CFI had unlimited jurisdiction to determine the amount of fines.

Judgment

'[*Breach of the principle that proceedings must be disposed of within a reasonable time*]

First, it must be noted that the proceedings being considered by the Court of Justice in this case, in order to determine whether a procedural irregularity was committed to the detriment of the appellant's interests, commenced on 20 October 1989, the date on which the application for annulment was lodged, and closed on 6 April 1995, the date on which the contested judgment was delivered. Consequently, the duration of the proceedings now being considered by the Court of Justice was about five years and six months.

It must first be stated that such a duration is, at first sight, considerable. However, the reasonableness of such a period must be appraised in the light of the circumstances specific to each case and, in particular, the importance of the case for the person concerned, its complexity and the conduct of the applicant and of the competent authorities.

As regards the importance of the proceedings to the appellant, it must be emphasised that its economic survival was not directly endangered by the proceedings. The fact nevertheless remains that, in the case of proceedings concerning infringement of competition rules, the fundamental requirement of legal certainty on which economic operators must be able to rely and the aim of ensuring that competition is not distorted in the internal market are of considerable importance not only for an applicant himself and his competitors but also for third parties in view of the large number of persons concerned and the financial interests involved.

It must be held that the procedure before the Court of First Instance was of genuine importance to the appellant.

As regards the complexity of the case, it must be borne in mind that, in its Decision, the Commission concluded that 14 manufacturers of welded steel mesh had infringed art 85 of the Treaty by a series of agreements or concerted practices concerning delivery quotas and the prices of that product. The appellant's application was one of 11, submitted in three different languages, which were formally joined for the purposes of the oral procedure.

In that regard, it is clear from the documents before the Court and from the contested judgment that the procedure concerning the appellant called for a detailed examination of relatively voluminous documents and points of fact and law of some complexity.

It has not been established that the appellant contributed, in any significant way, to the protraction of the proceedings.

As regards the conduct of the competent authorities, it must be borne in mind that the purpose of attaching the Court of First Instance to the Court of Justice and of introducing two levels of jurisdiction was, first, to improve the judicial protection of individual interests, in particular in proceedings necessitating close examination of complex facts, and, second, to maintain the quality and effectiveness of judicial review in the Community legal order, by enabling the Court of Justice to concentrate on its essential task, namely to ensure that in the interpretation and application of Community law the law is observed.

That is why the structure of the Community judicial system justifies, in certain respects, the Court of First Instance, which is responsible for establishing the facts and undertaking a substantive examination of the dispute, being allowed a relatively longer period to investigate actions calling for a close examination of complex facts. However, that task does not relieve the Community court established especially for that purpose from the obligation of observing reasonable time-limits in dealing with cases before it.

Account must also be taken of the constraints inherent in proceedings before the Community judicature, associated in particular with the use of languages provided for in art 35 of the Rules of Procedure of the Court of First Instance, and of the obligation, laid down in art 30(2) of those rules, to publish judgments in the languages referred to in art 1 of Regulation No 1 of the Council of 15 April 1958 determining the languages to be used by the European Economic Community.

However, it must be held that the circumstances of this case are not such as to indicate that constraints of that kind can provide justification for the time which the proceedings took before the Court of First Instance.

It must be emphasised, as far as the principle of a reasonable time is concerned, that two periods are of significance with respect to the proceedings before the Court of First Instance. Thus, about 32 months elapsed between the end of the written procedure and the decision to open the oral procedure. Admittedly, it was decided by order of 13 October 1992 to join the 11 cases for the purposes of the oral procedure. It must be pointed out, however, that, in that period, no other measure of organisation of procedure or of inquiry was adopted. In addition, 22 months elapsed between the close of the oral procedure and the delivery of the judgment of the Court of First Instance.

Even if account is taken of the constraints inherent in proceedings before the Community judicature, investigation and deliberations of such a duration can be justified only by exceptional circumstances.

Since there was no stay of the proceedings before the Court of First Instance, under arts 77 and 78 of its Rules of Procedure or otherwise, it must be concluded that no such circumstances exist in this case.

In the light of the foregoing considerations, it must be held, notwithstanding the relative complexity of the case, that the proceedings before the Court of First Instance did not satisfy the requirements concerning completion within a reasonable time.

For reasons of economy of procedure and in order to ensure an immediate and effective remedy regarding a procedural irregularity of that kind, it must be held that the plea alleging excessive duration of the proceedings is well founded for the purposes of setting aside the contested judgment in so far as it set the amount of the fine imposed on the appellant at ECU 3 million.

However, in the absence of any indication that the length of the proceedings affected their outcome in any way, that plea cannot result in the contested judgment being set aside in its entirety.

[Breach of the principle of promptitude]
It must be noted, first, that, contrary to the appellant's submission at the hearing, neither art 55(1) of the Rules of Procedure of the Court of First Instance nor any other provision of those rules or of the EC Statute of the Court of Justice provides that the judgments of the Court of First Instance must be delivered within a specified period after the oral procedure.

Also, it must be emphasised that the appellant has not established that the duration of the deliberations had any impact on the outcome of the proceedings before the Court of First Instance, in particular as far as any impairment of evidence is concerned.

In those circumstances, this plea must be rejected as unfounded.

[Breach of the principles applicable in the taking of evidence]
There is no ground for finding that the Court of First Instance failed to consider evidence submitted by the appellant when examining that submitted by the Commission.

The Court of First Instance was right in

considering that the offers of evidence submitted in the reply were out of time and in refusing them on the ground that the appellant had not given reasons for the delay in submitting them.

Consequently, the plea that the Court of First Instance infringed the rules of evidence must be rejected.

[*Infringement of the right to consult certain documents*]

The appellant claims that the Court of First Instance infringed the rights of the defence by refusing to accede to its request that all the documents in the administrative procedure be produced, even though the right of access to the file derives from a fundamental principle of Community law which must be observed in all circumstances.

It must be observed that access to the file in competition cases is intended in particular to enable the addressees of a statement of objections to acquaint themselves with the evidence in the Commission's file so that they can express their views effectively on the basis of that evidence on the conclusions reached by the Commission in its statement of objections.

However, contrary to the appellant's assertion, the general principles of Community law governing the right of access to the Commission's file do not apply, as such, to court proceedings, the latter being governed by the EC Statute of the Court of Justice and by the Rules of Procedure of the Court of First Instance.

The appellant was entitled to ask the Court of First Instance to order the opposite party to produce documents which were in its possession. Nevertheless, to enable the Court of First Instance to determine whether it was conducive to proper conduct of the procedure to order the production of certain documents, the party requesting production must identify the documents requested and provide the Court with at least minimum information indicating the utility of those documents for the purposes of the proceedings.

It must be held that it is clear from the contested judgment and from the documents before the Court of First Instance that, although the Commission submitted to it a list of all the documents in the file concerning it, the appellant did not sufficiently identify, in its request to the Court of First Instance, the documents in the file of which it sought production.

The Court of First Instance was therefore right to reject the request for the production of documents. Accordingly, this plea must be rejected as unfounded.

[*The pleas alleging infringement of art 15 of Regulation No 17*]

As regards the allegedly disproportionate nature of the fine, it must be borne in mind that it is not for the Court of Justice, when ruling on questions of law in the context of an appeal, to substitute, on grounds of fairness, its own assessment for that of the Court of First Instance exercising its unlimited jurisdiction to rule on the amount of fines imposed on undertakings for infringements of Community law.

As regards the finding that the appellant participated in the ... cartel, it need merely be stated that, since the appellant was penalised because of agreements which were not inseparably linked with constitution of the cartel and were intended to protect the German market against uncontrolled imports from other Member States, the Court of First Instance was fully entitled, in law, to conclude that the existence of that authorised cartel could not be regarded as a general mitigating circumstance in relation to that action by the appellant, which had assumed particular responsibility in that connection by reason of the functions exercised by its director.

The factors on the basis of which the gravity of an infringement may be assessed may include the volume and value of the goods in respect of which the infringement was committed and the size and economic power of the undertaking and, consequently, the influence which the undertaking was able to exert on the market.

Accordingly, this complaint must be rejected.

[*The consequences of annulment of the contested judgment to the extent to which it determines the amount of the fine*]

Having regard to all the circumstances of the case, the Court considers that a sum of EUR 50,000 constitutes reasonable satisfaction for the excessive duration of the proceedings.

Consequently, since the contested judgment is to be annulled to the extent to which it determined the fine ... the Court of Justice, giving final judgment, in accordance with art 54 of its Statute, sets that fine at EUR 2,950,000.'

Comment

In the present case, for the first time, the ECJ held that a Community court was in breach of the principle that the proceedings must be disposed of within a reasonable time. In order to determine whether or not the duration of the proceedings before the CFI had been excessive the ECJ made reference to art 6 of the European Convention on Human Rights and Fundamental Freedoms and the case law of the European Court of Human Rights in this area. Subsequently, the ECJ assessed the reasonableness of such period in the light of the circumstances of this case, in particular four criteria were taken into account: the importance of the case for the person concerned; its complexity; the conduct of the applicant; and the conduct of the competent authorities. The ECJ concluded the case was of considerable importance, not only to the applicant but also to third parties, in view of: the large number of persons concerned; the amount of the fine; the complexity of the case; and the fact that the applicant did not contribute to the protraction of the proceedings. Consequently, the ECJ implicitly confirmed that pecuniary sanctions imposed on legal persons for breach of EC Competition law are within the scope of criminal matters in the sense of art 6 of the ECHR.

In the present case, the ECJ for the first time held that it was entitled to award 'reasonable satisfaction' within the meaning of art 50 of the ECHR for the excessive duration of the proceedings and consequently reduced

the amount of the fine imposed on the applicants.

Commission of the European Communities v AssiDomän Kraft Products AB and Others Case C–310/97P [1999] 5 CMLR 1253 European Court of Justice

• *Appeal – effect of an ECJ judgment annulling a Commission Decision – the principle of legal certainty*

Facts

In *Ahlström and Others* v *EC Commission (Re Wood Pulp Cartel)* Joined Cases 89, 104, 114, 116, 117 and 125–129/85 [1994] ECR I–99 the Commission found more than 40 suppliers of wood pulp in violation of Community competition law despite the fact that none of these companies was resident within the European Community. Fines were imposed on 36 of those undertakings for violation of art 81(1) EC. Among those fined were nine Swedish undertakings, who paid their fines. Subsequently, 26 of the undertakings appealed to the ECJ against the Decision. They challenged the Commission's finding that they breached art 81(1) EC through concertation of prices for their products by means of a system of quarterly price announcements. However, the nine Swedish undertakings that had already paid fines, including AssiDomän Kraft Products, decided not to participate in the annulment proceedings.

The Court annulled the Decision of the Commission that the undertakings concerned infringed art 81(1) EC through concertation of prices for their products on the grounds that the Commission had not provided a firm, precise and consistent body of evidence in this respect. As a result the ECJ annulled most of the fines entirely, and reduced to Euro 20,000 the other fines imposed on the undertakings which had instituted proceedings.

AssiDomän Kraft Products and other undertakings which did not join in the annulment proceedings asked the Commission to reconsider their legal position in the light of the ECJ's judgment, and to refund to each of them the fines which they paid to the extent that they exceeded the sum of Euro 20,000. However, the undertakings in question were not the addressees of the judgment. The Commission refused to refund them on the grounds that it had already complied with the ECJ order by reducing the fines in respect of the undertakings participating in the proceedings, and that the decision of the ECJ had no necessary impact on the fines imposed upon the Swedish undertakings. The latter responded by challenging that decision before the Court of First Instance (CFI).

The CFI held that although the Commission issued one Decision in the *Wood Pulp* case, that Decision, in fact, consisted of a bundle of 43 separate Decisions, each of which was independent of the others. Consequently, the annulment or modification of 26 fines left the remaining fines unaffected. However, the CFI upheld the appeal of the Swedish undertakings on the ground of art 233 EC, which provides that when an act adopted by an EC institution has been declared void, that institution should take the necessary measures to comply with the judgment of the Court of Justice. The CFI decided that this obligation could extend to persons who were not party to any appeal before the ECJ, and thus the Commission should re-examine the legality of the unchallenged Decision in the light of the grounds of the annulling judgment, and determine whether, following such re-examination, the fines paid must be refunded. The CFI annulled the Commission's Decision refusing to refund the fines already paid by the Swedish undertakings. At that stage, the Commission challenged the Decision of the CFI, that challenge being the subject of the current appeal.

Held

The ECJ reversed the Decision of the CFI. The ECJ held that the Swedish undertakings were not entitled to have the fines reduced.

Judgment

'[*Findings of the Court*]
Essentially, the appeal raises the question whether, where several similar individual Decisions imposing fines have been adopted pursuant to a common procedure and only some addressees have taken legal action and obtained annulment, the institution which adopted them must, at the request of other addressees, re-examine the legality of the unchallenged Decisions in the light of the grounds of the annulling judgment and determine whether, following such a re-examination, the fines paid must be refunded.

Article 176 of the Treaty, which was the only provision relied on before the Court of First Instance by the respondents and on which the contested Decision is founded, requires the institution which adopted the annulled measure only to take the necessary measures to comply with the judgment annulling its measure.

The scope of that provision is limited in two respects.

First, since it would be ultra vires for the Community judicature to rule ultra petita (see the judgments in Joined Cases 46/59 and 47/59 *Meroni* v *High Authority* [1962] ECR 411, at p419, and the judgment in Case 37/71 *Jamet* v *Commission* [1972] ECR 483, para 12), the scope of the annulment which it pronounces may not go further than that sought by the applicant.

Consequently, if an addressee of a Decision decides to bring an action for annulment, the matter to be tried by the Community judicature relates only to those aspects of the Decision which concern that addressee. Unchallenged aspects concerning other addressees, on the other hand, do not form part of the matter to be tried by the Community judicature.

Furthermore, although the authority erga omnes exerted by an annulling judgment of a Court of the Community judicature (see, in particular, the judgments in Case 1/54 *France* v *High Authority* [1954–1956] ECR 1, at p17; Case 2/54 *Italy* v *High Authority* [1954–1956] ECR 37, at p55; and in Case

3/54 *ASSIDER* v *High Authority* [1954–1956] ECR 63) attaches to both the operative part and the ratio decidendi of the judgment, it cannot entail annulment of an act not challenged before the Community judicature but alleged to be vitiated by the same illegality.

The only purpose of considering the grounds of the judgment which set out the precise reasons for the illegality found by the Community Court is to determine the exact meaning of the ruling made in the operative part of the judgment. The authority of a ground of a judgment annulling a measure cannot apply to the situation of persons who were not parties to the proceedings and with regard to whom the judgment cannot therefore have decided anything whatever.

So, although art 176 of the Treaty requires the institution concerned to ensure that any act intended to replace the annulled act is not affected by the same irregularities as those identified in the judgment annulling the original act, that Article, contrary to what the Court of First Instance held in paras 69, 72 and 85, does not mean that the Commission must, at the request of interested parties, re-examine identical or similar Decisions allegedly affected by the same irregularity, addressed to addressees other than the applicant.

It is settled case law that a Decision which has not been challenged by the addressee within the time-limit laid down by art 173 of the Treaty becomes definitive as against him.

In view of that principle, the Court of Justice has repeatedly held that a Member State was no longer entitled, when defending infringement proceedings brought by the Commission, to challenge on the basis of art 184 of the EC Treaty (now art 241 EC) the validity of a Decision which had been addressed to it pursuant to art 93(2) of the Treaty (now art 88(2) EC) when it had allowed the period within which it could bring an action for annulment to expire (see, to this effect, Case 156/77 *EC Commission* v *Belgium* [1978] ECR 1881, para 20, and Case C–183/91 *EC Commission* v *Greece* [1993] ECR I–3131, para 10).

Similarly, the Court has held that, although a party may bring suit by means of an action for damages without being obliged by any provision of law to seek annulment of the unlawful measure which caused him damage, that party may not by those means circumvent the inadmissibility of an application for annulment concerning the same instance of illegality and having the same financial end in view (see, in particular, Case 543/79 *Birke* v *EC Commission and Council* [1981] ECR 2669, para 28; Case 799/79 *Bruckner* v *EC Commission and Council* [1981] ECR 2697, para 19; and Case 175/84 *Krohn* v *EC Commission* [1986] ECR 753, para 33).

Furthermore, in *TWD Textilwerke Deggendorf GmbH* [*TWD Textilwerke Deggendorf GmbH* v *Germany* Case C–188/92 [1994] ECR I–833], the Court held that art 173 of the Treaty precluded the recipient of State aid who could have challenged the Commission Decision declaring the aid unlawful and incompatible with the common market by bringing an action for annulment within the time-limit laid down in the fifth paragraph of art 173 of the Treaty and who did not bring such an action from challenging before the national court the measures implementing the Commission Decision by seeking to rely on the illegality of that Decision. A ruling to the opposite effect would give such a party the power to overcome the definitive nature which the Decision has in relation to him once the time-limit for bringing legal proceedings has expired.

Such a rule is based in particular on the consideration that the purpose of having time-limits for bringing legal proceedings is to ensure legal certainty by preventing Community measures which produce legal effects from being called in question indefinitely as well as on the requirements of good administration of justice and procedural economy.

Finally, it is settled case law that a judgment given by the Court of Justice or by the Court of First Instance annulling a measure can constitute a new fact causing time to start running again only with regard to the parties to the proceedings and to other persons directly affected by the measure which was annulled.

Where a number of similar individual Decisions imposing fines have been adopted pursuant to a common procedure and only some addressees have taken legal action against the Decisions concerning them and obtained their annulment, the principle of legal certainty underlying the explanations set forth in paras 57 to 62 above therefore precludes any necessity for the institution which adopted the Decisions to re-examine, at the request of other addressees, in the light of the grounds of the annulling judgment, the legality of the unchallenged Decisions and to determine, on the basis of that examination, whether the fines paid must be refunded.

In the respondents' submission, however, the Court of First Instance correctly applied the principles established in *Snupat* [*Snupat v High Authority* Joined Cases 42/59 and 49/59 [1959] ECR 127] and *Asteris* [*Asteris AE and Others* v *EC Commission* Joined Cases 97/86, 93/86, 99/86 and 215/86 [1988] ECR 2181], cited above.

Those two cases, however, concerned situations different from that which gave rise to these proceedings.

In Joined Cases 42/59 and 49/59 *Snupat v High Authority*, cited above, very particular circumstances led the Court to place an extensive interpretation on the obligations incumbent on the High Authority following the judgment it had given in Joined Cases 32/58 and 33/58 *Snupat v High Authority* [1959] ECR 127.

First of all, Snupat had systematically used the means of redress open to it, unlike the respondents in this case, who allowed the two-month time-limit laid down in the fifth paragraph of art 173 of the Treaty to expire. Snupat had initially asked to be exonerated from the obligation to contribute to an equalisation fund, relying on exemptions which had been granted by the High Authority to two other producers and then brought an action for the annulment of its decision refusing to grant it an exemption. After the Court had dismissed that action by

a judgment, cited above, which it gave on 17 July 1959, Snupat then asked the High Authority to revoke, with retroactive effect, the exemptions granted to the two other producers before finally bringing a new action, which was eventually upheld, before the Court against the High Authority's decision to refuse to accede to the second request.

Secondly, the exemptions granted to the two other producers were directly prejudicial to Snupat owing to the nature of the equalisation system which had been established, since they reduced the other two producers' production costs and increased Snupat's because the exemptions led to its own contribution being re-evaluated. This did not happen to the fines imposed on the various addressees of the *Wood Pulp* decision, since the annulment of some of the fines did not affect the amount of the fines which had not been challenged.

Nor can the respondents effectively rely on the judgment in *Asteris*, cited above, in which the Court held that, following the annulment, by a previous judgment, of an agricultural regulation applicable to a specific marketing year, the institution concerned was under an obligation to eliminate from the regulations already adopted when that latter judgment was delivered and governing subsequent marketing years any provisions with the same effect as the provision held to be illegal.

That case concerned the annulment of consecutive regulations so that the annulment of an earlier regulation necessarily obliged the enacting institution to take account of the judgment of the Court of Justice when drawing up the regulations subsequent to the annulled regulation.

The Court of First Instance therefore erred in law in holding that art 176 of the Treaty placed the Commission under a duty to re-examine, at the request of those concerned, the legality of the *Wood Pulp* decision in so far as it concerned them, in the light of the grounds of the *Wood Pulp* judgment, and to determine whether, on the basis of such an examination, it was necessary to refund the fines paid. The contested judgment must therefore be set aside.

In accordance with the second sentence of the first paragraph of art 54 of the EC Statute of the Court of Justice, where the Court sets aside the Decision of the Court of First Instance, it may itself give final judgment in the matter, where the state of the proceedings so permits. The Court considers that this is the case.

[*The application for annulment lodged at the Court of First Instance against the decision of 4 October 1995*]

In their action for annulment, the respondents raised a single plea alleging that, by its Decision of 4 October 1995, the Commission had disregarded the legal consequences of the *Wood Pulp* judgment.

In the first limb, they contended that the Commission infringed the principle of Community law according to which a judgment annulling a measure has the effect of rendering the contested measure null and void, erga omnes and ex tunc.

In the second limb, the respondents contended that the Commission had infringed the first paragraph of art 176 of the Treaty.

Since the first limb of the plea is unfounded for the reasons set out in paras 19, 20, 54 and 55 above and the second limb is unfounded for the reasons set out in paras 50 to 56 above, the application for annulment lodged at the Court of First Instance by the respondents on 15 December 1995 against the Commission's Decision of 4 October 1995 rejecting their request for a re-examination in the light of the *Wood Pulp* judgment must be dismissed as unfounded.'

Comment

In the above case the ECJ justified its judgment on two grounds. First, the Community judicature cannot rule ultra petita, that is to say the scope of the annulment which it pronounces may not go further than that sought by the applicant, and thus unchallenged aspects concerning other addressees did not form part of the matter to be tried by the Community judicature. Second, although the authority erga omnes exerted by an annulling judgment attaches to both the operative part

and the ratio decidendi of the judgment, it cannot entail annulment of an act not challenged before the Community judicature but alleged to be vitiated by the same illegality. Consequently, art 233 EC cannot be interpreted as requiring the institution concerned to re-examine identical or similar Decisions allegedly affected by the same irregularity addressed to addressees other than the applicant. The ECJ also added that the judgment of the CFI was contrary to art 230 EC, since it sidestepped the time-limit for bringing legal proceedings against acts adopted by EC institutions and thus undermined the principle of legal certainty. Furthermore, this principle also precluded the re-examination of unchallenged Decisions.

The judgment of the ECJ is fully justified in so far as the Commission's Decision is regarded as a bundle of individual Decisions against each participating undertaking, and not as a single Decision addressed to all of them. This solution has been confirmed in *Limburgse Vinyl Maatschappij NV and Others v EC Commission (Re PVC Cartel (No 2))* [1999] 5 CMLR 303, in which a number of undertakings successfully challenged the Commission's Decision on the ground that it had not been signed by the appropriate persons. The ECJ held that the challenged Decision was binding on those undertakings who had not appealed.

Although the solution consisting of considering the Commission's Decision as a bundle of separate Decisions addressed to each participating undertaking penalises undertakings which decide not to appeal it is, at the same time, fair. Undertakings may not challenge a Commission Decision in competition matters for a number of reasons, the most important being that the appeal procedure involves considerable investment in terms of time and money. Hindsight is very useful, but the fact is that if an undertaking has chosen to economise by not spending time and money on an appeal, and the judgment of the court in similar matters arrives after the limitation period has expired, it will by then be too late to jump on the bandwagon. Conversely, if the outcome goes against the appellant, the decision not to participate will be well justified.

Hoechst AG v *Commission* Cases 46/87 and 227/88 [1989] ECR 2859; [1991] 4 CMLR 10 European Court of Justice

• *Competition procedure – right of the Commission to enter premises and remove evidence – refusal of the undertaking to co-operate with the Commission – safeguards against abusive behaviour of the Commission – European Convention on Human Rights – assistance of national authorities – respect for the national procedural guarantees*

Facts
The Commission made Decisions authorising search and seizure operations at the headquarters and premises of the plaintiff under art 14 of Regulation 17/62, which concerns procedure for conducting investigations into infringements of Community competition policy. These Decisions were adopted after the plaintiff had refused to accede to the Commission's request to hand over certain confidential documentation. In response to the refusal to disclose information, the Commission also imposed fines against the plaintiff.

The plaintiff objected to the conduct of the search on the ground that it had infringed general principles of Community law. The plaintiff submitted a number of grounds in support of his contentions, the majority of which concerned the need to respect due process of law, particularly as enshrined in the European Convention on Human Rights.

Regulation 17/62 was silent on a number of important issues concerning the rights of the suspects in such investigations. The Commission was required to derive applicable rules from the general principles of Community law.

Held
The ECJ held that Regulation 17/62 must be interpreted in such a manner as to protect the rights of individuals against abuse of legal processes, particularly as regards the principles contained in the European Convention on Human Rights. Such rights included the protection of lawyer-client confidentiality, the privileged nature of legal correspondence between them, and the right to legal representation. The Court recognised that it was a general principle of Community law that individuals should be protected from arbitrary and disproportionate intervention by public authorities in the sphere of private activities.

Judgment
'The applicant considers that the contested Decision is unlawful inasmuch as it permitted the Commission's officials to take steps which the applicant describes as search, which are not provided for under art 14 of Regulation 17/62 and which infringe fundamental rights recognised by Community law. It adds that if that provision is to be interpreted as empowering the Commission to carry out searches, it is unlawful on the ground that it is incompatible with fundamental rights, for the protection of which it is necessary that searches should be carried out only on the basis of a judicial warrant issued in advance.

The Commission contends that its powers under art 14 of Regulation 17/62 extend to the adoption of measures which, under the law of some Member States, would be regarded as searches. It nonetheless considers that the requirements of judicial protection deriving from fundamental rights, which it does not contest in principle, are fulfilled in so far as the addressees of Decisions ordering investigations have an opportunity, on the one hand, to contest those Decisions before the Court and, on the other, to apply for suspension of their operation by way of interim order, which permits the Court to check rapidly that the investigations ordered are not arbitrary in nature. Such review is equivalent to a judicial warrant issued in advance.

It should be noted, before the nature and scope of the Commission's powers of investigation under art 14 of Regulation are examined, that that Article cannot be interpreted in such a way as to give rise to results which are incompatible with the general principles of Community law and in particular with fundamental rights.

The Court has consistently held that fundamental rights are an integral part of the general principles of law the observance of which the Court ensures, in accordance with the constitutional traditions common to the Member States, and the international treaties on which the Member States have collaborated or of which they are signatories. The European Convention for the Protection of Human Rights 1950 is of particular significance in that regard.

The interpreting art 14 of Regulation 17/62, regard must be had in particular to the rights of the defence, a principle whose fundamental nature has been stressed on numerous occasions in the Court's decisions (see in particular *Michelin* v *Commission* Case 322/81 [1983] ECR 3461).

In that judgment, the Court pointed out that the rights of the defence must be observed in administrative procedures which may lead to the imposition of penalties. But it is also necessary to prevent those rights from being irremediably impaired during preliminary inquiry procedures including, in particular, investigations which may be decisive in providing evidence of the unlawful nature of conduct engaged in by undertakings for which they may be liable.

Consequently, although certain rights of the defence relate only to the contentious proceedings which follow the delivery of the statement of objections, other rights, such as the right to legal representation and the privileged nature of correspondence between lawyer and client must be respected as from the preliminary-inquiry stage.

Since the applicant has also relied on the requirements stemming from the fundamental rights to the inviolability of the home, it should be observed that, although the existence of such a right must be recognised in

the Community legal order as a principle common to the laws of the Member States in regard to the private dwellings of natural persons, the same is not true in regard to undertakings, because there are not inconsiderable divergencies between the legal systems of the Member States in regard to the nature and degree of protection afforded to business premises against intervention by the public authorities.

No other inference is to be drawn from art 8(1) of the European Convention on Human Rights which provides that: "Everyone has the right to respect for his private and family life, his home and his correspondence." The protective scope of that Article is concerned with the development of man's personal freedom and may not therefore be extended to business premises. Furthermore, it should be noted that there is no case law of the European Court of Human Rights on that subject.

Nonetheless, in all the legal systems of the Member States, any intervention by the public authorities in the sphere of private activities of any person, whether natural or legal, must have a legal basis and be justified on the grounds laid down by law, and, consequently, those systems provide, albeit in different forms, protection against arbitrary or disproportionate intervention. The need for such protection must be recognised as a general principle of Community law. In that regard, it should be pointed out that the Court has held that it has the power to determine whether measures of investigation taken by the Commission under the ECSC Treaty are excessive (Joined Cases 5–11/62 *San Michele and ors* v *EC Commission* [1962] ECR 449).

The nature ans scope of the Commission's powers of investigation under art 14 of Regulation 17/62 should therefore be considered in the light of the general principles set out above.

Article 14(1) authorises the Commission to undertake all necessary investigations into undertakings and associations of undertakings and provide that:

To this end the officials authorised by the Commission are empowered:

a) to examine the books and other business records;

b) to take copies of or extracts from the books and business records;

c) to ask for oral explanations on the spot;

d) to enter any premises, land and means of transport of undertakings.

Article 14(2) and (3) provide that investigations may be carried out upon production of an authorisation in writing or of a Decision requiring undertakings to submit to the investigation. As the Court has already decided, the Commission may choose between those two possibilities in the light of the special features of each case (Case 136/79 *National Panasonic* v *Commission* [1980] ECR 2033). Both the written authorisation and the Decisions must specify the subject matter and purpose of the investigation. Whichever procedure is followed, the Commission is required to inform, in advance, the competent authority of the Member State in whose territory the investigation is to be carried out and, according to art 14(4), that authority must be consulted before the Decision ordering the investigation is adopted.

According to art 14(5), the Commission's officials may be assisted in carrying out their duties by officials of the competent authority of the Member State in whose territory the investigation is to be made. Such assistance may be provided either at the request of that authority or of the Commission.

Finally, according to art 14(6), the assistance of the national authorities is necessary for the carrying out of the investigation where it is opposed by an undertaking.

It follows from the seventh and eighth recitals in the preamble to Regulation 17/62 that the aim of the powers given to the Commission by art 14 of that Regulation is to enable it to carry out its duty under the [EC] Treaty of ensuring that the rules on competition are applied in the Common Market. The function of those rules is, as follows from the fourth recital in the preamble to the Treaty, art 3(f) and arts 85 and 86, to prevent competition being distorted to the detriment of the public interest, individual undertakings and consumers. The exercise of the power given to the Commission by Regulation 17 thus contributes to the maintenance of the system of competition intended by the Treaty with which undertakings are absolutely bound to comply. The eighth recital states that for that purpose the Commission must be empowered throughout the Common Market, to require such information to be supplied and to undertake such investigations "as are necessary" to bring to light any infringement of art 85 and 86.

Both the purpose of Regulation 17/62 and the list of powers conferred on the Commission's officials by art 14 thereof show that the scope of investigations may be very wide. In that regard, the right to enter any premises, land and means of transport of undertakings is of particular importance inasmuch as it is intended to permit the Commission to obtain evidence of infringements of the competition rules in the places in which such evidence is normally to be found, that is to say, on the business premises of undertakings.

That right of access would serve no useful purpose if the Commission's officials could do no more than ask for information or files which they could identify precisely in advance. On the contrary, such a right implies the power to search for various items of information which are not already known or fully identified. Without such a power, it would be impossible for the Commission to obtain information necessary to carry out the investigation if the undertakings concerned refused to co-operate or adopted an obstructive attitude.

Although art 14 of Regulation 17/62 thus confers wide powers of investigation on the Commission, the exercise of these powers is subject to conditions serving to ensure that the rights of the undertakings concerned are respected.

In that regard, it should be noted first that the Commission is required to specify the subject matter and purpose of the investigation. That obligation is a fundamental not merely in order to show that the investigation to be carried out on the premises of the undertaking concerned is justified but also to enable those undertakings to assess the scope of their duty to co-operate while at the same time safeguarding the rights of the defence.

It should be pointed out that the conditions for the exercise of the Commission's investigative powers vary according to the procedure which the Commission has chosen, the attitude of the undertakings concerned and the intervention of the national authorities.

Article 14 of Regulation 17/62 deals in the first place with investigations carried out without the co-operation of the undertakings concerned, either voluntarily, where there is a written authorisation, or by virtue of an obligation arising under a Decision ordering an investigation. In the latter case, which is the situation here, the Commission officials have, inter alia, the power to have shown to them the documents they request, to enter such premises as they choose, and to have shown to them the contents of any piece of furniture which they indicate. On the other hand, they may not obtain access to premises or furniture by force or oblige the staff of the undertaking to give them such access, or carry out search without the permission of the management of the undertaking.

The situation is completely different if the undertakings concerned oppose the Commission's investigation. In that case, the Commission's officials may, on the basis of art 14(6) and without the co-operation of the undertakings, search for any information necessary for the investigation with the assistance of the national authorities, which are required to afford them the assistance necessary for the performance of their duties. Although such assistance is required only if the undertaking expresses its opposition, it may also be requested as a precautionary measure, in order to overcome any opposition on the part of the undertaking.

It follows from art 14 (6) that it is for each Member State to determine the conditions under which the national authorities will afford assistance to the Commission's officials. In that regard, the Member States are required to ensure that the Commission's action is effective, while respecting the general principles set out above. It follows that, within those limits, the appropriate procedural rules designed to ensure respect for the rights of undertakings are those laid down by national law.

Consequently, if the Commission intends, with the assistance of the national authorities, to carry out an investigation other than with the co-operation of the undertakings concerned, it is required to respect the relevant procedural guarantees laid down by national law.'

Comment

The present case illustrates the relationship between national law and EC law in relation to enforcement powers conferred upon the Commission in competition matters. The Commission may decide to carry out investigations under an authorisation from the Commission or under a formal Decision, with or without prior notification to the undertaking concerned. The Commission officials may decide to carry out so called 'dawn raids' – that is arrive at the undertaking's premises without warning. In such event, the undertaking under investigation is entitled to refuse to submit to the investigation although this attitude is not sensible since, first, it implies that the undertaking under investigation has something to hide and, second, the obstruction of investigation will be taken into account in the determination of a fine. In the present case the Commission imposed a fine of EUR 55,000 on Hoechst. Under EC law alone, the Commission official are not entitled to enter the premises of the undertaking under investigation. They have to respect the relevant procedural guarantees laid down in the national law of the undertaking under investigation. For that reason, art 14(6) of Regulation 17/62 provides that when an undertaking refuses to submit to investigations national authorities are required to provide necessary assistance to enable the Commission to make their investigation. In the UK the Crown must obtain an injunction (for example a search order) from the commercial court to assist the Commission. National authorities are not entitled to call into question the need for the investigations since only the ECJ can review the acts of the Commission, but it is for them to decide upon the appropriate procedure to be applied in the investigations. The present case clarifies the rights of an undertaking in such investigations. The Commission is not permitted to carry out 'fishing expeditions'. The subject of the investigations must be specified in the above-mentioned authorisation or Decision, that is, the suspicion which the Commission is seeking to verify must be clearly indicated, but, as the ECJ held in the present case, the Commission is not obliged to provide the addressee with all information at its disposal in relation to the alleged infringement.

Masterfoods Ltd (T/A Mars Ireland) v HB Ice Cream Ltd Case C–344/98 [2000] ECR I–11369 European Court of Justice

* *Articles 81 and 82 EC – applications of arts 81 and 82 EC by national courts – parallel proceedings before national and Community courts*

Facts
HB (a wholly owned subsidiary of the Unilever group) was a leading manufacturer of ice cream in Ireland, and for a number of years supplied its ice cream retailers with freezer cabinets on the proviso that they were used exclusively for HB's products. Further, a condition was imposed that no other freezer cabinets, either provided by retailers or provided by another ice cream manufacturer, could be used in the retailer's premises. In 1989 Masterfoods, a subsidiary of the US corporation Mars Inc, entered the Irish ice cream market. From that time a number of HB's retailers began to stock and display Masterfoods' products in the freezer cabinets

belonging to HB. HB insisted that its retailers complied with the exclusivity clause contained in the agreements for the supply of freezer cabinets. Masterfoods commenced proceedings against HB before the High Court in Ireland challenging the validity of the exclusivity clause as being in breach of arts 81 and 82 EC. HB answered by bringing proceedings for an injunction to restrain Masterfoods from inducing retailers to breach the exclusivity clause. Both parties sought damages.

On 28 May 1992 the High Court dismissed the action brought by Masterfoods and granted HB a permanent injunction, but dismissed HB's claim for damages.

On 4 September 1992 Masterfoods appealed against that decision to the Irish Supreme Court. In parallel with those proceedings Masterfoods lodged a complaint against HB with the Commission. On 29 July 1993 the Commission in its statement of objections found HB in breach of arts 81 and 82 EC. In response HB submitted a proposal to alter the distribution agreements (which was never implemented).

On 11 March 1998 the Commission adopted Decision 98/531/EC (OJ (1998) L246) which found HB in breach of art 81(1) EC for imposing the exclusivity clause requiring that its retailers must, in their retail outlets, have only one or more freezer cabinets supplied by HB and must not have freezer cabinets procured from elsewhere, and in breach of art 82 EC for inducing its retailers to enter into the above freezer cabinet agreements.

HB, which in the meantime changed its name to Van Den Bergh Foods Ltd, brought an action under art 230 EC for annulment of that Decision (*Van den Bergh Foods Ltd v EC Commission* Case T–65/98 [1998] ECR II–2641) and an action for the suspension of the application of Decision 98/531/EC until the CFI had given a ruling on the subject matter.

Under those circumstances the Irish Supreme Court decided to stay proceedings and referred a number of questions to the ECJ for a preliminary ruling:

1. whether the Supreme Court should stay proceedings pending the disposal of the appeal to the CFI and any subsequent appeal to the ECJ;
2. whether or not the Decision of the Commission declaring a party in breach of EC competition law prevented such a party from seeking to uphold a contrary judgment of the national court in its favour where that judgment of a national court was subject to appeal to the national court of final appeal;
3. whether or not HB was in breach of arts 81 and 82 EC.

The CFI stayed proceedings pending the preliminary ruling delivered by the ECJ.

Held

The ECJ held that the duty of sincere co-operation between the national courts and the Community courts required that the national court stay proceedings pending final judgment in an action of annulment by the Community courts unless it considered that, in the circumstances of the case, a reference to the ECJ for a preliminary ruling on the validity of the Commission Decision is warranted. However, a national court, when staying proceedings, should examine whether it is necessary to order any interim measures in order to secure the interests of the parties pending final judgment.

Judgment

'[*Findings of the Court*]
First of all, the principles governing the division of powers between the Commission and the national courts in the application of the Community competition rules should be borne in mind.

The Commission, entrusted by art 89(1) of the EC Treaty (now, after amendment, art 85(1) EC) with the task of ensuring application of the principles laid down in arts 85 and 86 of the Treaty, is responsible for defining and implementing the orientation of Community competition policy. It is for the Commission to adopt, subject to

review by the Court of First Instance and the Court of Justice, individual decisions in accordance with the procedural rules in force and to adopt exemption regulations. In order effectively to perform that task, which necessarily entails complex economic assessments, it is entitled to give differing degrees of priority to the complaints brought before it (*Delimitis* v *Henninger Braü AG* [Case C–234/89 [1991] ECR I–935; [1992] 5 CMLR 210], para 44, and Case C–119/97P *Ufex and Others* v *EC Commission* [1999] ECR I–1341, para 88).

The Commission has exclusive competence to adopt Decisions in implementation of art 85(3) of the Treaty, pursuant to art 9(1) of Regulation No 17 (*Delimitis*, para 44). However, it shares competence to apply arts 85(1) and 86 of the Treaty with the national courts (*Delimitis*, para 45). The latter provisions produce direct effects in relations between individuals and create direct rights in respect of the individuals concerned which national courts must safeguard (*BRT* v *Sabam* [Case 127/73 [1974] ECR 313], para 16). The national courts thus continue to have jurisdiction to apply the provisions of arts 85(1) and 86 of the Treaty even after the Commission has initiated a procedure in application of arts 2, 3 or 6 of Regulation No 17 (*BRT*, paras 17 to 20).

Despite that division of powers, and in order to fulfil the role assigned to it by the Treaty, the Commission cannot be bound by a decision given by a national court in application of arts 85(1) and 86 of the Treaty. The Commission is therefore entitled to adopt at any time individual Decisions under arts 85 and 86 of the Treaty, even where an agreement or practice has already been the subject of a decision by a national court and the Decision contemplated by the Commission conflicts with that national court's decision.

It is also clear from the case law of the Court that the Member States' duty under art 5 of the EC Treaty to take all appropriate measures, whether general or particular, to ensure fulfilment of the obligations arising from Community law and to abstain from any measure which could jeopardise the attainment of the objectives of the Treaty is binding on all the authorities of Member States including, for matters within their jurisdiction, the courts (see, to that effect, Case C–2/97 *IP* v *Borsana Srl* [1998] ECR I–8597, para 26).

Under the fourth paragraph of art 189 of the Treaty, a Decision adopted by the Commission implementing arts 85(1), 85(3) or 86 of the Treaty is to be binding in its entirety upon those to whom it is addressed.

The Court has held, in para 47 of *Delimitis*, that in order not to breach the general principle of legal certainty, national courts must, when ruling on agreements or practices which may subsequently be the subject of a Decision by the Commission, avoid giving decisions which would conflict with a Decision contemplated by the Commission in the implementation of arts 85(1) and 86 and art 85(3) of the Treaty.

It is even more important that when national courts rule on agreements or practices which are already the subject of a Commision Decision they cannot take decisions running counter to that of the Commission, even if the latter's Decision conflicts with a decision given by a national court of first instance.

In that connection, the fact that the President of the Court of First Instance suspended the application of Decision 98/531 until the Court of First Instance has given judgment terminating the proceedings before it is irrelevant. Acts of the Community institutions are in principle presumed to be lawful until such time as they are annulled or withdrawn (Case C–137/92P *Commission* v *BASF and Others* [1994] ECR I–2555, para 48). The decision of the judge hearing an application to order the suspension of the operation of the contested act, pursuant to art 185 of the Treaty, has only provisional effect. It must not prejudge the points of law or fact in issue or neutralise in advance the effects of the decision subsequently to be given in the main action (order in Case C–149/95P(R) *EC Commission* v *Atlantic Container Line and Others* [1995] ECR I–2165, para 22).

Moreover, if a national court has doubts as to the validity or interpretation of an act of a Community institution it may, or must, in accordance with the second and third paragraphs of art 177 of the Treaty, refer a question to the Court of Justice for a preliminary ruling.

If, as here in the main proceedings, the addressee of a Commission Decision has, within the period prescribed in the fifth paragraph of art 173 of the Treaty, brought an action for annulment of that Decision pursuant to that Article, it is for the national court to decide whether to stay proceedings until a definitive decision has been given in the action for annulment or in order to refer a question to the Court for a preliminary ruling.

It should be borne in mind in that connection that application of the Community competition rules is based on an obligation of sincere cooperation between the national courts, on the one hand, and the Commission and the Community Courts, on the other, in the context of which each acts on the basis of the role assigned to it by the Treaty.

When the outcome of the dispute before the national court depends on the validity of the Commission Decision, it follows from the obligation of sincere cooperation that the national court should, in order to avoid reaching a decision that runs counter to that of the Commission, stay its proceedings pending final judgment in the action for annulment by the Community Courts, unless it considers that, in the circumstances of the case, a reference to the Court of Justice for a preliminary ruling on the validity of the Commission Decision is warranted.

If a national court stays proceedings, it is incumbent on it to examine whether it is necessary to order interim measures in order to safeguard the interests of the parties pending final judgment.

In this case it appears from the order for reference that the maintenance in force of the permanent injunction granted by the High Court restraining Masterfoods from inducing retailers to store its products in freezers belonging to HB depends on the validity of Decision 98/531. It therefore follows from the obligation of sincere co-operation that the national court should stay proceedings pending final judgment in the action for annulment by the Community Courts unless it considers that, in the circumstances of the case, a reference to the Court of Justice for a preliminary ruling on the validity of the Commission Decision is warranted.

The answer to Question 1 must therefore be that, where a national court is ruling on an agreement or practice the compatibility of which with arts 85(1) and 86 of the Treaty is already the subject of a Commission Decision, it cannot take a decision running counter to that of the Commission, even if the latter's Decision conflicts with a decision given by a national court of first instance. If the addressee of the Commission Decision has, within the period prescribed in the fifth paragraph of art 173 of the Treaty, brought an action for annulment of that Decision, it is for the national court to decide whether to stay proceedings pending final judgment in that action for annulment or in order to refer a question to the Court for a preliminary ruling.

[*Questions 2 and 3*]
Questions 2 and 3 were raised only in the event that Question 1 should be answered in the negative. In the light of the reply to Question 1, there is no need to answer the other questions.'

Comment
In the above case the ECJ delivered a very important judgment in respect of the duty imposed on national courts to sincerely co-operate with the Commission in the application of EC competition law. This case is particularly interesting, taking into account that the Irish High Court and the Commission reached diametrically opposed conclusions. Therefore, it was difficult for the Supreme Court of Ireland to decide the matter, although by virtue of the principle of supremacy of EC

law the only coherent solution consisted of giving priority to the Commission's Decision and consequently staying all national proceedings until a definite decision was given in proceedings before the Community courts. However, it is well established that national courts are not required to stay proceedings when the Commission has initiated investigating proceedings under arts 2, 3 or 6 of Regulation 17/62: *BRT* v *Sabam* Case 127/73 [1974] ECR 313. Indeed, the Commission and national courts share competence to apply arts 81(1) and 82 EC, although the Commission has exclusive competence to implement art 81(3) EC. Furthermore, both arts 81(1) and 82 EC are directly effective and thus create rights for individuals which national courts must safeguard.

The ECJ in *Masterfoods* established the principle that, in such circumstances, priority must be given to a decision adopted by the Community institutions.

The duty imposed on a national court to avoid any significant risk of conflict between its rulings and Decisions adopted by the Commission requires that, if the addressee of a Commission Decision brings proceedings for its annulment under art 230 EC, the national court has two options: it may decide to stay proceedings until a definitive decision has been given in the action for annulment, or it may decide to refer the matter to the ECJ for a preliminary ruling. However, if a national court exercises the first option it must examine whether it is necessary to order interim measures in order to safeguard the interests of the parties pending final decision.

This solution is not surprising in the light of the principle of the supremacy of EC law. Nevertheless, for the undertakings concerned it means long delays in obtaining a final decision. In the case under consideration the proceedings first commenced in 1992. The Supreme Court of Ireland, after obtaining a preliminary ruling from the ECJ, must, in order to avoid giving a decision inconsistent with a final decision of the Community court, stay the proceedings before it. A new reference to the ECJ on the validity of Decision 98/531/EC adopted by the Commission will serve no purpose, taking into account that this issue is already subject to the action for annulment before the CFI. There is no other solution compatible with the duty of sincere cooperation between national courts and the Community institutions which will ensure the application of the principle of legal certainty. Consequently, the undertakings concerned will have to wait at least two more years before their dispute is finally settled. Only large corporations, such as Masterfoods or HB, can afford to wait more than ten years for a final decision without experiencing financial and other difficulties.

Fines

Volkswagen v Commission Case T–62/98 [2000] 5 CMLR 948; [2000] ECR II–2707 Court of First Instance

• *Fines – appeal – principle of confidentiality of investigation – disclosure to the press – good administration*

Facts
On 28 January 1998 the Commission imposed the biggest ever fine on a single undertaking amounting to EUR 102 million on the German car manufacturer Volkswagen AG (VW): Volkswagen AG and Others Decision 98/273/EC of 28 January 1998 [1998] 5 CMLR 33. The fine represented 10 per cent of VW's net profit for the year preceding the commencement of proceedings. The circumstances were that VW and its subsidiaries, Audi AG and Autogerma SpA, were in persistent breach of arts 81 and 82 EC, as they prevented franchised dealers in Italy from selling VW models to German and Austrian nationals who wished to purchase them in Italy, where prices were lower than in Germany and Austria. The Commission stated that VW was in breach of the principle of the

prohibition of discrimination on the grounds of nationality as embodied in art 12 EC. VW appealed against that Decision.

Held
The CFI upheld the Decision of the Commission that the infringement committed by the applicant was of a particularly serious nature, both in terms of its impact on the internal market, taking into account the size of the Volkswagen group, and in the light of the well settled case law on parallel imports in the motor vehicle industry. Nevertheless, the Court reduced the total amount of fine impose on Volkswagen from EUR 102 million to EUR 90 million for two reasons. The CFI held that the Commission failed to prove that the infringement lasted after the period 1993–1996 and, second, the Commission failed to fully comply with the principle of confidentiality of an investigation, in that the fine was publicly announced to the press before the Commission had adopted a final Decision. The CFI stated that the principle of business secrecy requires that, until a final Decision is taken by the Commission, all proceedings relating to undertakings and their business relationships must remain confidential.

Judgment
'[*Alleged infringement of the principle of good administration in relation to art 214 of the Treaty*]
Article 214 of the EC Treaty lays down an obligation on the members, officials and servants of the institutions of the Community "not to disclose information of the kind covered by the obligation of professional secrecy, in particular information about undertakings, their business relations or their cost components". Although that provision primarily refers to information gathered from undertakings, the expression "in particular" shows that the principle in question is a general one which applies also to other confidential information (Case 145/83 *Adams v Commission (No 1)* [1985] ECR

3539, para 34; and Case T–353/94 *Postbank v EC Commission* [1996] ECR II–921, para 86).

In the present case, it is clear from the documents before the Court that prior to the adoption of the contested Decision a vital part of the draft Decision referred to the Advisory Committee and then, for final approval, to the College of Commissioners was the subject of several leaks to the press. As early as the beginning of January 1998 the press obtained information that the applicant would soon have a large fine imposed on it. Subsequently, the following information was published: "Volkswagen AG, Wolfsburg, will have to pay a fine of 'around' DEM 200 million on account of infringements of EU law. EU Commissioner Karel Van Miert announced this in an interview with the Hamburg weekly magazine *Die Zeit*. Until now, a fine of this amount had been confirmed only in well-informed circles. The decision is to be announced in Brussels on Wednesday." Likewise, the weekly magazine *Der Spiegel* stated: "On Wednesday this week [VW-boss] Piëch will receive further bad news: the EU Commission in Brussels will impose a fine of hundreds of millions on Piëch and Audi boss Herbert Demel". Moreover, as is apparent from an answer to a question put by the Court at the hearing in this case, the fact that a journalist from *Die Zeit* obtained, before adoption of the Decision, information that the fine provided for was around DEM 200 million is not disputed by the defendant.

It must be observed that those disclosures to the press were not restricted to expressing the personal views of the member of the Commission responsible for competition matters regarding the compatibility with Community law of the measures under examination, but also informed the public, extremely precisely, of the amount of the fine envisaged. In inter partes procedures which are liable to result in the imposition of a penalty, the nature and amount of the penalty proposed are by their very nature covered by business secrecy until the penalty has been finally approved and

announced. That principle ensues, in particular, from the need to have due regard for the reputation and standing of the person concerned during a period in which no penalty has been imposed on that person. In the present case, the Commission must be held to have harmed the standing of the undertaking charged by causing a situation to arise in which that undertaking learned from the press the exact nature of the penalty which, in all probability, was to be imposed on it. To that extent, the Commission's duty not to disclose to the press information on the specific penalty envisaged is not merely coterminous with its duty to respect business secrecy, but also with its duty of good administration. Finally, it should be borne in mind that the principle of the presumption of innocence applies to the procedures relating to infringements of the competition rules by undertakings that may result in the imposition of fines or periodic penalty payments. That presumption of innocence is clearly not respected by the Commission where, prior to formally imposing a penalty on the undertaking charged, it informs the press of the proposed finding which has been submitted to the Advisory Committee and the College of Commissioners for deliberation.

Moreover, in causing such sensitive aspects of the matters under deliberation to be disclosed to the press, the Commission acted in a manner injurious to the interests of good administration at the Community level precisely inasmuch as it enabled the public at large to have access, during the process of investigation and deliberation, to such information, internal to the administration.

It is settled case law that an irregularity of the type found above may lead to annulment of the Decision in question if it is established that the content of that Decision would have differed if that irregularity had not occurred. However, in the present case the applicant has not adduced such proof. There are no grounds for supposing that if the information at issue had not been disclosed the Advisory Committee or the College of Commissioners would have altered the proposed amount of the fine or the content of the Decision.

Consequently, this part of the third plea must also be rejected. The third plea must therefore be rejected in its entirety.'

Comment

The most interesting aspect of the above judgment is that the CFI clarified the scope of application of the principle of business secrecy in respect of infringement proceedings carried out by the Commission.

The CFI stated that art 287 EC requires that not only information gathered directly from undertakings, but also other confidential information, concerning the infringement proceedings carried out by the Commission within the framework of the enforcement of EC competition law are covered by the obligation of professional secrecy: *Adams* v *Commission (No 1)* Case 145/83 [1985] ECR 3539 and *Postbank* v *EC Commission* Case T–353/94 [1996] ECR II–921. The ECJ established in the commented case that the information disclosed to the public was very precise in nature, especially in respect of the amount of the fine envisaged, and therefore those disclosures could not be regarded as being an expression of personal views expressed by the members of the Commission in charge of competition matters on the compatibility with EC law of the measures taken by VW which were under examination. Consequently, the Commission, by disclosing to the press important information regarding the infringement proceedings (in particular concerning the amount of the intended fine) prior to the adoption of the challenged Decision, was in breach of three fundamental principles: the principle of business secrecy; the principle of good administration; and the principle of the presumption of innocence.

Appendix

Numbering of the Treaty on European Union and the EC Treaty Articles before and after entry into force of the Amsterdam Treaty

Treaty on European Union

Before	After	Before	After
TITLE I	TITLE I	Article J.16	Article 26
		Article J.17	Article 27
Article A	Article 1	Article J.18	Article 28
Article B	Article 2		
Article C	Article 3	TITLE VI (***)	TITLE VI*
Article D	Article 4		
Article E	Article 5	Article K.1	Article 29
Article F	Article 6	Article K.2	Article 30
Article F.1 (*)	Article 7	Article K.3	Article 31
		Article K.4	Article 32
TITLE II	TITLE II	Article K.5	Article 33
		Article K.6	Article 34
Article G	Article 8	Article K.7	Article 35
		Article K.8	Article 36
TITLE III	TITLE III	Article K.9	Article 37
		Article K.10	Article 38
Article H	Article 9	Article K.11	Article 39
		Article K.12	Article 40
TITLE IV	TITLE IV	Article K.13	Article 41
		Article K.14	Article 42
Article I	Article 10		
		TITLE VIa (**)	TITLE VII
TITLE V (***)	TITLE V		
		Article K.15 (*)	Article 43
Article J.1	Article 11	Article K.16 (*)	Article 44
Article J.2	Article 12	Article K.17 (*)	Article 45
Article J.3	Article 13		
Article J.4	Article 14	TITLE VII	TITLE VIII
Article J.5	Article 15		
Article J.6	Article 16	Article L	Article 46
Article J.7	Article 17	Article M	Article 47
Article J.8	Article 18	Article N	Article 48
Article J.9	Article 19	Article O	Article 49
Article J.10	Article 20	Article P	Article 50
Article J.11	Article 21	Article Q	Article 51
Article J.12	Article 22	Article R	Article 52
Article J.13	Article 23	Article S	Article 53
Article J.14	Article 24		
Article J.15	Article 25		

Treaty Establishing the European Community

Before	After	Before	After
PART ONE	PART ONE	Article 18 (repealed)	–
		Article 19 (repealed)	–
Article 1	Article 1	Article 20 (repealed)	–
Article 2	Article 2	Article 21 (repealed)	–
Article 3	Article 3	Article 22 (repealed)	–
Article 3a	Article 4	Article 23 (repealed)	–
Article 3b	Article 5	Article 24 (repealed)	–
Article 3c (*)	Article 6	Article 25 (repealed)	–
Article 4	Article 7	Article 26 (repealed)	–
Article 4a	Article 8	Article 27 (repealed)	–
Article 4b	Article 9	Article 28	Article 26
Article 5	Article 10	Article 29	Article 27
Article 5a (*)	Article 11		
Article 6	Article 12	CHAPTER 2	CHAPTER 2
Article 6a	Article 13		
Article 7 (repealed)	–	Article 30	Article 28
Article 7a	Article 14	Article 31 (repealed)	–
Article 7b (repealed)	–	Article 32 (repealed)	–
Article 7c	Article 15	Article 33 (repealed)	–
Article 7d (*)	Article 16	Article 34	Article 29
		Article 35 (repealed)	–
PART TWO	PART TWO	Article 36	Article 30
		Article 37	Article 31
Article 8	Article 17		
Article 8a	Article 18	TITLE II	TITLE II
Article 8b	Article 19		
Article 8c	Article 20	Article 38	Article 32
Article 8d	Article 21	Article 39	Article 33
Article 8e	Article 22	Article 40	Article 34
		Article 41	Article 35
PART THREE	PART THREE	Article 42	Article 36
		Article 43	Article 37
TITLE I	TITLE I	Article 44 (repealed)	–
		Article 45 (repealed)	–
Article 9	Article 23	Article 46	Article 38
Article 10	Article 24	Article 47 (repealed)	–
Article 11 (repealed)	–		
		TITLE III	TITLE III
CHAPTER 1	CHAPTER 1		
		CHAPTER 1	CHAPTER 1
SECTION 1 (deleted)	–		
		Article 48	Article 39
Article 12	Article 25	Article 49	Article 40
		Article 50	Article 41
Article 13 (repealed)	–	Article 51	Article 42
Article 14 (repealed)	–		
Article 15 (repealed)	–	CHAPTER 2	CHAPTER 2
Article 16 (repealed)	–		
Article 17 (repealed)	–	Article 52	Article 43
		Article 53 (repealed)	–
SECTION 2 (deleted)	–		

Before	After	Before	After
Article 54	Article 44	Article 76	Article 72
Article 55	Article 45	Article 77	Article 73
Article 56	Article 46	Article 78	Article 74
Article 57	Article 47	Article 79	Article 75
Article 58	Article 48	Article 80	Article 76
		Article 81	Article 77
CHAPTER 3	CHAPTER 3	Article 82	Article 78
Article 59	Article 49	Article 83	Article 79
Article 60	Article 50	Article 84	Article 80
Article 61	Article 51		
Article 62 (repealed)	–	TITLE V	TITLE VI
Article 63	Article 52	CHAPTER 1	CHAPTER 1
Article 64	Article 53	SECTION 1	SECTION 1
Article 65	Article 54	Article 85	Article 81
Article 56	Article 55	Article 86	Article 82
		Article 87	Article 83
CHAPTER 4	CHAPTER 4	Article 88	Article 84
Article 67 (repealed)	–	Article 89	Article 85
Article 68 (repealed)	–	Article 90	Article 86
Article 69 (repealed)	–		
Article 70 (repealed)	–	SECTION 2 (deleted)	–
Article 71 (repealed)	–	Article 91 (repealed)	–
Article 72 (repealed)	–		
Article 73 (repealed)	–	SECTION 3	SECTION 2
Article 73a (repealed)	–	Article 92	Article 87
Article 73b	Article 56	Article 93	Article 88
Article 73c	Article 57	Article 94	Article 89
Article 73d	Article 58		
Article 73e (repealed)	–	CHAPTER 2	CHAPTER 2
Article 73f	Article 59	Article 95	Article 90
Article 73g	Article 60	Article 96	Article 91
Article 73h (repealed)	–	Article 97 (repealed)	–
		Article 98	Article 92
TITLE IIIa (**)	TITLE IV	Article 99	Article 93
Article 73i (*)	Article 61		
Article 73j (*)	Article 62	CHAPTER 3	CHAPTER 3
Article 73k (*)	Article 63	Article 100	Article 94
Article 73l (*)	Article 64	Article 100a	Article 95
Article 73m (*)	Article 65	Article 100b (repealed)	–
Article 73n (*)	Article 66	Article 100c (repealed)	–
Article 73o (*)	Article 67	Article 100d (repealed)	–
Article 73p (*)	Article 68	Article 101	Article 96
Article 73q (*)	Article 69	Article 102	Article 97
TITLE IV (**)	TITLE V	TITLE VI	TITLE VII
Article 74	Article 70	CHAPTER 1	CHAPTER 1
Article 75	Article 71	Article 102a	Article 98

Before	After
Article 103	Article 99
Article 103a	Article 100
Article 104	Article 101
Article 104a	Article 102
Article 104b	Article 103
Article 104c	Article 104
CHAPTER 2	CHAPTER 2
Article 105	Article 105
Article 105a	Article 106
Article 106	Article 107
Article 107	Article 108
Article 108	Article 109
Article 108a	Article 110
Article 109	Article 111
CHAPTER 3	CHAPTER 3
Article 109a	Article 112
Article 109b	Article 113
Article 109c	Article 114
Article 109d	Article 115
CHAPTER 4	CHAPTER 4
Article 109e	Article 116
Article 109f	Article 117
Article 109g	Article 118
Article 109h	Article 119
Article 109i	Article 120
Article 109j	Article 121
Article 109k	Article 122
Article 109l	Article 123
Article 109m	Article 124
TITLE VIa (**)	TITLE VIII
Article 109n (*)	Article 125
Article 109o (*)	Article 126
Article 109p (*)	Article 127
Article 109q (*)	Article 128
Article 109r (*)	Article 129
Article 109s (*)	Article 130
TITLE VII	TITLE IX
Article 110	Article 131
Article 111 (repealed)	–
Article 112	Article 132
Article 113	Article 133
Article 114 (repealed)	–
Article 115	Article 134

Before	After
TITLE VIIa	TITLE X
Article 116 (*)	Article 135
TITLE VIII	TITLE XI
CHAPTER 1 (***)	CHAPTER 1
Article 117	Article 136
Article 118	Article 137
Article 118a	Article 138
Article 118b	Article 139
Article 118c	Article 140
Article 119	Article 141
Article 119a	Article 142
Article 120	Article 143
Article 121	Article 144
Article 122	Article 145
CHAPTER 2	CHAPTER 2
Article 123	Article 146
Article 124	Article 147
Article 125	Article 148
CHAPTER 3	CHAPTER 3
Article 126	Article 149
Article 127	Article 150
TITLE IX	TITLE XII
Article 128	Article 151
TITLE X	TITLE XIII
Article 129	Article 152
TITLE XI	TITLE XIV
Article 129a	Article 153
TITLE XII	TITLE XV
Article 129b	Article 154
Article 129c	Article 155
Article 129d	Article 156
TITLE XIII	TITLE XVI
Article 130	Article 157
TITLE XIV	TITLE XVII
Article 130a	Article 158
Article 130b	Article 159
Article 130c	Article 160

Before	After	Before	After
Article 130d	Article 161	Article 138c	Article 193
Article 130e	Article 162	Article 138d	Article 194
		Article 138e	Article 195
TITLE XV	TITLE XVIII	Article 139	Article 196
Article 130f	Article 163	Article 140	Article 197
Article 130g	Article 164	Article 141	Article 198
Article 130h	Article 165	Article 142	Article 199
Article 130i	Article 166	Article 143	Article 200
Article 130j	Article 167	Article 144	Article 201
Article 130k	Article 168		
Article 130l	Article 169	SECTION 2	SECTION 2
Article 130m	Article 170	Article 145	Article 202
Article 130n	Article 171	Article 146	Article 203
Article 130o	Article 172	Article 147	Article 204
Article 130p	Article 173	Article 148	Article 205
Article 130q (repealed)	–	Article 149 (repealed)	–
		Article 150	Article 206
TITLE XVI	TITLE XIX	Article 151	Article 207
Article 130r	Article 174	Article 152	Article 208
Article 130s	Article 175	Article 153	Article 209
Article 130t	Article 176	Article 154	Article 210
TITLE XVII	TITLE XX	SECTION 3	SECTION 3
Article 130u	Article 177	Article 155	Article 211
Article 130v	Article 178	Article 156	Article 212
Article 130w	Article 179	Article 157	Article 213
Article 130x	Article 180	Article 158	Article 214
Article 130y	Article 181	Article 159	Article 215
		Article 160	Article 216
PART FOUR	PART FOUR	Article 161	Article 217
Article 131	Article 182	Article 162	Article 218
Article 132	Article 183	Article 163	Article 219
Article 133	Article 184		
Article 134	Article 185	SECTION 4	SECTION 4
Article 135	Article 186	Article 164	Article 220
Article 136	Article 187	Article 165	Article 221
Article 136a	Article 188	Article 166	Article 222
		Article 167	Article 223
PART FIVE	PART FIVE	Article 168	Article 224
TITLE I	TITLE I	Article 168a	Article 225
CHAPTER 1	CHAPTER 1	Article 169	Article 226
SECTION 1	SECTION 1	Article 170	Article 227
		Article 171	Article 228
Article 137	Article 189	Article 172	Article 229
Article 138	Article 190	Article 173	Article 230
Article 138a	Article 191	Article 174	Article 231
Article 138b	Article 192	Article 175	Article 232

Before	*After*
Article 176	Article 233
Article 177	Article 234
Article 178	Article 235
Article 179	Article 236
Article 180	Article 237
Article 181	Article 238
Article 182	Article 239
Article 183	Article 240
Article 184	Article 241
Article 185	Article 242
Article 186	Article 243
Article 187	Article 244
Article 188	Article 245
SECTION 5	SECTION 5
Article 188a	Article 246
Article 188b	Article 247
Article 188c	Article 248
CHAPTER 2	CHAPTER 2
Article 189	Article 249
Article 189a	Article 250
Article 189b	Article 251
Article 189c	Article 252
Article 190	Article 253
Article 191	Article 254
Article 191a (*)	Article 255
Article 192	Article 256
CHAPTER 3	CHAPTER 3
Article 193	Article 257
Article 194	Article 258
Article 195	Article 259
Article 196	Article 260
Article 197	Article 261
Article 198	Article 262
CHAPTER 4	CHAPTER 4
Article 198a	Article 263
Article 198b	Article 264
Article 198c	Article 265
CHAPTER 5	CHAPTER 5
Article 198d	Article 266
Article 198e	Article 267

Before	*After*
TITLE II	TITLE II
Article 199	Article 268
Article 200 (repealed)	–
Article 201	Article 269
Article 201a	Article 270
Article 202	Article 271
Article 203	Article 272
Article 204	Article 273
Article 205	Article 274
Article 205a	Article 275
Article 206	Article 276
Article 206a (repealed)	–
Article 207	Article 277
Article 208	Article 278
Article 209	Article 279
Article 209a	Article 280
PART SIX	PART SIX
Article 210	Article 281
Article 211	Article 282
Article 212 (*)	Article 283
Article 213	Article 284
Article 213a (*)	Article 285
Article 213b (*)	Article 286
Article 214	Article 287
Article 215	Article 288
Article 216	Article 289
Article 217	Article 290
Article 218 (*)	Article 291
Article 219	Article 292
Article 220	Article 293
Article 221	Article 294
Article 222	Article 295
Article 223	Article 296
Article 224	Article 297
Article 225	Article 298
Article 226 (repealed)	–
Article 227	Article 299
Article 228	Article 300
Article 228a	Article 301
Article 229	Article 302
Article 230	Article 303
Article 231	Article 304
Article 232	Article 305
Article 233	Article 306
Article 234	Article 307
Article 235	Article 308

Before	After	Before	After
Article 236 (*)	Article 309	FINAL PROVISIONS	FINAL PROVISIONS
Article 237 (repealed)	–	Article 247	Article 313
Article 238	Article 310	Article 248	Article 314
Article 239	Article 311		
Article 240	Article 312		
Article 241 (repealed)	–		
Article 242 (repealed)	–		
Article 243 (repealed)	–		
Article 244 (repealed)	–		
Article 245 (repealed)	–		
Article 246 (repealed)	–		

(*)   New Article introduced by the Treaty of Amsterdam
(**)   New Title introduced by the Treaty of Amsterdam
(***)   Chapter 1 restructured by the Treaty of Amsterdam

Unannotated Cracknell's Statutes for use in Examinations

New Editions of Cracknell's Statutes

£11.95 due 2002

Cracknell's Statutes provide a comprehensive series of essential statutory provisions for each subject. Amendments are consolidated, avoiding the need to cross-refer to amending legislation. Unannotated, they are suitable for use in examinations, and provide the precise wording of vital Acts of Parliament for the diligent student.

Commercial Law
ISBN: 1 85836 472 8

European Community Legislation
ISBN: 1 85836 470 1

Conflict of Laws
ISBN: 1 85836 473 6

Family Law
ISBN: 1 85836 471 X

Criminal Law
ISBN: 1 85836 474 4

Public International Law
ISBN: 1 85836 476 0

Employment Law
ISBN: 1 85836 475 2

For further information on contents or to place an order, please contact:

Mail Order
Old Bailey Press
at Holborn College
Woolwich Road
Charlton
London
SE7 8LN

Telephone No: 020 8317 6039
Fax No: 020 8317 6004
Website: www.oldbaileypress.co.uk

Suggested Solutions to Past Examination Questions 2000–2001

The Suggested Solutions series provides examples of full answers to the questions regularly set by examiners. Each suggested solution has been broken down into three stages: general comment, skeleton solution and suggested solution. The examination questions included within the text are taken from past examination papers set by the London University. The full opinion answers will undoubtedly assist you with your research and further your understanding and appreciation of the subject in question.

Only £6.95 Due December 2002

Constitutional Law
ISBN: 1 85836 478 7

Jurisprudence and Legal Theory
ISBN: 1 85836 484 1

Criminal Law
ISBN: 1 85836 479 5

Land Law
ISBN: 1 85836 481 7

English Legal System
ISBN: 1 85836 482 5

Law of Tort
ISBN: 1 85836 483 3

Elements of the Law of Contract
ISBN: 1 85836 480 9

For further information on contents or to place an order, please contact:

Mail Order
Old Bailey Press
at Holborn College
Woolwich Road
Charlton
London
SE7 8LN

Telephone No: 020 8317 6039
Fax No: 020 8317 6004
Website: www.oldbaileypress.co.uk

Land Law

2000–2001 LLB Examination Questions
and Suggested Solutions

University of London
External Examinations

Solutions by Miss Coombes

Old Bailey Press

The Old Bailey Press integrated student law library is tailor-made to help you at every stage of your studies from the preliminaries of each subject through to the final examination. The series of Textbooks, Revision WorkBooks, 150 Leading Cases and Cracknell's Statutes are interrelated to provide you with a comprehensive set of study materials.

You can buy Old Bailey Press books from your University Bookshop, your local Bookshop, direct using this form, or you can order a free catalogue of our titles from the address shown overleaf.

The following subjects each have a Textbook, 150 Leading Cases/Casebook, Revision WorkBook and Cracknell's Statutes unless otherwise stated.

Administrative Law
Commercial Law
Company Law
Conflict of Laws
Constitutional Law
Conveyancing (Textbook and 150 Leading Cases)
Criminal Law
Criminology (Textbook and Sourcebook)
Employment Law (Textbook and Cracknell's Statutes)
English and European Legal Systems
Equity and Trusts
Evidence
Family Law
Jurisprudence: The Philosophy of Law (Textbook, Sourcebook and
    Revision WorkBook)
Land: The Law of Real Property
Law of International Trade
Law of the European Union
Legal Skills and System
    (Textbook)
Obligations: Contract Law
Obligations: The Law of Tort
Public International Law
Revenue Law (Textbook,
    Revision WorkBook and
    Cracknell's Statutes)
Succession

Mail order prices:	
Textbook	£14.95
150 Leading Cases	£11.95
Revision WorkBook	£9.95
Cracknell's Statutes	£11.95
Suggested Solutions 1998–1999	£6.95
Suggested Solutions 1999–2000	£6.95
Suggested Solutions 2000–2001	£6.95
Law Update 2002	£9.95
Law Update 2003	£10.95

Please note details and prices are subject to alteration.

To complete your order, please fill in the form below:

Module	Books required	Quantity	Price	Cost
		Postage		
		TOTAL		

For Europe, add 15% postage and packing (£20 maximum).
For the rest of the world, add 40% for airmail.

ORDERING

By telephone to Mail Order at 020 8317 6039, with your credit card to hand.

By fax to 020 8317 6004 (giving your credit card details).

Website: www.oldbaileypress.co.uk

By post to: Mail Order, Old Bailey Press at Holborn College, Woolwich Road, Charlton, London, SE7 8LN.

When ordering by post, please enclose full payment by cheque or banker's draft, or complete the credit card details below. You may also order a free catalogue of our complete range of titles from this address.

We aim to despatch your books within 3 working days of receiving your order.

Name

Address

Postcode   Telephone

Total value of order, including postage: £

I enclose a cheque/banker's draft for the above sum, or

charge my   ☐ Access/Mastercard   ☐ Visa   ☐ American Express
Card number

☐☐☐☐ ☐☐☐☐ ☐☐☐☐ ☐☐☐☐

Expiry date   ☐☐☐☐

Signature: ....Date: ....